Media Law and Practice

The College of Law
of England and Wales

LIBRARY SERVICES

Birmingham · Chester · Guildford · London · Manchester · York

Media Law and Practice

Edited by
David Goldberg,
Gavin Sutter, and Ian Walden

OXFORD
UNIVERSITY PRESS

OXFORD

UNIVERSITY PRESS

Great Clarendon Street, Oxford OX2 6DP

Oxford University Press is a department of the University of Oxford.
It furthers the University's objective of excellence in research, scholarship,
and education by publishing worldwide in

Oxford New York

Auckland Cape Town Dar es Salaam Hong Kong Karachi
Kuala Lumpur Madrid Melbourne Mexico City Nairobi
New Delhi Shanghai Taipei Toronto

With offices in

Argentina Austria Brazil Chile Czech Republic France Greece
Guatemala Hungary Italy Japan Poland Portugal Singapore
South Korea Switzerland Thailand Turkey Ukraine Vietnam

Oxford is a registered trade mark of Oxford University Press
in the UK and in certain other countries

Published in the United States
by Oxford University Press Inc., New York

© David Goldberg, Gavin Sutter, and Ian Walden, 2009

The moral rights of the authors have been asserted

Database right Oxford University Press (maker)

Crown copyright material is reproduced under Class Licence
Number C01P0000148 with the permission of OPSI
and the Queen's Printer for Scotland

First published 2009

British Library Cataloguing in Publication Data

Data available

Library of Congress Cataloging in Publication Data

Data available

Typeset by Cepha Imaging Private Ltd, Bangalore, India
Printed in Great Britain
on acid-free paper by
Ashford Colour Press Ltd,
Gosport, Hampshire

ISBN 978-0-19-955936-7

1 3 5 7 9 10 8 6 4 2

Contents—Summary

Contents

4. CONTEMPT OF COURT

Rosalind McInnes

5. Media, Democracy, and Reporting Elections

David Goldberg

8. Broadcasting

Tony Ballard

13. COMMERCIAL COMMUNICATIONS

John Enser

Preface

The media industry is undoubtedly one of the most dynamic areas of the economy, even during recession. While some sectors of the mass media, such as newspapers, are struggling to adapt to the current environment, new media forms, such as Twitter, are thriving and challenging the status quo. This book is our attempt to present and critically analyse the different areas of policy, law, and regulation of concern to those involved in the media industry, from creators and publishers, to distributors and consumers.

The contributors come from diverse backgrounds, insiders and outsiders, practitioners and academics. Each chapter is designed to be complete in itself, while as a whole the book should satisfy the needs of those coming new to the field, as well as hardened professionals seeking insight into areas related to their day job.

As with many books, *Media Law and Practice* was long in gestation. The editors have been teaching media law, on LLM and LLB courses as well as practitioner training courses, for many years. The idea of a book that addresses the range of media issues of interest to us was a constant topic of discussion between us during those years, until OUP kindly offered us the opportunity to realize those ideas. Coordinating editors and authors seemed at times an unnecessarily difficult task, while cajoling some to deliver their chapters became a constant refrain. We are incredibly grateful to all our authors for producing chapters of such high quality, with such good grace, and for continuing to talk to us!

We have attempted to state the law as correct to January 2009, although later developments have been incorporated wherever possible.

Finally, we hope that this book will simply be the first edition of an ongoing saga. The pace of change will demand it, we hope sales do too!

David Goldberg   Gavin Sutter   Ian Walden
Glasgow   London   Cambridge

January 2009

Table of Cases

Table of UK Legislation

Table of UK Secondary Legislation

Table of European and International Legislation

List of Abbreviations

ACA	Additional Costs Allowance (for MPs)
ACPO	Association of Chief Police Officers
ADI	Animal Defenders International
API	application program interface
ASA	Advertising Standards Authority
ATVOD	Association for Television On-Demand
AVMS Directive	Audiovisual Media Services Directive (EC) 2007/65
BACC	Broadcast Advertising Clearance Centre (now Clearcast)
BBFC	British Board of Film Classification
BLG	Broadcasters' Liaison Group
CAP Code	British Code of Advertising, Sales Promotion and Direct Marketing
CAS	conditional access system
CAT	Competition Appeal Tribunal
CDPA 1988	Copyright, Designs and Patents Act 1988
CJA 1988	Criminal Justice Act 1988
CJIA 2008	Criminal Justice and Immigration Act 2008
CJPA 2001	Criminal Justice and Police Act 2001
CLA	Copyright Licensing Agency
CPS	Crown Prosecution Service
CSPL	Committee on Standards in Public Life
DACS	Design and Artists Copyright Society
DCMS	Department for Culture, Media and Sport
DfES	Department for Education and Skills
DMA	designated market area
DPA 1988	Data Protection Act 1988
DPP	Director of Public Prosecutions
DTT	digital terrestrial television
ECHR	European Convention for the Protection of Human Rights and Fundamental Freedoms
ECJ	European Court of Justice
ECNs	electronic communications networks
ECSs	electronic communications services
ECtHR	European Court of Human Rights
ECU	Editorial Complaints Unit (BBC)
EIR 2004	Environmental Information Regulations 2004, SI 2004/3391
ELSPA	Entertainment Leisure Software Publishers Association
EPG	electronic programme guide

EPRA	European Platform of Regulatory Authorities
ESC	Editorial Standards Committee (BBC)
FCC	Federal Communication(s) Commission (US)
FCNM	Framework Convention for the Protection of National Minorities (1995)
FOIA 2000	Freedom of Information Act 2000
FOISA 2002	Freedom of Information (Scotland) Act 2002
IBA	Independent Broadcasting Authority
ICCPR	International Covenant on Economic, Social and Cultural Rights
ICO	Information Commissioner's Office
IMCB	Independent Mobile Classification Body
IP	intellectual property
IRIS	Legal Observations of the European Audiovisual Observatory
ISP	internet service provider
ITC	Independent Television Commission
IWF	Internet Watch Foundation
LGA 1972, 2000	Local Government Acts 1972, 2000
MBG	Mobile Broadband Group
MCPS	Mechanical Copyright Protection Society
MMC	Monopolies and Mergers Commission
MNO	mobile network operator
NRA	national regulatory authority
NTD	notice-and-take-down
NWICO	new world information and communication order
OCPA	Office of the Commissioner for Public Appointments
Ofcom	Office of Communications
OFT	Office of Fair Trading
OLAF	European Anti-Fraud Office
OPA 1959, 1964	Obscene Publications Acts 1959, 1964
OSCE	Organization for Security and Co-operation in Europe
P2P	peer-to-peer
PACE 1984	Police and Criminal Evidence Act 1984
PCA 1978	Protection of Children Act 1978
PCC	Press Complaints Commission
PEB	party election broadcast
PEGI	Pan-European Game Information age rating system
POA 1936	Public Order Act 1936
POCA 2002	Proceeds of Crime Act 2002
PPB	party political broadcast
PPP	PhonepayPlus
PRS	Performing Right Society
PSB	public sector broadcasting

PVT	public value test
RACC	Radio Advertising Clearance Centre
RIPA 2000	Regulation of Investigatory Powers Act 2000
RTTE Directive	Radio Equipment and Telecommunications Terminal Equipment Directive (EC) 1995/5
SFO	Serious Fraud Office
SLC	substantial lessening of competition
SOCPA 2005	Serious Organised Crime and Police Act 2005
SOPP	Statement of Programme Policy
TACT 2000, 2006	Terrorism Acts 2000, 2006
TLLS	television licensable content services
TWF Directive	Television without Frontiers Directive (EEC) 89/552, as amended by Directive (EC) 97/36
UGC	user-generated material
UNESCO	United Nations Educational, Scientific and Cultural Organization
VAC	Video Appeals Committee
VAT	value added tax
VOD	video-on-demand
VRA 1994	Video Recordings Act 1994
VSC	Video Standards Council
WIPO	World Intellectual Property Organization

List of Contributors

Editors

David Goldberg created the teaching of media law (in 1983) at the School of Law, University of Glasgow, having founded the Journal of Media Law and Practice in 1979. He is a Senior Visiting Fellow, Institute of Computers and Communications Law, Queen Mary, University of London. Goldberg is a regular contributor to the European Audiovisual Observatory's IRIS; an expert on access to information and media law for the Council of Europe; and an Associate Fellow, Centre for Socio-Legal Studies, Faculty of Law, University of Oxford. He teaches media law at Glasgow Caledonian University, Queen Mary (University of London), and the University of Stirling.

He is a founding member of the International Media Lawyers Association and sits on the UK Foreign and Commonwealth Office's Free Expression Panel. A Co-Convener of the Campaign for Freedom of Information in Scotland (1984–2008), he has been a co-external examiner for the LLM in Information Rights, Northumbria University.

Gavin Sutter is Lecturer in Media Law and a member of the Institute of Computer and Communications Law at the Centre for Commercial Law Studies, Queen Mary, University of London. He established, manages, and teaches on the LLB and LLM Media Law course for the ICCL, as well as writing in the field. His key areas of interest are in the regulation of content in both traditional and new media, with a particular emphasis on the issues of defamation and intermediary liability. He is Vice-Chairman of the executive board of BILETA (British and Irish Law, Education and Technology Association), and sits on the advisorial board of Tottel's Communications Law journal.

Dr Ian Walden is Professor of Information and Communications Law and head of the Institute of Computer and Communications Law in the Centre for Commercial Law Studies, Queen Mary, University of London. His publications include *EDI and the Law* (1989); *Information Technology and the Law* (1990); *EDI Audit and Control* (1993); *Cross-border Electronic Banking* (1995, 2000); *Telecommunications Law Handbook* (1997); *E-Commerce Law and Practice in Europe* (2001); *Telecommunications Law and Regulation* (2001, 2005, 2009); *Computer Crimes and Digital Investigations* (2007); and *Media Law and Practice* (2009). He has been involved in law reform projects for the World Bank, the European Commission, UNCTAD, UNECE, and the European Bank of Reconstruction and Development, as well as for a number of individual states. In 1995–96, he was seconded to the European Commission, as a national expert in electronic commerce law. He has held visiting positions at the Universities of Texas and Melbourne. He is a solicitor and is Of Counsel to the global law firm Baker &

McKenzie <http://www.bakernet.com> and is a Trustee and Vice-Chair of the Internet Watch Foundation <http://www.iwf.org.uk>.

Authors

Tony Ballard is a Partner in Harbottle & Lewis's Film and Television Group and he also works closely with the eCommerce and Technology Group. He is a prominent figure in communications law with extensive experience in the provision of electronic communication networks and the distribution of content over them. He has particular expertise in digital media and broadcasting; telecommunications; spectrum management; and copyright. His clients include major television broadcasters, fixed and mobile telecommunications operators, film producers and distributors, government bodies, and other organizations. He is a member of the International Bar Association and the Royal Television Society. Additionally he is an arbitrator on the international panel of the Independent Film and Television Alliance and is chairman of the UK branch of the European Centre for Space Law.

Siobhain Butterworth is *The Guardian*'s readers' editor—the newspaper's internal ombudsman. She qualified as a solicitor in 1991. Before taking up the post of readers' editor in April 2007, she was Legal Director for Guardian News & Media, publisher of *The Guardian* and *The Observer*. She held that role for ten years and had responsibility for all contentious and non-contentious legal matters relating to the company, including: pre-publication advice; libel and media-related litigation; intellectual property; contract and corporate work. She was also involved in lobbying and preparing responses to consultation papers in relation to matters such as freedom of information, conditional fees in libel cases, and the Data Protection Act. She was in private practice for six years before joining Guardian News & Media to set up its legal function from scratch. Reported cases in which she has been involved include: *Jonathan Aitken v Guardian Newspapers Ltd and ors* (1997); *Bennett and ors v Guardian Newspapers Ltd* (1998); *R v Hashemi, ex p Guardian Newspapers Ltd* (1998); *City of London Police v Guardian Newspapers Ltd and ors* (1999); *Attorney-General v Associated Newspapers and Guardian Newspapers Ltd* (1999); *Attorney-General v Guardian Newspapers Ltd* (1999); *R v Central Criminal Court, ex p Bright, Alton and Rusbridger* (2000); *James Mawdsley v Guardian Newspapers Ltd* (2002); *Financial Times and ors v Interbrew SA* (2002); *Sara Keays v Guardian Newspapers Ltd* (July 2003); and *Campbell James v Guardian Newspapers* (2005).

John Enser is a Partner in Olswang's Media, Communications and Technology Group and is Head of Music. He provides commercial and regulatory advice to clients active in all aspects of the media communications and technology business, particularly those offering audio and video content via digital platforms, whether TV, web, or mobile. His regulatory expertise extends to copyright law, content and advertising regulation, consumer protection, and the Broadcasting Acts.

Lindy Golding specializes in contentious and non-contentious intellectual property and information technology law primarily in the media, leisure, and entertainment fields.

She drafts and negotiates licences and other agreements of intellectual property and on copyright, trade mark and confidentiality issues, and all types of IT agreements.

She litigates and mediates trade mark, copyright, confidence, IT, and e-commerce disputes. She has worked on multimedia issues since 1994 and, more recently, on e-commerce-related issues, including domain name problems, internet start-up issues, setting up ISPs and business-to-business, and retaining e-commerce sites. She lectures as part of Bristol University's Diploma of Intellectual Property on Confidentiality and Intellectual Property and the Internet.

Jan Johannes is an in-house lawyer for Guardian News & Media. She advises on pre-publication issues, libel and contempt, protection of journalistic material, access to information, and data protection. Jan also trains journalists in these areas. She has prepared consultation papers and lobbied on matters such as freedom of information and police powers of search and seizure. She conducts litigation, in particular defending the newspaper in libel actions, challenging reporting restrictions, and protecting journalistic material from disclosure. She has successfully defended journalists, including Andrew Meldrum, the first foreign journalist to be prosecuted for 'abuse of journalistic privileges' in Zimbabwe in 2002 (on acquittal, he was deported).

Reported cases include *R v Central Criminal Court, ex p Bright, Alton and Rusbridger* (2000); *City of London Police v Guardian* (1999); *James Mawdsley v Guardian Newspapers Ltd* (2002); *Campbell James v Guardian Newspapers* (2005); *Attorney-General v Rusbridger* (2003). She has conducted appeals to the Information Tribunal, including *Guardian and Heather Brook v Information Commissioner (IC) and BBC* (2006) and *Guardian v IC and MoD* (2006).

Irini Katsirea studied at the Free University of Berlin, at the University of Leicester (LLM), and at Magdalene College, Cambridge (PhD). She is currently Lecturer in Law at Middlesex University, London. She is the author of *Cultural Diversity and European Integration in Conflict and in Harmony* (Athens: Ant N Sakkoulas, 2001) and of *Public Broadcasting and European Law. A Comparative Examination of Public Service Obligations in Six Member States* (Boston: Kluwer, 2008).

Rosalind McInnes graduated in law from the University of Glasgow in 1991. She qualified as a solicitor in private practice in Edinburgh and worked there for seven years, before joining the BBC in 1997, from Maclay, Murray and Spens, and is now Principal Solicitor at BBC Scotland. She is the author of *Contempt of Court in Scotland* and the co-author of *Scots Law for Journalists* and other media law texts. She annotated the Freedom of Information (Scotland) Act 2002 and teaches media law honours at the University of Glasgow.

Timothy Pitt-Payne was called to the Bar in 1989 and practises from 11 King's Bench Walk in London. He practises in information law, employment law, and related aspects of commercial, European, and human rights law. He has a broad-based employment law practice covering all aspects of employment litigation including privacy and data protection issues in the workplace. He has a particular interest in employment law issues specifically affecting the public sector. He has advised and represented a wide range of national public sector organizations, NHS employers, police bodies, and local authorities. In the public law field, his areas of interest include public sector pensions, various issues affecting local authorities, data protection and freedom of information, education, and community care.

He has trained a number of government departments and other public bodies on the Human Rights Act 1998 (in conjunction with JUSTICE) and on the Data Protection Act 1998. He is the joint author (with Michael Supperstone QC) of *Guide to the Freedom of Information Act 2000* (Butterworths 2001).

Lorna Woods (LLB (Hons) LLM), is a professor in the School of Law, City University, London. Prior to her arrival at City, she was Director of the LLM in Information Technology, Media and e-Commerce in the Department of Law at Essex University. Formerly a solicitor in the City of London, she has published widely in the field of media and new media regulation, as well as regularly taking part in a number of studies in the media field for a number of bodies, such as the European Commission, as well as advising NGOs on freedom of expression and media regulation.

1

THE MEDIA AND MEDIA LAW

Gavin Sutter and David Goldberg

1.1 INTRODUCTION

1.1.1 Nature of the book

This book—as its title suggests—is about media law. *Media Law and Practice* is a work about significant issues affecting media industries that will be useful both for academics and practitioners. This book is about the laws, rules, and regulations with which media industries should conform. The editors are academics at the Institute of Computer and Communications Law at the Centre for Commercial Law Studies, Queen Mary, University of London. The contributing authors are drawn from both academia and legal practice. Each chapter considers the law from the viewpoint of the practical realities of the media, with an emphasis on the day-to-day reality of how the law operates. It is intended that the reader will gain knowledge of the theoretical basis of legal concepts such as defamation. Also, of concern throughout the entire volume is the application of the law in the context of, for instance, the high-paced environment of daily newspapers, the changing reality of what constitutes 'broadcasting', or the implications for defamation law of the online, borderless world. The relevant articles of the European Convention on Human Rights and judgments of the European Court of Human Rights are mainstreamed throughout the book, discussed as and where suitable rather than dealt with in isolation.

1.1.2 Outline

The introductory chapter of the book explores the parameters of what is incorporated under the umbrella term 'media', and considers both traditional and new media alongside each other, exploring the shifting regulatory challenges affecting both. This is followed by a chapter which focuses on the policy and practice of laws regulating the ownership and control of media outlets—a further fundamental aspect of the practical delineation of who the media are.

The next chapters encompass the regulation of journalism and newsgathering alongside the practical regime which places restrictions on the material which the media are permitted to report, and also deals with relevant contempt of court issues. Topics about the regulation of distribution include: intellectual property (with specific emphasis upon the use made of copyright works, trade marks, and subsequent exploitation of intellectual property via licensing), and information law. Broadcasting law is considered both from the perspective of regulating the distribution channels, and regulating the distribution of material via those channels. The final chapters of the book tackle the self-regulation of media content. Topics covered include defamation, Chapter 11 covers both law and extra-legal regulation in the form of, for example, classification bodies like the BBFC, PCC, etc. This involves an analysis of how far extra-legal regulation in practice exists as an alternative and/or a complementary practice to strict legal control over content. The final chapters consider cultural protections (regulation of content on grounds of language, locality, and nature of productions) as well as of commercial communications (advertising, sponsorship, product placement, etc) both in print and on screen—an area which in practice has only become increasingly significant as the monetary value to the media of such communications rises. The UK in Europe is treated as a case study within which to explore these themes. However, inevitably references to other jurisdictions are made as and where appropriate.

1.2 WHAT IS 'THE MEDIA'?

1.2.1 Forms of media

Does this work have a fixed conception of what 'the media' actually is? Traditionally, the media is conceived as comprising print publications, radio, and television. One source on the UK media industry at the time of writing lists 844 radio stations, 550 television channels, 1,603 newspapers, and 1,972 magazines from 284 media owners, including many non-traditional outlets beyond the usual suspects.[1] These figures do not include the large and growing number of traditional media, mainly radio,

---

[1] See <http://www.mediauk.com>.

which aim to network individuals and groups into communities.[2] And what of cinema films (including home video and DVD), video and computer games (including those, such as Linden Labs' Second Life,[3] which are less a traditional game than an alternative means of social interaction in which different worlds bleed into each other), mobile telephone content, and—of course—the ubiquitous internet? Ofcom's November 2008 Report 'The International Communications Market 2008', emphasizes the significance and take-up of newer media.[4] It is now banal to note that the traditional conception of the media is increasingly outmoded. We now have to take account of two distinct emergent aspects: the development of new delivery channels for traditional content (see, for instance, the runaway success of the BBC's iPlayer, from which 22.8 million downloads were made in September 2008 alone),[5] and the advent of new forms of information delivery, such as blogs, wikis, and social networking websites.[6] More questionable is whether and to what extent they are part of the media.

'Blogs', a term derived from 'web-logs', first existed as a form of public electronic diary: personal, online spaces where even individuals with very little technological understanding can quickly and easily make regular posts of the details of their daily lives, thought, beliefs, interests, and attitudes. Blogs have now evolved to cover a wide range of subject matter used by individuals and professionals, as well as commercial media outlets. For lawyers generally, the most developed directory is Blawg,[7] which lists 2,330 law-themed blogs. As this evolutionary process continues, with more and more professional blogs, operated by journalists, but often associated via hyperlinks with mainstream media outlets, the line between these personal fiefdoms and traditional media blurs further, raising many complex regulatory questions. Reliable statistics about blogs are notoriously hard to come by. However, the authors offer the following:

In the context of the Blog World Expo (BWE) 20–21 September 2008, the organisers published some 'important blogging statistics'. However, Woan disagrees with the estimates, stating that, as at January 2008, the number of blogs being tracked by Technorati was in the order of 112.8 million with the daily addition of some 175,000. Significantly, however, BWE states that '22 of the 100 most popular websites in the world are blogs'. Just over 20% of the total is not an insignificant number. Nevertheless, Anne Helmond makes the point that Technorati's 112.8 million blogs obviously do not include the 72.82 million Chinese blogs as counted by The China Internet Network Information Center. Blog statistics often concern the English

---

[2] See <http://www.amarc.org/index.php?p=home&l=EN>.

[3] <http://www.secondlife.com>; see also the European Network and Information Security Agency's November 2008 Position Paper, 'Virtual Worlds. Real Money' at <http://www.enisa.europa.eu/doc/pdf/deliverables/enisa_pp_security_privacy_virtualworlds.pdf>.

[4] This report is available online at <http://www.ofcom.org.uk/research/cm/icmr08/overview/>.

[5] 'TV comes direct to your laptop' *The Times*, 20 November 2008.

[6] The best known of these include mySpace <http://www.myspace>; Facebook <http://www.facebook.com>; Friends Reunited <http://www.friendsreunited.com>; and Bebo <http://www.bebo.com>. Of course, these platforms raise legal issues: see New Media Knowledge, 'Rough Guide to: Social Media and the Law' at <http://www.nmk.co.uk/articles/1040>.

[7] <http://www.blawg.com> 21 January 2009.

language blogosphere, but we should not forget about the millions of other blogs omitted from such estimates.[8]

Viewing this explosion of blogging activity, the authors would contend that this is more than a phenomenon characterized by the facilitation of simple, exhibitionist availability of personal expressions. Indeed, the degree to which blogs, vlogs (video-blogs), and other myriad variants of the concept are a real and growing issue for media law is clearly illustrated by the volume of both civil and criminal actions sparked by specific blogs and bloggers.

In the University of Washington's *World Information Access Report*, a section on blogger arrests states that, since 2003, 64 citizens unaffiliated with news organisations have been arrested for their blogging activities. The Report concludes (somewhat lamely) that blogger arrests tend to increase and become more concentrated during sensitive times of political uncertainty.

A useful source of information for the USA is found in the Media Law Resource Centre's *Legal Actions against Bloggers*. As of 1 July 2008, 39 States had seen 149 personal injury law-suits and 11 criminal actions. Evidently, it's not just in the Third World that criminal law is deployed against bloggers and imprisonment can result, albeit indirectly, for example from refusing to reveal the identity of a source. The total damages awarded is said to be between $16–18.5 million, in judgements ranging from $7500 to $11.3 million. The largest was against a mother-blogger who was sued for defamatory statements concering a firm of removers (*Scheff v Bock*, Florida Circuit Court, September 2006). She blogged about the firm of removers taking her son's possessions from a boarding school in Costa Rica, using the terms 'crook', 'con artist' and 'fraud'.

. . .

A final data set is provided by the May 2008 YouGov survey for DLAPiper, London. Addressing 2006 internet users, it focused on their awareness and knowledge of their legal rights and responsibilities when posting comments online. Amongst its interesting findings are that 95% of internet users and 77% of posters were unclear about posting rules, 66% of posters had not read the terms and conditions, and 14% of users (rising to 28% of bloggers) had had comments removed. Furthermore, 42% of internet users (and 27% of bloggers) think that bloggers should be held to the same standards as journalists. In part, this is because of the view that not all standards that apply for journalists (e.g., libel laws) are good. In addition, some bloggers think that their standards are higher than journalists. Finally, the survey found that (only) 46% of users and 32% of bloggers supported the idea of a voluntary Code of Conduct for bloggers/postings. Indeed, 34% of bloggers opposed such a code.[9]

A 'wiki' is a type of website which is designed to permit users to add and edit material over time, typically with the aim of constructive collaboration leading to a useful product. The leading example of a 'wiki,' as is well known, is Wikipaedia.com, which defines itself as 'a multi-lingual web-based free-content encyclopaedia . . . written

---

[8] D Goldberg, *Blogging, Bloggers, Politics and Freedom of Expression* (Centre for Internet Development, forthcoming 2009).

[9] ibid; see also A Flanagan, 'Blogging: A Journal Need Not a Journalist Make' (Winter 2006) 16 Fordham Intellectual Property, Media and Entertainment Law Journal 395.

collaboratively by volunteers'.[10] Since its creation in 2001, Wikipedia has grown rapidly into one of the largest reference websites, attracting at least 684 million visitors yearly by 2008. There are more than 75,000 active contributors working on more than 10,000,000 articles in more than 250 languages. At the time of writing, there are 2,631,765 articles in English; every day hundreds of thousands of visitors from around the world make tens of thousands of edits and create thousands of new articles to enhance the knowledge held by the Wikipedia encyclopedia.[11] Readers of this book may be interested in contributing to the Wikipedia entry on 'Media Law'[12] or indeed the Online Ethics Wiki.[13]

A key feature of these technologies is that they bypass the editorial filter of the traditional media, and enable direct participation by the individual in providing information to a mass audience. This rebalances the roles involved in the delivery of content via the newer media, with greater emphasis being placed on the individual, now an active participant, rather than merely passive audience member. The role of the traditional intermediary between audience and content provider is eroded by a cultural shift towards such forms of information sharing: what may be termed a process of 'disintermediation'. In one of the leading texts, 'We the Media: Grassroots Journalism by the People, for the People', Dan Gillmor states: 'grassroots journalists are dismantling Big Media's monopoly on the news, transforming it from a lecture to a conversation'.[14]

Jay Rosen describes this process as the transformation of 'the people formerly known as the audience' via novel forms of technologically-driven empowerment.[15] The dynamic of the relationship between the traditional media and its audience is evolving. A new form of socio-political communications media is emerging, which deals in a novel combination of decentralized information provision. Different forms of media/speech have generated different forms of alternative new media, for example socio-political media is being recast through blogging, while entertainment media is being challenged by YouTube-style services.

Here it becomes essential to distinguish social conceptions of the media from their legal counterparts. The role of editors and their responsibility, from a legal perspective, are a fundamental feature of audio-visual media services as conceived of by the Audio Visual Media Services Directive.[16] Traditional media intermediaries may have to consider adapting and evolving. A key role for old media in the new environment will be as an assurance of quality. The complexity of this situation is highlighted by the current

---

[10] <http://en.wikipedia.org/wiki/Wikipaedia>.

[11] The most up to date figures may be found at the Wikipedia Statistics Page, at <http://en.wikipedia.org/wiki/Special:Statistics>.

[12] <http://en.wikipedia.org/wiki/Media_law>.

[13] <http://www.onlineethicswiki.com/index.php?title=Main_Page>.

[14] <http://www.wethemedia.oreilly.com>.

[15] <http://journalism.nyu.edu/pubzone/weblogs/pressthink>.

[16] Para 23 of the preamble to the Directive; see further section 1.3 below. See also IRIS Special Report, 'Editorial Responsibility' at <http://www.obs.coe.int/about/oea/pr/irisspecial2008_1.html> and IRIS, 'Legal Observations of the European Audiovisual Observatory' at <http://obs.coe.int/oea_publ/iris/index.html>.

stance adopted by Wikipedia. Despite exercising a limited degree of centralized editing by means of restricting the category of persons who may edit certain pages the
contents of which are prone to 'vandalism', Wikipedia explicitly states in its general
disclaimer that it is unable to offer any guarantee of accuracy, stressing in particular
that none of its articles are subject to any formalized peer-review.[17]

Also worthy of note is the new relationship between the traditional media intermediary and the individual citizen content provider.[18] What is referred to is the advent of
the use in televisual news broadcasts of photographs, information, and video footage
provided by individuals, typically captured and distributed by the use of the latest
generation of mobile telephone handsets. In an article on the BBC Online website,
Dr Jo Twist, a Senior Research Fellow leading the Digital Society and Media team at
the Institute of Public Policy Research, writes:

> 2005 was arguably the year citizens really started to do it for themselves. Raising mobiles aloft,
> they did not just talk and text, they snapped, shared and reported the world around them. Striking
> images of the 7 July bombings were taken by amateurs. Twelve months ago, it was clear the mass
> consumer was going to have at his or her disposal many more gadgets with greater capacity to
> record, store and share content. It was going to be a year in which people started to challenge
> those who traditionally provide us with content, be it news, music, or movies.[19]

In arguing that 'regulation needs to be clear about what its role is in this landscape
and that will be a long and intense process', Twist notes that: 'The UK has long worried
about the relationship between government, media and the public. The erosion of trust
and democracy is feared above all. The question is what happens to social cohesion in
this quickly evolving landscape and how can the government negotiate consumer-led
media.'[20]

The potential value in the information generated by individuals from within the
'empowered audience' of the new electronic media raises questions of content ownership. In the late 1990s, Yahoo Inc purchased the Geocities range of domains, which
had been one of the leaders in the provision of free webspace to individuals, enabling
them to express themselves in the new media environment. Following Yahoo's acquisition, users were expected to agree to new contractual terms that Yahoo Inc would own
outright any and all original information hosted. This policy was quickly reversed after
members removed their websites entirely rather than surrender ownership of their
content. This situation has given rise to new forms of enterprise such as Scoopt,[21]
which acts as an agent negotiating rights for the individual 'citizen journalist' to

---

[17] <http://en.wikipedia.org/wiki/Wikipedia:General_disclaimer>.

[18] See eg particularly in relation to the legal implications, the Citizen Media Law Project at
<http://www.citmedialaw.org>.

[19] <http://news.bbc.co.uk/1/hi/technology/4566712.stm>; the authors, while agreeing with Twist
generally, would make the point that the production of such content has changed more than the means of
distribution.

[20] ibid.

[21] <http://www.scoopt.com>; see n 2.3 below.

his content, for example the video images from a mobile telephone used by much of the mainstream broadcast media in its journalistic coverage of the 7 July 2005 terrorist attacks in London.[22] It remains to be seen how such developments will be affected by the general world economic downturn.[23]

1.3 LAW

Whatever the intellectual debate concludes as to what should or should not be included in the media, the key European legal framework norm defining it is the Audio Visual Media Services Directive (EC) 2007/65, amending Directive (EEC) 89/552.[24] Several preamble paragraphs cover the media. A major innovation of the AVMS Directive is the extension of European law, to broaden the scope of the legal framework for television content made available via the traditional, linear broadcasting delivery model. This is designed to embrace 'television-like' content made available in a non-linear manner, for example video on demand.[25] Nevertheless, the focus of the Directive is still very much upon a traditional media form—a clear case of new wine in old bottles.

Paragraph 16 states:

For the purposes of this Directive, the definition of an audiovisual media service should cover only audiovisual media services, whether television broadcasting or on-demand, which are mass media, that is, which are intended for reception by, and which could have a clear impact on, a significant proportion of the general public. Its scope should be limited to services as defined by the Treaty and therefore should cover any form of economic activity, including that of public service enterprises, but should not cover activities which are primarily non-economic and which are not in competition with television broadcasting, such as private websites and services consisting of the provision or distribution of audiovisual content generated by private users for the purposes of sharing and exchange within communities of interest.

Paragraph 17 continues:

It is characteristic of on-demand audiovisual media services that they are 'television-like', i.e. that they compete for the same audience as television broadcasts, and the nature and the means of access to the service would lead the user reasonably to expect regulatory protection within the scope of this Directive. In the light of this and in order to prevent disparities as regards free movement and competition, the notion of 'programme' should be interpreted in a dynamic way taking into account developments in television broadcasting.

---

[22] S Holmes and P Ganley, 'User-generated content and the law' (2007) 2(5) Journal of Intellectual Property Law & Practice 338.

[23] See 'Citizen journalism picture agency Scoopt closes,' *Press Gazette*, 3 February 2009 at <http://www.pressgazette.co.uk/story.asp?sectioncode=1&storycode=42994&c=1>.

[24] <http://ec.europa.eu/avpolicy/reg/avms/index_en.htm>. It should also be noted that in parallel the Council of Europe's Convention on Transfrontier Television is also expanding the scope of its coverage. <http://www.coe.int/t/dghl/standardsetting/media/T-TT/T-TT(2008)003Prov_en.pdf>.

[25] See further para 20; see also Ch 8 below.

Paragraph 18 makes clear that the media in the crosshairs of the AVMS is the *mass media*, including (but not limited to) commercial output. Consistent with this focus, private communications, for example e-mail, are explicitly excluded. Further excluded is audio-visual material which is 'merely incidental to the service e.g. websites containing animated graphical elements, short advertising spots or information related to a product or non-audiovisual service.'

While paragraph 22 makes clear that 'audio-visual media services' may include visual material with no sound; they are *not* to include material which is solely audio in content—in particular, radio transmissions. Clearly this reflects the focus on 'television-like' services. This includes text-only content insofar as it is sufficiently incorporated within a programme service, for example teletext, subtitling, and electronic programme guides.

Paragraph 21 specifically excludes from the ambit of the Directive 'electronic versions of newspapers and magazines'. This may very well require revision in the foreseeable future, as already many mainstream newspapers' websites carry video reportage and other audio-visual content which cannot be said to be easily accommodated by the examples of 'merely incidental' AV content as listed in paragraph 18. This blurring of the lines is yet another indication of the technological challenges presented by an evolving mass media. The UK government's consultation on this aspect of the AVMS closed at the end of October 2008.[26]

The media, then, form a rather nebulous creature. The popular conception of the media has a clear core which encapsulates the traditional mass media, and a rather less clear penumbra of doubt as to where exactly the boundary lines are drawn with respect to newer media.[27] For lawyers, a more concrete question is whether the media *per se* is a legal concept.[28] Whilst media law is increasingly established as a recognized legal category, law itself does not provide any all-encompassing, umbrella definition of just what exactly constitutes the media. There is a context for this, namely the opposition of the journalistic profession to seeing the media thus defined. To do so, it argues, risks legitimating certain modes of expression whilst excluding others.

1.4 THE DRIVERS OF MEDIA LAW

The drivers of media law are those factors, social, political, economic, and otherwise,[29] which shape media law as it exists at any point in time. Whilst some factors may be disposed towards encouraging new law and regulation, others act against it.

---

[26] <http://www.dcms.gov.uk/images/consultations/Part_2_Scope_the_definition_of_Audiovisual_Media_Services.pdf>; see also Ch 8 below.

[27] HLA Hart, *The Concept of Law* (Oxford University Press, 2nd edn, 1997).

[28] T Gibbons, 'Legal Status of the Media' in *Regulating the Media* (Sweet and Maxwell, 2nd edn, 1998) 26–9; see also M McGonagle, 'The Media and Media Law' in *Media Law* (Thomson Round Hall, 2nd edn, 2003) Ch 1, section 1.6: 'Media law is not a distinct division of the law . . . media law is that myriad of laws that relate to the media and affect media activities'.

[29] eg one should note the existence of corporate stakeholders coming together to collaborate across traditional boundaries and build a favourable 'media ecosystem', eg the World Economic Forum's Media

1.4.1 Technology

Devotees of *Trivial Pursuit* might not be surprised to be asked 'what was the first media that was felt to require regulation?' The authors posit that media law is a post-Gutenberg development. Whatever the answer, it remains a fact that from time to time new technological developments affecting social communication occasion new legislation. For instance, the Cinematograph Act 1909 was enacted not, as one might assume, to classify films on grounds of taste and decency, but for health and safety reasons in cinemas, owing to the fact that the chemicals in early film-stock had a tendency to ignite when heated up by the projector's light bulb. Another example would be the regulatory scheme for the use of the radio frequency spectrum. Over the years, regulating it has become less significant. Until recently, one might have said that 'as pulp is to the newsprint industry, so spectrum is to the broadcasting industry'. With the advent of digital broadcasting, spectrum is no longer the scarce resource it once was, and the prevalence of alternative, non-spectrum delivery platforms may require either another, or no, regulatory scheme.

1.4.2 Power and the fourth estate

The media considered as journalism, or 'the press', has long been referred to as 'the fourth estate'.[30] What is emphasized by this is that the media plays a vital 'watchdog' role not only in disseminating ideas about social and political life, but also facilitating the public's right to *receive* such information.[31] Of course, this does not rule out that a particular publisher may exercise this power to attempt to impose its own agenda upon the public. The significance of this driver presupposes conceiving of the media as having a, if not *the*, central role in holding the other estates to account. This aspect has been given most protection by the European Court of Human Rights (ECtHR) in its interpretation of Article 10 of the European Convention on Human Rights (ECHR).

1.4.3 Protecting the audience: individually and collectively

Media law protects different categories and categorizations of the audience. First, and picking up on the previous driver, there is the audience as citizen. Secondly, there is a group which comprises 'vulnerable' persons, including children and young people,[32]

---

and Entertainment Industry Partnership <http://www.wef.org>. See also K Sarikakis, *Powers in Media Policy*, (Peter Lang Academic Publishers, 2004).

[30] eg see Thomas Carlyle, *Reflections on the Revolution in France* (1790) Ch 39, section 5: 'A Fourth Estate, of Able Editors, springs up; increases and multiplies; irrepressible, incalculable. New Printers, new Journals, and ever new (so prurient is the world), let our Three Hundred curb and consolidate as they can!', at <http://www.worldwideschool.org/library/books/hst/european/TheFrenchRevolution/chap39.html>.

[31] *Sunday Times v UK* (1979–80) 2 EHRR 245, 26 April 1979.

[32] See Children and Young Persons (Harmful Publications) Act 1955; see also the Byron Review at <http://www.dcsf.gov.uk/byronreview>, and the ITU's Children Online Protection, at <http://www.itu.int/osg/csd/cybersecurity/gca/cop>.

ethnic and religious groups, adults of delicate sensibility,[33] speakers of non-dominant languages, and so on. On occasion, concerns that such groups should be protected can be pushed to a level of hysteria (usually by the popular tabloid press), leading to a moral panic.[34] Whilst often moral panics have their genesis in a reaction to genuine problems, they typically magnify the threat to such a degree that its true nature is distorted. Newer media are inevitably also susceptible to this phenomenon.[35] Thirdly, there is the audience as consumer, requiring protection from inaccurate, misleading and dishonest communications, both commercial and journalistic.[36] Conversely, consumers themselves may be a driver of media development; as Ross Biggam, Director-General of the Association of Commercial Television in Europe, has written:

The need for flexible thinking, the ability to see opportunities in every challenge (and maybe even vice versa?) is essential for broadcasters today. If only to respond to increasingly complex questions of 'what do our consumers want to watch, when, how, and on which platform?' . . . European politicians, rightly, worry about how to remain competitive in the global knowledge economy. If they can get the regulatory framework right, European media companies are ready to help build a new economy, based on consumer choice rather than paternalism.[37]

Members of the media's audience are further protected by a wide range of individual rights such as protection of reputation, a right to a fair trial, and ownership of one's own intellectual property and image. As it has become increasingly accepted, the individual right to respect for private life (Article 8 ECHR) has arguably become the new libel. There have been several high-profile cases involving the media and disgruntled litigants, for example *Mosley v News Group Newspapers Ltd*.[38] Media law may also be considered to be a bulwark protecting society itself. Illustrations are rules about newspapers and broadcasters uttering speech which constitutes incitement to violence; possession of extreme pornography; and the implications for freedom of expression and information of counter-terrorism legislation.[39]

---

[33] See AM Hargrave and S Livingstone, *Harm and Offence in Media Content* (Intellect Publishing, 2nd edn, 2009).

[34] 'A condition, episode, person or group of persons emerges to become defined as a threat to societal values and interests.' S Cohen, *Folk Devils and Moral Panics* (Paladin, 1973) 9.

[35] G Sutter, 'Nothing New Under The Sun: old fears and new media' (2000) 8(3) International Journal of Law and Information Technology 338.

[36] See, for instance, EU rules on misleading advertising at <http://europa.eu/rapid/pressReleasesAction. do?reference=IP/07/1915&format=HTML&aged=0&language=EN>; PCC, 'Report on Subterfuge and Newsgathering' at <http://www.pcc.org.uk/assets/218/PCC_subterfuge_report.pdf>; C Cramer, 'Trust and Integrity in the Modern Media' at <http://blogs.journalism.co.uk/editors/2008/11/18/trust-and-integrity-in-the-modern-media-chris-cramers-speech-to-nottingham-trent-university>; and Reuters Trust Principles at <http://www.thomsonreuters.com/about/reuters_trust_principles>.

[37] <http://www.pmcontent.com/web/thepulse/digitaltv.pdf>.

[38] [2008] EWHC 1777 (QB). See also J Rozenberg, 'Another Strap Across the Bottom' at <http://www.rozenberg.net/archives/1%20Keynote%20Address%20Joshua%20Rozenberg.pdf>.

[39] Case ICTR-99-52-A *Nahimana, Barayagwiza and Ngeze v The Prosecutor*, Appeals Decision of 28 November 2007 <http://www.ictr.org>; Criminal Justice and Immigration Act 2008, ss 63–71; <http://www.coe.int/t/dghl/standardsetting/media/ConfAntiTerrorism/Default_en.asp>. See further Ch 11 below.

1.4.4 Protecting the national heritage

The rationale behind such regulation is that a significant proportion of media output constitutes part of the national heritage, and should therefore be preserved. This notion of social repository holdings is as old in law as the ability to copy a document by mechanical means, and is also a further example of media law coming about in response to technological change. Under the UK Legal Deposit Libraries Act 2003 certain electronic and non-electronic media outputs are required to be deposited. The Explanatory Note to the Act states: 'The main purpose of the Legal Deposit Libraries Act 2003 is to give the Secretary of State power to extend the system of legal deposit progressively and selectively to cover various non-print media as they develop, including off-line publications (eg CD ROMS and microforms), on-line publications (eg e-journals) and other non-print materials.'[40]

As newer media evolve and occupy more of the informational space, surely this will pose increasing challenges in relation to what is to be preserved, and also how this will be achieved.[41]

1.4.5 Self-regulation and co-regulation[42]

The linkage between media law and freedom of expression has led to robust efforts on the part of the media to be free to regulate its own activities. Indeed, this approach has now gained official recognition in the recent European Audio Visual Media Services Directive, paragraph 16 of the preamble to which states that: 'Measures aimed at achieving public interest objectives in the emerging audiovisual media services sector are more effective if they are taken with the active support of the service providers themselves.'

In the UK there are numerous self- and co-regulatory bodies aiming to regulate the media. Among the most visible self-regulatory bodies is the Press Complaints Commission (PCC) with its code of practice and interpretative codebook published by the Editors' Code of Practice Committee.[43] Examples of co-regulatory bodies include the British Board of Film Classification (BBFC)[44] (which covers not only cinematographic exhibition, but also home video, DVD, video and computer games—both content and packaging), and the Advertising Standards Authority (ASA)(B).[45] Other less well

---

[40] Explanatory Note to the Act, para 6, at <http://www.opsi.gov.uk/acts/acts2003/en/ukpgaen_20030028_en_1>.

[41] See further L Brindley (Head of the British Library), 'We're in danger of losing our memories' *The Observer*, 25 January 2009; <http://www.guardian.co.uk/technology/2009/jan/25/internet-heritage>.

[42] See further Ch 9 below; see also <http://www.osce.org/documents/html/pdftohtml/30697_1117_en.pdf.html>.

[43] <http://www.pcc.org.uk>; see also <http://www.editorscode.org.uk>.

[44] <http://www.bbfc.co.uk>.

[45] <http://www.asa.org.uk/asa/ http://www.asa.org.uk/asa/codes>.

known examples of self- and co-regulatory bodies include: PhonepayPlus;[46] the Independent Mobile Classification Body (IMCB);[47] the Internet Watch Foundation;[48] the Teenage Magazine Arbitration Panel;[49] the Broadband Stakeholder Group;[50] and the Family Online Safety Institute.[51]

Another type of co-regulatory body is that whose existence and authority derives from statute law. Such bodies promulgate codes of practice and adjudicate complaints about infringements. Examples include the Video Appeals Committee established by the Video Appeals Provisions 1985,[52] and the Committee on Advertising Practice's Broadcast Committee.[53]

One of the oldest still-functioning bodies, namely the DA-Notice System,[54] represents yet another type. Originally established in 1912 by the Admiralty in the War Office, it is an administrative body with powers of persuasion only. The committee comprises five government representatives, and sixteen representatives nominated by the media, including, lately, Google.[55]

Finally, the authors note the role of Clearcast[56] and the Radio Advertising Clearance Centre,[57] which provide an advisory service to industry, giving their opinion on the compatibility of the content with the Broadcast Advertising Codes.

1.4.6 Other laws affecting the media

Laws affecting the media are not always media laws. A notable example is the role of fiscal law concerning the long-standing issue of whether core media products should be taxed or not. Currently in the UK, books and newspapers, as 'windows on the world', are VAT exempt. However, this position does not command universal assent. Indeed there is an ongoing debate at European level on whether such exemptions should exist. Further, the question of whether there should be some form of taxation imposed upon media products delivered digitally, or even use of the internet itself,

---

[46] Formerly The Independent Committee for the Supervision of Standards of Telephone Information Services <http://www.phonepayplus.org.uk>.

[47] <http://www.imcb.org.uk>; <http://www.imcb.org.uk/classificationframe>.

[48] <http://www.iwf.org.uk>.

[49] <http://www.ppa.co.uk/tmap>; <http://www.tmap.org.uk/cgi-bin/wms.pl/665>; <http://www.tmap.org.uk/public/downloads/tmap_guidelines.pdf>.

[50] <http://www.broadbanduk.org/content/view/65/43>.

[51] <http://www.fosi.org>.

[52] <http://www.bbfc.org.uk/policy/policy-appeals.php>.

[53] <http://www.cap.org.uk/cap/about/cap_broadcast>; New media advertising is currently under the jurisdiction of the Committee on Advertising Practice's non-broadcast advertising committee. As the line between broadcast and new media blurs, this is likely to lead to a degree of uncertainty as to the appropriate forum for a given dispute. There is also the issue of the disparity in enforcement powers held by the CAP Committees.

[54] <http://www.dnotice.org.uk>.

[55] <http://www.dnotice.org.uk/commitee.htm>.

[56] <http://www.clearcast.co.uk/clearcast>.

[57] <http://www.racc.co.uk/racc/showCategories.aspx?catID=1>.

remains open. Legislatures across the globe are considering introducing or banning digital taxes. A continuing tension is that between counter-terrorism laws and the media's freedom to publish. During the 1980s, several legal challenges were mounted against government restrictions on broadcasting oral statements by representatives of then-proscribed organizations. Post-9/11, the political focus may have changed, however, the legal issues persist.[58]

1.5 PARAMETERS OF MEDIA LAW

And so, we return to the question: just what is media law? What falls within this category? It is clear that the field of media law is dynamic, evolving, and fuzzy. A good example of this is the International Bar Association's Media Law Committee, which functions within the Intellectual Property, Communications and Technology Section.[59] This incorporates the following diverse group: Art, Cultural Institutions and Heritage Law; Communications Law; Intellectual Property and Entertainment Law; Space Law; Technology Law.[60] The field is additionally an intellectual construct, and it also has a history. At least in the UK, but arguably further afield, the first known use of the phrase appeared in the title of a law journal, The Journal of Media Law and Practice, published by Frank Cass & Company, London, from 1980.[61] Part of media law's development as a field has been a result of the drive towards academic specialisms, as opposed to any inherent essence of the field. This evolution also coincided with the explosion of the so-called information society and economy, and thus became attractive to publishers, academics, lawyers, and their clients alike. This phenomenon, of course, is far from unique. However, the authors, paradoxically perhaps, would still emphasize the reality and the importance of the media to which this field relates. As media law continues to develop as both an academic specialism and a distinct area of law in practice (including the lawyer's role in risk management), the authors of this chapter identify several ways of looking at the bigger picture.

1.5.1 The bottle analogy

It is now a truism to the point of cliché to speak of 'new wine in old bottles'. Nevertheless, it remains important to ask the question: the channel or mode of delivery may be new,

---

[58] 'Developments in anti-terrorism legislation in Council of Europe member states and their impact on freedom of expression and information', MCM (2009)011, <http://www.ministerialconference.is/media/images/MCM2009011_en_final_web.pdf>.

[59] See eg the International Bar Association's Media Law Committee at <http://www.ibanet.org/legalpractice/Media_Law.cfm>.

[60] See also the constantly evolving range of topics at <http://www.qlinks.net>.

[61] It is gratifying to note that this radical creation of a new field has spawned, even at a time of intellectual and political questioning of the scope of the area, a new publication dedicated to its core, The Journal of Media Law <http://www.hartjournals.co.uk/jml>.

but is it in point of fact a new regulatory issue? Or is it simply a matter of applying an existing legal approach in a new context? However, there is still the potential that the answer may very well be that in fact the new technology does indeed raise new legal issues as opposed to merely a question of enforcement. Even so, the conventional distinction between regulating media content and regulating the means of communication, ie the delivery platform, remains important.[62]

1.5.2 The nature of the regulation

There is a range of issues in media law that are considered to be of sufficient importance that the state, and in the UK, Parliament, will typically step in to actively regulate them. Examples include child pornography and extreme pornography.[63] Equally, there are a range of rights provided in law, such as intellectual property or the right to have one's own reputation protected, that are available to the individual, but which they themselves must actively pursue to enforce.[64] Which of these categories a given set of laws falls into may be indicative of distinct issues and difference in the application of the law in practice.

1.5.3 The implicit theory of communication in media law

Law students and media lawyers are not well versed in either the ever expanding field of 'media studies', or the literature concerning different theories of communication. The latter leads to tacit assumptions being made regarding the effects or impact that media messages are claimed to have. Arguably, many, if not most pertinent media laws assume the so-called Transmission Model of communication:

(1) an *information source*, which produces a message;

(2) a *transmitter*, which encodes the message into signals;

(3) a *channel*, to which signals are adapted for transmission;

(4) a *receiver*, which 'decodes' (reconstructs) the message from the signal;

(5) a *destination*, where the message arrives.[65]

Suppose media effects are not best described by the transmission model, but by constructivist theories?

Alternatives to transmissive models of communication are normally described as *constructivist*: such perspectives acknowledge that meanings are actively constructed by both initiators and interpreters rather than simply 'transmitted'. However, you will find no single, widely-accepted constructivist model of communication in a form like that of Shannon and Weaver's block diagram.

---

[62] See further Ch 8 below.
[63] See Ch 11 below.
[64] See Chs 6 and 10 below.
[65] CE Shannon and W Weaver, *A Mathematical Model of Communication* (University of Illinois Press, 1949).

This is partly because those who approach communication from the constructivist perspective often reject the very idea of attempting to produce a formal model of communication. Where such models are offered, they stress the centrality of the act of making meaning and the importance of the socio-cultural context.[66]

Would this have implications for media laws which purport to regulate content because of its perceived effects on its likely audience?[67]

1.5.4 Rights-based approach to media law

Every aspect of law has been affected by the Human Rights Act 1998, and media law is no exception. Section 12(4) of this Act states, *inter alia*, that: 'The court must have particular regard to the importance of the Convention right to freedom of expression . . . .'[68] Obviously, this section addresses the nexus between Articles 8 and 10 ECHR. However, the tension between the Article 10 right and Article 6 (the right to a fair trial) will also be important in the context of media law.[69] It should be noted that there is concern at the robustness which the European Court of Human Rights is exercising in relation to its core function of promoting and protecting freedom of expression under Article 10.[70]

Further, less robustly (or not at all) protected by the conventional rights regime, by which the authors mean political speech, is:

(1) The right of access to information which is so crucial for the newsgathering function of the media. The Strasbourg Court is inching its way towards hearing actions under Article 10 regarding this claimed right (which does not explicitly appear in Article 10, unlike Article 19 of the International Covenant on Civil and Political Rights). It remains to be seen what, if any, improvement in the situation will be gained from the coming into force of the Council of Europe's Convention on Access to Official Documents[71]—the world's first treaty providing rights of access to information.[72]

---

[66] D Chandler, 'The Transmission Model of Communication', at <http://www.aber.ac.uk/media/Documents/short/trans.html#M>.

[67] See n 32 above.

[68] <http://www.statutelaw.gov.uk/legResults.aspx?LegType=All+Legislation&title=Human+Rights+Act&searchEnacted=0&extentMatchOnly=0&confersPower=0&blanketAmendment=0&TYPE=QS&NavFrom=0&activeTextDocId=1851003&PageNumber=1&SortAlpha=0>.

[69] See further Ch 4 below. On the interplay between the Art 10 right and its exceptions, see further A Lester, 'Freedom of expression and its limits' in *Our Freedoms: A Decade's Reflection on the Advancement of Human Rights* (IBA Publications, 2007).

[70] <http://www-ircm.u-strasbg.fr/seminaire_oct2008/interventions_en.htm>.

[71] <http://wcd.coe.int/ViewDoc.jsp?id=1377737&Site=CM&BackColorInternet=9999CC&BackColorIntranet=FFBB55&BackColorLogged=FFAC75>; see eg, *Kenedi v Hungary* (Application 31475/05).

[72] W Hins and D Voorhoof, 'Access to State-Held Information as a Fundamental Right under the European Convention on Human Rights' at <http://www-ircm.u-strasbg.fr/seminaire_oct2008/docs/Hins_Voorhoof_Access_to_State_Held_Information.pdf>. See further on this issue: the Power of Information Taskforce <http://powerofinformation.wordpress.com> and Free Our Data <http://www.freeourdata.org.uk>.

(2) One should also be aware of the rights and interests of those who earn their livelihoods within media enterprises, and who campaign not only about wages and conditions, but also for the principles for which the media stand.[73] The Campaign for Press and Broadcasting Freedom in the UK[74] and the International Federation of Journalists globally champion these.[75]

(3) The conventional take on Article 10 is a hierarchical one. Expressing ideas and information about political institutions and theories is of undoubted general concern, and should be protected. However, a more inclusive notion of the media and its role would focus on social communication in general: for example entertainment media, as well as socio-political speech. Arguably, the vast bulk of communicative activity is social. The authors would encourage the development of a less hierarchical conception of media-related expression which values and reflects more accurately the significance of media content and its consumption in day-to-day life.

1.6 CONCLUDING REMARKS

This book is published at a moment when, in the authors' opinion, the market in practice, publication, and thinking about media law is at a mature phase of the cycle. Indeed, there are those already thinking about the next stage, for instance the Network Insight Institute's Future Communications Policy Matrix.[76] What will a new generation of thinkers and practitioners make of media law? Paradoxically, the subject is still not mainstreamed at undergraduate level, but much like the mainstreaming of intellectual property over the past decade, the authors urge that this field, which is connected so centrally to the sinews of modern society, receive a more centred and considered role in the knowledge base of current and future lawyers. Had Karl Marx been writing today, he would not have written *Das Kapital* but *Die Informationen*.

Parallel to the blue-sky thinking, a mix of socio-economic and technological factors is producing changes in and thinking about current media and in particular journalistic practices. Two emergent schools of thought are the evolutionists and those who perceive or prophesy the end of media as we know it. Blogs such as 'The end of journalism?'[77] reflect these positions. Meantime, the *Christian Science Monitor* has ceased hard copy publication in favour of an exclusively online presence.[78] Rupert Murdoch, clearly espoused an evolutionist thesis when he stated in November 2008: 'Among our

---

[73] H Thorgeirsdottir, *Journalism Worthy of the Name: Freedom Within the Press and the Affirmative Side of Article 10 of the European Convention on Human Rights* (The Raoul Wallenberg Institute Human Rights Library, Brill Academic, 2005).

[74] <http://www.cbpf.org.uk>.

[75] <http://www.ifj.org>.

[76] <http://www.networkinsight.org/the_future_communications_policy_matrix_main_page.html>.

[77] <http://www.end-of-journalism.org>.

[78] <http://www.csmonitor.com>; see in particular <http://www.csmonitor.com/2008/1029/p25s01-usgn.html>.

journalistic friends are some misguided cynics who are too busy writing their own obituary to be excited by the opportunity . . . Unlike the doom and gloomers, I believe that newspapers will reach new heights in the 21st century.'[79]

On the more day-to-day level, policy-makers and legislators continue to change media law and regulation. Current instances at the time of writing include the Culture, Media and Sport Committee's inquiry into 'Press Standards, Privacy and Libel';[80] the Westminster Hall debate on criminal libel;[81] and the House of Lords Communications Committee's report, 'The ownership of the news'.[82] Additionally, the UK government is involved in a flurry of thinking and policy formulation regarding the media. Examples of this include the Convergence Think Tank,[83] and the Digital Britain initiative.[84] In Australia, the Minister for Broadband, Communications and the Digital Economy has embarked upon a similar process, with the innovation of using online communication platforms to solicit the views of those with an interest in this field of regulation.[85] Whatever, by the time there is a second edition of this book, there is bound to have been a significant number of national and European decisions affecting the media. As Lord Carter of Barnes, in responding for the government during the debate on the Communications Committee's report, pertinently put it:

Digital technologies and the market . . . have created a profusion of new content. Production costs are lower and there are many more routes to the viewer and the user. We have seen, and will continue to see, thousands of flowers bloom, whether in user-generated content, local and special interest sites for information and social interaction, or 200-plus specialist channels on digital television . . .

We must look urgently at how best to secure a shared civic agenda—effective political debate, plural and impartial news, but in the changed circumstances of a fully digital world . . . If we want things to stay the same, or return to the quality they once were, they are going to have to change radically.[86]

That, we agree, suggests the agenda for UK media law during its next cycle.

---

[79] *The Guardian*, 17 November 2008; <http://www.guardian.co.uk/media/2008/nov/17/rupert-murdoch-internet-newspapers>.

[80] <http://www.parliament.uk/parliamentary_committees/culture__media_and_sport.cfm>.

[81] *Hansard* 17 December 2008: col 69WH; available at <http://www.publications.parliament.uk/pa/cm200809/cmhansrd/cm081217/halltext/81217h0001.htm#08121766000001>.

[82] HL-122, 27 June 2008; available at <http://www.publications.parliament.uk/pa/ld/ldcomuni.htm>.

[83] <http://www.culture.gov.uk/Convergence>.

[84] <http://www.culture.gov.uk/reference_library/media_releases/5548.aspx>; see for the interim report <http://www.culture.gov.uk/images/publications/digital_britain_interimreportjan09.pdf>.

[85] <http://www.dbcde.gov.au/communications_for_business/industry_development/digital_economy/future_directions_blog>.

[86] *Hansard* 5 November 2008: col 312; available at <http://www.publications.parliament.uk/pa/ld200708/ldhansrd/text/81105-0016.htm>. For the final report, see Digital Britain, <http://www.culture.gov.uk/images/publications/digitalbritain-finalreport-jun09.pdf>.

2

WHO OWNS THE MEDIA? PLURALITY, OWNERSHIP, COMPETITION AND ACCESS

Ian Walden

2.1 INTRODUCTION

As discussed in the previous chapter, part of the challenge faced by the editors and authors of this book is the fact that the historic and distinct sections of the media industry, radio and TV broadcasters and newspapers, are undergoing radical evolution in the face of technologically driven competitors for media consumption, such as YouTube and Blogs, which facilitate public access to communication platforms with a global reach. As such, part of the title's question may require us to recognize that the 'media' as an entity capable of being owned may become a less pertinent question over the coming years, in the face of such diversity of supply. The concept of 'ownership' is also somewhat misleading, since our concern lies not only with those that possess the assets that comprise the media entities, broadcasters, and newspapers, but also those that exercise some form of influence or control over such entities, through extra-legal or regulatory means.

The prevailing theme analysed in this chapter is that of plurality, the widely recognized value seen as emanating from having a variety of media providers and content for us to consume. If the media represent a powerful social instrument, then concentrating such power in the hands of the few, whether in economic or political terms, is seen as likely to constrain our freedom of expression, in terms of imparting and receiving information and ideas.[1] One important element of media law and regulation therefore consists of rules designed to strengthen pluralism, as a means of promoting freedom of expression, both politically and culturally, which states have a duty and right to protect and promote: 'Convinced that states have the duty to guard against infringements of the freedom of expression and information and should adopt policies designed to foster as much as possible a variety of media and a plurality of information sources, thereby allowing a plurality of ideas and opinions . . .'[2]

For the purposes of this chapter, pluralism is viewed from two distinct perspectives: commonly referred to as external and internal pluralism,[3] or structural and content regulation.[4] 'External' pluralism concerns the existence of media outlets and provision of media services and the market structure that exists to enable a diversity of provision and means of access for consumers. Government may adopt a range of different tools to facilitate a diversity of providers or 'speakers',[5] of which three areas will be examined in this chapter: licensing and authorization regimes; media ownership rules, including the role of public sector broadcasters; and competition law.

While the press tends to operate in a fully competitive marketplace in most Western nations, the broadcasting industry is more likely to be mixed, consisting of private and state-owned players, such as the BBC, which have asymmetric rights and obligations. Competition law can be further subdivided into *ex ante* and *ex post* measures, the former is used in respect of regulatory measures that proactively control the manner in which entities operate going forward; while the latter refers to measures that arise in reaction to the decisions and activities of entities, such as merger controls. The internet, as a global platform, is having a significant impact on the competitive nature of the media industry, dissolving local, national, and even regional markets, while at the same time offering opportunities for geographically diverse communities to be reconstituted and reinvigorated through global online media offerings.

Internal pluralism is concerned with regulatory mechanisms for ensuring a diversity of content made available for consumption. Diversity of ownership will not itself

---

[1] ECHR, Art 10(1).

[2] Council of Europe, Declaration of the Committee of Ministers 'on the Freedom of Expression and Information', 29 April 1982. See also the statement of the European Court of Justice in *Gouda* (1991) ECR I-4007, para 23.

[3] See eg Competition Commission Report, 'Acquisition by British Sky Broadcasting Group plc of 17.9 per cent of the shares of ITV plc', 14 December 2007, para 5.11: 'we also thought that it was appropriate to distinguish between the range of information and views that are provided across separate independent media groups ("external plurality") and the range that are provided within individual media groups ("internal plurality").'

[4] E Barendt, 'Structural and Content Regulation of the Media: United Kingdom and Some American Comparisons' in E Barendt (ed), *The Yearbook of Media and Entertainment Law 1997/98* (Clarendon Press, 1997).

[5] ibid.

ensure diversity of content where the sources of content are limited; the dependency of the newspaper industry on feeds from a few press agencies or the public relations industry represents a particular concern.[6] Content diversity may be driven by a variety of policy objectives, including the promotion of democratic discourse, the oft-quoted 'marketplace of ideas',[7] and cultural or economic protectionism. It can also be achieved through a range of mechanisms, from programming production quotas;[8] obligations concerning programming variety, quality, and integrity;[9] and access regimes for certain types of speaker; to controls placed on advertising.[10] Such rules form an adjunct to the content control regimes that are designed to limit the availability of harmful and illegal content.[11]

Finally, as noted in the introductory chapter, the focus of attention in this book is on UK law, with references to other jurisdictions as and when appropriate. As such, our consideration of media pluralism will inevitably shift back and forth between a discussion of high-level policy and principles, and detailed statutory rules and regulations. However, to better understand the approach to pluralism in the UK, we should first look briefly at the treatment of the issue as an element of European media policy.

2.2 EUROPEAN DEVELOPMENTS

Given that the notion of media pluralism is widely recognized within Europe as being intimately connected with the Convention right to freedom of expression,[12] it is not surprising that the Council of Europe has been the most influential intergovernmental institution in terms of delineating the scope of measures designed to facilitate media pluralism within Europe. A number of resolutions and recommendations have been adopted by the Parliamentary Assembly and Committee of Ministers addressing the issue,[13] although these 'soft law' instruments impose no legally binding obligation on Member States. Even the incorporation of an express provision on media pluralism in the Convention on Transfrontier Television[14] simply reminds states to take such matters into account. In addition to these measures, an ad hoc 'Group of Specialists on

---

[6] House of Lords, Select Committee on Communications, 'The Ownership of News', HL Paper 122-I, June 2008 (hereinafter 'Lords 2008') 6.

[7] Generally attributed to Justice Oliver Wendell Holmes Jr, in *Abrams v US* 250 US 616 (1919). See also Schauer, who talks about 'an open and unregulated market for the trade in ideas' in *Free Speech: A Philosophical Enquiry* (Cambridge University Press, 1982) 16.

[8] See further Ch 12 below.

[9] See further Ch 9 below.

[10] See further Ch 13 below.

[11] See further Ch 11 below.

[12] See J Raz, 'Free Expression and Personal Identification' (1991) 11(3) OJLS 303 and E Barendt, *Freedom of Speech* (Oxford University Press, 2nd edn, 2007) 34–6.

[13] eg Recommendation No R (1999) 1 'on measures to promote media pluralism' and Recommendation No R (2007) 2 'on media pluralism and diversity of media content'.

[14] Protocol amending the European Convention on Transfrontier Television, ETS No 171, 1 October 1998, inserting a new article 10*bis*, 'Media Pluralism'.

Media Diversity' has been in existence since 2005 to monitor and advise on policy in the area.[15]

At an EU level, while the European Parliament has adopted a number of resolutions calling for measures to control media ownership and promote pluralism over the years,[16] such calls have yet to be heeded by the Commission in terms of specific regulatory measures. Various public consultations have led the Commission to conclude that such an initiative would be inappropriate at the current time, most recently within the context of the revision of the 'Television without Frontiers' Directive;[17] although it continues to monitor the situation.[18] This stance also reflects both a legal constraint, in terms of subsidiarity and property ownership, and the complex political dimension of such issues.

What is perhaps somewhat surprising is that concerns about pluralism have only relatively recently come to the fore as a component of European media policy; 'since the early nineties' according to a Commission working paper.[19] This at a time when the media marketplace is being transformed through technological, regulatory, and market developments to contain many new players, platforms, and opportunities. So what reasons lie behind this renewed concern with media pluralism in Europe?

Four key factors would seem discernible within the policy discourse. First, the emergence of a liberated media sector within central and east european states following the end of the Soviet era has generated a public debate about pluralism and media independence that has surfaced less often within Western Europe;[20] Italy perhaps being the exception to the rule.[21] Secondly, while new technologies have greatly enhanced our ability to disseminate and access information, progressive convergence between historically distinct market sectors, ie media, telecommunications, and IT, has meant that existing industry players have been keen to consolidate their market position, exploiting the benefits of vertical integration and the emergence of so-called 'gatekeeper' technologies.[22] As well as recognizing the opportunities these developments present for enhancing pluralism, such rapid market convergence and realignment has inevitably been of concern to policy-makers and governments.[23] Thirdly, the liberalization of the broadcasting sector over the past two decades has seen the rise of private

---

[15] See <http://www.coe.int/t/dghl/standardsetting/media/MC-S-MD/default_en.asp>.

[16] eg Resolution 'on media takeovers and mergers' [1990] OJ C68/137; Resolution 'on media concentration and diversity of opinions' [1992] OJ C284/44; Resolution 'on concentration of the media and pluralism' [1994] OJ C323/157; and Resolution 'on pluralism and media concentration' [1995] OJ C166/133.

[17] See Commission Issue Paper for the Liverpool Audiovisual Conference, 'Media Pluralism—What should be the European Union's role?', July 2005.

[18] n 14 above, at 4.

[19] Commission Staff Working Document, 'Media Pluralism in the Member States of the European Union', SEC (2007) 32, 16 January 2007, 4.

[20] See A Richter, 'Restrictions on media ownership in post-Soviet countries' (2008) 13(6) Communications Law, 197.

[21] eg see the Venice Commission documents concerning the 'Frattini' and 'Gasparri' laws, available at <http://www.venice.coe.int/site/dynamics/N_Opinion_ef.asp?L=E&OID=309>.

[22] See further section 2.5.3 below.

[23] eg Commission 2007 (n 19 above) 5.

media entities with the capability of fully rivalling public sector broadcasters, reviving concerns about the influential and powerful nature of visual media, when in private hands as much as in the hands of governments. Fourthly, globalization revives concerns about the impact that foreign ownership and the prevalence of foreign content may have on domestic politics and culture.[24]

2.3 LICENSING AND AUTHORISATION

The most basic form of *ex ante* regulatory control of any market is the imposition of a licensing or authorization regime on suppliers; a requirement to obtain permission from the state to engage in the activity.[25] Licensing the right to supply services has obvious market entry implications, but also directly affects media pluralism from a structural perspective. Where licensing or authorization is a pre-condition for the provision of a media outlet or service, then the licensing authority, whether as part of government or an independent authority, will need to determine to what extent the regime should be used to facilitate media pluralism. The licensing authority may have the ability to grant licences to specific minority groups and interests that are seen as promoting diversity, or withhold the granting of a licence to an entity considered to have too large a market share or representing interests considered unsuitable, such as political parties.[26]

Radio and television broadcasting are distinct from the newspaper industry in that they are subject to an *ex ante* licensing scheme governing the provision of such services.[27] Licensing regimes for radio and television broadcasting do, however, constitute an indirect form of press licensing, to the extent that cross-media ownership rules are predicated on the granting of a broadcast licence to entities owning both papers and broadcast stations.[28]

In the past, the newspaper industry has been subject to something akin to an authorization regime, through a 'stamp tax' payable on every copy sold. The tax was first introduced in 1712, but was raised to politically significant levels by the Stamp Act 1815; the duty making newspapers inaccessible to the vast majority of the population.[29] There was considerable opposition to this so-called 'tax on knowledge'[30] and it was ignored by a number of radical publications, resulting in fines and imprisonment.

---

[24] ibid section 2.4.
[25] For a general discussion of licensing, see A Flanagan, 'Authorization and Licensing' in I Walden (ed) *Telecommunications Law and Regulation*, (Oxford University Press, 2009).
[26] eg UK law disqualifies local authorities, political parties, religious bodies, and advertising agencies from holding a broadcasting licence. See further 8.3.8 below.
[27] See further Ch 8 below.
[28] eg US cross-media ownership rules, Code of Federal Regulations, Title 47, section 73.3555(c).
[29] See S Lang, *Parliamentary Reform 1785–1928* (Routledge, 1999).
[30] A phrase coined by John and Leigh Hunt, publishers of the *Examiner*, a weekly magazine founded in 1808.

The scope of the tax was subsequently extended to any journal containing any 'public news, intelligence or occurrences, or any remarks or observations thereon, or upon any matter in Church or State' and based on frequency of publication,[31] as well as requiring the pre-payment of a bond.[32] Opposition to the tax continued to grow and it was eventually abolished in 1855. While such *ex ante* intervention seems inconceivable in a modern democratic state, it took place in the context of considerable political unrest at home and throughout Europe and the statutory language used terminology that would be recognizable to modern media lawyers, ie libel, excitement of hatred, and contempt!

The mere existence of licensing and authorisation regimes for media outlets could be construed as an unnecessary restriction on a person's right to freedom of expression. To forestall such an argument, the European Convention on Human Rights expressly qualifies the right to freedom of expression by recognizing the right of states to license: 'This article shall not prevent States from requiring the licensing of broadcasting, television or cinema enterprises.'[33] This qualification is distinct from the grounds for derogation permissible under Article 10(2). Similarly, in the US, the Supreme Court has maintained that it would be nonsense to consider an 'unabridgeable First Amendment right to broadcast comparable to the right of every individual to speak, write, or publish'.[34]

These sentiments reflect one of the historic rationales for broadcast licensing, the need to manage access to the electromagnetic spectrum, a scarce resource that is itself a market access limiting factor.[35] Regulated access is justified primarily by the need to optimize the use of this scarce resource and to prevent or minimize harmful interference between different equipment and types of usage. This reasoning is manifest in the applicable rules operable at a national, European, and international level.[36] Scarcity constraints have declined in importance over recent years, as a result of technological developments that have dramatically improved the efficiency with which the available spectrum is used, as well as the emergence of alternative predominantly non-spectrum platforms, particularly the internet. Such changes have indeed called into question the continuing need for a licensing regime at all.[37] However, spectrum continues to be a valuable resource and decisions made about how certain segments are allocated for

---

[31] An Act to subject certain Publications to the Duties of Stamps upon Newspapers, and to make other Regulations for restraining the Abuses arising from the Publication of blasphemous and seditious Libels (30 December 1819), 60° GEO III & 1° GEO IV, C 9.

[32] ibid VIII.

[33] Art 10(1).

[34] *Red Lion Broadcasting Co v FCC* 395 US 367 (1969) 388.

[35] See further Ch 8 below. See also L Hitchens, *Broadcasting Pluralism and Diversity* (Hart, 2006) 46, and E Barendt, *Broadcasting Law* (Clarendon Press, 1995) 3–10.

[36] In the UK, the governing statute is the Wireless Telegraphy Act 2006; within Europe, see Decision 676/2002/EC on a regulatory framework for radio spectrum policy in the European Community [2002] CJ L08/1; internationally, see the ITU's Radio Regulations (Geneva, 2008).

[37] eg Hitchens (n 35 above).

use, at a national, regional, and international level,[38] will have implications for media providers and consequentially pluralism.[39]

2.4 MEDIA OWNERSHIP

Member states should consider the adoption of rules aimed at limiting the influence which a single person, company or group may have in one or more media sectors as well as ensuring a sufficient number of diverse media outlets.[40]

As stated in this Council of Europe Recommendation, media ownership rules are concerned with controls over influence and determining the number of market players. Achieving these objectives will involve the operation of both an effective licensing regime, discussed at section 2.3 above, and a competition law regime, discussed at section 2.5 below. This section, however, briefly considers four different aspects of a media ownership regime: the similarities and differences between ownership rules and competition law; the unique role of public sector broadcasters; the different types of influence that require regulation; and concerns over foreign ownership.

In terms of implementing a media ownership policy, jurisdictions may vary as to whether such issues are seen as a concern of government, the executive branch of state, or a regulatory tool to be wielded by the national regulatory authority. Rules in the US, for example, are partly determined by statute,[41] but primarily fall to the Federal Communications Commission (FCC) for determination and review.[42] By contrast, in the UK, while Ofcom has a duty to secure 'the maintenance of a sufficient plurality of providers of different television and radio services',[43] it is simply required to keep the statutory rules under review and report to the Minister on any recommendations for change.[44]

2.4.1 Ownership and competition

While competition law is concerned with market power, rules on media ownership are concerned with the power of mass media. The two overlap and are obviously related,

---

[38] eg in the UK, Ofcom is currently engaged in its Digital Dividend Review, examining the use of the spectrum that will become available from the switch to all digital terrestrial television; the Commission has adopted various decisions harmonizing the use of various frequency bands (see <http://ec.europa. eu/information_society/policy/radio_spectrum/ref_documents/index_en.htm>); while at the ITU World Radiocommunications Conference 2007, broadcasters lost spectrum to the mobile telecommunications sector.

[39] See R (1991) 1, Explanatory Report, para 26.

[40] R (2007) 2, para 2.1.

[41] ie the 'national television ownership limit' prohibits a licensee from having an aggregate reach exceeding 39%.

[42] 47 USC § 303. Although subject to judicial review, eg *Prometheus Radio Project v FCC* 373 F 3d 372 (3d Cir 2004).

[43] Communications Act 2003, s 3(2)(d).

[44] ibid s 391. See Ofcom, 'Review of Media Ownership Rules'.

although the nature of that relationship will vary. For some, facilitating a competitive marketplace is seen as a sufficient tool for achieving media pluralism; a fully competitive market being virtually synonymous with pluralism. For others, external pluralism requires a more interventionist approach to media ownership, a competitive market being neither sufficient nor necessarily always supportive of pluralism. Under US law, for example, the FCC is tasked with keeping under review television ownership rules precisely because such rules may be 'necessary in the public interest *as the result of* competition'.[45] Both policies, however, often deploy similar language, such as using market share as a proxy threshold for triggering regulatory intervention.

From a traditional competition law perspective, sustained market power is viewed as having a detrimental economic impact in a number of ways, including inefficient use of resources, excessive pricing, and consequential consumer harm. Under European law, such market power, or dominance, is defined in the following terms: 'a position of economic strength enjoyed by an undertaking which enables it to prevent effective competition being maintained in the relevant market by giving it the power to behave to an appreciable extent independently of its competitors, customers and ultimately of its consumers.'[46]

Competition regulation, both *ex ante* and *ex post*, is designed to prevent such market power or control it where it exists. Facilitating market entry is seen as playing a critical role in achieving this objective, as new entrants should seek to enter a monopolistic market and compete away the detrimental consequences. However, a market may contain structural constraints that restrict entry and may therefore require ongoing *ex ante* regulatory intervention. In the broadcasting sector, for example, access to scarce spectrum for terrestrial television has historically been a justification for the licensing of broadcasters.[47]

In terms of media pluralism, economic concerns augment a regulatory objective couched in democratic concerns and the media as a 'cultural service'.[48] However, as a consequence of the inevitable overlap, it can be the case that pluralistic claims are used as a disguised form of economic protectionism. Programming quotas in particular, such as those concerning 'European works' in the 'Television without Frontiers' Directive,[49] can be seen as measures to promote pluralism and/or, as protectionism vis-à-vis the US media industry, depending on your viewpoint.

One element of any market power analysis is the criteria used to measure such a position. Traditional competition law operates on a three-stage process: market definition, market analysis, and the imposition of remedies against any undertaking found to exercise market power. Market definition is usually carried out using demand and supply substitutability and the state of potential competition. Certain categories of media content, for example, may be considered to constitute distinct markets, such as

---

[45] 47 USC § 303.
[46] Case 27/76 *United Brands v Commission* [1978] ECR 207.
[47] See further Ch 8 below.
[48] Directive (EC) 07/65 [2007] OJ L332/27.
[49] Directive (EEC) 89/552, art 6.

premium sports events and movies for television.[50] Identifying market power involves a range of considerations, with market share usually being adopted as a proxy.[51] Conversely, assessing media power will generally require a more complex set of measurement criteria. Readership or audience share figures provide an obvious and favoured quantitative basis for making an assessment in the media industry, coupled to any geographical limitations within the market or jurisdiction.[52] However, other factors that may also require consideration would include revenues, the number of licences held, and network capacity.[53]

The ability of an entity to leverage market power from one market into another is obviously pertinent as the media industry continues to converge with the telecommunications and IT sectors. 'Cross-media' ownership rules relate to entities within different sectors of the media industry, eg press and broadcasting. Rules restricting media ownership and 'cross-media' ownership often utilize a market share approach akin to competition law for a pluralistic policy objective. Under the Communications Act 2003, for example, a person is not allowed to hold a Channel 3 licence if he runs a national newspaper, or newspapers, with a national market share of 20 per cent; based on the percentage of the total number of copies of all newspapers sold in the UK over a six-month period.[54] In the US, the FCC's cross-ownership rules utilize the concept of a 'Designated Market Area' (DMA) when assessing media concentrations,[55] although the concept does not reflect a traditional market analysis under competition law but a demarcation employed by the advertising company Nielson Media Research.[56]

In terms of numbers of market players, *ex post* competition law is relatively neutral, being primarily concerned with abuses of dominant position rather than dominant positions *per se*;[57] while merger regulations are designed to pre-empt only those concentrations that would 'significantly impede effective competition'.[58] Media ownership rules, by contrast, necessarily involve some form of statutory, ministerial, or regulatory decision detailing a minimum number of desired entities for a pluralistic market. In the US, for example, the FCC prescribes how many independent 'media voices' must be present within a DMA when a merger is proposed between a TV and radio station or in the newspaper sector.[59] While the Council of Europe does not prescribe any threshold, it is suggested that a 30 per cent audience share limit is appropriate within a particular media sector and 10 per cent of the market for total media

---

[50] See Ofcom Pay-TV Consultation, para 1.25.

[51] See Commission guidelines on market analysis and the assessment of significant market power under the Community regulatory framework for electronic communications networks and services [2002] OJ C165/6.

[52] See R (1999) 1, Explanatory Memorandum, para 6.

[53] See R (2007) 2, para 2.3.

[54] eg Communications Act 2003, Sch 14, para 1.

[55] Code of Federal Regulations, Title 47, section 73.3555, which took effect on 15 July 2008.

[56] ibid at section 73.3555(b). A similar scheme is used for radio broadcasting, ie Aribtron.

[57] EC Treaty, Art 82.

[58] Council Regulation (EC) 139/2004, on the control of concentrations between undertakings (the EC Merger Regulations) [2008] OJ L24/1.

[59] Code of Federal Regulations, Title 47, section 73.3555, applicable from 15 July 2008.

ownership, which should ensure at least four providers in the radio, TV, and press sectors and at least ten different providers in the market as a whole.[60] However, the complex nature of the relationship between external and internal pluralism means that neither is the guarantor of the other and therefore a too rigid maintenance and reliance on maintaining a certain number of providers may fail to promote or sustain effective pluralism.

The third component of a competition law process is the imposition of one or more remedies upon the entity(ies). Similar measures will be used to curb media power, from denying the grant of a licence to broadcast, a structural remedy, to the obtaining of guarantees concerning the independence of the editorial process, a behavioural undertaking. As with competition law, however, the policing and enforcement of structural remedies will generally be more practicable than behavioural remedies, resulting in a bias against the latter approach.

2.4.2 Public sector broadcasting

Although matters of external and internal pluralism can be treated separately, they are obviously intimately related, no more so than under the system of public sector broadcasting (PSB). As stated in the Amsterdam protocol, 'the system of public broadcasting in the Member States is directly related to the democratic, social and cultural needs of each society and to the need to preserve media pluralism'.[61] However, the extent to which that PSB system is characterized by the funding of broadcast entities (external pluralism) and/or, certain types of content (internal pluralism), will vary between and within Member States over time, particularly in the face of a rapidly evolving sector.[62] To date, however, PSB systems within Europe continue to be embodied in one or more specific entities and, as such, comprise an important aspect of our media ownership regime.

In stark comparison with the newspaper industry, the radio and TV broadcasting market is unique in having the continued presence in most jurisdictions of entities in some form of public ownership, competing with private companies for audiences; although this itself represents a radical shift from the historic position of exclusive state monopolies. While the reasons for this liberalization of the broadcasting market over the past thirty years are varied, it has been expressly recognized by the European Court of Human Rights (ECtHR) that the sole existence of state monopolies is an obstacle to plurality and free expression: 'Of all the means of ensuring that these values are respected, a public monopoly is the one which imposes the greatest restrictions on the freedom of expression . . . The far-reaching character of such restrictions means that they can only be justified where they correspond to a pressing need.'[63]

---

[60] R (1999) 1, Explanatory Report, para 7.
[61] Protocol on the system of public broadcasting in the Member States, annexed to the Treaty of Amsterdam [1997] OJ C340.
[62] See generally T Gardam and D Levy, 'The Price of Plurality: Choice Diversity and Broadcasting Institutions in the Digital Age', Reuters Institute for the Study of Journalism, 2008.
[63] *Informationsverein Lentia v Austria* (1994) 17 EHRR 93, para 39.

The financing of the PSB system can obviously impact on competition and plurality in a number of ways. In terms of the acquisition and sale of programming rights, for example, a PSB may, on the one hand, be able to outbid commercial broadcasters when obtaining rights to broadcast premium content, such as Premiership football, while at the same time financing and selling its in-house productions at non-market rates. The mixed nature of broadcast markets, with state-owned or state-funded entities competing with wholly private entities, may significantly distort market economics. The Channel 3 licensee, ITV, for example, primarily competes in the terrestrial television sector with the BBC; although the BBC can rely on licence fees for its core funding, while ITV must primarily look to advertising revenues, 'a single, highly cyclical, revenue source',[64] where it is competing with new online entrants, such as Google, who recently surpassed ITV in terms of UK revenues,[65] while also being subject to regulatory controls over the price it may charge advertisers.[66]

Conversely, it is widely accepted that the private sector public sector broadcasters in the UK, particularly ITV and Channel 4, are likely to experience a funding shortfall over the coming years that will mean they may struggle to sustain current levels of PSB. This has led the government, Ofcom, and others to consider alternative solutions, including a merger of Channels 4 and 5; a deal between Channel 4 and BBC Worldwide, the commercial arm of the BBC;[67] or the granting of franchises that were previously auctioned off.[68] Although the options are still under consideration, the government has expressed a desire to establish a public sector broadcaster capable of 'providing competition for quality to the BBC'.[69] Such a solution would clearly have a significant impact on market structure, essentially reducing the number of players in order to safeguard the PSB system, which in turn supports content pluralism.

State-owned or state-funded enterprises are subject to European competition law,[70] although they may be protected from the full application of the rules to the extent that they are providing 'services of general economic interest',[71] which includes PSB.[72] Indeed, the European Court of Justice has held that such protection can mean completely removing an entity from competition jurisdiction through the granting of an

---

[64] Stated in the BSkyB response to the 'Digital Britain Review—Interim Report' (March 2009) 3.

[65] Reported in 'Google shows ITV a vision of the future' *The Times*, 30 October 2007.

[66] Under the Contract Rights Renewal (CRR) scheme; a remedy imposed by the Competition Commission in 2003, when it approved the merger of Carlton and Granada to form ITV plc, to address concerns about ITV's market power. See further Ch 13 below.

[67] See eg Mark Thompson, Director-General of the BBC, 'Broadcasting must restructure to survive' *Financial Times,* 11 January 2009.

[68] Ofcom's Second Public Service Broadcasting Review, 'Putting Viewers First' (21 January 2009).

[69] DCMS and BERR, *Digital Britain: The Interim Report* (Cm 7548, 29 January 2009) (hereinafter 'Carter Report') Action 16.

[70] Case 41/83 *Re British Telecommunications: Italy v Commission* [1985] 2 CMLR 368 and Case 311/84 *Centre Belge d'Etudes de Marché-Télé-Marketing v Compagnie Luxembourgeoise de Telediffusion SA and Information Publicite Benelux SA* [1986] 2 CMLR 558.

[71] EC Treaty, art 86(2).

[72] Communication 'on the application of state aid rules to public service broadcasting' [2001] OJ C320/5 (hereinafter 'PSB Communication') para 9, n 3.

exclusive right to broadcast.[73] The funding of the BBC News 24 channel from the licence fee, for example, was considered by the Commission to be a legitimate means of facilitating the provision of 'services of general economic interest', in response to a complaint from BSkyB, producers of Sky News.[74] However, to the extent that the presence of publicly-owned media entities or private media entities receiving public financing in the market may skew the playing field to the detriment of the private sector, media pluralism may be compromised with the spectre of the state being dominant.

While the PSB system is entity-based, those entities are obliged to meet a public service remit in respect of the programmes they broadcast; promoting content pluralism. In the UK, for example, Channels 3 and 5 are required to provide 'a range of high quality and diverse programming'; while Channel 4's remit is more detailed, including the need to appeal 'to the tastes and interests of a culturally diverse society'.[75] Such remits are generally extremely high-level in nature, lacking regulatory precision, which offers public sector broadcasters substantial flexibility and latitude in meeting their obligations. While such generalities can be criticized as being effectively meaningless, as well as largely overlapping the programming practices of mainstream commercial broadcasters, more detailed criteria, laid down in statute or by regulators, could be perceived as state interference in the editorial independence of broadcasters.[76]

A current issue in the debate over the future of PSB is the means and legitimacy of extending its scope to cover the variety of platforms used by viewers to access broadcast content, from digital terrestrial television to IPTV and mobile services, as well as the evolving modes of consumption, from scheduled programming to on-demand catalogues.[77] The European Commission has stated, for example, that it does not consider 'advertising, e-commerce, teleshopping, sponsorship or merchandising' to form part of a public service remit,[78] although some pay services, such as premium rate telephone voting, may be acceptable.

2.4.3 Ownership, influence, and control

If there is to be democratic discourse, it is important who controls the forum. A fairly universal belief exists in the link between ownership of media and the social narrative of their content.[79]

When considering questions of media ownership, the words 'influence' and 'control' are often used in overlapping but different senses in respect of pluralism. In terms of

---

[73] Case 155/73 *Sacchi* [1974] ECR 409.
[74] State aid N88/98, SG(99) D/10201, 14 December 1999.
[75] Communications Act 2003, s 265.
[76] See the CFI's comments in *TV 2/Danmark A/S and ors v Commission* Judgment of 22 October 2008, paras 117–123.
[77] These changes have also required to be addressed as a matter of general broadcast regulation; see further Ch 8 below.
[78] Commission revised draft communication for consultation (November 2008) para 47.
[79] M Price, *Television, The Public Sphere, and National Identity* (Clarendon Press, 1996) 196.

external pluralism, it is possible to exercise control over a commercial entity without legally owning the entity; such 'corporate control' represents a concern for regulators and is directly addressed in ownership rules. In terms of internal pluralism, influence and control is used in respect of two distinct relationships: that between the owner of a media enterprise and the person responsible for the content output of that enterprise, generally referred to as 'editorial control'; and that between government and the media service provider, a question of political influence.

In terms of corporate control, as stated under UK competition law: 'A person or group of persons able, directly or indirectly, to control or materially to influence the policy of a body corporate, or the policy of any person in carrying on an enterprise but without having a controlling interest in that body corporate or in that enterprise, may . . . be treated as having control of it.'[80]

UK law therefore distinguishes between three levels of corporate control: 'material influence', '*de facto* control', and 'legal control'.[81] A material influence can exist even where an entity has no equity interest in the target, but has commercial or financial agreements on which the target is dependent.[82] The nature of such influence was recently considered by the Competition Commission in its report on the acquisition by BSkyB of a 17.9 per cent shareholding in ITV.[83] The Commission found that BSkyB would be able to block special resolutions proposed by ITV's management, which would in turn limit the latter's strategic options, as well as being able to influence other shareholders as the largest single shareholder.[84] In addition, Ofcom has the power, under certain circumstances, to determine that a person owning less than 50 per cent of the share capital in a company is deemed to control that company.[85]

In terms of private ownership, there is a concern that the concentration of media entities in the hands of a few private companies and persons may have an adverse and invidious impact on a nation's democratic life: 'power without responsibility', in the words of Stanley Baldwin.[86] Concerns with the ability of 'press barons' and 'media moguls' to influence, and potentially subvert, a nation's political and cultural life has been an ongoing issue in media law: from the Lords Beaverbrook, Northcliffe, and Rothermere in the 1920s and 1930s; to Orson Welles' film *Citizen Kane* (1941), based on the life of the US newspaper magnate William Randolph Hearst; and to the current controversies that surround Rupert Murdoch and Silvio Berlusconi.

Through such powerful figures, the 'media' become both an outlet and channel for the expression of information and ideas that constitute the democratic process, and a

---

[80] Enterprise Act 2002, s 26(3).
[81] OFT, 'Mergers—Substantive assessment guidance' (May 2003) para 2.9.
[82] ibid para 2.10.
[83] See n 3 above.
[84] ibid para 11.
[85] Communications Act 2003, s 357(2).
[86] The complete phrase, 'power without responsibility—the prerogative of the harlot throughout the ages' was borrowed by the then leader of the Conservative Party from his cousin Rudyard Kipling, during an attack on Lord Beaverbrook's *Daily Express* in 1931.

participant itself.[87] The media's role as participant is sometimes referred to as the 'Fourth Estate'.[88] To try to limit such influence, pluralistic concerns tend to favour an environment where ownership and editorial control are kept separate.[89] To date, these latter matters have tended to be left to self-regulation in the UK; although editorial independence may comprise an undertaking given by an entity when seeking approval of a media merger or acquisition.[90]

Restricting the ability of governments and politicians to exercise undue influence and control over media outlets and service providers is a central theme within media law,[91] as in other areas of activity. The establishment of an 'independent' sectoral regulatory authority, such as Ofcom, is designed, in large part, to minimize such influences; maintained by clear statutory demarcations between those areas in which governments can intervene and those that are left to the regulator.

2.4.4 Foreign ownership

Allied to concerns about media concentration are rules designed to prevent or limit foreign ownership of domestic media enterprises. In the US, for example, a broadcast licence may not be granted to an alien or a 'foreign corporation'.[92] Within the European Union, Community rules prevent restrictions on intra-EU investments, although concerns have been expressed that this is having an adverse impact on domestic pluralism, particularly within central and eastern EU Member States.[93]

Rules governing the liberalization of trade restrictions on the cross-border supply of media services are also being addressed within a broader trade liberalization agenda under the World Trade Organisation and the multilateral negotiations to extend the applicability of the General Agreement on Trade in Services.[94] However, the current round of negotiations, formally commenced at Doha in November 2001, has made little progress in terms of substantial new commitments to liberalize the 'audiovisual' sector.

Foreign investment in domestic media entities can raise a range of concerns and, similar to quotas, rules restricting such investment may be viewed variously as legitimate mechanisms to protect domestic culture, and therefore part of a pluralism agenda; a national security issue; or as non-tariff trade barriers preventing market entry and a fully competitive marketplace.

---

[87] Hitchens, (n 35 above) 32.
[88] See eg J Lloyd, 'The fourth estate's coup d'etat' *Observer*, 13 June 2004.
[89] R (1999) 1, Explanatory Report, para 32 and Commission 2007, para 2.1.
[90] See MMC Report, HC 378, 1980–81, para 8.53 (29 June 1981) and further 2.5.1 below.
[91] See Council of Europe Recommendation (2000) 23 'on the independence and functions of regulatory authorities for the broadcasting sector', adopted 20 December 2000.
[92] 47 USC § 310 'Licence ownership restrictions'.
[93] See Council of Europe, Transnational media concentration in Europe (Strasbourg, 2004).
[94] See generally <http://www.wto.org/english/tratop_e/serv_e/audiovisual_e/audiovisual_e.htm>.

2.5 COMPETITION LAW

An *ex post* competition law regime is generally concerned with four types of behaviour: anti-competitive agreements and concerted practices between market participants; abuses of dominant position; anti-competitive mergers or acquisitions; and unlawful state aids given to market participants. Such behaviours may occur within a distinct media market segment—often vertically within the supply chain, such as a deal between a content producer and broadcaster; or horizontally across different media markets, as arises in cross-media ownership deals, or in a non-media sector that has an indirect impact on a sector of the media, at the wholesale or retail level.

Any overview of the competitive state of a sector requires an understanding of the different elements that comprise the supply chain of the sector. In television broadcasting, for example, 'content origination' can be seen as being at the top of the supply chain, with control over the intellectual property (IP) rights embodied in such content being the primary mechanism for controlling market entry.[95] The exercise of such IP rights by rights-holders may be subject to regulatory intervention on competition law grounds, which effectively require the grant of usage rights in respect of certain content in order to facilitate a competitive marketplace.[96] In terms of rights to broadcast football, for example, both UEFA[97] and the Premier League[98] were required by the Competition Directorate-General of the European Commission to redesign the way in which they jointly sold rights, prohibiting exclusive deals with a single broadcaster, implementing a competitive bidding process, limiting the duration of the deals, and unbundling the rights into several packages.[99]

The next level of the broadcast supply chain is channel provision, the aggregation of programme content into bundles or packages of channels. The deals done to secure certain content may give rise to competition concerns beyond the licensing of IP rights. Under the Broadcasting Act 1990,[100] for example, an agreement between the Channel 3 licensees for the appointment of a 'news provider' may be declared as being either acceptable or anti-competitive. If the latter, the declaration must state that any restrictive provisions are necessary to achieve the conditions imposed upon Channel 3 licensees in respect of the provision of nationwide news programmes capable of competing effectively with other such programming, ie the BBC, an element of an internal pluralism policy.[101]

---

[95] See further Ch 6 below.

[96] eg *RTE and Independent Television Publications Ltd v Commission* [1995] 4 CMLR 718.

[97] See Commission press release, 'Commission clears UEFA's new policy regarding the sale of the media rights to the Champions League', IP/03/1105, 24 July 2003.

[98] See Commission press release, 'Commission reaches provisional agreement with FA Premier League and BSkyB over football rights', IP/03/1748, 16 December 2003.

[99] See further Ch 6 below.

[100] Broadcasting Act 1990, s 194A.

[101] Communications Act 2003, s 280.

A market distinction can be made between free,[102] pay-per-view, and subscription-based programme services, the latter often being tiered. These channels are then distributed across different platforms—terrestrial, cable, satellite, internet, and mobile—although each platform is not necessarily substitutable for another. In the UK, the provision of broadcast transmission services for the terrestrial platform is a further distinct link in the supply chain, which gave rise to its own competition concerns when the two dominant service providers merged during 2008.[103] At the retail end of the supply chain, users require terminal equipment in order to receive broadcasts, from satellite dishes to televisions and set-top boxes, and such devices provide a potential market bottleneck that may require regulatory intervention.[104]

In terms of mergers and acquisitions, regulators have intervened in a number of cases to prevent what were seen as deals that would have had an anti-competitive impact. At an EU level, for example, the Commission blocked a proposed joint venture to supply digital pay-TV services under the name MSG Media Service, which would have involved the leading German media group, Bertelsmann; the incumbent telecommunications company, Deutsche Telekom; and a leading supplier of films and television programmes, part of the Kirch group.[105] The Commission held that the consortium would have resulted in a strengthening of existing dominant positions and a lessening of competition. In the UK, in 2003, the Competition Commission held that the acquisition of two regional radio stations by a leading commercial national radio station, GWR, was against the public interest as it risked reducing competition in the market for local advertising services in particular geographical areas.[106] Conversely, in 2008, the Competition Commission approved, subject to various undertakings, the merger of the two leading providers of transmission services for terrestrial television and radio broadcasters.[107] This latter case is a good example of a case involving parties ostensibly outside the 'media' sector, but whose transaction had significant implications for UK broadcasters.[108]

Media enterprises may obviously be subject to multiple competition law regimes, depending on the scale of the business activity, but the primary governing statutes in the UK are the Competition Act 1998 and the Enterprise Act 2002. UK-based activity

---

[102] In the UK, such 'free' at the point of delivery services are either funded through a licence regime or advertising revenues.

[103] Macquarie UK Broadcast Ventures Ltd and National Grid Wireless Group. The Competition Commission initially found against the acquisition, but subsequently approved it after various undertakings were made by the parties.

[104] See section 2.5.3 below.

[105] Commission Decision of 9 November 1994 relating to a proceeding pursuant to Council Regulation (EEC) 4064/89 (IV/M.469 - MSG Media Service) [1994] OJ L364/1.

[106] Competition Commission, 'Scottish Radio Holdings plc and GWR Group plc and Galaxy Radio Wales and the West Limited: A report on the merger situation' (2003).

[107] See Competition Commission, 'Macquarie UK Broadcast Ventures Ltd./National Grid Wireless Group', Final Report (11 March 2008) and Notice of acceptance of final Undertakings pursuant to section 82 of and Schedule 10 to the Enterprise Act 2002 (1 September 2008).

[108] See eg the third party submissions at <http://www.competition-commission.org.uk/inquiries/ref2007/macquarie/third_party_submissions.htm>.

may also be subject to EU competition law to the extent that it may 'affect trade between Member States'[109] or has a 'Community dimension'.[110] It is beyond the scope of this chapter to review UK and EU competition law, except to the extent that special rules are applicable to activities within the media sector and/or, that non-competition issues, specifically media pluralism, constitute an explicit additional dimension to the operation of competition law rules.

2.5.1 The UK media merger regime

Until 2003, the UK had two distinct merger regimes: general competition law controls over mergers and a special regime for newspapers. Under this special regime, a transfer of a newspaper or its assets required the prior consent of the Secretary of State where the newspapers of the purchasing proprietor had an average paid for circulation of half a million copies or more.[111] Failure to obtain such consent was an offence.[112] The two regimes have since been merged into one under the Enterprise Act 2002, with adaptations to the general regime to reflect the unique plurality concerns raised in the media sector.

Under the general merger regime, the government has been removed from the vast majority of transactions, leaving the decision-making to the relevant competition authorities, ie the Office of Fair Trading (OFT) and the Office of Communications (Ofcom) in the case of media-related deals. A recent example is a proposed joint venture, known as 'Project Kangaroo', between the BBC, Channel 4, and ITV to provide video-on-demand services. The OFT, exercising its powers under the Enterprise Act 2002, referred the deal to the Competition Commission for investigation and report (section 33(1)). The Commission found that the proposed joint venture would result in a 'substantial lessening of competition' in the supply of video-on-demand content at the wholesale and retail levels in the UK, as well as in the online UK advertising market and the market for content acquisition in the UK.[113] The Commission considered whether any remedial action could satisfactorily address the competition concerns, but concluded that prohibiting the joint venture was the only suitable remedy.[114]

While the general regime resides with the competition authorities, the Secretary of State does have the power to intervene in a 'relevant merger situation' (section 23(1) of the 2002 Act) that he considers raises public interest considerations (section 45). Such considerations are specified in the Enterprise Act 2002 and were initially limited to national security concerns; although, media mergers and the stability of the UK

---

[109] See Council Regulation (EC) 1/2003 on the implementation of the rules on competition laid down in Articles 81 and 82 of the Treaty ([2003] OJ L1/1) art 3(1).
[110] EC Merger Regulations (n 58 above) Art 1.
[111] Fair Trading Act 1973, ss 57–62. These provisions largely replicated provisions first introduced in the Monopolies and Mergers Act 1965.
[112] ibid s 62.
[113] Competition Commission, 'Summary of Provisional Findings' (3 December 2008).
[114] Competition Commission, 'Final Report' (4 February 2009).

financial system have subsequently been included (section 58).[115] In respect of media mergers, three different concerns are elaborated:

(2A) The need for—
    (a) accurate presentation of news; and
    (b) free expression of opinion;
in newspapers is specified in this section.

(2B) The need for, to the extent that it is reasonable and practicable, a sufficient plurality of views in newspapers in each market for newspapers in the United Kingdom or a part of the United Kingdom is specified in this section.

(2C) The following are specified in this section—
    (a) the need, in relation to every different audience in the United Kingdom or in a particular area or locality of the United Kingdom, for there to be a sufficient plurality of persons with control of the media enterprises serving that audience;

    (b) the need for the availability throughout the United Kingdom of a wide range of broadcasting which (taken as a whole) is both of high quality and calculated to appeal to a wide variety of tastes and interests; and

    (c) the need for persons carrying on media enterprises, and for those with control of such enterprises, to have a genuine commitment to the attainment in relation to broadcasting of the standards objectives set out in section 319 of the Communications Act 2003. (section 58 (2A)–(2C))

The first subsection is a restatement of the considerations detailed under the previous Fair Trading Act regime[116] and focuses on 'internal pluralism' concerns in respect of 'newspapers'.[117] Under the previous regime, such editorial issues were relevant in five adverse decisions made by the Competition Commission.[118] When Lonrho purchased *The Observer* in 1981, for example, the Monopolies and Mergers Commision (MMC) recommended that the Secretary of State's consent be subject to a number of conditions designed to safeguard *The Observer*'s editorial independence.[119] Subsequently, in 1990, David Sullivan's acquisition of a controlling interest in the *Bristol Evening Post* was held likely to harm the section 58(2A) objectives, as well as the paper's standing in the community and its circulation.[120]

Section 58(2B) is also limited to newspapers, but addresses structural considerations to ensure 'external pluralism'; shifting from the need for a variety of views to the need

[115] The media mergers provisions were inserted into the Enterprise Act 2002, s 58 by the Communications Act 2003, s 375; while the UK financial system was inserted by SI 2008/2645, in response to the proposed merger between Lloyds TSB Group plc and HBOS plc.

[116] Fair Trading Act 1973, s 59(3).

[117] 'Newspaper' means 'a daily, Sunday or local (other than daily or Sunday) newspaper circulating wholly or mainly in the United Kingdom or in a part of the United Kingdom' (Enterprise Act 2002, s 44(10)).

[118] BERR, Guidance on the operation of the public interest merger provisions relating to newspaper and other media mergers (May 2004) para 5.4.

[119] MMC Report, HC 378, 1980–81, para 8.53 (29 June 1981).

[120] MMC Report (Cm 1083, 1990).

for 'a variety of outlets and publications in which they can be expressed'.[121] Such considerations arose in two cases under the Fair Trading Act regime in respect of the proposed merger of Century Newspapers/TRN and Trinity plc/Mirror Group plc.[122] Both were seen as resulting in the loss of distinctive Unionist opinion within Northern Ireland's newspapers. While in the MMC's adverse decision in DMGT/TBF,[123] a clear distinction was made between the anti-competitive implications of the proposed acquisition and the impact that the concentration would have on free and diverse expression in the press.

Section 58(2C) of the Enterprise Act 2002 covers any media enterprise that 'consists in or involves broadcasting' (section 58A(a)), although the term extends to newspapers if at least one of the entities involved in the proposed merger is a broadcaster, ie it is a cross-media merger. Section 58(a) addresses external pluralism, while (b) and (c) address pluralism of content.

In making an intervention and determining the applicability of any of these 'public interest considerations', the Secretary of State shall be assisted and advised by Ofcom (section 44A of the 2002 Act).[124] The Secretary of State can then decide whether to refer the merger to the Competition Commission for consideration on the grounds that the merger will, or is expected to, result in a 'substantial lessening of competition' (SLC) and a relevant public interest consideration is engaged (section 45(2)). During the course of its deliberations, the Commission has an obligation to consult with the public (section 104A), which is not the case for other types of merger. The Commission also has a specialist newspaper panel, from which the Commission Chairman must nominate one or more members when a group is established to consider a 'newspaper merger reference'.[125] When reporting, the Commission makes recommendations to the Secretary of State about any actions that he should take for the purpose of 'remedying, mitigating or preventing' any of the identified adverse effects (section 47(7)).

In addition, the Enterprise Act 2002 also details a similar but separate procedure for so-called 'special public interest cases' (sections 62 to 66) and cases where there is a need to protect 'legitimate interests' under the EU Merger Regulations (sections 67 to 68). In the case of the former, the Communications Act 2003 amended the original provisions to specifically provide for three media-related scenarios where the Secretary of State can intervene and serve a 'special intervention notice' for the merger to be scrutinized on public interest considerations alone, ie competition considerations would not be relevant. The first is where the criteria for a relevant merger situation have not been met in respect of the turnover threshold or share of supply criteria (section 59(3B)),[126] enabling intervention in small-scale media mergers, such as

---

[121] Communications Act 2002, Explanatory Note, para 800.
[122] MMC Report (Cm 677, 1989) and MMC Report (Cm 4393, 1999).
[123] MMC Report (Cm 2693, 1994).
[124] Advice and assistance may also be sought from the OFT (s 44). See Ofcom guidance for the public interest test for media mergers (May 2004).
[125] Competition Act 1998, Sch 7, para 1.
[126] The criteria being where turnover exceeds £70m (Enterprise Act 2002, s 23(1)(b)) and where at least one-quarter of the supply of services is provided by one person (s 23(2)(b) and (4)).

local newspapers. The second concerns a derogation from the share of supply criteria in respect of newspapers, to the extent that one of the parties has at least a 25 per cent share of the UK market, or a substantial part, regardless of the impact of the merger (section 59(3C)). The third scenario is similar to the second, but concerns the provision of broadcasting (section 59(3D). For these latter situations, the basis upon which the 'share of supply' is determined may utilize a range of criteria, such as circulation, capacity, numbers of viewers or listeners, or advertising revenues (section 59A).[127]

In respect of mergers that have a Community dimension, as defined under the EC Merger Regulations,[128] the Secretary of State may issue a 'European intervention notice' asking the OFT to examine whether any public interest considerations are present that would require measures to protect 'legitimate interests' under the EC Merger Regulation, which includes the 'plurality of media'.[129]

On enforcement, the Enterprise Act 2002 contains a distinct regime for public interest and special public interest cases (section 85 and Schedule 7), permitting the Secretary of State to accept undertakings to prevent pre-emptive actions (Schedule 7, paragraphs 1 to 2) or undertakings that remove the need to make a reference to the Competition Commission (Schedule 7, paragraphs 3 to 6). In addition, under the general remedies that may be imposed on the parties, specifically the issuance of an enforcement order (section 86), distinct remedies are detailed that may be required in cases involving a newspaper enterprise, including 'attaching conditions to the operation of a newspaper' (Schedule 8, paragraph 20A(4)(c)), which would include the implementation of procedures to ensure editorial independence. These tailored remedies reflect the experience of cases decided under the previous Fair Trading Act regime.[130]

Both the government and Ofcom have published guidance on the application of the public interest test in media mergers.[131] The government's guidance lists factors that it considers may be relevant to public interest considerations in respect of newspaper mergers, including the volume of adverse third party comments and mergers occurring within the same or overlapping markets.[132]

The first case of an anti-competitive acquisition considered under the media merger control rules has been the ongoing case against BSkyB's acquisition of a 17.9 per cent shareholding in ITV. The Secretary of State referred the case to the Competition Commission, which reported back in December 2007.[133] The Commission concluded that the acquisition would result in an SLC in the 'all-TV market' through BSkyB's ability to influence the strategic direction of ITV. However, in respect of the 'Pay-TV market', the market for television advertising, and the provision of wholesale national

---

[127] See also BERR Guidance (n 118 above) para 3.10.
[128] n 58 above.
[129] ibid art 21(4).
[130] Communications Act 2003, Explanatory Note, para 845.
[131] See nn 118 and 124 above respectively. The Secretary of State's guidance is published under the Enterprise Act 2002, s 106A.
[132] BERR Guidance (n 118 above) paras 6.5–6.10.
[133] n 3 above.

news provision, no SLC would result.[134] In respect of media plurality, however, the Commission held that the acquisition would not materially impact on 'the sufficiency of plurality of persons with control of media enterprises servicing audiences for news'.[135] The remedies recommended by the Commission were to require BSkyB to reduce its shareholding from 17.9 per cent to below 7.5 per cent, coupled with certain behavioural undertakings, including not disposing of the shares to an associated person, not seeking or accepting representation on the Board of ITV, and not reacquiring shares in ITV.[136] These recommendations were accepted in full by the Secretary of State.[137]

BSkyB subsequently appealed the Competition Commission's findings to the Competition Appeal Tribunal (CAT). In addition, one of BSkyB's major competitors, Virgin Media, also asked for a review of the Commission's findings regarding its finding on the plurality considerations.[138] BSkyB's appeal was dismissed,[139] although at the time of writing the Court of Appeal has subsequently given permission to BSkyB to appeal. In respect of Virgin Media's claims, however, the CAT upheld the complaint and quashed aspects of the Competition Commission's report and decision that related to the plurality considerations at section 58(2C)(a). The CAT held that the Competition Commission had misdirected itself as to interpretation of the relevant provisions and had therefore taken into account irrelevant considerations. In particular, the Commission had held that BSkyB and ITV were not under the control of one person for the purposes of the plurality assessment and had given consideration to 'internal plurality' factors which were not relevant to the assessment.[140] However, after further hearings, the CAT concluded that the Commission's misdirection did not affect the existing remedy and therefore the original decision would not be remitted to the Commission or the Secretary of State.[141]

The government has recently announced its intention to ask the OFT and Ofcom to review the current merger regime, particularly as it applies to the local and regional media sector.[142] The review is partly in response to the economic downturn and the resultant shrinking advertising revenues being experienced by media entities; the recognition that these entities need to transform themselves for an online digital environment; and to the increasing competitive threat from international media sources.[143] A report from a House of Lords Committee has called for a review of the

---

[134] ibid paras 19–28. However, Ofcom is currently engaged in a separate investigation into the competitive state of the UK's pay-TV market.

[135] ibid para 41.

[136] ibid para 49.

[137] BERR News Release, 'Final decision on BSkyB's stake in ITV', 2008/020 (29 January 2008).

[138] Any person aggrieved by a decision under Part 3 has the right to apply to the CAT for a review (Enterprise Act 2002, s 120).

[139] [2008] CAT 25.

[140] ibid para 266.

[141] [2008] CAT 32.

[142] Carter Report (n 69 above) 51–2.

[143] ibid.

'public interest test' for media mergers, to include matters such as the likely impact of a merger on newsgathering and investigative journalism.[144] The Committee also recommended that Ofcom be granted the power to issue public interest intervention notices (at paragraph 261), as well as stating the need for a clear separation between the investigation of a media merger by Ofcom, in respect of the public interest issues, and the Competition Commission, in respect of the competition issues (at paragraph 271). The government has rejected these recommendations; although it has accepted the need to review local cross-media rules.[145]

2.5.2 State aids

In terms of competition, the public financing of any media undertaking, whether in the form of direct subsidies or indirect tax relief, raises issues as to whether such benefits constitute a form of unlawful state aid or subsidy. Under EU law, state aids are generally considered to be incompatible with the common market to the extent that they distort competition and affect trade within the common market.[146] However, one area where the Treaty considers that state aid 'may be' compatible, is for the 'promotion of culture and heritage conservation', which is pertinent to the media sector (Article 87(3)(d)). Aid may also be legitimated under the derogation in Article 86(2), if it can be shown that the application of Community competition law would obstruct the discharge of a 'service of general economic interest'. Within the European Union, state aid concerns have primarily arisen in respect of public service broadcasting and the film industry, which has resulted in the European Commission issuing communications detailing its views on the lawfulness of state financing in both sectors.[147]

The financing of public sector broadcasting clearly falls within the concept of state aid and therefore EU law has had to address the potential conflict between these objectives.[148] Such reconciliation is achieved in a number of ways. First, state aids that precede the coming into force of the Treaty obligations, 'systems of aid existing in those states',[149] are not subject to the Article 87 prohibition, which would include the BBC's licensing fee arrangement.[150] Secondly, the European Court of Justice in the *Altmark* case[151] has defined certain conditions when public service compensation is not

---

[144] Lords 2008 (n 6 above) para 243.

[145] DCMS, Government Response to the Report of the House of Lords Select Committee on Communications on the Ownership of the News (Cm 7486, October 2008).

[146] EC Treaty, Art 87(1).

[147] PSB Communication (n 72 above) and Communication 'on certain legal aspects relating to cinematographic and other audiovisual works, [2002] OJ C43/6 (hereinafter 'Film Communication').

[148] See generally H Hobbelen, V Harris and I Dominguez, 'The increasing importance of EC state aid rules in the communications and media sectors' (2007) 28(2) European Competition Law Review 101.

[149] EC Treaty Art 88(1). See also Council Regulation (EC) 659/1999 ([1999] OJ L83/1) Art 1(b)(i).

[150] See State aid N631/01, C(2002)1886fin, 22.5.2002, concerning the UK Government's approval for the BBC to offer 9 new digital services, which it considered to be part of existing public service remit rather than an alteration of existing aid.

[151] *Altmark Trans GmbH and anor v Nahverkehrsgesellschaft Altmark GmbH* [2003] 3 CMLR 12.

considered to constitute a 'state aid' within the meaning of Article 87. These cumulative conditions are that the entity has clearly defined public service obligations to discharge; the compensation is calculated in an objective and transparent manner; the compensation appropriately reflects the net cost of provision; and the cost analysis reflects that of a 'typical undertaking, well run'.[152] Where these conditions are not met, the European Commission may order the recovery of any sums not considered appropriate.[153] The third approach is the issuance by the Commission of guidance about the conditions under which state aid to public service broadcasters will be considered acceptable.[154]

In addition to the substantive criteria that must be met when funding the provision of public broadcast services, the European Commission also recognizes the need for procedural safeguards. These include the need for an independent regulator, independent both in respect of the market players, and government in its role as funder. The regulator should supervise the public service regime and intervene when necessary to prevent inappropriate state aid. The manner in which such independent regulation is achieved is inevitably left to the Member State concerned. In the UK, Ofcom and the BBC Trust are entrusted with this role. In November 2008, for example, the BBC Trust rejected a proposal from the Corporation to offer online local news services. It held that the proposal, costing in the region of £68 million, would not sufficiently improve public services, while at the same time having a negative impact on the commercial media sector.[155]

The Commission's Film Communication encompasses both film and TV programme production, therefore impacting on content pluralism as well as the broader cultural objectives recognized under Article 87, the so-called 'cultural derogation'. The quota provisions for 'European' and 'independent' works under the Television without Frontiers Directive (TWF Directive) are also an element in achieving these objectives.[156] The Commission has laid down four specific criteria by which state funding schemes supporting film and TV production are evaluated as falling under the 'cultural derogation':

- The aid must be directed to a 'cultural product', which should be verifiable according to national criteria. In the UK, for example, a 'Cultural Test' has been developed that is applicable to films, documentaries, and animations.[157]

- Only 80 per cent of the production costs can be directed by the terms of the funding scheme to be spent in the territory of the Member State.

---

[152] ibid para 13.

[153] See *TV 2/Danmark A/S & ors v Commission* Judgment of the Court of First Instance, 22 October 2008, where the Commission decision was annulled for inadequate reasoning.

[154] PSB Communication (n 72 above). Draft 2008 Communication (see n 78 above); see Commission Press Release IP/08/1626.

[155] BBC Trust press release, 'BBC Trust rejects local video proposals', 21 November 2008.

[156] See further section 12.3.1 below.

[157] Films Act 1985, Sch 1, paras 4B–4D. The test is based around four elements: (a) cultural content (eg set in the UK); (b) cultural contribution (eg representation of British heritage); (c) cultural hubs (eg use of UK creative industries); and (d) cultural practitioners (eg UK director or actors).

• Aid should be limited to 50 per cent of the production budget, except in respect of 'difficult and low budget' films.

• Aid supplements should not be directed at specific film-making activities, such as post-production, since this may result in unnecessary market distortions.[158]

The Commission has examined the validity and given approval for three UK schemes:[159] a film tax incentive scheme for film productions;[160] funding support for digital projection facilities in a network of cinemas to encourage the showing of 'specialised' films that involve innovative techniques or challenging subject matter;[161] and the establishment of a regional investment fund for SMEs in the film and media sector in the East Midlands region.[162]

In other European countries, the newspaper industry has also received state financial support over the years. In the Netherlands, for example, the state has given financial support to the newspaper industry for investments in IT; the retention of senior journalists, and a foundation for investigative journalism.[163] In January 2009, the French government announced a package of €600 million emergency aid for the French newspaper industry, in addition to its existing estimated annual support of €1.5 billion, including proposals for the subsidizing of newspaper subscriptions for 18-year-olds; doubling the state's spending on print advertising; and tax breaks for investors in online journalism.[164] The proposed measures are designed to safeguard the French newspaper industry, although they were coupled with government criticism of current content, which must clearly raise concerns about state interference. While such state support for the newspaper industry is unheard of in the UK, and would be likely to be perceived as a threat to press freedom, such financial support, particularly during times of economic recession, must be recognized as an element of a pluralistic policy.

2.5.3 Access technologies

In addition to the licensing regime discussed above, there are other forms of *ex ante* regulation that impact on broadcast pluralism, based on competition law principles and designed to facilitate access, specifically controls over so-called 'access technologies'. These controls fall outside the broadcast regime, comprising elements of EU communications law that impose obligations on those providing 'electronic

---

[158] Film Communication, s 2.3(b).
[159] See generally Competition Commission's page on media cases at <http://ec.europa.eu/competition/sectors/media/cases.html#1>.
[160] State aid N461/05 [2007] OJ C9/1. See Commission Press release IP/06/1611 of 22 November 2006.
[161] State aid N477/04, C (2005) 45 final, 19 January 2005.
[162] State aid N73/05, C (2006) 168, 23 January 2006.
[163] Interview with Professor Dirk Voorhoof, University of Ghent, 20 March 2009.
[164] See 'Sarkozy pledges €600m to newspapers' *The Guardian*, 23 January 2009.

communication networks and services' but they relate directly to the issue of both external and internal pluralism.[165]

There are two key forms of access technology that impact on digital radio and television, particularly those received over terrestrial or satellite broadcasting platforms: conditional access systems and electronic programming guides (EPGs). Conditional access systems govern the ability of a user to obtain access to the digital signal, which comprises encrypted and multiplexed channels.[166] An EPG is the primary navigation tool to enable the user to access the multitude of available channels. Both are essentially software applications that are installed in hardware that is either stand-alone, commonly referred to as a 'set-top box', or forms an integrated part of the radio or TV receiver.[167] A third regulated element of access technologies are so-called 'application program interfaces' (APIs), the information transmitted alongside the video signal that is required to enable the various software applications, such as interactivity, to operate together and seamlessly with the range of content made available via digital broadcast services.

The driver behind *ex ante* regulation of these technologies arises from the fact that they are generally seen as 'gatekeeper' or 'bottleneck' technologies through which the user receives digital radio or television services. Under EU law, the provision of these access technologies may be made subject to *ex ante* regulatory controls. Obligations were first imposed on providers under a measure specifically addressing the standardization of television signals[168] but in 2002 these rules were merged into the general access regime for the provision of electronic communications networks and services.[169]

Providers of conditional access systems are subject to mandatory conditions of supply, including offering all broadcasters 'on a fair, reasonable and non-discriminatory basis' the technical services necessary to enable viewer/listener reception, as well as maintaining separate accounts in respect of the provision of such services (Article 6(1) and Annex I, Part 1(b)). However, in contrast to the treatment of other access markets, the default position in respect of conditional access systems is one requiring the imposition of *ex ante* obligations on all market players, regardless of the existence of market dominance (Article 6(1)). Member States, national regulatory authorities (NRAs) *may* then be obliged to carry out a market review in respect of the conditional access market, rather than *shall* be required to (Article 7(3)); and as a result of such review *may*, rather than must (Article 8(3)), withdraw these conditions where dominance is found not to be present, and *only* if such withdrawal would not adversely

---

[165] Directive (EC) 2002/21 on a common regulatory framework for electronic communications networks and services [2002] OJ L108/33 (hereinafter 'Framework Directive').

[166] For the regulatory definition, see ibid Art 2(f).

[167] Referred to as 'enhanced digital television equipment', ibid Art 2(o).

[168] Directive (EC) 95/47 on the use of standards for the transmission of television signals [1995] OJ L281/51 (hereinafter 'Television Standards Directive').

[169] Directive (EC) 02/19 on access to, and interconnection of, electronic communications networks and associated facilities [2002] OJ L108/7 (hereinafter 'Access Directive').

impact on end-user accessibility or the prospects for effective competition in the market (Article 6(3)). Such differential treatment for conditional access systems results from an express recognition that 'competition rules alone many not be sufficient to ensure cultural diversity and media pluralism' (recital 10).

The Access Directive similarly enables Member States to impose access conditions on providers of EPGs and APIs, regardless of the existence of market dominance, for the purpose of ensuring end-user access to digital television and radio services. Providers may be required to offer such facilities on 'fair, reasonable and non-discriminatory terms' (Article 5(1)(b) and Annex I, Part II). In addition, the interoperability of digital television equipment is detailed under the Universal Service Directive.[170] These regulations require that such equipment use a standard encryption algorithm for scrambling signals and have an 'open interface socket' that is compliant with either a European or industry-wide standard specification, enabling the connection of peripherals and 'interactive and conditionally accessed services'.[171]

A third layer of regulation, in the Framework Directive, also obliges Member States to encourage providers of 'digital interactive television services' and 'digital television equipment' to use or comply with an 'open API', in order 'to promote the free flow of information, media pluralism and cultural diversity' by facilitating interoperability and the widest customer choice.[172] This also reflects the broader EU policy of facilitating interoperability between various types of computer software.[173] Where such open standards have not been achieved, the European Commission was given the right to make appropriate standards mandatory.[174] As required under the Directive,[175] the Commission has subsequently issued two communications examining progress towards the adoption of open APIs, concluding in both cases that the imposition of mandatory standards would not be appropriate, as this would have a negative impact on legacy equipment, stifling innovation and creating a barrier to market entry; while also conceding that full interoperability and the use of open APIs has not been achieved within the Union.[176] This experience can be seen as illustrative of the limitations of regulating for standards in a rapidly evolving marketplace, as well as the tenuous nature of the link with the promotion of pluralism as a policy objective.

In the UK, the regulation of these access technologies arose initially under secondary legislation transposing the Television Standards Directive[177] and the issuance of a

---

[170] Directive (EC) 2002/22 on universal service and users' rights relating to electronic communications networks and services [2002] OJ L108/7 (hereinafter 'Universal Services Directive').

[171] ibid Art 24 and Annex VI.

[172] Framework Directive, Art 18(1).

[173] See Council Directive (EEC) 91/250 on the legal protection of computer programs [1991] OJ L122/42, 17 Art 6(1).

[174] ibid Art 18(3), in accordance with the procedure under Art 17(3) and (4).

[175] ibid.

[176] Communication COM (2004) 541 final, 30 July 2004 and COM (2006) 37 final, 2 February 2006.

[177] Advanced Television Services Regulations 1996 (SI 1996/3151) and the Advanced Television Services (Amendment) Regulations 1996 (SI 1996/3197).

class licence under the Telecommunications Act 1984.[178] The only suppliers offering such services were Sky Subscriber Services Limited (SSSL) and ITV Digital.[179] In addition, a class licence was issued for the regulation of so-called 'access control systems'—which fell outside the scope of EU law but are related to the other access technologies—by governing the manner in which certain interactive communication services, such as shopping channels, were made available through digital television receivers. Similar to the conditional access rules, 'Regulated Suppliers' of access control systems, of which SSSL was the only provider, were required to offer their services on fair, reasonable, and non-discriminatory terms. In terms of the pricing of such services, the then regulator, Oftel, refrained from dictating what constituted fair, reasonable, and non-discriminatory tariffs, preferring instead to leave it to market negotiations; although also issuing guidance on the pricing of such services[180] and retaining a power of intervention.[181]

With the transposition of the Access Directive by Part 2 of the Communications Act 2003, the class licence for conditional access systems (CASs) was replaced by 'access-related conditions',[182] reflecting the provisions detailed in the Access Directive. The following conditions continue to be imposed only upon SSSL in respect of the digital satellite platform:

- requirement to provide conditional access services;
- requirement to ensure that conditional access services have the necessary technical capability for cost-effective transcontrol;[183]
- requirement to keep separate financial accounts;
- requirement to ensure that holders of industrial property rights to conditional access products and systems ensure that this is done on fair, reasonable, and non-discriminatory terms;
- obligation to not unduly discriminate in the provision of conditional access services; and
- obligation to publish charges, terms, and conditions.[184]

The digital terrestrial platform, Freeview, does not utilize conditional access systems, while the digital cable platform, offered by Virgin Media, only enables broadcasters to access customers through the bundled cable service, rather than as individual channels, thereby not requiring an access service.[185]

---

[178] Issued by the Secretary of State under Telecommunications Act 1984, s 7.
[179] ITV Digital, originally known as ONdigital, subsequently went into administration in March 2002 and the service was relaunched as a free-to-air platform by Freeview.
[180] Oftel statement, 'Terms of supply of conditional access', 22 October 2002.
[181] Oftel statement, 'The pricing of conditional access services and related issues', 8 May 2002.
[182] Promulgated under the Communications Act 2003, ss 45(5), 73(5), and 75(2).
[183] 'Transcontrol' is the ability of a programme service to be protected under the CAS of one platform (eg satellite), but still be retransmitted over a different platform (eg cable) using its CAS.
[184] Oftel statement, 'The regulation of conditional access' (24 July 2003) para 1.10.
[185] ibid paras 2.6–2.9.

For EPGs and access control systems, the existing class licences currently continue in operation.[186] In addition, the Communications Act 2003 also provides for the drafting and issuance by Ofcom of a code of practice to govern providers of EPGs.[187] The Code addresses three main issues: the prominence that should be given to public service broadcasting channels; access for disabled users; and ensuring effective competition.[188]

In October 2006, Ofcom carried out a market review of 'wholesale digital platform services', which included the access technologies (ie CASs, EPGs, and access control), referred to generically as 'technical platform services', to determine whether there was a need to modify the access conditions in respect of CASs or introduce such conditions for the other services.[189] In addition to the conditions, Ofcom has issued a statement and revised guidelines detailing how it interprets the obligation on SSSL to provide its technical platform services on fair, reasonable, and non-discriminatory terms.[190] One of the main reasons for revising the guidelines was to reflect the changing market conditions, from a position where Sky was keen to attract content during its start-up phase, to Sky having over 8 million customers in the UK and being the leading market player for digital television services.[191] In 2007, Ofcom also consulted on the imposition of access-related conditions on a second provider of CASs, Top Up TV.[192] The market review and decision on Top Up TV have been delayed, however, by Ofcom's decision, in March 2007, to launch a market investigation into the UK pay-TV market, to consider whether it was operating competitively and whether there is a need to make a 'market reference' to the Competition Commission under the Enterprise Act 2002.[193] The decision to investigate was triggered by submissions received from a number of market entrants alleging that the pay-TV market was not competitive.[194]

2.6 INTERNAL PLURALISM

Media law is primarily concerned with content rather than provision. Content rules are designed to address a wide range of policy objectives, including controls over advertising, harmful and illegal content, production quotas, access for political parties, and impartiality and cultural diversity, all of which are examined in detail in other

---

[186] Continuation notices were issued by Oftel, under the Communications Act 2003, Sch 18, para 9, effective from 25 July 2003.

[187] ibid ss 310–311.

[188] Ofcom, 'Code of practice on electronic programme guides' (2004).

[189] Ofcom, 'Review of wholesale digital platform services' (10 October 2006).

[190] Ofcom, 'Provision of Technical Platform Services—Guidelines and Explanatory Statement' (21 September 2006) effective 1 January 2007.

[191] ibid paras 2.22–2.27.

[192] Ofcom, 'The setting of access-related conditions upon Top Up TV Limited' (15 February 2007).

[193] Enterprise Act, s 131. Ofcom has concurrent functions with the OFT, by virtue of the Communications Act 2003, s 370.

[194] The submissions were made by BT, Setanta, Top Up TV, and Virgin Media on 16 January 2007.

chapters of this book and are therefore not reiterated in this chapter.[195] However, it is worth noting that the pursuance of internal pluralism is a central objective in a number of these diverse content rules, such as quota obligations for the broadcasting of 'independent' productions.[196]

This part of the chapter is concerned with other media law rules that can be seen as addressing internal or content pluralism objectives, either by ensuring that certain types of person are given access to a media outlet or that certain types of content are made accessible to the public, either through rules governing its usage or the imposition of content carrying obligations. An example of the former would be the granting of a right of reply to persons who have been subject to media attention; in terms of the latter, there are content carrying obligations that can be imposed on those providing transmission services.

2.6.1 Right of reply

One means by which media law addresses our ability to obtain access to the media is through rules offering a person a right of reply. Such a right could be characterized either as an element of an individual's right to freedom of expression, or as a derogation from that right, in terms of 'protection of the reputation or rights of others'.[197] From the latter perspective, offering a right of reply can be seen as a remedial mechanism to protect a person's legitimate interests, reducing the need to resort to more onerous legal measures restricting speech.

In terms of broadcasting, a right of reply is an element of the European legal framework under the 'TWF' Directive, which has been retained and extended under the 2007 amendment. As originally stated, all broadcasters must offer a right of reply or equivalent remedies to those who have been damaged by 'an assertion of incorrect facts in a television programme'.[198] Under the amendment, this right is extended to those providing 'on-demand' audiovisual media services. Under UK broadcasting law, a right to reply has been incorporated into the Broadcasting Code, with which licensees are required to comply: 'If a programme alleges wrongdoing or incompetence or makes other significant allegations, those concerned should normally be given an appropriate and timely opportunity to respond.'[199]

For the press, a right of reply is part of the Press Complaints Commission's self-regulatory Code: 'A fair opportunity for reply to inaccuracies must be given when reasonably called for.'[200] Numerous Commission adjudications address this issue, generally in relation to claims under clause 1, obliging the publication of accurate

---

[195] See further Chs 5, 9, 11, 12, and 13 below.
[196] See Ch 12 below.
[197] ECHR, Art 10(2).
[198] TWF Directive, Art 23.
[199] Ofcom Broadcast Code, para 7.11. See further Ch 8 below.
[200] PCC Code, para 2 'Opportunity to reply'. See further Ch 9 below.

information as the remedy for the complainant.[201] A recent example concerned Paul Burrell, the former royal butler, and accusations about the nature of his relationship with Princes Diana. The *News of the World* was found in breach of clause 1 in respect of the article it had published, but the Commission noted that the paper's offer 'to include the denial on the website, made at the end of the PCC investigation, was neither prompt nor proportionate'.[202]

2.6.2 Content carriage rules

Under EU law an attempt has been made to draw a clear regulatory distinction between the provision of transmission networks and services and the content services that are carried over such networks, from television programmes to internet traffic. As a logical consequence, the obligations placed upon providers of transmission services should not need to address the nature of the content being carried, as the transmission medium should be content neutral. From the beginning, however, this regulatory distinction has never been clear cut, with regulatory obligations requiring that certain content be carried on certain distribution platforms, specifically the rules concerning 'must-carry' and 'listed events'. Such rules are largely driven by a concern to facilitate pluralism, through ensuring public access to content that cannot be guaranteed through pure free market mechanisms. Recent debates around the concept of 'network neutrality' are a further manifestation of the integral link between carriage and content.

2.6.2.1 *'Must-carry'*

As noted already, the proliferation of alternative distribution platforms within an increasingly liberalized and competitive marketplace would appear to be the perfect environment for facilitating media pluralism. However, periods of transition can generate unique regulatory concerns not present during relatively stable developmental periods. 'Must-carry' rules can be seen as an example of what can be labelled 'transitional' media regulation. The policy concern is that as new platforms emerge certain content services may not be made available over these platforms, which will harm the promotion of diverse content across all platforms.[203] Regulatory intervention to require carriage, a radical departure from freely negotiated commercial arrangements between producers and distributors, would ensure the availability of specified content.

Under the Universal Services Directive, Member States have the right to impose on certain electronic communication networks an obligation to carry 'specified radio or television broadcast channels and services' (Article 31), in the 'interest of legitimate public policy considerations',[204] such as media pluralism. Such obligations may only

---

[201] A search of the PCC site revealed 78 hits on a search under the Clause title (dated 17 December 2008).
[202] Decision available at <http://www.pcc.org.uk/news/index.html?article=NTQwNQ>.
[203] See eg Recommendation (1999) 1, at Appendix V, para 4.
[204] ibid Recital (43).

be imposed on providers 'where a significant number of end-users of such networks use them as their principal means to receive radio and television broadcasts'.[205] The providers can be remunerated for such transmission services, but only on a non-discriminatory, transparent, and proportionate basis.[206]

These 'must-carry' rules are transposed into UK law under the Communications Act 2003 (section 64(1)). Ofcom has the responsibility for implementing them through the General Conditions of Entitlement, applicable to all providers of networks, although only in respect of a designated 'Appropriate Network'.[207] The list of services that comprise the 'must-carry' services are the digital format channel versions of the public service broadcasters, ie the BBC, Channels 3, 4, 5, and S4C, and the public teletext service (section 64(3)). 'Must-carry' obligations are therefore designed to ensure that certain types of content are made available to the public by ensuring that particular channels or packages of content are made available by broadcasters that have a specified 'public service' remit that includes diverse content.[208]

Ofcom may also impose conditions upon these public service broadcasters to ensure that their services are available for broadcasting or distributing over the transmission networks, so-called 'must-offer' or 'most-provide' obligations (sections 272 to 275).[209] The Secretary of State has the power to issue an order concerning the making available of capacity to carry such services, or concerning the terms under which the services are carried, or to add services to the list; although no such order has yet been promulgated. To date, Ofcom has not imposed the 'must-carry' condition upon any provider, primarily because the nature of such public service channels makes them highly desirable for any platform provider and therefore the policy concern has not materialized.

2.6.2.2 'Listed events'
While the 'must-carry' rules operate at a relatively high level of abstraction in terms of facilitating internal pluralism, the 'listed events' regime directly mandates that specific content be made available on certain distribution platforms on certain terms.

The regime originated in UK law under in the Broadcasting Act 1990.[210] It was then adopted at a European level through an amendment to the 'Television without frontiers' Directive in 1997, which requires Member States to take measures to ensure that broadcasters do not obtain exclusive rights to events that are regarded as 'being of major importance for society' and thereby deprive a 'substantial proportion of the public' from viewing the event on 'free' television, ie non-subscription television.[211]

---

[205] ibid Art 31(1).
[206] ibid Art 31(2).
[207] General Conditions of Entitlement, 7.
[208] See 2.4.2 above.
[209] These obligations extend to a 'satellite television service' (Communications Act 2003, s 273) and 'certain areas' (s 274).
[210] Section 182, 'Certain events not to be shown on pay-per-view terms'.
[211] Directive (EC) 97/36 of 30 June 1997 amending Council Directive (EEC) 89/552 on the co-ordination of certain provisions laid down by law, regulation or administrative action in Member States concerning the pursuit of television broadcasting activities ([1997] OJ L202/60) at 3a(1).

These events may take place within the jurisdiction or may be international in nature, such as the Olympics. Although not directly promoting pluralism *per se*, it constitutes another derogation from a non-regulatory free market approach to the broadcast sector by recognizing that the exercise of exclusive rights can undermine the achievement of plurality of content. Indeed, the recitals to the 1997 Directive describe the measure in terms of protecting 'the right to information';[212] the right to receive information within the context of the right to freedom of expression.[213] The provision has been retained in the Audiovisual Media Services Directive, but has not been extended to on-demand service providers.[214]

As a derogation from the general right of freedom to provide services under European law, the 'listed-events' regime is subject to a notification procedure whereby each Member State is required to notify the European Commission of the measures it has taken, and the Commission will then verify the compatibility of such measures with Community law and notify the other Member States.[215] The operation of this procedure was subject to the scrutiny of the European Court of Justice, when a rights-holder successfully challenged the Commission's approval of the measures adopted by the UK government in respect of the World Cup football finals in 2002 and 2006.[216] The Commission tried to argue, unsuccessfully, that its role in verifying the measures of a Member State, under Article 3(a)(2), did not constitute an 'decision' with binding legal effects under Article 249 of the EC Treaty.

In addition, Member States have an obligation to ensure that broadcasters under their jurisdiction do not exercise exclusive rights to content in a manner which will prevent the public in another Member State from obtaining access to content that has been designated in that other Member State in accordance with the previous procedure.[217] The application of this provision has been subject to judicial consideration by the House of Lords in the UK, which noted that this obligation to protect access to designated public interest content on behalf of other jurisdictions was not qualified 'by considerations of competition, free market economics, sanctity of contract and so forth'[218] and that the UK regulatory authority had therefore been right to refuse consent to broadcast based on considerations of the Danish system of regulation, despite the fact that the broadcaster had obtained the exclusive rights through an open and transparent auction.

---

[212] ibid Recital (18).

[213] Although the ECtHR has made it clear that Art 10 does not confer on individuals a general right of access to information (*Leander v Sweden* (1987) 9 EHRR 433, para 74).

[214] AVMS Directive, Art 3j.

[215] TWF Directive, Art 3a(2), (3) and AVMS Directive, Art 3j(2), (3).

[216] See *Infront WM AG (formerly Kirchmedia WM AG) v Commission* [2005] ECR II-5897 (CFI) and *Commission v Infront WMAG* [2008] 2 CMLR 28.

[217] TWF Directive, Art 3a(3), and AVMS Directive, Art 3j(3).

[218] *R v ITC, ex p TVD Danmark 1 Ltd* [2001] UKHL 42 para 33.

The EU regime was transposed into UK law by the Broadcasting Act 1996, as amended,[219] and the Communications Act 2003.[220] Under these provisions, the Secretary of State has the power to draw up a list 'of sporting and other events of national interest';[221] while Ofcom has the responsibility for issuing regulations, publishing a Code in respect of such events, and enforcement.[222] Those events which have been designated have been divided into Group A and Group B events. Group A events are those which cannot be covered live on an exclusive basis, unless certain criteria are met; while Group B events cannot be broadcast live on an exclusive basis 'unless adequate provision has been made for secondary coverage'.[223] The government is currently reviewing the list, with fierce lobbying from those wanting to expand the list, such as the BBC, and those wanting it to be abolished altogether, such as BSkyB.[224]

Although jurisdiction to 'list' an event could extend beyond sporting events, for instance to the opening of Parliament, the UK list is currently exclusively concerned with sporting events; a similar position is reflected throughout Europe, with a few exceptions made for music events.[225] It is perhaps somewhat ironic that a plurality measure justified using the rhetoric of 'free speech' should focus so directly on entertainment rather than any contribution to democratic discourse!

2.6.2.3 *'Network neutrality'*

A final example of content carriage rules impacting on internal pluralism concerns the developing policy debate over the concept of 'network neutrality'. The phrase is used in a variety of ways, but generally relates to the use of the internet as a distribution platform for content, whether media-related or otherwise, and the treatment given to the different forms of data traffic being transmitted over that platform. In brief, the debate reflects the evolving nature of the internet, as a network of networks, from a historically academic-orientated, content-neutral environment providing a 'best efforts' and non-discriminatory transmission service, to a major commercial communications infrastructure for content distribution in the twenty-first century. As users exchange and consume greater volumes of content over the internet, there is a concurrent need to upgrade the capacity of the various components of the network, particularly the local access network, for example that connecting a domestic user to the local exchange of the main transport network. However, investment in that infrastructure, specifically the laying of optical fibre to homes, will be constrained by the revenues

---

[219] ie by the Television Broadcasting Regulations 2000 (SI 2000/54).

[220] However, certain amendments to the Broadcasting Act 1996 made under the Communications Act 2003 have still to be commenced, eg Communications Act 2003, s 299(1).

[221] Broadcasting Act 1996, s 97(1).

[222] ibid s 104 ('Code of guidance'), s 104ZA ('Regulations about coverage of listed events'), and s 102 ('Power of Ofcom to impose penalty').

[223] Ofcom, 'Code on Sports and Other Listed and Designated Events' (2 September 2008).

[224] See eg, 'Sky to fight for right to screen crown jewels' *The Guardian*, 6 March 2009.

[225] eg Austria lists the Vienna Philharmonic Orchestra's New Year Concert, while Italy lists the San Remo music festival. See generally the consolidated list of measures [2008] OJ C17/7.

that can be generated from customers, which are in turn constrained by the competitive environment for such transmission services.

The BBC's iPlayer service, launched in December 2007, is an example of a tremendously successful content service, which has persuaded large numbers of new people to watch TV-like content over the internet.[226] While from the consumer's perspective such new content is a great new free source of high quality programming, for the transmission provider, such content has significantly increased usage of network capacity, placing strains on the existing infrastructure and bringing forward the timetable for investment in network upgrades.[227] The question this raises is: who will pay for such network development? In the short term, the internet service providers (ISPs) may have to place limits or caps on the usage made of the internet by customers, effectively constraining the consumption of certain types of content service. In the longer term, either customers will have to pay more for the transmission services they consume, possibly tiered to reflect different types of content services; or those providing high bandwidth content services may be required to contribute towards the cost of carriage. In both the short and long term, however, the internet may no longer be considered 'neutral' in respect of the content it carries.

As these are relatively recent developments, policy-makers are generally still pondering whether and how to intervene. The Council of Europe made some general remarks, back in 1999, about the need to 'ensure fair access by service and content providers to the networks', which can be seen as indicative of an emerging concern about network neutrality.[228] However, it was not until November 2007 that the European Commission proposed regulatory measures designed to address aspects of the 'network neutrality' issue. The first is a consumer protection measure obliging service providers to notify customers prior to signing-up to a service, as well as regularly during the term of the contract, of 'any limitations imposed by the provider on their ability to access or distribute lawful content or run any lawful applications and services of their choice'.[229] The second measure would give the Commission the power to set 'minimum quality of service' requirements that NRAs would impose on certain public networks.[230] The European Parliament has supported these proposals;[231] while three major service providers, Google, Yahoo!, and Skype, most likely to be adversely impacted by a move away from net neutrality, have published a survey indicating overwhelming support by EU consumers for open and unrestricted access, while also

---

[226] Other similar services include 4OD, Sky Anytime, and Joost.

[227] See 'BBC iPlayer "risks overloading the internet"' *The Times*, 10 April 2008.

[228] R (1999) 1, at Appendix II, 1.

[229] Proposal amending Directive (EC) 2002/22 on universal service and users' rights relating to electronic communications networks, Directive (EC) 2002/58 concerning the processing of personal data and the protection of privacy in the electronic communications sector, and Regulation (EC) No 2006/2004 on consumer protection cooperation, COM (2007) 698, Art 1(12), introducing a new Art 20(5).

[230] ibid Art 1(13)(b), introducing a new Art 22(3).

[231] See COM (2008) 723 final, 6 November 2008.

calling for laws to prohibit traffic management practices that 'constitute unnecessary, discriminatory and/or anti-competitive behaviour'.[232]

In the US, the FCC has issued a decision requiring Comcast, a large provider of broadband internet services, to stop its 'discriminatory and arbitrary' traffic management practices by interfering with its customers' use of the BitTorrent P2P file-sharing application, which is used for the distribution of video programming by companies such as Twentieth Century Fox and CBS.[233] Comcast initially denied such practices; then claimed that such actions were only carried out during peak times of network congestion, before eventually admitting that such actions were carried out on a general basis.[234] Comcast has been ordered to disclose details of all such practices and implement instead 'protocol-agnostic' network management techniques; although Comcast has appealed the decision.

The 'network neutrality' debate in the US has also reflected a slightly different concern from that about who bears the cost of network investment, relating to the competitive behaviour of networks. There is a concern that network providers may discriminate between the treatment given to different content services in order to promote their own content services, or those of their preferred suppliers, from other non-affiliated content services; as noted by the then Presidential candidate Barack Obama: 'carriers are tempted to impose a toll charge on content and services, discriminating against websites that are unwilling to pay for equal treatment. This could create a two-tier Internet in which websites with the best relationships with network providers can get the fastest access to consumers, while all competing websites remain in a slower lane.'[235]

Such a scenario creates an obvious tension with a free and competitive marketplace. From a competition law perspective, discriminatory treatment is only actionable if certain other conditions are present, such as the existence of a dominant position. However, the sentiments being expressed by Barack Obama are suggestive of a more interventionist approach to network access; which, as with the rationales for broadcasting regulation, are more likely to be 'explained by history than by coherent theory'.[236]

As with the role of public service broadcasting in media pluralism, some commentators have called upon governments to invest public moneys in network upgrades, on the ground that it is a key infrastructure supporting economic growth, eg: 'If we are looking for a government project that would stimulate the economy in the short term and help combat the impact of the credit crunch, while also bringing long-lasting improvements to the nation's infrastructure, then we could do no better than rewire the

---

[232] Reuters, 'Consumers want unrestricted Internet access: survey', 18 March 2009.

[233] FCC 08–183, 1 August 2008. Comcast has appealed the decision.

[234] ibid para 9.

[235] 'Connecting and Empowering all Americans through Technology and Innovation' (November 2007), available at <http://www.barackobama.com>. See also the comments of Neil Berkett, CEO of Virgin Media, who was reported as stating that content companies that are unwilling to pay for access 'might end up in slower "bus lanes"', in 'Pay-per-voom TV' (2008) 45(4) *Television*.

[236] Hitchens (n 35 above) 47, based on LC Bollinger, cited in Barendt (n 35 above) 8, n 24.

nation with fibre optics.'[237] Some governments, particularly in some Asian countries,[238] have enthusiastically accepted this role. Where such public investment takes place, however, the resultant infrastructure is likely to be subject to usage rules that necessarily reflect the public nature of the funding and therefore may be likely to tend towards a network neutrality stance. The public funding of network build can also be seen as having a long-term impact on external pluralism, ie the diversity of media services, to the extent that it will facilitate the use of one broadcast delivery platform, which may in the long term impact on the use of other modes of delivery, specifically the digital terrestrial and satellite platforms.

'Network neutrality' raises issues above and beyond the scope of this chapter. However, as noted above, obligations concerning the carriage of certain types of content are an essential component of a media pluralism policy and, therefore, debates over the appropriate response to 'network neutrality' are simply the latest manifestation of a perceived need for regulatory intervention to promote access to a diverse variety of content.

2.7 CONCLUDING REMARKS

As noted throughout this chapter, and indeed the book as a whole, the development of the internet is causing a fundamental shift in the nature of the media industry and, as a consequence, calling into focus the suitability of existing governing laws and regulation, including media ownership rules. It can be argued, for example, that given an individual's potential capability to reach a global audience through the internet, ownership controls no longer make sense as a tool of pluralism. However, while it is appropriate to raise such questions, when responding it is necessary to take account of the actual state of change rather than the mere possibility or potential. In the US Court of Appeals decision in the *Prometheus* case, for example, the court held that the FCC had given too much weight to the internet as a 'media outlet' when revising its ownership rules, which was not justifiable considering that 'media outlets have an entirely different character from individual or organizations' websites and thus contribute to viewpoint diversity in an entirely different way'.[239] Data presented to the Court also indicated that users were primarily using the internet to access online versions of the major press and broadcast brands, rather than taking advantage of the array of new sources.[240]

Media ownership rules, as a barrier to market entry, can be viewed as a restriction on a person's ability to obtain access to the media, in the sense of being able to impart expression or speech. In contrast, *ex ante* regulatory regimes control the importation,

---

[237] Professor Chris Bishop, Chief Scientist at Microsoft Research, Cambridge, 'UK behind in global rush to broadband' *The Observer*, 28 December 2008.
[238] eg South Korea's Information Infrastructure Plan.
[239] *Promethius Radio Project and ors v FCC* 373 F 3d 372, 395–7 (3d Cir 2004) 407.
[240] ibid 406.

distribution, or dissemination of expression, in the form of licensing requirements; as well as our ability to receive such expression, from the access technologies to content requirements.

It should be noted that policies concerning media literacy can also be seen as an element of a comprehensive media pluralism policy, on the grounds that the freedom to receive information, a component of a person's right to freedom of expression, can only be meaningfully exercised if the recipient has the necessary skills and knowledge to be able to understand the nature of what is being received. Media literacy is defined in the AVMS Directive in the following terms: 'skills, knowledge and understanding that allow consumers to use media effectively and safely. Media-literate people are able to exercise informed choices, understand the nature of content and services and take advantage of the full range of opportunities offered by new communications technologies.'[241] In the UK, Ofcom already has a duty to promote media literacy.[242] The ability to use media 'effectively' would seem to be a critical final element of the various strands of pluralism examined in this chapter, from a multiplicity of providers to a diversity of content. While using media 'safely' concerns the ability of recipients to control illegal and harmful content, such as the use of filters.

Finally, it must be reiterated that the current economic downturn, resulting from the so-called 'credit crunch', is already having a significant impact on the attitude of policy-makers towards external pluralism. The need for measures to help media companies weather the recession is likely to result in a weakening in the application of rules designed to ensure pluralism through competition, facilitating sectoral restructuring in favour of the substantial few over the insubstantial many, as well as direct governmental intervention in the structure of the public sector broadcasting sector.

---

[241] AVMS Directive, Recital (37).
[242] Communications Act 2003, s 11.

3

REGULATING JOURNALISM AND NEWSGATHERING

Siobhain Butterworth and Jan Johannes

3.1 PROTECTION OF JOURNALISTS' SOURCES

Journalists have a moral obligation and a professional duty, recognized by the Press Complaints Commission code of practice, not to disclose the identity of their sources of confidential information.[1]

Disclosing a source's identity can have serious consequences as *The Guardian* learned in 1984 when Sarah Tisdall, a clerical officer with the Foreign and Commonwealth Office (FCO), was jailed for leaking information to the newspaper. After *The Guardian* published a story based on information she had given to it

---

[1] Press Complaints Commission Code of Practice, cl 14.

(anonymously), about the delivery of Cruise missiles to RAF Greenham Common air base, the government obtained an order for disclosure.[2] When *The Guardian* handed over the documents the FCO was able to identify Tisdall as the source of the leak because the copies she made could be traced to a particular photocopying machine.

The Guardian's editor at the time, Peter Preston, saw no option but to comply with the order because the publisher faced fines for non-compliance and he thought the newspaper should not put itself on the wrong side of the law: 'Could companies that believed in the rule of law, owning papers that championed it, duck when the going got tough?' he asked in an article published more than two decades later.[3]

The issue of non-disclosure of sources is more than an ethical issue for journalists. As the European Court of Human Rights made clear in *Goodwin v UK*, it is linked to the right of freedom of expression and the need to protect the free flow of information.[4] Case law and statutes such as the Contempt of Court Act 1981, the Police and Criminal Evidence Act 1984, and the Terrorism Act 2000 (discussed below) acknowledge the special role journalists play in a democratic society, but the legal privileges journalists enjoy in relation to their sources are not absolute.

3.2 WHO IS A JOURNALIST IN THE NEW MEDIA WORLD?

Phrases such as 'journalistic material',[5] 'journalistic privilege',[6] and 'freedom of the press'[7] make regular appearances in legislation and legal judgments, but these terms are more difficult to define in an era of mass self-publishing, when the demarcation between journalists and everyone else is unclear. A proliferation of websites and bloggers means that it is becoming harder to say who is a journalist and to describe what journalism is, with the result that there is room for doubt about who can avail themselves of the legal protections that have developed for the media.

In *Here Comes Everybody*, Clay Shirky points out that while the traditional definition of 'journalist' (someone who writes for a newspaper or prepares news stories for broadcast) is closely linked to ideas about employment, the employer and means of production of news are less relevant in the digital world.[8] You don't need to be employed by a newspaper or broadcaster to commit an act of journalism.

---

[2] *Secretary of State for Defence v Guardian Newspapers Ltd* [1984] 3 All ER 601. Note that a group of news organizations including *The Guardian* took a different view in 2002, when disclosure orders were made against them in *Interbrew SA v Financial Times and ors* [2002] EWCA Civ 274 and upheld by the Court of Appeal; they did not comply and the claimant backed down leaving it to the Financial Services Authority to pursue the information.

[3] Preston, 'How not to defend your Source' (2005) 16(3) *British Journalism Review* 47.

[4] *Goodwin v UK* [1996] 22 EHRR 123.

[5] See eg the Police and Criminal Evidence Act 1984, s 13 and the Terrorism Act 2000, 5, para 4.

[6] See eg *X Ltd and anor v Morgan-Grampian (Publishers) Ltd and ors* [1990] 2 All ER 1, 14.

[7] See eg *Goodwin* (n 4 above) 39.

[8] C Shirky, *Here Comes Everybody* (Penguin, 2008) 71.

Shirky mentions the problems members of the US Congress encountered when they tried to frame a Federal shield law allowing reporters to protect their confidential sources. 'If anyone can be a publisher, then anyone can be a journalist', he says. 'And if anyone can be a journalist, then journalistic privilege suddenly becomes a loophole too large to be borne by society.' He suggests that there may be good public policy reasons why the privileges that journalists currently claim should not be enjoyed by everybody: 'Journalistic privilege has to be applied to a minority of people, in order to preserve the law's ability to uncover and prosecute wrongdoing while allowing a safety valve for investigative reporting.' [9]

Depriving bloggers of the protections available to journalists is neither practical (some bloggers are also journalists) nor attractive. As Shirky says: 'The simple answer is that there is no simple answer.' [10] Nevertheless it seems likely that the courts will be asked to come up with one sooner or later. [11]

3.3 FREEDOM OF THE PRESS

The digital publishing revolution reminds us that freedom of speech is not synonymous with freedom of the press. Nevertheless the law has continued to place considerable emphasis on protecting press freedom. It has, for example, recognized the media's special role as the 'eyes and ears of the public' enabling other citizens to take part in public life by reporting events such as press conferences and public meetings. [12] The courts have also been keen to stress the importance of journalistic investigations. [13] In *Reynolds v Times Newspapers Ltd* the House of Lords developed common law qualified privilege to provide a defence of responsible journalism in libel cases where allegations about matters of public interest turn out to be false or cannot be proved to be true. Lord Nicholls explained the approach to be taken in such cases:

Above all, the court should have particular regard to the importance of freedom of expression. The press discharges vital functions as a bloodhound as well as a watchdog. The court should be slow to conclude that a publication was not in the public interest and, therefore, the public had no right to know, especially when the information is in the field of political discussion. Any lingering doubts should be resolved in favour of publication. [14]

---

[9] ibid.

[10] ibid 72.

[11] Bloggers may argue that they are entitled to use the shield provided by the Contempt of Court Act 1981, s 10, which gives protection to 'any person' in relation to 'a publication for which he is responsible'. In *Secretary of State for Defence v Guardian Newspapers Ltd* [1984] 3 All ER 601, Lord Diplock said at 604 that the section 10 protection is not exclusive to the media. The protection was sought in *Totalise plc v Motley Fool Ltd* [2001] EWCA Civ 1897, but not in *Sheffield Wednesday Football Club Ltd and ors v Hargreaves* [2007] EWHC 2375 (QB).

[12] *McCartan Turkington Breen (a firm) v Times Newspapers Ltd* [2000] 4 All ER 913, 923, 924, 928.

[13] See eg *Reynolds v Times Newspapers Ltd* [1999] 4 All ER 609; *R v Central Criminal Court, ex p Bright* [2001] 2 All ER 244; and *Jameel and anor v Wall Street Journal Europe Sprl* [2006] UKHL 44.

[14] *Reynolds* (n 13 above) 626.

Decisions of the lower courts in the following seven years meant that the *Reynolds* qualified privilege defence was in danger of becoming merely theoretical until the House of Lords restated its nature and purpose in *Jameel v Wall Street Journal* as 'a public interest' defence.[15] The *Reynolds* and *Jameel* cases are relevant to discussions about orders for disclosure of the identity of leaks because in both cases the right of journalists to protect their sources was considered to be beyond question. In *Reynolds* Lord Nicholls said that the unwillingness to disclose the identity of a source should not weigh against a media defendant who claims qualified privilege and, in *Jameel*, the *Wall Street Journal*'s reliance on five anonymous sources did not operate to defeat its qualified privilege defence.[16]

In the *Reynolds* case the presumption in favour of non-disclosure of journalistic sources granted by section 10 of the Contempt of Court Act 1981 was one of the reasons given for rejecting a new, generic, qualified privilege defence for political speech. Lord Nicholls said that malice would not be a sufficient safeguard for claimants in such cases because, faced with a media defendant who is unwilling to disclose its source, a claimant may be unable to prove that information has been published recklessly or maliciously.[17]

On the same point Lord Hope had this to say: 'The importance which must be attached to the principle which justifies the protection of their sources by the media . . . carries with it certain penalties. One of these, I believe, is the discipline of having to justify each claim to the benefit of qualified privilege should the statements of fact which are made by the media turn out to be defamatory.'[18] Seen from this perspective, more stringent libel laws are the price paid for the shield the Contempt of Court Act 1981 provides for journalists.

In *R v Central Criminal Court, ex parte Bright* the Court reviewed production orders granted in favour of the police.[19] The orders were made following publication of a letter in *The Guardian* from ex-MI5 officer David Shayler and an article in *The Observer* by journalist Martin Bright, relating to Shayler's allegations that in 1996 the British Security Services were involved in a failed bomb plot to assassinate Libyan head of state Colonel Gadaffi. At the time *The Guardian* letter and *The Observer* article were published, Shayler was under investigation for breaches of the Official Secrets Act 1989 and was wanted by the police.[20]

The production orders required the journalist and the newspapers to hand over all files, documents, and records relating to the letter and the journalist's article. Notwithstanding that Shayler was evading the police, and despite the fact that the case involved

---

[15] *Jameel* (n 13 above) *per* Lord Hoffman, para 46.
[16] *Reynolds* (n 13 above) 626.
[17] ibid 623, 631.
[18] ibid 654.
[19] *R v Central Criminal Court, ex p Bright* [2001] 2 All ER 244. The orders were granted under the Police and Criminal Evidence Act 1984, s 9, Sch 1, para 4.
[20] He was believed to be resident in France and earlier extradition proceedings had failed.

issues of national security, the Queen's Bench Divisional Court held that the orders should not have been made. Judge LJ said:

Inconvenient or embarrassing revelations, whether for the Security Services or for public authorities, should not be suppressed. Legal proceedings directed toward the seizure of the working papers of an individual journalist or the premises of the newspaper or television programme publishing his or her reports, or the threat of such proceedings, tends to inhibit discussion. When a genuine investigation into possible corrupt or reprehensible activities by a public authority is being investigated by the media, compelling evidence would normally be needed to demonstrate that the public interest is served by such proceedings. Otherwise, to the public disadvantage, legitimate enquiry and discussion . . . would be discouraged, perhaps stifled.[21]

3.4 SECTION 10 OF THE CONTEMPT OF COURT ACT AND ARTICLE 10 ECHR

Media defendants faced with an order for disclosure may rely on the shield provided by section 10 of the Contempt of Court Act and on Article 10 of the European Convention on Human Rights.[22]

Article 10(1) of the European Convention on Human Rights provides: 'Everyone has the right to freedom of expression. This right shall include freedom to hold opinions and to receive and impart information and ideas without interference by public authority and regardless of frontiers.' This right is subject to the qualifications set out in Article 10(2):

The exercise of these freedoms, since it carries with it duties and responsibilities, may be subject to such formalities, conditions, restrictions or penalties as are prescribed by law and are necessary in a democratic society, in the interests of national security, territorial integrity or public safety, for the prevention of disorder or crime, for the protection of health or morals, for the protection of the reputation or rights of others, for preventing the disclosure of information received in confidence, or for maintaining the authority and impartiality of the judiciary.

The European Court of Human Rights set out its views on the importance of journalists' sources in *Goodwin v UK*:

Protection of journalistic sources is one of the basic conditions for press freedom, as is reflected in the laws and the professional codes of conduct in a number of contracting states and is affirmed in several international instruments on journalistic freedoms . . . Without such protection, sources may be deterred from assisting the press in informing the public on matters of public interest. As a result the vital public watchdog role of the press may be undermined and the ability of the press to provide accurate and reliable information may be adversely affected.[23]

---

[21] *R v Central Criminal Court, ex p Bright,* (n 13 above) para 98.

[22] Some statutes are designed to prevent reliance on the section.

[23] *Goodwin v UK* [1996] 22 EHRR 123, para 39.

It has been said that the principles found in Article 10 are 'bred in the bone of the common law' and that decisions of the Strasbourg Court simply repeat in a different language the principles of common law.[24] Nevertheless, even before the Human Rights Act 1998 came into force in October 2000 and required the domestic courts to take the European decisions into account, the Convention was called on in support of arguments concerned with freedom of expression.[25]

The Contempt of Court Act 1981 was intended to bring domestic law in line with the Convention.[26] It followed the decision of the Strasbourg Court in *Sunday Times v UK*, that an order restraining publication of a newspaper article breached Article 10.[27] The structure of section 10 echoes that of Article 10 but is not identical to it. Section 10 provides:

No court may require a person to disclose, nor is any person guilty of contempt of court for refus-ing to disclose, the source of information contained in a publication for which he is responsible, unless it be established to the satisfaction of the court that disclosure is necessary in the interests of justice or national security or for the prevention of disorder or crime.

Section 10 creates a presumption in favour of non-disclosure of sources, which can be defeated if the claimant can bring itself within one of the four listed exceptions and can show that the order is 'necessary' for those purposes.[28] The effect of the Human Rights Act 1998 is that section 10 must be read and applied by the courts in such a way as to ensure compatibility with Convention rights.[29] In *Ashworth Hospital Authority v MGN Ltd* the House of Lords noted that while judicial opinions differ about the extent to which section 10 was intended by Parliament to reflect Article 10, it is clear that they have a common purpose of enhancing the freedom of the press by protecting journal-istic sources and courts should approach them in the same way. Lord Woolf, referring to the European Court's approach to the concept of necessity in the *Goodwin* case, said: 'The same approach can be applied equally to section 10 now that Article 10 is part of our domestic law.'[30]

Section 10 and Article 10 provide protection regardless of whether a story contain-ing information from the source has been published.[31] The section 10 shield can be

---

[24] *R v Central Criminal Court, ex p Bright* (n 13 above) para 87. Geoffrey Robertson and Andrew Nicol make a similar observation: 'The advent of art.10 does not open a new era so much as spell out, and provide a framework for, the operation in law of the principle that in a democracy infringements on free speech can only be justified in cases of overriding necessity to prevent demonstrable harm to citizens.' See, *Media Law* (Thomson/Sweet and Maxwell, 5th edn, 2007) ix.

[25] See eg *Attorney-General v Guardian Newspapers Ltd* [1987] 1 WLR 1248 and *Derbyshire County Council v Times Newspapers Ltd* [1993] 1 All ER 1011.

[26] MW Janis, RS Kay *et al*, *European Human Rights Law* (Oxford University Press, 2008) 105.

[27] *Sunday Times v UK* [1979] 2 EHRR 245.

[28] The party seeking the order has the burden of showing that it comes within one of the exceptions and of proving necessity, see *X Ltd v Morgan-Grampian (Publishers) Ltd* [1990] 2 All ER 1, *per* Lord Bridge, 6.

[29] Human Rights Act 1998, s 3(1).

[30] *Ashworth Hospital Authority v MGN Ltd* [2002] UKHL 29, *per* Lord Woolf, para 38, referring to *Goodwin v UK* (1996) 22 EHRR 123, para 39.

[31] *X Ltd v Morgan-Grampian (Publishers) Ltd* [1990] 2 All ER 1, *per* Lord Bridge, 6.

used even where there is no explicit agreement between the journalist and the source that the identity of the source will remain confidential and even where a journalist receives unsolicited material from an anonymous source.[32] Note that there is no requirement for the material to be in the public interest.[33] However, as we will come to see when we look at the balancing exercise to be undertaken by the court in these cases, the (presumed) purpose of the source and the absence of any public interest in the information provided by him or her may weigh in favour of an order for disclosure.[34]

3.5 *NORWICH PHARMACAL* JURISDICTION

Section 10 creates a shield for journalists who seek protection for their sources of confidential information but it does not establish the jurisdiction under which courts can make orders for disclosure between parties in civil proceedings. That jurisdiction exists at common law. Orders for disclosure in the context of criminal investigations and criminal proceedings are discussed below. In other cases, for example where a company wants to trace the source of a leak of confidential information in order to dismiss an employee or bring legal proceedings against a third party, the disclosure jurisdiction is based on the principles established in *Norwich Pharmacal Co v Commissioners of Customs and Excise*.[35]

In the *Norwich Pharmacal* case a chemicals company, which owned a patent for a chemical compound called furazolidone, brought an action against the Commissioners of Customs and Excise who had seized consignments of furazolidone that were unlawfully imported into the UK without a licence. The chemicals company wanted to know the identity of the importers so that they could bring legal proceedings against them. However, Customs and Excise refused to supply the details.

As a general rule, an action for discovery cannot be brought against a person who is merely a witness and not a party or potential party to legal proceedings. In the *Norwich Pharmacal* case, however, the Commissioners of Customs and Excise were ordered to provide information about the importers on the grounds that they had, in performing their duties, become mixed up in the importers' wrongful acts. Lord Reid outlined the principle:

. . . if through no fault of his own a person gets mixed up in the tortious acts of others so as to facilitate their wrongdoing he may incur no personal liability but he comes under a duty to assist the person who has been wronged by giving him full information and disclosing the identity of

---

[32] See *Secretary of State for Defence v Guardian Newspapers Ltd* [1984] 3 All ER 601; *X Ltd v Morgan-Grampian (Publishers) Ltd* [1990] 2 All ER 1; and *Interbrew SA v Financial Times and ors* [2002] EWCA Civ 274.
[33] *Secretary of State for Defence v Guardian Newspapers Ltd* [1984] 3 All ER 601, *per* Lord Diplock.
[34] See *Mersey Care NHS Trust v Ackroyd* [2006] EWHC 107 (QB) and *Interbrew SA v Financial Times and ors* [2002] EWCA Civ 274.
[35] *Norwich Pharmacal Co v Commissioners of Customs and Excise* [1973] 2 All ER 943.

the wrongdoers. I do not think that it matters whether he became so mixed up by voluntary action on his part or because it was his duty to do what he did. It may be that if this causes him expense the person seeking the information ought to reimburse him. But justice requires that he should co-operate in righting the wrong if he unwittingly facilitated its perpetration.[36]

In *Ashworth Hospital Authority v MGN* the House of Lords confirmed and extended the application of the *Norwich Pharmacal* jurisdiction in relation to journalistic sources. It held that an order for disclosure can be made notwithstanding that it is sought in order to dismiss an employee rather than for the purpose of bringing legal proceedings against him or her.[37] In that case, the *Daily Mirror* published a story based on extracts from the medical records of serial killer Ian Brady, a patient at Ashworth security hospital, who was on hunger strike at the time and undergoing forced feeding.

The information did not come to the paper directly through the source but through an intermediary whose identity was known to the publisher and who was paid £1,500. The newspaper did not know the source's identity but accepted that he or she was probably a hospital authority employee. An order requiring the defendant to explain how it came into the possession of Brady's medical records and to identify any employee of the authority involved in publication was upheld both by the Court of Appeal and the House of Lords.

Ashworth had carried out an investigation to discover the source of the leak and claimed that the source could not be uncovered unless an order for disclosure was made. One of the grounds on which the newspaper opposed the order was that the claimant wanted to identify the source, not for the purpose of bringing proceedings but so that it could dismiss him or her. The newspaper argued that the *Norwich Pharmacal* disclosure jurisdiction (and the 'interests of justice' exception to section 10 of the Contempt of Court Act 1981, discussed below) is limited to cases where disclosure is required for existing or intended proceedings.

The House of Lords in the *Ashworth* case held that it is not a precondition of the disclosure jurisdiction that the applicant should either have begun or have an intention to bring legal proceedings against the wrongdoer. The Court said that no such limitation on the disclosure jurisdiction had been contemplated by the House of Lords in *Norwich Pharmacal* and the imposition of such a restriction would encourage proceedings to be brought for purely technical reasons.[38]

In *Interbrew SA v Financial Times*, decided shortly before the *Ashworth* case, the Court of Appeal had held that the *Norwich Pharmacal* jurisdiction was confined to civil wrongs and could not be used in relation to criminal matters. Sedley LJ said the job of identifying criminals should generally be left to prosecuting authorities equipped with statutory powers of search and seizure.[39] However, in *Ashworth* the House of Lords

---

[36] ibid.
[37] *Ashworth Hospital Authority v MGN* [2002] UKHL 29.
[38] ibid *per* Lord Woolf CJ, paras 44–49.
[39] *Interbrew* (n 32 above) *per* Sedley J, paras 18–23.

dismissed this view as 'too restrictive'. Lord Woolf emphasized that while *Norwich Pharmacal* is an 'exceptional jurisdiction', it is also a developing jurisdiction.[40]

In summary, the *Norwich Pharmacal* disclosure jurisdiction does not depend on whether the media defendant has committed a tort, a breach of contract, or other civil or criminal wrong. The party against whom the order is made does not have to be a wrongdoer, all that is needed is for him or her to have participated or been mixed up in some way in the source's wrongdoing.[41] The need for involvement in wrongdoing is a 'threshold requirement' said the Court in the *Ashworth* case, but the *Norwich Pharmacal* jurisdiction is discretionary and an order for disclosure should not be made unless it is a 'necessary and proportionate response in all the circumstances'.[42]

A question may arise as to whether a source has been involved in any wrongdoing, for example the media defendant may be able to argue that the information is no longer secret, or it may claim that there is a public interest defence in relation to breach of confidence.[43] In the *Ashworth* case the newspaper argued that there was no breach of confidence (and therefore no wrongdoing) because Ian Brady had put similar information about his medical treatment into the public domain. However, the House of Lords said there was wrongdoing on the part of the source who, it was presumed, was an employee who had breached his or her contract of employment.[44] In any case, the Court said, Ashworth hospital had an independent interest in the confidentiality of the material.[45]

How do journalists get 'mixed up' in the wrongdoing of sources? In the *Ashworth* case the answer to this question was considered to be reasonably straightforward: 'It is sufficient if, in the words of Viscount Dilhorne in the *Norwich Pharmacal* case . . . that there was "involvement or participation". As MGN published the information which was wrongfully obtained, the answer as to whether there was involvement or participation must be an emphatic Yes.'[46]

Did the House of Lords intend to suggest that a media defendant's involvement in wrongdoing *only* occurs if the information is published?[47] Would the outcome have been different if the newspaper had received the information but had not published it? The *Ashworth* decision appears to leave room to argue that the *Norwich Pharmacal* jurisdiction does not extend to cases in which a party seeks an order for disclosure before the journalist has been able to publish a story. In this respect it appears to contradict the principle expounded by Lord Bridge in *X Ltd v Morgan-Grampian* that the jurisdiction may apply in cases where an order for disclosure is sought in connection

---

[40] *Ashworth* (n 37 above) *per* Lord Woolf CJ, para 57. He gave the example of *P v T Ltd* [1997] 1 WLR 309 in which relief was granted because it was necessary in the interests of justice even though the claimant could not identify the appropriate cause of action without discovery.

[41] *Ashworth* (n 37 above) *per* Lord Slynn, para 1, Lord Woolf CJ, para 34.

[42] ibid *per* Lord Woolf CJ, para 36.

[43] *Mersey Care NHS Trust v Robin Ackroyd* [2003] EWCA Civ 663.

[44] *Ashworth* (n 37 above) *per* Lord Woolf CJ, paras 31–32.

[45] ibid *per* Lord Woolf CJ, para 22.

[46] ibid *per* Lord Woolf CJ, para 34. See also *Interbrew* (n 32 above) *per* Sedley LJ, para 14.

[47] Sedley LJ made a similar suggestion in ibid, para 29.

with information from a source that was never published because publication of the story was restrained by a court order.[48]

3.6 PIERCING THE SHIELD PROVIDED BY SECTION 10 OF THE CONTEMPT OF COURT ACT 1981

An order for disclosure cannot be made unless the person seeking it can satisfy the court that one of the four exceptions in section 10 applies and that the order is 'necessary'. The exceptional purposes for which an order for disclosure may be made are, as noted above, in the interests of justice; in the interests of national security; for the prevention of disorder; and for the prevention of crime.

3.6.1 Prevention of disorder

There are no decided cases on the meaning of prevention of disorder and in practice this is probably not a separate exception to the prevention of crime exception. The factors required to establish both purposes are likely to be the same because serious disorder is likely to involve criminal activity.[49]

3.6.2 Prevention of crime

Prevention of crime in section 10 need not be taken literally. In *Re an Inquiry* the House of Lords held that this exception is not limited to future identifiable crimes but can mean the prevention of crime generally.[50]

The court may refuse to order disclosure under this head if the applicant is the victim of a crime who has no public duty to investigate or prosecute.[51] In *Interbrew SA v Financial Times* the Court of Appeal ordered delivery up of documents to enable Interbrew to identify the potential defendant in a breach of confidence action: 'disclosure is necessary in the interests of justice', said Sedley J. He added: 'That it may also go to the prevention of crime cannot be ruled out as irrelevant, but it is peripheral because it is not a purpose for which Interbrew themselves are entitled to disclosure.'[52]

3.6.3 In the interests of national security

In *Secretary of State for Defence v Guardian Newspapers Ltd* (the Tisdall case) the House of Lords held that the burden of proof lies with the party seeking the order

---

[48] *X Ltd v Morgan-Grampian (Publishers) Ltd* [1990] 2 All ER 1, *per* Lord Bridge, 6.
[49] See Robertson and Nicol (n 24 above) 331, n 24.
[50] *Re an Inquiry under the Company Securities (Insider Dealing) Act 1985* [1988] 1 All ER 203.
[51] *X v Y* [1988] 2 All ER 648, discussed by Robertson and Nicol (n 24 above) 331. See also *Interbrew* (n 32 above) *per* Sedley J, paras 18–23.
[52] ibid para 51.

(in this case the government) to show that one of the section 10 of the Contempt of Court Act 1981 exceptions applies, and, in relation to national security, it said that the party seeking the disclosure must provide as much specific information as possible as to why disclosure is necessary in the interests of justice.[53] The Court upheld the order for disclosure even though there was only a reasonable chance that delivery up of the documents would reveal the source.

3.6.4 In the interests of justice

In several cases the effectiveness of the section 10 shield depended on the court's interpretation of the phrase 'interests of justice'. When the Court of Appeal considered the issue in the *Ashworth* case Lord Phillips MR held that the 'interests of justice' in section 10 is not limited to the administration of justice in the course of legal proceedings.[54] Instead, the phrase should be given the broader interpretation recommended by Lord Bridge in *X Ltd v Morgan-Grampian (Publishers) Ltd*:

> It is, in my opinion, 'in the interests of justice', in the sense in which this phrase is used in s10, that persons should be enabled to exercise important legal rights and to protect themselves from serious legal wrongs whether or not resort to legal proceedings in a court of law will be necessary to attain these objectives. Thus, to take a very obvious example, if an employer of a large staff is suffering grave damage from the activities of an unidentified disloyal servant, it is undoubtedly in the interests of justice that he should be able to identify him in order to terminate his contract of employment, notwithstanding that no legal proceedings may be necessary to achieve that end.[55]

3.7 NECESSITY AND PROPORTIONALITY

Section 10 and Article 10 require that the disclosure must be necessary, otherwise the presumption in favour of protection of sources cannot be overridden.[56] There are two aspects to necessity. First, as discussed above, there is no necessity if the party seeking the order cannot bring itself within one of the four exceptions set out in section 10.[57] In such cases the journalist's statutory right to refuse to disclose the source is preserved intact. Secondly, it is not enough to establish that the facts of the case fit within one of the exceptions and that the disclosure of the source is necessary to meet

---

[53] *Secretary of State for Defence v Guardian Newspapers Ltd* [1984] 3 All ER 601, *per* Lord Diplock, 604. Lord Fraser at 604 said that sufficient evidence is required to establish that disclosure is necessary, including information about the seriousness of the leak—a bare assertion in an affidavit is not sufficient.

[54] This was the narrow interpretation given to the phrase by Lord Diplock in *Secretary of State for Defence v Guardian Newspapers Ltd*.

[55] *X Ltd v Morgan-Grampian* (n 28 above) *per* Lord Bridge, 6 cited in *Ashworth* (n 37 above) para 84.

[56] Contempt of Court Act 1981, s 10 requires disclosure to be necessary for one of the listed purposes and Art 10(2) requires disclosure to be 'necessary in a democratic society'.

[57] *X Ltd v Morgan-Grampian* (n 28 above) *per* Lord Bridge, at 6.

one of those legitimate aims; the disclosure order must be a 'necessary and proportionate' response.[58]

In the *Ashcroft* case, the House of Lords endorsed the approach outlined by Lord Bridge (supported by Lord Oliver and Lord Lowry) in *X Ltd v Morgan Grampian-Publishers Ltd* that the 'balancing exercise' required to be undertaken in order to establish that disclosure is necessary in the interests of justice under section 10 is the same as that required for Article 10(2).[59] The court's job is to weigh competing public interests against each other:

It will not be sufficient, per se, for a party seeking disclosure of a source protected by s 10 to show merely that he will be unable without disclosure to exercise the legal right or avert the threatened legal wrong on which he bases his claim in order to establish the necessity of disclosure. The judge's task will always be to weigh in the scales the importance of enabling the ends of justice to be attained in the circumstances of the particular case on the one hand against the importance of protecting the source on the other hand. In this balancing exercise it is only if the judge is satisfied that disclosure in the interests of justice is of such preponderating importance as to override the statutory privilege against disclosure that the threshold of necessity will be reached.[60]

The Court of Appeal in the *Ashworth* case had highlighted the need to reconcile section 10 and Article 10. Whilst the two provisions are similar, Article 10(2) does not include 'interests of justice' as an exception to the presumption in favour of free speech.[61] The House of Lords in *Ashworth* said that the same approach should be applied to both now that Article 10 is part of our domestic law.[62]

In *Mersey Care NHS Trust v Ackroyd*—the sequel to *Ashworth*—Tugendhat J refined the balancing exercise with reference to the later decision of the House of Lords in *Re S* about the approach required when dealing with conflicting Convention rights.[63] In *Re S* Lord Steyn said:

The interplay between articles 8 and 10 has been illuminated by the opinions of the House of Lords in *Campbell v MGN Ltd* [2004] 2 WLR 1232. For the present purposes the decision of the House on the facts of *Campbell* and the differences between the majority and the minority are not material. What does, however, emerge clearly from the opinions are four propositions. First, neither article has as such precedence over the other. Secondly, where the values under the two articles are in conflict an intense focus on the comparative importance of the specific rights being claimed in the individual case is necessary. Thirdly, the justifications for interfering with or restricting each right must be taken into account. Finally the proportionality test must be applied to each. For convenience I will call this the ultimate balancing test.[64]

---

[58] *Ashworth* (n 37 above) *per* Lord Woolf CJ, para 36.
[59] ibid para 39.
[60] *X Ltd v Morgan-Grampian* (n 28 above) 8–9.
[61] *Ashworth* (n 37 above) *per* Lord Phillips MR, paras 77 and 78.
[62] ibid *per* Lord Woolf CJ, para 39.
[63] *Mersey Care NHS Trust v Ackroyd* [2006] EWHC 107, para 103. This approach was endorsed by the Court of Appeal in that case, see *Mersey Care NHS Trust v Robin Ackroyd* [2007] EWCA Civ 101, para 29.
[64] *Re S (A Child)* [2005] 1 AC 593, para 17. The case is about reporting restrictions.

The House of Lords in the *Ashworth* case said that the requirements of necessity and proportionality are separate concepts which cover substantially the same area and that the Strasbourg Court's decision in *Goodwin* should be followed. [65] The test for necessity in section 10 is 'an overriding requirement in the public interest' as set out in *Goodwin*:

Having regard to the importance of the protection of journalistic sources for press freedom in a democratic society and the potentially chilling effect an order of source disclosure has on the exercise of that freedom, such a measure [an order for disclosure] cannot be compatible with art 10 of the convention unless it is justified by an overriding requirement in the public interest.[66]

Following the *Goodwin* case, the 'necessity' for any restriction of freedom of expression must be convincingly established and the limitations on the confidentiality of journalistic sources call for the most careful scrutiny by the court.[67] In addition, in order to comply with the requirements of Article 10(2) the exercise of the disclosure jurisdiction must meet a 'pressing social need' and the restriction must be proportionate to a legitimate aim that is being pursued.[68]

3.7.1 Factors relevant to necessity and proportionality

The factors to be put in the balance when deciding whether it has been convincingly established that there is a pressing social need to require a journalist to reveal his or her source will, to a very great extent, depend on the facts each case. In the *Ashworth* case Lord Woolf described the *Norwich Pharmacal* jurisdiction as a 'discretionary jurisdiction'.[69] The varying outcomes, in cases that are similar, or closely related, support that analysis of the disclosure jurisdiction.[70] Some of the factors the courts have considered relevant to the issues of necessity and proportionality in recent cases are discussed below.

3.7.1.1 *Other avenues of inquiry*
The disclosure order may not be necessary if other means of obtaining the information have not been pursued.[71] But, does this mean that the party seeking the order must show that all other avenues have been exhausted before an approach is made to the

---

[65] *Ashworth Hospital Authority v MGN Ltd* [2002] UKHL 29, para 63.

[66] *Goodwin v UK* (1996) 22 EHRR 123, para 39.

[67] *Ashworth* (n 65 above) para 63.

[68] ibid para 62; *Goodwin* (n 66 above) para 40. See also *Sunday Times v UK* (1979) 2 EHRR para 59.

[69] *Ashworth* (n 65 above) *per* Lord Woolf CJ, para 36. But see *Mersey Care NHS Trust v Robin Ackroyd* [2007] EWCA Civ 101, *per* Sir Anthony Clarke MR, paras 33–36 and also *Interbrew SA v Financial Times Ltd and ors* [2002] EWCA Civ 274, *per* Sedley J paras 44–47: 'Deciding whether disclosure is necessary for one of the listed purposes is a matter of hard-edged judgment, albeit one of both fact and law, and none the less so for having to respect the principles of proportionality . . .'

[70] cf *Ashworth* (n 65 above) with *Mersey Care NHS Trust v Ackroyd* [2006] EWHC 107, and *Goodwin* (n 66 above) with *X Ltd v Morgan-Grampian (Publishers) Ltd* [1990] 2 All ER1.

[71] In *John v Express Newspapers plc* [2000] All ER (D) 575, the Court of Appeal overturned an order for disclosure because no attempt had been made to trace the source of the leak.

media defendant? In *Secretary of State for Defence v Guardian Newspapers Ltd* Lord Roskill said that such a principle would place the applicant 'on the horns of a dilemma': if it delayed the application in order to pursue all other lines of inquiry then a subsequent application for a disclosure order against the media defendant might be defeated on grounds that the order should have been made earlier.[72]

The question of whether the *Norwich Pharmacal* jurisdiction is a remedy of last resort has been debated more recently. In some cases it has been suggested that the disclosure jurisdiction can only be exercised when the party against whom an order is sought is the only practicable source of information and the missing piece of the puzzle.[73] However, in *R (on the application of Mohamed) v Secretary of State for Commonwealth Affairs* the Divisional Court said that to suggest that the disclosure order must be the last piece of the jigsaw puts the test of necessity too high. The court should consider matters such as the size and resources of the applicant, the urgency of its need to identify the source, and the public interest in the disclosure of the source.[74]

3.7.1.2 *The type of information*

The threshold for establishing necessity and proportionality is high. In the *Goodwin* case information from a source about the financial status of the claimant company was never published because an injunction was granted when the journalist put allegations to the company in advance of publishing a story. The Strasbourg Court held that since an order had already been made prohibiting publication of confidential information the order for disclosure was not necessary and breached Article 10: 'The Court does not therefore consider that the further purposes [tracing the source] served by the disclosure order, when measured against the standards imposed by the Convention, amount to an overriding requirement in the public interest.'[75] On the facts of the case the proportionality requirement in Article 10(2) had not been satisfied:

... there was not, in the Court's view, a reasonable relationship of proportionality between the legitimate aim pursued by the disclosure order and the means deployed to achieve that aim. The restriction which the disclosure order entailed on the applicant journalist's exercise of his freedom of expression cannot therefore be regarded as having been necessary in a democratic society, within the meaning of paragraph 2 of Article 10 (art. 10.2), for the protection of [the applicants] under English law, notwithstanding the margin of appreciation available to the national authorities.[76]

---

[72] *Secretary of State for Defence v Guardian Newspapers Ltd* (n 53 above), see also Lord Bridge at 624.

[73] *Mitsui v Nexen Petroleum* [2005] EWHC 625 CH, *per* Lightman J paras 19–24 and *Nikitin and ors v Richards Butler LLP* [2007] EWHC 173 QB in which Langley J said, at para 24, that the party seeking the order for disclosure should show that the information sought is vital to a decision to sue, or an ability to plead, and cannot be obtained from other sources.

[74] *R (on the application of Mohamed) v Secretary of State for Commonweath Affairs* [2008] EWHC 2048 (Admin), paras 93–94. See also *Interbrew* (n 69 above) *per* Sedley J, para 53.

[75] *Goodwin* (n 66 above) para 45.

[76] ibid para 46.

In contrast, the House of Lords decided that, on its facts, the case of *Ashworth* was 'exceptional' and an order for disclosure should be made. A great deal hung on the fact that these were medical records:

The situation here is exceptional ... as it has to be, if disclosure of sources is to be justified. The care of patients at Ashworth is fraught with difficulty and danger. The disclosure of the patients' records increases that difficulty and danger and to deter the same or similar wrongdoing in the future it was essential that the source should be identified and punished. This was what made the orders to disclose necessary and proportionate and justified.[77]

The Court found that the leak would have an inhibiting effect on the doctor/patient relationship and that there was a cloud of suspicion over other employees at the hospital. It is worth noting that the passage quoted above includes the suggestion that the general deterrent effect of a disclosure order on those who might be tempted to leak information is relevant to the question of necessity and proportionality.

The House of Lords took into account the decision of the European Court in the case of *Z v Finland*, which was not concerned with disclosure of journalistic sources but with the need to preserve confidentiality of medical records and the Article 8 rights of a patient.[78] In that case the Strasbourg Court held that domestic law should afford appropriate safeguards to prevent disclosure of health data because it is critical, not only to the issue of respect for patient privacy but also for the purpose of preserving confidence in the medical profession and healthcare systems.

3.7.1.3 *The source's conduct and nature of the wrongdoing*
The source's conduct and the nature of the wrongdoing are also relevant to the issues of necessity and proportionality.[79] In the *Ashworth* case the fact that Ian Brady had himself disclosed information about his medical treatment did not detract from the need to prevent staff from revealing patient records.[80]

Mersey Care NHS Trust v Ackroyd, as noted, was the sequel to *Ashworth*.[81] Following the House of Lords' judgment in *Ashworth*, the *Daily Mirror*, in compliance with the disclosure order, gave the hospital authority details of the intermediary who had provided the newspaper with information for its story, but this did not lead to the source. The intermediary was another journalist, Robin Ackroyd, who refused to identify his source. Consequently there was another trial about the events. However, this time the Court declined to make an order for disclosure.[82]

The Court of Appeal in the *Ackroyd* case upheld the decision of Tugendhat J and said that the question of whether or not it was necessary and proportionate to order the disclosure of the source was a matter for the trial judge who had the task of balancing

---

[77] *Ashworth* (n 65 above) para 66.
[78] *Z v Finland* [1998] 25 EHRR 371.
[79] *Ashworth* (n 65 above) *per* Lord Woolf CJ, paras 65 and 66.
[80] ibid para 66.
[81] *Mersey Care NHS Trust v Ackroyd* [2006] EWHC 107 (QB).
[82] ibid.

the conflicting interests of the parties. An appellate court should not interfere 'unless it is persuaded he erred in principle or reached a conclusion that was plainly wrong; that is a conclusion outside the ambit of conclusions which a judge could reasonably reach'.[83]

In his closing remarks, Tugendhat J was careful to say that, although he reached the opposite conclusion to the House of Lords in *Ashworth*, he had followed its decision on all points of law.[84] Nor did he consider that medical records were less deserving of protection, however, he had arrived at other findings of fact based on different (new) evidence—including the evidence of Robin Ackroyd. Among other things, he found that only parts of the notes had been disclosed and that medical information of extreme sensitivity had been left out. He also found that it was not possible to say that the information had been disclosed without Ian Brady's consent—it was similar to information he had put in the public domain. There was also the passage of time to consider.[85]

3.7.1.4 *Public interest in the information disclosed*
The presumption in favour of the protection of journalistic sources does not depend on whether the material disclosed by the source is in the public interest.[86] In *Interbrew SA v Financial Times* Sedley J described the public interest in the confidentiality of journalists' sources as 'constant'.[87] Indeed, there is no mention of public interest in either section 10 or Article 10. However, information disclosed by a source about matters of public interest may obtain a higher degree of protection and tip the balance in favour of freedom of expression.[88]

3.7.1.5 *Source's motive*
On the one hand, the public interest in disclosure of source is 'constant'—whatever the merits of the information or the motives and character of the source.[89] On the other hand, the source's purpose, while not a deciding factor, may weigh against the presumption in favour of non-disclosure in section 10.[90] In *Interbrew SA v Financial Times* the purpose of the source was considered to be an important factor. Sedley LJ asked: 'Is the necessity of disclosure affected by the source's motive?'[91] He made a distinction between the motive of the source, which is 'ordinarily pure guesswork' and 'immaterial

---

[83] *Mersey Care NHS Trust v Robin Ackroyd* [2007] EWCA Civ 101, paras 33–36.
[84] *Mersey Care NHS Trust v Ackroyd* (n 81 above) para 196.
[85] ibid paras 134, 135, 144, 147, and 193.
[86] *Secretary of State for Defence v Guardian Newspapers Ltd* (n 53 above) *per* Lord Diplock, 605 and *Ashworth* (n 65 above) *per* Laws LJ, para 101: 'The public interest in the non-disclosure of press sources is constant, whatever the merits of the particular publication, and the particular source.'
[87] *Interbrew* (n 69 above) *per* Sedley LJ, para 53.
[88] *Mersey Care NHS Trust v Ackroyd* (n 81 above) paras 105–119 and *Mersey Care NHS Trust v Robin Ackroyd* (n 83 above) para 30. See also *Sunday Times v UK* (n 68 above) para 65.
[89] *Ashworth* (n 65 above) *per* Laws LJ, para 101.
[90] *Interbrew* (n 65 above).
[91] ibid para 15.

to the legal issues' and the source's purpose in leaking the information, which he considered to be 'highly material':

If it [the purpose of the leak] is to bring wrongdoing to public notice it will deserve a high degree of protection, and it will not matter—assuming that it could anyway be ascertained—whether the motive is conscience or spite. If the purpose of the leak is to wreck legitimate commercial activity, again it will not matter whether it is done for political motives or personal gain: it will be less deserving of protection. For these reasons the court of first instance, while not speculating about motive, needs to form the best view it can of the source's purpose . . . where a case for overriding the privilege against disclosure is made out, the consequent chilling effect, as Lord Phillips MR said in *Ashworth*, may be no bad thing.[92]

The idea that the motive of the source is critical in deciding whether an order should be made goes to the heart of a fundamental, but rarely explored, question about section 10. Does it exist to protect journalists' sources or to protect the journalists' newsgathering activities and therefore the free flow of information? The different approaches of the Court of Appeal in *Interbrew* and *Ashworth* suggest there is some confusion about this issue.[93]

In the *Ashworth* case the assumption that the source had been paid was considered to be relevant to the issue of necessity, but when the facts about the leak of Ian Brady's medical information were considered afresh in the *Ackroyd* case, Tugendhat J found that the source did not have a financial motive and was probably involved in a misguided attempt to act in the public interest and that this was a significant factor:

If the motive were financial there would be the obvious risk of repetition referred to in the MGN case. And the fact that no repetition has occurred so far would be little indication to the contrary. It would be consistent with the source lying low . . . But a source who misguidedly thought he or she was acting in the public interest in the extraordinary circumstances of October 1999 (when Ian Brady had a well founded complaint of mistreatment by the hospital which followed the dreadful history set out in the Fallon report) is not a person who can be said to present a significant risk of disclosure . . .[94]

3.7.1.6 *Journalist's conduct*
In the *Ackroyd* case Tugendhat J put into the scales the journalist's conduct on the basis that this reflected the approach taken in other cases relating to journalists' exercise of their rights of free speech, such as *Reynolds*.[95] The journalist had a record of investigative reporting and it was not in the public interest that his sources should be discouraged from speaking to him.[96]

---

[92] ibid para 42.
[93] Contrast Sedley LJ in *Interbrew* (n 69 above) para 42 with Laws LJ in *Ashworth* (n 65 above) para 101.
[94] *Mersey Care NHS Trust v Ackroyd* (n 81 above) para 188
[95] *Reynolds v Times Newspapers Ltd* [1999] 4 All ER 609, 626.
[96] *Mersey Care NHS Trust v Ackroyd* (n 81 above) paras 174 and 196.

3.7.1.7 *Truth or falsity of the information*

In *Interbrew SA v Financial Times* it was alleged that parts of a document disclosed by an anonymous source about the takeover of the brewery had been forged. Whilst that was not a deciding factor, Sedley LJ said: 'if this were a case in which the falsehood of the nub of the story had been established . . . it would in my judgement be an additional reason for overriding the protection accorded to the source'. He added: 'If, as the Court stressed in *Goodwin* . . . the central purpose of the shielding of journalists' sources is to enable the press to provide accurate and reliable information, to the extent that that purpose is departed from the rationale of the protection recedes . . .'[97]

Sedley LJ recognized, however, that if the claimant asserts that the source's information is false or claims that the documents have been falsified the media defendant is at a distinct disadvantage because it may not be in a position to prove otherwise:

I have to say that I find this aspect of the *Norwich Pharmacal* procedure troubling. A commercial enterprise which may very well have its own reasons for denying the authenticity of a document gets a clear run against a media defendant which can only, save in rare cases, take a neutral stand on the question. The court of first instance needs to be extremely circumspect before accepting evidence, especially when, as here it is second or third-hand.[98]

The courts need to scrutinize carefully evidence given by applicants for source information from media defendants in all contexts, including criminal investigations. Journalists will often be at a disadvantage when faced with assertions about the need for disclosure of journalistic material in order to progress a criminal investigation.

3.8 CRIMINAL INVESTIGATIONS

3.8.1 Police powers to breach journalistic privacy

Police powers to search for, and seize, journalistic material have widened in scope since the Police and Criminal Evidence Act 1984 (PACE 1984) came into force. New criminal offences have been created for failing to disclose information in relation to terrorism and serious organized crime and fraud.[99] Statutory powers not only to obtain documents, but also to compel the disclosure of information have increased in scope.

Police powers of search and seizure are set out in PACE 1984. Similar powers are contained in the Terrorism Act 2000, the Official Secrets Act 1989, and statutes such as the Serious Organized Crime and Police Act 2000 that create additional powers to compel disclosure of information. The Regulation of Investigatory Powers Act 2000 allows investigators to obtain journalists' material through covert means, including the interception of e-mails and telephone calls.

---

[97] *Interbrew* (n 69 above) para 42.
[98] ibid para 41.
[99] See the Financial Services and Markets Act 2000; the Police Act 1997; the Criminal Justice Act 1997.

The use of coercive powers by the state to obtain information from journalists and media organizations must be viewed as a potential threat to the freedom to investigate and report to the public in a democracy, and there must be strong safeguards of the right to freedom of expression.[100]

These are serious powers, with serious consequences: penalties for failure to comply include imprisonment, and if a journalist or newspaper fails to comply with a production order by refusing to hand over material, police may obtain a warrant to enter media premises to search for and seize material. In other circumstances entry to premises to seize material would be unlawful or tortious: 'By the law of England every invasion of private property, be it ever so minute, is a trespass. No man can set foot upon my ground without my licence, but he is liable to an action though the damage be nothing.'[101]

The image of police raids on news organizations sits uneasily with our view of a liberal democracy. Such events are rare, but they happen: in 1987, the police raided BBC Scotland's offices in connection with a proposed broadcast of a film about Zircon, the spy satellite.[102] More recently (in 2007 and 2008) police searched the offices of a local newspaper, seizing a journalist's notebooks, e-mails, and contact books. They also placed a listening device in the journalist's car to 'bug' conversations.[103]

Media organizations often face police requests and applications for the production of journalistic material under PACE 1984. In most, but not all, cases requests from the police for journalistic material are resisted unless there is a court order requiring the documents to be produced.[104] However, it is difficult to establish accurate data on how often police powers are used to seize journalistic material in connection with terrorism or other serious crimes[105]—in many cases it may be a criminal offence even to disclose that an application for disclosure has been made.[106]

It is accepted that the use of compulsion to disclose documents is an incursion on individual rights—Lord Scarman described the powers of Customs and Revenue officials to obtain a search warrant where they suspected a serious tax fraud was being, or was about to be committed[107] as 'a breathtaking inroad on the individual's right of

---

[100] 'Without such protection, sources may be deterred from assisting the press in informing the public in matters of public interest. As a result the vital public-watchdog role of the press may be undermined and the ability of the press to provide accurate and reliable information may be adversely affected.' (*Goodwin v UK* 17488/90 [1996] ECHR 16, 27 March 1996).

[101] *Entick & Carrington* 1765 19 St Tr 1030, 1066.

[102] Offices of the *New Statesman* were raided by Special Branch in connection with journalistic investigation into the Zircon affair in 1987, see 'BBC gag on £500m Defence Secret' *The Observer*, 18 January 1987 and D Campbell, 'The day Cook saved the New Statesman' *New Statesman*, 22 August 2005.

[103] *R v Sally Murrer and ors*, Crown Court, Kingston upon Thames, November 2008; the case was stayed under PACE 1984, s 78 as the covert surveillance was a breach of Art 10 ECHR.

[104] Material may be surrendered voluntarily by a person who holds it without the consent of the person to whom it relates: *R v Singelton* [1995] 1 Cr App R 431.

[105] Around 700 applications each year, mostly uncontested (*per* Gavin Millar QC and Heather Rogers QC, Seminar held at Matrix Chambers, 2008).

[106] Terrorism Act 2000; Proceeds of Crime Act 2002, Pt 7.

[107] The Taxes Management Act 1970, s 20 conferred powers on HMRC officials to obtain a search warrant from a circuit judge where there were reasonable grounds to suspect that a serious tax fraud is

privacy and right of property'. [108] When such powers are used against the press they represent both a breach of privacy and a threat to freedom of expression: both the freedom to conduct journalistic investigations and to report on matters of public interest. As discussed above, Article 10 of the ECHR provides journalists and media organizations with a strong presumptive right to protect sources from disclosure. [109] In *Ex parte Simms and O'Brien* the prison service refused to allow journalists to visit and interview prisoners in order to investigate alleged miscarriages of justice. The House of Lords overturned the refusal, pointing out the key role of the media in contributing to the free flow of information that is the lifeblood of democracy.[110]

It has been accepted that the danger of exposing sources is that it may inhibit future whistleblowers from disclosing information, and therefore prevent journalists from reporting on matters of public interest. But the personal safety of frontline reporters and photographers is also a vital issue. If the press is seen to be freely passing on information to investigating authorities then reporters and photographers will be at risk of becoming targets at public events and demonstrations.[111] This risk is at its most obvious in war zones: 'in order to do their jobs effectively, war correspondents must be perceived as independent observers rather than potential witnesses for the prosecution'.[112]

In 2007, the Council of Europe's guidelines to Member States (following its Recommendation No R (2000) 7) were that, to ensure their safety, journalists should not be required to hand over notes, photographs, audio, or video in crisis situations.[113] What is at risk is 'the impartiality and independence of the press, the importance of ensuring that members of the press can photograph and report what is going on without fear of their personal safety'.[114]

An application under PACE 1984 brings into the arena the competing public interest in the investigation and prevention of crime, and the public interest in the press being free to report and photograph 'as much as they can of what is going on in our great cities'.[115] Any interference with the right to freedom of expression must be justified as being an overriding requirement or fulfilling a pressing social need, and must be necessary and proportionate.[116]

---

being, had been, or was about to be committed, and that there would be evidence on the premises specified in the application.

[108] *R v IRC, ex p Rossminster Ltd* [1980] AC 952, 1022; these powers were amended in 1989.

[109] *Goodwin v UK* (n 100 above).

[110] *R v Secretary of State for Home Department, ex p Simms and O'Brien* [1999] 3 All ER 100, HL.

[111] Evidence of Chris Elliott, Managing Editor, *The Guardian*, in *City of London Police v The Guardian, The Times, The Independent and ors* (Central Criminal Court, 2 July 1999): police application for photos of demonstrators, 'Carnival Against Capitalism', 18 June 1998.

[112] Case IT-99-36-AR73.9 *Prosecutor v Radoslav Brdjanin and Momir Talic* Decision on Interlocutory Appeal, ICTY, 11 December 2002.

[113] Recommendation No R 2000 7 of the Committee of Ministers of Council of Europe. See also Guidelines of the Committee of Ministers on protecting freedom of expression and information in times of crisis, para III(13) and (14). Adopted by Committee of Ministers 26 September 2007.

[114] *R v Bristol Crown Court, ex p Bristol Press and Picture Agency* (1987) 85 Cr App R.

[115] ibid.

[116] Art 10 ECHR.

3.8.2 Production orders: Police and Criminal Evidence Act 1984

Police powers to search and seize material are based in both common law and statutory principles. Before PACE 1984 the law on police powers was 'haphazard and irrational':[117] around fifty statutes included various powers to issue search warrants. PACE 1984 (and its Code of Practice B) simultaneously created new powers to search for evidence and limited existing statutory and common law powers.

It is important to consider PACE 1984 in detail, as it has provided a template for subsequent legislation on search and seizure powers, although the limited protections under the Act have been diluted in later statutes.

Journalistic material is one of the categories of privileged material recognized under PACE 1984. While magistrates have the general power to grant a search warrant to the police, as set out in section 8, this does not extend to legally privileged material (which is exempt from disclosure),[118] 'excluded material', or 'special procedure material'. The latter two categories, set out in sections 11 and 14 of PACE 1984, include 'journalistic material'.

While there is some attempt to define 'journalistic material', it is, perhaps intentionally, a very broad definition: 'material acquired or created for the purposes of journalism'.[119] The courts have accepted that journalistic material extends to a range of forms of publication such as books and photographs.[120] However, 'journalism' itself is not defined. The definition of journalistic material would protect self-publishing bloggers from disclosure applications, only if they could show that they held the 'material' (for example notes about a source, or a source's e-mail address) for journalistic purposes. Note that once the material is passed to another person, for a purpose other than journalism (for example to avoid disclosure), it ceases to be journalistic material.

Journalistic material is 'excluded material' under section 11 if it comprises documents or records held in confidence.[121] It must have been held continuously subject to an express or implied undertaking to hold it in confidence or to a statutory restriction on disclosure or obligation of secrecy since it was first acquired or created for the purposes of journalism.[122] So, if at any stage a source no longer requires confidentiality, their details may no longer constitute excluded material under section 11 (although the material might still be protected as 'special procedure material', see below).

Alternatively, journalistic material may be 'special procedure' material under section 14, which includes: (a) material created or acquired by a person in their work and held in confidence and (b) journalistic material (ie not held subject to the continuous confidentiality requirement in section 11). It includes material such as photographs

---

[117] AW Bradley, *Constitutional and Administrative Law* (Langman, 14th edn, 2009) 495.
[118] This includes legal advice and litigation privilege. Items held with the intention of furthering a criminal purpose are not subject to legal privilege.
[119] PACE 1984, s 13.
[120] *Malik v Manchester Crown Court and ors* [2008] EWHC 1362 (Admin) (19 June 2008) and *R v Bristol Crown Court, ex p Bristol Press and Picture Agency* (n 114 above).
[121] PACE 1984, s 11(c).
[122] ibid s 11(3).

and film. Amendments introduced by the Criminal Justice and Police Act 2001 (CJPA 2001) allow the police to seize 'mixed' material, for example by seizing a computer, and to 'search and sift' the material off the premises to determine which is special procedure material (requiring an application under Schedule 1) and which is not. [123]

In order to obtain journalistic material, an *inter partes* (on notice) application must be made to a circuit judge.[124] The judge may make an order requiring the material to be delivered to a police constable or investigating officer within seven days.[125] The judge may only order the handing over of such material if the first or second set of 'access conditions' in Schedule 1 to the Act are met.

3.8.2.1 *Access conditions*

Access conditions are set out in Schedule 1. The first set of access conditions is fulfilled if there are reasonable grounds for believing that:

- an indictable offence has been committed;
- the material is likely to be of substantial value; or
- the material is likely to be relevant evidence.

Other means of obtaining the material should have been tried without success, or not tried because it appeared that such means were bound to fail.

The court must also consider the public interest, in particular whether handing over the material is in the public interest. Schedule 1.2(c) says that the court must have regard to the likely benefit to the investigation if the material is obtained, and 'the circumstances under which the person in possession of the material holds the material'.[126]

The second set of access conditions apply if there are reasonable grounds for believing that there is material which consists of or includes excluded material on the premises specified, and a search of the premises could have been authorized by the issue of a warrant prior to PACE 1984, and the issue of such a warrant would have been appropriate.

Even if the access conditions are met in full, the court retains a discretion as to whether or not to make the order sought, bearing in mind wider public interest considerations, such as the principle against self-incrimination, and wider freedom of expression issues.[127] The judge exercises a vital role in scrutinizing the evidence and assessing whether the access conditions are met and whether the making of an order is in the public interest. It is not enough to proceed on the basis of unsubstantiated police statements: 'the judge cannot proceed on the basis of bare assertion by a police officer'; there is a

---

[123] CJPA 2001, ss 50 and 51 re additional powers of seizure—lawful search—to sift material off premises and return if excluded, special procedure, or legally privileged.

[124] Amendments not yet in force extend this jurisdiction to include a High Court Judge, Recorder, and District Judge (Magistrates Court).

[125] PACE 1984, s 9(1) authorizes production/access orders.

[126] PACE 1984, Sch 1, para 2(c)(i) and (ii).

[127] *R v Central Criminal Court, ex p Bright, Alton and Rusbridger* [2001] All ER 244, *per* Judge LJ.

duty on the part of the applicant to make full and frank disclosure.[128] This includes setting out what steps have been taken to seek the material from other sources and whether the application is necessary and proportionate. A fishing expedition is not justified.[129] Other reasonable steps should be taken before seeking information from the media.[130]

There must be reasonable grounds for believing an indictable offence has been committed and that there is special procedure material which is 'likely to be of substantial value to the investigation and is likely to be relevant evidence'. While the investigation must concern specific incidents the application does not need to link any particular document to any particular incident of violence or criminal offence.[131]

PACE 1984 provides two routes for police officers to gain access to special procedure material, and excluded material through a warrant.[132] Following the first route, an on notice *inter partes* application is made to a circuit judge who determines whether the grounds for making a production order ('access conditions' in Schedule 1) are satisfied. This is the usual route, as set out in paragraph 7.

A notice must be served on the person holding the material (it may not be the suspect). The notice must set out the offences being investigated, describe the material, and give the address(es) of premises at which it is believed the material is held (or all premises specified which are occupied or controlled by a specified person).[133] Once on notice, it is a contempt for the holder of material to conceal, alter, or destroy it, or to pass the material sought to a third party.

While the usual application must be on notice,[134] it is possible (but rare) to make an *ex parte* application for a search warrant on the grounds that (a) the access conditions are met and (b) one of four further conditions set out in paragraph 14 of Schedule 1, can be established:

(1) it is not practicable to communicate with the person entitled to grant entry to the relevant premises;

(2) it is not practicable to communicate with the person entitled to grant access to the relevant material;

---

[128] ibid. 'This application demanded full and proper disclosure. All these matters would be relevant to the exercise of the judge's discretion, but more important, they are also directly relevant to the question whether the access conditions were established.'

[129] *R v Bristol Crown Court, ex p Bristol Press and Picture Agency* (n 114 above).

[130] *R v Central Criminal Court, ex p Bright, Alton and Rusbridger* (n 127 above) *per* Judge LJ, para 50: police officer did not address whether Shayler's e-mail was already known to government.

[131] 'A whole series of possible offences arising out of disturbances such as these, he says, are too wide to come within the ambit and thus, unless in some way the material is identified as relating particularly to the throwing of a petrol bomb or the committing of an offence of violence or something of that sort, it does not fall within the section.' Judge at first instance: '—the inference I would draw in the absence of evidence is that photographers would take pictures (if they could) of assaults and other violence or damage for the very good reason that these are newsworthy'. *R v Bristol Crown Court, ex p Bristol Press and Picture Agency* (n 114 above).

[132] It makes no provision for access to legally privileged material—ie it is not obtainable.

[133] Serious Organised Crime and Police Act 2005 (SOCPA 2005) ss 113 and 114 amend PACE 1984 to allow 'all premises' warrants to be granted under that Act: a number of premises may be specified.

[134] PACE 1984, Sch 1, para 7.

(3) the material sought is in danger of being disclosed in breach of a restriction on disclosure (for example the Official Secrets Act 1911);

(4) proceedings *inter partes* might 'seriously prejudice the investigation'.

This practice was strongly disapproved of in *R v Maidstone Crown Court, ex parte Waitt*:[135] 'An ex parte application under paragraph 12 must never become a matter of common form'.[136] Nonetheless, the *ex parte* procedure continues to be used in circumstances that fall outside the above provisions, as in the police investigation into Sally Murrer, a *Milton Keynes Citizen* reporter, in order to discover her sources.[137]

The judge must be personally satisfied that the statutory requirements—one of the sets of access conditions—have been met, interposing his judgment between the opinion of the police officer seeking the order, and the consequences to the journalist or media organization. He is not simply asking whether the decision of the constable making an application is reasonable, or whether it might be susceptible to judicial review. He is required to act as a safeguard, given that 'an order will force or oblige the individual against who it is made to act under compulsion when, without the order, he would be free to do otherwise'.[138]

The police officer must therefore produce evidence to satisfy the court that there exist reasonable grounds to suspect that there is likely to be material of substantial value to an investigation into indictable offences.[139] It is not enough to simply assert the fact in the application notice.

Grounds for belief, not merely grounds for suspicion, are required, and the material to be produced or disclosed must be more than general information which might be helpful to police inquiries, but evidence in the sense in which that term is applied in the Crown Court, 'relevant and admissible' at a trial.[140]

If the judge is persuaded that the 'access conditions' under Schedule 1 are satisfied, as required under section 9 of PACE 1984, he may make the order. He still retains discretion as to whether or not to make the order. Whilst neither section 9 nor Schedule 1 of PACE 1984 contain a statutory requirement to weigh press freedom against the public interest in facilitating a criminal investigation, they make provision for the court to consider the public interest, in the light of all the circumstances under which the person holds the material.

---

[135] *R v Waitt* [1988] Crim LR 384: 'The special procedure under section 9 and schedule 1 is a serious inroad upon the liberty of the subject. The responsibility for ensuring that the procedure is not abused lies with circuit judges . . . The responsibility is greatest when the circuit judge is asked to issue a search warrant under paragraph 12. It is essential that the reason for authorising the seizure is always made clear.'

[136] ibid, see also *R v Soton Crown Court, ex p J and P* [1999] 30 Crim LR 961 and *R v CCC, ex p AJD Holdings Ltd* [1992] Crim LR 669.

[137] 'Meet Sally. Her case should scare us all.' *The Observer*, 21 November 2008.

[138] *R v Central Criminal Court, ex p Bright, Alton and Rusbridger* (n 127 above) para 78.

[139] ibid, with reference to Lord Diplock's reasoning in *R v IRC, ex p Rossminster* (n 108 above) 1011 (e)–(f): 'the onus would be upon the officer to satisfy the court that there did in fact exist reasonable grounds.'

[140] *R v Central Criminal Court* (n 127 above) para 78.

This residual discretion, which remains even after the access conditions are met, should allow the court to consider other issues and interests concerning criminal justice and human rights, for example the privilege against self-incrimination.[141] As *per* Lord Justice Judge in *R v Central Criminal Court, ex parte Bright, Alton and Rusbridger*: 'This provision, as it seems to me, is the final safeguard against an oppressive order, and in an appropriate case, provides the judge with the opportunity to reflect on and take account of matters which are not expressly referred to in the set of relevant access conditions.'

What consequences follow? A successful application results in a production order which is directed to the person who appears to be in possession of the relevant material. Entry to premises is not immediately authorized. The order imposes a personal obligation on the individual to whom it is addressed to hand over or give access to the material.[142]

If the respondent does not comply with the production order, a judge may issue a search warrant. The warrant authorizes a police officer or a designated investigating officer to enter and search the premises and seize the material in question (Schedule 1, paragraph 12). This can either be a specific premises or an all premises warrants.[143]

The person who fails to comply not only faces the possibility of a search of the relevant premises, but also faces penalties as if he had committed a contempt (Schedule 1, paragraph 15): 'non-compliance . . . may have serious consequences, including an order of imprisonment. On this basis alone it therefore behoves a judge to act with great circumspection before making an order.'[144]

3.9 JOURNALISTIC PRIVILEGE IN PRACTICE

The fact that journalistic material receives some protection in PACE 1984 reflects the fact that the right to freedom of expression is engaged when police powers are used against media organizations. The court, in the person of the circuit judge (or other judge, see n 124 above), plays a vital role in assessing whether a production order, which engages Article 10 and constitutes a breach thereof, is justified: whether there is an overriding requirement or a pressing social need for the order, and if it is both necessary and proportionate.

---

[141] ibid. Judge LJ concludes: 'special procedure orders do not exclude the privilege against self-incrimination'; if not dealt with as part of the access conditions, this would be dealt with as matter of public interest as defined in para (c) and fall to be considered when the judge decides whether to exercise his discretion.

[142] ibid para 77.

[143] Note, *Khan v Commissioner of Police of the Metropolis* [2008] WLR (D) 182 CA (Pill, May, and Moses LJJ): 4 June 2008. PACE 1984, s 18 (as amended by SOCPA 2005, s 111, Sch 7, Pt 3), which gave the police the power to enter and search a premises occupied or controlled by a person under arrest without a warrant, should be construed literally so that the power could only be used where the premises were, in fact, occupied or controlled by a person who was under arrest.

[144] *R v Central Criminal Court ex parte Bright, Alton and Rusbridger* (n 127 above) para 77.

The access conditions should provide protections to journalistic material, but there is a danger that the case law is interpreted so that they are seen merely as technical hurdles. This has led to a somewhat sterile debate as to whether Article 10 issues should be considered at the 'access condition' stage, or whether the judge can put such issues to one side until he is asked to exercise his discretion, after having decided that the access conditions have been met.[145]

In 'Secrets, Spies and Whistleblowers: Freedom of Expression in the UK' (November 2000), the organizations Article 19 and Liberty, whilst welcoming the judgment of Judge LJ in *R v CCC, ex p Alton, Bright and Rusbridger*, expressed their concern that the decision focused on 'primarily procedural errors, not the balancing of freedom of expression in the context of a national security interest'.

Procedures do matter: police compliance provides a basic safeguard which is an essential first hurdle given that, if an order is made, they will be given the power to search premises and all that follows. It may be argued that the procedural hurdles themselves reflect the balancing of freedom of expression against the interests of the prevention and detection of crime. But this depends on the quality of the scrutiny of procedures: media organizations complain that too often the courts have treated these applications routinely, issuing production orders once the police applicant appears to have 'ticked the right boxes'. And there are other factors that may need to be considered when the judge exercises his discretion, such as the protection against self-incrimination (see below).

Procedures should reflect principles, and recent European cases have returned to the language of principles. *Roemen and Schmidt v Luxembourg*,[146] and *Ernst v Belgium*,[147] are important examples. In *Roemen*, searches of journalists' offices and homes were technically lawful under domestic law but the ECtHR found that they amounted to breaches of Article 10 and Article 8. In the *Ernst* case a search by 160 police officers of the offices and homes of four journalists to identify confidential sources was found to have violated Article 10 and Article 8. Perhaps not surprisingly, the European Court ruled that the searches were disproportionate, and that this infringement of freedom of expression was not 'necessary' in the sense of corresponding to a pressing social need.

In *Voskuil v the Netherlands* the ECtHR assessed the conduct of Dutch police against standards set out by the Council of Europe Committee of Ministers on the right of journalists not to disclose their sources of information.[148] The Dutch court had ordered the journalist, in criminal proceedings, to reveal the identity of a police source. He refused, and was imprisoned for thirty days. He complained to Strasbourg that the purpose of his detention was to compel him to reveal a source, and it was therefore unlawful. While the Court accepted that the state had a legitimate interest in identifying

[145] ibid, and see *Malik v Manchester Crown Court and ors* (n 120 above).
[146] *Roemen and Schmidt v Luxembourg* 51772/99 ECtHR (25 February 2003).
[147] *Ernst and ors v Belgium* B33400/96 (15 July 2003).
[148] Recommendation R (2000) 7.

the source to establish whether there had been a miscarriage of justice (police officers had allegedly fabricated evidence in a criminal case), in the light of the principles set out in the Recommendation, the Court found that even this important interest did not justify the action taken against the journalist.

In another case a journalist, Hans-Martin Tillack, complained of a violation by Belgian authorities of his right to protect his sources. Following his publication of articles about corruption in European institutions, based on confidential documents from the European Anti-Fraud Office, OLAF, Belgian judicial authorities opened an investigation for breach of confidence and bribery involving a civil servant. The Belgian police raided Hans-Martin Tillack's home and workplace and seized sixteen crates of papers, two boxes of files, two computers, four mobile phones and a metal cabinet. The ECtHR decided that the searches and seizures were a violation of Hans-Martin Tillack's right to freedom of expression under Article 10. While the Court accepted that the reasons given by Belgian courts were 'relevant', they could not be considered 'sufficient' to justify the searches. The investigation was based on uncorroborated rumours about the source. And the Court stressed that a journalist's right not to reveal sources was not 'a mere privilege' to be granted or taken away depending on the lawfulness or unlawfulness of the source's actions but was a fundamental part of the right to freedom of expression.[149]

In England, in *R v Kearney, Webb, Murrer* ('the Sally Murrer case'), the circuit judge viewed *Voskuil v Netherlands* as authority for the proposition that the Committee of Ministers' Recommendation 7 on journalistic sources is effectively binding.[150] Whether or not this is right, the Recommendation sets out principles fundamental to Article 10 and must be taken into account in any decisions on whether it is legitimate to take measures against journalists in order to obtain journalistic material for criminal proceedings.

In the Sally Murrer case, concerning the leaking of information from a police officer to a journalist and others, the police had placed a listening and tracking device in the journalist's car (and seized journalistic material from the newspaper's offices). Even though the covert surveillance had been authorized under the Police Act 1997 and the Regulation of Investigatory Powers Act 2000, the court decided, in the light of Recommendation 7, that the evidence had been obtained unlawfully and should be excluded. There had been an unwarranted interference with the right to freedom of expression under Article 10 that had not met the standards of being 'necessary'.[151]

---

[149] *Tillack v Belgium* 20477/05 ECtHR (27 November 2007).
[150] Recommendation R (2000) 7 of the Committee of Ministers of the Council of Europe.
[151] The prosecution then dropped the charges. *R v Kearney, Webb, Murrer*, Crown Court at Kingston Upon Thames, Case No T20077479, 25 November 2008.

3.10 TERRORISM, DISCLOSURE, AND SURVEILLANCE

There has been a raft of legislation connected to terrorism. The adoption of new laws prohibiting speech considered 'extremist' or supporting terrorism has an impact on journalists, as well as the wide powers given to authorities to seize material and conduct surveillance. The right to protect sources is recognized in law, but is often undermined by anti-terrorism laws.

The key statutes that impact on obtaining journalistic information are the Terrorism Acts 2000 and 2006 ('TACT 2000' and 'TACT 2006').

The breadth of the concept of 'terrorism' and the variety of political contexts in which terrorism occurs were heavily debated during the Bill's passage. It was pointed out that the definition was so wide it could include hunt saboteurs and community charge protesters in Trafalgar Square, and cover the activities of political leaders such as Nelson Mandela in the fight against apartheid in South Africa.[152] Journalists interviewing all sorts of political activists risk having notebooks seized under the terrorism legislation.

TACT 2000 potentially widens considerably the scope of material that might be recovered through an order, compared with PACE 1984. There are several features that distinguish the procedure for production orders under TACT 2000 from that set out in PACE 1984.

The statute creates similar categories of protected material to those set out in PACE 1984, but the breadth of its scope means that it is much easier for the police to obtain a wide range of journalistic material. Where the material sought consists of or includes excluded or special procedure material as defined in PACE 1984, an application should be made under Schedule 5 to TACT 2000—a police officer may apply to court for an order for the purposes of a 'terrorist investigation'.[153] As in PACE 1984, material that is legally privileged is exempt from disclosure.[154]

A terrorist investigation is defined under section 32 of TACT 2000 as the investigation of:

- the commission, preparation, or instigation of acts of terrorism;
- an act which appears to have been done for the purposes of terrorism;
- the resources of a proscribed organization;
- the possibility of making an order proscribing an organization (section 3(3));
- the commission, preparation, or instigation of an offence under TACT 2000 (or particular offences under TACT 2006).

In section 1 of TACT 2000 'terrorism' is defined as the use or threat of action where:

(1) the action:

    (a) involves serious violence against a person,

---

[152] *Hansard* HC Deb, 15 March 2000 vol 346 cols 381–419.
[153] TACT 2000, Sch 5(1).
[154] ibid 5(2).

(b) involves serious damage to property,

(c) endangers a person's life (other than that of the person committing the action),

(d) creates serious risk to the health or safety of the public or a section of the public, or

(e) is designed seriously to interfere with or disrupt an electronic system;

(2) the use or threat is designed to influence the government (or international governmental organizations) or to intimidate the public or a section of the public; and

(3) the use or threat is made for the purposes of advancing a political, religious, or ideological cause.

The definition of terrorism is not limited to events in the UK, and 'public' can be the public of a country other than the UK (TACT 2000, section 1(4)). In addition, 'government' is not limited to the central government of the UK, but can also mean a government of part of the UK (for example Scotland) and a foreign government.[155] The definition of property includes property wherever situated.[156]

An order for the production of journalistic material,[157] for the purposes of a terrorist investigation, may not only require a person to produce or make the material accessible to a constable, but may also require the person to state to the best of his knowledge and belief the location of material to which the application relates if it is not in, and it will not come into his possession, custody, or power within the period specified under (1) or (1). In other words, a journalist may be compelled to provide information (even if it is uncertain or speculative) to police authorities.

Schedule 5 sets out the access conditions, in similar terms to PACE 1984, but the order is sought for the purposes of an investigation only, and there is no need for the applicant to show that there are reasonable grounds to believe that the material is likely to be relevant, admissible evidence. The applicant need only show that the material is likely to be of substantial value either by itself, or together with other material, to a terrorist investigation. This is a much less clear and lower hurdle than in PACE 1984. The second access condition, in section 6(3), simply refers to 'the benefit likely to accrue to the terrorist investigation if the material is obtained'.[158]

If the order is not complied with, a circuit judge may grant an application for a warrant. This may be a specific premises or 'all premises' warrant.[159] The judge may also grant an application for a warrant if satisfied that there are reasonable grounds

---

[155] ibid s 1(4)(d).

[156] ibid s 121.

[157] ibid Sch 5, para 5(3)(c). (Note Criminal Procedure Rules may make provision about proceedings relating to an order, including the variation or discharge of an order: TACT 2000, Sch 5.)

[158] A judge may order any person who appears to be entitled to grant entry to premises to allow any constable to enter the premises to obtain access to the material (TACT 2000, Sch 5, para 5(5)).

[159] TACT 2006, s 26 amends Sch 5 to allow all premises warrants to be issued. These provisions are based on SOCPA 2025, ss 113 and 114, which amended PACE 1984 to allow all premises warrants to be granted under that Act.

for believing that there is material on premises specified in the application which consists of or includes excluded or special procedure material (but not legally privileged material) and that specified conditions are satisfied.[160]

The terrorism legislation includes the power to compel answers to questions: a constable may apply to a circuit judge for an order requiring any specified person to provide an explanation of any material handed over or seized in pursuance of a warrant, or made available under relevant provisions of TACT 2000.[161] The only ground on which refusal to disclose is allowed is legal professional privilege—although a lawyer may be required to provide the name and address of his client. The matter has not yet been tested, but it is likely that a journalist would rely on section 10 of the Contempt of Court Act 1981 to refuse to comply with the order.[162]

Disturbingly, the power to order urgent searches of media premises is delegated to the police themselves. In urgent applications, under section 37 and paragraph 15(1) and (2) of Schedule 5, a police officer, of at least the rank of superintendent, who has reasonable grounds to believe that immediate action is necessary, may, by written order signed by him, give to any constable the authority of a search warrant, under the relevant provisions of TACT 2000. Particulars of the case must be notified as soon as is reasonably practicable to the Secretary of State. It is an offence to wilfully obstruct a search under such an order. Similarly, a police officer (superintendent or above) may by written notice require an explanation of material.

In 2008, Shiv Malik, a freelance journalist, was ordered to hand over notes and other material in connection with a book he had written about Hassan Butt—a self-confessed reformed terrorist.[163] The High Court in a judicial review found that the order had been properly made, but it was too broad—Greater Manchester Police appeared to have been on a fishing expedition. The High Court decided that disclosure did not have to include information that might identify other sources. As Hassan Butt had already identified himself as involved in serious criminal activities, and as the material had been requested by 'A' in connection with another criminal trial in order to exonerate himself, the balance weighed against the protection of Butt as a source.[164]

---

[160] TACT 2000, Sch 5.

[161] ibid Sch 5, para 13.

[162] It is an offence to make a false or misleading statement either knowingly or recklessly. Penalty—indictment—2 years or a fine or both, summary—term not exceeding 6 months or fine not exceeding statutory max or both.

[163] Draft production orders were also served on CBS, the BBC and *The Sunday Times* but in the former case it was argued that it was outside the jurisdiction, and after the *Shiv Malik* judicial review there were no court proceedings involving the latter two organizations. *Malik v Manchester Crown Court and ors* [2008] EWHC 1362 (Admin) (19 June 2008).

[164] TACT 2000, Sch 5, para 12(2) as amended—a warrant is sought for purposes of terrorist investigation where material is likely to be of substantial value, whether by itself or together with other material, to a terrorist investigation, and it is not appropriate to make an order for the production of excluded material because:

(a) It is not practicable to communicate with any person entitled to produce the material;

(b) it is not practicable to communicate with any person entitled to grant access to the material, or entry to premises;

In resisting the production order application, Shiv Malik's lawyers raised the privilege against self-incrimination, and the court set out five factors which should be taken into account when making orders in such circumstances:

- the material should be of true benefit to investigation of material sought;
- the court should take into account the importance of privilege against self-incrimination: convincing justification is required if the court is to override it;
- the gravity of offence with which the person required to surrender material might be charged is relevant and should be considered;
- is there a real risk of prosecution—has immunity been given to the subject?
- the court should also take into account the power under section 78 of PACE 1984 to exclude evidence at trial.

While it is valuable to have some judicial consideration of these factors, the definitions remain vague and therefore the scope of orders under TACT 2000 remains wide. It is difficult to know what 'true benefit' means: it is much less clear than 'relevant and admissible', and inevitably this will be a problem with police searches for material in cases where there may be no intention to consider prosecution. It is right that the risk of prosecution may be lower if evidence is excluded under section 78, but at the stage of an application for disclosure this is an unknown and uncertain factor. It is right that in the Sally Murrer case (see below) the Court decided to exclude the evidence under section 78 and the prosecution dropped the charges against the journalist. Nevertheless, this is an 'after-the-event' matter, and the obtaining of the journalistic material in the first instance may still be an unjustifiable interference within Article 10.

The *Shiv Malik* case raises important questions about how journalists can investigate and the public learn about why people become attracted to organizations espousing terrorism. There is an inherent tension between public safety and press freedom, but the interests are not always contradictory. The press has a role to play in maintaining and improving public awareness and safety: investigating and reporting on the ways in which individuals become terrorists and therefore providing the community as a whole with some understanding of how to recognize risks and develop ways to divert young people from terrorism.

The creation of offences of encouragement of terrorism, including glorification of terrorism, also impacts on journalists. It restricts their ability to investigate and conduct research.[165] Since the terrorist attacks on the World Trade Center in New York,

---

(c) a terrorist investigation may be seriously prejudiced unless a constable can secure immediate access to the material.

[165] See eg the news report: 'Student was studying terrorism', BBC News, 23 May 2008. TACT 2006 uses the definition of 'terrorism' in TACT 2000, s 1 and creates offences of encouragement of terrorism (TACT 2006, s 1): 'the indirect encouragement or inducement to commit, prepare or instigate an offence of terrorism. This is subject to an objective test as to the likelihood of a statement to have the effect of encouraging terrorism. There is no need to prove intention—recklessness suffices. Encouragement includes glorification of the commission or preparation of terrorist acts or the praise or celebration of

September 11 2001, we have seen an increase in legislation that impacts on journalism. Many European nation states have adopted new legislation based on the need to investigate and detect terrorist activities.[166] But the increased requirements to disclose information, under threat of prosecution, and the relaxation of measures to protect journalistic material[167] are part of a process that began before then, and is likely to continue even after this period of a perceived heightened threat of terrorism.

3.10.1 Self-incrimination and reasonable excuses

The way that TACT 2000 is drafted means that there is a risk of self-incrimination whenever a journalist is ordered to hand over material connected to terrorism investigations: sections 19 and 58 create offences of failing to disclose information about terrorist activities to a police constable.[168] The duty to disclose information may well be justified in situations of real emergency (information that a bomb has been planted, for example), but the vagueness and breadth of the definition of terrorism means that a 'failure to disclose' offence can be committed in the course of all sorts of journalistic investigations, for example an investigation into environmental protests that lead to the occupation and perhaps damage of power stations, or interviews with hunt saboteurs.

---

such acts. The acts in question can be 'acts of terrorism of a particular description or acts of terrorism generally'. Section 2 creates an offence of dissemination of terrorist publications (objective test: publications deemed likely to be an indirect encouragement to preparation of terrorist acts), and internet activity. Other offences include training for terrorism.

Section 15 amends the Regulation of Investigatory Powers Act 2000 (RIPA 2000) s 53—increases the maximum penalty on indictment of contravening a notice issued on national security grounds from 2 to 5 years' imprisonment. RIPA 2000, Pt 3 provides power to enable properly authorized persons (law enforcement, security, intelligence agencies) to serve notices on persons requiring disclosure of protected (eg encrypted) information in an intelligible form.

[166] eg Russia: Federal Law No 148-FZ of 27 July 2006 amending arts 1 and 15 of the federal law 'On Countering Extremist Activity'; Spain: Criminal Code amended in 2000 to prohibit glorification of terrorism and also 'the commission of acts tending to discredit, demean or humiliate the victims of terrorist offences or their families'; France: internal security law: Loi No 2003-239 du 18 mars 2003 and Loi No 2004-204 du 9 mars 2004, Loi portant adaptation de la justice aux évolutions de la criminalité, JO No 59 du 10 mars 2004; Luxembourg: 2004 Law on Freedom of Expression in the Media (re forced disclosure of sources). For full details see D Banisar, 'Speaking of terror' (Council of Europe, November 2008).

[167] Search and seizure powers and procedures under PACE 1984 are currently the subject of governmental review. See 'PACE Review, Government proposals in response to the Review of the Police and Criminal Evidence Act 1984' (Home Office, August 2008). Following public consultation in 2008, the government published a summary of proposals. An interdepartmental working group is considering a new statutory scheme for third-party disclosure (para 9.10) and particularly has recommended that 'subject to an overriding public interest test and judicial oversight, the police should be able to obtain access during a criminal investigation to material held by third parties that is currently barred to them by the Police and Criminal Evidence Act 1984, such as medical, social services or educational records'. Although not explicitly referred to, this would appear to include other forms of excluded material such as journalistic material. The Working Group's findings are currently under consideration with a view to a possible further public consultation exercise (para 9.12).

[168] *Malik v Manchester Crown Court and ors* [2008] EWHC 1362 (Admin), 19 June 2008.

Section 38b of TACT 2006 creates an offence if a person has information they know or believe might be of material assistance (a) in preventing the commission by another person of an act of terrorism, or (b) in securing the apprehension, prosecution or conviction of another person, in the UK, for an offence involving the commission, preparation or instigation of an act of terrorism. The information must be disclosed 'as soon as reasonably practicable' to a police officer.

There is a defence of having a 'reasonable excuse' for not making the disclosure and this may provide journalists with a defence, particularly if the information requested concerns confidential sources. This has not been tested yet.[169]

The operation of sections 19 and 58 means that when there is an application for the handover of journalistic material, the journalist risks handing over material that might lead to his prosecution for a failure to disclose information that might benefit a terrorist investigation. In effect, as soon as a journalist or media organization is on notice that the material is sought in connection with a terrorist investigation, they are aware that the police consider that it is likely to benefit their investigation and that they will be committing an offence if they fail to disclose the information. Any disclosure in response to a production order under the terrorism legislation involves a risk of self-incrimination.

The privilege against self-incrimination must also be considered in connection with offences under the Official Secrets Act 1989.[170] Self-incrimination also becomes an issue where the disclosure of journalistic material is ordered in an investigation into breaches of the Official Secrets Act 1989. Journalists who disclose to others information that is damaging to national security, (for example other journalists), without authority are potentially in breach of section 5 of the Official Secrets Act 1989, as in the Martin Bright case: 'The Observer newspaper appears to be in possession of material covered by the OSA. The disclosure of this information in the article of the 27th February may constitute a breach of Section 5 OSA 1989.'

Judge LJ decided that an element of compulsion was the key issue in deciding whether the risk of self-incrimination arose: if the material is only available to a police officer by some action from the person (such as copying, printing, handing over), the risk of self-incrimination arises. A production order requires the journalist to hand over or give a constable access to the material. In this situation, assurances not to

---

[169] TACT 2000: s 19 offence:

If a person—
   (a) believes or suspects that another person has committed an offence under any of sections 15 to 18 [ie various offences relating to funding of terrorism], and
   (b) bases their belief or suspicion on information which comes to his attention in the course of a trade, profession, business or employment.

That person commits an offence if they do not disclose to a police officer 'as soon as is reasonably practicable' (a) their 'belief or suspicion' and (b) the 'information on which it is based'.

They have a defence if they prove that they had a 'reasonable excuse for not making the disclosure'.

[170] Official Secrets Act 1989, s 5; *R v Central Criminal Court, ex p Bright Alton and Rusbridger* [2001] 2 All ER 244.

prosecute are not enough—only an undertaking not to prosecute would remove the risk of self-incrimination.[171]

Under section 9 of the Official Secrets Act 1911 a magistrate may issue a warrant authorizing the search of premises and persons found there and the 'seizure of anything which is evidence of an offence under this Act having been or about to be committed'; where interests of state require immediate action, a police superintendent may authorize such a search. The offences concern information which is or might be useful to an enemy. These powers were used to search the premises of BBC Scotland in Glasgow, following government concern about the proposed broadcast of a television programme about a British spy satellite (Zircon).

The Official Secrets Act 1989 creates offences relating to disclosures by Crown servants and by anyone notified that they are subject to the Act. Section 5 makes it an offence to disclose information where the person making the disclosure suspects that it would be damaging to national security.[172]

In addition, under section 8(4) it is an offence for a journalist to fail to comply with an 'official direction' by a Crown servant or government contractor for the return or disposal of information subject to section 5 of the Official Secrets Act 1989 which is in their possession or control. The penalty may be three months' imprisonment and/or an unlimited fine.[173]

The UN Human Rights Committee commented critically on the UK government's use of the Official Secrets Act in 2001:

The committee is concerned that powers under the Official Secrets Act 1989 have been exercised to frustrate former employees of the Crown from bringing into the public domain issues of genuine public concern, and to prevent journalists from publishing such matters. The State Party should ensure that its powers to protect information genuinely related to matters of national security are narrowly utilised, and limited to instances where it has been shown to be necessary to suppress release of the information.[174]

3.11 COVERT SURVEILLANCE

The Regulation of Investigatory Powers Act 2000 (RIPA 2000) provides a regulatory regime which authorizes the executive to undertake interception of electronic communications on grounds of threats to national security and economic well-being, and to compel access to decryption keys.[175] It legitimates official surveillance of e-mail correspondence and internet use by private individuals (surveillance by private

---

[171] *R v Central Criminal Court, ex parte Bright Alton and Rusbridger* [2001] 2 All ER 244, para 35.

[172] In *Ex parte Bright, Alton and Rusbridger* it was suggested that the *Observer* journalist (Martin Bright) may have committed an offence under s 5.

[173] Official Secrets Act 1989, s 10(2).

[174] Concluding Observations of the Human Rights Committee: United Kingdom of Great Britain and Northern Ireland 5 November 2001, CCPR/CO/73/UK, CCPR/CO/73/UKOT.

[175] RIPA 2000, s 49—such orders usually need to be made by a circuit judge.

organizations or individuals—other than interception of communications is not covered by RIPA 2000).

RIPA 2000 also provides for the disclosure of 'comunications data', for example data such as the date and time when telephone calls were made or e-mails sent and received. A warrant is not required, but a 'designated person' may serve a notice requiring an organization to obtain or disclose the material. The person must believe that obtaining the data is proportionate to what is sought to be achieved in obtaining the data, and that it is necessary on grounds set out in RIPA 2000.[176]

The interception of communications (and use of several other forms of surveillance under RIPA 2000) to obtain information about journalists' sources or journalistic material threatens to undermine the protection of sources provided in other statutes, and Article 10 ECHR itself. These methods can be used to bypass judicial oversight of measures used by investigating authorities to obtain journalistic material.

Surveillance can be carried out covertly on orders of the executive without prior judicial authorization. In the case of telephone intercepts, information obtained in this way is inadmissible in court proceedings.[177] However, other forms of covert surveillance are admissible. We do not know how often surveillance of journalists takes place—the journalist would be unaware of the covert surveillance. The issue has arisen recently in the *Murrer* case where the journalist found out that she had been bugged: evidence obtained by placing microphones and tracking devices in the journalist's car formed the basis of a prosecution of the journalist. If the journalist herself had not been prosecuted, she might never have discovered the extent of police surveillance.

RIPA 2000 was introduced in response to the Human Rights Act 1998, in order to make lawful measures such as the interception of private phone calls: actions which clearly breach the subject's right to privacy under Article 8 ECHR (Alison Halford case)[178] and, if the subject is a journalist, under Article 10 too. It is now accepted that the fact that surveillance is authorized under RIPA 2000 does not prevent it being challenged as a breach of human rights. The court in the Sally Murrer case adopted Principle 6 of Recommendation (2000) 7: 'interception orders or actions concerning communications or correspondence of journalists should not be applied if their purpose is to circumvent the right of journalists . . . not to disclose information identifying a source'.[179]

In principle, this is good guidance, but in practice (as noted above) it is impossible to know whether, or how often, covert surveillance of journalists is taking place. Authorizations of surveillance under RIPA 2000 can be made by executive officers of a public authority. While it is possible, if one is able to obtain evidence of surveillance

---

[176] ibid ss 21 and 22.
[177] ibid s 17.
[178] *Halford v UK* [1997] IRLR 471, ECtHR.
[179] Recommendation R (2000) 7 of the Committee of Ministers of the Council of Europe.

or the interception of communications, to complain to the RIPA Tribunal, meetings and minutes of the Tribunal are usually secret.[180]

3.12 SERIOUS ORGANIZED CRIME AND COMPULSORY QUESTIONS AND ANSWERS

The power to compel answers to questions is found in a number of statutes dealing with organized crime or investigations into serious fraud.[181]

A very wide range of investigators are empowered to compel answers to questions. Section 60 of the Serious Organised Crime and Police Act 2005 (SOCPA 2005) confers compulsory powers relating to the investigation of particular crimes on investigating authorities (the DPP, Director Revenue and Customs Prosecutions, and the Lord Advocate). These powers may be delegated to Crown or Revenue and Customs prosecutors and procurators fiscal. This means, for example, that it is possible for more than 2,500 Crown prosecutors to authorize compulsory questioning.

Similarly, the powers under section 2(ii) of the Criminal Justice Act 1987 to direct or to require a person to answer questions, provide information, or produce documents for the purposes of an investigation can be exercised by a 'competent investigator (other than a constable)' even one who is not a member of the Serious Fraud Office (SFO). Under the Financial Services and Markets Act 2000 regulatory investigators may require a person to attend and answer questions and produce documents. A failure (or refusal) to do so may be treated as contempt—a journalist is likely to seek to rely on section 10 of the Contempt of Court Act 1981 in these circumstances.[182]

SOCPA 2005 does not require judicial authorization for compulsory questioning using section 62 disclosure notices, of a person's lawyer, accountant, banker, or other professional adviser—or, for example, of a financial journalist. Warrants to enter, search, and seize documents may be made by a Justice of the Peace, and there is no special protection for journalistic material. There are only three restrictions on the following types of material:

- material or information that is legally privileged;
- excluded material, defined in PACE 1984 (but not special procedure material);
- confidential banking material.

---

[180] See Investigatory Powers Tribunals Preliminary Rulings: Applications IPT/01/62 and IPT/01/77, 2003 (Liberty and Guardian Newspapers Ltd application to the Tribunal to publish its ruling): under the Investigatory Powers Tribunals Rules 2000, rule 9(6), the Tribunal's proceedings, including any oral hearings, shall be conducted in private. However, the Tribunal may determine its own proceedings under s 68(1) and has a discretion to hear matters in public and/or to publish its reasons.

[181] Enterprise Act 2002, Financial Services and Markets Act 2000, Financial Services Act 1986—see *Re an Inquiry under the Company Securities (Insider Dealing) Act 1985* [1988] AC 66, HL.

[182] They may also obtain search warrants from a Justice of the Peace where there are reasonable grounds to believe that access conditions have been met.

There is no statutory right of appeal against an authorization to disclose information.

SOCPA 2005 allows for the use of these compulsory powers in connection with offences listed under section 61: these include 'lifestyle' offences under the Proceeds of Crime Act 2002, offences under sections 15 to 18 of the Terrorism Act 2000 (fundraising, money laundering), and section 170 of the Customs and Excise Management Act 1979. But there are more than 30 statutory provisions that also include comparatively minor offences, such as keeping a brothel, or trade mark and copyright offences. Coercive investigations are permitted in relation to these and other offences such as fraudulent evasion of duty or evasion of VAT, or cheating in relation to the public revenue, where the loss is not less than £5,000. [183]

The powers cannot be used to obtain 'excluded material', which would include journalistic material held in confidence.[184] However, some journalistic material may fall outside the continuous confidentiality requirements.

3.13 CITIZENS AND JOURNALISTS

Powers to require the retention of data and to seize communications traffic data are increasing. These provisions affect us all, citizens or journalists.

In 2006, the European Union adopted the Directive on Data Retention, which requires telecommunications providers to automatically collect and retain all information on all users' activities.[185] The Directive is currently being challenged by the Irish government and forty civil liberties groups including Statewatch, Open Rights Group, and Privacy International, in the European Court of Justice (ECJ). The Irish government did not oppose the principle of data retention, but argued that the wrong procedure had been used—this was a matter concerning security, rather than commerce and trade, and required a unanimous vote rather than a majority. The ECJ decided, on 11 February 2009, that the procedure had been correct: as an 'internal market measure' which only requires qualified majority voting. However, the question of whether it is compatible with Article 8 and Article 10 protections under the ECHR remains a live issue for the civil liberty groups involved.[186] In the UK, the Anti-Terrorism, Crime and Security Act 2001 allowed the Home Secretary to issue a code of practice for the 'voluntary' retention of communications data by communications providers. While most communications providers have complied already, following the 2006 Directive the requirement is due to become mandatory from 6 April 2009.

---

[183] SOCPA 2005, s 61.
[184] ibid s 64(5).
[185] Directive (EC) 2006/24 of 15 March 2006 on retention of data.
[186] Submission to the Court of Justice of the European Communities from Patrick Breyer, Arbeitskreis Vorratsdatenspeicherung (Working Group on Data Retention) on behalf of 43 European human rights groups concerned with data retention, 8 April 2008, in Case C-301/06 *Ireland v Council of the European Union*, European Parliament, 6 July 2006.

As global communications increase so, too, do powerful legal weapons that cross borders: in October 2004, two UK servers for Indymedia, an independent 'alternative' media organization, were seized at the request of US authorities on behalf of Swiss and Italian authorities. In the UK, Caroline Flint MP responded to a question in the House of Commons about what, if any, involvement the Home Office had with the seizure: 'I can confirm that no UK law enforcement agencies were involved in the matter referred to in the question posed by the Hon Member for Sheffield, Hallam.'[187]

Difficulties arise in protecting journalistic material when important 'intermediaries' between journalists and others, such as internet service providers are involved. The internet hosting company, Rackspace Managed Hosting, delivered copied drives to the FBI. The two servers hosted by RMH (located in London) provided space to more than twenty Independent Media Centres in the US, and around the world, that were taken offline. These represent collectives of independent media organizations and thousands of individuals writing 'grassroots, non-corporate coverage of news events'.[188]

Global communications depend on technology provided by commercial organizations that may not want—or have the opportunity—to argue with investigators about journalistic privilege. Where they do, the courts may not recognize that they have any right to journalistic protection. In a case brought against Motley Fool, an interactive investors' website, the court ordered the dislosure of the identity of *Zeddust*, who posted defamatory comments on the site. Mr Justice Robert Owen adopted a narrow definition of 'publication': as the website operator took no responsibility for what was put on its message boards, and exercised no editorial control, it could not rely on section 10 of the Contempt of Court Act 1981, which provides protection for 'the source of information contained in a publication *for which he is responsible*'.[189]

The growth of independent 'alternative' sites such as Indymedia, and the increasing reliance of mainstream media organizations on ordinary citizens who send photographs and other content to their news websites, illustrate how difficult it has become to define who is a journalist and whether journalistic privilege attaches to such material. In the past it may have been more straightforward, as journalism was clearly a trade or profession. Indeed it still is, and has its own professional bodies, rules, and standards, but now we are all encouraged to join in.

No UK statute clearly sets out a definition of journalism or who may be regarded as a journalist. In contrast, Belgium has a fairly comprehensive definition: 'any self-employed or non-self-employed person and any natural person who contributes regularly and directly to the acquisition, editing, production and dissemination of information by way of a medium in the public interest'.[190]

In 2006, a California state appeals court ruled (in response to a petition brought by the Electronic Frontier Foundation), that three anonymous individuals who allegedly

---

[187] *Indymedia Server Takedown* (Electronic Frontier Foundation, August 2005).
[188] ibid.
[189] *Totalise plc v Motley Fool Ltd and anor*, *The Times*, 19 February 2001.
[190] Arrêt No 91/2006 du 7 juin 2006, Constitutional Court, Belgium. See <http://www.arbitrage.be>.

had posted leaked information about new Apple Computer products onto several online news sites, should be entitled to journalistic privilege. In its judgment the court reflected on the difficulties of identifying what is 'proper' journalism: 'We can think of no workable test or principle that would distinguish "legitimate" from "illegitimate" news.'[191]

Attempts to define what deserves protection as journalistic material are not straightforward. A survey of journalism 'Silencing sources', published by Privacy International,[192] shows that in some countries the legal system only protects journalistic material if it is published in certain kinds of media; in other jurisdictions the protection only applies if the journalist is officially recognized as such under press law, or is licensed to operate as a journalist. Such measures, while they provide clearer boundaries and might help to maintain and preserve professional standards, would be highly restrictive to freedom of expression in an era of global communication via the internet. In the Apple case referred to above, the court responded to the difficulty in drawing such boundaries by abandoning the attempt, saying that 'any attempt by courts to draw such a distinction [between 'legitimate' and 'illegitimate' news] would imperil a fundamental purpose of the First Amendment, which is to identify the best, most important, and most valuable ideas not by any sociological or economic formula, rule of law, or process of government, but through the rough and tumble competition of the memetic marketplace.' [193]

We have seen how, at the same time as the boundaries of journalism become less clear, the investigative powers of police and other statutory bodies increase, on the grounds that such powers are needed to defeat terrorism and serious crime. While these powers may well play an important role in investigating serious crime, it is a matter of concern that they are often used to investigate and collect data about journalists themselves. Journalists reporting on the Kingsnorth Climate Change camp in 2008 were targeted by police intelligence officers who filmed them at the camp and while filing their reports from a café nearby. [194] While state powers to retain data and conduct surveillance increase, reporters fear that their own ability to investigate and collect data on the police or armed forces—even, for example, to photograph the police at an incident—will be curtailed by section 76 of the Counter-Terrorism Act 2008, which creates an offence of eliciting or attempting to elicit information about a member of the armed forces, intelligence services, or a police constable 'which is of a kind likely to be useful to a person committing or preparing an act of terrorism', or publishing or communicating such information.[195] It is not yet clear whether the offence includes the taking of a photograph of a police constable, but this section is clearly capable of

---

[191] *O'Grady v Superior Court* 139 Cal App 4th 1423 (Cal App 2006).
[192] D Banisa, 'Silencing Sources: An International Survey of Protections and Threats to Journalists' Sources' (Privacy International, November 2007).
[193] *O'Grady v Superior Court* (n 191 above).
[194] 'Revealed, Police databank on thousands of protestors: Films and details of campaigners and journalists may have breached Human Rights Act' *The Guardian*, 7 March 2009.
[195] Counter-Terrorism Act 2008, s 76 amends the Terrorism Act 2000 to include a new s 58A that sets out this offence.

covering photography, and the National Union of Journalists has organized a series of protests against section 76.[196]

What kind of legal protection should be provided to journalistic material in the future in criminal or civil proceedings? As mentioned earlier in this chapter, debates continue, particularly in the US, about whether the 'shield law' for sources should apply to bloggers as well as professional journalists. The answers depend on where the emphasis lies—is it to protect the profession of journalism, the individual journalist (accredited or not?), the material itself, or the medium of communication? If journalistic privilege applies to news published on a blog, would it also apply to information disseminated in a leaflet, graffiti painted on a wall, content published on a mobile phone?

---

[196] 'Is it a crime to take pictures?' BBC, 16 February 2009, see <http://news.bbc/1/hi/uk/7888301.stm>.

4

CONTEMPT OF COURT

Rosalind McInnes

4.1 WHAT IS CONTEMPT?

Contempt is a broad notion covering a number of different acts and omissions, tending to interfere with the administration of justice. Journalists, like any citizen, are required to obey a court's order, to comply with any undertakings they give to the court, to behave with propriety in court, not to commit perjury, and so on. However, the type of contempt of most concern to the media is publication contempt, ie publishing matter likely to impinge upon court proceedings.

4.2 THE 1981 ACT

The traditional approach of the British judiciary was militantly against what has been called 'trial by media'. For at least some judges in the past, 'trial by media' apparently encompassed any publication running the risk that a juror would turn up in court having heard from the media about the case.

The Contempt of Court Act 1981 was supposed to change all that. It was prompted, in part, by the UK's defeat in the European Court of Human Rights (ECtHR) in the Thalidomide case.[1] The *Sunday Times* had published an article campaigning for more generous offers by the manufacturers of the Thalidomide drug to the victims of birth defects, who had pending personal injury actions against the drugs company. The House of Lords did not actually punish the newspaper for contempt, but restored an injunction against publication of an article suggesting that the drug company had been negligent. Strasbourg decided, by a narrow majority, that the restriction breached the Article 10 freedom of expression right of the newspaper. In response to this decision, and other pressure to reform contempt law, the Contempt of Court Act 1981 was enacted.

4.3 IS PUBLICATION CONTEMPT IN DECLINE?

The 1981 Act was certainly, from the media's perspective, an advance. Intended as a liberalizing measure in favour of freedom of expression, its most immediate practical benefit was a better definition of when and how the publication contempt risk began.

Although the Act is UK-wide, there are significant differences within the jurisdictions of the UK, with a perceived greater severity over publication contempt in Scotland. The numbers of contempt prosecutions and findings have been dropping, however, since the 1981 Act came into force, with a pronounced decline over the past couple of years, even in the teeth of some provocative reporting. Richard Danbury's

---

[1] *Sunday Times v UK*, 26 April 1979, ECtHR Series A No 30.

Reuters Fellowship Paper for Michaelmas 2007[2] is entitled 'Can I Really Report That? The Decline of Contempt'.

Suggested factors behind this trend include not only the 1981 Act itself, but the general support from the ECtHR for responsible journalism, entrenched in domestic thinking by the passing of the Human Rights Act 1998; the pushing back of the boundaries of judicial tolerance by very high-profile cases, such as the West murders;[3] the increasing empirical support for the robustness of juror independence;[4] more controversially, the anti-terrorism agenda, where it has been said in some quarters that unfettered reporting of arrests and trials is politically expedient; and, finally, the growth of the internet.

However, complacency on the part of the media would be premature. Contempt remains penal. ITV received a sharp reminder of this in July 2008 when it was fined £25,000 and voluntarily accepted costs of £37,014 for publishing the previous murder conviction of an accused on the morning of the trial.[5]

4.4 WHAT IS A COURT?

Section 19 of the 1981 Act defines a court as 'any tribunal or body exercising the judicial power of the State'. The courts-martial appeal court and employment appeal tribunals are explicitly covered by the statutory contempt regime.

In *Attorney-General v BBC*[6] the question was whether the BBC, by broadcasting a programme dealing with matters relating to an appeal pending before a local valuation court, could be in contempt. The House of Lords held that the body was not a court for contempt purposes. In the interests of freedom of expression, the contempt jurisdiction should not be extended to the plethora of modern tribunals. Lord Scarman said that: 'Judicial power is to be contrasted with legislative and executive (ie administrative) power. If the body under review is established for a purely legislative or administrative purpose, it is part of the legislative or administrative system of the state, even though it has to perform duties which are judicial in character.'

In *General Medical Council v BBC*[7] the Court of Appeal held that the General Medical Council's Professional Conduct Committee was not part of the judicial process of the state and accordingly was not subject to the Contempt of Court Act 1981. Mental health review tribunals are 'courts' for contempt purposes, according to the

---

[2] <http:reutersinstitute.politics.ox.ac.uk/fileadmin/documents/publications/fellows-papers/Richard_Danbury/01.pdp>.

[3] *R v West* [1996] 2 Cr App R 374.

[4] See eg New Zealand Law Commission preliminary paper no 37, November 1999, or 'Managing Prejudicial Publicity: An Empirical Study of Criminal Jury Trials in New South Wales' (2001), available at <http://www.lawfoundation.net.au>.

[5] *Attorney-General v ITV Central Ltd* [2008] EWHC 1984 (Admin) Pill LJ, King J.

[6] [1981] AC 303. See also *Badry v DPP of Mauritius* [1983] 2 AC 297.

[7] (1998) 3 All ER 426.

House of Lords in *Pickering v Liverpool Daily Post and Echo Newspapers plc* [8]—not surprisingly, given that they deal with the liberty of the subject. So are employment tribunals: *Peach Grey & Co v Sommers*.[9] In the different context of the Regulation of Investigatory Powers Act 2000, it was held in *Ewing v Security Service*[10] that the Investigatory Powers Tribunal was a court.

4.5 THE STRICT LIABILITY RULE

The 'strict liability rule' is defined in section 1 of the 1981 Act as 'the rule of law whereby conduct may be treated as a contempt of court as tending to interfere with the course of justice in particular legal proceedings regardless of intent to do so'.

However, the applicability of the strict liability rule is limited in a number of ways. First, within section 1 itself, the tendency to interfere with the course of justice is confined to 'particular legal proceedings'. It does not, therefore, cover, for example, behaviour which might have a deterrent effect on the willingness of witnesses to come forward in general. Moreover, under section 2, the strict liability rule applies only to publications as defined;[11] 'only to a publication which creates a substantial risk that the course of justice in the proceedings in question will be seriously impeded or prejudiced';[12] and only where the proceedings in question are active.[13]

4.5.1 When does a case become active?

Criminal proceedings [14] become active when there is an arrest, a warrant for an arrest, the issue of a summons to appear, or the service of an indictment or other document specifying the charge. Except in Scotland, an oral charge also makes a case active. In Scotland, the grant of a warrant to cite is the equivalent of the issue of a summons to appear.[15]

Appellate proceedings [16] are active from the point of application for leave to appeal or to apply for review, or by notice of such an application; by notice of appeal or of application for review; or by other originated process.[17]

---

[8] [1991] 2 AC 370. See also *Birmingham Post & Mail Ltd v Birmingham City Council* [1994] 158 JP 307, 158 LG Rev 523, *The Times*, 25 November 1993, *The Independent*, 25 November 1993, DC, where a magistrate considering the power of compulsorily removing a possible TB sufferer to hospital was held to constitute a court.

[9] [1995] 2 All ER 513.

[10] QBD, Brown J, 30 July 2003.

[11] Contempt of Court Act 1981, s 2(1).

[12] ibid s 2(2).

[13] ibid s 2(3).

[14] As defined in Sch 1, para 1 of the 1981 Act.

[15] ibid Sch 1, para 4.

[16] Defined in Sch 1, para 1.

[17] ibid Sch 1, para 15.

In *criminal appeal* cases, where the court remits the case to the court below, orders a new trial or, in Scotland, grants authority to bring a new prosecution, 'any further or new proceedings which result shall be treated as active from the conclusion of the appellate proceedings'.[18]

First instance *civil proceedings* begin in England, Wales, or Northern Ireland when the case is set down for trial in the High Court or, elsewhere, when a date for the trial or hearing is fixed.[19] In Scotland, in the case of an ordinary action in the Court of Session or Sheriff Court, proceedings become active when the Record is closed, ie when the document setting out the parties' pleadings is finalized, or when a motion or application is enrolled or made or, in any other case, when the date for a hearing is fixed or a hearing is allowed.[20] Throughout the UK, motions or applications made in or for the purpose of the proceedings are treated as distinct proceedings, as is a pre-trial review in the county court.[21] If a hearing begins without any arrangement having been previously made for it—for example an interlocutory injunction in England, or interim interdict in Scotland—those proceedings become active from the time when the hearing begins.[22] In practice, the media are unlikely to know about the latter proceedings unless they are themselves party.

4.5.2 When does a case cease to be active?

Criminal proceedings stop being active when there is an acquittal; a sentence; any other verdict, finding, order or decision which puts an end to the proceedings; or by discontinuance or by operation of law.[23] 'Sentence' is broadly defined at paragraph 6 of Schedule 1 to the 1981 Act and would include a deferred sentence. Practically speaking, in the ordinary case, the contempt risk ends once the jury has given its verdict and sentencing is in the hands of a judge.[24] Proceedings are discontinued in England and Wales or Northern Ireland by the withdrawal of the charge or summons or the entry of a *nolle prosequi*. They can also be discontinued by virtue of section 23 of the Prosecution of Offences Act 1985, or by the release without charge of a person arrested without warrant.

In Scotland, discontinuance of proceedings can only take place if the prosecutor expressly abandons them or if they are deserted *simpliciter*. Journalists should be very careful to note that, in Scotland, desertion *pro loco et tempore* (ie for the time being) does not end the contempt risk, as Express Newspapers found in Scotland, to their cost—a £50,000 fine.[25]

---

[18] ibid sch 1, para 16.
[19] ibid sch 1, para 13.
[20] ibid sch 1, para 14.
[21] ibid sch 1, para 12.
[22] ibid.
[23] ibid sch 1, para 5.
[24] See section 4.6 below.
[25] *Express Newspapers, Petitioners*, 1999 SCCR 262.

There are certain events which 'pause' the contempt risk. Where proceedings in England and Wales have been discontinued by virtue of section 23 of the 1985 Act, but notice is given by the accused that he wants the proceedings to continue, that notice triggers the operation of the strict liability rule again.[26] Similarly, criminal proceedings in England and Wales or Northern Ireland cease to be active if an order is made for the charge to lie on the file, but become active again if leave is later given for the proceedings to continue.[27] Criminal proceedings also cease to be active where the accused is unfit to plead or, in Scotland, insane in bar of trial, or if there is a hospital order or the Scottish equivalent, but become active again if the proceedings are later resumed.[28] Where a warrant has been outstanding for a year without an arrest, then again, proceedings cease to be active at the end of the period of twelve months, but become active again on a subsequent arrest.[29] This happened in relation to the Lockerbie bombing case.[30]

Service offences, including service discipline and civil offences, dealt with by the Court Martial, are treated as 'criminal offences'.[31]

First instance civil proceedings cease to be active for strict liability contempt purposes when 'the proceedings are disposed of or discontinued or withdrawn'.[32] Similarly, civil appellate proceedings continue 'until disposed of or abandoned, discontinued or withdrawn'.[33] Criminal appellate proceedings end at the same point, except where there has been a remit to the court below, order of a new trial, or, in Scotland, authority to bring a new prosecution. Thus, the appellate proceedings cease to be active, but the new proceedings become active instead.

4.5.3 Meaning of 'substantial risk of serious prejudice'

To fall foul of the strict liability rule, a publication must create 'a substantial risk that the course of justice in the proceedings in question will be seriously impeded or prejudiced'. The wording of this test perhaps suggests a misleadingly high bar. In *Attorney-General v Express Newspapers*[34] Lord Justice Rose summarized the relevant case law: ' "Substantial risk" in Section 2(2) means a risk which is more than remote . . . or "not insubstantial" . . . or, as Mr Caldecott prefers to express it, "real". The risk must be practical and not theoretical . . . '

Finding the newspaper in contempt for publishing information which could have affected a rape complainer's identification evidence, he said:[35] 'When, uniquely, the

[26] Contempt of Court Act 1981, Sch 1, para 9a.
[27] ibid Sch 1, para 9.
[28] ibid Sch 1, para 10.
[29] ibid Sch 1, para 11.
[30] See section 4.10 below.
[31] Contempt of Court Act 1981, Sch 1, para 8, repealed by Armed Forces Act 2006, Sch 16, para 92.
[32] ibid Sch 1, para 12.
[33] ibid Sch 1, para 15(c).
[34] [2004] EWHC 2859 (Admin), para 5.
[35] ibid para 14.

respondents published in a national newspaper, with a readership of millions, these items . . . created a real, substantial, more than remote practical risk that the course of justice would be seriously impeded or prejudiced.'

Sir John Donaldson MR said in *Attorney-General v News Group Newspapers:*[36]

There has to be a *substantial* risk that the course of justice in the proceedings will be *seriously* impeded or prejudiced. This is a double test. First, there has to be some risk that the proceedings in question will be affected at all. Second, there has to be a prospect that, if affected, the effect will be serious . . . I accept the submission of counsel for the defendants that 'substantial' as a qualification of 'risk' does not have the meaning of 'weighty' but rather means 'not insubstantial' or 'not minimal'. The 'risk' part of the test will usually be of importance in the context of the width of the publication . . . Proximity in time between the publication and the proceedings would probably have a greater bearing on the risk limb than on the seriousness limb, but could go to both.

In one of the earliest decisions on the 1981 Act, Lord Diplock said in *Attorney-General v English:*[37]

The public policy that underlies the strict liability rule . . . is deterrence. Trial by newspaper . . . is not to be permitted in this country. That the risk that was created by the publication when it was actually published does not ultimately affect the outcome of the proceedings is . . . neither here nor there. Next for consideration is the concatenation in the sub-section of the adjective 'substantial' and the adverb 'seriously', the former to describe the degree of risk, the latter to describe the degree of impediment or prejudice to the course of justice. In combination I take the two words to be intended to exclude a risk that is only remote. With regard to the adverb 'seriously' . . . the adjective 'serious' has from time to time been used as an alternative to 'real' to describe the degree of risk of interfering with the course of justice, but not the degree of interference itself . . .

In *Attorney-General v ITN*[38] Lord Justice Leggatt said that the jury in that case was unlikely to hear that the accused had been convicted of murdering an SAS officer:

If, therefore, that information had come to the attention of the jury because one or more of their number remembered having already heard about it in the broadcast or articles complained of, there can be no doubt that the course of justice in those proceedings would have been seriously prejudiced. The question therefore for us is . . . whether there was a substantial or more than minimal risk of that happening, judged at the time of broadcast or of publication . . .

All these dicta suggest a low bar, from the media's point of view, falling to be assessed at the time of publication. It does not follow that contempt findings are readily made. In the above case, for instance, Lord Justice Leggatt found no contempt had been committed. He said: 'When the long odds against the potential juror reading any of the publications is multiplied against the long odds of any reader remembering it, the risk of prejudice is, in my judgment, remote.'

---

[36] [1986] 2 All ER 833, 841.
[37] [1982] 2 All ER 903, 918–19.
[38] [1995] 2 All ER 370.

Any lawyer defending a client accused of publication contempt should also cherish the words of Schiemann LJ in *Attorney-General v MGN Ltd*.[39] The then boyfriend of *Eastenders* actress Gillian Taylforth was facing criminal charges, widely reported in various newspapers, in a manner to which the Attorney-General took exception. The Divisional Court dismissed the latter's application for committal. After a very detailed analysis of the principles governing assessment of the risk of prejudice, Schiemann LJ observed: 'One must remember that . . . a small risk multiplied by a small risk results in an even smaller risk.'

4.6 SUSCEPTIBILITY TO INFLUENCE

The risk of contempt of court varies according to the presumed or feared audience for the publication. Different considerations arise as to whether the reader or viewer is a judge, magistrate, juror—hypothetical or actual—witness, or party.

4.6.1 Judges

It is generally recognized that a judge is, or ought to be, beyond being influenced by what the media says: 'If he were, he would not be fit to be a judge.'[40] A similar point has been made in Scotland in relation to magistrates[41] though their position in England and Wales is more equivocal.[42] Traditionally, most publication contempt cases have related to apprehended impact upon jurors.

4.6.2 Parties

The impact on parties is a still rarer consideration, but not unknown. Lord Bridge said in *Re Lonrho plc*:[43]

Whether the course of justice in particular proceedings will be impeded or prejudiced by a publication must depend primarily on whether the publication will bring influence to bear which is likely to divert the proceedings in some way from the course which they would otherwise have followed. The influence may affect the conduct of witnesses, the parties or the court. Before proceedings have come to trial and before the facts have been found, it is easy to see how critical

---

[39] [1997] 1 All ER 456.

[40] *A-G v BBC* [1981] AC 303 *per* Lord Salmon, 342. See, though, Viscount Dilhorne's caveat at 335. See also the observations of the Lord Justice-Clerk in *Al Megrahi and Khalifa Fhima v Times Newspapers Ltd* 1999 SCCR 824, 838. Note, too, the possible common law contempt implications. In *HMA v JT*, Appeal Court, High Court of Justiciary, 24 September 2004, it was said of critical media comment on a sentence: 'The denigration of a judge . . . tends to harm the administration of justice.'

[41] *Aitchison v Bernardi* 1984 SLT 343.

[42] See *Martyn Johnson v Leicestershire Constabulary*, *The Times*, 7 October 1998 and *R (Mahfouz) v General Medical Council* [2004] EWCA Civ 431, *The Times*, 19 March 2004, CA, for a 'spectrum' approach to influence.

[43] [1990] 2 AC 154, 208.

public discussion of the issues and criticism of the conduct of the parties, particularly if a party is held up to public obloquy, may impede or prejudice the course of the proceedings by influencing the conduct of witnesses or parties in relation to the proceedings.

In *Attorney-General v Hislop*[44] the Court of Appeal held that it was contempt when *Private Eye* published articles about Sonia Sutcliffe, who was married to the Yorkshire Ripper, which might have deterred her from pursuing her defamation action against them, due to come to trial in a couple of months. There was also possible jury influence there. *Attorney-General v Times Newspapers Ltd and ors*[45] and *Attorney-General v Unger and ors*[46] both dealt with impact on parties.[47]

In the *Lonrho* case,[48] the House of Lords concluded: 'In the ordinary [appellate] case . . . there will be no question of influencing witnesses. In general terms the possibility that the parties will be influenced is remote. When a case has proceeded so far it is unlikely, save in exceptional circumstances, that criticism would deter [parties].'

4.6.3 Witnesses

In *R v West*[49] the Court of Appeal dismissed Rosemary West's appeal against her ten convictions for murder, based on the fact that five prosecution witnesses had been paid sums, varying from £750 to £30,000, by the media for their stories.[50] In principle, publication damaging to the credibility of witnesses, or appearing to trench upon evidence they may give, can endanger a trial: see *HMA v Andrew McGhee*;[51] *R v Solicitor-General, ex p Taylor*;[52] *Attorney-General v BBC*.[53]

In *Ex p HTV Cymru*[54] an injunction was granted to restrain HTV from interviewing Crown witnesses in a murder trial until the start of closing submissions. The judge was influenced by his view that several of the prosecution witnesses were 'clearly vulnerable and impressionable'.[55] Some had said that they were frightened to give evidence and more than one had given different versions of their stories. At least one Crown witness would need to be recalled. The judge said (at 197):

. . . If a witness who has already given evidence thereafter reconsiders it or is unwilling to give further evidence at all as a result of what has been said or done by an outside party, that must be

---

[44] [1991] 1 AB 514.
[45] *The Times*, 12 February 1983.
[46] [1998] 1 Cr App Rep 308, [1998] EMLR 280.
[47] See section 4.15 below.
[48] [1990] 2 AC 154.
[49] (1996) 2 Cr App R 374.
[50] Though the judges did express some disquiet about the practice, leading to a wider political debate about chequebook journalism in murder trials.
[51] 12 October 2005, High Court of Justiciary, Lord Abernethy.
[52] 1 FCR 206, TLR, 14 August 1995.
[53] [2001] EWHC Admin 1202.
[54] [2002] EMLR 11, Aikens J, 27 and 29 November 2000.
[55] Contrast the Scottish approach in *HMA v Slonaker*, 13 September 2005, where Lady Paton refused to grant a s 4(2) order to postpone reporting until all child witnesses had given their evidence.

'serious prejudice' to the trial . . . On what I have seen of certain witnesses and given the general difficulty of this trial so far, I must conclude that there is a risk of such serious prejudice . . . at the least . . . that the conduct of the trial might be delayed . . .

In *Attorney-General v Express Newspapers*, in 2004,[56] the *Daily Star* was fined £60,000 for identifying footballers in connection with an alleged gang rape. The Court took the view that this could have affected the complainer's identification evidence.[57] The newspaper accepted that it had not heeded repeated advice by the Attorney-General and the Metropolitan Police that identification was an issue. The newspaper had used a partly pixellated photograph of one suspect. The background to this finding was 'a series of media pieces published . . . by newspapers and television, on an almost daily basis . . . frequently in florid terms . . . ' and the complainant's having hired the publicist Max Clifford. However, only the *Daily Star* identified potential defendants. The complainant had not been able to identify her alleged attackers to the police 'by name or effective description'. It was held that she would be 'highly vulnerable to cross-examination on the basis that her identification . . . was tainted by what she had read, or had been told that others had read . . . .' The suggestion that she could already have worked out their identities from other sources was rejected as speculative.

In *Chief Constable of Greater Manchester Police v Channel Five Broadcast Ltd*, in 2005,[58] by contrast, the Court of Appeal refused to restrain a Channel Five documentary called 'Gangsters' which featured Desmond Noonan, a violent offender, discussing his 'violence, interference with witnesses [and indifference to the law]'. The Chief Constable was concerned that broadcast of the programme would deter witnesses from coming forward when Desmond Noonan was killed and a man arrested in that connection. Lord Justice Auld considered that both the Noonan family and this sort of behaviour were notorious in Manchester.

In *R v Bieber*, in 2006,[59] unsuccessful appeal arguments were made on behalf of a convicted murderer, *inter alia*, on the grounds that the media had published photographs of him and that a documentary had been screened shortly after the verdict which had included interviews with a number of witnesses. The Court of Appeal rejected the photograph-based ground, visual identification not having been an issue at trial. As to the documentary:

Those acting for the applicant had sought from the makers of the programme full information as to all material that they had available . . . and as to the manner in which the programme was put together . . . [The applicant's counsel] suggests that it is possible that the making of this programme might in some unspecified way have contaminated the evidence that was given at the trial. This is pure speculation.

---

[56] [2004] EWHC 2859 (Admin), 25 November 2004, (2005) EMLR 13, (2005) ACD 41.
[57] In the event, there was insufficient evidence to bring any criminal charges at all.
[58] [2005] EWCA Civ 739, 22 March 2005.
[59] [2006] EWCA Crim 2776.

In *Attorney-General v BBC*, in 2007,[60] the Court of Appeal discharged an order restraining the BBC from broadcasting any document in which is was alleged by Ruth Turner that she was asked to lie for Lord Levy about the 'cash for honours' investigation. The first instance judge had said that: 'Depriving the police of the ability to reveal [a central] document to the current suspects or witnesses at the time and circumstances of their choosing . . . would give rise to a substantial risk that this investigation was seriously prejudiced.'

There, the Court of Appeal took the view that, in the light of what had gradually been published, all those named would anticipate questions about the document and there was no evidence that anyone would not receive a fair trial in consequence. That comes down to public domain considerations, rather than assumptions about witness robustness.

4.7 CIRCULATION

The scope of circulation matters in assessing whether a substantial risk of serious prejudice has been created. The extent of the circulation in breadth and depth, its circulation in or close to the neighbourhood of the trial, the number of media outlets publishing the material, and the amount of republication are all salient factors. Lord Donaldson MR said in *Attorney-General v News Group Newspapers Ltd*, a case arising out of a libel action brought by cricketer Ian Botham:

The 'risk' part of the test will usually be of importance in the context of the width of the publication. To declare in a speech at a public meeting in Cornwall that a man about to be tried in Durham is guilty of the offence charged and has many previous convictions for the same offence may well carry no substantial risk of affecting his trial but, if it occurred, the prejudice would be most serious. By contrast, a nationwide television broadcast at peak viewing time of some far more innocuous statement would certainly involve a substantial risk of having some effect on a trial anywhere in the country . . . [61]

Attorney-General v ITN[62] is a good illustration. A broadcaster and four newspapers published damaging information about a man arrested on a murder charge. In deciding not to make contempt findings, the Court paid attention to the fact that the articles had appeared only in the first edition of each newspaper. Their circulation within the trial area, London, was in the low thousands.

The Court in this case did a very detailed analysis of the distribution within the UK of the newspapers, even looking at the numbers unsold and considering the precise location of the sales: 'It may be said in relation to railway stations that the newspapers may be expected to be bought mainly by people leaving the London area for

---

[60] [2007] EWCA Civ 280, 12 March 2007.
[61] [1986] 2 All ER 833, 841.
[62] [1995] 2 All ER 370.

destinations outside', remarked Lord Justice Leggatt. An ingenious argument was made in this case about the so-called 'leakage' or indirect effect,

> ... that is to say the effect that a newspaper may have upon persons not living in the area in which it is distributed ... supported by the argument that the larger the distribution, the more likely it is that a potential juror might be visiting friends outside his own area ... or alternatively he might encounter, for example, commuters coming into his own area ...

The court regarded the possibility of 'leakage' in this case as minimal, given the very small distributions in London. The scope of the ITN broadcast, by contrast, was both geographically and numerically large. However, Mr Justice Buxton pointed out that: 'The broadcast, although striking, was brief. It was contained in one bulletin only ... ' This case also suggests that the medium matters. Lord Justice Leggatt attached some lenitive importance to the nature of television: 'However horrible the incident that was described, this medium is in its nature ephemeral ... In the case of each of the newspapers, the article would have been somewhat more likely to be remembered, since even a casual reader has the opportunity of reading a particular passage twice ... '

Broadcast journalists would be unwise, however, to rely over much on this comforting dictum, in the era of the I-player and online archives. Even in 1997, a very different view was taken by the Divisional Court in *Attorney-General v BBC and Hat Trick Productions Ltd*,[63] where the broadcast had been shown throughout the UK twice at peak viewing time on one of the most popular programmes on BBC 2. The combined audience was estimated at over 6 million. There was a reference by Lord Justice Auld to 'the impermanent medium of television', but it was undercut by his later statement that 'the offending publicity is great ... because of its medium and repetition ... '. A contempt finding resulted.

4.8 PROXIMITY TO TRIAL

Probably the single biggest factor influencing the judges in strict liability contempt is chronological. The greater the lapse in time between the controversial publication and the trial, the less likely a finding of contempt. The highest point of risk occurs during the trial, with the crescendo being while the jury is out. In *Attorney-General v MGN*[64] the *Sunday Mirror* was fined £75,000, plus Attorney-General's costs of £54,160.37. Its article suggesting a racist motive was published whilst the jury (directed that this was not a racist crime) was considering its verdict. This led to the collapse of the trial against two Leeds United footballers.

In *Attorney-General v ITN*[65] the judges clearly regarded 'the lapse of time as being the single element in this unfortunate incident most likely to avail [the media

---

[63] [1997] EMLR 76.
[64] [2002] EWHC 907 (Admin).
[65] [1995] 2 All ER 370.

defendant]'. It was estimated at nine months. That avoided a contempt finding, despite acceptance by the court that 'if even one juror at Mr McGhee's trial for a terrorist murder had in mind Mr McGhee's criminal record . . . the effect on the course of justice in those proceedings would without doubt be serious'. Given the highly prejudicial nature of the information and, in the case of the broadcast, its penetration and geographical extent, the *ITN* case suggests that a contempt finding where there is a probable gap of nine months, must be most unlikely. In the *Botham* case,[66] where the likely interval was ten months, Lord Donaldson MR said that by that time 'many wickets will have fallen, not to mention much water having flowed under many bridges, all of which would blunt any impact of the publication.'

That said, all contempt cases are fact-sensitive. Some publicity may be so prejudicial that nine months would be insufficient to sterilize it, though it is submitted that, in most cases, if something is not forgotten after nine months, it is unforgettable altogether. A shorter period has sufficed to absolve the media, see, for example, *HMA v Caledonian Newspapers Ltd*,[67] where the period between publication and trial was likely to be about three months.

The question of revival is also of interest in this regard. The phrase 'the fade factor' for the presumed impact of the passage of time on memories comes from Simon Brown LJ in *Attorney-General v Unger*.[68] In the *Sherwood* case, which concerned a decision to impose reporting restrictions over a trial to protect a subsequent trial, the Court of Appeal said: '[The fade factor] can be very significant in low profile cases . . . where the story is of passing interest only to general readers. This is hardly such a case . . . the striking facts of this police raid are such that they are not likely to fade quickly from people's minds; it would in any event be easily revived once the second trial got under way.'[69]

4.9 VENUE

As in *Attorney-General v ITN*,[70] the venue of the trial can be important in considering the impact of publication. In *R v Sherwood, ex p Telegraph Group*, in 2001,[71] the Court of Appeal made the caveat that: 'A change of venue can often be salutary in cases of only local or regional interest. Unfortunately, where the facts of a particular case are striking or unique, and are naturally likely to attract national interest, the location of the trial is not going to be a critical factor.'

---

[66] [1986] 2 All ER 833, 842.
[67] 1995 SLT 926. There was a contempt finding against *The Evening Times* there, but because it used a photograph.
[68] [1998] 1 Cr App R 308.
[69] (2001) 1 WLR 1983, *The Times*, 12 June 2001, [2001] EWCA Crim 1075.
[70] [1995] 2 All ER 370.
[71] (2001) 1 WLR 1983, (2002) EMLR 10.

Local publicity is unlikely to blight a trial which is taking place hundreds of miles away, in the absence of special circumstances.[72] National publicity, however, could clearly prejudice a trial anywhere. In *Attorney-General v Newsgroup Newspapers Ltd* in 1986 ('the Botham case'),[73] Parker LJ said: 'An article in a newspaper circulating in a part of Devon would . . . be far less likely, if likely at all, to create a substantial risk of prejudice to proceedings which were due to be tried in Newcastle than would the same article contained in a national newspaper or a local Newcastle newspaper. The converse is equally true.'

In the same case, Sir John Donaldson MR added psychologically subtler observations:

Furthermore, whilst I have never been a great believer in the efficacy of a conscious effort to put something out of one's mind, an acceptance of the fact that it is likely to remain there, but a determination not to take it into account, is more effective . . . For one reason or another, a trial, by its very nature, seems to cause all concerned to become progressively more inward looking . . . [74]

4.10 MEMORABLE FACTS

Any criminal case which attracts widespread media coverage is likely to be memorable one way or another. However, the memorability of a case, or of potentially damaging information about a player in the drama, will be on a continuum. The most memorable details are presumed most resistant to 'the fade factor'.

In *Attorney-General v ITN*,[75] Leggatt LJ said that, in assessing how memorable these facts were, it was 'permissible to pay regard to the frequency of reported IRA outrages, which, although they are not, on that account, less untoward, do tend on the other hand to be individually less memorable'. This may resonate with the numerous alleged terrorism offences at the time of writing. Buxton LJ, concurring that there should be no finding of contempt, nonetheless put emphasis on the nature of the reporting: 'Although I accept entirely that the broadcast itself was not couched in sensational terms, the information that it conveyed was sensational or . . . certainly very noteworthy. It took an already notorious and much-discussed murder and added to it striking and significant information prejudicial to the man accused . . . '

In *Attorney-General v Sport Newspapers*,[76] although the newspaper was not found in contempt because the case was not active,[77] it was held that publication did indeed create a real risk, giving 'sensational publicity to information which may never . . . be disclosed to jurors . . . The disappearance of Anna Humphries was an event of great

---

[72] It is possible, eg, to imagine a situation in which a large number of witnesses would be drawn from an area remote from the trial venue.
[73] [1986] 2 All ER 833, 843.
[74] ibid 842.
[75] [1995] 2 All ER 370.
[76] [1992] 1 All ER 503.
[77] See section 4.15 below.

notoriety, particularly in the area where it occurred . . . The fact that Evans had a record of serious sexual violence was simple, easy to grasp and likely to be remembered . . . '.

In the *Sherwood* case,[78] which turned on reporting restrictions rather than a contempt finding, the two linked trials arose out of the fatal shooting by a police officer of a naked and unarmed man in his bedroom.[79] The Court of Appeal clearly attached significance to the dramatic facts.

4.11 SECURITY

The reporting of security arrangements for a trial initially led to a Scottish contempt finding in the *Cox and Griffiths* case,[80] quashed on appeal. The article, which did not name the accused, spoke of 'a dozen high-risk prisoners . . . a massive armed police guard . . . motorcycle outriders', etc. The men were referred to as 'heavy-duty guys' and a 'police insider' was quoted as saying: 'Security was extremely tight because we had to work on the premise that someone might try to bust them free.' The Appeal Court took the view that, whilst a juror on the trial might well make the connection to the unnamed prisoners: 'Juries will often see that some accused are on bail, while others are held in custody, while still others are taken to and from court under conditions of particular security. There is nothing to suggest that jurors' awareness of those particular facts affects their ability to return a proper verdict based on the evidence . . . '

In *R v Bieber*[81] ('the Nathan Coleman case'), in 2006, the existence of allegedly 'unprecedented and highly visible security' at the Crown Court during the trial was similarly rejected as a ground of appeal: 'It seems to us that if the jury noticed security at the trial, the likely conclusion that they would have drawn would have been that with a trial of a man accused of these particular crimes, security at the trial was only to be expected.'

4.12 EMOTIVITY

In an initially unsuccessful appeal by Barry George, acquitted on retrial of the murder of television presenter Jill Dando, the Court of Appeal rejected a ground of appeal based on 'lurid headlines'. In *R v West*[82] the Court of Appeal again rejected an appeal by Rosemary West in relation to the Cromwell Street murders, saying:

There is no doubt that [the press coverage before the trial] was extensive and hostile to the Wests . . . It is true that there were also reports which were adverse to the applicant, referring to her as a nymphomaniac and a prostitute. But, however lurid the reporting, there can scarcely ever

---

[78] *R v Sherwood, ex p The Telegraph Group and ors* (2001) 1 WLR 1983, (2002) EMLR 10, *The Times*, 12 June 2001.

[79] See section 4.18 below.

[80] 1998 SLT 1172.

[81] [2006] EWCA Crim 2776, para 19.

[82] 2 April 1996, Court of Appeal.

have been a case more calculated to shock the public who were entitled to know the facts. To hold [that a fair trial was impossible because of intensive, hostile publicity] would mean that if allegations of murder are sufficiently horrendous so as inevitably to shock the nation, the accused cannot be tried. That would be absurd.

In that case, the emotivity arose from content, as much as from editorializing by the press. The coverage of the Taylor sisters case, on the other hand, which resulted in the quashing of murder convictions, featured a distorted freeze-frame from a wedding video suggesting that the accused and the victim's husband had been kissing each other on the mouth, captioned 'Cheat's Kiss'. The trial judge described the media coverage as 'unremitting, extensive, sensational, inaccurate and misleading'.[83] Refusing a judicial review application to override the decision of the Attorney-General not to institute contempt proceedings, Stuart-Smith LJ said: 'It is . . . true that coverage was sensational and extensive; it does no credit to the tabloid press. But the facts alleged by the Crown and to a large extent accepted . . . were of a sensational nature.'[84]

The considerations facing an Appeal Court when considering the impact of publicity are practically different from those facing a court considering whether or not to make a contempt finding; however, it should not be assumed that the tone of coverage (as distinct from its content) can never be a risk factor. In *Attorney-General v MGN*,[85] with regard to the contempt finding following the abandonment of a trial against Leeds United footballers, the trial judge had said: 'In my judgment, justice cannot be done in the sort of atmosphere created by a publication such as this. The whole misleading issue of a racial motivation, which Prosecution, Defence and the Court have sought to exorcise, has been revived and brought before the Jury, potentially, in highly emotive terms.' The publication consisted of an interview with the victim's father, in which he made it clear he considered that his son had suffered a racially-motivated attack.

Even contemporaneous court reporting requires to be 'fair and accurate' to get the benefit of statutory contempt protection.[86]

4.13 IDENTIFICATION AND PHOTOGRAPHS

Identification may be crucial to a trial. Thus, photographs or video footage of someone whose identification is likely to be the subject of evidence in court—typically, the accused—can create a substantial risk of serious prejudice.

This is particularly so in Scotland. There, photographs of an accused will only exceptionally be used during the course of evidence, although there are occasions where the accused is visually well known, for instance (although see the Derek Riordan case, below), or where the circumstances of the alleged crime or the nature of

---

[83] 1993 TLR 15 June.
[84] *The Times*, 14 August 1995.
[85] [2002] EWHC 907 (Admin).
[86] See at section 4.17 below.

the defence make it obvious that identification is unlikely to be a practical issue. Photographs of the MP Mohammed Sarwar were used during his trial for electoral offences, of which he was acquitted, partly because Mr Sarwar is very well known in Scotland and partly because he wished publicly to protest his innocence. Although other elements of the coverage of the *Sarwar* case led to a contempt finding against *The Scotsman*,[87] the use of photographs did not. Similarly, photographs of the two men accused of the Lockerbie bombing were used, because their images had gone all around the world by the time the trial in Zeist was in the offing.[88]

In the rest of the UK, photographs of criminal defendants are commonly used, but may still create a contempt risk where identification is an issue—see *R v Bieber*, also known as the Nathan Coleman case.[89]

The use of a poor quality or 'probably unrecognisable' photograph will mitigate the risk—*Attorney-General v ITN News Ltd*.[90] Similarly, the use of pixellation, dorsal views, very old photographs, and so on may do so, but each risk still turns on its own facts. If height or race is an issue in a trial, such techniques may be useless.

In *Attorney-General v Express Newspapers*, in 2004,[91] even a partly pixillated photograph of a Newcastle United footballer—in the teeth of a request by the Attorney-General and the Metropolitan Police not to use photographs—contributed to a contempt finding against *The Daily Star*. Although the 17-year-old girl who had complained of gang rape may have known the club, age, and colour of her alleged attackers, she had not identified them to the police either by name or effective description. The identification issues in that case were rather unusual and complex, not hingeing on visual identification alone, but the point remains that a photograph even of a well-known footballer who is implicated in a criminal trial may create a difficulty.

So the *Scottish Sun*, *Daily Record*, and Scottish Television recently found. They were held in contempt entirely because they published a photograph of Derek Riordan, a well-known footballer, facing trial for assault.[92] In that case, the issue was the impact of the photograph upon civilian witnesses who said that they did not, in fact, know who Riordan was or what he looked like. As the Sheriff said: 'The fact that the name of Derek Riordan and his photograph might be well-known to many persons who follow football is nothing to the point . . . If, as turned out to be the case here, neither of the two civilian witnesses knew or were ever aware of having previously seen or heard of Derek Riordan, the risk of prejudice or impediment to the course of justice was substantial . . . '

---

[87] See *HMA v The Scotsman Publications* 1999 SLT 466. The publishers were fined £10,000, the editor £3,000, the journalists £1,000 each. Mr Sarwar was found not guilty.

[88] See section 4.5.2 above.

[89] [2006] EWCA Crim 2776, where the sole issue for the jury was the identification of the murderer (see n 59 above) though his appeal failed. His more recent appeal against a whole life term was more successful, although the Court of Appeal held on 23 July 2008 that he must serve 37 years before being considered for release on licence.

[90] [1995] 2 All ER 370.

[91] [2004] EWHC 2859 (Admin), (2005) EMLR 13, (2005) ACD 41.

[92] 4 September 2007, Sheriff Douglas Allan, Edinburgh.

The *Daily Record* unsuccessfully appealed, the Appeal Court of the High Court of Justiciary holding:

Recognition of a person is a notoriously subtle process, one which is best described by psychologists; but our own experience in the criminal courts justifies the description. It is common experience that one may fail to recognise a person, familiar in a particular context, when seen out of context. The only safe course, where identification is in issue, is not to publish any photograph . . . There may be cases in which publication of the photograph of an accused person may not give rise to a risk of substantial prejudice, but such cases are likely to be rare . . .[93] [in the course of a trial if identification is an issue].

Riordan was acquitted.

It was also clear in the Mags Haney case[94] that, well known or notorious as this Scottish gangland matriarch was, the Appeal Court nonetheless felt that a photograph of her 'clearly constituted contempt' and expressed surprise that the Lord Advocate had not proceeded against the newspaper. One of the photographs showed her seated on a chair captioned 'Mags' drug throne', so the content and presentation of the photograph was also significant here. Plainly, content or presentation can create a contempt risk, independently of identification issues, as with the Taylor sisters' 'wedding kiss' photograph.

As well as the issues of identification or oblique editorializing, photographs can give greater prominence or impact to a report. In the case of *HMA v Andrew McGhee*[95] a trial which had been due to start was adjourned because of a two-page spread in *The Sun* less than a week before the start of the trial containing 'strong allegations of sexual and physical abuse by the accused against both his wife and his daughter, all of whom were named . . . the article had sensationalist headlines and was illustrated with photographs of the three individuals. In all there were two photographs of the accused, three of his wife and two of his stepdaughter', although the article did not mention the outstanding charges. McGhee's wife was a former co-accused, the step-daughter was on the Crown list of witnesses. Note was made of the fact that one of the photographs was an almost full-length photograph of all three. Again, there were no contempt proceedings in this case, and the photographs were almost certainly less significant in the judge's eyes than the allegations made against McGhee.

In *Attorney-General v MGN*, in 2002, where the *Sunday Mirror* was found in contempt principally for creating the impression that an attack was racist, note was made that 'the article is lavishly illustrated with photographs of the victim's family and also photographs of the three defendants'.[96] In *Attorney-General v BBC and Hat Trick*[97] the Divisional Court was also influenced by the fact that a photograph of the *Mirror* pensioners remained on display for one-and-a-half minutes. A photograph of a

---

[93] [2009] HCJAC 24, 12 March 2009, 2009 GWD 11–171.
[94] 5 February 2003, Appeal Court, High Court of Judiciary.
[95] 12 October 2005, [2005] HCJAB01.
[96] [2002] EWHC 907(Admin), para 12.
[97] [1997] EMLR 76, *The Times*, 26 July 1996, DC.

particular landlord was a factor in the court's deciding that the section 5 defence was not available in *Attorney-General v TVS Television Ltd.*[98] In Barry George's original, albeit unsuccessful, appeal against his conviction for Jill Dando's murder, much attention was given to the consequences of the judges lifting a Section 11 Order preventing publication of photographs or drawings of him, with a view to protecting the integrity of identification parades:

They published numerous pictures of the appellant spanning 30 years under what the Judge himself described as 'lurid headlines' and the accompanying publication of background information, which for example spoke of the appellant's habit of changing his appearance . . . The Judge looked at every sketch of the proceedings before sanctioning its use. None of the sketches showed the face of the appellant.[99]

In summary, then, photographs can prejudice identification, distort reporting, implicitly criticize an accused, and raise the impact of a publication. They require especial care, and particularly in Scotland.

4.14 PUBLIC FIGURE

While the existing notoriety of someone accused of crime might not stop a contempt finding, it is recognized that a celebrity is in a somewhat unusual position, and not merely as regards identification.

In *Lord Advocate v Scottish Media Newspapers*[100] *The Evening Times*, about nine months before any likely trial, had described an actor accused of threatening Sheriff Officers[101] with an axe, as 'troubled', and having 'a well-documented history of personal setbacks, including drink problems'. Three Court of Session judges unanimously dismissed the Lord Advocate's Petition that the newspaper be found in contempt of court. The court said:

Where personalities, whether from the world of politics, sport or entertainment, are tried by a jury, the jurors may often know more about their way of life and the background to any charge than they would in an ordinary case. That in itself may perhaps mean that the judge presiding at any trial would think it appropriate to give a more pointed direction about the need for the jury to reach their verdict solely on the evidence . . .

So, more is already known about the well known. The flipside, however, can be that new information can be more memorable. In *HMA v Scotsman*[102] a newspaper was found to be in contempt for publishing an article headed 'Sarwar Charge Witnesses

---

[98] *The Times*, 7 July 1989 (Lexis).
[99] Court of Appeal, 29 July 2002: [2002] EWCA Crim 1923, *The Times*, 30 August 2002. Barry George was acquitted on a retrial, with new forensic evidence.
[100] 2000 SLT 331.
[101] The Scottish equivalent of bailiffs.
[102] 1999 SLT 466.

Ask For Protection', when electoral fraud charges were active against the ultimately acquitted Govan MP Mohammed Sarwar. Lord Marnoch said: 'Once the ordinary reader has formed [the impression that an accused person would intimidate witnesses] I do not consider that he is likely to forget it, particularly when applied to someone as well-known as Mr Sarwar.'

In *Attorney-General v News Group Newspapers Ltd* [103] the Court of Appeal discharged an injunction granted by a judge to restrain a newspaper from publishing allegations about the cricketer Ian Botham at a time when Botham's libel action against another newspaper had been set down for trial. Mr Justice Leggatt had said, granting the injunction:

Mr Botham is a public figure. For that reason, if for no other, people are likely to remember what they hear about him . . . [Counsel] says Mr Botham's activities have attracted considerable publicity, in relation to New Zealand, this country, the current tour of the West Indies, his charity walk and the allegations made or alleged to have been made by his manager. And the temerarious submission is made that this article could add little. I find that extremely unattractive . . . . Some attempt was made to say that because Mr Botham is a public figure the newspaper has a duty to show that he has feet of clay. And that, irrespective of the effect it will have on the trial. But this could not apply to an attempt to reiterate allegations made some two years ago in another newspaper.

Although the Appeal Court lifted the injunction, they did not comment upon Leggatt J's reasoning in this respect.

Similar thinking can be traced in the Divisional Court's decision in *Attorney-General v BBC and Hat Trick Productions Ltd* [104] to make a contempt finding over the reference in the comedy quiz *Have I Got News For You* to Robert Maxwell's sons as 'heartless scheming bastards'. [105] The Attorney-General:

. . . referred to the enormous publicity which had already surrounded the alleged fraud on the pensioners by their father and their, the brothers', alleged part in it. He allied to that publicity the impact of the broadcast of the prejudicial words on a national and highly popular television programme featuring well-known television celebrities . . . He added that the fact that the comments were made in a humorous and irreverent programme did not diminish that risk; on the contrary, their source being a well-known and highly popular television presenter, the general and lasting impression was likely to have been that they were guilty . . .

Lord Justice Auld said:

At the very least, they constituted a readily-memorable encouragement to viewers to regard the Maxwell brothers as guilty of defrauding the Mirror pensioners, the very subject matter of their well-publicised forthcoming trial. The allegation was made by a well-known television personality about the equally well-known sons of a notorious man . . . The offending publicity is great

---

[103] [1986] 2 All ER.
[104] [1997] EMLR 76.
[105] For some reason, Lord Justice Auld's judgment puts the word 'celebrities' into inverted commas in relation to the participant teams, as it does the word 'presenter'.

both because of its medium and repetition, and because both the speakers and the victims are already much in the public eye.

It is perhaps hard to imagine a judge today taking such a decision.

4.15 PREVIOUS CONVICTIONS AND BAD CHARACTER

The revelation of previous convictions is probably the classic teaching example to journalists about what one must *not* do. In one of the few recent English publication contempt findings, ITV Central Ltd was fined £25,000 for broadcasting, on the morning of the trial, the fact that one of the accused had been convicted for murder. The trial was postponed. ITV immediately apologized and offered to pay the third-party costs of the postponement. The journalist was sacked. The television company's Counsel said that his client 'recognised that there had been a serious breach, as serious as it is basic'. It was a simple oversight, handled by ITV Central with dispatch, zeal, and contrition, as the court acknowledged: 'We accept that this was a mistake made by a normally responsible company in an industry which in this respect is normally responsible.' However: 'The charge to be heard by the trial court—one of murder—was a most serious one. The conviction disclosed was also an offence of murder. . . . [It] should be known universally in the journalistic profession that previous convictions of persons being tried must not be disclosed.'[106]

That said, there will be circumstances where reference to a previous conviction is legitimate or, at any rate, may not result in a finding of contempt: for instance, if the fact of the previous conviction is so widely known as to be in the public domain. In the retrials of, for instance, Barry George or Sion Jenkins for murder, there was no attempt to conceal the fact that these men had, during their first trials, been convicted of murder. Barry George was acquitted on retrial, Sion Jenkins was acquitted after two successive juries failed to reach a majority verdict—intriguing examples, both, of the possibility of acquittal after prolonged and sometimes highly hostile reporting.[107] Reference to a previous conviction might be, in context, harmless—for instance, if the facts and gravity of the previous conviction would be irrelevant to the upcoming trial. Even there, though, it is submitted that caution needs to be exercised. A conviction for drunk-driving might not be strictly relevant to an allegation of fraud, but it still tends to cast the accused in a bad light. Reference to a previous conviction without reference to an active charge may also be acceptable.[108]

In *Attorney-General v ITN News Ltd*[109] the court did decline to make a contempt finding when they published a previous murder conviction, but the factors saving them

---

[106] [2008] EWHC 1984 (Admin).
[107] The doctors in *Attorney-General v English* and *Attorney-General v News Group Newspapers plc* were both, like Mohammad Sarwar, Derek Riordan, and the accused in *AG v BBC* 1991, acquitted in their trials, despite the newspapers' contempts.
[108] *HMA v Caledonian Newspapers Ltd* 1995 SLT 926.
[109] [1995] 2 All ER 370.

related to circulation, the evanescent nature of the broadcast medium, and the passage of time.[110] In *Attorney-General v Sport Newspapers Ltd*[111] the newspaper published a sensational account of previous rape convictions of a man who was wanted in connection with the murder of Anna-Louise Humphries. Since the case was not active, and there had been no specific intent to cause a risk to the administration of justice, there was no contempt finding there, either. Had the suspect been arrested, that would have been a different matter.

It is clear that the Scottish court regarded the reference to Mags Haney's previous convictions and those of her family as at least potentially contemptuous. Publication of suggestions that the accused had substance addiction problems and 'demons' to fight posed an issue in the Big Tam case, albeit that the newspaper was not found to be in contempt there. Similarly, a *Sunday Mail* article depicting the accused as physically and sexually abusive, which did not result in a contempt prosecution, nonetheless resulted in a trial being moved.[112]

4.16 'SERIOUSLY IMPEDED OR PREJUDICED'

The strict liability test is wide enough to encompass not just a publication which risks prejudicing the outcome of proceedings. It also covers a substantial risk that the course of justice be seriously impeded, although, in practice, the boundary between impediment and prejudice seems fluid. In *Attorney-General v Times Newspapers Ltd*[113] Oliver LJ said:

> The course of justice is not just concerned with the outcome of proceedings. It is concerned with the whole process of law, including the freedom of a person accused of a crime . . . to conduct his defence in the way which seems best to him . . . Any extraneous factor or external pressure which impedes or restricts that election or that conduct, or which impels a person accused to adopt a course in the conduct of his own defence which he does not wish to adopt, deprives him . . .

This should not be taken to mean that an accused person can keep his or her options open until the eleventh hour. In *Attorney-General v Unger and ors*[114] the defendant, a home help, had been caught on video stealing money from a pensioner. The *Daily Mail* ran an article headlined 'The Home Help Who Was Busy Helping Herself' and contained a quotation from the home help: 'I won't be denying [the theft allegations]. I don't know why I took it. I have just been ill.' The *Manchester Evening News* also reported that the home help had said that she would not be denying the allegations and threatened suicide. The *Daily Mail* had received legal advice that, since the home help

---

[110] See section at 4.6.3 above.
[111] [1992] 1 All ER 503, [1991] 1 WLR 1194.
[112] *HMA v Andrew McGhee*, 12 October 2005, [2005] HCJA B01.
[113] *The Times*, 12 February 1983.
[114] [1998] 1 Cr App R 308, [1998] EMLR 280.

had confessed and was caught red-handed on video, she would be bound to plead guilty, which eventually she did.

Although the Divisional Court did not hold the newspapers to be in contempt of court, Simon Brown LJ regarded the *Daily Mail*'s assumptions as:

... wholly misguided ... It is not to be assumed that because someone has 'confessed' to a crime they will necessarily plead guilty to it, or indeed that they necessarily are guilty ... Still less is it for the newspapers to assess the strength of the evidence against an accused and to second-guess a jury's verdict ... I do not go so far as to say that [the home help's] intimation to the respondents that she would not be denying these theft allegations was immaterial. In my judgment, however, ... it was only of the most limited materiality. There is always a chance that an accused ... however apparently strong the evidence against him, will plead not guilty and elect trial by jury ...

The decision not to find the newspapers in contempt was principally predicated on the 'fade' factor, plus the presumption that juries would decide according to the evidence, and their oath. Simon Brown LJ also stated that it was 'important ... that the Courts do not speak with two voices, one used to dismiss Criminal appeals with the Court roundly rejecting any suggestion that prejudice resulted from media publications, the other holding comparable publications to be in contempt'. However, the Court implied in the *Unger* case that, if the trial had to be moved or delayed, or required directions from the court 'well beyond those ordinarily required and routinely given to juries' or created a seriously arguable ground for an appeal, that could fall foul of the strict liability rule.

The Attorney-General argued that there was a real chance that the home help might have elected for trial by jury. Alternatively, the publications could have affected her, for example by making her conclude that there was no point in defending herself. The Divisional Court said: 'That articles of the nature published here, which plainly pre-judge guilt, are capable of influencing an accused and thus constituting a contempt cannot be doubted,'[115] although the court admitted that there was only one case in which influence on the accused was a major factor in a contempt finding. That was the case where Michael Fagan had broken into Buckingham Palace and had a conversation with the Queen in her bedroom.[116] Oliver LJ found that *The Times* appeared to have been 'gunning' for Fagan, resulting in his solicitor recommending that he be tried on indictment, rather than a summary trial, which would have enabled his case to come to court more quickly.

In *Attorney-General v Birmingham Post & Mail Ltd*[117] a newspaper had published an article suggesting that a murder had been carried out by members of a notorious drug-dealing gang. The publication occurred during the trial of a number of defendants who were not identified in the article nor stood accused of drug-dealing or gang-related offences. The judge stayed the proceedings and the trial recommenced at a different venue, where the defendants were convicted. The article was inaccurate, inflammatory, attributed motives to the defendants which formed no part of the proper deliberation of

---

[115] ibid.
[116] *Attorney-General v Times Newspapers and ors*, *The Times*, 12 February 1983.
[117] [1998] 4 All ER 49.

the case, and, although it did not name them as individuals, gave a detailed account of events. There, David Pannick submitted that 'impeded' added nothing to the scope or proper understanding of the strict liability rule, which Simon Brown LJ appeared to accept—at least to the extent that the mere fact that a stay had been ordered was not *ipso facto* proof of contempt having been committed. However, the Divisional Court did find the newspaper in contempt.

In *Attorney-General v Associated Newspapers Ltd*[118] Kennedy LJ noted that 'For present purposes it is agreed that we should not trouble with the word 'impede'.' However, in *Attorney-General v BBC*,[119] Watkins LJ said—of a case where there had been no stay of the criminal proceedings, only an interruption of a couple of hours, and where the accused was ultimately acquitted:

... the question of whether there was a similar risk of the course of justice being seriously impeded also requires to be answered . . . There would have existed in the words of the statute a substantial risk that the course of justice would be seriously impeded, with the additional consequence, I would add, of possible prejudice to the defendants through having to wait for a fresh trial and being tried by another jury.

Similarly, in *R v Attorney-General, ex p BBC*[120] the accused pleaded guilty before a relevant broadcast came to his attention and before any decision had been taken as to a stay. Contempt was nonetheless found established, on the basis that the broadcast might have occasioned an application for a stay. Rougier J said in that case:

Another practical consideration is that . . . no judge would wish to create a gratuitous ground of appeal based on procedural irregularity unconnected with the merits of the case, therefore in all probability arrangements would have been made to transfer the case off circuit . . . . I do not think that it could be said that the chance of [the accused] having a fair trial would have been seriously prejudiced [by delay] but some impediment to the course of justice . . . was . . . inevitable.

In practice, the courts tend to concentrate on the notion of prejudice, rather than impediment. By most contemporary views, the *Unger* case notwithstanding, the mere need to give a special direction to the jury would not *per se* ground a finding of contempt.[121]

4.17 INNOCENT PUBLICATION AND DISTRIBUTION

Section 3(1) of the Contempt of Court Act 1981 reads: 'A person is not guilty of contempt of court under the strict liability rule as the publisher of any matter to which that rule applies if at the time of publication (having taken all reasonable care) he does

---

[118] *Independent*, 6 November 1997.
[119] [1992] COD 264.
[120] 1 December 1995, unreported.
[121] *Attorney-General v Birmingham Post and Mail Ltd* [1998] 4 All ER 49; see also, in a slightly different vein, *HMA v Scottish Media Newspapers* 2000 SLT 331.

not know and has no reason to suspect that relevant proceedings are active' with a similar protection for distributors at section 3(2).

Section 3 is not an easy defence. The publisher must have 'taken all reasonable care' and have 'no reason to suspect the relevant proceedings are active'. He or she bears the burden of proof (section 3(4)), though recent commentators have queried how this should be approached in the light of the Human Rights Act 1998.[122] As the Divisional Court said in *R v Duffy*:[123]

Section 3 expects of journalists a high standard of care before they are in a position to avail themselves of that defence . . . It would be rare, indeed, for a journalist, who writes an article suggesting that an identifiable person has committed a criminal offence, to be able to avail themselves of the statutory defence without specifically asking those in a position to know if there are any active criminal proceedings but, as this case shows, even that rule cannot be absolute.

In *R v Duffy* the journalist in question had been in extensive contact with the senior police officer dealing with the case. It was felt that he was entitled to assume proceedings were not active, even though he had not expressly asked the police, the Crown, or the courts.

Section 3 has been successfully used in Scotland by the editors of the *Scottish Daily Mail* and *Daily Record* to cover garbled reporting by a freelance, who was found in contempt,[124] and another attempt was abandoned in mid-stream by the *News of the World*.[125]

4.18 DISCUSSION OF PUBLIC AFFAIRS—SECTION 5

Section 5 of the Contempt of Court Act 1981 says: 'A publication made as or as part of a discussion in good faith of public affairs or other matters of general public interest is not to be treated as a contempt of court under the strict liability rule if the risk of impediment or prejudice to particular legal proceedings is merely incidental to the discussion.'

In *Attorney-General v English* the *Daily Mail* had published an article about pro-life issues, referring to a doctor charged with murdering a baby who had Down's Syndrome. Lord Diplock said that an article which did not contain the statement that doctors had left babies with such a handicap to die 'would be emasculated into a mere contribution to a purely hypothetical debate'. The defence must be established on the

---

[122] See A Arlidge, D Eady, and A Smith, *Arlidge, Eady & Smith on Contempt* (Sweet & Maxwell, 3rd edn, 2005) paras 4-261–4-262.

[123] 9 February 1996 (Lexis).

[124] See (1997) 2(3) Communications Law, for a further report on this case and on *HMA v Belmonte*, 24 October 1996, where no contempt finding was made because of the limited distribution of the *Dumfries and Galloway Standard* in the trial area, Glasgow, but where Lord Weir said obiter that the newspaper should have contacted the Crown Office.

[125] *Solicitor-General v Henry*, 20 March 1990 (Lexis), [1990] COD 307. See also *R v Home Secretary, ex p Westminster Press Ltd* (1991) 4 Admin LR 445. In *Attorney-General v Channel 4 Television Ltd*, 14 April 1987, QBD, Kerr LJ, Simon Brown LJ, the broadcaster explicitly accepted that s 3 could not be used, although the mitigatory circumstances of that case meant that the fine was only £2,500.

balance of probabilities.[126] 'Discussion' has been given a fairly wide definition.[127] The test is not whether the publication could readily have done without reference to the case, but rather whether the risk created was 'no more than an incidental consequence of expounding [the author's or publication's] main theme'.[128]

In *Attorney-General v TVS Television Ltd*,[129] where a television programme about bad landlords ultimately caused a trial to be aborted, it was held necessary to look at the subject matter of the discussion and to see how closely it related to the proceedings. The closer the relationship, the greater the risk. The section 5 defence failed because it was held that the risk of prejudice to the impending trial was not merely incidental to the public discussion.

Section 5 was also used in *Leary v BBC*[130] to ward off injunction of a television programme concerning the disbandment of the West Midland Serious Crime Squad. It was held that the programme would not infringe the strict liability rule. In *Attorney-General v Associated Newspapers Group plc and ors*[131] Mann LJ rejected a section 5 defence in relation to articles about a patient sent to a secure hospital after killing a young girl, saying that the discussion in the *Liverpool Echo* was limited to that case.[132] Section 5 also failed ignominiously in *Attorney-General v Hislop*,[133] which concerned *Private Eye* publications about the former wife of the Yorkshire Ripper: 'One of the pre-requisites to the application of section 5 is that the publication was a part of a discussion "in good faith" . . . Mr Hislop's intention negatived the existence of good faith.'[134]

Section 5 was raised in the 1990 case of *Re Lonrho*,[135] but not decided, because the House of Lords took the view that the publication there posed no risk.

4.19 COMMON LAW CONTEMPT—SECTION 6

Section 6 of the Contempt of Court Act 1981 reads:

Nothing in the foregoing provisions of this Act—

(a) prejudices any defence available at common law to a charge of contempt of court under the strict liability rule;

---

[126] *Attorney-General v English* [1983] AC 116.

[127] ibid *per* Lord Diplock, 143.

[128] ibid *per* Lord Diplock, 143B.

[129] DC 6 July 1989, *Independent*, 7 July 1989. Contrast the approach of the Scottish court in the (non-s 5) case of *HMA v Wilson* 2000, 15 June 2001, High Court of Justiciary—see text accompanying n 181 below.

[130] 29 September 1989 (Lexis).

[131] [1989] All ER 604, [1989] 1WLR 322.

[132] The House of Lords took a different view of the status of the mental health review tribunal as a 'court' in *Pickering v Liverpool Daily Post and Echo plc and ors* [1991] 2 AC 370, [1991] 1 All ER 622.

[133] [1991] 1 QB 514.

[134] Asserted want of good faith was also an issue in the *TVS Television* case, see n 129 above.

[135] [1989] 2 All ER 1100.

(b) implies that any publication is punishable as contempt of court under that rule which would not be so punishable apart from those provisions;

(c) restricts liability for contempt of court in respect of conduct intended to impede or prejudice the administration of justice.

The 1981 Act applies the strict liability rule from the point at which proceedings become active. However, there remains a risk of a publication contempt finding if the court can be convinced that the risk of prejudice was deliberately created. Intent is not motive or desire.[136] As Sir John Donaldson MR said in *Attorney-General v Newspaper Publishing Ltd*:[137] 'Such intent need not be expressly avowed or admitted, but can be inferred from all the circumstances, including the foreseeability of the consequences . . . Nor need it be the sole intention of the contemnor.' As to intent, Lord Justice Bingham added in *Attorney-General v Sport Newspapers*[138] that, 'the probability of the consequence taken to have been foreseen must be little short of overwhelming before it will suffice to establish the necessary intent.'[139]

Attorney-General v News Group Newspapers plc[140] concerned *The Sun*'s offer to fund a private prosecution against a doctor accused (and ultimately acquitted) of raping an 8-year-old. *The Sun* ran a series of 'lurid and garish' articles, with headlines like 'Doc Groped Me, Says Girl'. The 'girl' in question was a woman who claimed that the doctor had assaulted her on a cruise, evidence which, according to the contempt judges, would have been inadmissible.

Lord Justice Watkins said:

I simply cannot accept that an experienced editor such as Mr Mackenzie could have failed to have foreseen that the material which he published . . . and the steps he announced he was taking to assist the mother to prosecute would incur a real risk of prejudicing the fairness of a trial of Dr B. The inescapable inference is, in my judgment, that Mr Mackenzie became so convinced of Dr B's guilt and incensed by that and the failure to prosecute him that he endeavoured to persuade readers of 'The Sun' to take a similar view.

He also took the view that a criminal contempt at common law could be committed even where proceedings were not pending or imminent but added: 'If it is necessary for the Attorney-General to establish that proceedings were imminent, he has, I think done so. In my judgment, where a prosecution is virtually certain to be commenced and particularly where it is to be commenced in the near future, it is proper to describe such proceedings as imminent.'

---

[136] Lord Bridge of Harwich in *R v Moloney* [1985] AC 905, 926.
[137] [1988] CH 333, 374.
[138] [1991] WLR 1194, 1208.
[139] ibid.
[140] [1988] 3 WLR 163, [1989] QB 110.

Lord Justice Watkins's view of common law contempt was doubted in the later case of *Attorney-General v Sport Newspapers Ltd*[141] by Hodgson J, who observed that *The Sun* case was:

. . . undoubtedly complicated by the fact that there was not only publication of material but also active support given to the proceedings which the newspaper's editor wanted to happen. But it is plain authority for the proposition that publication of material prior to proceedings being pending can amount to publication contempt. In my judgment . . . that was a wrong decision . . . Many of the 'targets' of investigative journalism are rich and powerful and who is to say that they, when attacked, will not respond by seeking leave to move for contempt?[142]

The *Sport* newpaper's case concerned an article entitled 'Evans Was Given Ten Years For Rape', published at the time Evans was sought in connection with the disappearance of the 15-year-old schoolgirl Anna-Louise Humphries.[143] Bingham LJ, unlike Hodgson J, considered that there was:

. . . a growing consensus that a publication could be contemptuous if proceedings were at the time of publication imminent though not in existence . . . Section 6(3) was intended to preserve what was understood to be the existing law, that a publisher was liable in contempt for an intentionally prejudicial publication made at a time when proceedings were imminent.[144]

He also stated that, had it not been for *The Sun*/doctor case, he would have been much more hesitant in considering whether merely imminent proceedings could give rise to liability for common law contempt: 'It is a decision with very serious implications in those cases . . . where reporters are concerned to highlight an alleged crime, to point an accusing finger at an identified culprit and to stimulate a demand for prosecution.'[145] It might, then, be doubted whether we will ever see a prosecution for common law contempt where proceedings are merely 'imminent', especially since Hodgson J pointed out some significant authorities apparently not considered by the court in *The Sun*/doctor case.

Although scathing as to the priority which the editor gave his avowed motive (of alerting the public to the danger of a violent and habitual sexual predator), Bingham LJ saw 'no reason to doubt that it played a part in his thinking', furthermore that the editor had genuinely 'worried whether the police were seeking to cover up their own failure to question a rather obvious local suspect before he slipped through the net' in asking the press not to reveal the previous convictions. He also accepted that, as at publication, the editor regarded criminal proceedings against Evans as speculative and remote since Evans had disappeared, possibly abroad: 'With the benefit of hindsight, of course, we know that a warrant was issued shortly after publication and an arrest made shortly after that. But these facts were not known when the newspaper was published.'

---

[141] [1991] WLR 1194.
[142] ibid 1229–30.
[143] He was ultimately convicted of her murder.
[144] ibid 1206–7.
[145] ibid 1207.

Therefore, Bingham LJ concluded that it had not been shown beyond reasonable doubt that the newspaper had the 'specific intention' which must be proved against it. Recklessness alone was not enough.[146]

In *Re Lonrho plc and ors*,[147] which concerned a failed Harrods takeover bid, the court also rejected an argument that the publication of an *Observer* special edition campaigning in favour of Lonhro (of which *The Observer* was a wholly-owned subsidiary) amounted to common law contempt in terms of section 6. The special edition had been distributed, *inter alia*, to members of both Houses of Parliament, including four of the five Lords of Appeal in Ordinary who were to hear the appeals in related judicial review proceedings concerning the takeover bids. The House of Lords Appellate Committee said:

If the publication of the Observer special edition did create a risk that the course of justice in Lonhro's appeal would be impeded or prejudiced, there would be no difficulty in inferring that those responsible for the publication intended that consequence. But if the publication created no such risk, as we concluded in considering the question of statutory contempt, common law contempt . . . could only be established if those responsible for the publication intended it to have consequences . . . which it neither achieved nor was ever likely to achieve.

Though the strict liability rule tends to be the focus of journalistic concern, common law contempt is famously protean. Nor is it either/or. In *Attorney-General v Hislop*[148] the Court of Appeal considered that *Private Eye* and its editor were guilty *both* of common law and strict liability contempt for articles about the Yorkshire Ripper's ex-wife, when her defamation trial against *Private Eye* was two or three months away.

Direct disobedience of a court order is plainly contempt.[149] Third-party publishers may also be liable for 'Spycatcher'-type contempt[150] when they intentionally interfere with the administration of justice in a way which undermines a court order directed against a party to proceedings. In *Attorney-General v Punch*[151] the House of Lords, overturning the Court of Appeal, held that *Punch*'s editor was in contempt for publishing an article by David Shayler, a former member of the Security Service, which undermined the interlocutory injunction against Shayler himself. The editor argued that he did not have the requisite intention to undermine national security. The House of Lords took the view that he nonetheless wilfully undermined the court's intention

---

[146] Watkins LJ took a similar approach to the inadequacy of recklessness in the Sun/doctor case. For a different view taken by Lord Dawson in Scotland, see the *Scottish Daily Mail* and *Daily Record* case, 7 February 1997, (1997) 2(3) Communications Law, where a freelance reporter who filed inaccurate copy was fined £750 on the basis that the report was so reckless that there was no need to establish intention. This seems questionable.

[147] [1989] 2 All ER 1100.

[148] (1991) 1 QB 514, (1991) 1 All ER 911.

[149] *Times Newspapers Ltd and ors v R*, 30 July 2007, (2008) 1 All ER 343, (2008) 1 Cr App R 16, (2008) 1 WLR 234.

[150] *A-G v Newspaper Publishing plc* [1998] Ch 333, [1987] 3 All ER 276.

[151] [2002] UKHL 50, (2003) 1 All ER 289.

in granting the interlocutory injunction, ie to avoid pre-empting the court's ultimate decision on confidentiality. Lord Nicholls said:

> He knew that the action against Mr Shayler raised confidentiality issues . . . He must, inevitably, have appreciated that by publishing the article he was doing precisely what the order was intended to prevent, namely, pre-empting the court's decision on these confidentiality issues. That is knowing interference with the administration of justice . . . He may have had, as he says, no intention of damaging national security. Those beliefs and intentions are not inconsistent with an intention to take it upon himself to make a decision which, as he knew, the court had reserved to itself . . . He frankly admitted, as is obvious, that he was not qualified to assess whether disclosure of any particular information would damage national security. Despite this he proceeded to publish information whose disclosure was, as he knew, asserted by the Attorney-General to be damaging to national security.[152]

4.20 COURT REPORTING

Section 4(1) of the Contempt of Court Act 1981 reads: 'Subject to this section a person is not guilty of contempt of court under the strict liability rule in respect of a fair and accurate report of legal proceedings held in public, published contemporaneously and in good faith.'

4.20.1 What is 'fair and accurate'?

A fair and accurate report does not have to be exhaustive and can be selective. Media court reporting would be almost impossible otherwise. A typical press report of a trial will involve compressing hours of evidence into a few hundred words and penning a headline summarizing 'the top line'—the most newsworthy element. This is neither malicious nor, necessarily, salacious; it is a practical necessity. In criminal trials, in particular, where the accused will frequently not give evidence, an arithmetical balance of the space given to each side of adversarial proceedings would be impossible without distortion. Apart from that, editorial decisions as to covering a trial on any given day will depend upon the other news stories requiring to be covered.

In general, the courts have been tolerant of editorial paraphrases. As far back as 1925, in *R v Evening News, ex p Hobbs*[153] the recorder's charge to the jury of: 'There can be no doubt I should say—it is for you to judge—that Hobbs was a party to a gigantic fraud, as monumental and perhaps as impudent a fraud as has ever been perpetrated' was recorded in the evening headlines as 'no doubt party to a monumental fraud', omitting the words 'it is for you to judge'. A contempt application against the *Evening News* and its editor failed. The article was held to be a fair and accurate report of judicial proceedings.[154]

---

[152] ibid para 523.
[153] [1925] 2 KB 158.
[154] This, obviously, was before the 1981 Act.

Courts have also supported the positive facilitation of accurate court reporting. In *Harman v Secretary of State for the Home Department*[155] the House of Lords (*per* Lord Roskill) approved the practice of showing documents disclosed on discovery, which were otherwise subject to an implied undertaking not to be used other than for the purposes of litigation, to those engaged in court reporting: 'I would prefer to regard the assistance long given to press agencies, representatives of the media, and law reporters concerned with what I have called day-by-day reporting, in the interests of fair and accurate reporting, as being for the immediate purpose of the litigation . . . '

For while omitting, summarizing, and selective emphasis are all excusable, flat out inaccuracy is perilous. In *Attorney-General v British Broadcasting Corporation*[156] the BBC was fined £5,000 in relation to a report of a trial at Shrewsbury Crown Court said to be misleading and inaccurate and to contain matters which were not put before the jury. Four jurors saw it. The trial proceeded, after the judge had warned the jury to ignore the programme, and the defendants were acquitted. The BBC admitted errors but argued unsuccessfully that a reasonable juror would have been able to spot them. The reporting of extraneous matter was also a problem here. In attempting to summarize Prosecuting Counsel's speech, the report included a number of matters he had deliberately omitted which had come from an earlier police briefing.

In *R v Solicitor General, ex p Taylor & Taylor*[157] there was a judicial review of the Solicitor-General's decision not to take contempt proceedings over newspaper coverage of the Taylor sisters' trial. Scrutiny was given to the misleading 'wedding video' photograph used extensively in the newspaper coverage of the murder trial. Although there were no contempt proceedings against the newspapers ultimately, and the judicial review application failed, the Attorney-General had originally told the newspapers that:

> . . . these reports did not represent a fair and accurate report of the proceedings as neither the video recording of the wedding of John and Alison Shaughnessy nor any of the still photographs . . . were presented to the jury . . . He considers that these pictures and accompanying captions provided a wholly unwarranted sense of emphasis to the secret relationship between Mr Shaughnessy and Miss Taylor and thereby to the motive alleged . . .

The decision not to raise contempt proceedings was taken against a background that the jury had heard much evidence of an illicit relationship between the accused and the victim's husband. There can be little doubt that it could have gone the other way. In quashing the Taylor sisters' convictions, McCowan LJ said the newspaper coverage 'was not reporting at all; it was comment, and comment which assumed guilt on the part of the girls in the dock'.[158]

---

[155] [1982] 1 All ER 532.
[156] Divisional Court CO/411/91, 10 December 1991, Watkins and Mann LJJ and Roch J [1992] COD 265, *The Independent*, 3 January 1992, *The Guardian*, 18 December 1991.
[157] 31 July 1995, *The Times,* 14 August 1995.
[158] (1993) 98 Cr App R 361, 369.

The courts have traditionally regarded court reports done as reconstructions in a similar light,[159] or as positively dangerous.[160]

Inaccurate reporting was an issue in the Fagan case[161] and in *Attorney-General v Birmingham Post & Mail Ltd*.[162] In *Attorney-General v Unger*[163] Simon Brown LJ observed: 'The risk . . . is heightened, the more vulnerable the accused, the more high-profile the case, and the less accurate the reporting.' If that is correct, then inaccuracy not only loses the media its shield, but sharpens the sword against it.

The court in *R v Sherwood*[164] rejected the notion of a limited reporting restriction, designed to safeguard a later trial, on the basis that it would give a one-sided and incomplete picture of his defence:

Mr Tugendhat responded by saying that no-one is entitled to a full report and that summarising is inevitable. So stated, that is clearly right. Here, however, the problem is that there would be certain forbidden areas, which could not be reported even by way of summary . . . The court needs, therefore, to be very careful about sanctioning any course that would lead to information about a criminal trial being presented to the public in a way that actually distorted what was taking place, rather than merely summarising it.

Substantial accuracy is, therefore, the principal goal of court reporting and a primary safeguard against contempt.

4.20.2 What does 'contemporaneous' mean?

The purpose of confining protection given by section 4(1) to contemporaneous court reports is, presumably, that there is no urgency about reporting proceedings which are past and gone. There may, indeed, be particular prejudice if, say, fresh proceedings are in train against the same accused. In practice, of course, the media's interest lies mainly in reporting current stories. The Act does not define 'contemporaneous' and there is a paucity of case law on the topic. Section 4(3)(a) does provide that, once a reporting restriction under section 4(2) is lifted, a report which is 'published as soon as practicable after that order expires' counts as 'contemporaneous'.

Obviously, publication 'as soon as practicable' is always the safe, as well as the jour-nalistically desirable, course. An interpretation of the meaning of contemporaneous publication in the different context of defamation suggests that a fairly generous view may be taken of 'contemporaneous'.[165]

---

[159] *Peacock v London Weekend Television* (1986) 150 JP 71, *per* Croom-Johnson LJ, 83.
[160] *A-G v Channel Four Television Co Ltd* [1988] Crim LR 237.
[161] *A-G v Times Newspapers* The Times, 12 February 1983 (Lexis).
[162] [1998] 4 All ER 49.
[163] (1998) 1 Cr App R 308, Independent, 8 July 1997, DC 3/7/97. Inaccurate inclusion of an older charge, dropped from the indictment, led to the abandonment of a Glasgow murder trial in June 2009, but not, so far, to contempt proceedings.
[164] *R v Sherwood, ex p The Telegraph Group and ors* [2001] EWCA Crim 1075, (2001) 1 WLR 1983, (2002) EMLR 10, The Times, 12 June 2001. A similar view was taken by Lord Philip in the High Court of Justiciary in Scotland in *HMA v Zahid and Mohammed*, 3 November 2004, when he refused to grant a s 4(2) order which would have concealed that 3 missing co-accused had participated in the fatal attack on Kriss Donald.
[165] *Arthur Bennett v Newsquest (London) Ltd*, 22 February 2006, Claim HQ 05X03743, Eady J, QBD.

4.21 REPORTING RESTRICTIONS UNDER THE 1981 ACT: SECTION 4(2)

Section 4(2) reads:

In any such proceedings [ie legal proceedings held in public] the court may, where it appears necessary for avoiding a substantial risk of prejudice to the administration of justice in those proceedings, or in any other proceedings pending or imminent, order that the publication of any report of the proceedings, or any part of the proceedings, be postponed for such period as the court thinks necessary for that purpose.

Section 4(2) orders are the most commonly experienced barriers to court reporting in the daily newsroom. It might therefore be thought that section 4 gives with one hand and takes away with another. That, however, was not the analysis of the House of Lords when it first came to consider section 4(2). In *R v Horsham Justice, ex p Farquharson and anor*[166] Lord Denning said:

Section 4(2) retains the common law about the occasions when a report (otherwise fair and accurate) may be a contempt of court—but with this improvement: nothing is to be left to implication . . . Thus, when the jury is sent out, the judge should tell the newspaper reporters, 'You are not to publish anything of what takes place whilst the jury are out . . . ' It applies only to a very limited type of case. So read, the statute is not a measure for restricting the freedom of the press. It is a measure for liberating it. It is intended to remove the uncertainties which previously troubled editors.

He added that:

The ordinary folk who sit on juries . . . are good, sensible people. They go by the evidence that is adduced before them and not by what they may have read in the newspapers. The risk of their being influenced is so slight that it can usually be disregarded as insubstantial—and therefore not the subject of an order under Section 4(2).

Ackner LJ, in the same case, pointed to the limits of section 4(2):

First of all, the power is a power to postpone, not to prohibit totally, publication. Secondly, the power may be exercised in relation to only a part of the proceedings. Thirdly, that in order for the jurisdiction to be exercised the court must be satisfied that an order is necessary for avoiding a substantial risk of prejudice to the administration of justice. The obvious case for the postponement of a report of proceedings is where the substantive trial or a retrial has yet to take place, or where a fair and accurate report might still prejudice another trial still to be heard . . . What the court is generally concerned with is the position of a jury man . . .

Lord Denning had also emphasized: '[When] an application is made by one party for an order under Section 4(2) the magistrates must remember that there is a third party to be considered who is neither seen nor heard . . . the public at large.'

---

[166] [1982] 2 All ER 269.

According to Horsham Magistrates, then, section 4(2) has the following characteristics:

(1) It is a power to postpone only, not permanently to prevent reporting.

(2) It supersedes the common law position whereby certain sections of court proceedings were implicitly unreportable at the time, for instance trial-within-a-trial proceedings or proceedings taking place deliberately outwith the presence of the jury.

(3) Orders should be granted only where necessary.

(4) They should be no wider than necessary.

(5) They should not be granted in order to prevent 'embarrassing revelations'.

In the intervening quarter of a century, such parameters have not always been respected. However, the coming into force of the Human Rights Act 1998 has sharpened the courts' awareness of the always-accepted Benthamite truism that publicity is the soul of justice.[167]

Two cases are of particular interest. First, *R v Sherwood, ex p The Telegraph Group and ors*,[168] in which the Court of Appeal upheld a section 4(2) order in a murder trial at the Central Criminal Court. The order postponed any reporting whatsoever of the case until after the conclusion of another trial arising out of the same incident. The trials concerned the shooting dead of an unarmed man in his own bedroom, based on inaccurate information. The trial of the police officer who did the shooting, and in relation to which the section 4(2) order was upheld by the Court of Appeal, was due to be followed by a trial against three more senior officers who had been charged in respect of the shooting with 'misconduct in public office'. The trials had been severed because the police officer was going to rely not only on self-defence but on alleged failures on the part of the more senior officers. As the Court of Appeal put it:[169] 'It is thus obvious that the three senior officers will be comprehensively criticised by both sides in the murder trial without anyone to defend them or put their point of view.' Although the senior officers would be tried at a different venue with a different jury, there was 'a clear danger that an impression will have become irretrievably embedded in the public consciousness as to where the blame lies in the tragic turn of events. . . . [Even] fair and accurate coverage of Mr Sherwood's trial could easily generate a powerful head of steam in the form of public resentment . . .'[170]

It was readily accepted by the court that the media had 'the right (and indeed duty)' to report court proceedings. The contemplated news blackout of two to three months in relation to a murder trial was 'a very striking set of circumstances', not to be contemplated unless necessary. The Court of Appeal used a three-stage approach (at paragraph 22 of the judgment):

(1) The first question is whether reporting would give rise to a 'not insubstantial' risk of prejudice to the administration of justice in the relevant proceedings. If not, that will be the end of the matter.

---

[167] *Scott v Scott* [1913] AC 417, HL.
[168] (2001) 1 WLR 1983.
[169] ibid para 7.
[170] All 4 officers were ultimately acquitted.

(2) If such a risk is perceived to exist, then the second question arises: would a Section 4(2) order eliminate it? If not, obviously there could be no necessity to impose such a ban . . . On the other hand, even if the judge is satisfied that an order would achieve the objective, he or she would still have to consider whether the risk could satisfactorily be overcome by some less restrictive means . . .

(3) Suppose that the judge concludes that there is indeed no other way of eliminating the perceived risk of prejudice; it still does not follow *necessarily* that an order has to be made. The judge may still have to ask whether the degree of risk contemplated should be regarded as tolerable in the sense of being 'the lesser of two evils'.

However, the Court of Appeal pointed out that the public was not going to be excluded from either trial, that many journalists would be attending the later trial, and that it was a postponement only. They did concede that an important aspect of freedom of speech was reporting when, as well as what, one wished. Whilst accepting that jurors must be regarded as robust, the court held that the facts were very memorable, there were questions of admissibility of evidence, and, ultimately, charges of misfeasance in public office which involved 'more nebulous issues' than a conventional murder case. The two trials had been severed in the interests of justice and publicity would inevitably defeat the object of that order.

A more robust approach was taken earlier in *Re Saunders*[171] and later in *R v B*.[172] There, one defendant, Barot, had pleaded guilty to conspiracy to murder. His co-defendants were still to be tried. His conviction would be admissible as evidence against them. An order had been granted preventing reporting of Barot's sentencing, and the judge's explanatory remarks. The judge was concerned because:

Whatever sentence I impose, and the observations I make when imposing it, are likely to be the subject, quite legitimately, of public discussion and debate . . . It is likely to be prolonged. Because the case of Barot will, by virtue of its timing, be a benchmark for later cases it is unlikely that the sentence and the reasons for that sentence will simply fade from public consciousness . . .

The Court of Appeal lifted the reporting restriction. It cited the Scottish case of *Galbraith v Her Majesty's Advocate*,[173] where a section 4(2) order which would have postponed reporting of the appeal of a woman convicted of murder was refused. She admitted having shot her husband, but claimed diminished responsibility.[174] Her Counsel argued that appeal coverage would be hostile, which might create the appearance that the Appeal Court could not address the issues in an impartial manner; might

---

[171] (1990) 7 February 1990, Court of Appeal, *The Times*, 8 February 1990. The Court of Appeal declined to interfere with the trial judge's decision not to ban reporting of the proceedings against Ernest Saunders until conclusion of the second, related trial under s 4(2) in the case of *Re Saunders*.

[172] (2007) HRLR 1, The Times, 6 November 2006. Also of interest, although not dealing with order under the 1981 Act, is the House of Lords' unanimous decision in *Re Attorney-General's Reference (No 3 of 1999) sub num BBC's application* [2009] UKHL 34.

[173] 2001 SLT 465, 2000 SCCR 935.

[174] Ultimately her conviction was quashed and she pleaded guilty to culpable homicide instead of going to retrial. Since the Kim Galbraith case, the practice in Scotland has been to circulate s 4(2) orders to interested media organizations and their agents. Such orders become effective immediately, but do not become final until 48 hours after they are circulated, to give the media a chance to oppose them where desired.

affect jurors in any retrial; and might 'bring the (somewhat sensational) evidence and events in the case back to the attention of the public', including prospective jurors, in a way which would damage her credibility. The Lord Justice-General said:

> The court's power in Section 4(2) is not intended to be used to deal with [prejudicial] publications but to deal, rather, with reports of its proceedings which are fair and accurate but should nonetheless be postponed. It would accordingly be an abuse of this particular power to pronounce an order . . . for the purpose of warding off prejudicial comment which those proceedings might prompt.

Although the Court of Appeal in *Barot* gave thought to the argument that 'an as yet unchosen jury, all of whom (it was suggested) were potential victims of the charge which the co-defendants faced . . . would have great difficulty putting out of their minds the material which would derive from the publicity', it laid emphasis on two factors. First, the sentencing of Barot would 'be of true and genuine public interest, not gawping regard of a prurient nature'. Secondly 'the collective experience . . . has demonstrated to us time and time again, that juries up and down the country have a passionate and profound belief in, and a commitment to, the right of a defendant to be given a fair trial.'

In *Times Newspapers Ltd and ors v R* [175] a section 4(2) order had been made after, by accident, a question and answer slipped out in public, which should have been heard in private. The trial judge had taken the view that a section 4(2) order could be used to 'postpone' permanently reporting of something which had happened in open court. The Court of Appeal disagreed: 'The section permits postponement and the need for postponement cannot subsist beyond the end of the proceedings . . .' The order was also lifted as unnecessary to avoid prejudice to the administration of justice in the case the judge had been trying, since that trial had already finished. The Court of Appeal agreed that: 'Such orders may, however, be necessary for the general administration of justice. If the consequence of bringing prosecutions for breach of the [Official Secrets Act 1989] is that the secrets to which they relate become public, it will not, in practice, be possible to bring such prosecutions.' The court suggested a slightly amended version of the order should be re-cast as an order under section 11 of the 1981 Act [176] and warned that publication of information which the judge had ordered was to be heard in private might be common law contempt. [177]

In *BBC Petitioners* [178] two men had been separately indicted in Scotland for the murder of a shopkeeper, Mr Basra. The Crown was proceeding with the trial of only one, Graeme Donaldson, but reserving its position on the prosecution of the other, William Ward. Donaldson's defence was to incriminate Ward. A section 4(2) order was initially granted to postpone any reporting of Donaldson's trial. This was subsequently

---

[175]   [2007] EWCA Crim 1925.
[176]   See section 4.20 above.
[177]   See section 4.15 above.
[178]   2001 SCCR 440.

amended to postpone the reporting of 'any matter showing or tending to show the participation of William Ward' in the fatal incident. BBC Scotland broadcast a report of the trial which did not mention Ward by name, but to which Counsel for the accused and the Advocate Depute both took exception. After a hearing on contempt, at which the court held that the broadcasting of the news item did not constitute a contempt, the BBC successfully petitioned for the lifting of the order altogether. The Appeal Court observed that a section 4(2) order was an exception to the general rule favouring publication. The public interest in court proceedings:[179]

... is distinct from the interest of the parties in having the proceedings conducted under the eyes of the public. A court must be careful to bear that wider public interest in mind, especially in those cases where—for whatever reason—the parties themselves would wish the court to make an order postponing publication or where, as here, one of the parties adopts a neutral stance. Even in these situations, the court must consider not only whether such an order is 'necessary' but also what the appropriate scope of any order might be . . . Even where publication of a report of proceedings would give rise to a substantial risk of prejudice to proceedings which are pending or imminent, there may be other means of eliminating or reducing the risk.

Ultimately, although accepting that this was likely to be a widely-reported trial where criticism would be made of Ward in his absence, the Appeal Court made it clear that they did not think any order should have been made; any evidence incriminating Ward would be replicated or supplemented at any trial of Ward:

The jury would therefore be likely to base their decision on the version of the evidence led at that trial, which would be fresh in their minds, rather than on their recollection of a report of what had been said in the accused's trial. In these circumstances we are satisfied that this is a case where directions by the judge at any trial of Ward could deal perfectly adequately with any risk of prejudice to Ward . . .

Proceedings against William Ward were much less probable than were the proceedings against the senior officers in the *Sherwood* case, but neither the uncertainty nor the timing appear to have been factors in the judges' decision that no order in the *Donaldson* trial was appropriate. A similar view was taken by Lord Reed in *HMA v Wilson and ors*:[180]

It was not immediately apparent to me that publication of a report of the hearing [about allegations of child sexual abuse] would give rise to a substantial risk of prejudice to the administration of justice. In particular, I was not so persuaded on the basis of the article to which my attention was drawn.[181] That article was a feature article . . . concerned with the treatment by the legal system of the victims of child sexual abuse . . . The article seemed to me to be legitimate reporting of a matter of public interest. It did not contain any details which would enable jurors readily to identify the present case as being one of those discussed . . . Even if there were such

---

[179] In the middle of the hearing, Donaldson was found guilty, at which point the matter became academic.

[180] 15 June 2001, High Court of Justiciary.

[181] A *Scotsman* article referring, on an anonymized basis, to the facts of the present case and describing its history as 'a story of delay and evasion'.

a risk, it seemed to me that it would be likely to be possible to eliminate the risk by the usual directions . . . and if necessary by giving the jury special directions . . .

In *Beggs No 1*[182] Lord Osborne was asked by Counsel for William Beggs, who was later convicted of murdering Barry Wallace, to place a section 4(2) order over the whole murder trial on the basis 'that even responsible, contemporaneous, fair and accurate reporting of the trial proceedings would be likely to start . . . a "feeding frenzy" on the part of the less responsible elements of the media'. Lord Osborne declined: 'Senior Counsel for the accused himself said that he had "no problem" with fair and accurate reporting; his concern lay elsewhere. That acceptance that fair and accurate reporting did not create a problem is plainly fatal to the motion.' The judge said that if a feeding frenzy were to emerge, that could be dealt with as a contempt of court. Following the *Galbraith* case, it would be an abuse of the section 4(2) power to impose such a reporting restriction merely for the purpose of warding off apprehended hostile publicity.

The Scottish courts have also declined section 4(2) orders in civil proceedings in recent years. Lady Smith refused one in preliminary proceedings concerning the defamation trial brought by the then MSP Tommy Sheridan against the *News of the World*. The proceedings involved the attempt to recover an SSP document, which its holder was refusing to produce. It was argued for Tommy Sheridan that, given that the defamation trial was to be heard by a jury, it would be inappropriate to have a court report touching on the merits of the case. Lady Smith said that, even taking into account that there was a jury trial in a little under six weeks, counsel had expressed no more specific concern than that the merits of the action might be discussed in the press. Bearing in mind the public interest in open justice and the fact that the jury were bound to be directed to decide only on the facts, she was not satisfied that normal reporting would give rise to a substantial risk of prejudice and refused the motion.[183] The Inner House of the Court of Session later refused to grant a section 4(2) order in a judicial review brought by William Beggs against the Scottish Ministers, reporting of which might, he argued, affect the mind of jurors taking part in any retrial of him. The Inner House not only rejected the idea that any such retrial could be said to be 'pending or imminent' but also that such reporting would be prejudicial at all.[184]

Although tribunals of various kinds can be classed as courts for contempt purposes,[185] it is generally thought that they have no power to grant section 4(2) orders,[186] although some, including employment tribunals, have statutory powers of their own to regulate reporting.

---

[182] 2002 SLT 135, 2002 SCCR 869.
[183] Outer House, Court of Session, 25 May 2006.
[184] Extra Division, Inner House, Court of Session, 10 March 2006, [2006] CSIH 17.
[185] See section 4.4 above.
[186] See Arlidge, Eady, and Smith (n 122 above) para 7–109, n 19.

4.22 SECTION 11 OF THE CONTEMPT OF COURT ACT 1981

Section 11 reads: 'In any case where a court (having power to do so) allows a name or other matter to be withheld from the public in proceedings before the court, the court may give such directions prohibiting the publication of that name or matter in connection with the proceedings as appear to the court to be necessary for the purpose for which it was so withheld.'

Section 11 can be difficult to construe, because it implicitly preserves common law powers without specifying what those powers are or were.[187] It is perhaps easier to give examples of use of the power than to delineate its parameters. Orders have been made preventing the identification of a man believed to be suffering from tuberculosis;[188] of another man who had undergone a penectomy when he was expecting a skin-graft;[189] of a claimant for criminal injuries compensation who alleged psychological damage as a result of sexual abuse by her stepfather;[190] and a Brazilian national with advanced HIV who was not lawfully present in the UK, on the basis of medical evidence that he would be psychologically endangered were anonymity not granted.[191]

There has never been a properly-argued reported decision about the role, if any, of section 11 in the Scottish jurisdiction, but see *HMA v Giovanni Mola*,[192] where such an order was granted to anonymize a woman whose former partner was ultimately convicted of culpable and reckless conduct for knowingly infecting his former partner with HIV and Hepatitis C. In *Re C (Adult Patient: Publicity)*[193] a section 11 order granted in relation to a hearing over whether life-sustaining treatment for a brain-damaged

---

[187] In the teeth of the recommendation of the Phillimore Report which pre-dated the 1981 Act.

[188] *Birmingham Post & Mail Ltd v Birmingham City Council* [1994] 158 JP307, 158 LG Rev 523, *The Times*, 25 November 1993, *The Independent*, 25 November 1993, DC.

[189] That judgment does not specifically mention s 11. *H v Ministry of Defence* [1991] 2 QB 103, [1991] 2 WLR 1192, [1991] 2 All ER 834, 141 NLJ 420, *The Independent*, 22 March 1991, *The Guardian*, 27 March 1991, *The Daily Telegraph*, 1 April 1991, *The Times*, 1 April 1991, CA.

[190] *R v Criminal Injuries Compensation Board, ex p A* [1992] COD 379. *R v Central Criminal Court, ex p Crook and anor*,[191] where the NUJ sought to review an order made under s 11 prohibiting the naming of a witness who had been abducted for the purposes of unlawful sexual intercourse. This was rejected, apparently on a rather technical basis. Anonymity for alleged witnesses of sexual offences in England and Wales would now fall within the Sexual Offences (Amendment) Act 1992 (see *Marie O'Riordan v Director of Public Prosecutions*[191] and *Gazette Media Co Ltd v Teesside Crown Court*).[191] There has been unanimous self-constraint by the Scottish media whereby victims of sexual offences are routinely anonymized.

[191] *The Matter of D*, 17 November 1997 (1997–98) 1 CCL Rep 1909, (1999) 45 BMLR 191.

[192] [2007] HCJ02, 7 February 2007, High Court of Justiciary, Glasgow, Lord Hodge. Since then, orders have also been granted, unopposed, to anonymize the rape victims in a case attracting interest outwith Scotland—*HMA v Harcar*, 18 March 2009, High Court of Justiciary, Glasgow, Lord Bracadale—and to anonymize the complainer in a case involving an element of sexual torture—*HMA v Ellis, Gallacher and McKay*, 12 December 2008, High Court of Justiciary, Glasgow, Lord Brailsford. The Scottish media are not statutorily banned from naming victims or alleged victims of sexual offences, but have never done so without consent.

[193] (1996) 2 FLR 251.

man was continued after the patient's death. Sir Stephen Brown, the President of the Family Division, held that it could because there were possible detrimental future consequences for medical staff, family members, and decision-makers. Again, however, this case was not fully argued.

A strong medical flavour helps, therefore, but is not necessarily enough: two HIV sufferers bringing a judicial review in a housing case were denied anonymity.[194] Section 11 orders have also been denied to a former MP charged with a minor MOT-related offence, who had wanted to avoid renewed harassment from his ex-wife;[195] to anonymize a person charged with public health offences on the basis that it might lead to the closure of his restaurant business;[196] to prevent the publication of the name and address of a defendant charged with indecent assault who was fearful of attack;[197] by a firm of solicitors who did not wish to be tarnished by publicity.[198] There, the Court of Appeal, quite predictably, said that solicitors were in the same position as anyone else, although in a later case, Ferris J granted anonymity to a barrister in an interlocutory application concerning professional negligence claims. The application was unopposed, and the judge commented that he would probably have been unwilling to grant anonymity in the trial.[199]

Anonymity was refused in two separate cases in 2008 where convicted men, one a high-profile barrister, sought it, it was said, to protect their children. In *R v Croydon County Court, ex p Trinity Mirror plc*[200] the Court of Appeal lifted an order purporting to restrain the media from identifying a man convicted of child pornography offences on the basis that his children, who were neither witnesses nor victims, would be likely to suffer significant harm through his identification. The trial judge claimed that, as the names of the children had not been mentioned, section 11 provided jurisdiction to prohibit publication of any facts leading to their identification, such as their father's name. The Court of Appeal rejected this:

The judge accepted that the court had not allowed the defendant's name to be 'withheld', or indeed 'exempted' it from disclosure. Nevertheless he seems to have approached the problem as if permission had been given for the names, address and school of the children to be withheld. However, the stark reality was that these facts were quite irrelevant to the proceedings . . . Unless the court deliberately exercises its power to allow a name or other matter to be withheld, Section 11 of the 1981 Act is not engaged . . .

---

[194] *R v Westminster City Council, ex p Castelli and Tristram-Garcia* [1996] 1 FLR 534.
[195] *R v Evesham Justices, ex p McDonagh* [1988] 1 QB 553—address-only case, he did not object to being named.
[196] *R v Dover Justices, ex p Dover District Council and Wells* (1991) 156 JP 433, *The Independent*, 21 October 1991, *The Times*, 21 October 1991.
[197] *Re Belfast Telegraph Newspaper Ltd's Application* [1997] NI 309.
[198] *R v Legal Aid Board, ex p Kaim Todner* (1998) 3 All ER 541, (1998) 3 WLR 925. One was also recently refused when sought by a man accused of assaulting his alleged love rival at a recording of the *Tricia* show; *Press Gazette*, 22 June 2009.
[199] *Green v Hancocks*, 11 July 2000, High Court of Justiciary, Chancery Division.
[200] 1 February 2008 [2008] EWCA Crim 50.

This decision was followed in *Crawford v Crown Prosecution Service*,[201] where a high-profile barrister and judge was convicted of harassing his ex-wife and her partner, though in that case the orders successfully appealed against were under section 39 of the Children and Young Persons Act 1933.

Section 11 orders cannot be granted where the information has already been revealed in open court.[202] The existence of earlier publicity may impact on the decision as to whether or not to grant a section 11 order.[203] So will the relative degree of legitimate public interest in the information suppressed.[204]

Section 11 orders cannot prohibit publication which *might* reveal information heard in camera.[205] Whilst such orders, unlike section 4(2) orders, are potentially permanent, in *R v Barry Michael George*[206] the Court of Appeal observed that an order under section 11 should only remain in force for the time necessary to fulfil its purpose.[207]

It has been suggested that applications for an order under section 11 should be heard in camera.[208] It has also been suggested that all section 11 orders, and indeed rulings under any statutory power which involve a departure from open justice, should be noted.[209]

The court has to have the power to withhold, and must have exercised that power, in order for a section 11 order to be granted. However, it does not follow that the withholding must have been effectual or the order obeyed[210]—though doubtless questions of public domain would affect the appropriateness of continuing a prohibition which had been ineffectual.

Bearing in mind the words of the House of Lords in *Re S*[211] as to the undesirability of further restrictions on open justice given the plethora which already exist under

---

[201] [2008] EWHC 854 (Admin), Thomas LJ, Dobbs LJ, *The Times*, 20 February 2008.

[202] *R v Arundel Justices, ex p Westminster Press Ltd* (1985) 2 All ER 390, 1 WLR 708; *The Times*, 15 February 1985—*R v Reigate Justices, ex p Argus Newspapers Ltd* [1983] Crim LR 564, doubted in this respect. See also *Belfast Telegraph Newspapers Ltd's application, re sub nom R v Newtonabbey Magistrates' Court, ex p Belfast Telegraph Newspapers Ltd* [1997] NI 309, *The Times*, 27 August 1997. In Scotland, a s 11 order was lifted on this basis in *HMA v Brian Johnstone*, 25 November 2008, Sheriff Norman Ritchie QC, Glasgow Sheriff Court (unreported).

[203] *R v Westminster City Council, ex p Castelli and Tristram-Garcia* [1996] 1 FLR 534; *The Matter of D*, 17 November 1997, Dyson J, 45 BMLR 191.

[204] *CICB, ex p A* [1992] COD 379; *H v Ministry of Defence* [1991] 2 QB 103, [1991] 2 WLR 1192, [1991] 2 All ER 834, 141 NLJ 420, *The Independent*, 22 March 1991, *The Guardian*, 27 March 1991, *The Daily Telegraph*, 1 April 1991, *The Times*, 1 April 1991, CA.

[205] *R v Times Newspapers Ltd and ors* (2008) 1 All ER 343, (2008) 1 Cr App R16, (2008) 1 WLR 237, *The Times*, 31 July 2007.

[206] [2002] EWCA Crim 1923, *The Times*, 30 August 2002.

[207] See also *Birmingham Post & Mail Ltd v Birmingham City Council* [1994] 158 JP 307, 158 LG Rev 523, *The Times*, 25 November 1993, DC, where it was held that the s 11 order should have been time-limited.

[208] See *R v Tower Bridge Magistrates Court, ex p Osborne* [1987] 88 Cr App R 28 and *R v Westminster City Council, ex p Castelli and Tristram-Garcia* [1996] 1 FLR 534.

[209] *Belfast Telegraph Newspaper Ltd's application, re sub nom R v Newtonabbey Magistrates' Court, ex p Belfast Telegraph Newspapers Ltd* [1997] NI 309, *The Times*, 27 August 1997.

[210] *Times Newspapers Ltd v R* [2007] EWCA Crim 1925.

[211] [2004] 4 All ER 683, (2005) 1 AC 593, (2004) 3 WLR 1129, (2005) EMLR 551.

statute, an applicant seeking an order under section 11 ought normally to be able to point to a pre-1981 instance of a court having made such a restriction order in a parallel situation. The impact of the Human Rights Act 1998 on section 11, however, remains to be played out; whilst obviously Articles 6, 8, and 10 are likely to feature prominently, it would not be surprising if Articles 2 and 3 were raised, as happened recently in the *Times Newspapers* case.[212]

In *Birmingham Post & Mail Ltd v Birmingham City Council*[213] Mann LJ said: 'The court wishes to emphasise how important it is that those who exercise their powers under S11 of the 1981 Act should give immediate and written reasons for doing so . . . Open justice demands of them no less.' The reasons, to a critical ear, can sound a little limp and general, for example in the *Birmingham Post* case itself: 'The administration of justice requires that courts should act in a manner which is fair.' Once all opportunity to challenge the compulsory hospitalization for tuberculosis which was contemplated in the *Birmingham Post* case had passed: 'No interest of justice is any longer involved. Any wish to protect privacy or avoid embarrassment is not a ground for the further continuance of an order.'

Despite the amorphousness of the use of section 11, the courts, when dealing with claims for anonymity of various types, have uniformly emphasized that granting them should be a rarity. In *R v Evesham Justices, ex p McDonagh*[214] Watkins LJ said: 'I go so far to say that in the vast majority of cases . . . defendants would like their identity to be unrevealed and would be capable of advancing seemingly plausible reasons why that should be so. But Section 11 was not enacted for the benefit of the comfort and feelings of defendants.' Approving references to the administration of justice, in a rather mantra-like fashion, and disapproving references to individual embarrassment, tend to be a feature of section 11 cases.

In *R v Westminster City Council, ex p Castelli & Tristram-Garcia*[215] Latham J dismissed the claims as 'no more than a plea for privacy', saying the test was 'that the failure to grant anonymity would render the attainment of justice really doubtful or, in effect, impracticable. The power cannot be used simply to protect privacy or avoid embarrassment.'

In *Re D*[216] Mr Justice Dyson J said:

In my judgment the test is the same in all these cases, namely whether the proposed derogation from open justice is necessary in order to prevent a real risk that the administration of justice will be rendered impracticable. In my judgment it is right that the test for according anonymity should be strict, and that the power to grant anonymity should be exercised sparingly.

---

[212] *Times Newspapers Ltd and Guardian News & Media v R* [2008] EWCA Crim 2396. s 11 was used to anonymize soldiers accused of conspiracy to defraud, the Court of Appeal extended the anonymity because of the real and immediate risk of the threat to the lives of some of the soldiers were they identified.

[213] [1994] 158 JP 307, 158 LG Rev 523, *The Times*, 25 November 1993, *The Independent*, 25 November 1993, DC.

[214] [1988] 1 QB 553.

[215] [1996] 1 FLR 534.

[216] 17 November 1997.

It was not suggested that D—of whose identity there had already been 'limited disclosure' (not in court)—would abandon the proceedings if he lost anonymity, nor was there evidence about the impact on other similarly situated applications. It was simply a question of whether he would suffer physical or mental harm. Dyson J rejected the evidence of the possibility of a physical attack, but accepted that D might suffer significant psychological harm:

I emphasise that this is not to spare him the embarrassment, discomfort or even the distress that would almost certainly be occasioned by the glare of publicity. It is because, on the medical evidence, public knowledge of his situation would, to quote Dr Reid, 'be extremely destructive to him . . . and would endanger him psychologically'.

In *R v Legal Aid Board, ex p Kaim Todner*[217] a firm of solicitors, whose franchise from the Legal Aid Board had been terminated on the basis of denied allegations involving dishonesty, was denied anonymity. The Court of Appeal summarized the importance of vigilance when the principle of open justice was under attack, because of:

. . . the natural tendency for the general principle to be eroded and for exceptions to grow by accretion as the exceptions are applied by analogy to existing cases . . . Any interference with the public nature of court proceedings is therefore to be avoided unless justice requires it . . . It is not unreasonable to regard the person who initiates proceedings as having accepted the normal incidence of the public nature of court proceedings . . . Although the foundation of the exceptions is the need to avoid frustrating the ability of the courts to do justice, a party cannot be allowed to achieve anonymity by insisting upon it as a condition for being involved in the proceedings irrespective of whether the demand is reasonable. There must be some objective foundation for the claim which is being made.

The Court of Appeal in that case suggested that a plaintiff was in the weakest position to seek anonymity and a witness in the strongest position:

In general, however, parties and witnesses have to accept the embarrassment and damage to their reputation and the possible consequential loss which can be inherent in being involved in litigation. The protection to which they are entitled is normally provided by a judgment delivered in public which will refute unfounded allegations. Any other approach would result in wholly unacceptable inroads on the general rule.

The Court of Appeal also suggested that the nature of the proceedings was relevant, with interlocutory hearings, financial and other family disputes being less likely to be of public interest.

4.23 INJUNCTIONS AGAINST APPREHENDED CONTEMPTS

In 1987, the Attorney-General obtained an injunction restraining the re-enactment on television of the Birmingham Six appeal currently before the Court of Appeal, on the

---

[217] (1998) 3 All ER 541, (1998) 3 WLR 925.

basis that the programme was likely to undermine public confidence in the administration of justice. The portrayal of witnesses by actors troubled the Court of Appeal, which said such a re-enactment was not truly analogous to a press report, even though the exact words would be used. The injunction was lifted, with the consent of the Attorney-General, just over a month later and its reasoning later criticized by a three-judge Bench of the High Court of Justiciary,[218] though the broadcaster's application to Strasbourg failed.[219] Similarly, in *Attorney-General v Steadman*,[220] Bell J granted an injunction restraining the respondent from staging a musical about Robert Maxwell whilst his sons were awaiting trial. Whilst there remains a perceptible judicial distaste for the reconstructed or the staged, it is less likely, perhaps, that such injunctions would be granted today.

Certainly, in *Chief Constable of Greater Manchester Police v Channel Five Broadcast Ltd*[221] the Court of Appeal lifted an injunction restraining Channel Five from broadcasting the programme *Gangsters* following the fatal shooting of one of the gangsters featured. Auld LJ, lifting the injunction, said: 'The burden on the Chief Constable even at this early stage is a heavy one . . . it is one of a high standard of persuasion that there will be a substantial risk that the course of justice in the proceedings in question will be seriously impeded or prejudiced.'

In the earlier case of *Ex parte HTV Cymru (Wales) Ltd*,[222] where the Crown and defendant got an injunction prohibiting the media from contacting or interviewing witnesses, for a documentary to be transmitted after the verdict, Aitkens J, although exercising what he termed 'this draconian power', concluded: 'I have kept in mind . . . that injunctions restraining threatened contempts are rarely appropriate . . . In my judgement . . . this is one of those rare cases . . . '

The Attorney-General obtained an injunction against the BBC in 2007 over the 'cash for honours' investigation, arguing that there was a substantial risk that the police investigation would be impeded or prejudiced. Ultimately, this injunction was lifted, largely because of what had come into the public domain: *Attorney-General v BBC*.[223] The Scottish equivalent of injunction is interdict. It appears to be more easily granted against apprehended contempts.

In *Muir v BBC*,[224] the High Court of Justiciary granted an interim interdict against a *Frontline Scotland* documentary, taking the view that it had power to do so even if the broadcast would not amount to a statutory contempt. An application to Strasbourg was declared inadmissible.[225] The court also—unlike the English court in *Leary v BBC*[226]— refused to take account of a possible section 5 defence at this stage.

---

[218] *Al Megrahi and Fhima v Times Newspapers Ltd* 1999 SCCR 824.
[219] *C Ltd v UK*, 13 April 1989, App No 14132188.
[220] 7 February 1994 (unreported).
[221] [2005] EWCA Civ 739.
[222] [2002] EMLR 11.
[223] [2007] EWCA Civ 280.
[224] 1997 SLT 425, SCCR 584.
[225] 23/10/97, App No 34324196, HUDOC Ref 00003829.
[226] 29 September 1989 (Lexis).

A petition by a convicted drug-smuggler with a pending appeal, which attempted to stop another *Frontline Scotland* documentary from broadcasting at its scheduled time, was refused by the High Court the next year in *Forbes Duncan Cowan, Petitioner*.[227] However, interdicts of this sort still occur from time to time. On 4 February 2005, in *Paterson, Petitioner*, Lord Bracadale granted an interim interdict in relation to *Tonight With Trevor McDonald* on what was, perforce and by the judge's own description, a relatively superficial consideration of the law. The proposal was to broadcast a sequence which might well have formed part of the evidence at Paterson's trial, albeit with pixellation and without identification of the locus of the incident.

4.24 JURY RESEARCH

Under section 8 of the Contempt of Court Act 1981: 'It is a contempt of court to obtain, disclose or solicit any particulars of statements made, opinions expressed, arguments advanced or votes cast by members of a jury in the course of their deliberations of any legal proceedings.'

Section 8 poses two problems for the media. First, the thoughts and reactions of jurors in high-profile (and sometimes other) cases are often of great interest. Furthermore, the section is a barrier to empirical, contextualized research into whether in fact jurors are prejudiced by what they read in or hear through the media. As regards the first issue, where, as happens, an unhappy juror contacts a journalist to tell him or her about such matters, it is a contempt of court, potentially, even to listen.

That said, the embargo is only on 'particulars of statements made, opinions expressed, arguments advanced or votes cast . . . in the course of . . . deliberations'. 'Deliberations' was defined in *Re Scottish Criminal Cases Review Commission*[228] as applying to what occurred in the jury-room after the retiral of the jury to consider the verdict. Thus, for example, it would not be contempt to broadcast an interview with a juror about emotional reactions to sitting through the evidence of a brutal murder, or the impression made by adversarial court proceedings.

Even before section 8, there was what Criminal Law Committee described in its 10th Report in 1968 as 'a rule of conduct that what passes in the jury-room during discussion by the jury of what their verdict should be ought to be treated as private and confidential'. (See Lord Justice Bankes in *Ellis v Deheer*,[229] and the Morris Report (1965)[230] at paragraph 355.) Yet another consideration in the 1968 Report was the idea that it was 'contrary to the public interest that the issue before the jury should

---

[227] 17 March 1998.
[228] 2001 SCCR 775.
[229] [1922] 2 KB 113, 118.
[230] CMMD 2627.

be "retried" in public with the use of information supplied by one or more of the jurors'.

The policy of section 8, therefore, appears to rest on twin pillars of protecting jurors and preventing a rehashing of matters after the verdict. According to *Hansard*, the enacted clause was deliberately extended to prohibit the publication of anonymous reminiscences plus all publication of the results of research. In the case of *Attorney-General v Associated Newspapers Ltd*,[231] which arose out of the 'Blue Arrow Trial', a year-long trial concerning serious frauds, the House of Lords made short work of the suggestion that section 8 applied only to the jurors and not to the media.

In *R v Mizra*[232] it was held that section 8 did *not* apply to the trial court and the Court of Appeal when they were investigating the conduct of a trial; however, evidence of the jurors' deliberations was inadmissible, in order to protect the confidentiality of the jurors' deliberations and the finality of their verdict. Only evidence directed to matters intrinsic to the jurors' deliberations was inadmissible. In the later House of Lords case, *Attorney-General v Scotcher*,[233] where a juror had written to a convicted defendant's mother, expressing concerns about his fellow jurors' reasoning and commitment, the House had to accept, though, that the line between 'intrinsic' and 'extrinsic' is not clear-cut. In *Attorney-General v Michael Seckerson and Times Newspapers Ltd* [2009] EWHC 1023 (Admin), Pill LJ and Sweeney J, in the Divisional Court on 13 May 2009, held *The Times* and a jury foreman in breach of section 8. The disclosure was that the jury consensus was 10–2 three minutes after the foreman was voted in, on account of overwhelming medical evidence and 'that despicable enemy of correct and logical thinking . . . commonsense'.

It is perhaps worth noting that such research as exists from other jurisdictions with juries does not tend to support media influence as a major factor.[234]

4.25 SOUND RECORDING

Section 9 of the Contempt of Court Act 1981 makes it a contempt of court: '(a) to use in court, or bring into court for use, any tape recorder or other instrument for recording sound, except with leave of the court; (b) to publish a recording of legal proceedings made . . . '

Offending recording instruments or recordings can be forfeited (section 9(3)). The section does not apply to recordings for the making of official transcripts (section 9(4)). A sentence of four months' imprisonment for breach of this section was recently

---

[231] [1994] 2 AC 238, [1994] 1 All ER 556.
[232] (2004) 1 All ER 925.
[233] [2005] UKHL 36.
[234] See eg New Zealand Law Commission preliminary paper no 37, November 1999; or 'Managing Prejudicial Publicity: An Empirical Study of Criminal Jury Trials in New South Wales' (2001), available at <http://www.lawfoundation.net.au>.

quashed (*R v Patrick Cullinane*)[235] but the Court of Appeal took the view that some sanction was undoubtedly appropriate (paragraph 6):

The Recorder believed that the appellant may have intended to publish the recordings in due course 'on a website'. Such publication—that is, of the recordings themselves as opposed to any transcript—would be a further contempt (see section 9(1)(b) . . .) . . . It would not however by itself be likely to prejudice the administration of justice . . . It would also be a different matter if the recordings contained, or were made in the hope that they would contain, not something that was said in open court but the private conversations of those involved in the court process.

The Court of Appeal also mentioned in *Cullinane* that there was no exact analogy between the taking of photographs in court and recordings of the Cullinane sort. *Mens rea* is probably not requisite to a finding of contempt under section 9, but innocent technical contempts are unlikely to lead to severe censure.[236]

4.26 CONTEMPT AND THE CRIMINAL STANDARD OF PROOF

In order to make a finding of contempt, the court must be satisfied beyond reasonable doubt (see, for example *X v Dempster*;[237] *Official Solicitor v News Group Newspapers*;[238] *Scottish Daily Record and Sunday Mail Ltd v Procurator-Fiscal, Edinburgh*).[239] It was accepted in *Attorney-General v BBC*[240] that, to grant an injunction, the court should be satisfied to the same standard.[241]

4.27 INTERNET ARCHIVES AND CONTEMPT

The impact of the internet on contempt law remains to be developed, but clearly the existence of a vast amount of readily traceable, internationally available, ultimately ineradicable material about (among others) people accused of crime will affect the practicability of keeping information from jurors and witnesses. Lord Justice Leggatt's statement in *Attorney-General v ITN*[242] that a broadcast revealing previous convictions was not a contempt—because 'however horrible the incident that was described, this medium is in its nature ephemeral' is now less true; broadcasters' news websites, often based on broadcasts or incorporating them, are widely used.

---

[235] 4 October 2007, CA, [2007] EWCA Crim 2682.
[236] See *In the matter of Patricia Hooker* [1993] COD 190, where both the fine and the forfeiture order re the offending tape recorder were quashed. The Divisional Court was plainly unimpressed by the magistrate's behaviour here.
[237] [1999] 1 FLR 894, [1999] 3 FCR 759, [1999] Fam Law 300.
[238] [1994] 2 FLR 174, [1994] 2 FCR 552.
[239] [2009] HCJAC 24, 12 March 2009.
[240] 12 March 2007, [2007] EWCA Civ 280.
[241] Although see Sir Anthony Clarke MR's comments at para 24 on orders made under rules of court.
[242] [1995] 2 All ER 370, [1995] 1 Cr App R 204, [1994] COD 370.

In the Scottish case of *HMA v Beggs*[243] Lord Osborne opined that information on an internet archive was, in effect, continuously republished:

It appears to me unrealistic to make a distinction between the moment when the material is first published on the Website and the succeeding period of time when it is available for access on demand by members of the public . . . [The] better view is that the situation affecting the Website may be compared with the situation in which a book or other printed material is continuously on sale and available to the public. During that whole period, I consider that it would be proper to conclude that that material was being published.

However he concluded that the material objected to did not create a substantial risk of serious prejudice to the proceedings, despite the fact that it referred, *inter alia*, to previous convictions of the panel, called him the 'gay ripper', and compared him to Fred West. Lord Osborne said:

I recognise immediately that the use of computers by members of the public to access Websites is relatively commonplace . . . However, in this connection, it is necessary, in my view, to take account of the manner in which the material concerned is now available . . . The material concerned was originally published in December 1999 and . . . is accessible only in the form of archive material forming part of the information available at the Websites of the publications concerned . . .

Thus, availability of information is not to be equated with general knowledge. Similarly, finding the Express Newspapers[244] in contempt in 2004, the Court of Appeal rejected the argument that a young woman complaining of rape by a number of footballers, but unable to identify the attackers by name, must have known their identity from the Web. The Court of Appeal rejected that: 'What has been demonstrated . . . is a probability that newspaper editors were aware of the identity of the footballers, that gossip and rumour were available on the Internet, and the complainant could, if she was so inclined, have carried out research to work out identities by a process of elimination.' The Court of Appeal declined 'to elevate the material placed before us to the status of a working possibility of actual foreknowledge' of the identity of the alleged assailants. However, online material is not beneath that court's notice: in declining to uphold an injunction against the programme *Gangsters* following a killing, it made reference to the degree of publicity concerning the victim, including 'an online entry which puts in words the sort of behaviour and bragging . . . that is a feature of the television programme about the Noonan family.'

As the High Court of Justiciary said in *Angus Sinclair v HMA*:[245]

The availability of the Internet and its increasingly wide use by members of the public, including potential and serving jurors, presents a challenge for the administration of justice. While news reported and opinions expressed in the press or broadcasting media on a daily basis are themselves ephemeral, the Internet provides ready access to historical material, including media

---

[243] Lord Osborne, Opinion (No 2) 21 September 2001, 2002 SLT 139, 2001 SCCR 879.
[244] *A-G v Express Newspapers* [2004] EWHC 2859, [2005] EMLR 13, QBD (Admin).
[245] 25 April 2007, [2007] HCJ AC 27, para 14.

items. At one time a person seeking reported information about a past event or about a particular individual would require to spend significant time, and possibly expense, in retrieving it from a public library or similar institution; now such information can be accessed by the pressing at home of a few controls on a computer. Moreover, persons with interests in particular fields, including criminal investigations and criminal histories, may choose to set up websites which provide links to historical and other materials.

In this case, Angus Sinclair, who was serving the second of two life sentences for crimes including rape and murder, was about to stand trial for the World's End murders, which arose out of the deaths of two young women in the 1970s.[246] Sinclair's previous crimes and possible connection to the World's End killings had been the subject of extensive media speculation for a number of years; a book which claimed he was so responsible was withdrawn from sale before his trial. However, his particular concern was the number of references to him, his previous convictions, and possible future convictions, available on the internet. One site, entitled 'Murder, United Kingdom', blamed him for the World's End murders. There had been over a million hits on that site. The website owner was apparently cooperating in removing that element, but Sinclair argued that access to prejudicial information on the internet could not realistically be controlled either before or during the trial.

Referring to the statutory provision in Queensland that a person sworn as a juror must not inquire, including through the internet, about the defendant until the trial was over, the Appeal Court acknowledged that 'the chances of selected jurors actively seeking in the course of the trial material on the Internet about the circumstances of the murders and about the appellant may require to be managed by the court. That, if appropriate, can be done . . . by a suitably framed instruction by the trial judge.'

The jury system, the Appeal Court said in *Sinclair*, depended on there being trust between judge and jury,

. . . including an understanding that jurors will not deliberately disobey the instructions on law or procedure . . . It is customary . . . for judges at the outset of the trial . . . to tell the jurors that if any of them knows the accused or the victim on any charge or if there is any other good reason why he or she should not serve on the jury, that juror should so advise . . . In appropriate cases . . . a reference to knowledge acquired by use of the internet might usefully be added to that instruction. This is no more than a development of existing practice in the context of technological advances.

The Appeal Court fought shy of being more specific, saying that it was for the trial judge to determine what needed to be done. They did, however, suggest that the parties get together with the judge to discuss the terms of any instruction.[247] In *HMA v Bermingham*,[248] Lord Hamilton commented, in response to the accused's advocate's

---

[246] Ultimately, the case against him for these murders was dismissed by the trial judge on the basis of an insufficiency of evidence.

[247] This was done in chambers and, since the trial never happened, we cannot be sure what form, if any, the instruction might have taken.

[248] 13 June 2002 (unreported). It has to be said that use of the internet has much increased even since 2002.

arguing that website material revealed prejudicial information about his client in the course of a trial, that it was speculative whether a juror was computer literate, had access to the internet site, and how often a juror would use a search engine which could throw up information about an accused person.[249]

While Peter Tobin was being tried in Scotland for the murder of Vicky Hamilton, the jury were reported to have been instructed to disregard any 'past, present or future' publication. Wikipedia acceded to a request to remove an item concerning Peter Tobin. Other media outlets made differing accommodations to requests.

In *Stuart Bray v Deutsche Bank*[250] Tugendhat J said—in the admittedly very different context of qualified privilege as a defamation defence—that:

> If qualified privilege . . . can be lost by passage of time, then that would have far reaching consequences . . . [B]ack copies of newspapers held in libraries and websites would have to be regularly reviewed and edited. But there would be no way for the holder of the information to know when or in what form the editing was required . . . It is hard to see how the keeper of a library or database can guard against the risk of liability for defamation where there is a publication of a statement written at a time when it was protected by common law privilege . . . but where the same reciprocal duty and interest may not subsist at some subsequent date upon which the document is read . . .

Although the law of defamation radically differs from the law of contempt, the practical difficulties for archives are the same. The historical consequences of stripping out archives might be seen as using a sledgehammer to crack a pine-nut.

In a recent New Zealand decision from Judge David Harvey,[251] it was held that names and images of two men charged with murder could be reported in print or on the television news, but not on the news websites. Judge Harvey said:

> The intent of the limited order was to ensure that at a later stage, any concerns about a fair trial would not be prejudiced as a result of the availability of information stored on the internet . . . Contemporaneous or what might be called 'traditional' publication is not prohibited. However, digital technologies introduce the concept of the 'information that does not die' . . . A quality of [traditional] media is that of immediacy . . . If for any reason the attention of the audience member is distracted, the level of comprehension of the information may be less. In the case of a newspaper story, the ability to read and comprehend the information depends upon the length of time that the newspaper is available to the reader . . . But in the main the adage that today's newspaper is tomorrow's fish and chip wrapping applies . . . Given the present technology . . . information . . . is . . . available for days, weeks and months later enhanced by search facilities that are built in to the TV or newspaper website . . . Although prior to the internet the focus was upon the open justice system with the news media as the surrogates of the public . . . there was as a property of pre-digital news media a form of 'partial obscurity'.

---

[249] Bermingham was jailed for 12 years and, though he appealed, it was not on the grounds of prejudicial publicity. The appeal failed. According to the *Daily Record*, William Beggs was giving him legal advice: 8 September 2008.

[250] 12 June 2008, [2008] EWHC 1263 (QB).

[251] In Manukau District Court, 25 August 2008.

However, this order was recalled within less than a month.[252]

It is difficult to see how any jurisdiction could attempt to control potentially prejudicial publicity which is built up either over a long time or over a number of jurisdictions by way of reporting restrictions. In *Coia v HMA*[253] the Appeal Court of the High Court of Justiciary recognized 'innumerable difficulties in connection with controlling information accessible on the internet . . . In our opinion, criminal trials in our jurisdiction are not and cannot be conducted in a prophylactic vacuum. They are, and must be, conducted in the real world, of which [the Financial Services Authority] . . . and the internet are parts'. The obvious point of control is the juror or witness, whether by vetting, sequestration, instruction, or reliance on oath.

What is clear is that the notion of publication contempt will have to adapt or die in the teeth of the evidence, the internet, and international terrorism.

---

[252] 19 September 2008.
[253] 18 December 2007, [2007] HCJ 17 IN 219/06.

5

MEDIA, DEMOCRACY, AND REPORTING ELECTIONS

David Goldberg[1]

5.1 INTRODUCTION

The media play an important role in the construction and sustainability of democratic societies. This chapter concentrates on a couple of core topics: the access by registered UK political parties to the mainstream electronic media (in particular broadcasters) around and during the cornerstone of the democratic process, elections[2] (including

---

[1] The author wishes to acknowledge the assistance of Keith Clement in the preparation of the this chapter.
[2] See Ofcom's Broadcast Code, October 2008, Section 6, for the meanings of election, referendum, major party, election period, candidate, referendum period, designated organisation, and permitted participants <http://www.ofcom.org.uk/tv/ifi/codes/bcode/elections/>. Traditionally, UK elections have been thought to be above criticism—but no more; see, 'Purity of Elections in the UK: Causes for

referendums) and rules about media coverage of elections; and the increasingly contentious issue of political advertisements. Whilst mainly focusing on the UK, the chapter sets out pertinent European framework norms and standards and refers to some comparative material.[3] As well as pointing to conventional normative inputs—statutes and court decisions—the chapter draws readers' attention to the applicable 'soft law', such as broadcasters' guidelines; the informal rules on party political and election broadcasts (including referenda); and the important role of the relatively low-key Broadcasters Liaison Group.[4]

5.1.1 Impartiality

The important editorial standard for broadcasters in this area—due impartiality—must be mentioned. It is not easily defined. A recent BBC Report, 'From Seesaw to Wagon Wheel: safeguarding impartiality in the 21st century'[5] sums it up as follows: 'In recent years, the BBC Editorial Guidelines, as well as the Neil Report of 2004, have attempted an explanation and a description. But it remains an elusive, almost magical substance, which is often more evident in its absence than in its presence.'

Impartiality is prescribed by the Communications Act 2003, in particular, in section 319(2)(c), (d) and (8), and section 320. Section 6(1) of the Ofcom Broadcast Code states that: 'The rules in Section Five, in particular the rules relating to matters of major political or industrial controversy and major matters relating to current public policy, apply to the coverage of elections and referendums.' Rule 5.5 deals with due impartiality on matters of political or industrial controversy and matters relating to current public policy and requires that it 'must be preserved on the part of any person providing a service . . . This may be achieved within a programme or over a series of programmes taken as a whole'.[6]

Concern', <http://image.guardian.co.uk/sys-files/Politics/documents/2008/04/28/JRRTstudy.pdf> (last accessed 7 March 2009). More generally, see 'Political Debate and the Role of the Media - The Fragility of Free Speech' (Strasbourg: IRIS Special, 2004). See also,C Christophorou (ed), 'Media and Elections: Case Studies', at <http://aceproject.org/ero-en/topics/media-and-elections/media-and-elections-final-19052003_4_pdf/view> (last accessed 7 March 2009).

[3] See, generally, the ACE project, at <http//www.aceproject.org> (last accessed 7 March 2009). Key documents promoting electoral standards include IDEA's 'International Electoral Standards: Guidelines for reviewing the legal framework of elections', at < http://www.idea.int/publications/ies/> (last accessed 7 March 2009) and the OSCE's 'Existing Commitments for Democratic Elections in OSCE Participating States', at <http://www.osce.org/documents/odihr/2003/10/772_en.pdf> (last accessed 7 March 2009).

[4] See, BBC, 'Guidelines on party election broadcasts', at <http://www.bbc.co.uk/info/policies/blg.shtml> (last accessed 7 March 2009); 'Ofcom Rules on Party Political and Referendum Broadcasts', at < http://www.ofcom.org.uk/tv/ifi/guidance/ppbrules/> (last accessed 7 March 2009); and the Broadcasters Liason Group, at <http://www.broadcastersliaisongroup.org.uk/index.html> (last accessed 7 March 2009).

[5] See <http://news.bbc.co.uk/1/shared/bsp/hi/pdfs/18_06_07impartialitybbc.pdf > (last accessed 7 March 2009).

[6] See <http://www.ofcom.org.uk/tv/ifi/codes/bcode/elections/> (last accessed 7 March 2009).

The parallel obligation for the BBC's output can be found in its Editorial Guidelines.[7] Section Four states that:

The Agreement accompanying the BBC's Charter requires us to produce comprehensive, authoritative and impartial coverage of news and current affairs in the UK and throughout the world to support fair and informed debate. It specifies that we should do all we can to treat controversial subjects with due accuracy and impartiality in our news services and other programmes dealing with matters of public policy or of political or industrial controversy. It also states that the BBC is forbidden from expressing an opinion on current affairs or matters of public policy other than broadcasting.

A recent decision of the BBC's Editorial Standards Committee (ESC) upholding a breach of impartiality ruling by the Editorial Complaints Unit illustrates the issue. The matter arose from the programme *People and Power—Back to the Future*. Specifically, the ESC found that statements about Lady Thatcher 'were not inaccurate, [but] ... they were highly contentious'. The ESC also stated that it was wrong to use images of violence at Orgreave near Sheffield during the Miners' Strike in 1984 without making it clear that the footage was from England, whereas viewers might have assumed the events had taken place in Wales. Commentary that encouraged people to vote in the elections was also criticized, on the basis that it was 'not the role of BBC presenters to encourage audiences to exercise their right to vote on particular occasions'.[8]

There is a specific section in the BBC's Editorial Guidelines concerning impartiality and broadcasting during election campaigns: 'Our commitment to impartiality and fairness is under intense scrutiny when we report election campaigns. All political parties will seek to influence editorial decisions. . . . We should make, and be able to defend, our editorial decisions on the basis that they are reasonable and carefully and impartially reached.' To achieve this, the BBC aims to ensure that:

- news judgements at election time are made within a *framework of democratic debate* which ensures that due weight is given to hearing the views and examining and challenging the policies of all parties. Significant minor parties should also receive some network coverage during the campaign.

- they are aware the *different political structures* in the four nations of the United Kingdom and that they are reflected in the election coverage of each nation. Programmes shown across the UK should also take this into account.

The way in which due accuracy and impartiality is achieved between parties will vary. It may be done in a single item, a single programme, a series of programmes, or over the course of the campaign as a whole. But content producers must take responsibility

---

[7] See <http://www.bbc.co.uk/guidelines/editorialguidelines/edguide/impariality/> (last accessed 7 March 2009).

[8] See ESC Bulletin, September 2008, Wales: 'Power and the People—Back to the Future', BBC Two Wales, 23 July 2007, at <http://www.bbc.co.uk/bbctrust/assets/files/pdf/appeals/esc_bulletins/2008/september.txt> p 43 (last accessed 7 March 2009).

for achieving due accuracy and impartiality in their own output and not rely on other BBC services to redress any imbalance for them.[9]

5.2 POLITICAL ADVERTISEMENTS

5.2.1 Broadcast advertisements

The long-standing general prohibition on broadcasting 'political' advertisements is now being increasingly challenged. At the time of writing, the principal legal dispute in the UK concerns Animal Defenders International and the UK government.[10] The topics are actually interrelated. The general ban on political advertising in the UK means that offering parties free airtime to broadcast about themselves and what they offer the electorate is, in effect, the functional equivalent of permitting political parties direct access to the electorate. It also, to some extent, justifies, or at least explains, the ban. The argument, though, is broader. Emmanuelle Machet notes, with respect to Europe generally:

Basically . . . Europe can be split in two with regard to the legal status of political advertising. On the one hand, political advertising is statutorily forbidden in the vast majority of Western European countries (e.g. Germany, France, Ireland, Sweden, UK, Malta, Norway, Denmark etc.). The traditional justification for this prohibition is that rich or well-established parties would be able to afford significantly more advertising time than new or minority parties. In this context, paid political advertising is considered as a discriminatory practice. However, parties are usually granted free airtime, often but not exclusively on public service broadcasters to present their programmes, sometimes in the format of short advertising spots. The broadcasters are usually reimbursed for their technical costs either by the State or directly by the parties.[11]

5.2.2 Non-broadcast advertisements

Generally, in the UK, oversight of non-broadcast political advertising is carried out by the Advertising Standards Authority (ASA).[12] It is not always appreciated, however, that if the message is aimed at 'influencing' voters in elections, it is exempt from the provisions of the British Code of Advertising, Sales Promotion and Direct Marketing (CAP Code). Clause 12.1 of the Code states: 'Any advertisement or direct marketing communication, whenever published or distributed, whose principal

---

[9] See <http://www.bbc.co.uk/guidelines/editorialguidelines/edguide/politics/broadcastingdur.shtml> (last accessed 7 March 2009).

[10] See section 5.11.3 below.

[11] 'Political Advertising', 16th EPRA Meeting, Ljubljana, 24–25 October 2002, Working Group 2, EPRA/2002/09, at <http://www.epra.org/content/english/press/back.html> (last accessed 7 March 2009).

[12] See <http://www.asa.org.uk/asa/news/news/2005/Control+of+Political+Advertising.htm> (last accessed 7 March 2009) and <http://www.asa.org.uk/asa/codes/cap_code/ShowCode.htm?clause_id=1514> (last accessed 7 March 2009).

function is to influence voters in local, regional, national or international elections or referendums is exempt from the Code.'

The justification is that political parties are occasional advertisers and have never signed up to the CAP Code. In particular, the parties have never agreed to be judged against the CAP Code's requirement that marketers should hold documentary evidence to prove all claims capable of objective substantiation. However, this exemption does not apply to marketing communications by central or local government, the Code stating in Clause 12.2: 'There is a formal distinction between Government policy and that of political parties. Marketing communications (see clauses 1.1 and 1.2) by central or local government, as distinct from those concerning party policy, are subject to the Code.'

The Electoral Commission published a report in 2004, 'Political Advertising', which considered the argument for a specific code of practice in relation to non-broadcast political advertising.[13] The report concluded that difficulties in implementing a code would make it impractical, but it recommended that political advertisers abide by the fundamental principle in the existing advertising code—that adverts should be prepared with 'a sense of responsibility to consumers and society'.

Thus, during or around elections there remains the fundamental difference between electronic and print media, the latter being 'entitled to be (and frequently are) extremely selective and biased in their reporting of events', and broadcasters, which must be 'particularly aware of the obligations imposed on them to be impartial'.[14] One rarely noted ploy is the use made by political parties of 'letters to the editor' pages in newspapers:

During election campaigns, local parties may become highly influential in shaping the contents of letters pages as part of their broader media-based campaigning strategy. For their part, editors select letters not simply according to their newsworthiness but to reflect the identity of the newspaper, to meet the perceived preferences of readers, as well as the more prosaic requirements of availability of space and editorial imperatives concerning balance.[15]

5.3 OTHER TOPICS

Whilst this chapter focuses on the above-mentioned topics, there are, of course, many other pertinent matters that could have been discussed in detail. Several are briefly considered here.

---

[13] See <http://www.electoralcommission.org.uk/news-and-media/news-releases/electoral-commission-media-centre/news-releases-reviews-and-research/the-electoral-commission-publishes-report-on-political-advertising> (last accessed 7 March 2009).

[14] B Mckain, A Bonnington, and R McInnes, *Scots Law for Journalists* (W. Green, 7th revised edn, 2000) para 24.46.

[15] See J Richardson and B Franklin, 'Letters of Intent: Election Campaigning and Orchestrated Public Debate in Local Newspapers' Letters to the Editor', <http://www-staff.lboro.ac.uk/~ssjer/Publications/letters,%20pol%20comm.pdf> (last accessed 7 March 2009).

5.3.1 Publication of polling information

Article 19 has published a general guide to the issue of laws and regulations restricting the publication of electoral opinion polls.[16] Council of Europe Recommendation CM/ Rec 2007)15 (see below) opens the door to the legitimacy of a 'day of reflection', meaning that Member States may consider the merits of including a provision in their regulatory framework prohibiting the dissemination of partisan electoral messages on the day preceding voting.

The European Platform of Regulatory Authorities, in 'Political Communication on Television' (EPRA/2000/02),[17] makes the point that:

> The specific issue of opinion polls is worth mentioning because of its potential influence on the election results. Opinion polls are a useful tool to inform the audience of the voting intentions. However, they can also be used as a tool of manipulation of the electorate—especially if they are published on the last days before an election. As a consequence, most European countries have introduced specific rules dealing with opinion polls—the most usual being the determination of a cut-off time for reporting of opinion poll results. The length of this cut-off time varies from one day to one week according to the different countries. In France, no opinion polls can be published in the week preceding the election. This cut-off time may be statutorily determined as in France (Art. 11 of the law of 11 July 1977) . . . One question is how effective bans of polls will be given the emergence of new means of communication. In France, during the 1997 legislative elections, election-poll results were made available on the Internet through the website of the Tribune de Genève in Switzerland.

In the UK, the matter is regulated by section 15(1) of, and Schedule 6, paragraph 6 to, the Representation of the People Act 2000, inserting section 66A into the Representation of the People Act 1983, on the prohibition on publication of exit polls.[18] Thus:

- No person shall, in the case of an election to which this section applies, publish before the poll is closed any statement relating to the way in which voters have voted at the election where that statement is (or might reasonably be taken to be) based on information given by voters after they have voted, or any forecast as to the result of the election which is (or might reasonably be taken to be) based on information so given.

- This section applies to any parliamentary election; and any local government election in England or Wales.

- In this section, 'forecast' includes estimate; 'publish' means make available to the public at large, or any section of the public, in whatever form and by whatever means; and any reference to the result of an election is a reference to the result of the election either as a whole or so far as any particular candidate or candidates at the election is or are concerned.

According to the BBC's Editorial Guidelines, no opinion poll may be published on the day of the election until the polls close, or, in the case of a European election, until all the

---

[16] See 'Laws and Regulations Restricting the Publication of Electoral Opinion Polls', at <http://www. article19.org/pdfs/publications/opinion-polls-paper.pdf> (last accessed 7 March 2009).

[17] See < http://www.epra.org/>, click on Background Papers (last accessed 7 March 2009).

[18] Representation of the People Act 1983, s 66A, inserted by Representation of the People Act 2000, s 15(1), Sch 6, para 6 (3 September 2000).

polls have closed across the European Union. And on the polling day itself, the BBC, in common with other broadcasters, will cease reporting the substance of campaigns from 6.00 am until polls close. Coverage is restricted to factual accounts, for example turnout; politicians' appearances at polling stations; and the weather. This is so as to ensure that, while the polls are open, nothing might be construed as influencing the ballot.[19]

The effectiveness of such rules, owing to the nature of online publication, needs to be questioned. If 'publish' means make available to the public at large, or any section of the public, in whatever form and by whatever means, does this also include by the internet, whether on blogs, social networking sites, or via online versions of traditional media? And if so, would such measures be practically enforceable?

In France, the issue of the possibility of French voters accessing 'foreign' websites whilst polls in France were still open (so that French voters should not have had legally at that time the information being published lawfully in other jursidictions) occurred notably during the 2007 Presidential elections:

To be among the first to know the result of France's presidential election, you had to be … surfing Web sites in Switzerland or Belgium, or watching British TV. A French law that even officials admit is becoming outdated for the Internet age barred results from being published in France until polls closed Sunday night. But by then, it was already an open secret abroad that Segolene Royal and Nicolas Sarkozy had qualified for the May 6 runoff. Some estimates popped up on the Web two hours before polls closed, when thousands of voters were still waiting.[20]

In, Canada, the Supreme Court dealt with this issue in *R v Bryan*. During the 2000 federal election, Mr Bryan published the election results from thirty-two ridings in Atlantic Canada by posting the information on a website. However, polling stations remained open elsewhere in Canada. He was charged with contravening section 329 of the Canada Elections Act 2000. This prohibits the transmission of election results in one electoral district to another electoral district before the close of all polling stations in that other district. The Supreme Court upheld (by 5 to 4) the legal ban on reporting early vote results on federal election nights in regions of the country where the polls are still open. The court ruled that section 329 of the Canada Elections Act does not violate the Canadian Charter of Rights.[21]

Finally, in 1999, in Russia, the website www.election99.com published the results of exit polls during the day of elections to the State Duma (see section 5.12.1 below). At the time, Russian election law forbade such publication. However, the law applied only to the mass media. Access to the site was eventually blocked, and a debate raged

---

[19] See <http://www.bbc.co.uk/guidelines/editorialguidelines/edguide/politics/pollsatelection.shtml> (last accessed 7 March 2009).

[20] See 'French bloggers fight law that gives foreign media edge in political reporting', at <http://www.foxnews.com/story/0,2933,267901,00.html> (last accessed 7 March 2009).

[21] See 'Supreme Court upholds blackout on early election night results', at <http://www.cbc.ca/canada/story/2007/03/15/election-law.html> (last accessed 7 March 2009); *R v Bryan* [2007] 1 SCR 527, 2007 SCC 12, at <http://scc.lexum.umontreal.ca/en/2007/2007scc12/2007scc12.html> (last accessed 7 March 2009).

about the legitimacy of the action:

In the opinion of the Moscow Media Law and Policy Center (MMLPC), the most adequate way to resolve this collision would be to declare the applicable standards null and void. In accordance with general legal practice, one of the grounds for declaring legal norms null and void is the appearance of new relationships other than those which lawmakers had intended to regulate. In the current case, the Internet, which was only a theory in 1991, had become a completely real and common phenomenon by the end of the decade. For this reason, the relationships that have developed in connection with the Internet can be seen as principally new, and therefore to apply the provisions of Article 24 to the Internet would be legally incorrect. In other words, calling Internet sites a type of mass media is unlawful.[22]

5.3.2 Reporting foreign elections

According to the BBC, the principles of fairness and impartiality that underlie its coverage of UK elections should also inform its election reporting about other countries. When reporting such elections, it may be necessary to take into account the circumstances under which the particular election is being held, especially where serious questions are raised about the openness or fairness of the electoral process. Additional issues may arise when broadcasting to the actual country in which an election is taking place. There is a special responsibility to audiences who are about to vote, and this means considering the timing of the re-transmission on international services of programmes originally made for the UK audience. The closer the election date, the greater the need for care. If it is considered that a programme could have an undue and unfair influence on the election, then transmission should be delayed until after polling.[23]

5.3.3 Participation of candidates at a parliamentary or local government election in local items about the constituency or electoral area in question

In 1979, at the time when *Marshall v BBC* (see section 5.8.1 below) was heard, a candidate had a right of veto vis-à-vis any election programme in which he took part. This has now been altered by the amendment to the Representation of the People Act 1983.[24] With regard to broadcasting of local items during an election period, the rules are that:

• Each broadcasting authority shall adopt a code of practice with respect to the participation of candidates at a parliamentary or local government election in items

---

[22] See <http://www.medialaw.ru/e_pages/research/commentary4.htm> (last accessed 7 March 2009).

[23] <http://www.bbc.co.uk/guidelines/editorialguidelines/edguide/politics/reportingoverse.shtml> (last accessed 7 March 2009); see also 'Coverage of the election by the Media', at <http://www.dfid.gov.uk/pubs/files/elections.pdf> (last accessed 7 March 2009).

[24] Representation of the People Act 1983, s 93 substituted (on 16 February 2001 for specified purposes and otherwise on 16 March 2001) by Representation of the People Act 2000, s 144; Political Parties, Elections and Referendums Act 2000 (Commencement No 1 and Transitional Provisions) Order 2001, SI 2001/222, art 3.

about the constituency or electoral area in question which are included in relevant services during the election period.

- The code for the time being adopted by a broadcasting authority under this section shall be either a code drawn up by that authority, whether on their own or jointly with one or more other broadcasting authorities, or a code drawn up by one or more other such authorities; and a broadcasting authority shall from time to time consider whether the code for the time being so adopted by them should be replaced by a further code falling within the above two categories.

- Before drawing up a code under this section a broadcasting authority shall have regard to any views expressed by the Electoral Commission for the purposes of this subsection; and any such code may make different provision for different cases.

- 'The election period', in relation to an election, means the period beginning (a) (if a parliamentary general election) with the date of the dissolution of Parliament or any earlier time at which Her Majesty's intention to dissolve Parliament is announced, (b) (if a parliamentary by-election) with the date of the issue of the writ for the election or any earlier date on which a certificate of the vacancy is notified in the London Gazette in accordance with the Recess Elections Act 1975, or (c) (if a local government election) with the last date for publication of notice of the election, and ending with the close of the poll.

5.3.3.1 *The BBC's Editorial Guidelines*

The Guidelines state that the BBC is required by law to adopt a code of practice at each election to govern the participation of candidates in each constituency or electoral area. Before drawing up a code the BBC is required to have regard to any views expressed by the Electoral Commission. Election and referendum guidelines will be agreed by the Board of Governors and issued by the Chief Adviser, Politics before each election or referendum.

5.3.3.2 *Ofcom Broadcast Code*

Section 6 of the code provides the following rules:

6.8 Due impartiality must be strictly maintained in a constituency report or discussion and in an electoral area report or discussion.

6.9 If a candidate takes part in an item about his/her particular constituency, or electoral area, then candidates of each of the major parties must be offered the opportunity to take part. (However, if they refuse or are unable to participate, the item may nevertheless go ahead.)

6.10 In addition to Rule 6.9, broadcasters must offer the opportunity to take part in constituency or electoral area reports and discussions, to all candidates within the constituency or electoral area representing parties with previous significant electoral support or where there is evidence of significant current support.

6.11 Any constituency or electoral area report or discussion after the close of nominations must include a list of all candidates standing, giving first names, surnames and the name of the party they represent or, if they are standing independently, the fact that they are an independent candidate. This must be conveyed in sound and/or vision.

6.12   Where a candidate is taking part in a programme on any matter, after the election has been called, s/he must not be given the opportunity to make constituency points, or electoral area points about the constituency or electoral area in which s/he is standing, when no other candidates will be given a similar opportunity.

5.4   GENERAL PRINCIPLE(S) REGARDING DISSEMINATION OF OPINION AND INFORMATION AT ELECTION TIME

5.4.1   European Court of Human Rights

The European Court of Human Rights (ECtHR) has reviewed several cases recently in the course of which it has affirmed the general principle of the right to freedom of expression in the context of the 'dissemination of pertinent election opinion and information'.

5.4.1.1   Filatenko v Russia

In *Filatenko v Russia* the Court noted the specific context of the case: a live television show, broadcast four days ahead of general and regional elections, with three prospective candidates taking questions put by viewers by phone to the programme's editors. Mr Filatenko asked a question about the tearing-off of the Tyva Republic flag from the car which had campaigned in support of Mrs Salchak, the Otechestvo party candidate. The incident had taken place somewhere near the campaign headquarters of the Edinstvo political movement, the main competitor of the Otechestvo party. Filatenko was successfully sued for defamation. Having regard to the context—the forthcoming elections—the Strasbourg Court stated that:

As a general rule, any opinions and information pertinent to elections, both local and national, which are disseminated during the electoral campaign should be considered as forming part of a debate on questions of public interest . . . According to its constant case-law, there is little scope under Article 10 § 2 of the Convention for restrictions on political speech or on debate on questions of public interest and very strong reasons are required for justifying such restrictions.[25]

5.4.1.2   Kwiecień v Poland

In *Kwiecień v Poland*, indirectly relevant for media law, the Head of the Dzierżoniów District Office, Mr SL, was due to stand for election to the district council (*rada powiatu*) in the local elections scheduled for 11 October 1998. On 21 September 1998, the applicant sent Mr SL an open letter calling on him to withdraw from the election. The applicant sent copies of his letter to the Wałbrzych Governor, the Wałbrzych Regional Assembly, the Dzierżoniów Municipal Council, local mayors, the Prime Minister's

---

[25] Application No 73219/01.

Office, and a number of local newspapers. A thousand copies of the letter were to be made available to local inhabitants—although, according to the applicant, as a matter of fact, no newspapers published the letter. The Court observed that:

> The general aim of the applicant's open letter was to attract the voters' attention to the suitability of Mr S.L. as a candidate for local public office. It accordingly finds that the statements in the letter concerned a matter of public interest for the local community, even if some of them might appear harsh or far-fetched. As a general rule, the Court considers that opinions and information pertinent to elections, both local and national, which are disseminated during the electoral campaign should be considered as forming part of a debate on questions of public interest, unless proof to the contrary is offered.[26]

5.4.1.3 Krasulya v Russia

Finally, in *Krasulya v Russia* (No 12365/03, § 38, 22 February 2007) the Court dealt with publication about 'the decision of the town legislature to abolish mayoral elections in the regional capital and the applicant's supposition that the regional governor had unduly interfered in the legislative process'. The article also commented on the results of the governor's election and criticized the governor's managerial abilities:

> The issues raised in the article were of paramount importance for the regional community. That was a matter of public concern and the article contributed to an on-going political debate. The Court reiterates that there is little scope under Article 10 § 2 of the Convention for restrictions on political speech or debates on questions of public interest. It has been the Court's constant approach to require very strong reasons for justifying restrictions on political speech, for broad restrictions imposed in individual cases would undoubtedly affect respect for the freedom of expression in general in the State concerned.[27]

5.4.2 Main Framework norm: Recommendation CM/Rec (2007)

The Main Framework norm is Recommendation CM/Rec (2007) 15 on measures concerning media coverage of election campaigns.[28] This updates Recommendation No R (99) 15 on measures concerning media coverage of election campaigns. There does not appear to be an Explanatory Memorandum for the 2007 version, so the reader's attention is drawn to the one for the earlier Recommendation.[29]

The scope of the Recommendation encompasses all types of elections taking place in Member States, including presidential, legislative, regional, and, where practicable, local elections and referenda; media reporting on elections taking place abroad, especially when these media address persons in the country where the election is taking

---

[26] Application No 51744/99.

[27] Application No 12365/03.

[28] <https://wcd.coe.int/ViewDoc.jsp?id=1207243&Site=CM&BackColorInternet=9999CC&BackColorIntranet=FFBB55&BackColorLogged=FFAC75> (last accessed 7 March 2009).

[29] <https://wcd.coe.int/ViewDoc.jsp?Ref=ExpRec(99)15&Language=lanEnglish&Ver=original&Site=CM&BackColorInternet=9999CC&BackColorIntranet=FFBB55&BackColorLogged=FFAC75> (last accessed 7 March 2009).

place; and, where the notion of the 'pre-election period' is defined under domestic legislation, the principles contained in the Recommendation should also apply.

5.4.2.1 *General framework principles*

Various general principles are set out: non-interference by public authorities; protection against attacks, intimidation or other types of unlawful pressure on the media; editorial independence; ownership by public authorities; professional and ethical standards of the media; transparency of, and access to, the media; the right of reply or equivalent remedies; opinion polls; and 'day of reflection'. The general principles are followed by a set of specific principles applicable to broadcast media, as follows.

During election campaigns, regulatory frameworks should encourage and facilitate the pluralistic expression of opinions via the broadcast media. With due respect for the editorial independence of broadcasters, regulatory frameworks should also provide for the obligation to cover election campaigns in a fair, balanced, and impartial manner in the overall programme services of broadcasters. Such an obligation should apply to both public service media and private broadcasters in their relevant transmission areas. Member States may derogate from these measures with respect to those broadcast media services exclusively devoted to, and clearly identified as, the self-promotion of a political party or candidate.

5.4.2.2 *News and current affairs programmes*

Where self-regulation does not provide for this, Member States should adopt measures whereby public service media and private broadcasters, during the election period, should in particular be fair, balanced, and impartial in their news and current affairs programmes, including discussion programmes such as interviews or debates. No privileged treatment should be given by broadcasters to public authorities during such programmes. This matter should primarily be addressed via appropriate self-regulatory measures. In this connection, Member States might examine whether, where practicable, the relevant authorities monitoring the coverage of elections should be given the power to intervene in order to remedy possible shortcomings.

5.4.2.3 *Non-linear audiovisual services of public service media*

Member States should apply the principles contained in the points made in section 5.4.2 above or similar provisions to non-linear audiovisual media services of public service media.

5.4.2.4 *Free airtime and equivalent presence for political parties/candidates on public service media*

Member States may examine the advisability of including in their regulatory frameworks provisions whereby public service media may make available free airtime on their broadcast and other linear audiovisual media services and/or an equivalent presence on their non-linear audiovisual media services to political parties/candidates during the election period. Wherever such airtime and/or equivalent presence is granted, this should be done in a fair and non-discriminatory manner, on the basis of transparent and objective criteria.

5.5 MONITORING REPORTS

Whether such norms (and other, more general, freedom of expression standards) are actually implemented is, as ever, another question. However, institutions, such as the OSCE's Representative on Freedom of the Media and other ad hoc missions, regularly produce reports after conducting specific election monitoring missions.

Two recent examples are (1) the report on the 2 December 2007 Duma elections in Russia. Concerning the implementation of press freedom commitments, it found that there had been harassment of media outlets; undue legislative limitations; and arbitrary application of the rules by the authorities, thus preventing equal access to the media for the political parties; and (2) the report on the Presidential election in Azerbaijan. It found that Azerbaijan did not meet all its commitments. Thus, the election process was characterized by a lack of 'vibrant political discourse facilitated by media', and did not reflect all the principles of a meaningful and pluralistic democratic election.[30]

5.6 BROADCASTING AT ELECTION TIME

5.6.1 BBC Editorial Guidelines and Ofcom Broadcast Code

The BBC Guidelines on election broadcasting, and the parallel Ofcom Broadcast Code provisions, are the source of the day-to-day norms.

The BBC materials relate to elections; the BBC code of practice; broadcasting during elections; impartiality; interviewing party leaders; interviewing politicians; overseas legal issues; polls; and reporting UK election and referendum campaigns.

As to commercial broadcasters, the main day-to-day source of their obligations is to be found in Ofcom's Broadcast Code: Section 6 on Elections and Referendums. The basic principle is to ensure that the special impartiality requirements in the Communications Act 2003 and other legislation relating to broadcasting on elections and referendums are applied at the time of elections and referendums.

---

[30] See 'Press freedom commitments not met during Russian electoral campaign, says OSCE media freedom watchdog', at <http://www.osce.org/item/28670.html> (last accessed 7 March 2009); see also, The International Election Observation Mission (IEOM) for the 15 October 2008 Presidential election in the Republic of Azerbaijan, at<http://www.osce.org/documents/html/pdftohtml/34414_en.pdf.htm> (last accessed 7 March 2009).

5.6.2 Party political and election broadcasts[31]

The rationale for the system of free party political broadcasts (PPBs) is to offset the differential ability and/or capacity of political parties to attract campaign funds. So, free airtime is provided prior to elections, and other significant events, allowing 'qualifying' parties an opportunity to deliver their messages directly to the electorate through the broadcast media.[32]

Election broadcasts are often referred to as 'PPBs'. However, one should distinguish between party political broadcasts (PPBs) in general and party election broadcasts (PEBs), as they are or can be subject to different rules, regulations and legislation: 'It is worth noting that party election broadcasts are different from party political broadcasts which are shown at other times of the year. The terminology can be confusing as PPBs is often used as a generic term to describe both types of broadcasts.'[33]

A party election broadcast is defined, by the BBC, as 'broadcasts made by the parties and transmitted on TV or radio. By agreement with the broadcasters, each party is allowed a certain number according to its election strength and number of candidates fielded.'[34]

There are also other broadcasts: ministerial broadcasts; Budget broadcasts; and broadcasts around the Queen's Speech.

With regard to PPBs, the current arrangements apply only to broadcasters who use the terrestrial radio spectrum (although the obligation extends to those same channels on other platforms) and are the so-called 'public service broadcasters': BBC, Channel 3, Channel 4, and Five, and national radio services: the BBC, Classic FM, Virgin Radio, and TalkSPORT. Allocation is a matter for individual broadcasters. However, in practice, the Broadcasters' Liaison Group (BLG see section 5.10.1 below) plays the significant, coordinating role. Political parties are invited to make representations to the BLG about matters of concern as well as practical arrangements. The broadcasting regulators, however, determine disputes between the parties and the broadcasters.[35] Generally:

- PPBs and PEBs are allocated in accordance with rules agreed by the broadcasting authorities. Commercial channels are required by the Communications Act 2003, under powers derived from the Broadcasting Act 1990, to follow the rules set by the

---

[31] For the history of such broadcasts, see the Broadcasters' Liaison Group, at <http://www.broadcast-ersliaisongroup.org.uk/history.html> (last accessed 7 March 2009). See also, 'The Funding of Political Parties in the United Kingdom' in Standards in Public Life, Vol 1: Report, at <http://www.archive.official-documents.co.uk/document/cm40/4057/volume-1/volume-1.pdf> (last accessed 7 March 2009).

[32] See, Electoral Commission Fact Sheet 04-05, 'Party Political Broadcasts', at <http://www.electoral-commission.org.uk/__data/assets/electoral_commission_pdf_file/0020/13268/Partypoliticalbroadcasts_17063-6138__E__N__S__W__.pdf> (last accessed 8 March 2009).

[33] See O Gay, 'Party Election Broadcasts' (updated, February 2009), at <http://www.parliament.uk/commons/lib/research/briefings/snpc-03354.pdf> (last accessed 7 March 2009).

[34] BBC, 'Glossary of Election Terms', at < http://news.bbc.co.uk/2/hi/uk_news/politics/vote_2005/basics/4346975.stm> (last accessed 7 March 2009).

[35] See <http://www.culture.gov.uk/reference_library/media_releases/2380.aspx> (last accessed 8 March 2009).

relevant licensing body (currently Ofcom). There is no parallel duty on the BBC, but the Corporation acts along similar lines. General arrangements for allocating broadcasting times are devised jointly by Ofcom, the BBC, S4C, and the Radio Authority.

• In order for political parties to qualify for a party election broadcast they must contest one-sixth of seats or more at an election. For a general election, parties must contest at least 110 seats to gain access to a political broadcast.

• Parties contesting one-sixth of seats or more in Scotland or Wales will also qualify for a political broadcast but this will be limited to the respective countries where their candidates are standing only.[36]

The content is determined (provided it is within the law) by the parties themselves and they retain copyright, although extracts may be used without consent. The cost is borne by the parties. The BBC and Ofcom, being themselves bound by law and their own guidelines, may have to take a view as to what is sought to be broadcast (see below).

5.6.3 Referendum broadcasts

A newer category, which may be of more importance in the future (although there have been cases already in Scotland, see section 5.7.2 below) is the referendum broadcast. Section 127 of the Political Parties, Elections and Referendum Act 2000 provides that a broadcaster shall not include in its broadcasting services any referendum campaign broadcast made on behalf of any person or body other than one designated in respect of the referendum in question (under section 108). 'Referendum campaign broadcast' is defined as any broadcast whose purpose (or main purpose) is or may reasonably be assumed to be: (1) to further any campaign conducted with a view to promoting or procuring a particular outcome in relation to any question asked in a referendum to which this regulation applies; or (2) otherwise to promote or procure any such outcome.

5.6.4 Legal basis and rules

Election reporting in general is covered by the Representation of the People Act 1983, the Political Parties, Elections and Referendums Act 2000, and the Local Government Act 1986.[37] Specific legal obligation on broadcasters to carry PPBs was first prescribed in sections 36 and 107 of the Broadcasting Act 1990, as amended by section 333 of the Communication Act 2003. This provides that the regulatory regime for every licensed public service channel, and the regulatory regime for every national radio service, includes (a) conditions requiring the inclusion in that channel or service of PPBs and of referendum campaign broadcasts; and (b) conditions requiring that licence-holders

[36] See 'General Election May 2005 Briefing Information', at <http://www.dca.gov.uk/elections/gen-elec-brief-info.pdf> (last accessed 7 March 2009).
[37] See, *Blackstone's Statutes*: 'Media Law', at <http://fds.oup.com/www.oup.co.uk/pdf/statutes06_caddell_contents.pdf> (last accessed 8 March 2009).

observe such rules with respect to PPBs and referendum campaign broadcasts as may be made by Ofcom.

The BBC is party to an Agreement made with HM Secretary of State for Culture, Media and Sport. Clause 48 of the current Agreement, on party political broadcasts, makes the following provisions:

- The BBC must include, in some or all of the UK Public Broadcasting Services, party political broadcasts and referendum campaign broadcasts.

- The Trust must determine which of the UK Public Broadcasting Services are in principle to include party political broadcasts and referendum campaign broadcasts; and the basis on which, and the terms and conditions subject to which, such broadcasts are to be included in them.

- In particular, the Trust may determine, so far as they are permitted so to do by sections 37 and 127 of the Political Parties, Elections and Referendums Act 2000 (only registered parties and designated organisations to be entitled to party political broadcasts or referendum campaign broadcasts) the political parties on whose behalf party political broadcasts may be made; and the length and frequency of party political broadcasts and referendum campaign broadcasts.

In this clause, 'referendum campaign broadcast' has the meaning given by section 127 of the Political Parties, Elections and Referendums Act 2000.[38]

5.6.5 Rules on PPBs, etc [39]

Rules made under section 333 of the Communications Act 2003 (regarding PEBs, PPBs, and referendum campaign broadcasts) and paragraph 18 of Schedule 12 are contained in the Ofcom Rules on Party Political and Referendum Broadcasts.

Such broadcasts are also required to comply with the relevant provisions of the Broadcast Code, for example the provisions regarding harm and offence, notwithstanding that the content is normally the responsibility of the relevant political parties. Within the terms of these rules, the precise allocation of broadcasts is the responsibility of the licensees (note, though, the rules 'reflect minimum requirements'. They are not intended to 'fetter broadcasters' discretion, e.g., to make additional allocations'). Unresolved disputes between any licensee and any political party, as to the length, frequency, allocation, or scheduling of broadcasts, are to be referred by the party or the licensee to Ofcom for resolution. The Ofcom Board has delegated the adjudication on such disputes to the Election Committee.

What do the Rules cover?—services carrying broadcasts; allocation of broadcasts; length of broadcasts; and scheduling of broadcasts. Under 'services', when it comes to

---

[38] See 'An Agreement Between Her Majesty's Secretary of State for Culture, Media and Sport and the British Broadcasting Corporation', at <http://www.bbc.co.uk/bbctrust/assets/files/pdf/regulatory_framework/charter_agreement/bbcagreement_july06.pdf> (last accessed 8 March 2009).
[39] See 'Rules on Party Political and Referendum Broadcasts', at <http://www.ofcom.org.uk/tv/ifi/guidance/ppbrules> (last accessed 8 March 2009).

European Parliamentary elections, only ITV and Five will carry broadcasts and ITV will also carry local election broadcasts in those UK nations/regions where such elections are taking place; broadcasts in the relevant nations/regions for Scottish Parliament, Welsh Assembly, Northern Ireland Assembly and Greater London Authority elections; and broadcasts for the major parties in Great Britain around other key events in the political calendar, such as the Queen's Speech, the Budget, and party conferences.

'Major parties' include the Scottish National Party on Channel 4 and SNP and Plaid Cymru on Five. How do other, non-'major parties' qualify for a party election broadcast? The basis is:

. . . contesting one sixth or more of the seats up for election, modified as appropriate for proportional representation systems. The four nations of the UK will be considered separately. Parties which qualify in one or two of the nations of England, Scotland and Wales will be offered broadcasts on ITV, in the appropriate regions of those nations. Parties which qualify in all of these three nations will additionally be offered broadcasts on Channel 4, Five and national commercial radio.

In relation to 'other key events', major parties will be offered 'one broadcast on each occasion'. Before each referendum, each 'designated referendum organisation will be allocated one or more broadcasts . . . The allocation should be equal for both sides.'

Given that the broadcasts in question are not being paid for, it is perhaps not surprising that parties are circumscribed in the amount of airtime on offer. So, parties and referendum organizations have the option of choosing 'a length of 2'40", 3'40" or 4'40" on TV. For radio, parties and organizations may choose any length up to 2'30"'. Finally, another restriction concerns when the broadcasts may or may not go out:

TV election broadcasts by the Conservatives, Labour, the Liberal Democrats and Northern Ireland major parties must be carried in peak time (6.00pm–10.30pm), as must SNP and Plaid Cymru broadcasts on ITV in Scotland and Wales, and all referendum broadcasts. Other broadcasts should normally be carried in the period 5.30pm to 11.30pm. UK referendum broadcasts and general election broadcasts by the Conservatives, Labour and Liberal Democrats must be carried on national radio between 5.00pm and 9.00pm. Other broadcasts must be transmitted between 6.00am and 10.00pm.

Despite the apparent precision of these rules (and parallel BBC rules), it is an open question whether the system as a whole is 'prescribed by law' and thus Article 10 compliant. This issue has been considered by the Electoral Commission (see section 5.10.5 below).

5.7 HIGH PROFILE CASES

There have been several significant cases concerning broadcasting in the run-up to, or during, elections.

5.7.1 *R v BBC and Independent Television Commission, ex p the Referendum Party*[40]

The case concerned an application by the Referendum Party (RF) claiming that the BBC and the then regulator, the Independent Television Commission, had decided irrationally to allocate it one five-minute party election broadcast during the 1997 General Election campaign. This compared, in the RF's view unfavourably, to the Conservative and Labour Parties' allocations of five ten-minute television party election broadcasts each, and the Liberal Democrats four such broadcasts, on each network. The RF argued that the broadcasters: 'wrongly included in the criteria for their decisions past electoral support, something that a new party could not show; [and] failed to take account of its electoral size and support, especially the large number of candidates it is fielding in the election'. The court dismissed the first argument, holding that neither the broadcasters' inclusion of past electoral support as part of their general criteria for allocating PEBs, nor their treatment of the lack of it in this case, was irrational.

The court accepted that broadcasters had to exercise a duty of impartiality but said that:

> . . . in this context [impartiality] is not to be equated with parity or balance as between political parties of different strengths, popular support and appeal . . . It means fairness of allocation having regard to those factors, yet making allowance for any significant current changes in the political arena and for the potential effect of the powerful medium of television itself in advancing or hindering such changes. Where it exists, past electoral support is obviously a relevant consideration, though only one, and an imprecise one at that, for assessing for this purpose the current strength of a political party relative to that of others. Clearly it would be absurd for broadcasters to allow it to be determinative or to regard it as a pre-condition for allocation of more than one party election broadcast.

As regards the second main argument—the disproportionate nature of the allocations in the light of the Party's strength at the time, mainly evidenced by the number of candidates it was fielding—the court found that the RF had:

> . . . made full representations to the broadcasters about its strength and support and that the broadcasters considered those representations. The broadcasters' criteria for allocation of further party election broadcasts where the threshold condition of 50 candidates is established are, in our view, reasonable—a combination of past electoral support, where there is any, and the present number of candidates. Their application of those criteria to the present case so as to take account both of the number of candidates and the other indications of support on which the Referendum Party relied seems to us reasonable. The weight that they gave to those various matters, in particular the significance of the number of candidates as a mark of overall support, was for them. This Court should not intervene unless it is of the view that they were irrational in not giving enough weight to those matters in allocating it only one broadcast.[41]

---

[40] EWHC 406 (Admin) (24 April 1997) QBD.

[41] See 'Only one broadcast for Referendum Party', at <http://findarticles.com/p/articles/mi_qn4158/is_19970430/ai_n14110223?tag=content;coll> (last accessed 8 March 2009).

5.7.2 *R v BBC, ex p Prolife Alliance*[42]

In *R v British Broadcasting Corporation, ex p Prolife Alliance* the court was asked to review the BBC's decision not to air a party election broadcast prepared by the ProLife Alliance (PLA). For the 2001 General Election, the PLA had fielded six candidates in Wales, thus securing the allocation of one 4'40" PEB in that region.

The film primarily consisted of footage depicting 'the products of a suction abortion: tiny limbs, bloodied and dismembered, a separated head, their human shape and form clearly recognizable'. The broadcasters refused to screen the PEB saying that it engaged their general taste and decency obligations. Importantly, it was accepted that such obligations do apply to PEBs as well as any other genre of programming. Thus, the case turned merely on whether or not the BBC had exercised its discretion in that regard reasonably. The court noted that 'The present case concerns a broadcast on behalf of a party opposed to abortion. Such a programme can be expected to be illustrated, to a strictly limited extent, by disturbing pictures of an abortion.' But the PLA tapes went much further. In its decision letter dated 17 May 2001, the BBC noted that some images of aborted foetuses could be acceptable depending on the context: 'what is unacceptable is the cumulative effect of several minutes primarily devoted to such images'. None of the broadcasters to whom the tape had been submitted regarded the case as at the margin. Each regarded it as a 'clear case in which it would plainly be a breach of our obligations to transmit this broadcast'. In reaching their decisions, the broadcasters stated they had taken into account the importance of the images to the political campaign of the PLA.

The Court held that: 'The broadcasters' application of the statutory criteria cannot be faulted. There is nothing, either in their reasoning or in their overall decisions, to suggest they applied an inappropriate standard when assessing whether transmission of the pictures in question would be likely to be offensive to public feeling.'[43]

5.8 OTHER CASES

5.8.1 *Marshall v BBC* [1979] 3 All ER 80

At the time when this case was heard, a candidate had a right of veto vis-à-vis any election programme in which he took part. The court held that a candidate, James Marshall, had not taken part, since there had only been pictures of him canvassing. The programme did not therefore require his consent before being broadcast. Lord Denning also noted the BBC's duty to be impartial in its programmes, especially during an election campaign, when one candidate or party should not be favoured more than another candidate or party.

---

[42] [2003] UKHL 23.
[43] See <http://www.1cor.com/1315/?form_1155.replyids=677> (last accessed 8 March 2009).

5.8.2 *Wilson v IBA* (1979) SC 351

The issue in this case was the distribution of access to airtime in the context of the first referendum on UK devolution. The four main political parties were given equal time. However, this meant that three out of four broadcasts would be focused on the same side of what in reality was a 50/50, yes/no question. Wilson, the Scottish National Party leader, argued that there should be an equal number of broadcasts for the 'yes' and the 'no' sides. It was held that the allocation was unlawful[44] and an interdict was granted preventing the programmes from being broadcast. Lord Ross said: 'It will be necessary however to ensure that the same time is given to the proponents of the "yes" as is given to the proponents of the "no".'

5.8.3 *McAliskey v BBC* [1980] NI 44

A European Parliament election was the context for this case. Ms McAliskey claimed that the treatment she was to receive in a programme implied she was a more minor candidate than others also standing. Her rationale was that the programme divided the candidates into two groups and proposed to allocate less time to one (in which she had been placed). She refused to give her consent to the programme and sought an injunction. Mr Justice Murray held that, despite thinking that the division was not unfair in terms of section 9(1) of the Representation of the People Act 1969, the BBC did have to obtain the consent of all candidates prior to the item being broadcast and if such consent was not forthcoming, the broadcast would be illegal in terms of section 9(1).

5.8.4 *Lynch v BBC* (1983) 6 NIJB

As one aspect of election programming, the BBC held a series of phone-in discussions. The Northern Ireland Workers' Party sought an injunction because it was not featured. The BBC argued that the WP (NI) had not fielded candidates in at least five constituencies and had not secured a reasonable percentage of votes in previous elections (percentage of the first preference votes in the election for the Assembly a year earlier). The BBC affirmed that the WP (NI) would obtain coverage in other programmes. It was held that the BBC was probably not under a legal duty to be impartial; that its rules were adequate to secure that goal; and that impartiality was not equivalent to giving an equal allocation to all parties in an election.

5.8.5 *Wilson v IBA (No 2)* (1988) SLT 276

The IBA allocation in Scotland to the SNP was challenged, it having received two broadcasts as compared with five for the other main parties. It was held that, since of the five, two would go out in Scotland, the SNP had parity of access 'as regards Scottish issues'.

---

[44] Independent Broadcasting Authority Act 1973, s 2(2)(b)—programmes broadcast shall maintain a 'proper balance in their subject matter'.

5.8.6 *Houston v BBC The Times*, 9 May 1995

This case concerns the successful application by a local election candidate to postpone the broadcast of a forty-minute interview with the Prime Minister on *Panorama*, due to go out on 2 April 1995. It was the subject of an interim interdict until after the Scottish local elections on 6 April 1995. The BBC accepted that its duty to be impartial raised an arguable case that showing the programme shortly before the election could breach that obligation as the views of other national leaders would not have been so aired before the election. However, Colin Munro is critical of the decision:

One wonders if the Court of Session did not act rather precipitously in banning a single programme of uncertain influence when, apart from other considerations, there was still a period of two clear days in which perceived imbalances might have been redressed. In the result the Courts have cast themselves in the role of censors, and their actions have formed an unattractive precedent.[45]

5.8.7 *The Queen on the Application of Craig v BBC* [2008] EWHC 1369 (Admin)[46]

The case concerns an action for judicial review against the BBC because it changed words in a party election broadcast. This, in the claimant's opinion, amounted to a breach of the principle that 'there must be no improper censorship . . . of what a particular party or individual wishes to say in a pre-election broadcast'.

Alan Craig, London Newham councillor and representative of the Christian Peoples Alliance, standing for the London Mayoral election of 2008, was entitled to a pre-election PPB. It was produced by Quirky Motion and scheduled for airing on 23 April. In the broadcast, Mr Craig wished to say: 'You may know about plans for a separatist Islamic group to build Europe's biggest mosque next to the Olympic site in West Ham. I think it is a bad idea that will bring division. I am glad moderate Muslims support my stance in opposing it.'

The chief political adviser at the BBC contacted Quirky Motion, expressing BBC lawyers' concerns about the words 'separatist' and 'moderate'. It was suggested they might be potentially defamatory and that the former be replaced by 'controversial' and the latter by 'Muslim leaders'. A version of events is that the BBC demanded the change. Mr Justice Collins expressed his surprise (in paragraph 8 of the judgment) 'at the thought that that could be in fact something which was defamatory or that there was anyone who could, in reality, be likely to sue'.

The claimant's lawyer argued, on the basis of Article 10 ECHR that, in such circumstances as this, the words sought to be used be permitted and no media organization has any business 'to try to dictate what a particular party or individual in these

---

[45] cf T Gibbons, *Regulating the Media* (Sweet & Maxwell, 2nd revised edn, 1998) 118; See also, C Munro, 'SNP v BBC' (1996) 146 NLJ 1433 and 'Party Politics and the Broadcasters—Round Three' (1977) 147 NLJ 528.

[46] Unreported; copy of judgment on file with author.

circumstances should say'. The court, however, acknowledged that in principle, as publisher, the BBC would be responsible, and that when dealing with major parties, would obtain an indemnity. Further, the court was satisfied that any media organization is entitled to raise any matter because of concerns that it might be infringing law and/or its own guidelines if it broadcast matter that a third party required it to, as in this case: 'The point is whether there was at the time a belief in good faith that there might be a danger that [the content] was defamatory.' Normally, a claimant in such a case would get a lawyer's letter sent to the BBC, saying that if the BBC did not change its mind the claimant would go before a judge to seek an order that the objections be not maintained. But, in this instance, the requested changes were made and the broadcast was aired on 23 April 2008.

On 24 April 2008, a decision was made to act against ITV, which had obtained even more changes ('You may know about controversial plans by an Islamic group to build Europe's largest mosque next to the Olympic site in West Ham. I think it is a bad idea and I'm glad some Muslim leaders support my stance in opposing it.')

The BBC was ultimately challenged in the instant case on the basis that there might have been 'considerable difficulties in persuading the court that ITV was a public body and thus amenable to judicial review'. Collins J had no doubt that 'nowadays it would be unlikely that the BBC would be able to persuade a court that it was not a public body for the purposes of judicial review'.

The remedy sought in the instant case—to broadcast on the news on the night of the hearing the content before the amendments had been made—was said by the court to be 'inappropriate', quite apart from the point about breaking the embargo on publishing pre-election broadcasts the day before the poll. And, if such a remedy had been granted, 'other candidates might have something to say if it was felt that extra publicity is being given in the circumstances to a particular candidate'.

The judge was clear that in all the circumstances, there was no claim that could be pursued in this case. The matter was not about the media's views: 'It is about what they are required to publish at the instance of another party.'

In essence, this case raises the same issue as that of *ProLife Alliance*, related to the balance between allowing election broadcasts to be transmitted unfettered in their content (text or images) and the right/duty of the broadcaster to ensure that content does not breach general obligations applicable to PEBs as well.

5.9 REGULATORS' DECISIONS

5.9.1 Jason Donovan and Invicta FM

Jason Donovan made the following comment about the (then) forthcoming London Mayoral election: 'It's time for a change. It's definitely time for a change. Boris Johnson. I have to say it. That's my political message.' A listener to Invicta FM objected.[47]

---

[47] 'Sunday Night with Jason Donovan', Invicta FM and 36 other radio stations owned by GCap, 27 April 2008, Broadcast Bulletin Issue number 113–07|07|08, at <http://www.ofcom.org.uk/tv/obb/prog_cb/obb113> (last accessed 8 March 2009).

Ofcom determined that the matter engaged Rule 6.1 of the Broadcast Code, which states that the rules in Section Five of the Code, specifically concerning due impartiality, apply to coverage of elections. Rules concerning material broadcast at or around the time of elections are applicable during the official election period up to the election ballot. In this case, the London Mayoral elections were held on 1 May 2008, and the official election period with respect this ballot began on 18 March 2008.

Ofcom considered Donovan's remarks a very serious breach of the Code. A presenter, albeit one relatively new to the role, had been allowed to use, or had used, his programme to promote an unchallenged political message in favour of a candidate for the 2008 London Mayoral elections. It is, said Ofcom, the responsibility of the licensee to ensure that all those involved in programming are familiar with, and adhere to, the requirements of the Code.

However, Ofcom decided not to take any further regulatory action, finding *in casu* that:

- Jason Donovan's comment about Boris Johnson was isolated;
- it was a message of general political support rather than actively encouraging listeners to vote for Boris Johnson;
- GCap had recognized that the content of this programme had clearly breached the Code and had taken subsequent measures not only to strengthen and improve compliance in the future, but also to broadcast an on-air apology.

5.9.2 James Whale and TalkSPORT

Ofcom imposed a statutory sanction on TalkSPORT Ltd for infringing Rule 6.1 of the Code (due impartiality in coverage of elections and referendums). Ofcom found that, during an edition of 'The James Whale Show' (20 March 2008), Mr Whale had 'directly encouraged listeners to vote for Boris Johnson in the upcoming London mayoral elections and criticised Ken Livingston'. Ofcom imposed a fine of £20,000 (a sum payable to HM Paymaster General). TalkSPORT was also directed to broadcast a statement of Ofcom's findings, agreed with the regulator, on one occasion. Ofcom judged the level of the fine as not so high that it would have imposed 'an inappropriate and restricting effect on live discussion and phone-in programmes on TalkSPORT and similar channels, hosted by presenters with controversial and outspoken views'.[48]

5.9.3 George Lamb and the BBC

The BBC's Guidelines on due impartiality were infringed by BBC 6 music presenter George Lamb, after he told listeners, regarding the London Mayoral elections, that he would vote for 'the candidate with blond hair', on 1 May—the day of the election. Six listeners complained to the BBC Complaints Unit. The Guidelines state that there

---

[48] See, <http://www.ofcom.org.uk/tv/obb/ocsc_adjud/TalkSPORT.pdf> (last accessed 8 March 2009).

should be impartiality and fairness in reporting election campaigns and that content producers must take responsibility for achieving due accuracy and impartiality in their own output. The BBC issued a warning to Mr Lamb.[49]

5.9.4 Channel S

Ofcom fined Channel S World Limited, Channel S Plus Limited and Channel S Global Limited £40,000 for breaching the TV Advertising Code by repeatedly broadcasting a political advertisement. Under the Communications Act 2003, political advertising is prohibited (see section 5.11.2 below). During April 2008, the Channels broadcast, on forty-four occasions, an advertisement that called on electors to vote for Liberal Democratic candidates in the London mayoral and London Assembly elections held on 1 May 2008. The broadcasts infringed Section 4(a) and (b) of the TV Advertising Code (which prohibits advertisements by or on behalf of any body whose objects are of a political nature, and prohibits advertisements that are directed towards a political end). Ofcom considered this to be 'a very serious breach of the Code and a flagrant breach of the statutory ban on political advertising'. The Channels were also ordered to broadcast a statement of Ofcom's findings, twice on each channel.[50]

5.10 BODIES REGULATING ELECTION BROADCASTING

In this section, the role and/or input of various UK bodies regulating broadcasting and elections are described: principally, the Broadcasters' Liaison Group (BLG), but also the BBC Trust; Ofcom; the Department for Culture, Media and Sport (DCMS); and the Electoral Commission.

5.10.1 Broadcasters' Liaison Group [51]

The BLG was established in 1997. It is composed of representatives from each of the broadcasters (but not radio) who make airtime available to registered political parties, namely the BBC, ITV, STV, UTV, Channel 4, Five, Sky, and S4C. Ofcom and the Electoral Commission attend as observers. A main purpose is to coordinate and har-monize the criteria for allocating PPBs, PEBs, Budget and ministerial broadcasts which, in principle, are at the disposal of each broadcaster. It is chaired by the BBC's Chief Adviser, Politics. The BLG considers as the 'main political parties', the Conservatives, Labour, and the Liberal Democrats. In Scotland, the SNP is also

---

[49] See '6Music's Lamb warned over Boris Gaffe', at <http://www.guardian.co.uk/media/2008/may/13/bbc.radio1> (last accessed 8 March 2009).

[50] See <http://www.ofcom.org.uk/tv/obb/ocsc_adjud/channel_s.pdf> (last accessed 8 March 2009).

[51] See <http://www.broadcastersliaisongroup.org.uk/index.htmll> (last accessed 8 March 2009).

included as is Plaid Cymru in Wales. In Northern Ireland, the main political parties are considered to be the DUP, Sinn Fein, the SDLP, and the Ulster Unionists.

The BLG has elaborated a set of 'Production Guidelines', which are designed to cover compliance issues and the political 'rules' to be observed by all parties. It also prescribes practical and technical matters such as format for the broadcasts: 'Broadcasts should be delivered on digi-beta tapes in widescreen format (16x9 full height anamorphic). The sound can be in mono or stereo. Two digi-beta tapes should be delivered together with two VHS copies. 'Broadcasts can be one of three lengths, 2'40", 3'40" or 4'40". The Broadcasters must be informed of the duration selection a minimum of 2 weeks in advance of the broadcast date'. Two other matters are when to deliver.[52]

The BLG also sets out its approach to Broadcast Allocations and Qualification Criteria.[53]

Finally, in the interests of transparency, it publishes minutes of its meetings, from 2005 to 2007. The website notes that, at the time of writing, the last meeting took place on 12 January 2009.[54]

5.10.2 The BBC Trust

The BBC Trust retains regulatory responsibility in relation to PPBs. One of its duties is to approve proposed election guidelines for each election. The BBC was required, by a 2003 amendment to section 93 of the Representation of the People Act 1983, to draw up a code of practice for each election, detailing the BBC's proposals for covering the election with due impartiality and appropriate balance between candidates. The guidelines are updated from previous (equivalent) elections to ensure increased consistency across the UK and to respond to developments such as interactivity. At its 2007 meeting, the Chair of the Editorial Standards Committee (ESC) noted the ESC had reviewed the guidelines in detail and was satisfied they covered all necessary areas. The Trust discussed the implementation of the election guidelines, and approved the guidelines.[55] Other parts of the BBC may be involved too, in particular as regards other nations, for example the Audience Council for Scotland and Head of Programmes and Services have discussed recent output, notably coverage of the Scottish parliament and council elections. Council members felt the quality of

---

[52] Note that the requirements for programmes delivered in Scotland are different to those delivered to London, see, generally <http://www.bbc.co.uk/guidelines/dq/contents/television.shtml> (last accessed 8 March 2009).

[53] See <http://www.broadcastersliaisongroup.org.uk/allocations.html> and < http://www.broadcasters-liaisongroup.org.uk/criteria.html > (last accessed 8 March 2009).

[54] See <http://www.broadcastersliaisongroup.org.uk/meetings.html> and <http://www.broadcasters-liaisongroup.org.uk/index.html> (last accessed 8 March).

[55] See <http://www.bbc.co.uk/bbctrust/assets/files/pdf/about/minutes/21_Mar07.txt>, (last accessed 8 March 2009); see, for the 2005 Guidelines <http://news.bbc.co.uk/newswatch/ifs/hi/newsid_4370000/newsid_4371200/4371227.stm> (last accessed 8 March 2009).

election programming was high and noted that presenters had coped well with the 'unexpected challenges'.[56]

5.10.3 Ofcom Election Committee

The Election Committee meets, as and when required.[57] It is chaired by the Chair of Ofcom's Content Board and is composed of up to five members drawn from the Ofcom Board, the Content Board, and/or Ofcom colleagues, as determined by the Chair of the Committee (subject to quorum requirements). Its duties are:

• to consider and adjudicate on complaints received with regard to the allocation by broadcasters of party election broadcasts, the scheduling of party election broadcasts, or their duration;

• to consider and adjudicate on complaints received in relation to due impartiality during an election period where the Content and Standards Group considers that a substantive issue is raised and where the complaint, if upheld, might require redress before the election; and

• other matters as directed by the Ofcom Board.

Practically speaking, it is not clear that the Election Committee does much. A response to the author, following a freedom of information request for information about its activities, stated that the Election Committee was dormant but would be activated in the event of an election. The Election Committee has met once—on 3 March 2005—but it seems as if nothing about this meeting has been published on the Ofcom website.

5.10.4 Department of Culture, Media and Sport

In 2004, the DCMS launched a public consultation on proposed changes to modernize the Party Political Broadcasting system. The consultation aimed to ensure that the current system was right for the multi-channel age (and was part of a wider cross-Government drive to engage voters more fully with the political process). It was set up in response to the Electoral Commission's 2003 report 'Voting for Change', as well as an earlier report on Party Political Broadcasting. The consultation sought views on the Commission's recommendations, as well as alternative ways of better engaging the viewing and listening public.[58]

---

[56] See <http://www.bbc.co.uk/scotland/aboutus/acs/content/meetings/minutes.shtml?minutes=minutes20070601> (last accessed 8 March 2009).
[57] See <http://www.ofcom.org.uk/about/csg/election_cmmt> (last accessed 8 March 2009).
[58] See, for the Consultation Paper <http://www.culture.gov.uk/images/consultations/Partypoliticalconsultation.pdf> (last accessed 8 March 2009) and the responses at <http://www.culture.gov.uk/ppb_responses/default.htm> (last accessed 8 March 2009).

5.10.5 Electoral Commission

Under the Political Parties, Elections and Referendums Act 2000, broadcasting authorities must have regard to any views of the Electoral Commission, but it is for each
broadcasting authority to adopt a code of practice with respect to the participation
of candidates at a parliamentary or local government election. Accordingly, the
Electoral Commission is not responsible for regulating media coverage at elections/
referenda and party political broadcasts.

The Electoral Commission is independent of government and aims to ensure
openness and transparency in the financial affairs of Britain's political parties, and
to increase public confidence and participation in the democratic process. The Electoral
Commission issued a discussion paper in December 2001 that invited comments on
a range of issues relating to arrangements for PPBs, their effectiveness, the media
environment, and arrangements in other countries. The Commission consulted political parties, broadcasting authorities, broadcasters, and other stakeholders in conducting this review. The final report was submitted to the Secretary of State for Culture,
Media and Sport. The Commission has no powers to implement any recommendations
the report makes.

In 2003, as noted in section 5.6.2 above, following its consultation, the Electoral
Commission published its report and recommendations for improvements to PPB
arrangements.[59] It backed the continuation of the broadcasts as well as the ban on paid
political advertising in the broadcast media. PPBs, the report says, offer political
parties their only opportunity to present an unmediated broadcast message directly to
the electorate. Surveys show that, at election time, they are among the most effective
direct campaigning tools available to parties. However, the Commission argued that
the current system for allocating broadcasts needed to be overhauled and made more
robust and transparent. It also recommended that it should be more clearly defined in
law to strengthen the argument for sustaining the ban on paid political advertising.
As part of the new system, the Commission recommended that all the broadcasters
who carry PPBs should come within a single system under the authority of the new
communications regulator, Ofcom.

Recognizing the changing media environment, the report also urged that the system
should be modernized to take account of the growth of non-terrestrial channels, to
ensure that PPBs reach as broad an audience as possible. Any TV or radio channel with
a significant audience share should be required to air the broadcasts. The Commission
stated that the qualification for election broadcasts should continue to be based on the
number of candidates put forward and the number of broadcasts should be related to
proven electoral support. However, it did propose that greater flexibility should be
provided to parties on the length of broadcasts.

---

[59] See n 32 above.

5.11 POLITICAL ADVERTISING

In its report, 'Political Communication on Television: Matters for debate', the European Platform of Regulatory Authorities (EPRA) noted that political parties paying for advertisements in the form of short broadcasts is 'common practice in the US . . . [but] is statutorily forbidden in most of the European countries'.[60] Counter-examples given are Italy and Greece, under certain conditions.

The rationale is that, otherwise, 'rich or well-established parties would be able to afford significantly more advertising time than new or minority parties'. Counter-arguments are that the prohibition is an unwarranted infringement of the right to freedom of expression (argued by Bulgaria, Macedonia, Hungary, Poland, and Ukraine); that new organizations and candidates could become better known more quickly if they were able to purchase such publicity; and that the non-discrimination point is answered by regulating matters such as duration, frequency, and/or rates charged.

The definition of a 'political advertisement' is not straightforward. Emmanuelle Machet notes: 'The term political advertising is widely used in practice and in various publications. However, it is not always clear what is meant by this term.'[61] Paid-for political advertisements are clearly distinguishable from free PPBs. But, a key question is: are they 'advertisements' at all (for example for the purposes of the AVMS Directive)? Or are they, since they are not aimed at persuading people to purchase goods or services, *sui generis*, being, in reality, 'political propaganda'?

One small step for clarity at least is to differentiate between party political, political, and advocacy/issue advertising:

In many (Western) European countries, the most burning topic at present seems to be 'issue advertising', i.e. messages with a political end emanating from organizations which are not political parties, such as interest or societal groups. Further to the ECHR ruling, a few countries have restricted the scope of the ban of political advertising and now allow such spots—outside election periods. Are the current total bans (including issue advertising) justified in a 'relevant and sufficient manner' so that they would survive scrutiny under the ECHR? Do they constitute a disproportionate restriction on the freedom of expression? [62]

---

[60] See EPRA/2000/02; see also, 'Political advertising: case studies and monitoring' (EPRA/2006/02).

[61] See 'Political advertising: case studies and monitoring', Annex 1: Some definitions of Political Advertising; see also, the Lords debate seeking to legalize political (ie not party political) advertisements—the so-called 'Amnesty amendment', at <http://www.publications.parliament.uk/pa/ld199596/ldhansrd/vo960307/text/60307-20.htm> (last accessed 8 March 2009).

[62] ibid. Andrew Scott has written robustly on the 'legality of the broadcasting prohibition on "advocacy advertising"—the use of advertising space to communicate social, political and moral arguments to a wider public—in the light of the growing jurisprudence on the freedom of political expression'. He concludes that 'the purported justifications sit ill against existing legal rulings, and evidence a poor understanding of the critical sophistication of the public as a broadcasting audience' and he suggests that 'a continuation of the prohibition would be unlawful'; see A Scott, 'A Monstrous and Unjustifiable Infringement: Political Expression and the Broadcasting Ban on Advocacy Advertising' (2003) 66(2) MLR 224.

5.11.1 Regional framework: Council of Europe

Because there is no uniformity across European countries, the Council of Europe has not come down on one side or other of the debate. The 2007 Recommendation on media and election coverage, regarding paid political advertising, states:

> In member states where political parties and candidates are permitted to buy advertising space for election purposes, regulatory frameworks should ensure that all contending parties have the possibility of buying advertising space on and according to equal conditions and rates of payment. Member states may consider introducing a provision in their regulatory frameworks to limit the amount of political advertising space and time which a given party or candidate can purchase. Regular presenters of news and current affairs programmes should not take part in paid political advertising.

The Explanatory Memorandum to Recommendation Rec (99) 15, acknowledges that:

> Paid political advertising in the broadcast media has traditionally been prohibited in many Council of Europe member States, whilst it has been accepted in others. One of its major advantages is the opportunity which it provides for all political forces to widely disseminate their messages/programmes. On the other hand, it may give an unfair advantage to those parties or candidates who can purchase important amounts of airtime.

The Recommendation 'does not take a stance on whether this practice should be accepted or not, and simply limits itself to saying that if paid advertising is allowed it should be subject to some minimum rules.' The two main ones are (1) that equal treatment (in terms of access and rates) be given to all parties requesting airtime; and (2) that the public be made aware that the message has been paid for. In addition, setting limits on the amount of paid advertising that can be purchased by a single party should also be considered. Such decisions should be taken at the national level.

5.11.1.1 Vgt Verein gegen Tierfabriken v Switzerland

In *Vgt Verein gegen Tierfabriken v Switzerland* (at the first of two hearings), the European Court of Human Rights (ECtHR) stated that it 'cannot exclude that a prohibition of political advertising may be compatible with the requirements of Article 10 of the Convention in certain situations', but that any interference has to be 'necessary in a democratic society', which means that there has to be a 'pressing social need'.[63]

---

[63] Application No 24699/94: Final Judgment 28 September 2001. The Court's press release describing the case summarizes it as follows: 'The applicant, Verein Gegen Tierfabriken Schweiz (VGT), is a Swiss-registered animal-protection association which campaigns against experiments on animals and battery farming. In response to various advertisements produced by the meat industry, it made a television commercial which showed a noisy hall with pigs in small pens and compared the conditions to those in concentration camps. Permission to broadcast the commercial was refused on 24 January 1994 by the Commercial Television Company (*AG für das Werbefernsehen*—now Publisuisse S.A.) and at final instance by the Federal Court, which dismissed an administrative-law appeal by the applicant association on 20 August 1997. The applicant association lodged an initial application (no. 24699/94) with the European Court of Human Rights, which, in its Chamber judgment of 28 June 2001, held that the Swiss

The EPRA's analysis of the case[64] highlights the following points. With regard to the *concept of political advertising*, the Court observed that the commercial could be regarded as 'political', as it reflected controversial opinions pertaining to modern society in general, lying at the heart of various political debates—rather than inciting the public to purchase a particular product. Regarding the *impact of the different regulatory treatment of political advertising for broadcasting and the press*: Further to Article 10(2), the exercise of the right to freedom of expression may be subject to restrictions if several conditions are met. In particular, the interference with the rights must be prescribed by law and *necessary in a democratic society*. This implies that the existence of a 'pressing social need' is necessary to refuse to broadcast the commercial. The Court found that a prohibition of political advertising, which applied only to certain media (ie to broadcasting but not to the press), did not appear to be a particularly pressing need.

The ECtHR did not exclude that a prohibition of 'political advertising' may be compatible with the requirements of Article 10 in certain situations. Nevertheless, the interference in the freedom of expression must be justified in a 'relevant and sufficient manner': in the Court's opinion, the domestic authorities had not justified the interference in VgT's freedom of expression in a 'relevant and sufficient' manner. It had not been argued that VgT itself constituted a powerful financial group which, with its proposed commercial, sought to endanger the independence of the broadcaster, to unduly influence public opinion, or to endanger the equality of opportunity between the different forces of society. The Court considered that, rather than abusing a competitive advantage, the association intended only to participate in an ongoing general debate on animal protection.

5.11.1.2 TV Vest AS and Rogaland Pensjonistparti v Norway

A new element has been injected into the debate by the December 2008 decision, *TV Vest AS and Rogaland Pensjonistparti v Norway*.[65] The Court considered whether a general ban was necessary in a democratic society. It concluded that all the supportive arguments in Norway, as elsewhere, safeguarding quality of political debate,

authorities' refusal to broadcast the commercial in question was in violation of Article 10 (freedom of expression) of the European Convention on Human Rights. On 1 December 2001, on the basis of the Court's judgment, the applicant association applied to the Federal Court for revision of the final domestic judgment prohibiting the commercial from being broadcast. On 29 April 2002 the Federal Court refused that request. The Committee of Ministers of the Council of Europe—which is responsible for supervising execution of the Court's judgments—was not informed that the Federal Court had refused the request for revision and accordingly ended its examination of the applicant association's initial application (no. 24699/94) by adopting a resolution in July 2003. However, the resolution noted the possibility of lodging a request for revision with the Federal Court. In July 2002 the applicant association lodged a second application (no. 32772/02) with the Court, complaining about the continued prohibition on broadcasting the television commercial in question. In its Chamber judgment of 4 October 2007 in that case, the Court held, by five votes to two, that there had been a violation of Article 10.'

[64] See EPRA/2002/09.

[65] See <http://cmiskp.echr.coe.int/tkp197/view.asp?action=html&documentId=844220&portal=hbkm &source=externalbydocnumber&table=F69A27FD8FB86142BF01C1166DEA398649> (last accessed 8 March 2009).

promoting pluralism, preventing financially powerful political groups buying airtime, pushing up election campaign costs, etc, were 'relevant but not sufficient' to justify such a prohibition. The Court looked at the effect of a ban and concluded that it was:

. . . not persuaded that the ban had the desired effect. In contrast to the major political parties, which were given a large amount of attention in the edited television coverage, the Pensioners Party was hardly mentioned. Therefore, paid advertising on television became the only way for the Pensioners Party to get its message across to the public through that type of medium. By being denied this possibility under the law, the Pensioners Party's position was at a disadvantage, compared to that of major parties which had obtained edited broadcasting coverage that could not be offset by the possibility available to it to use other but less potent media.

Further, the Court asserted that:

. . . the fact that the audio-visual media has a more immediate and powerful effect than other media . . . albeit an important consideration in the assessment of proportionality . . . could not justify the disputed prohibition and fine imposed in respect of the broadcasting of the political advertising at issue . . .

However, cautioning against jumping to the conclusion that states such as the UK will have to amend their law, Dirk Voorhoof[66] suggests that the decision was influenced by Norway's lack of a 'system of fair, equal and transparent access to free political broadcasts', as in the UK or in Belgium and some other states upholding a ban on paid political advertisements on TV. Further, the Court made it clear that 'if a general prohibition is applied in a way which still gives some possibilities of access to relevant "political" advertising to small groups or parties, or to NGOs or other organisations who otherwise are not sufficiently heard in society, there might be no violation of Article 10 of the Convention'.

The upshot of the case is, arguably, that a 'rigorous, strict application of a blanket ban on political advertising on television (and other audiovisual media services) however seems no longer in accordance with Article 10 of the European Convention'.

5.11.2 The prohibition in the UK[67]

The current statutory basis for the prohibition is to be found in sections 319(1) and (2)(g) and 321(2) and (3) of the Communications Act 2003, as well as the Committee

---

[66] See 'Blanket ban on political advertising on television violates Article 10 of the European Convention on Human Rights', at <http://www.psw.ugent.be/Cms_global/uploads/publicaties/dv/05recente_publicaties/TVVest.DV.EN.12.12.doc> (last accessed 8 March 2009).

[67] For examples of how this issue is dealt with in other jurisdictions, see the section on 'Case Studies in Political advertising: case studies and monitoring' in EPRA/2006/02; see also for other countries experiences—India: <http://www.indianexpress.com/news/decks-cleared-for-political-ads-on-air/389150> (last accessed 8 March 2009); Malta: <http://merlin.obs.coe.int/iris/2007/2/article28.en.html> (last accessed 8 March 2009); Norway: <http://merlin.obs.coe.int/iris/2005/7/article26.en.html> (last accessed 8 March 2009); Ireland: <http://merlin.obs.coe.int/iris/2008/5/article22.en.html and http://www.amnesty.ie/amnesty/live/irish/news-events/article.asp?id=25799&page=2156> (both last accessed 8 March); Cyprus: <http://merlin.obs.coe.int/iris/2005/10/article12.en.html> (last accessed 8 March 2009).

of Advertising Practice (Broadcast) Television Advertising Standards Code, Section 4.[68] It is a fact of some interest that the then Secretary of State for Culture, Media and Sport, Tessa Jowell, made the following declaration when introducing the Bill: 'Human Rights Act 1998: I am unable (but only because of clause 309) to make a statement that, in my view, the provisions of the Communications Bill are compatible with the Convention rights. However, the Government nevertheless wishes the House to proceed with the Bill.'[69]

The CAP(B) Television Advertising Code explains:

The term 'political' here is used in a wider sense than 'party political'. The rule prevents, for example, issue campaigning for the purpose of influencing legislation or executive action by legislatures either at home or abroad. Where there is a risk that advertising could breach this rule, prospective advertisers should seek guidance from licensees before developing specific proposals.

Notes to the Code, Section 4, interpret some of the provisions. Thus, the overall purpose is said to be 'to prevent well-funded organisations from using the power of television advertising to distort the balance of political debate'. Any public service advertisement by or on behalf of a government department having 'any relation to any industrial dispute' is exempt from the prohibition.

In its 2003 review of PPBs, the Electoral Commission considered whether the ban on paid political advertising should continue and concluded that it should: 'The case for retaining the ban on paid advertising is persuasive. The ban is in the interests of the electorate and therefore the public interest. It is also in the interests of political

---

[68] Communications Act 2003, s 319 states: '(1) It shall be the duty of OFCOM to set, and from time to time to review and revise, such standards for the content of programmes to be included in television and radio services as appear to them best calculated to secure the standards objectives. (2) The standards objectives are . . . (g) that advertising that contravenes the prohibition on political advertising set out in section 321(2) is not included in television or radio services'; s 321 states: '(2) For the purposes of section 319(2)(g) an advertisement contravenes the prohibition on political advertising if it is—(a) an advertisement which is inserted by or on behalf of a body whose objects are wholly or mainly of a political nature; (b) an advertisement which is directed towards a political end; or (c) an advertisement which has a connection with an industrial dispute. (3) For the purposes of this section objects of a political nature and political ends include each of the following—(a) influencing the outcome of elections or referendums, whether in the United Kingdom or elsewhere; (b) bringing about changes of the law in the whole or a part of the United Kingdom or elsewhere, or otherwise influencing the legislative process in any country or territory; (c) influencing the policies or decisions of local, regional or national governments, either in the United Kingdom or elsewhere; (d) influencing the policies or decisions of persons on whom public functions are conferred by or under the law of the United Kingdom or of a country or territory outside the United Kingdom; (e) influencing the policies or decisions of persons on whom functions are conferred by or under international agreements; (f) influencing public opinion on a matter which, in the United Kingdom, is a matter of public controversy; (g) promoting the interests of a party or other group of persons organised, in the United Kingdom or elsewhere, for political ends.' The CAP(B) Television Advertising Standards Code, Section 4 states that: 'No advertisement: (a) may be inserted by or on behalf of any body whose objects are wholly or mainly of a political nature. (b) may be directed towards any political end. (c) may have any relation to any industrial dispute (with limited exceptions).'

[69] <http://www.parliament.the-stationery-office.co.uk/pa/cm200203/cmbills/006/03006.i-viii.html> (last accessed 8 March 2009).

parties and broadcasters.' The conclusion was based on the by now familiar reasons: access to such advertising would be restricted to parties and candidates who had access to sufficient financial resources which would also lead to a 'spending race' and a concern that 'such spending could not realistically be accommodated within the current limits on campaign expenditure.' If small(er) parties were to be excluded on cost grounds, 'the electorate would receive information only from a very small number of political parties which could afford to advertise'. Further, broadcasters' duty to maintain balance ('due impartiality is preserved on the part of the person providing the service as respects matters of political or industrial controversy or relating to current public policy', section 6(1)(c) of the Broadcasting Act 1990 for television and section 90(3)(a) for national radio) would be hard to maintain. Whilst sympathetic to the case for radio advertising, as basically less costly, the Electoral Commission still felt 'that the case for retaining the ban on political advertising in broadcast media would be more difficult to sustain if certain media were excluded from the ban'.

However, the Electoral Commission also said that: 'Clause 309 re-enacts the ban on paid political advertising. While we consider that the case for retaining the ban on paid political advertising is persuasive, we share the government's concern that this ban might be incompatible with human rights law.'

5.11.2.1 *UK decisions: courts and regulators*

There have been several decisions in the UK, including well-documented cases concerning Animal Defenders International (ADI), Amnesty International (British Section), and the Make Poverty History campaign.[70]

(a) *Animal Defenders International* Recently, the House of Lords considered the appeal by ADI against the refusal to transmit its 'My mate's a primate' advertisements.[71] The present author has commented on the case:[72]

On 12 March 2008, the House of Lords announced its decision, upholding the view of the Broadcast Advertising Clearance Centre (now 'Clearcast'), that an advertisement submitted on behalf of Animal Defenders International for broadcast clearance would infringe Section 321(2) of the Communications Act 2003, i.e. the prohibition on political advertising. There was no disagreement that the content of the advertisement was inoffensive. It was intended as part of a campaign, entitled "My Mate's a Primate", which sought to draw the public's attention to the exploitative (in ADI's eyes) use of primates by humans, coupled with the threat to their survival. In part, it was a riposte to the use of a chimpanzee in a Pepsi Cola advertisement.

---

[70] See, for the Amnesty case, 'R v Radio Authority, ex.p Bull and Anor', at <http://www.bailii.org/ew/cases/EWCA/Civ/1996/1230.html> (last accessed 8 March 2009) and for the MPH decision < http://www.ofcom.org.uk/tv/obb/prog_cb/pcb52/issue43a.pdf#xml> (last accessed 8 March 2009). In both, the general prohibition was judged to apply to their attempt to purchase airtime (on radio as well as television) to publicize messages—despite the acknowledged worthiness and/or morality of the messages' substance.

[71] See *R (On The Application of Animal Defenders International) v Secretary of State For Culture, Media and Sport (Respondent)*, at <http://www.publications.parliament.uk/pa/ld200708/ldjudgmt/jd080312/animal-1.htm> (last accessed 8 March 2009).

[72] See <http://merlin.obs.coe.int/iris/2008/5/article16.en.html> (last accessed 8 March 2009).

In enacting Section 321(2), the UK Parliament and its Joint Committee on Human Rights had regard to the decision of the European Court of Human Rights in *VgT Verein gegen Tierfabriken v Switzerland* (2001). Both bodies were aware that the UK legislation might fall foul of that case. However, the impracticality of a more limited ban, in addition to the fear, noted as well in VgT, of 'the annexation of the democratic process by the rich and powerful' persuaded the Government and Parliament that the law would be compatible with the Convention.

Essentially, the House of Lords decided to give more weight to the argument that '[T]he rights of others which a restriction on the exercise of the right to free expression may properly be designed to protect must . . . include a right to be protected against the potential mischief of partial political advertising' than was accorded to it by the European Court of Human Rights. Furthermore, the House of Lords stated that there is a pressing social need for such a ban on television and radio (as compared to the press, cinema, etc), because of the ' . . . greater immediacy and impact of television and radio advertising.' In addition, the lack of a European consensus on the matter led the House of Lords to accept that the United Kingdom had a wide margin of appreciation in this matter.

It should be noted that, although the House of Lords distinguished *VgT Verein gegen Tierfabriken v Switzerland* from the instant case, this was on the basis of the 2001 decision. On 4 October 2007, a second decision of the European Court of Human Rights on the same matter was published, again finding that the decision of the Swiss Federal Court constituted an infringement of VgT's Article 10 rights.

Developments at the time of writing include that: (1) on 19 December 2007, the Swiss government requested that the case be referred to the Grand Chamber and the request was accepted on 31 March 2008; and (2) ADI has decided to ask the Strasbourg Court to review its claim against the UK's ban on political advertising; and (3) there will be reverberations after the decision in *TV Vest AS and Rogaland Pensjonistparti v Norway*.

(b) *RSPCA* In 2001, the Broadcast Advertising Clearance Centre (BACC, now Clearcast, see section 5.11.1.2 above) refused to pass an RSPCA advertising campaign aimed at improving the production conditions of broiler chickens for eating: 'The charity said the Broadcasting Advertising Clearance Centre's decision was "extra-ordinary" and claimed a 30 second clip comparing the growth rate of a broiler over six weeks with that of an egg-laying hen had been refused "on the basis it was controversial and seen to attack the [poultry] industry".'[73]

The point made earlier in this chapter about the availability of alternative media platforms to circumvent prohibitions on specific ones is pertinent here. But, the point is not only relevant regarding newer technologies outwitting old-fashioned legislation. For example, in the *RSPCA* case, as the BACC (as was) only has jurisdiction over broadcast television, the organization said that the 'campaign will be featured in newspapers and cinemas' albeit, in the latter, 'it can only be shown in programmes with

---

[73] See, 'Television ban on "political" ad to improve poultry rearing', at <http://www.guardian.co.uk/media/2001/nov/23/advertising.broadcasting> (last accessed 8 March 2009).

15 or 18 certificate films'.[74]

(c) *Shelter* In 2007, Shelter was told that an advertisement it wanted to have broadcast on radio about council housing waiting lists was refused clearance by the Radio Advertising Clearance Centre (RACC). The content was found to be 'too political' and also it was deemed to 'denigrate' local authorities. The charity's website points out that the RACC has no jurisdiction over the internet—and it offers a link to listen to the advertisement on that platform.[75]

(d) *ITV 1 (Granada)* In 2008, Ofcom was asked to adjudicate on seven complaints against ITV 1 (Granada) transmitting a local poll advertisement[76] which had been passed by Clearcast. It publicized a local opinion poll on a proposed transport plan for the area, including a congestion charge. The advertisement featured a presenter in a studio, referring to the poll and summarizing the consequences of 'yes' and 'no' outcomes. During the advertisement there was a call to action to vote and the name and logo: Greater Manchester Future Transport (GMFT), and GMFT's website address were all prominently displayed.

Interestingly, some of the finding is taken up with describing the content of the website of one of the groups making up the body which was the subject of the complaint in order to assess the degree of political orientation and focus of the advertiser.

---

[74] Indeed, in the context of prohibitions on religious advertisements, the ECtHR said in *Murphy v Ireland*, *inter alia*, that because the claimant had alternative means of advertising the meeting, eg by taking out newspaper ads, the refusal to broadcast could be upheld, see <http://www.echr.coe.int/eng/Press/2003/july/JudgmentMurphyvIreland10July2003.htm> (last accessed 8 March 2009).

[75] See, 'Banned radio ads spark row', at <http://england.shelter.org.uk/news/previous_years/2007/july_2007/banned_radio_ads_spark_row> (last accessed 8 March 2009); see also Clearcast's Guidance, Section 4.11.1 Advertisements and Section 4.11.2. Section 4.11.1 states that: 'Clearcast will seek to investigate the activities of organizations that appear prima facie to be involved in political activity in order to establish whether the political activity is the main or whole extent of their activity. A degree of involvement will not necessarily debar an organization from advertising. There is some precedent that 75% may be an appropriate threshold in this connection but each case will be considered on its merits', at<http://www.clearcast.co.uk/clearcast/notes_of_guidance/4.%20Unacceptable%20Products#4.11%20Political%20and%20Controversial%20Issues> (last accessed 8 March 2009). The Radio Advertisement Clearance Centre (RACC) has parallel provisons, thus: 'Advertisements by central Government (eg COI) and by councils are only acceptable where they consist of factual information about Government's/councils' executive (rather than political) functions within existing legislation. Copy must be neutral in content, tone and style. Whilst 'Vote for change in local Government' is unacceptable, "*Call X to find out how you can register your vote in the local elections*" is acceptable.' Or 'RACC can only accept campaigns that consist of neutral, impartial information and do not "sell" a government policy, show any partiality or make the facts in the copy "promotional" for government; neutral, non-partisan information about a current/decided policy would be acceptable, but references to future policy would probably be unacceptable; RACC will need to take into consideration the production of the draft copy and may need to hear "dummy" ads; RACC may need to "time limit" some campaigns to ensure that clearances concerning matters which are not politically controversial at clearance stage are not broadcast if they have since become politically controversial matters', <http://www.racc.co.uk/racc/showContent.aspx?pubid=18> (last accessed 8 March 2009).

[76] See, 'ITV1 (Granada) in breach of political advertising rules', at <http://www.ofcom.org.uk/media/features/manadvert> (last accessed 8 March 2009).

Ofcom found that the advertisement was in breach of Section 4 of the CAP(B) Television Advertising Code: Section 4(b) which prohibits advertisements that may be directed towards a political end and Section 4(d) which prohibits advertisements that show partiality as respects matters of political or industrial controversy or relating to current public policy.

5.11.2.2 *Clearances*

The process of obtaining pre-transmission clearance for advertisements is, perhaps, not as well known as it should be. In fairness, the RACC and Clearcast websites have become more informative of late. However, it is important to stress the point, made by Ofcom in a recent adjudication, that the ultimate responsibility rests with the licensee, whatever the judgment of the pre-clearance bodies:

Ofcom noted that in line with the normal process for placing an advertisement on ITV, the advertiser had sought, and obtained, clearance from Clearcast. Further, Clearcast had recognised in this case the particular need for the advertisement to meet the requirements of Section 4 of the TV Advertising Code. Ofcom takes this opportunity to remind licensees and advertisers that discharging the licence obligation for pre-transmission scrutiny of advertising (whether through Clearcast or by other means) does not guarantee the compliance of advertising to the advertising codes. The broadcaster itself is obliged under its licence to ensure that any advertising it broadcasts is so compliant.[77]

5.12 CONCLUDING REMARKS

A major focus of this chapter has been the system of PPB and PEBs, now some eighty-plus years old. Another has been political advertisements. Unsurprisingly, the online world poses a significant challenge to both the continuing relevance of the arrangements and rules about PPBs and for political advertising generally.

5.12.1 Internet and newer technologies

As early as 2000, an article appeared on the website of the Moscow Media Law and Policy Centre entitled 'Is the Internet Independent of the Law on Elections?'. At issue was the online publication of exit poll data during elections for the State Duma. Did this infringe the Law on the Mass Media?[78] In the UK, in 2002, it was noted that, despite the legal prohibition, political advertising was entering 'British homes'.[79]

Even earlier—in the late 1990s—in thinking about political parties, the media and advertising, the 1998 Neill Report was seised of the new developments, such as digital broadcasting and the internet:

---

[77] See n 75 above.
[78] See <http://www.medialaw.ru/e_pages/research/commentary4.htm> (last accessed 7 March 2009).
[79] See A Mayer, 'Towards a digital democracy: political advertising in the interactive age', at <http://www.opendemocracy.net/media-digitaltv/article_24.jsp> (last accessed 7 March 2009).

The advent of satellite and cable television and of digital broadcasting means that the current arrangements governing political broadcasting may soon no longer be relevant. The increasing use of the Internet, and the widespread availability of desktop publishing, raise similar kinds of issues. Indeed, the various technologies are increasingly converging to convey electronic information services into people's homes through a variety of sources. We have no doubt that political parties, special interest groups and others who wish to influence the political process will increasingly be seeking ways to use these technologies . . . In addition to its overall duty of keeping election and finding arrangements under review, the Election Commission should be specifically charged with monitoring the working of the current arrangements for the provision of party political and election broadcasts and the effect on political advertising generally of developing communications technologies.[80]

Despite the Neill Committee's charge to the Electoral Commission, the author was notified in an e-mail from it in 2008 that: 'Whilst the Electoral Commission did look at this area in the past, we are currently not conducting any work at this time. The Commission believes that although we may review this process periodically, we are not seeking to drive the policy direction on broadcasting and online party political activity and any input has been completely advisory.'[81]

Another illustration of the current disconnect between traditional legal rules and newer technological realities is the publication, and continuing availability on YouTube,[82] of the '(Uncensored) Christian Choice London Election Broadcast' which had been 'toned down' by the broadcasters prior to transmission of Alan Craig's London Mayoral PEB (see section 5.8.7 above).

5.12.2 PPBs: allocation and transparency

Since the 1990 Broadcasting Act, there has been a statutory footing for PPBs—indeed, there is a duty on public service broadcasters to carry them. Prescribing a general duty to make airtime available is not considerped tantamount to interfering with the principle of broadcaster independence vis-à-vis scheduling and content. As was discussed (see section 5.6.2 above), the system is something of a *quid pro quo* for the long-standing prohibition on political—including party political—broadcasting in the UK. However, is the system, even with the degree of transparency now offered by the Broadcasters' Liaison Group, vulnerable to a Human Rights Act challenge, as being inadequately 'prescribed by law'? Also: 'The system has come under criticism for favouring big parties over smaller, newer ones (which could be said to reflect the political representation on the committee). A different type of criticism is that, with the

---

[80] Fifth Report of the Committee on Standards in Public Life, 'The Funding of Political Parties in the United Kingdom' in *Standards in Public Life* Vol 1: Report at <http://www.archive.official-documents. co.uk/document/cm40/4057/volume-1/volume-1.pdf> (last accessed 7 March 2009).

[81] Election Commission e-mail to the author, 1 August 2008.

[82] See '(Uncensored) Christian Choice London Election Broadcast', at <http://uk.youtube.com/ watch?v=6Lq_2k79QFc > (last accessed 7 March 2009).

proliferation of different types of broadcasting—such as cable and satellite—the system will no longer work.'[83]

The Electoral Commission has also criticized the system of party political broadcasts in the light of the Human Rights Act 1998. Its 2003 publication, 'Party Political Broadcasts: Report and Recommendations', emphasizes the dual/hybrid nature of the UK's regime. It concludes, as regards the ban on political advertisements, that 'we are firmly of the view . . . that the ban is in the public interest in a democratic society'. But this is so only insofar as the UK system 'would survive scrutiny under the ECHR and the HRA, at least if the regime of free and unmediated broadcasts is robust. Any restriction on freedom of expression must be justified under Article 10(2) of the ECHR. Not only must the restriction be defensible in substance, but there is also a requirement that it be "prescribed by law"'. So, the justifiability of the one depends on the other. That means showing that the PPBs system is capable of withstanding a Human Rights Act challenge. But:

> . . . if the regime of free and unmediated broadcasts is to be robust as a counterbalance to the ban on paid political advertising, it should satisfy the same requirement. We doubt whether the existing arrangements for free broadcasts are sufficiently clear, formalised and predictable, as expressed in law, to satisfy this requirement as it has now been elaborated in the Strasbourg case law.

Whilst the Broadcasters' Liaison Group lays a beneficial coordinating role, ' . . . there is a lack of transparency in the way decisions are made by the broadcasters . . . [they] have too much discretion in making their determinations and accordingly there is a lack of predictability regarding the broadcasters' decisions'. The counter-argument (put by the Neill Committee) is that broadcasters should not be ordered to provide time for PPBs.

The Electoral Commission's central recommendation to enhance transparency and predictability is that Ofcom should organize a committee composed of broadcasters but with an independent Chair. Further, whilst the BLG does meet political parties, there is scope for enhancing the transparency of procedures for consultation with parties. Also, the Commission recommends legislation to include criteria to which the regulator should have regard in making rules regarding qualification for PPBs and length and frequency of PPBs. The aim of the Commission's proposals is in effect to retain the broadcasters' flexibility whilst formalizing the current practice—thus, ensuring that PPBs are 'prescribed by law' and are thus immunized against a Human Rights Act challenge. This is because it is necessary in itself and also because having the system of PPBs is bound up with the current prohibition on (party) political advertising.

5.12.3 Political advertising

A final point concerns the general ban on political advertising. Whatever the outcome of ADI's application to Strasbourg, it is worth mentioning the challenge to the ban on

---

[83] See R Carver, 'United Kingdom: Self-Regulation for election broadcasting', at <http://aceproject.org/ero-en/topics/media-and-elections/ukselfregulation> (last accessed 8 March 2009).

non-political party advertising coming from another, non-legal quarter. This is the argument that the ban inhibits the effectiveness of the voluntary sector in the life of the country and has recently been put forward by the influential 'Report of the Advisory Group on Campaigning and the Voluntary Sector', chaired by Baroness Helena Kennedy.

Chapter 3 of the Report concludes that the Communications Act 2003 has a censoring effect on the voluntary sector and the Report makes several Recommendations.[84] These are, in Section 3—Broadcast Law, as follows:

- The Communications Act 2003 currently imposes an unreasonable prohibition on advertising by charities and NGOs. Ofcom and the BACC [sic] should immediately recognise that registered charities are not permitted to have a political purpose and apply a rebuttable presumption that charities are not political bodies.

- The ban in the Communications Act 2003 on all advertising by 'political' organisations should be repealed.

- A new legislative framework should permit in principle non-political advertising by NGOs and charities.

- The definition of political in s.321 (3) b–f of the Communications Act 2003 should be amended so as to permit the broadcast of social advocacy advertisements on radio and television but restrict the broadcast of advertising for political parties.

- A new regulatory framework for broadcast media advertising should be imposed in which any 'political' (excluding party political) advertising by NGOs should state that it contains political content and represents the opinion of the advertiser and should state the source of funding for the advertisement. Consideration should be given to a moratorium on all political and social advocacy advertising in the broadcast media during local and national election periods.

It does seems as if, one way or another, whether as a result of the impact of newer technologies, the Human Rights Act 1998, or political/governmental will, the UK's dual regime of a general prohibition on political advertising and a substantially self-regulatory regime of free and unmediated PPBs may not survive for much longer, at least in its present form.

As a concluding point, and whatever the complexities and complications attending political advertising and broadcasting during or around the time of elections, it is worth bearing in mind the statement of principle (albeit qualified) expressed by Collins J during the case involving Alan Craig and the BBC (see section 5.8.7 above): 'It is of the utmost importance, particularly in the contexts of elections and public opinion, that the right [to freedom of expression] should not be circumscribed in any way which is not in accordance with the law.'

---

[84] See <http://www.bateswells.co.uk/Files/News/CampaigningReport.doc> (last accessed 8 March 2009); see also the point about helping charities to 'better campaign' in 'The Governance of Britain', at <http://www.official-documents.gov.uk/document/cm71/7170/7170.pdf> (last accessed 8 March 2009).

6

INTELLECTUAL PROPERTY AND THE MEDIA

Lindy Golding[1]

6.1 INTRODUCTION

Intellectual property and, in particular, copyright, underpins the media industries' creative output. The media are both creators of copyright material and users of copyright material created by others. This chapter begins with an outline of the key aspects of copyright and then deals in more detail with some issues which most often arise. There are several aspects of copyright which concern only a section of a particular media industry. This chapter does not seek to deal with those aspects, but rather provide an overview with some detail on issues in copyright law which have attracted most attention in the courts. The chapter also deals with database rights, trade marks, and passing off.[2]

---

[1] Louise Zafer, a Partner at Lovells, wrote the trade mark section. The author would also like to acknowledge the assistance from other colleagues at Lovells.
[2] The protection of confidential information belonging to or held by the media is dealt with in Ch 7 below.

6.2 COPYRIGHT

6.2.1 Summary of key aspects of copyright

The Copyright, Designs and Patents Act 1988 (CDPA 1988), which has been sub-stantially amended[3] and updated since its introduction, principally governs the UK copyright position. In many cases international conventions provide international protection subject to national laws.

6.2.1.1 *What works attract copyright protection?*
Copyright subsists in works such as:

(1) original literary, dramatic, musical, or artistic works;

(2) sound recordings, films, or broadcasts; and

(3) typographical arrangements of published editions.[4]

Copyright subsists in such works upon creation. No formalities, such as registration of the work, are required to obtain protection. The author must be a qualifying person or the work must be first published in a qualifying place to attract protection.

6.2.1.2 *What does copyright protection confer?*
Copyright protection confers on the owner the exclusive right to do, or to authorize others to do, certain acts in relation to that copyright work in the UK (or to do nothing with the work).[5] Third parties exploiting the work or a substantial part of the work either directly or indirectly will be infringers unless the copyright owner has granted permission or the third party can rely upon one of several defences.

In many cases the creator of a copyright work will have the right to be identified as the author and to object to certain treatment of his or her work.

There are a substantial number of defences or exceptions to copyright infringement. Many of these apply in limited circumstances.[6] The exceptions or defences most widely relevant to the media industries are the 'fair dealing' defences set out in section 30 of CDPA 1988 (see section 6.2.6 below).

6.2.1.3 *What is the term of protection?*
Copyright protection lasts for a varying degree of time depending on the type of work, but typically the term of literary, musical, dramatic and artistic copyright lasts for the life of the author plus seventy years. Copyright in films lasts for the life of the last to

---

[3] A review of copyright law is currently underway. See <http://www.ipo.gov.uk> for details.

[4] CDPA 1988, s 1.

[5] This is one of the principal differences between copyright and other forms of IP where protection is given by the law in return for exploitation.

[6] It is always worth reviewing all the defences and exceptions if faced with allegations of infringement.

survive of the principal director, or the creator of the screenplay or dialogue or any specially created music, plus seventy years. Protection for sound recordings and broadcasts lasts for fifty years from the date the sound recording or broadcast was made.[7]

6.2.2 Some common issues

The most common issues arising in the creation and exploitation of copyright material in the media industries are:

(1) Is the work protected by copyright? This is important to both the owner—when considering exploiting or licensing the work or preventing others from doing so—and to a third party considering exploiting that work.

(2) Which entity owns the copyright or has an exclusive licence to use the work? This is important when seeking to take a licence for use of the material or, as owner, to license it yourself to a third party or when seeking to take action against someone else.

(3) Can the copyright material be used in a particular way? Will the proposed use infringe or can an exception or defence be relied upon?

6.2.2.1 *Work protected by copyright*

Is the work itself protected? The work must fall into a category of protectable works as identified in CDPA 1988 and set out above. The work must also have been created by a 'qualifying' person or first published in a 'qualifying' place.[8] Copyright protects the expression of ideas and the work must be recorded in writing or some other form.[9]

Literary, artistic, dramatic, and musical works must also meet the requirement of originality. This means that a degree of skill and labour must be involved in their creation. A single unstylized word is thought not to be protectable (but may be protected by trade mark law and the law of passing off). There is no requirement of originality for sound recordings, films, and broadcasts. However CDPA 1988 states that copyright does not subsist in films or sound recordings 'to the extent' the film or sound recording

---

[7] CDPA 1988, ss 13A and 13B. There is a move to extend the term of copyright in sound recordings from 50 years to 95 years: the Copyright in Sound Recordings and Performers' Rights (Term Extension) Bill had its first reading in the House of Commons in February 2008 and proposed a 95-year term of protection for sound recordings. The Bill's second reading was scheduled for 7 March 2008 but was subsequently dropped. The Bill superseded a previous Bill introduced (as a ballot Bill) in the House of Commons in December 2007. The call for an extension of this copyright term has received support at EU level and in July 2008 the European Commission published a proposal to extend the term to 95 years. In April 2009 the European Parliament voted to endorse the Commission proposal, but for a lesser term of 70 years. The proposed amendment to the Copyright Term Directive ((EC) 2006/116) would also include a series of measures aimed at ensuring that session musicians benefit from the extended term.

[8] CDPA 1988, ss 153 onwards deal with qualifying for protection. It can be very complex particularly in relation to older works. What is described here is a very basic outline which will cover most recently created works. For more information see K M Garnett, G Davies, and G Harbottle, *Copinger and Skone James on Copyright* (Sweet & Maxwell, 15th edn 2005), Part I (Copyright), (hereinafter '*Copinger*').

[9] However, care must be taken with the statement that there is 'no protection of ideas' as there have been some cases where the line between ideas and expression of ideas has been blurred.

is a copy of another film or sound recording[10] or in a broadcast which 'infringes, or to the extent that it infringes, the copyright in another broadcast'.[11]

(a) *Literary and artistic works* Computer programs and databases fall within the definition of a literary work, as do song lyrics, manuscripts, poems, articles, reviews, classified ads, scripts, stage directions, written treatments and outlines for shows, production bibles and manuals, and most other written documents.

Photographs, paintings, sculptures, a work of architecture, works of artistic crafts-manship, technical drawings, logos, cartoons, and other design work fall within the definition of artistic works. Of these, the courts have most struggled to define what should be included in the definition of sculpture, particularly where the article in-volved is a toy or has some other commercial application such as three-dimensional articles developed as part of a merchandising programme. CDPA 1988 states that 'sculpture' includes a cast or model made for purposes of sculpture.[12] In addition, something can be a sculpture 'irrespective of [its] artistic quality'.[13]

In the *Star Wars* case[14] the judge had to decide whether helmets and other props made for the first *Star Wars* film and toys made to those designs were sculptures within the meaning of CDPA 1988. He provided guidelines to determine whether an article should also be considered a sculpture for the purposes of attracting copyright protec-tion. He said that, while notice should be taken of the ordinary meaning of the word, sculpture could encompass articles one would not normally expect to find in an art gallery. Not every three-dimensional article could be a sculpture—it should have, as part of its purpose, a visual appeal whether or not it might have another purpose as well. 'An artist (in the realm of the visual arts) creates something because it has visual appeal which he wishes to be enjoyed as such. He may fail, but that does not matter (no judgments are to be made about artistic merit).' So, 'a pile of bricks, temporarily on display at the Tate Modern for two weeks, is plainly capable of being a sculpture. The identical pile of bricks dumped at the end of my driveway for two weeks preparatory to a building project is equally plainly not . . . One is created by the hand of an artist, for artistic purposes, and the other is created by a builder, for building purposes.' He concluded that the props were not sculptures because their primary functions were utilitarian. The toys were not sculptures as their primary purpose was for play.

(b) *Dramatic works* Dramatic works are not exhaustively defined and are said to 'include' a work of dance or mime. A television programme format, if it is a dramatic work and meets the requirement of originality, could be protected within this cate-gory of work (see (f) below).

---

[10] This statement has come under some scrutiny recently as the copyrights in some famous sound recordings have expired and record companies consider whether re-mastered or digitized recordings attract a separate copyright which is still in existence.

[11] CDPA 1988, ss 5A(2), 5B(4), and 6(6).

[12] ibid s 4(2).

[13] ibid s 4(1)(a).

[14] *Lucasfilm Ltd v Ainsworth* [2009] FSR 2.

(c) *Musical works* 'Musical work' is defined to mean a work consisting of music, exclusive of any words or action intended to be sung, spoken, or performed with the music. Again, the work must be original. The extent of the originality needed to attract copyright protection often arises when considering whether a new arrangement or adaptation of an existing piece of music is entitled to separate copyright protection. In *Sawkins v Hyperion Records Ltd* [15] it was held that an edited version of existing musical arrangements (which had fallen out of copyright) attracted its own copyright. The judge concluded that, even though the adaptation was based on an existing score, sufficient skill and labour had been used to produce the adaptation to satisfy the originality requirement of section 1 of CDPA 1988.

(d) *Broadcast works* A broadcast protected under CDPA 1988 is an electronic transmission of visual images, sound, or other information transmitted by wireless means or by cable, transmitted for reception by the public (section 6(1)). [16] Internet transmissions are excluded (unless of a broadcast nature such as those which take place simultaneously by other means, for example webcasting). Whether a transmission over the internet will qualify for protection will depend on the nature of the transmission and whether it is made 'on-demand', referred to in CDPA 1988 as one of the categories of protectable work. [17]

(e) *Computer games* Computer games are not expressly referred to in CDPA 1988. However, there are various categories of protectable works, which will protect elements of computer games, such as:

(1) computer programs (as literary works);

(2) graphic works (as artistic works);

(3) films;

(4) other literary works, such as the story board;

(5) musical works; and

(6) sound recordings.

---

[15] *Sawkins v Hyperion Records Ltd* [2004] EWHC 1530 (Ch), upheld on appeal.

[16] As amended by the Copyright and Related Rights Regulations 2003, SI 2003/2498, regs 4 and 5. 'Broadcast' was originally defined under CDPA 1988 s 6(1)(a) as 'a transmission by wireless telegraphy . . . capable of being received by members of the public'. The definition was altered in the course of implementing the EU Copyright Directive (Directive (EC) 2001/29— Harmonisation of Certain Aspects of Copyright and Related Rights in the Information Society). With effect from 31 October 2003, the reference to 'wireless telegraphy' was removed and replaced with the requirement for the transmission to be 'electronic', thereby allowing cable programmes (transmissions by wire) to fall under the wider broadcast category as defined by CDPA 1988. Electronic is defined as meaning 'actuated by electric, magnetic, electro-magnetic, electro-chemical or electro-mechanical energy' (ibid s 178). For further detail see *Copinger* (n 8 above) Part I, Ch 3 (Requirements for Copyright Protection) Broadcasts, paras 3.82–3.85, 3.89–3.101.

[17] CDPA 1988, s 6(1A) CDPA excludes 'internet transmissions' from the definition of 'broadcast' unless they fall within one of the listed exceptions, which cover internet transmissions that take place simultaneously with broadcasts made by other means, concurrent transmissions of live events, and programmed services. 'On-demand' services are not covered. For further detail see *Copinger* (n 8 above) Part I (Copyright), Ch 3 (Requirements for Copyright Protection) Broadcasts, paras 3.98–3.99.

In *Nova Productions Ltd v Mazooma Games Ltd*[18] the court accepted that copyright subsisted in the computer games' graphics generated on screen (as artistic works), the underlying computer program and preparatory design notes (as literary works), and the film itself as a film copyright. The court did not accept that the computer game was protectable as a dramatic work as it was not a work of action which was intended to be, or capable of being, performed before an audience. Although the game had a set of rules, the particular sequence of images displayed on the screen would depend on the manner in which it was played. That sequence of images would not be the same from one game to another, even if the game was played by the same individual.

(f) *Television programme formats* As with computer games, CDPA 1988 does not expressly confer protection on 'format rights', ie the structure and content of television programmes. Protection must be sought within the listed categories of protected works. The name of a television show may be protectable under trade mark law or the law of passing off. The ideas for the format itself may have a sufficient quality of confidence to be protected from disclosure by an equitable duty of confidence.[19] The components of the programme, such as written treatments and outlines, presenters' scripts, camera instructions (for live shows), theme music and incidental music, set design graphics, and programme logos/idents, may be protected by copyright because they are each literary, musical or artistic works, or sound recordings. However, whether there will be protection for the programme as a whole will depend on whether it qualifies as a film and/or dramatic copyright work. Copyright does not protect general ideas[20] but the expression of ideas. However, as the judge noted in *IPC v Highbury*,[21] it is often difficult to define the boundary between the taking of general ideas and concepts on the one hand and copying in the copyright sense on the other.

If recorded for or during transmission, the resulting material will amount to a film for the purposes of CDPA 1988 and will be protected accordingly. But the scope of protection for film copyright is limited in the sense that to infringe the film copyright requires exact copying of the images and sounds recorded in the film.[22] However, if a film (or a broadcast) is also a dramatic work, the copyright will be infringed if a substantial part of the original dramatic work is used, without the need for exact copying of the images and sounds. Therefore, if a television programme format is an original dramatic copyright work, then the format will be protected by copyright.

In the only decided case in the UK on formats, *Green v Broadcasting Corporation of New Zealand*,[23] Hughie Green, the presenter of the game show *Opportunity Knocks*, sued a New Zealand broadcaster for copyright infringement. Green claimed to be the author of copyright in the 'dramatic format' (certain signature elements of the show

---

[18] *Nova Productions Ltd v Mazooma Games Ltd* [2006] All ER 131, upheld on appeal.
[19] *Fraser v Thames Television Ltd* [1983] 2 WLR 917.
[20] *Designers Guild Ltd v Russell Williams (Textiles) Ltd* [2001] FSR 11.
[21] *IPC Media Ltd v Highbury-SPL Publishing Ltd* [2004] EWHC 2985 (Ch).
[22] CDPA 1988, ss 17(1) and (4).
[23] *Green v Broadcasting Corporation of New Zealand* [1989] RPC 469 (NZ CA); on appeal [1989] RPC 700, PC.

repeated in each performance of the show), which he alleged were copied, including the title, the use of particular catchphrases and the use of a 'clap o meter' to measure the audience's level of applause. The Privy Council[24] considered these unifying features (the programme's 'format') to be a general idea and not sufficient to be a copyright work: 'The protection which copyright gives creates a monopoly and there must be certainty in the subject matter of such monopoly in order to avoid injustice to the rest of the world.' However, the case was decided in 1989 and Counsel for Green has said that dramatic work copyright was not argued before the Privy Council.

In *Norowzian v Arks Ltd*[25] the claimant made a short unscripted film, called 'Joy', of an individual performing a dance. The film was heavily edited so that the film gave the impression that the actor was performing movements impossible for any human being. The defendant used the idea of jump-cutting, which had been used in the film 'Joy', to produce an advertisement for Guinness, called 'Anticipation', also showing a man doing a dance which no ordinary person could perform. The claimant argued that the film 'Joy' should be protected by copyright as a dramatic work. At first instance the judge held that a film could not be a dramatic work and that the film of the dance depicted in 'Joy' was not a recording of a dramatic work because a dramatic work had to be capable of being physically performed. This part of the judgment was overturned by the Court of Appeal, which held that a film could be a dramatic work and was capable of physical performance: to an audience viewing the film. This case suggests that television programme formats, recorded in film (or broadcast), can be protected by dramatic work copyright as well as by film copyright. The key question is whether the programme is of dramatic quality and meets the threshold of originality.

6.2.2.2 *Qualifying person*
Is the author a 'qualifying' person or has the work been first published in a 'qualifying' country? The author is the person who creates the work and he or she (or it) must be a qualifying person or the work must first be published in the UK or a country to which CDPA 1988 'extends'. In most cases this requirement will be met as qualifying persons include British citizens, persons resident or domiciled in the UK, and a person who is domiciled or resident in any country of the world to which CDPA 1988 'extends'. CDPA 1988 now 'extends' for this purpose, to most countries of the world but care must be taken with old foreign-produced works, which may have been created by someone who is not a qualifying person.

6.2.3 Ownership of a copyright work

6.2.3.1 *Authorship*
It is often important to identify the author of a copyright work because the general rule is that the author is the first owner of any copyright in the work.[26] The major exception

---

[24] The Privy Council at that time acted as the final court of appeal for New Zealand.
[25] *Norowzian v Arks Ltd (No 2)* [2000] FSR 363.
[26] CDPA 1988, s 11(1).

to this rule applies to works made by a person in the course of employment, where the employer will be the first owner subject to any agreement to the contrary.[27] Other exceptions apply to works controlled by the Crown,[28] by Parliament,[29] and by international organizations.[30]

It is also often important to identify the author of a work to ensure that he or she is a qualifying person, to assist in determining whether copyright has expired, and to determine whether title to copyright has been transferred or licensed correctly.[31] Any prospective licensee may want to ensure that it has obtained a licence from the person properly entitled to grant a licence either as first owner of the copyright or as someone who has obtained the copyright by assignment, or a properly authorized licensee.[32] It is no defence to infringement to say that a licence was obtained from someone who was believed (erroneously) to be the copyright owner or authorized licensee. Identifying the author and owner of copyright also often becomes important when selling the business or asset or when trying to raise finance against an asset which is largely protected by copyright.

The 'author' is defined as the person who creates the work.[33] For a literary, dramatic, musical, or artistic work, the author will be the writer of the poem or play, the composer of the song, or the painter or sculptor who has created the art. For other categories of works, where authorship is not so clear, the author is specifically defined.[34] For a sound recording, the author is the producer. For a film, it is the producer and principal director. For a broadcast, the author is the person who makes the broadcast, which is defined to mean the person transmitting the programme (if he has responsibility to any extent for its content) or any person providing the programme who makes, with the person transmitting it, the arrangements necessary for its transmission. For a typographical arrangement, the author is the publisher. In the case of computer-generated works, where there is no human author, the author is the person who makes the necessary arrangements for creating the work.[35] This may be the owner of the computer, or the person who has invested in the set-up and operation of the IT systems.

---

[27] ibid s 11(2). This is the case for literary, dramatic, musical, or artistic works made after 1 August 1989, and sound recordings or films made after 1 July 1994 (CDPA 1988, s 11(2), as amended by the Copyright and Related Rights Regulations 1996 (SI 1996/2967), regs 18 and 36). There is no such exception in relation to sounds recordings or films made before 1 July 1994, nor for broadcasts, cable programmes, or typographical arrangements.

[28] ibid s 163.

[29] ibid s 165.

[30] ibid s 168.

[31] Although the CDPA 1988 specifies when copyright should be taken to have expired where the author cannot be identified. See s 13B(4).

[32] Sometimes prospective licensees or assignees of copyright will rely on contractual assurances or warranties instead, although this will only usually give rise to a claim in contract against the contracting party if the assurance is demonstrated to be untrue.

[33] CDPA 1988, s 9(1).

[34] ibid s 9(2).

[35] ibid s 9(3).

6.2.3.2 *Joint authors and co-authors*

In the case of the sometimes complex collaborations which can be involved in the creation of works, particularly dramatic works, determining who is or are the author(s) can be problematic. If the work has arisen from the effort of one or more persons it will be a matter of fact and degree as to whether a person has contributed sufficient skill or effort of the necessary type (for example in relation to a dramatic work, the contribution must be to the dramatic qualities) to be regarded as the author or one of the authors.[36]

A work of joint authorship is a work produced by the collaboration of two or more authors in which the contribution of each author is not distinct from the contribution of the other author or authors.[37] A work may, however, have co-authors where the efforts of the individual authors are distinct.

There have been a number of cases involving stage plays which demonstrate the issues well:

(1) providing stage directions and dealing with scenic effects is not the right kind of contribution to a dramatic work for the person to be considered an author of the dramatic work copyright;[38]

(2) providing an outline of a plot to a playwright who in turn produces a one-act sketch following that plot is not sufficient for joint authorship when the ideas for the plot elements were not original;[39]

(3) neither plot changes implemented at the suggestion of a director nor contributions as to interpretation and theatrical presentation of the play by the director during rehearsals were contributions sufficient to give rise to joint authorship.[40]

In other works, such as live television shows, establishing who made the contributions necessary for a claim for authorship can be complex—it might be the director and producer, but junior production staff and those in the editing suite might also make a contribution to authorship of the work in question. Written contracts with those involved at all levels in a project, and which vest copyright in or grant an exclusive licence to the production company, obviously overcome such issues.

There can be serious problems with exploitation of joint works or works where there are two or more owners of copyright. Whilst each author will generally have the same rights as a sole owner, they cannot exploit the work without the licence of their co-owners or assign ownership of the work without their prior consent.[41] If they do so,

---

[36] In *Nova Productions Ltd v Mazooma* [2006] All ER 131, Kitchin J found that, even though the player of a computer game generated the images on screen, he was not an author or co-author because his input was not artistic in nature and he contributed no skill or labour of an artistic kind.

[37] CDPA 1988, s 10(1).

[38] *Tate v Fulbrook* [1908] 1 KB 821.

[39] *Bagge v Miller* (1917–23) MCC 179.

[40] *Brighton v Jones* [2004] EWHC 1157 (Ch), [2004] EMLR 26.

[41] See *Brighton v Jones* [2004] EWHC 1157 (Ch) and *Fisher v Brooker* [2008] EWCA Civ 287 on the joint authorship of a dramatic ('Stones in his Pockets') and musical work ('A Whiter Shade of Pale'), respectively. See also *Ray v Classic FM plc* [1998] FSR 622.

they are at risk of an infringement action from their co-owners and accounting for a share of the profits made may not be sufficient remedy.[42] Similarly, a person looking to exploit the work created by more than one person must take a licence from all the owners of copyright to avoid a potential infringement claim or be satisfied that one person is authorized to license on behalf of all owners.

6.2.3.3 *Works of employees*

An employer will own the copyright of work created by his or her employees provided the 'employee' was acting in 'the course of employment'. An 'employee' is defined as someone employed under a contract of service or apprenticeship.[43] Independent contractors may not be considered employees and may own the copyright in work they create. Established common law principles will apply to determine whether someone is an employee with a contract of service or an independent contractor with a contract for services. Factors to be considered include the degree of control being exercised over the employee and whether the employee's work is done as an integral part of the business (a contract of service), or merely as an accessory to it (a contract for services).[44]

The work must be created by the employee in the normal 'course of employment'. This has been interpreted to mean within the scope of the employee's duties, or being typical of the kind of work that the employee was engaged by the employer to do. The result is that copyright can vest in the employer where work relates to the employment, even where such work is carried out by the employee at home, but an employee may own copyright in work completed during office hours which is entirely unrelated to their duties as an employee.[45]

These provisions are subject to any contrary agreement between the employer and employee, provided that the agreement is concluded before the work is created.[46] But, of course, rights may be transferred later by agreement.

6.2.4 Dealing in or using a copyright work—assignment and licensing

6.2.4.1 *Transferring rights*

Copyright can be transferred by assignment or by a will and such transfer can be for a limited time or in respect of some or all of the owner's rights. Any transfer must be in writing and signed by the owner. The new owner of copyright is bound by the terms of any existing licences granted by the previous owner unless the new owner had knowledge (actual or constructive) of the licences and paid money for the transfer of rights.[47]

---

[42] See *Ray v Classic FM plc* [1998] FSR 622.

[43] CDPA 1988, s 178.

[44] *Stephenson, Jordan and Harrison v Macdonald and Evans* (1952) 69 RPC 10, later approved in *Market Investigations Ltd v Minister of Social Security* [1969] 2 QB 173.

[45] The two leading cases in this area are *Stephenson, Jordan and Harrison v Macdonald and Evans* (n 44 above) and *Noah v Shuba* [1991] FSR 14. See also *Copinger* (n 8 above) Part 1 (Copyright) Ch 5 (Requirements for Copyright Protection) The Chain of Title, para 5-19.

[46] *Noah v Shuba* (n 45 above).

[47] CDPA 1998, s 90. In *R Griggs Group v Evans (No 1)* [2005] FSR 31, the court found that the assignee of copyright had notice of the prior rights of the claimant to that action and if they had not had

6.2.4.2 *Licensing rights*

The author of a copyright work retains certain moral rights, discussed in section 6.2.9 below.[48] The owner of the copyright (who may also be the author) can choose to exploit the work by assigning the copyright in the work, through a sale or other transfer, or by licensing use of the work to another party.[49] Different rights may be granted to different licensees. Licences are usually expressed to be exclusive, sole, or non-exclusive. An exclusive licence permits the licensee and no other person, including the owner of copyright, to exploit the work. CDPA 1988 requires exclusive licences to be in writing and signed by or on behalf of the copyright owner.[50] A sole licence means that the owner may have retained the right to exploit the copyright him- or herself but will grant no other licences. A non-exclusive licence means that the owner and other licensees may exploit the rights. Licences may be for the term of copyright or for a period limited in time.

Typically media companies grant many licences in respect of the same work and care must be taken to ensure that rights do not overlap where that is not intended. For example, it is possible for a television production company (which has ensured, through contracts with all working on a particular programme, that it has acquired all the necessary rights): to grant an exclusive right to a UK terrestrial television broadcaster to permit first broadcast of a work (and a second airing showing within a particular term); to grant a satellite broadcaster a right to air the programme on UK satellite television after the expiry of the first broadcaster's exclusivity; to grant a computer games company an exclusive right to make a game based on the programme; to grant an advertising agency an exclusive right to use an excerpt from the programme to make a particular advertisement for broadcast at cinemas only; to grant a television distribution company an exclusive right to distribute copies of the programme outside the UK for exclusive broadcast on television in each country of the world or a part of the world; and to grant to someone else the right to use excerpts of the programme as part of advertising merchandising associated with the programme. There are many variations on what might be granted and rights may be exclusive, non-exclusive, limited in time, very specifically limited to what use can be made of the copyright work, whether use can be made on the internet, and so on.[51]

6.2.4.3 *Collecting Societies*

In order to facilitate the use of a number of songs, sound recordings, and music videos and to streamline the effective licensing of such works, owners of the rights in these

---

actual notice, thought that the fact that they were purporting to take an assignment of a 'famous' logo (in which artistic copyright subsisted) would have been enough for constructive notice to be found.

[48] CDPA 1988, s 94 onwards. The moral rights of authors only apply in the case of literary, dramatic, musical, or artistic works and films. Similar rights do not apply for the author of a sound recording, broadcast, cable programme, or typographical arrangement.

[49] ibid s 90.

[50] ibid s 92.

[51] Another important consideration in licensing is competition law and the extent to which some exclusive licences, in particular, fall foul of competition law.

works are often members of Collecting Societies. Collecting Societies acquire by assignment or licence the right to license third parties to use the works and to administer royalties from these arrangements. In practice this means that entities such as television and radio broadcasters, retailers, restaurants, and bars can enter into a single licence covering the use of works owned by a large group of rights owners. The rights owners benefit from being able to exploit their works more widely and cost-effectively than in negotiating and executing individual licences.

In the UK, the major Collecting Societies are the alliance between the Mechanical Copyright Protection Society and Performing Right Society (now called 'PRS for Music'), Phonographic Performance Limited ('PPL'), and Video Performance Limited ('VPL'). PRS for Music represents writers and publishers of copyright in musical compositions and can authorize the reproduction in physical form, the public performance and the communication to the public of music copyright works. PPL and VPL respectively represent the rights of the record labels in relation to copyright in sound recordings and music videos and can authorize the public performance and broadcasting of a sound recording.

The licence terms are generally negotiated and agreed between the licensees and the Collecting Societies. However, under CDPA 1988 the Collecting Societies are controlled and subject to the jurisdiction of the Copyright Tribunal. Any licensee who is refused a licence or considers the terms unreasonable (including disputing the amount of the licence fee) for exploiting the Collecting Societies' works, can seek independent adjudication on the matter from the Copyright Tribunal. The Copyright Tribunal also has the power to decide matters referred to it by the Secretary of State. It also has limited powers in matters which do not relate to Collecting Societies but still concern a dispute over royalties paid on the distribution of copyright protected works.

Other Collecting Societies, such as the Copyright Licensing Agency (CLA), issue licences to enable organizations to copy from magazines, books, and journals within their remit, and the Design and Artists Copyright Society (DACS) licenses, more typically on an individual rather than collective basis, the right to use artistic works.[52]

6.2.4.4 *Failing to comply with legal formalities and commissioned works and works written by freelance workers*
Following the general principle in copyright law that the author will be the first owner of copyright, any independent contractor or freelancer will be the first owner of the copyright unless there is a term in his or her contract to the contrary effect. Assignments and exclusive licences must be in writing and signed to be effective under CDPA 1988, so sometimes issues arise because the parties have not complied with the formalities at the time of commission.

If there is no written document signed by the copyright owner transferring the copyright or granting an exclusive licence, the court may consider that, nonetheless,

---

[52] <http://www.ppluk.com>; <http://www.cla.co.uk>; <http://www.dacs.org.uk>.

an exclusive licence has been granted or the equitable title to copyright has been transferred, and order that the parties comply with the legal requirements (ie execute a signed written transfer or licence) to ensure copyright or an exclusive licence is vested properly in the new owner. The most common examples are where the parties clearly intended to transfer the copyright or to grant an exclusive licence but failed to use the appropriate language in the contract or where a commissioning contract is silent on the question of copyright.

In *R Griggs Group Ltd v Evans* [53] the owner of 'Doc Martens', Griggs, had commissioned its advertising agency to design a new logo incorporating its old logos. The agency, in turn, commissioned a freelance designer to design the logo. Later the designer, Evans, assigned the copyright in the new design to a competitor third party. The court found that neither Griggs nor Evans had given any thought to copyright at the time of the commission. The parties agreed that, as the author and an independent contractor, Evans was the first owner of the copyright. The question the court had to consider was whether the formal owner of the copyright, the third-party competitor, was holding the copyright on behalf of Griggs (or, in legal terms, was Griggs the owner of copyright in equity and entitled to a formal assignment of the legal title?). In practical terms this meant that the court had to decide whether there were any implied terms in the contract between Evans and the agency which commissioned the work from him on behalf of Griggs. The court referred to the well-known principles governing the circumstances when a term would be implied into a contract: (1) it must be reasonable and equitable to do so; (2) it must be necessary to give business efficacy to the contract; (3) it must be so obvious that 'it goes without saying'; (4) the term must be capable of clear expression; and (5) the term must not contradict any express term of a contract.

While recognizing that, if it is necessary to imply some grant of rights between the client and the author of the work in question, the grant of rights should be limited to what is necessary in the circumstances, the court concluded that on the facts of the case an assignment should be ordered to prevent the designer assigning copyright in the design work to a competitor. The court concluded that if a bystander had asked whether Evans would retain rights in the logo he had been asked to design which could be used against Griggs, by Evans or anyone he sold the rights to anywhere in the world, the answer would have been 'of course not'.

6.2.5 Dealing in or using a copyright work—infringement

The copyright owner has the exclusive right to do certain acts in relation to the work or to license others to carry out those acts. The acts include, among other things, the exclusive right to:

(1) copy the work;

(2) issue copies of the work to the public;

---

[53] *R Griggs Group Ltd v Evans (No 1)* [2005] FSR 31.

(3) rent or lend the work to the public;

(4) perform, show, or play the work in public;

(5) communicate the work to the public; and

(6) adapt the work.[54]

These acts are commonly referred to as the 'restricted acts'. If a third party carries out those acts without permission or authorizes someone else to carry out those acts and cannot rely on a defence then he or she infringes the copyright.

6.2.5.1 *Copying*

The right to copy the work raises a number of issues. It is an infringement to copy a substantial part of a copyright work. Whether a potential infringer has taken a substantial part of a work will be determined taking into account all the circumstances but will be assessed looking at the quality or importance of what has been taken as well as the amount.[55]

There must be copying to infringe. Copying is usually demonstrated by showing that the defendant had the means to copy the work and that the two works are sufficiently similar to justify the inference of copying. However, care must be taken not to ignore the differences as an indication that there has been no copying. It is not an infringement for one author independently to create a substantially similar work to the copyright work in question. The copying must be of a substantial part of the work and the part of the work that is copied must be the part which attracts copyright protection.

Copying in relation to a literary, dramatic, musical, or artistic work means reproducing the work in any material form, including storing the work in any medium by electronic means. In relation to an artistic work, copying includes the making of a copy in three dimensions of a two-dimensional work and the making of a copy in two dimensions of a three-dimensional work. Copying in relation to a film or broadcast includes making a photograph of the whole or any substantial part of any image forming part of the film or broadcast. Copying in relation to the typographical arrangement of a published edition means making a facsimile copy of the arrangement. Copying in relation to any description of work includes the making of copies which are transient or are incidental to some other use of the work.[56]

Copyright protects the expression of ideas rather than the ideas themselves; however, it is often difficult to tell where the dividing line falls. For example, copyright

---

[54] CDPA 1988, s 16 lists the acts restricted by copyright in a work.

[55] See *Designers Guild Ltd v Russell Williams (Textiles) Ltd* [2001] FSR 11, and *HRH Prince of Wales v Associated Newspapers Ltd* [2006] EWHC 522.

[56] Currently in the UK there is no provision that allows private copying or format shifting of music. It is therefore illegal to copy music from a CD that one has legally purchased onto one's own computer. In July 2009 the Government produced its Digital Britain White Paper which considers time and format shifting, at paras 62–66. See <http://www.culture.gov.uk/images/publications/digitalbritain-finalreport-jun09.pdf>.

may be infringed by copying the original elements in the plot of a play or novel without reproducing a single sentence of the original work.

The issue of substantial copying can be very complex and the courts have said that each case must be decided on the merits. A maxim often used in case law is, 'what is worth copying is worth protecting'.[57] Works which fuse commonplace ideas so that the originality and therefore the protected work is in the finished work or parts of the whole of the work (such as programme formats or magazine covers) raise particular difficulties. The question to be determined is has the defendant taken a substantial part of the independent skill and effort expended by the author?

In *IPC Media Ltd v Highbury-SPL Publishing Ltd*[58] IPC claimed that its copyright in the 'design, subject matter, theme and presentational style' in its magazine cover 'Ideal Home' had been infringed by Highbury in its magazine cover 'Home'. Highbury argued, and the court accepted, that most of the design aspects relied on by IPC were commonplace in the field of magazine covers and were therefore not sufficiently original to form part of the artistic work relied on. Furthermore, the court should not infer copying because of their widespread use in the magazine industry.

In the case concerning *The Da Vinci Code*[59] the Court of Appeal upheld the first instance decision and concluded that the author of the popular novel of that name, Dan Brown, had not infringed the copyright in a book called *The Holy Blood and the Holy Grail* which had been published earlier. The claimants, authors of *The Holy Blood and the Holy Grail*, had sued Random House, publisher of both books, arguing that Dan Brown had copied their book's central theme. The Court of Appeal agreed that although Dan Brown had access to the earlier book and based relevant parts of *The Da Vinci Code* on it, he only took generalized propositions which were too abstract to qualify for copyright protection. They were not the product of the application of skill and labour by the claimants in the creation of their literary work. Although the relevant 'central theme elements' identified by the claimants were present in both books, the Court of Appeal found that elements (if any) which had been copied from the earlier book were insufficient to qualify as a substantial part. The 'central theme' elements identified by the claimants were merely a selection of features of the earlier book collated by Dan Brown for research purposes rather than a theme emerging from the reading of the book as a whole.

In *Nova v Mazooma*,[60] in which the court had to decide whether one computer game infringed another, the court stated that in deciding whether to infer copying, the court would:

... consider the similarities and differences between the works and whether or not the particular similarities relied on are sufficiently close, numerous or extensive to be more likely to be the

---

[57] A summary of Peterson J's remarks in *University of London Press Ltd v University Tutorial Press Ltd* [1916] 2 Ch 601 approved in a number of later cases.

[58] *IPC Media Ltd v Highbury-SPL Publishing Ltd* [2004] All ER 342.

[59] *Baigent v The Random House Group Ltd* [2006] FSR 44.

[60] *Nova Productions Ltd v Mazooma Games Ltd* [2006] All ER 131, upheld on appeal.

result of copying than coincidence. Similarities may be disregarded because they are common-place, unoriginal, or consist of general ideas . . . once copying is established then the question arises whether what has been taken constitutes all or a substantial part of the copyright work. At this point the only issue is whether or not the features which have been taken represent a substantial part of the copyright work. A visual comparison of the two designs to see the extent to which they may differ in appearance is unnecessary and liable to mislead . . . in assessing whether or not a substantial part has been taken it is important not to deal with the copied features piece-meal. Rather, it is the cumulative effect of the copied features which is important. The court must consider whether, taken as a whole, they constitute a substantial part of the copyright work.

In the *Nova* case an additional point was raised: the claimants contended that the defendants infringed the copyright in the program by copying the outputs which appeared on the screen. The judge concluded that similarities in output did not mean that the underlying software had been copied. What had been taken was essentially a number of generalized ideas which did not form part of the program itself (the Software Directive having excluded specifically the notion that ideas would be protected).

6.2.5.2 *Typographical arrangements*
There is copyright in the typographical arrangements of published editions of literary works, such as novels or textbooks, separate from any copyright in the underlying liter-ary work. Its purpose is to protect the investment in typesetting against exact copying by photocopying or other methods. Therefore, copyright in the typographical arrange-ment is only infringed if an exact copy of the typeface is reproduced. If a journalist is proposing to reproduce exactly the typeface of a published work, even if the underly-ing work itself is out of copyright, the copyright in the typographical arrangement may subsist and permission from the publisher would be required.

6.2.5.3 *Secondary infringement*
CDPA 1988 also lists a number of other acts of infringement, which are entitled 'secondary' acts of infringement in which an element of knowledge or reason to believe is required. They are (in summary form):

(a) importing (other than for private and domestic use) an article which one knows or has reason to believe is an infringing copy;

(b) possessing in the course of business, selling or hiring or offering or exposing for sale or hire, distributing an article which one knows or has reason to believe is an infringing copy;

(c) providing the means for making infringing copies knowing or having reason to believe that such use would be made;

(d) permitting the use of premises for an infringing performance of a literary, dra-matic, or musical work unless when permission was given it was believed on reason-able grounds that the performance would not infringe copyright; and

(e) where copyright is infringed by a public performance or the playing of the work in public by means of apparatus for playing sound recordings, showing films or receiving images or sounds, supplying apparatus, allowing the apparatus to be brought onto premises, and supplying the sound recording or film used to infringe copyright in each case knowing or reasonably believing the apparatus or sound recording or film was to be used to infringe copyright.[61]

An article is an infringing copy if its making constituted an infringement or it is, has been, or is proposed to be imported into the UK, and its making in the UK would have constituted an infringement of copyright or breach of an exclusive licence (subject to the free movement of goods principles of the European Union). 'Reason to believe' is to be construed as being in possession of facts which would lead a reasonable person to arrive at the belief, having had time to evaluate the facts.[62]

6.2.5.4 *The circumvention of effective technological measures*

Many rights owners install protection mechanisms to prevent unauthorized use of the copyright work like pirating (unauthorized copying), computer games being played on different platforms, and audio visual content being watched in countries other than was intended at the point of sale. The protection mechanisms used tend to be embedded in the audio visual material itself or, in the case of computer games, in the games software or the consoles, or both (such as to have a lock and key effect). CDPA 1988 seeks to protect such measures in a complicated set of provisions at sections 296 and 296ZA to 296ZF. Briefly, the most relevant civil law[63] sections can be summarized as follows:

(1) where a technical device has been attached to a computer and someone manufactures, distributes, or has in his possession for commercial purposes, etc means for, or publishes information to assist in, the circumvention or removal of the device knowing or having reason to believe that it will be used to make infringing copies, section 296 applies;

(2) where effective technological measures have been applied to a copyright work other than a computer program and

(a) a person does anything which circumvents those measures knowing, or with reasonable grounds to know, that he is pursuing that objective, section 296ZB applies; or

(b) a person manufactures, distributes, or has in his possession for commercial purposes any device or provides services which (i) are marketed for the purpose of the circumvention of, or (ii) have only a limited commercially significant purpose or use other than to circumvent, or (iii) are primarily designed or performed for the purpose of enabling or facilitating the circumvention of, those measures, section 296ZD applies.

---

[61] CDPA 1988, ss 21–27.
[62] *LA Gear Inc v Hi-Tec Sports plc* [1992] FSR 121.
[63] There are criminal offences set out in CDPA 1988, s 296ZC.

Those provisions referred to (ie sections 296, 296ZB, and 296ZD) give the owner of intellectual property rights in the protection device (or someone issuing copies of or communicating to the public the computer program or work to which the device has been applied) the same rights against the person carrying out those acts as the copyright owner has.

In *Sony v Owen*,[64] which involved the application of a chip to a games console allowing the console to bypass the copy protection codes embedded in the games CD/DVD (decided under the previous section 296), the judge concluded that it did not matter whether the chip had purposes other than to assist in copyright infringement and whether once circumvented the machine may read non-infringing copyright material.

In *Sony v Ball*[65] the Judge accepted that a technical protection measure applied to a games console fell within the provisions of sections 296 and 296ZA to 296ZF. An infringing article was made, although transiently, when an unauthorized copy was stored in the RAM of the console.

6.2.5.5 *Free movement of goods principles and copyright*

One important element of the European Union is the notion of free movement of goods and services throughout the Union. Once an item has been placed on a market of a country within the European Union it must be allowed to move across borders. This is generally referred to as the 'exhaustion of rights' principle. The European Union promotes a single market within the Union. Copyright, on the other hand, is a right granted by each country of the Union (and the world) on a territorial basis. How do these principles co-exist? The Treaty which established the European Union recognized the potential conflict and provided that the principle of free movement of goods was subject to the protection of intellectual property, provided any such prohibitions or restrictions were justified.[66] This caveat, however, has generated a lot of case law at national and EU level. Early on it was recognized that exhaustion of rights in goods applies to the distribution of articles which embody a copyright work. So the right to issue copies of the work is a right which is exhausted in respect of the physical embodiment of that work once an article containing the copyright work (for example a CD) is placed

---

[64] *Sony Computer Entertainment v Paul Owen and others* [2002] EWHC 45.

[65] *Kabushiki Kaisha Sony Computer Entertainment Inc. Also Trading As Sony Computer Entertainment Inc. (A Company Incorporated Under The Law Of Japan), Sony Computer Entertainment Europe Ltd, Sony Computer Entertainment UK Ltd v Gaynor David Ball* [2004] EWHC 1738 (Ch). In *R v Higgs* [2008] EWCA Crim 1324, Mr Higgs was convicted under s 296ZB of offences of manufacturing and selling devices designed to circumvent effective technological measures (ie modchips). This was quashed by the Court of Appeal as it was held that Mr Higgs was not, by his activities, encouraging a market for pirate games and thereby circumventing an effective technological measure. The Court required evidence that the technological measures prevented copyright infringement. However, the Crown had not relied on the case of *Sony v Ball* and had not run the argument that an infringing copy of the game is created when the pirated copy is played on the console. The Court of Appeal has warned Mr Higgs that had the Crown relied on the arguments run in *Sony v Ball* it would have been successful.

[66] The Treaty on European Union [1992] OJ C191.

on the market in one EU territory with the copyright owner's consent.[67] This principle does not cover copies put into circulation for rental since otherwise the rental right would have no force.[68] The copyright owner's rights are not exhausted by the communication of the work to the public.[69]

6.2.6 Exceptions and defences to copyright infringement

Chapter III of CDPA 1988 entitled 'Acts Permitted in relation to Copyright Works' largely contains the exceptions or defences to copyright infringement spread out over fifty-two sections. The wide variety of uses of copyright material permitted in Chapter III is directed at achieving a proper balance between the protection of rights of the creative author and the wider public interest.[70]

The 'fair dealing' defences for criticism, review, and news reporting contained in section 30 of CDPA 1988 have probably been most closely scrutinized by the courts in cases involving the media but there are many other defences which might be relevant in certain situations (such as the use of a record of spoken words[71] and the representation of certain artistic works such as buildings and sculptures on public display) as well as incidental inclusion (see below).[72]

---

[67] *Deutsche Grammophon Gesellschaft mbH v Metro, SB Grossmarkte GmbH* [1971] CMLR 631. The justification is said to be that the rights owner can ensure fair compensation by determining a fair price for the exploitation at the time he or she places the work on the market.

[68] *Metronome Musik GmbH v Music Point Hokamp GmbH* (C-200/96) European Court of Justice, 28 April 1998, [1998] ECR I-1953.

[69] *Coditel SA v Ciné-Vog Films SA* [1982] ECR 3381.

[70] The Court of Appeal and first instance judge in *Pro Sieben Media AG v Carlton UK Television Ltd* [1999] 1 WLR 605.

[71] CDPA 1988, s 58—Use of notes or recordings of spoken words in certain cases:
  (1) Where a record of spoken words is made, in writing or otherwise, for the purpose:
    (a) of reporting current events, or
    (b) of [communicating to the public] the whole or part of the work,
    it is not an infringement of any copyright in the words as a literary work to use the record or material taken from it (or to copy the record, or any such material, and use the copy) for that purpose, provided the following conditions are met.
  (2) The conditions are that:
    (a) the record is a direct record of the spoken words and is not taken from a previous record or from a broadcast [. . .];
    (b) the making of the record was not prohibited by the speaker and, where copyright already subsisted in the work, did not infringe copyright;
    (c) the use made of the record or material taken from it is not of a kind prohibited by or on behalf of the speaker or copyright owner before the record was made; and
    (d) the use is by or with the authority of a person who is lawfully in possession of the record.

[72] CDPA 1988, s 62—Representation of certain artistic works on public display:
  (1) This section applies to:
    (a) buildings, and
    (b) sculptures, models for buildings and works of artistic craftsmanship, if permanently situated in a public place or in premises open to the public.
  (2) The copyright in such a work is not infringed by:
    (a) making a graphic work representing it,
    (b) making a photograph or film of it, or
    (c) [making a broadcast of] a visual image of it.

6.2.6.1 *Criticism or review*

'Fair dealing' with the work for the purpose of criticism or review, of that or another work or of a performance of a work, does not infringe any copyright in the work provided that it is accompanied by a sufficient acknowledgement and provided that the work has been made available to the public. Whether the purpose is for criticism or review is to be interpreted liberally and objectively. Criticism may be strongly expressed and unbalanced without forfeiting the fair dealing defence.[73]

The criticism or review need not be of the work used; a substantial part of a copyright work may be used for criticism or review of another work or the underlying ideas or philosophy represented by another work, and not amount to copyright infringement.

In *IPC Media Ltd v News Group Newspapers Ltd*[74] *The Sun* newspaper, in promoting its own TV listings guide, published an advertisement in which it reproduced the front cover and logo of a rival weekly listings magazine produced by IPC Media, along with the slogan 'get more for less'. The judge concluded that the criticism or review did not have to be of the work itself, it could be criticism of the product represented by the work (ie the rival TV listings magazine).

In *Fraser-Woodward Ltd v BBC*[75] the claimant objected to the use of fourteen photographs by the defendants. The photographs were of a celebrity and his family and were originally published in various tabloid newspapers by licence. The second defendant television production company used the images of the newspaper pages in which the photographs were published in a programme which it made for the first defendant. The photographs were shown for no more than two or three seconds, apart from one which was on screen for about four seconds. The defendants said that the programme was intended to criticize tabloid journalism and the way in which certain celebrities exploited the press to increase their fame. The court stated that while it was not sufficient merely to criticize something to invoke section 30, there was no requirement that the criticism or review be of the copyright work or another work—it could extend to the ideas and philosophy behind that other work.

6.2.6.2 *Sufficient acknowledgement*

In order to rely successfully on the defence of fair dealing, the person using the copyright work must accompany it with a sufficient acknowledgement. This means identifying the copyright work in question by its title or other description, and identifying the author.[76] In the *Pro Sieben* case, in which a television production company

---

(3) Nor is the copyright infringed by the issue to the public of copies, or the [communication to the public], of anything whose making was, by virtue of this section, not an infringement of the copyright.

[73] *Pro Sieben v Carlton* [1998] FSR 43, the court taking the view that any remedy in such cases was to be found in defamation law.

[74] *IPC Media Ltd v News Group Newspapers Ltd* [2005] FSR 35.

[75] *Fraser-Woodward Ltd v BBC* [2005] FSR 36.

[76] CDPA 1988, s 178 and unless, in the case of published work, it is published anonymously, or in the case of an unpublished work, it is not possible for a person to ascertain the identity of the author by reasonable inquiry.

used footage of an interview in a programme about 'cheque book' journalism, the Court of Appeal accepted that the appearance of the programme name and the television company logo was enough to meet the 'sufficient acknowledgement' requirement.[77]

In the *Fraser-Woodward* case, the court held that it was not necessary expressly to identify the author: it was enough for it to be obvious who the author was from the circumstances. In that case the judge thought it was enough that the photographer was being interviewed at the time the photographs could be seen.[78]

6.2.6.3 *Made available to the public*
The criticism or review must be of a work which has been lawfully made available to the public (the rationale being that it cannot be 'fair' to deal in a work which has not yet been made available to the public).[79] A work has been made available to the public if it has been made available by any means, including:

(a) the issue of copies to the public;

(b) making the work available by means of an electronic retrieval system;

(c) the rental or lending of copies of the work to the public;

(d) the performance, exhibition, playing or showing of the work in public;

(e) the communication to the public of the work,

provided that the means of making the work available has not been by way of an unauthorized act.[80]

6.2.6.4 *News reporting*
Under CDPA 1988 section 30(2), fair dealing with a work (other than a photograph) for the purpose of reporting current events does not infringe any copyright in the work provided that it is accompanied by a sufficient acknowledgement.

(a) *Current events* Events reported do not have to be recent provided they are of current interest to the public at the time of reporting. In *Ashdown v Telegraph Group Ltd*[81] the *Sunday Telegraph* published substantial parts of a leaked minute of a meeting between the former leader of the Liberal Democrats, Paddy Ashdown, and the then Prime Minister, which Paddy Ashdown had been intending to publish himself as part of his diary of his political career. The Court of Appeal held that 'reporting current events' should be interpreted liberally and that, although the meeting had taken place two years prior to publication of the minute by *The Telegraph*, the information about a deal between the Liberal Democrats and the Labour Party was of legitimate

---

[77] *Pro Sieben v Carlton* [1998] FSR 43.
[78] *Fraser-Woodward Ltd v BBC* [2005] FSR 36, paras 71 *et seq.*
[79] Directive (EC) 2001/29 of 22 May 2001 on the harmonisation of copyright and related rights in the information society, Art 5(3)(d).
[80] CDPA 1988, s 30.
[81] *Ashdown v Telegraph Group Ltd* [2001] EWCA Civ 1142.

and continuing public interest. However, the Court held that there was no justification for the reproduction of a substantial part of Paddy Ashdown's own words as such use was not 'fair'.

(b) *Sufficient acknowledgement* Under section 30(3), no acknowledgement is required in connection with the reporting of current events by means of a sound recording, film, or broadcast, where this would be impossible for reasons of practicality or otherwise.

(c) *Fair dealing* There is no statutory definition of what amounts to 'fair' dealing for the purposes of section 30 of CDPA 1988. However, the Court of Appeal in *Ashdown v Telegraph Group* considered the key factors to be:

(a) whether the use of the copyright work is in fact competing commercially with the copyright owner's exploitation of the work (in that case Paddy Ashdown was preparing his own memoirs which would have included the minute); and

(b) the amount and importance of the copyright work which has been taken.[82]

The Telegraph Group's publication of a substantial part of a confidential, leaked minute, published in that form, in order to further the commercial interests of the Telegraph Group, rather than for the public interest was not considered 'fair' dealing. The fact that the minute had been obtained by the newspaper without the knowledge of the copyright owner was also a material consideration. In the *Fraser-Woodward*[83] case the court found that the defendant's use of fourteen photographs for mostly one or two seconds, in circumstances where the defendants were not competing with the commercial interests of the photographer, was fair.

In *Hyde Park Residence Ltd v Yelland*[84] the Court of Appeal decided that *The Sun* newspaper, having published photographs of Princess Diana and Dodi Fayed in breach of copyright which it had paid for knowing the footage had been dishonestly obtained, was not 'fair'.

In *BBC v British Satellite Broadcasting Ltd*[85] BSB included excerpts taken from BBC broadcasts of football matches played during the 1990 World Cup in its sports news programmes. Each excerpt was between 14 and 37 seconds in length, was used in successive bulletins in a 24-hour period following the match, and accompanied by an attribution to the BBC.[86] The BBC brought a claim for copyright infringement and BSB relied on the fair dealing defence. The BBC argued that BSB had an 'oblique' motive in using the excerpts 'to compete with the BBC for a sports audience by making BSB's programme attractive' thus making it unfair. The judge disagreed.

---

[82] The Court also a third consideration, namely whether the work had been made available to the public. However, this element has since been enshrined in CDPA 1988.

[83] *Fraser-Woodward Ltd v BBC* [2005] FSR 36.

[84] *Hyde Park Residence Ltd v Yelland* [2000] 3 WLR 215.

[85] *BBC v British Satellite Broadcasting Ltd* [1992] Ch 141.

[86] Except on one occasion, which was said to have been a mistake.

He quoted Lord Denning in *Hubbard v Vosper*[87] when he said: 'It is impossible to define what is "fair dealing". It must be a question of degree.' Having viewed the excerpts in question during the course of the trial, the judge commented that: 'The impression I formed . . . was that each of them fell squarely within the fair dealing defence . . . the matches were current events for the purposes of section 30(2). The Sportsdesk programmes seemed to me to be genuine news reports . . . The quality and quantity of BBC copyright material used in each programme seemed to me consistent with the nature of a news report.'[88]

(d) *Photographs* Photographs are given special treatment under CDPA 1988. Photographs are specifically excluded from the fair dealing for news reporting exception. Furthermore, a person who commissions a photograph for private and domestic purposes has the right to prevent copies of the photograph being issued, shown, or exhibited to the public.[89] It is possible therefore to obtain consent from the copyright owner (for example the photographer) but be prevented from publishing a photograph which has been commissioned for private and domestic purposes, for example a wedding photograph.

However, the definition of 'photograph' in section 4(2) of CDPA 1988 excludes stills from a film from the definition. The fair dealing exception was therefore considered in *Hyde Park Residence Ltd v Yelland*,[90] in which *The Sun* newspaper printed a series of stills shots of Princess Diana taken from CCTV images. Although the court ultimately held that the defence of fair dealing failed for other reasons, film stills are capable of attracting the defence of fair dealing.

6.2.6.5 *Incidental inclusion*
Another exception often relied on is that of 'incidental inclusion'. Copyright in a work is not infringed by its incidental inclusion in an artistic work, sound recording, film, or broadcast.[91] CDPA 1988 also states that the inclusion of a musical work and words spoken or sung is not to be regarded as incidental if deliberately included.[92] Clearly, this exception is intended to capture, for example, songs sung by football supporters

---

[87] *Hubbard v Vosper* [1972] 2 QB 84.

[88] The AVMS Directive (EC) 2007/65 or the Audio Visual Media Services (AVMS) Directive amends and renames the Television Without Frontiers Directive. The Directive must be transposed into national law by 19 December 2009. At the time of writing a public consultation on its implementation has been concluded but the results have not been published. The Directive permits broadcasters to take short extracts of other broadcasters' exclusive coverage of events for the purpose of including them in news reports and allowing limited subsequent use in on-demand services. However, there will be a number of important caveats on this right: the extracts must be used in general news programmes and Member States are required to 'ensure . . . that . . . conditions regarding the provision of such short extracts are defined, in particular, any compensation arrangements, the maximum length of short extracts and the time limits regarding their transmission.'

[89] CDPA 1988, s 85.

[90] *Hyde Park Residence Ltd v Yelland* [2000] 3 WLR 215.

[91] CDPA 1988, s 31(1).

[92] ibid s 31(3).

at a match, which are included in the broadcast of the match on television. In the *Panini* case,[93] the defendant distributed a football sticker album, which contained stickers of players wearing their club strips on which appeared the club logos and (sometimes) the Football Association's lion logo. The defendant argued that the inclusion of such works was incidental. The Court of Appeal, confirming the judgment below, disagreed. 'Incidental' did not mean only unintentional or non-deliberate inclusion. In order to test whether the use of one work in another was incidental, it was proper to ask why it had been included in the other, considering both commercial and aesthetic reasons. In this case, the use of the logos was to make the stickers more attractive to collectors and was essential to the object for which the image of the player, as it appeared on the sticker or album, had been created.

In the *Fraser-Woodward* case[94] the judge concluded that the inclusion of one of the photographs in a television programme could benefit from the incidental inclusion exception. This photograph was included in one of the tabloid headlines which in itself was used in the programme; the judge concluded that this part of the television programme was concerned with tabloid headlines and the photograph contained in the headline was incidental to the inclusion of the headline.

6.2.6.6 *'Public interest'*
Section 171 of CDPA 1988 states that nothing in this part 'affects any rule of law preventing or restricting the enforcement of copyright, on grounds of public interest or otherwise'. The courts have been keen to emphasize that this section merely acknowledges the court's inherent jurisdiction to refuse to enforce copyright where it would 'offend against public policy' to do so. Copyright, being a property right conferring on the owner the right to do or not to do certain acts is not to be treated as aligned with confidential information, where the interest in keeping something secret is to be balanced against the public interest.[95]

6.2.7 Remedies for infringement

The owner of copyright (and/or the exclusive licensee of copyright) may be entitled to an injunction, damages, or an account of profits and delivery up or destruction of infringing articles. The action is available to the owner, or the exclusive licensee, or both but all parties with an interest in the copyright (ie all owners and any exclusive licensees) must be joined in the action (as claimant) or added (as defendant), except when the owner or exclusive licensee is seeking an interim injunction. An interim injunction may be granted to the owner of the copyright in equity only (in other words to someone who has only a beneficial interest in the copyright and not yet the legal title, although the legal title must be obtained before a final injunction can be granted).

[93] *Football Association Premier League Ltd v Panini UK Ltd* [2004] 1 WLR 1147.
[94] *Fraser-Woodward Ltd v BBC* [2005] FSR 36, paras 79 *et seq.*
[95] See in particular the judgments of Aldous LJ and Mance LJ in *Hyde Park Residence Ltd v Yelland* (n 84 above).

A person who has authorized acts of infringement may be an infringer under CDPA 1988.[96] However, even someone who has not committed acts of infringement himself but who has procured and intended those acts be done by another or has joined with an infringer in concerted action to secure that those acts were done may be liable as a joint tortfeasor.

A successful claimant is entitled to an inquiry as to damages or may take an account of the infringer's profits. The claimant is entitled to some information first before electing for an inquiry as to damages or an account of profit.

An innocent infringer has limited protection against damages for infringement. If a defendant proves that at the date of the infringement he was not aware, and had no reasonable ground for suspecting, that copyright subsisted in the work, the claimant is not entitled to damages for infringement, although he is still entitled to an injunction, an account of profits, and delivery up of infringing copies.[97] A mistake as to the ownership of copyright is not enough to bring the defendant within the protection of this provision.

Most forms of infringement of copyright, when committed knowingly, are offences triable by a court of summary jurisdiction or on indictment.

6.2.8 Copyright and the internet

The internet is an increasingly dominant medium in which media companies can exploit their goods and services. Newspapers and television programmes can be viewed, games played, and music downloaded, all online. Similarly, the internet opens up opportunity for infringement, sometimes on a large scale, by, for example, accessing material and file sharing. The internet, being a global medium, presents challenges for copyright law, which is essentially territorial by nature. Copyright law in the UK has been adapted and amended over many years to deal with technological challenges, from the development of printing presses to films, broadcasts, and sound recordings. Owning or using copyright material on the internet is dealt with in the same way as works in any other medium. CDPA 1988 contains a number of provisions which cover much of the unlawful use of copyright material on the internet—the greater challenge is often one of enforcement.

One of the restricted acts reserved to the owner of copyright is the right to make copies or authorize others to make copies.[98] CDPA 1988 provides that the making of transient copies of a copyright work infringes copyright in that work.[99] So even a temporary copy, created for merely a few seconds, infringes copyright if it was not permitted.[100] A fleeting image shown on a television monitor could also infringe.[101]

---

[96] CDPA 1988, s 16(2), and see more generally *Clerk and Lindsell on Torts*.
[97] ibid s 233.
[98] ibid s 16(1) and (2).
[99] ibid s 17(6).
[100] A permitted act in this context will be an act which conforms with CDPA 1988, s 28A.
[101] *Bookmakers' Afternoon Greyhound Services v Wilf Gilbert (Staffordshire) Ltd* [1994] FSR 723.

In relation to literary, dramatic, musical, and artistic works, copying expressly includes the storing of the work in any medium by electronic means.[102]

So accessing and viewing copyright material on the internet is an infringement of copyright if done without consent of the copyright owner. Clearly, if the rights-holder has authorized the display of a work on a webpage there must be at least an implied licence for authorized users to make temporary copies for the purposes of accessing and viewing the page. Popular social networking websites, such as Facebook and MySpace, require users to agree to allow others to copy their work before users upload the work.[103] The user usually retains the copyright but grants a royalty-free, worldwide, non-exclusive licence for the work to be copied. The terms and conditions of membership of such sites also often contain similar provisions. Many websites have terms and conditions of use which attempt to circumscribe the use to which copyright material can be put.

6.2.8.1 *The position of ISPs*

The E-Commerce Directive[104] provides that 'information society service providers', for example internet service providers (ISPs), will not be liable in respect of activities of 'caching' and 'hosting'.[105] Copies made during 'hosting' or 'caching' may be permanent or temporary. If the copies are temporary, they may come within the exception provided for in section 28A of CDPA 1988. This section provides that copyright in a literary work is not infringed by the making of a temporary copy which is 'transient or incidental' where the temporary copy must be an 'integral and essential part of a technological process' and made for the sole purpose of enabling 'a transmission of the work in a network between third parties'. The copy must also have no independent economic significance.[106]

(a) *Hosting* Websites are often hosted by an ISP. The ISP, as host, saves files that make up a website onto a server which can then be accessed by others via the internet. The website saved by the server may include infringing copies of a third party's material. Although the host has not set up the website, it will have provided the means for the infringing material to be published. The ISP will also have a copy of the work saved on its server and which would, in itself, be a breach of copyright. Therefore, the ISP may be liable for copyright infringement by hosting the site on which the infringing work appears.

In order for an ISP to claim immunity for hosting copyright protected work under the E-Commerce Regulations, it must show that it did not have actual knowledge of the

---

    [102] CDPA 1988, s 17(2).
    [103] J Miles, 'Distributing user-generated content: risks and rewards' (2007) 18(1) Entertainment Law Review 28, 29.
    [104] Directive (EC) 2000/31. The Directive was implemented in the UK by the Electronic Commerce (EC Directive) Regulations 2002, SI 2002/2013. It has been in effect since 21 August 2002.
    [105] E-Commerce Directive, arts 13 and 14, E-Commerce Regulations 2002, reg 18.
    [106] CDPA 1988, s 28A.

unlawful activity or information held on the website. Where a claim for damages is made, it must be shown that the ISP was not aware of facts or circumstances from which it would have been apparent to the ISP that the activity or information was unlawful. If the ISP did have such knowledge or awareness, it must show that it acted expeditiously to remove or disable access to the information.[107]

(b) *Caching* Caching is the temporary storage on a local computer of digital information, especially from a website. The purpose of this is to enable users to reload webpages more quickly by removing the need to reconnect to a remote web server each time a website is accessed. It is generally recognized that without caching, the internet would not be able to cope with the huge volume of users. In addition to caching by end-users, ISPs also use caching to store previously delivered webpages temporarily on their servers. This enhances the speed which the server can retrieve information and so ultimately enhances the speed of the ISP's internet service. Caching therefore requires a temporary copy on the files constituting a website to be made and so, similarly to hosting, could infringe an owner's copyright. Caching is usually seen as a technical and automatic process.

In order for an ISP to claim immunity for caching copyright protected work, it must be able to show that the information was copied as part of an automatic, intermediate, and temporary storage process which was for the sole purpose of making the onward transmission of the information more efficient. The ISP must have complied with conditions on access to the information[108] and industry rules regarding updating the information. The ISP must also not have modified the information and must not interfere with the lawful use of technology. The ISP must act expeditiously to remove or disable access to the information stored if it obtains actual knowledge that the information has been removed or access has been disabled at the initial source.[109]

(c) *Limitations* The immunities outlined above only apply to damages and criminal sanctions. There is no immunity against other legal remedies or associated legal costs. It is therefore possible for a copyright owner to obtain an injunction against an ISP, if it can be shown that the ISP has actual knowledge of another person using the service to infringe copyright.[110]

The immunities also apply only to ISPs or similar providers. They give no protection to individual internet browsers. Most web browsing software (such as Explorer or Netscape) has a caching facility[111] and so it is possible, and often the case in theory, that web-users make copies of internet sites without their knowledge. These copies could in theory render them liable for copyright infringement.

---

[107] E-Commerce Regulations 2002, reg 19. This is currently a contentious area of law. The position is not helped by contradictory case law in continental Europe.

[108] This is not defined by the Directive, although it is thought that it means the conditions imposed by the website owner: *Copinger* (n 8 above) para 22-98.

[109] E-Commerce Regulations 2002, reg 18.

[110] CDPA 1998, s 97A.

[111] M Hart, 'Caching: UK issues', Practical Law Company, Intellectual Property, IT and Communications.

6.2.8.2 *File Sharing and P2P*

There has been much publicity about file sharing and the liability of those who provide file sharing software or services and ISPs involved in the file sharing process. There is no doubt that users who make available copyright material for download by others and those who upload such content infringe copyright (by copying the material, for example) unless they have permission from the owner of copyright. Enforcement against individual file sharers has been slow and piecemeal and rights owners argue that such actions are ineffective against a wave of illegal action. More effective action can be taken if those offering file sharing/P2P software and/or services can be found to be infringing either as facilitating or authorizing someone else's infringing act or as joint tortfeasors themselves. There have been a number of high-profile cases in a number of countries in which the courts have had to determine to what extent such providers are infringing, if at all, depending on the way in which such software and/or services are provided.[112] In the *Napster* case, Napster distributed P2P software and maintained a centrally held server containing an index of files held by users. Registered users could access and search the index and download a file directly from another user's computer. The court rejected the argument that Napster had no liability because its software had legitimate uses and held that Napster was a 'contributory infringer' under US law since it had reasonable knowledge of specific infringing acts. In the *Grokster* case, the architecture of the P2P technology was decentralized and so there was no centrally held index. The court held that, nonetheless, Grokster could be sued for infringement because it had taken active steps to encourage users to infringe. In the Australian case against Kazaa (which operated a type of P2P decentralized service, although it was argued in court that it was not a true P2P system) the court decided that Kazaa was itself infringing because it authorized others to infringe copyright (under a section similar to that in CDPA 1988). In the *Kazaa* case the court held that, even though there were warnings about infringing copyright and the end-user licence agreement required users to agree not to infringe, it had been known for some time that such measures were ineffective and Kazaa had done nothing to curtail the illegal sharing and had even encouraged it in other ways. One of the current issues before the courts is the extent to which those who operate so called 'BitTorrent' systems, which allow users to search and download small files that contain metadata necessary to download data files from other users, infringe.

Rights owners, such as the music and film rights owners, have also looked at the role of ISPs to try to help them stem the tide of piracy. In July 2008, various content owner associations and six of the UK's largest ISPs reached a Memorandum of Understanding which outlines codes of practice for identifying and dealing with illegal uploaders or downloaders.[113]

---

[112] See the *Napster* case—*A&M Records Inc v Napster, Inc* 239 F 3d 1004 (9th Cir 2001); the *Grokster* case—*MGM Studios, Inc v Grokster, Ltd* 545 US 913 (2005); and the *Kazaa* case—*Universal Music Australia Pty Ltd v Sharman Licence Holdings Ltd* (with Corrigendum dated 22 September 2005) [2005] FCA 1242.

[113] The Joint Memorandum of Understanding on an Approach to Reduce Unlawful File Sharing is attached as Annex D to the Department for Business, Enterprise and Regulatory Reform

The Memorandum of Understanding, which was backed by the UK government, was part of a consultation intended to 'gather views on a proposal for a co-regulatory approach that could be adopted in order to facilitate and ensure co-operation between Internet Service Providers (ISPs) and rights holders to address the problem of illicit use of Peer-to-Peer (P2P) file-sharing technology to exchange unlawful copies of copyright material'.[114]

6.2.9 Moral rights

Moral rights are non-proprietary rights relating to a copyright work. They include:

(1) For the author of a copyright literary, dramatic, musical or artistic work, and the director of a copyright film:
  (a) the right to be identified as the author or director;[115] and
  (b) the right to object to derogatory treatment of the work.[116] 'Treatment' covers addition, alteration, deletion or adaptation of the work (other than a translation or transcription) and the treatment is 'derogatory' if it amounts to distortion, mutilation, or is otherwise prejudicial to the honour and reputation of the author or director.[117]
  Copyright must subsist in the work for such moral rights to apply.

(2) In relation to literary, dramatic, musical, artistic works, or films, the right of a person not to have such a work falsely attributed to that person[118] (ie the person created a particular work when in fact they did not).
  Copyright does not need to subsist for such a moral right.

(3) In relation to a photographs or a film (where copyright subsists in the resulting work) the right not to have such a work issued to the public where the work was commissioned for private and domestic purposes.[119]

(4) For a performer:
  (a) the right to be identified;[120] and
  (b) the right to object to derogatory treatment of performance.[121]

(BERR) 'Consultation on Legislative Options to Address Illicit Peer-to-Peer (P2P) File-Sharing' (July 2008).

[114] The Consultation takes forward the recommendation from the Gowers Review of Intellectual Property, dated November 2006. See also the June 2009 *Digital Britain Report*.

[115] CDPA 1988, s 77.

[116] There are exceptions set out in ibid s 81. For example, the right does not apply to a computer program or to any computer-generated work; any work made for the purpose of reporting; publication in a newspaper, magazine or similar periodical; an encyclopaedia, dictionary, yearbook, or other collective work of reference for the purposes of such publication or with the author's consent (*inter alia*).

[117] CDPA 1988, s 80(2).

[118] ibid s 84.

[119] ibid s 85.

[120] ibid s 205C.

[121] ibid s 205F.

If moral rights are infringed, the author will be entitled to an injunction to prevent or stop the infringing act and also to damages.[122] Damages may be awarded to cover specific financial losses suffered by the author, as well as damages for his or her loss of reputation or goodwill and possibly also compensation for hurt feelings.

A moral right will not be infringed if the moral right-holder has given consent to the doing of an act which would otherwise infringe such a moral right. Also, a moral right can be waived by an instrument in writing signed by the person giving up the moral right[123] in the work, such as the right to be identified as the author and the right to object to derogatory treatment of the work.[124] Moral rights are not assignable but, unless waived, remain with the author until death. There are circumstances in which the owner of moral rights may be different from the owner of the copyright.

6.3 DATABASES

Databases are used in all types of media industry in one form or another. For example, customer lists, television programme schedules, lists of songs on an internet music website, and a list of football player statistics in a computer game are all databases. Databases are defined as collections of material that are arranged in a systematic or methodical way, where each item is individually accessible by electronic or other means.[125]

Before the implementation of the EC Directive on the Legal Protection of Databases ((EC) 96/9) (the Database Directive) the intellectual property in compilations of data could only be protected in the UK by copyright as a type of literary work.[126] This meant that the usual conditions for originality and the qualification requirements for the author had to be satisfied before the database could be protected under CDPA 1988 and a substantial part of the database had to be copied to meet the test of infringement.[127]

The Database Directive, which aimed to harmonize the protection and exploitation of databases within the European Union, was implemented in the UK by the Copyright and Rights in Databases Regulations in 1996 (the Database Regulations).[128] The Database Regulations amended the existing provisions under CDPA 1988 to include a specific protection for databases (the 'Database Right').[129]

---

[122] ibid s 103(2).
[123] ibid s 87 in relation to moral rights in literary, dramatic, musical, artistic work, photographs, and film, s 205J in relation to performances.
[124] ibid ss 77 and 80.
[125] ibid s 3A(1).
[126] *Ladbroke (Football) Ltd v William Hill (Football) Ltd* [1964] 1 WLR 273, HL (originality arising in skilful arrangement of the materials in a football pools coupon. Some members of the House of Lords based their decision on the selection of bets, others on the layout of the coupon); *Independent Television Publications Ltd v Time Out Ltd* [1984] FSR 64 (sequence of broadcast programmes).
[127] CDPA 1988, ss 1(1)(a) and 153.
[128] SI 1997/3032.
[129] A database will only be original if 'by reason of the selection or arrangement of the contents of the database the database constitutes the author's own intellectual creation' (CDPA 1988, s 3A).

Compilations of data that do not meet the definition of a database may continue to be protected as literary works, as before, subject to the usual originality threshold of the author having shown sufficient skill, judgment, or labour in the work.[130] The Database Right entitles the maker of a database to prevent the extraction or re-utilization of all or a substantial part of its database, as well as the repeated and systematic extraction or re-utilization of insubstantial parts (evaluated qualitatively and/or quantitatively).[131] The 'maker' of the database is defined as the person who takes the initiative and assumes the risk of investing in obtaining, verifying, or presenting the content of the database.[132] The Database Right is an EU-only right in that the maker must be the national of an EU Member State or have their habitual residence in the European Union in order to qualify for protection.

In 2004, the European Court of Justice (ECJ) was asked to interpret what is meant by the maker 'investing in obtaining' the content of its database, in *British Horseracing Board Ltd and ors v William Hill Organisation Ltd*.[133] This case concerned the alleged infringement by the bookmaker, William Hill, of BHB's horseracing database, and three joined cases involving a UK football fixture database and its alleged infringement by companies in Finland, Sweden, and Greece. The ECJ held that the phrase 'investing in obtaining' referred to resources which were used to find existing, independently-created materials and to collate those materials into a database. It did not extend to the resources used to create the materials themselves.

The decision was seen as a disappointment for database owners since it meant that the Database Right might not apply where a maker has not invested in finding or presenting the contents of its database, regardless of how much time or money has been spent in creating the content. Nevertheless, the decision means that, provided the right exists in the first place, the protection is broad. For example, the ECJ ruled that the right protected against the taking of a substantial part of the contents of a database, not only by direct access, but by taking indirectly from publicly available material, such as that in newspapers or accessible on websites.

In *Directmedia Publishing GmbH v Albert-Ludwigs-Universität Freiburg*[134] the ECJ did not alter its assessment as to when protection is available, but confirmed that, for the purposes of infringement of a protected database, 'extraction' of

---

[130] *BAGS Ltd v Wilf Gilbert (Staffordshire) Ltd* [1994] FSR 723 (greyhound race cards).

[131] Database Regulations, SI 1997/3032 regs 13 and 16. The right lasts for 15 years from the end of the year in which the database was made. Where a change to the contents of the database constitutes a 'substantial new investment', the amended database will qualify for a new 15-year term (reg 17).

[132] ibid reg 14.

[133] Case C-203/02 *British Horseracing Board Ltd and ors v William Hill Organisation Ltd*; Case C-444/02 *Fixtures Marketing Ltd v Organismos Prognostikon Agonon Podosfairou*; Case C-338/02 *Fixtures Marketing Ltd v Svenska Spel AB*; Case C-46/02 *Fixtures Marketing Ltd v OV Veikkaus Ab*, 9 November 2004.

[134] Case C-304/07 *Directmedia Publishing GmbH v Albert-Ludwigs-Universität Freiburg*, 9 October 2008.

data should be interpreted broadly.[135] It held that the Database Right would not be affected by:

(a) the method used in appropriating the content—manual recopying constitutes extraction in the same way as direct copying through photocopying or downloading;

(b) the extracting party consulting the database and then using its own judgment to compile a new database containing some of the material;

(c) whether the purpose of the extraction was to create another database for commercial or non-commercial purposes.

In interpreting broadly the protection given by the Database Right, the ECJ followed its reasoning in the *William Hill* case that the right was introduced to protect investment (whether human, technical, or financial) in producing a database. Therefore, acts prejudicing that investment will generally infringe; 'extraction' covers any unauthorized appropriation of all or part of the database's contents.

6.4 PASSING OFF AND PERSONALITY RIGHTS

Passing off is judge-made law which protects the goodwill of a trader from misappropriation by another. It is akin to unfair competition. The classic test for a successful action in passing off, formulated in the Advocaat case by Lord Diplock,[136] provides that a misrepresentation must be made in the course of trade to prospective or ultimate customers which is likely to injure the goodwill of another and which causes that trader's goodwill or business actual damage. The test has been re-stated since then but does not differ greatly in these elements: the claimant must establish that he or she has goodwill, that there is a relevant misrepresentation by the defendant, and that damage or a real likelihood of it will follow.

Much depends on the facts of a particular case. The publishers of the *Daily Mail* and *Mail on Sunday* were able to prevent the launch of a free evening newspaper with 'Mail' in the title because the judge was satisfied that the publishers had acquired sufficient reputation and goodwill in the name 'Mail' so that the public would be confused if a new paper launched bearing that name. While other newspapers existed with the word 'Mail' in the title, the publishers in this action were able to show that the majority of readers in its heartland referred to the papers as 'The Mail'.

In *Clark v Associated Newspapers Ltd*, the *Evening Standard* published a series of articles which were parodies of the journals of the then MP and author, Alan Clark. The judge decided, on the basis of significant evidence of confusion, that a substantial

---

[135] 'Extraction' is defined under Database Directive, 96/9/EC, Art 7(2) (and repeated in the Database Regulations, reg 12) as the permanent or temporary transfer of the database content to another medium by any means or in any form. 'Re-utilisation' is defined as making the database content available to the public by any means.

[136] *Erven Warnink BV v J Townend & Sons (Hull) Ltd (No 1)* [1979] AC 731, HL.

body of readers of the newspaper were misled or likely to be misled into thinking that the diaries were in fact written by Mr Clark.[137]

Given the likely evidential difficulties of proving damage, historically the courts would not recognize passing off unless there was a 'common field of activity' between the claimant and the defendant. This was seen as the bar to using passing off to protect the goodwill of personalities. The Court departed from such a narrow interpretation in *Irvine v Talksport*, a case involving the use in an advertisement by Talksport radio of a photograph of the racing driver, Eddie Irvine, which implied that Mr Irvine had endorsed the station.[138] The Court held that if someone acquires a valuable reputation or goodwill, the law of passing off may protect it from unlicensed use by other parties irrespective of a common field of activities.

Although the Court in *Irvine v Talksport* stated that it is not necessary to show that the claimant and the defendant share a common field of activity, there is still a need to demonstrate misrepresentation in the sense that third parties will gain a false impression of a connection with the defendant's products or business with the claimant. The requirements for passing off in relation to a false endorsement were set out by the Court as follows:

(a) that at the time of the acts complained of the complainant[139] had a significant reputation or goodwill;

(b) that the actions of the defendant gave rise to a false message which would be understood by a not insignificant section of the defendant's market;

(c) that the defendant's goods have been endorsed, recommended, or are approved of by the claimant.

It is important to note that the Court did not merely require reputation or goodwill, as is the case for normal passing off, but 'significant' reputation or goodwill. Put simply, the action only extends to 'famous' people or those who might be understood by the public as having a reputation or goodwill that is capable of being commercially exploited in such a way.[140]

---

[137] [1998] 1WLR 1558. (This case does not mean that parodies are unlawful—the presentation of the articles in this case was considered by the judge to be too realistic.)

[138] *Irvine v Talksport* [2002] 2 All ER 414.

[139] Crucially, this may not be the claimant as the goodwill may vest in another entity, eg a company of which the complainant is an employee. See *Globelegance v Sarkissian* [1974] RPC 603, where the proper claimant was the company that employed the fashion designer Valentino Garavani, commonly known as Valentino, even though the company's goodwill was wholly attributable to Mr Garavani's talent and reputation as a fashion designer.

[140] The British Code of Advertising, Sales Promotion and Direct Marketing (CAP Code) states that marketers should not unfairly portray or refer to people in an adverse or offensive way. Although not legally binding, a breach may result in an advertisement being withdrawn if the individual portrayed in the image makes a complaint. The CAP Code recommends that marketers obtain written permission before:

(a) referring to or portraying members of the public or their identifiable possessions, although the use of crowd scenes or general public locations without permission may be acceptable; or

6.5 TRADE MARKS

When looking at all forms of media the trade marks at stake often consist of an attractive name or slogan that may be combined with design elements, and potentially the images and names of famous personalities. The questions applicable to those different marks are essentially the same:

- Can I use it?
- Can I protect it?
- Can I exploit and enforce it, ideally to the exclusion of everyone else?

Taking, for example, a new name or brand for a television format or a new publication, the name selected should be cleared before it is used. This not only ensures that there are no third-party prior rights, which could prevent use of the name, but also ascertains whether it may be possible to secure trade mark registration for the name. The purpose of seeking trade mark registration is to obtain exclusive rights to directly or indirectly exploit the protected television format name within that same territory. The registered trade mark may subsequently be enforced against third parties exploiting without consent an identical or similar name for a television format in the territory where the mark is protected.

6.5.1 Trade mark use

Ensuring that this protection is in place on an international basis is more complex, as it is to a large extent dependent on national rights. A clearance search should therefore be conducted in each of the jurisdictions where the television format or publication is intended to be exploited, to ensure that there are no local prior rights which could prevent the trade mark's immediate or future use. Prior trade mark rights could prevent one obtaining the appropriate trade mark protection and, as a worst case scenario, lead to trade mark infringement proceedings and an injunction prohibiting use of the later trade mark.

The effectiveness of clearance searches will depend on the identification of the mark of interest and of the goods and/or services in respect of which that mark is going to be used. A clearance search in respect of a television format would need to cover 'entertainment programmes' in class 41 of the Nice Classification[141] as well as any

---

(b) referring to people with a public profile, however, references that accurately reflect the contents of books, articles, or films may be acceptable without permission; or

(c) implying any personal approval of an advertised product. The guidance states that marketers should realize that those who do not want to be associated with a product may have a legal claim.

[141] The International (NICE) Classification of Goods and Services for the Purposes of the Registration of Marks (9th edn) is specified by the World Intellectual Property Organisation and serves to determine the scope of protection of trade marks. It is divided into classes of Goods (classes 1–34) and Services (classes 35–45).

other goods or services in which the mark may be used in future. For example, the trade mark owner may wish to use the mark exclusively for merchandised products such as computer game programs (found in class 9) or t-shirts and clothing (found in class 25). Ideally, the trade mark clearance should be conducted within all the classes relevant to the products or services of current or future interest, and in all the territories where the mark is intended to be used.

Such clearance searches ought to disclose prior titles, slogans, or designs registered as trade marks, but would not disclose titles, slogans, or designs protected by other registered or unregistered rights, including copyright, designs, or passing off. Such earlier rights can constitute potential obstacles to the intended trade mark. In some jurisdictions, such as France, earlier rights in company names, commercial names, shop signs, or domain names can also be problematic. The clearance searches conducted nationally should therefore cover all prior rights locally enforceable against the proposed mark's use and registration.

Whilst conducting full searches in all relevant classes in all relevant jurisdictions will provide the trade mark owner with some comfort that there is no unknown third party who could enjoin use or registration of his proposed mark, it can end up being costly. A balance may need to be found between the certainty surrounding the trade mark's intended use, and the acceptable time and cost for the clearance searches. In addition, searching for unregistered rights is never conclusive.

6.5.2 Trade mark protection

The mark can be protected at different levels: national, European, and international. All jurisdictions retain their national system, where the conditions and time taken to obtain registration vary from one jurisdiction to another. The Community Trade Mark registration system has the advantage of granting protection throughout the European Union with a single registration. The systems of the Madrid Agreement or Protocol enable the World Intellectual Property Organization (WIPO) to ease the application process for a chosen set of national protections across the world. Which system is chosen will depend on the scope of the protection sought and the demands of the different systems, which tends to mean that the costs of registering the mark will vary.

The trade mark's protection is dependent on its distinctiveness for the products or services of interest. A trade mark is distinctive when it enables the relevant public to identify goods and services as being from a single origin, and to distinguish them from similar goods or services of a different origin. What is distinctive in one country may not be in another. This can depend on the language or the alphabet used for the mark in each country and upon other local circumstances. Thus, whether the mark is translated in the local language or used in a single language in all countries can impact on the mark's local distinctiveness, and hence on its protection. For example, the mark CHOCOLATE may be distinctive for chocolate if it is used in Mandarin in the UK, but would be descriptive when used in English.

The trade mark can consist of a slogan or a publication title, but it must not be descriptive in relation to the product's subject matter or characteristics, or else it would be entitled to little or no trade mark protection. If a word or phrase is not considered as distinctive, an option may be to incorporate additional design elements, but bearing in mind that the scope of protection for devices incorporating words would not be as broad as a registration for word only. As an example, the television format name *Who Wants to be a Millionaire?* can be regarded as descriptive of the well-known television show's subject matter—at least in the absence of distinctiveness acquired through use—but combined with stylized elements and colours it can be seen as distinctive.

The trade mark can also consist of 'personality rights', such as a name, signature, image, or likeness. A famous personality or group, either real or fictional, may indeed wish to exploit their name and image. One means of doing this is through registered trade mark protection.[142]

The distinctiveness of such trade marks can, however, be questioned. The name and image of famous personalities often become so widespread that the public may perceive their use as indicating that relevant goods or services are about the identified person as opposed to the name or image indicating that the goods or services originate from or are authorized by the personality. The goods at stake may also be perceived by the public as linked to the activities for which that person is famous, for example, sporting goods in relation to a famous sporting personality.

Finally, trade mark protection can involve timing issues. With some exceptions based on unregistered rights obtained through use, trade mark protection in a number of jurisdictions is on a first-come-first-served basis and applications for trade mark registration should therefore be filed as soon as possible. However, the publication of the trade mark application is a prerequisite, which may interfere with a wish for confidentiality as competitors may then become aware of the applicant's plans.

6.5.3 Trade mark exploitation and enforcement

Exploiting a trade mark successfully involves stopping others from exploiting the same without authorization, hence enforcing the trade mark against them. A balance needs to be found between exploitation and enforcement. For example, in the case involving the memorial fund of the late Princess of Wales,[143] some argued that more time and money was spent trying to stop (ultimately unsuccessfully) third parties using the Princess's famous name and image for merchandise, than fundraising through exploitation.

---

[142] The racing car driver, Lewis Hamilton, has, for example, registered his name as a UK trade mark, No 2258089.

[143] *The Franklin Mint Co v The Diana Princess of Wales Memorial Fund* (Oppositions 49400 and 49431) Decision of the Appointed Person dated 1 May 2003.

A more positive example is the successful game show *Who Wants to be a Millionaire?* The trade mark protection for this name covers a wide variety of goods such as toys, games, playthings, clothing, and computer games. If there was originally any doubt about the distinctiveness of the name *Who Wants to be a Millionaire?* there is now little doubt that it is one of the most successful game shows ever in commercial terms. The proliferation of associated merchandise, and its use in an Oscar-winning film,[144] supports this contention.

Character merchandising consists of licensing the use of a name or likeness of a real or fictional character in relation to the marketing of goods or services. The name of a story may be taken as a sign indicating the goods or services of one trade. However, there is a danger that the name in question, if long-established and well known, may have passed into common language. In that case it will become a characteristic of the goods or services simply indicating that the goods and services feature the story or character concerned rather than the story or character functioning as an indicator of origin. The most typical defence against the enforcement of a trade mark consisting of a famous name would be that the name or character is not being used in a trade mark sense, ie as an indicator of origin, but to describe the subject matter of the products or services at stake.

Whilst quite a few celebrities have managed to get their names and images registered, there remain doubts regarding the extent to which such rights can be enforced against third parties. Third parties may seek to challenge the trade mark registration itself. A third party may claim the mark's invalidity for lack of distinctiveness, on the basis that the mark has become generic or descriptive, or its revocation, when it has not been used during a five-year period for all or part of the goods and services covered by the mark's registration. Indeed, marks which are not used will become vulnerable to cancellation.

In addition, where the third party's mark is only similar to the earlier mark, or where it covers products or services only similar to those covered by the latter (as opposed to being identical thereto), there will be no infringement unless it is proved that the relevant public is likely to confuse the two marks. Well-known trade marks are usually afforded a greater protection, even when the marks or the goods at stake are only similar, but case law indicates that there is some doubt as to whether trade marks in relation to the names or images of famous people are afforded that level of protection.[145] It appears that courts are inclined to believe that the name of someone famous is less likely to be confused with a similar name or mark. The same will also go for the name and image of a real or fictitious well-known personality.[146]

Nonetheless, in relation to character merchandising (as well as to celebrity endorsement), even if the name or image of a character has not been registered there is a

---

[144] *Slumdog Millionaire*, 2008.

[145] Court of First Instance (CFI), Case T-185/02 *PICASSO/PICARO*, 22 June 2004; European Court of Justice (ECJ), case C-361/04 *PICASSO/PICARO*, 12 January 2006.

[146] ECJ, Case C-16/06 P *OBELIX/MOBILIX*, 18 December 2008.

possibility of bringing a passing off action, where there is a misrepresentation that the goods are in fact 'official' (ie produced by or under licence of the celebrity/character).[147]

Finally, the inter-relationship between trade marks and domain names should be considered. Domain names are essentially a contractual right and can be registered whether distinctive or not. The obvious difficulty arises when a third party seeks to register domain names containing a prior trade mark. Whilst domain names themselves do not afford trade mark rights it is therefore sensible to acquire the rights to obvious domain names when seeking to obtain trade mark protection and to take prompt action against cybersquatters.

---

[147] See section 6.4 above.

7

INFORMATION LAW[1]

Timothy Pitt-Payne

7.1 INFORMATION LAW AND THE MEDIA

Information is essential to the work of the media. This is an obvious point, and it applies with equal force to internet-based media and to traditional print and broadcast journalism. Hence it is not surprising that information law is a central aspect of media law. It involves questions such as these:

• What are the limits of permissible information-gathering by the media—either in terms of the information that can be collected, or in terms of the techniques that can be used?

• What legal rights of access to information are available to assist the media in their work?

• How much control do media organizations have over their own information? Can they ever be forced to disclose information that they would prefer to withhold?

• What are the constraints on the freedom of the media to publish information?

An obvious focal point in any discussion of information law is the 'information Acts': ie the Data Protection Act 1998 (DPA 1998) and the Freedom of Information Act 2000

---

[1] This chapter includes a revised and updated version of material that previously appeared in C Reed and J Angel (eds), *Computer Law* (OUP, 6th edn, 2007) Ch 11.

(FOIA 2000).[2] These Acts share a common regulator (the Information Commissioner) and a common specialist Tribunal (the Information Tribunal). DPA 1998 governs the acquisition, use, and disclosure of personal information about identifiable individuals. FOIA 2000 provides a general right of access on request (subject to exceptions) to information held by public authorities.

However, information law is by no means just about the information Acts. It has a strong human rights component. Hence this chapter begins with a consideration of the European Convention on Human Rights ('the Convention'), as given further effect by the Human Rights Act 1998 (HRA 1998). The Convention provisions relating to privacy (Article 8) and freedom of expression (Article 10) are particularly important in this context. Attempts have been made—with varying degrees of success—to use both provisions as the basis for a positive right of access to information held by public authorities. More fundamentally, Article 8 and Article 10 are in obvious tension: unrestricted free expression for the media would inevitably impinge at times on individual privacy, in cases where the media wished to publish details of an individual's private life. In English law that tension is now accommodated within the action for breach of confidence, which has developed rapidly as a result of HRA 1998. Breach of confidence, particularly in its post-HRA 1998 version, is discussed in section 7.3 below. The chapter then goes on to consider DPA 1998 and FOIA 2000, together with other statutory rights of access to information.

7.2 THE HUMAN RIGHTS CONTEXT[3]

7.2.1 The European Convention on Human Rights and the Human Rights Act 1998

The Convention was opened for signature in November 1950, was ratified by the UK on 8 March 1951, and came into force on 3 September 1953. The UK adopted Article 34 of the Convention (giving individual citizens the right to bring claims against their own government before the European Court of Human Rights)[4] in 1966. However, the importance of the Convention in UK law has considerably increased since the passage of HRA 1998 (which came into force on 2 October 2000). The Act is sometimes referred to as having incorporated the Convention into UK law. Technically speaking this is not accurate:[5] a more precise description is in the long title to the Act, which

---

[2] DPA 1998 and FOIA 2000 are collectively defined as 'the information Acts' by DPA 1998, s 59(5).

[3] See generally A Nicol, G Millar and A Sharland, *Media Law and Human Rights* (OUP, 2nd edn, 2009).

[4] The procedures for enforcing the Convention were radically changed on 1 November 1998 when Protocol 11 to the Convention came into force. Before that date, 2 institutions were involved: the European Commission and the European Court of Human Rights. Protocol 11 abolished both institutions and replaced them with a newly constituted, full-time European Court of Human Rights.

[5] For instance, the Act's references to 'Convention rights' do not extend to the whole of the Convention and its Protocols.

describes the Act's purpose as being 'to give further effect to rights and freedoms guaranteed under the European Convention on Human Rights'.

A detailed account of HRA 1998 is outside the scope of this chapter,[6] but in very broad terms the most important provisions are these:

• so far as it is possible to do so, primary and subordinate legislation must be read and given effect in a way which is compatible with Convention rights (section 3(1));

• the UK courts may make a declaration of incompatibility if satisfied that a provision in primary legislation is incompatible with a Convention right (section 4(2));

• the UK courts may also make a declaration of incompatibility in respect of a provision of subordinate legislation, made in the exercise of a power conferred by primary legislation, in cases where the primary legislation concerned prevents removal of the incompatibility (section 4(4));

• it is unlawful for a public authority to act in a way which is incompatible with a Convention right (section 6(1));

• a person who claims that a public authority has acted or proposes to act in a way which is made unlawful by section 6(1) may bring proceedings under HRA 1998 in the appropriate court or tribunal, or may rely on the Convention right(s) concerns in any legal proceedings, but only if he is or would be a victim of the unlawful act (section 7(1)); and

• in relation to any act or proposed act of a public authority which the court finds is (or would be) unlawful, the court may grant such relief or remedy, or make such order, within its powers as it considers just and appropriate (section 8(1)).

As already indicated, the most important Convention articles, as far as information law issues affecting the media are concerned, are Article 8 (dealing with privacy) and Article 10 (dealing with freedom of expression). Two issues about these articles are discussed below: the extent to which either article provides a positive right to access official information (section 7.2.2); and the way in which HRA 1998 deals with the potential for conflict between privacy and freedom of expression (section 7.2.3).

7.2.2 Articles 8 and 10 as a source of positive rights to access information

Article 8.1 provides that everyone has the right to respect for his private and family life, his home, and his correspondence. This is qualified by Article 8.2, which reads:

There shall be no interference by a public authority with the exercise of this right except such as is in accordance with the law and is necessary in a democratic society in the interests of national security, public safety or the economic well-being of the country, for the prevention of disorder

---

[6] The literature on HRA 1998 is very extensive indeed. The leading practitioner text is the magisterial work by R Clayton QC and H Tomlinson QC, *The Law of Human Rights* (OUP, 2nd edn, 2009). Chs 2–5 deal with general principles under HRA 1998. Chs 12 (on privacy) and 15 (on freedom of expression) are especially relevant to the subject matter of this chapter.

or crime, for the protection of health or morals, or for the protection of the rights and freedoms of others.

Article 10.1 provides that everyone has the right to freedom of expression, and continues:

That right shall include freedom to hold opinions and to receive and impart information and ideas without interference by public authorities and regardless of frontiers.[7]

Article 10.(2) qualifies this right, and is in similar (though not identical) terms to Article 8.2:

The exercise of these freedoms, since it carries with it duties and responsibilities, may be subject to such formalities, conditions, restrictions or penalties as are prescribed by law and are necessary in a democratic society, in the interests of national security, territorial integrity or public safety, for the prevention of disorder or crime, for the protection of health or morals, for the protection of the reputation or rights of others, for preventing the disclosure of information received in confidence, or for maintaining the authority or impartiality of the judiciary.

Attempts have been made, both before the Strasbourg Court and in the UK courts, to use each of these articles as the basis for a positive right of access to information held by public authorities. Those attempts have enjoyed rather more success in relation to Article 8 than in relation to Article 10.

Clearly, Article 8 does not create any general right of access to official information. However, on occasion it has been used as the basis for a positive obligation to supply information to individuals where that information has a bearing on their own home or private life. Thus in *Gaskin v UK*[8] the Strasbourg Court held that an individual who had been fostered as a child had a right under Article 8 to obtain access to his own records. In *Guerra v Italy*[9] the Strasbourg Court held that respect for private and family life carried with it a right of access to information that would enable the applicants to assess the risks involved in continuing to live near a particular factory.[10] In *R (on the application of S) v Plymouth City Council*[11] the Court of Appeal held that information about a man who was in the guardianship of the local authority under the Mental Health Act 1983 should be disclosed to his mother, so that the mother could decide whether to take steps to end the guardianship. One of the matters relied upon by the Court was the Article 8 right to family life of both mother and son.[12]

This use of Article 8 is of limited interest to media organizations, as it is based on the claimants' contention that their own private or family life requires that certain information be disclosed to them. Far more interesting from a media point of view is

---

[7] The final sentence of Art 10.1 provides that the article shall not prevent states from requiring the licensing of broadcasting, television, or cinema enterprises.

[8] (1989) 12 EHRR 36.

[9] (1998) 26 EHRR 357.

[10] See also *McGinley and Egan v UK* (1998) 27 EHRR 1; *Roche v UK* (2006) EHRR 30; *Smith v UK*, Decision of 4 January 2007.

[11] [2002] EWCA Civ 388, [2002] 1 WLR 2583.

[12] See Hale LJ, para 46 of the decision.

the question whether Article 10 can be used as the basis for a positive right of access to information held by public authorities. In general, both the Strasbourg Court and the UK courts have rejected attempts to use Article 10 in this way. The right to receive information under Article 10 means that public authorities may not interfere with communication between a willing speaker and a willing recipient of information, unless the interference is justified under Article 10.(2): see for instance *Open Door Counselling v Ireland* (where the Strasbourg Court held that an injunction preventing abortion clinics from providing information to pregnant women was a breach of the Article 10 rights of both parties). However, it appears that the right to receive information does not entail that public authorities are under a duty to *provide* information to those wishing to receive it. Hence in *Gaskin v UK*, above, the individual's claim for access to the information on the basis of Article 10 was rejected. Similarly in *Leander v Sweden*[13] the Strasbourg Court held that Article 10 did not confer any right of access to confidential government information, in the context of a claim arising out of an unsuccessful job application. The UK courts have taken a similar approach, in a series of cases involving public inquiries.[14]

By way of contrast, the corresponding provision of the American Convention on Human Rights (Article 13 of the American Convention) has been construed by the Inter-American Court of Human Rights as creating a positive state obligation to supply information on request, subject only to the restrictions set out in the American Convention itself: see *Claude-Reyes and ors v Chile*.[15] Admittedly Article 13 of the American Convention is differently worded from Article 10 of the European Convention, referring to a right to *seek* information, as well as a right to receive and impart information. The case is nevertheless of considerable interest.

Sedley LJ, writing extra-judicially, has suggested that the current orthodoxy in respect of the Convention is anomalous: 'There is something odd about discovering a right to information in the entrails of Article 8, which says nothing about information, and refusing to discern it in Article 10.'[16] As yet, however, there is no sign of shift in interpretation on this point, either at European or UK level. Any change would be of considerable importance to the media, as it would potentially widen or supplement the information access rights conferred under FOIA 2000.

---

[13] (1987) 9 EHRR 433.

[14] See *Persey v Secretary of State for the Environment, Food and Rural Affairs* [2002] EWHC 371 (Admin); *Howard v Secretary of State for Health* [2002] EWHC 396 (Admin); and *Decision on Application by CNN* (Dame Janet Smith, unreported, 25 October 2001). *R (on the application of Wagstaff) v Secretary of State for Health* [2001] 1 WLR 292 takes a different approach, but was disapproved in *Howard* and is unlikely to be followed.

[15] Judgment of 19 September 2006 (Series C No 151). The decision is available at <http://www.corteidh.or.cr/docs/casos/articulos/seriec_151_ing.pdf>.

[16] S Sedley, 'Information as a Human Right' in *Freedom of Information and Freedom of Expression: Essays in Honour of Sir David Williams* (OUP, 2000). For discussion by Sedley LJ in his judicial capacity of the relationship between Art 10 and rights of access to public authority information, see *London Regional Transport and anor v Mayor of London and anor* [2001] EWCA Civ 1491.

7.2.3 Balancing privacy and freedom of expression: HRA 1998, section 12

The previous section discussed the extent to which Articles 8 and 10 of the Convention could be used as the basis for a positive right of access to information. Prior to the passage of HRA 1998, media organizations were rather more concerned about the potential implications of Article 8 of the Convention as a basis for *limiting* the dissemination of information by the media themselves. The concern was that the courts would use Article 8 as the basis for developing a fully-fledged right to privacy, capable of being asserted not merely against public authorities but against private sector bodies (such as media organizations)—and that such a right would then be used by individuals to control the publication of stories affecting their private lives.

A right to privacy could in theory give rise to a number of different remedies. It could, for example, give rise to a claim for damages for invasion of privacy: and such a claim might be made both in relation to the *content* of a news story, and in relation to the *process* by which the story had been obtained (for instance, if it involved intrusive techniques such as covert surveillance). However, much of the concern about the implications of HRA 1998 was focused on the possibility that individuals would obtain injunctions in order to prevent information from being published, rather than seeking damages after publication. Such injunctions, it was feared, might be granted on an interim basis (in order to preserve the status quo until such time as a full trial could take place), even in cases where the claimant's case was a weak one. Widespread use of interim injunctions, pre-publication, could constitute a significant limitation on the media. There is an important difference between remedies that can be claimed after publication has taken place, and remedies that can be used to prevent publication in the first place; 'prior restraints' have generally been viewed as a particularly serious incursion on media freedom.[17]

At first sight it might appear that HRA 1998 should have had no impact whatsoever on the privacy rights of private individuals against media organizations. Article 8 prohibits interference with privacy by public authorities (see Article 8(2)), and very few media organizations will be public authorities. However, the European Court of Human Rights has treated Article 8 as extending to a positive obligation on the state to protect individuals against media intrusion into their private lives. Moreover, HRA 1998 provides that courts and tribunals are themselves 'public authorities' for the purposes of the Act (see section 6(3)(a)). So the concern was that once HRA 1998 came into force the courts would develop remedies for private individuals against media organizations, in order to give effect to the positive obligations imposed by Article 8.[18]

These concerns about the possible impact of HRA 1998 led to the adoption of what is now section 12 of the Act. The section was introduced by way of amendment to the

---

[17] See eg *Holley v Smyth* [1998] QB 726, 737, citing *Blackstone's Commentaries*.
[18] There has been vigorous academic debate about the extent to which HRA 1998 should have 'horizontal' effect, ie the extent to which Convention rights will be binding as between private individuals and organizations. For exhaustive citation, see Clayton and Tomlinson (n 6 above) para 5.92, n 299.

Human Rights Bill by the then Home Secretary, Jack Straw, who stated that it was 'specifically designed to safeguard press freedom'.[19] The section reads as follows.

12 Freedom of expression

(1) This section applies if a court is considering whether to grant any relief which, if granted, might affect the exercise of the Convention right to freedom of expression.

(2) If the person against whom the application for relief is made ('the respondent') is neither present nor represented, no such relief is to be granted unless the court is satisfied—

(a) that the applicant has taken all practicable steps to notify the respondent; or

(b) that there are compelling reasons why the respondent should not be notified.

(3) No such relief is to be granted so as to restrain publication before trial unless the court is satisfied that the applicant is likely to establish that publication should not be allowed.

(4) The court must have particular regard to the importance of the Convention right to freedom of expression and, where the proceedings relate to material which the respondent claims, or which appears to the court, to be journalistic, literary or artistic material (or to conduct connected with such material), to—

(a) the extent to which—

(i) the material has, or is about to, become available to the public; or

(ii) it is, or would be, in the public interest for the material to be published;

(b) any relevant privacy code.

(5) In this section—

• 'court' includes a tribunal; and

• 'relief' includes any remedy or order (other than in criminal proceedings).

Section 12(2) is clearly intended to limit the possibility for interim injunctions to be given on a 'without notice' basis (ie without the defendant being present in order to resist the application). Section 12(3) is intended to make it more difficult to obtain interim injunctions, by requiring the courts to scrutinize carefully the merits of the claimant's case, even at the interim stage (though its precise significance depends on how the word 'likely' is interpreted).[20] Section 12(4) requires the court to have full regard to Article 10 in cases where Article 8 is used as a basis for restraining publication.

Section 12 thus recognizes the potential for conflict between the right to freedom of expression and other Convention rights—in particular, the privacy right protected by Article 8. The next section of this chapter looks at how that conflict has been played out in practice since HRA 1998 came into force. It focuses on the law about privacy and breach of confidence, and how this area has developed in the light of HRA 1998. As will be apparent, the courts have been very conscious of the need to strike a balance between privacy and freedom of expression; but they certainly have not interpreted

---

[19] Hansard, HC, cols 534–563 (2 July 1998). For discussion of the Parliamentary history, see generally H Rogers and H Tomlinson, 'Privacy and Expression: Convention Rights and Interim Injunctions' [2003] European Human Rights Law Review Special Issue, 37.

[20] The meaning of the word will depend on the context, and there is no single standard of likelihood that is applicable in every case: see *Cream Holdings v Banerjee* [2005] 1 AC 253, paras 15 and 22.

section 12 of HRA 1998 as requiring them to treat freedom of expression as being intrinsically more significant than privacy.

7.3 CONFIDENTIAL AND PRIVATE INFORMATION IN THE LIGHT OF HRA 1998

Prior to the coming into force of HRA 1998, it was well-established that English law did not recognize any cause of action specifically for breach of privacy. An individual complaining of what was, in substance, an invasion of their privacy could only bring a claim if they relied upon some other recognized cause of action. This did not mean that privacy interests were wholly unprotected in English law; but any protection that was available was piecemeal and incomplete.

A notorious illustration is the case of *Kaye v Robertson*.[21] A TV actor was in hospital recovering from a serious head injury. Journalists from the *Sunday Sport* entered his hospital room without permission, interviewed him, and took photographs. An attempt to obtain an interim injunction restraining any publication of the interview and the photographs was unsuccessful, though the Court of Appeal made a more limited order restraining publication of any material suggesting that the actor had consented to be interviewed or photographed. Glidewell LJ stated:[22] 'It is well-known that in English law there is no right to privacy, and accordingly there is no right of action for breach of a person's privacy. The facts of the present case are a graphic illustration of the desirability of Parliament considering whether and in what circumstances statutory provision can be made to protect the privacy of individuals.' Instead, the Court of Appeal considered whether any causes of action were available on the basis of libel, malicious falsehood, trespass to the person, or passing off.[23]

This chapter is not concerned with privacy generally, but with one specific aspect of it: the wrongful use or disclosure of private information. Even before HRA 1998, the law of breach of confidence to some extent provided a remedy for this. Since HRA 1998 came into force breach of confidence has come to encompass what is, in substance, a cause of action for misuse of private information; and in the context of this cause of action the courts have explicitly addressed the balance between Article 8 and Article 10.

In its origins, the claim for breach of confidence was based on the improper use of information disclosed by one person to another in confidence. It was intended to prevent the misuse of certain kinds of relationship, rather than of certain kinds of information. The cause of action depended on there being a confidential relationship between the person who imparted the information and the person who received it.[24] By extension, a remedy could be granted not simply against the person who originally

---

[21] [1991] FSR 62. See also eg *Malone v Metropolitan Police Commissioner* [1979] Ch 344.
[22] [1991] FSR 62, 66.
[23] The limited relief granted by the Court was based on the tort of malicious falsehood.
[24] See *Campbell v MGN Ltd* [2004] UKHL 22, [2004] 2 AC 457, para 13 (Lord Nicholls).

obtained the information in confidence, but upon anyone else who received it with actual or constructive knowledge of the duty of confidence.[25] Even in that extended situation, the claimant would still need to establish that there was some initial confidential relationship between himself and a third party, and that the defendant had received the information via that third party in circumstances where he knew or should have known of the duty of confidence. For as long as breach of confidence was formulated in this way, it could provide only a limited remedy for publication of private information by the media. The claimant would need to show a confidential relationship between himself and the media or their source. Some of the most objectionable cases— where private information was obtained by covert or intrusive means[26]—would be precisely the cases that fell outside the scope of breach of confidence.

Even before HRA 1998 came into force there were indications that the courts were willing to take a wider view of the claim for breach of confidence. For example, in *Attorney-General v Guardian Newspapers Ltd (No 2)*[27] Lord Goff suggested that it would be illogical to insist on violation of a confidential relationship in circumstances where an obviously confidential document was blown from a window on to a crowded street, or dropped in a public place. In *Hellewell v Chief Constable of Derbyshire*[28] Law J (as he then was) suggested that if someone with a telephoto lens took a photograph from a distance and with no authority of another person engaged in some private act, then subsequent disclosure of the photograph would be a breach of confidence. In *Earl Spencer v UK*[29] the European Court of Human Rights accepted that a claim for breach of confidence was available in the UK even without a prior confidential relationship.

HRA 1998 has affected the development of the law as to breach of confidence in two main ways. First, in cases where the action is used as a remedy for the unjustified publication of personal information, as one judge has put it[30] the 'centre of gravity' has shifted, with the focus being on the nature of the information protected rather on the nature of the relationship in which it was disclosed. Secondly, within the framework of the law of breach of confidence there is now an explicit recognition of the need to balance Article 8 and Article 10; in effect, the rights protected by both Articles have been absorbed into the framework of this cause of action.[31]

These developments can be illustrated by three well-known cases involving the unauthorized publication of newspaper photographs about celebrities or their families: *Douglas and ors v Hello! Ltd*; *Campbell v MGN Ltd*; and *Murray v Express Newspapers plc and anor*.

---

[25] See ibid para 44 (Lord Hoffman).
[26] See eg the facts of *Kaye v Robertson* above.
[27] [1990] 1 AC 109, 281.
[28] [1995] 1 WLR 804, 807H.
[29] (1998) 25 EHRR CD 105.
[30] See *Campbell* (n 24 above) para 51 (Lord Hoffman).
[31] See *A v B plc* [2003] QB 195, 202, para 4 (Lord Woolf CJ).

The *Douglas* case became something of a legal saga.[32] The claimants were a celebrity couple (Michael Douglas and Catherine Zeta-Jones), together with *OK!* magazine. The couple had sold exclusive rights to the magazine to publish photographs of their wedding. All three claimants sought an interim injunction to restrain a rival magazine, *Hello!*, from publishing unauthorized photographs of the event. Those photographs had been taken without the knowledge or consent of the couple, who had tried to ensure that nobody other than *OK!* magazine took photographs. The claim was brought before publication of the unauthorized photographs by *Hello!*; so this was a 'prior restraint' case. An interim injunction was granted at first instance, but the decision was overturned in the Court of Appeal.[33]

The case was put partly on the basis of an orthodox breach of confidence analysis. It had been made clear to those attending the wedding (whether as guests or employees) that photography was prohibited. Hence it was argued that any unauthorized photographs were therefore taken in breach of a duty of confidence, and that *Hello!* was on notice that this was so. The case was also put, however, on the basis that the proposed publication by *OK!* amounted to a wrongful use of private information.

The Court took a range of approaches to the privacy issue. The strongest statement in favour of an explicit recognition of a right of privacy was in the judgment of Sedley LJ:[34]

I would conclude, at lowest, that [the Claimants have] a powerfully arguable case to advance at trial that [the couple] have a right of privacy which English law will today recognise and, where appropriate, protect . . .

What a concept of privacy does . . . is to accord recognition to the fact that the law has to protect not only those people whose trust has been abused but those who simply find themselves subjected to an unwanted intrusion into their personal lives. The law no longer needs to construct an artificial relationship of confidentiality between intruder and victim; it can recognise privacy itself as a legal principle drawn from the fundamental value of personal autonomy.

The Court considered the significance of section 12 of HRA 1998. All three judges agreed that, in considering the merits of the case, section 12(3) required a more stringent threshold for the grant of interim relief than the familiar *American Cyanamid* test of whether there was a serious issue to be tried.[35] This did not mean that the Article 10 right took priority over other Convention rights—in assessing prospects of success for the purpose of section 12(3), it was necessary to consider both Article 10 itself and any conflicting Convention rights.[36] Nor did section 12(4) mean that Article 10 took priority over other Convention rights. In applying section 12(4) the Court had to give full weight both to the right protected by Article 10(1) and to the limitations on that right set out in Article 10(2); and those limitations included the requirement to take account of the Article 8 privacy right.[37]

---

[32] On the Westlaw site (accessed 24 March 2009) there are now 9 separate judgments under this title.
[33] [2001] QB 967.
[34] At paras 125–126.
[35] See paras 50–54 (Brooke LJ); paras 136 (Sedley LJ); paras 148–154 (Keene LJ).
[36] Paras 135–137 (Sedley LJ).
[37] ibid.

All members of the Court agreed that an injunction should not be granted, essentially because the balance of convenience was in favour of allowing publication to go ahead and leaving the claimants to their remedy in damages at trial if it was held that publication had been unlawful. As between the two magazines this was essentially a commercial dispute, and it would much easier for *OK!* to compute its losses if publication was allowed than for *Hello!* to compute its own losses if publication was refused.[38] The couple had effectively made their privacy rights the subject of a commercial transaction with *OK!* and were in no better position than the magazine as far as interlocutory relief was concerned.[39]

At trial the couple were awarded modest amounts by way of damages; *OK!* was awarded a substantial sum. On appeal, the Court of Appeal[40] upheld the award of damages to the couple, but overturned the award in favour of the magazine. The Court also considered that an interlocutory injunction ought to have been granted to the couple, as the only effective way of satisfactorily protecting their rights.

The leading case on the interaction between privacy and the claim for breach of confidence is now the decision of the House of Lords in *Campbell v MGN Ltd.*[41] The claimant was an internationally famous supermodel. The *Mirror* newspaper published a story about her which, as analysed in the House of Lords,[42] consisted of five elements: (1) the fact that she had a drug addiction; (2) the fact that she was receiving treatment; (3) the fact that she was receiving treatment at Narcotics Anonymous; (4) the details of the treatment, including such matter as the duration and frequency of her attendance at meetings; and (5) a photograph of her leaving a specific meeting. Following the publication she brought a claim for breach of confidence. She succeeded at trial, and was awarded £3,500 damages, but the decision was overturned by the Court of Appeal.

In the House of Lords it was accepted that the newspaper was entitled to publish elements (1) and (2) above, as Ms Campbell had falsely claimed in public that she did not take drugs and the newspaper was entitled to set the record straight. The question was whether publication of the remaining elements of the story was actionable.

The House of Lords approached the case as being essentially about the misuse of private information,[43] and analysed it within the framework of Articles 8 and 10, in two stages. The first stage was to ask whether the right to privacy under Article 8(1) was engaged, and that turned on whether the claimant had a reasonable expectation of privacy in relation to the disclosed facts. The reasonable expectation was that of the person affected by the publicity. As Lord Hope expressed it, the question was what a

---

[38] See para 99 (Brooke LJ); para 144 (Sedley LJ); para 171 (Keene LJ).
[39] See para 101 (Brooke LJ); para 142 (Sedley LJ).
[40] See *Douglas and ors v Hello! Ltd and ors (No 3)* [2005] EWCA Civ 595, [2006] QB 125.
[41] [2004] UKHL 22, [2004] 2 AC 457.
[42] See eg at para 23 (Lord Nicholls).
[43] The clearest statement of this is in the speech of Lords Nicholls, at para 14. However, although the language of the speeches varies, the principles set out in the 5 speeches do not differ significantly: see *per* Lord Hoffman, para 26.

reasonable person of ordinary sensibilities would feel if placed in the same position as the claimant and faced with the same publicity.[44] If yes, the second stage was to balance the right to privacy against the right to freedom of expression, asking: (1) how serious was the interference with the right to privacy, by reason of publication of the photographs; and (2) how serious an interference would it be with freedom of expression if the claim were to succeed.[45] This balancing test would determine whether the claim succeeded or failed. Baroness Hale stated that there were different types of private information, some more deserving of protection than others; and likewise there were different types of freedom of expression, with political, educational, and artistic speech attracting a higher degree of protection than celebrity gossip.[46]

Their Lordships differed as to how these principles applied to the facts of the case. The majority (Lords Hope and Carswell, and Baroness Hale) upheld Ms Campbell's claim, considering that the information about the nature of the treatment, together with the photograph, added something of real significance to the disclosure that Ms Campbell was a drug addict and receiving treatment. The minority (Lords Nicholls and Hoffman) considered that—given that it was agreed that the newspaper was entitled to publish the fact that Ms Campbell was a drug addict and receiving treatment—the additional information was peripheral. As Lord Hoffman put it,[47] publication was within the margin of editorial judgment and something for which appropriate latitude should be allowed.

The facts of *Murray v Express Newspapers plc and anor*[48] are a striking illustration of how far breach of confidence in its post-HRA version can now reach. The author JK Rowling and her husband were out walking with their child. A photograph of the family group was taken and subsequently published in the *Sunday Express* magazine. A claim for damages and other relief was brought by the parents, on behalf of the child, against both the newspaper and the photographic agency that took the picture. The claim against the newspaper was settled. The photographic agency applied to strike out the claim; it was successful at first instance, but the decision was reversed by the Court of Appeal.

The Court of Appeal approached the case by reference to the two-stage analysis set out in *Campbell*, above. They considered that it was arguable both that the child's right to privacy under Article 8 was engaged, and that the balance between privacy and freedom of expression should be struck in his favour. This was so, even though the pictures were innocuous in their content, and showed the family group on a public street. The Court of Appeal took account of the fact that the claimant was a child, that the pictures had been taken and sold to the press without the parents' knowledge or consent, and

---

[44] See para 99. In *Murray* (n 45 below) para 35, the Court of Appeal stated that it could not detect any difference in this regard between Lord Hope's opinion and that of the other Law Lords in *Campbell*.

[45] For a similar two-stage analysis of the reasoning in the case, see *Murray v Express Newspapers* [2008] EWCA Civ 446, [2008] 3 WLR 1360, paras 24–41.

[46] Paras 148–149 (Baroness Hale).

[47] See para 77.

[48] [2008] EWCA Civ 446, [2008] 3 WLR 1360.

that the pictures had been targeted at the parents and the child (rather than showing a street scene with the family in the background). In order for Article 8 to be engaged it was not necessary to show that the publication of the photograph would be regarded as offensive by reasonable people; though the degree of any incursion into privacy would be relevant at the second stage of the analysis, when balancing privacy against freedom of expression.

What these three cases illustrate is the far-reaching way in which the claim for breach of confidence has developed under the influence of HRA 1998 and the Convention. Lord Nicholls was surely correct to say in the *Campbell* case[49] that there is now a cause of action for misuse of private information (though sometimes still labelled as breach of confidence). When it comes to shaping the development of the substantive law, section 12 of HRA 1998 would seem to have had little effect.[50] However, section 12(3) is still an important procedural protection against excessive readiness to grant interim injunctions prior to publication.

These UK developments will be further encouraged by *Von Hannover v Germany*,[51] which is now the leading Strasbourg case. The claimant was a member of the Monaco royal family. She complained about the publication of various photographs (mostly taken while she was in public) showing her carrying out innocuous activities such as shopping or horse-riding. Her claim failed before the German court. The Strasbourg Court held that even though she was a public figure she was still entitled to a private life; and there was no value in the publication of this material, which did not in any way contribute to public debate on matters of importance. Her claim under Article 8 was upheld, on the basis that the German state had failed to provide her with an adequate remedy to protect her privacy.

No doubt the law in this area will continue to develop rapidly, both in the UK and in Strasbourg. Issues where the scope of privacy protection remains unclear include the following:

• To what extent is there legal protection against the dissemination of information or photographs recording activities that are both innocuous in themselves and carried out in public?

• To what extent should the publication of photographs be regarded as intrinsically a more serious incursion of privacy than is the written word?

• How far will the courts develop the idea that there is a hierarchy both of invasions of privacy and of free expression? In future, will there be lengthy controversy as to whether or not particular newspaper articles fall into one of the categories that receive closer protection (such as political or artistic expression)?

---

[49] See *Campbell* (n 24 above) para 14.
[50] It certainly has not led the courts to treat Art 10 as having priority over any other Convention right: see eg *Lord Browne of Madingley v Associated Newspapers* [2008] QB 103.
[51] (2005) 40 EHRR 1.

7.4 DATA PROTECTION AND THE MEDIA

7.4.1 Data Protection Act 1998 in outline

The Data Protection Act 1998 (DPA 1998) is a complex piece of legislation, and a comprehensive treatment would be well beyond the scope of this chapter.[52] It builds on and replaces an earlier piece of UK legislation (the Data Protection Act 1984), and it gives effect in the UK to Directive (EC) 95/46 ('the Data Processing Directive'). In broad terms, both the Data Processing Directive and DPA 1998 are intended to protect the privacy of individuals in relation to the use that is made of their personal information, particularly when such information is held on computer or in some other automated form.

The potential impact on media organizations of legislation of this nature should be immediately apparent. Many news stories are stories about identifiable individuals. Journalism involves researching and publishing information about individuals, often without their knowledge or consent, and indeed sometimes in the face of their active opposition. A legal regime that controls the right to obtain and disseminate information about individuals has obvious potential for serious impact on these activities. Indeed, it appears that before publication of the Bill that ultimately became DPA 1998 there was considerable concern about its implications for journalism.[53] The Act recognizes this potential impact, and includes specific exceptions in relation to information that is processed for the 'special purposes' of journalism, and artistic and literary work. There are also exceptions for information processed for research purposes. However, although these exceptions limit the impact of DPA 1998 on journalistic organizations, they fall well short of a blanket exemption. Moreover, in order to make sense of the exemptions it is necessary to have an understanding of the Act as a whole. Hence this section gives a general outline of the Act's main provisions. The following section goes on to deal with the specific aspects of the Act that are most directly relevant to the media, including some of the exemptions from the Act.

7.4.1.1 *General issues of interpretation in relation to DPA 1998*
A fundamental point about the 1998 Act is that it is intended to give effect to the Data Processing Directive. The courts will therefore apply a purposive approach to its construction, interpreting it so far as possible in a manner that is consistent with the Directive and that gives effect to its purpose.[54] In ascertaining the purpose of the Directive it is relevant to take account of the recitals to the Directive, and also the background papers (or *travaux préparatoires*) on which the Directive was based.

---

[52] The leading practitioner text is R Jay, *Data Protection Law and Practice* (Sweet and Maxwell, 3rd edn, 2007). For anyone requiring a more detailed discussion of the Act, this is the obvious starting-point.

[53] See generally ibid para 17-02.

[54] See *Campbell v MGN Ltd* [2002] EWCA Civ 1373, [2003] 2 WLR 80, para 96 (Court of Appeal). On the general principles of interpretation applicable to domestic legislation that implements a European Directive, see eg *Von Colson* [1984] ECR 1891.

The construction of DPA 1998 has also been heavily influenced by Article 8 of the European Convention. There are two reasons for taking Article 8 into account. One is that the Directive is intended to give effect to Article 8.[55] The other is that HRA 1998 requires the courts, so far as it is possible to do so, to read and give effect to legislation in a way which is compatible with Convention rights (see section 3(1) of HRA 1998). However, it should not be assumed that Article 8 and DPA 1998 are coterminous, so that there will be no breach of DPA 1998 in circumstances where there would not be an infringement of Article 8. That would be to treat Article 8 as a limitation on the Act rather than as an aid to its interpretation.[56]

DPA 1998 confers rights on *data subjects*, and imposes duties on *data controllers* in relation to the *processing* of *personal data*. Each of the italicized terms is specifically defined in section 1(1) of the Act. These concepts are fundamental to an understanding of the Act.

(a) *The definition of 'data'* Data means information which:

(a) is being processed by means of equipment operating automatically in response to instructions given for that purpose,

(b) is recorded with the intention that it should be processed by means of such equipment,

(c) is recorded as part of a relevant filing system or with the intention that it should form part of a relevant filing system,

(d) does not fall within paragraph (a), (b) or (c) but forms part of an accessible record as defined by section 68; or

(e) is recorded information held by a public authority and does not fall within any of paragraphs (a) to (d).

Limb (a) of the definition will cover information that is held on computer or in some other automated form, and limb (b) will cover information that is recorded with the intention that it should be automatically processed. A considerable amount of information held by media organizations will fall within limb (a) or (b).

Limb (c) will cover some manual data (ie paper records), but its scope is limited. A relevant filing system is defined in section 1(1) of DPA 1998 as being:

. . . any set of information relating to individuals to the extent that, although the information is not processed by means of equipment operating automatically in response to instructions given for that purpose, the set is structured, either by reference to individuals or by reference to criteria relating to individuals, in such a way that specific information relating to a particular individual is readily ascertainable.

The Court of Appeal considered this definition in the leading case of *Durant v Financial Services Association* [2003] EWCA Civ 1746, and concluded that limb (c) would only cover paper records that are organized with sufficient sophistication to provide the same or similar ready accessibility to specific personal information as

---

[55] As the recitals in the Preamble make clear: see eg Recital (10).
[56] cf Jay (n 52 above), para 3-04.

would a computerized filing system (see at paragraphs 45 to 50 of the judgment). This is a demanding standard; and, precisely because of the widespread availability of computer systems, it is very difficult to see why many organizations would now go the trouble of maintaining paper-based records of this kind. It is unlikely that much information held by media organizations will fall within this limb.

Limb (d) relates to certain health, educational, housing, and social services records: see section 68 of DPA 1998, and the provisions cross-referred in that section. Essentially limb (d) covers various sorts of information held by public bodies, and so it is of limited significance to media organizations.

Limb (e) covers all recorded information held by public authorities and not falling within any of limbs (a) to (d). The term 'public authority' for this purpose bears the same meaning as in FOIA 2000.[57] However, information falling within limb (e) is only covered by a very limited part of DPA 1998; virtually all of the Act is excluded, except for the right of subject access under section 7 (discussed below). The practical effect of limb (e), in conjunction with section 7, is to give individuals a right of access to personal information about themselves that is held by public authorities, regardless of how that information is held. The journalistic significance of this is limited.[58]

(b) *What is personal data?* DPA 1998 provides (section 1(1)) that:

'personal data' means data which relate to a living individual who can be identified—

(a) from those data, or

(b) from those data and other information which is in the possession of, or is likely to come into the possession of, the data controller.

Note that the definition does not cover information about companies and other organizations,[59] or about the dead.[60] The main controversy about the scope of the definition has been about when information should be regarded as 'relating to' an individual: how close must the proximity be between an individual, and a particular item of information, in order for that information to constitute the individual's personal data? In the *Durant* case, referred to above, a narrow approach was adopted by the Court of Appeal (see in particular at paragraph 28 of the decision). Two notions were identified as being of assistance: whether the information was biographical in any significant sense, and whether it had the putative data subject as its focus. The Court of Appeal suggested that in general terms personal data was intended to be data that affected an individual's privacy.

---

[57] It would also cover a Scottish public authority, as defined by the Freedom of Information (Scotland) Act 2002.

[58] Though there may be occasions when a journalist researching a story may wish to obtain access to their own personal information held by public authorities, in which case the extended limb (e) definition of 'data' will assist them.

[59] See also *Smith v Lloyds TSB Bank plc* [2005] EWHC 246 (Ch), paras 30–32.

[60] In relation to information about the dead, see generally *Bluck v Information Commissioner* EA/2006/0090.

The *Durant* decision has proved controversial.[61] It is understood that the European Commission has raised questions as to whether this approach is compatible with the Data Protection Directive.[62] The notion that personal data is confined to information that affects individual privacy is difficult to reconcile with European authority on the construction of the Directive.[63] The Information Commissioner has issued detailed technical guidance on the meaning of 'personal data', taking a wider approach than has been adopted by many practitioners in the light of *Durant*.[64] It remains to be seen what weight will be given to this guidance by the Information Tribunal and the courts.[65]

(c) *Other key definitions in DPA 1998* DPA 1998 draws a distinction between personal data generally, and sensitive personal data. The latter is defined by section 2 of the Act. It means personal data consisting of information as to any of the following:

(a) the racial or ethnic origin of the data subject;
(b) his political opinions;
(c) his religious beliefs or other beliefs of a similar nature;
(d) whether he is a member of a trade union (within the meaning of the Trade Union and Labour Relations (Consolidation) Act 1992);
(e) his physical or mental health or condition;
(f) his sexual life;
(g) the commission or alleged commission by him of any offence; or
(h) any proceedings for any offence committed or alleged to have been committed by him, the disposal of such proceedings or the sentence of any court in such proceedings.

Many of the provisions of the Act relate to the *processing* of personal data. Section 1(1) provides that:

'processing', in relation to information or data, means obtaining, recording or holding the information or data or carrying out any operation or set of operations on the information or data, including—

(a) organization, adaptation or alteration of the information or data,

---

[61] For a valuable discussion see S Lorber, 'Data Protection and Subject Access Requests' (2004) 33 Industrial Law Journal 179.

[62] See Jay (n 52 above) para 3–33.

[63] See eg Case (C-101/01) *Lindqvist* [2004] QB 1014. See also the judgment of the European Court of First Instance in the *Bavarian Lager* case, 8 November 2008 (Case T-194/04), which treats as separate the questions (a) whether information is personal data, and (b) whether that information engages the Art 8 right to privacy.

[64] The guidance was issued in August 2007. It is available at <http://www.ico.gov.uk/upload/documents/library/data_protection/detailed_specialist_guides/personal_data_flowchart_v1_with_preface001.pdf>.

[65] In *Common Services Agency v Scottish Information Commissioner* [2008] UKHL 47 the House of Lords was invited to address the status and legal correctness of the guidance, but chose not to do so. The Information Tribunal in *Harcup v Information Commissioner and Yorkshire Forward* EA/2007/0058 suggested that *Durant* and the guidance were inconsistent, and that *Durant* should be followed, not the guidance: see paras 18–27 of the decision. See also the Information Tribunal decisions in *Department for Business Enterprise and Regulatory Reform v Information Commissioner and Friends of the Earth* EA/2007/0072, paras 89–101, *and Kelway v Information Commissioner and Chief Constable of Northumbria Police* EA/2008/0037, paras 55–60.

(b) retrieval, consultation or use of the information or data,

(c) disclosure of the information or data by transmission, dissemination or otherwise making available, or

(d) alignment, combination, blocking, erasure or destruction of the information or data.

Hence—among other matters—collecting, holding, and retaining personal data will constitute processing of the data. Likewise, its disclosure will also constitute processing.

In general terms, the Act imposes duties on data controllers and confers rights on data subjects. A data controller is:[66] 'a person who (either alone or jointly or in common with other persons) determines the purposes for which and the manner in which any personal data are, or are to be, processed'. A data subject is 'an individual who is the subject of personal data.'

Note that a data subject must be an individual (ie an actual human being, or what lawyers sometimes call a 'natural person'). A data controller must be a 'person', but this term is wide enough to cover a legal person (for example a company) or a body of persons (such as an unincorporated association).[67]

Not everyone who is involved in dealing with personal data will be a data controller. A person (other than an employee of the data controller) who processes data on behalf of a data controller is a 'data processor': see section 1(1) of DPA 1998.

(d) *Rights of data subjects* DPA 1978 confers a number of rights on data subjects.

First, there is a right of access to one's own personal data, under section 7. Data subjects are entitled on written request to be informed by any data controller whether their personal data is being processed by or on behalf of the data controller. If that is the case, then they are entitled to be given a description of that personal data, of the purposes for which it is being processed, and of the recipients or classes of recipient to whom the data is or may be disclosed. More importantly, perhaps, data subjects also have the right to have communicated to them, in an intelligible form, the information constituting any personal data of which they are the data subject (together with any information available to the data controller as to the source of that data). The right conferred by section 7 is often referred to as the 'subject access right'.

The subject access right is of limited value to media organizations as an information-gathering tool. It can only be exercised by individuals in relation to their own personal data; contrast the right of information access under FOIA 2000, discussed in section 7.5 below, which is not dependent on there being any link between the information requested and the person seeking access to that information. Where section 7 is potentially of importance, of course, is as a basis on which individuals can obtain access to information held by media organizations.

One important qualification on the subject access right is that in some cases it may be impossible to comply with the request without disclosing information about

---

[66] This is subject to qualification by DPA 1998, s 1(4), which is of little relevance to media organizations.

[67] See the Interpretation Act 1978, Sch 1 (definition of 'person').

another individual who can be identified from that information. The data controller is not obliged to disclose third-party information of this kind, unless either the third party consents or it is reasonable in all the circumstances to disclose without consent.[68] This does not excuse the data controller from complying with the request to the extent that he can do so without disclosing the identity of the third party.[69]

Other rights of data subjects include:

- a right to prevent processing likely to cause damage or distress (section 10);
- a right to prevent processing for the purposes of direct marketing (section 11);
- certain rights in relation to automated decision-taking (section 12);
- a right to compensation for damage, or damage and distress, caused by contravention by a data controller of any of the requirements of the Act (section 13); and
- a right to rectification, blocking, erasure, or destruction of inaccurate personal data (section 14).

(e) *Duties of data controllers: the data protection principles* Subject to limited exceptions,[70] personal data must not be processed unless the data controller is included in a register maintained by the Information Commissioner.[71] In order to be included in the register, a data controller must give a notification to the Commissioner together with certain prescribed information (including a general description of the purposes for which personal data is processed).[72]

The main duty on data controllers is to comply with the eight data protection principles set out in Schedule 1 to the Act.[73] The most complex principle is the first principle, which states that personal data shall be processed fairly and lawfully and, in particular, shall not be processed unless at least one of the conditions in Schedule 2 to the Act is met, and, and in case of sensitive personal data, at least one of the conditions in Schedule 3 is also met.

In order to comply with the fairness requirement of the first principle, certain information in most circumstances must be provided to or made readily available to the data subject, so far as it is practicable to do so.[74] The prescribed information is: the identity of the data controller; the identity of the data controller's nominated representative for the purposes of the Act (if any); the purpose(s) for which the data is intended to be processed; and any further information which is necessary in the specific circumstance to enable processing in respect of the data subject to be fair.[75] A notification setting out this information is often referred to as a 'fair processing notice', although this

---

[68] See DPA 1998, s 7(4).
[69] ibid s 7(5).
[70] eg under DPA 1998, s 36, in respect of information processed for domestic purposes.
[71] ibid s 17.
[72] ibid s 18.
[73] See ibid s 4(4).
[74] See ibid Sch 1, part II, para 3 for exceptions.
[75] See ibid Sch 1, part II, para 2(3).

term does not appear in the Act. As well as the issue of whether a suitable fair process-ing notice has been provided, the first principle requires that the question of fairness must be considered in general terms.[76]

Schedules 2 and 3 are complex. There are six conditions in Schedule 2,[77] including:

* that the data subject has given his consent to the processing (condition 1); or

* that the processing is necessary for the purposes of legitimate interests pursued by the data controller or by the third party or parties to whom the data is disclosed, except where the processing is unwarranted in any particular case by reason of prejudice to the rights and freedoms or legitimate interests of the data subject (condition 6).

There are ten conditions in Schedule 3, including:

* that the data subject has give his explicit consent to the processing of the personal data (condition 1).

Schedules 2 and 3 are perhaps the source of the persistent data protection myth that nothing whatsoever can be done with anyone's personal data without that individual's express consent.[78] The true position is that consent is one way of satisfying Schedules 2 and 3, but it is by no means the only way.

The other data protection principles in Schedule 1 are these:

* Principle 2, requiring that personal data shall be obtained only for one or more specified and lawful purposes, and shall not be further processed in any manner incompatible with those purpose(s).

* Principle 3, requiring that personal data shall be adequate, relevant, and not excessive in relation to the purpose(s) for which it is processed.

* Principle 4, requiring that personal data shall be accurate and, where necessary, kept up to date.

* Principle 5, requiring that personal data processed for any purpose(s) shall not be kept for longer than is necessary for such purpose(s).

* Principle 6, requiring that personal data shall be processed in accordance with the rights of data subjects under the Act.

* Principle 7, requiring that appropriate technical and organizational measures shall be taken against unauthorized or unlawful processing of personal data and against accidental loss or destruction of, or damage to, personal data.

---

[76] See *Johnson v Medical Defence Union* [2006] EWHC 321(Ch), paras 114 et seq.

[77] The conditions in DPA 1998 Sch 2 are separate, not cumulative: that is to say, it is only necessary to comply with one of the conditions, not all of them. The same point applies to Sch 3 (in cases where that Schedule is applicable).

[78] Hence the stories that periodically appear in the press, about petty organizational obstructiveness supposedly justified by the requirements of DPA 1998. For instance, in September 2008 it was reported in the press that a Marks & Spencer employee told the mother of a 7-year-old boy that they could not discuss with her the delivery of a Superman suit for her son, because of DPA 1998: see <http://www.ico.gov.uk/upload/documents/pressreleases/2008/statement_mands_superman.pdf>.

- Principle 8, limiting the circumstances in which personal data may be transferred outside the European Economic Area.

(f) *Exemptions to the rights and duties set out above* The rights and duties set out above are subject to a number of exemptions: see in particular sections 27 to 39 of DPA 1998. The exemptions that are of most direct relevance to the media (those in sections 32 and 33 of the Act) are discussed in section 7.4.2 below. Other exemptions to note are the following:

- Section 28 of the Act creates a wide-ranging exemption in relation to national security. The section empowers a Minister of the Crown to certify, in respect of any personal data, that exemption from the main provisions of the Act is required for the purpose of safeguarding national security.[79] Such a certificate may apply to a general description of personal data, and may be prospective in effect.[80] A person 'directly affected' by the issuing of such a certificate may appeal to the Information Tribunal.[81] There is also a right of appeal to the Information Tribunal against a data controller's assertion, in any proceedings under the Act, that specific personal data falls within the scope of a ministerial certificate.[82] Appeals of this nature are determined by a specially constituted National Security Panel of the Information Tribunal.[83]

- Section 29 provides a complex exception for certain personal data processed for the purposes of the prevention or detection of crime, the apprehension or prosecution of offenders, or the assessment or collection of any tax, duty, or similar imposition.

- Section 30 permits information in relation to health, education, and social work to be exempted from the Act by order.

- Section 31 creates a complex exemption in relation to information processed for various forms of regulatory activity.

(g) *Criminal offences and enforcement* DPA 1998 creates the office of Information Commissioner, and also creates a specialist Tribunal, the Information Tribunal.[84] The Information Commissioner has a range of enforcement powers: for example he can issue enforcement notices requiring data controllers to remedy contraventions of the data protection principles,[85] and he can serve information notices requiring data controllers to provide him with information to assist him in determining whether they are complying with the principles.[86] Persons who are directly affected by the processing of personal data can request the Commissioner to carry out an assessment as to whether the processing is likely to comply with the requirements of the Act.[87]

---

[79] DPA 1998, s 28(2).
[80] ibid s 28(3).
[81] ibid s 28(4).
[82] ibid s 28(6).
[83] See ibid s 28(12) and Sch 6.
[84] See ibid s 6 and Sch 5.
[85] ibid s 40.
[86] ibid s 43.
[87] ibid s 42.

The Commissioner's power to serve enforcement notices can have far-reaching effects. For example, in March 2009 the Commissioner served an enforcement notice on a company that was operating an unlawful blacklist of employees working in the construction industry, effectively putting the company out of business.[88]

A person on whom an enforcement notice, information notice, or special information notice[89] is served by the Commissioner may appeal to the Information Tribunal against the notice.[90]

Processing personal data without complying with the requirement to register with the Information Commissioner is a criminal offence.[91] There is also an important provision in section 55, relating to the unlawful obtaining of personal data (discussed further in section 7.4.2 below).

Section 144 of the Criminal Justice and Immigration Act 2008 inserts important new provisions into DPA 1998 (sections 55A to 55E), giving the Information Commissioner the power to impose fines for serious breaches of the Act. These provisions are not yet in force and at the time of writing no date for them to come into force has been given.

7.4.2 Application of DPA 1998 to the media

It should be clear from the above outline that DPA 1998 potentially has very considerable implications for media organizations. For instance, do journalists have to provide all relevant data subjects with a fair processing notice before they embark upon their research? Do they have to consider whether their use of personal information satisfies a Schedule 2 condition (and where appropriate a Schedule 3 condition also)? Can they be required, by a subject access request under section 7, to disclose their research material, and indeed their sources?

The answer to these questions is no, or at any rate, not necessarily. The application of the DPA is significantly modified in respect of the 'special purposes', which section 3 of DPA 1998 defines as meaning any one or more of the following:

(a) the purposes of journalism,

(b) artistic purposes, and

(c) literary purposes.

There is no specific definition of any of these terms in the DPA 1998. They are derived from Article 9 of the Data Processing Directive, which does not contain a definition either. However, the main purpose of the Act's provisions about the special purposes is to be to reconcile data protection with freedom of expression[92] and it is

---

[88] See the *Guardian*, 6 March 2009: article available at <http://www.guardian.co.uk/uk/2009/mar/06/ian-kerr-data-protection> (site accessed 28 March 2009).
[89] Under DPA 1998 s 44, discussed at section 7.4.2 below.
[90] ibid s 48.
[91] ibid s 21.
[92] cf Recommendation 1/97 of the Working Party set up under Directive (EC) 95/46, Art 24.

suggested that a wide interpretation of section 3 is therefore appropriate. For example, it is suggested that 'journalism' should not be limited to writing that is done for payment; and that no test of literary merit should be imposed in determining whether work is done for literary purposes.

This section goes on to discuss a number of provisions of the Act that are especially relevant to the media, and in particular those provisions that deal specifically with the 'special purposes'.

7.4.2.1 *Section 13*

Section 13 of DPA 1998 entitles an individual to compensation from a data controller, if that individual suffers damage by reason of any contravention by the data controller of any of the requirements of the DPA. An individual who suffers distress is also entitled to compensation for that distress, if:

- the individual also suffers damage by reason of the contravention; or
- the contravention relates to the processing of data for the special purposes.

It is a defence for the data controller to prove that he took such care as was reasonably required in the circumstances to comply with the requirement concerned (section 13(3)).

There is authority that 'damage' means financial loss and not damage to reputation.[93] In the absence of damage (in this narrow sense) there is no right to compensation for distress, *unless* the contravention relates to the processing of data for the special purposes. This means that an individual who brought a successful claim under section 13, arising out of a media disclosure of personal information about him, could claim compensation for distress alone (even if he had suffered no financial loss). However, in the light of section 32 of DPA 1998, discussed below, there may well be serious obstacles to the success of such a claim.

7.4.2.2 *Section 32*

Section 32(1) of DPA 1998 provides that personal data which is processed only for the special purposes are exempt from any provision to which the subsection relates, provided that three conditions are satisfied. These are: (1) that the processing is undertaken with a view to the publication by any person of any journalistic, literary, or artistic material; (2) that the data controller reasonably believes that, having regard in particular to the special importance of the public interest in freedom of expression, publication would be in the public interest; and (3) that the data controller reasonably believes that, in all the circumstances, compliance with that provision would be incompatible with the special purposes.

The provisions to which this exemption applies are set out at section 32(2). They include most of the provisions in the Act that confer rights on data subjects or impose duties on data controllers. All of the data protection principles are covered, with the

---

[93] *Johnson v Medical Defence Union* [2007] EWCA Civ 262, paras 72–78.

exception of the seventh principle (which relates to data security). The following are also covered: section 7 (the subject access right); section 10 (right to prevent processing likely to cause damage or distress); section 12 (rights in relation to automated decision-taking); section 12A (rights of data subjects in relation to certain manual data); and section 14(1) to (3) (rights to require rectification, blocking, erasure, or destruction of inaccurate data).[94]

One of the conditions for this exemption, as explained above, is that the data controller must *reasonably* believe that publication would be in the public interest. Section 32(3) makes further provision as to how the reasonableness of that belief is to be tested. It provides that regard may be had to the data controller's compliance with any code of practice that is relevant to the publication in question, and that is designated by the Secretary of State by order.[95]

The provisions discussed so far are substantive: they confer exemption from various provisions of the DPA 1998. The remainder of section 32 sets out procedural rules in relation to certain litigation under the Act involving the special purposes. Section 32(4) applies, broadly speaking, to all of the provisions that would be likely to give a right of action under the Act to a data subject against a data controller. In any case where the data controller claims that any personal data to which the proceedings relate are being processed:

• only for the special purposes; and

• with a view to the publication by any person of any journalistic, literary or artistic material which (up until 24 hours previously) had not been published by the data controller

the court must stay the proceedings. The stay is to continue until one of two conditions is met (see section 32(5)). The first condition (section 32(5)(a)) is that a determination of the Commissioner under section 45 of the Act takes effect: ie a determination that the personal data is not being processed only for the special purposes, or are not being processed with a view to the publication by any person of any journalistic, literary, or artistic material which had not been previously published by the data controller. The second condition (section 32(5)(b)) is that the claim is withdrawn.

Finally, section 32(6) defines the term 'publish' for these purposes as meaning to make available to the public or to any section of the public.

In summary then, section 32 affects media organizations in two different ways. There is a substantive exemption from various provisions of the Act, on certain conditions: section 32(2) and (3). There is also a procedural right to stay certain kinds of proceedings: section 32(4) and (5). When the procedural right is exercised, the effect

---

[94] DPA 1998, s 13 (right to compensation) is not listed in s 32(2). However, to the extent that there is an exemption from the duties imposed by the Act, there can be no question of a claim of compensation for breach of those duties.

[95] Codes have been designated for this purpose by the Data Protection (Designated Codes of Practice) (No 2) Order 2000 (SI 2000/1864). They include the Press Complaints Commission Code of Practice, and the Broadcasting Standards Commission Code on Fairness and Privacy.

is that the Information Commissioner[96] (not the court) is to determine the purposes for which the personal data is being processed. The purpose of the procedural provisions in section 32(4) and (5) is clearly to prevent the provisions of DPA 1998 from being used as a prior restraint on publication: hence these provisions only operate in relation to material not previously published by the data controller.

The application of DPA 1998 to media organizations, and the scope of section 32, was extensively considered in the *Naomi Campbell* litigation (discussed in section 7.3 above). As well as relying on breach of confidence, the claimant brought a claim under section 13 of DPA 1998. She contended that the publication constituted processing of sensitive personal data, in breach of the first data protection principle (since the processing was unfair, and no Schedule 2 or Schedule 3 condition was satisfied), and that section 13 entitled her to compensation for these breaches of the Act.

The judgments in the Court of Appeal[97] considered the DPA issues at some length.[98] The Court of Appeal held that the newspaper had not breached the Act, and dismissed the claim under section 13. Publication of the story in question constituted the processing of personal data, and thus fell within the scope of the Act.[99] However, the newspaper could rely on section 32 in its defence. An argument that section 32(1) to (3) only applied up to the moment of publication was rejected,[100] and the Court accepted that section 32(1) to (3) could apply to a claim arising out of the fact of publication itself.[101] On the facts of the case the Court considered that the newspaper satisfied the conditions in section 32(1).[102] The newspaper reasonably believed that publication was in the public interest; and it would not have been possible to make the publication while complying with the provisions of the Act on which the claimant relied.

As discussed above, the claim for breach of confidence succeeded in the House of Lords (by a 3–2 majority). The House of Lords did not consider the DPA issues (the parties having agreed that the DPA claim would stand or fall with the claim for breach of confidence). The decision of the Court of Appeal remains the leading authority on the construction of section 32.

However, despite the wide view taken by the Court of Appeal as to the scope of section 32, it should not be assumed that all activity for journalistic, artistic, or literary purposes will inevitably be covered by the exemption in section 32(1). The three conditions set out in section 32(1) need to be considered by reference to the circumstances of each individual case, and also with respect to the particular provision in DPA 1998 from which exemption is sought.

---

[96] And potentially the Information Tribunal on appeal from the Information Commissioner's determination under section 45: see DPA 1998, ss 45(2) and 48(4). There could then be a further appeal to the Court from the Information Tribunal, on a point of law: ibid s 49(6).

[97] [2002] EWCA Civ 1373, [2003] QB 633.

[98] The Court of Appeal described the Act as a cumbersome and inelegant piece of legislation: see at para 72. Any regular user of the Act will sympathize.

[99] See *Campbell* (n 97 above) paras 96–106 of the judgment.

[100] ibid paras 107–127 of the judgment.

[101] ibid paras 128–130 of the judgment.

[102] ibid paras 131–137 of the judgment.

To illustrate the practical application of section 32, consider the following scenario. A journalist is investigating a story about corruption in a local authority planning department. She has obtained material from a number of sources indicating that planning officers and councillors have been taking bribes. One of the individuals that she is investigating makes a subject access request under section 7, seeking to find out what information the journalist has obtained about him and from what sources.

The journalist is almost certainly processing personal data within the meaning of DPA 1998[103] (not just for the purposes of this particular story, but generally): so either the journalist or her employer should have provided a notification to the Commissioner under section 18.[104] The journalist (or her employer) will need to consider the application of the tests in section 32(1). The processing is clearly undertaken with a view to the publication of journalistic material (section 32(1)(a)). Given the nature of the story, there are very good grounds to believe that publication would be in the public interest (section 32(1)(b)). If the journalist had to disclose her research material at this stage, then there would be an obvious risk of impeding her research; hence there are reasonable grounds to believe that compliance with the particular provision of DPA 1998 (ie section 7) would be incompatible with the journalistic purposes for which the data is being processed. On the facts discussed, it is suggested that the journalist would probably be entitled to refuse to answer the subject access request. Further, if before publication the data subject brought a claim under section 7(9) or section 13, arising out of the refusal to answer the subject access request, then the journalist would be entitled to a stay of the proceedings under section 32(5).

Even if section 32 did not apply on the facts of this scenario, section 7 would not necessarily require the journalist to identify her sources. Where a subject access request is made, the data controller does not have to disclose third party personal data (ie personal data about someone other than the requester) unless either the third party consents or it is reasonable to disclose without consent: see section 7(4) to (6). In determining whether it was reasonable to disclose without consent in this scenario, it would be necessary to take into account that requiring a journalist to identify her sources is potentially an infringement of her right of freedom of expression under Article 10.[105]

7.4.2.3 *Section 33*
Section 33 creates an exemption for information that is processed for research purposes. 'Research purposes' are defined in section 33(1) as including statistical or historical purposes. In order for data processing to come within the section 33

---

[103] Unless perhaps she makes no use whatsoever of modern information technology, so that none of the information that she holds counts as 'data'.

[104] The notification would cover the fact that personal data was being processed, and the general nature of the data concerned. It is not, of course, suggested that the Commissioner would need to be notified about this specific story, or its content: notification under s 18 operates in far more general terms.

[105] See eg *Ashworth Hospital Authority v MGN* [2002] 1 WLR 2033.

exemption, it must satisfy two conditions (defined in section 33(1), and referred to as 'the relevant conditions'):

- that the data is not processed to support measures or decisions with respect to particular individuals; and
- that the data are not processed in such a way that substantial damage or substantial distress is or is likely to be caused to any data subject.

Section 33(2) modifies the second data protection principle: it states that, in applying that principle, the further processing of personal data only for research purposes in compliance with the relevant conditions is not to be regarded as incompatible with the purposes for which the data was obtained. Section 33(3) provides that personal data processed only for research purposes in compliance with the relevant conditions may be kept indefinitely, notwithstanding the fifth data protection principle. Section 33(4) provides that personal data processed only for research purposes and in compliance with the relevant conditions is exempt from section 7 (the right of subject access), provided that the results of the research or any resulting statistics are not made available in a form which identifies data subjects or any of them. Section 32(5) provides that data is not to be treated as processed otherwise than for research purposes, merely because it is disclosed in various specified circumstances.

Section 33 is much more limited in scope than section 32. In particular, it does not confer any exemption from the first data protection principle. Hence if the publication of research material constitutes the processing of personal data, then that processing must be fair, and must satisfy a Schedule 2 condition, together with (in the case of sensitive personal data) a Schedule 3 condition.

7.4.2.4 *Sections 44 to 46: the Commissioner's role in relation to the 'special purposes'*

The Commissioner's enforcement role was set out, in general terms, in section 7.4.1 above; and his role in assessing whether data is being processed for the special purposes was referred to above, in relation to the procedural aspects of section 32.

The Commissioner has the power, under section 45 of the Act, to make a determination as to the special purposes. Section 45(1) provides that he may make a determination in writing that any personal data:

- is not being processed only for the special purposes; or
- is not being processed with a view to the publication by any person of any journalistic, literary, or artistic material which has not previously been published by the data controller.

There is a right of appeal to the Information Tribunal against any such determination (section 48 of DPA 1998).[106]

---

[106] The author is not aware that any such appeal has ever been brought. There are no decisions on the Information Tribunal website dealing with appeals against s 45 determinations: see <http://www.informationtribunal.gov.uk/> (site accessed 28 March 2009).

If the Information Commissioner determines that personal data is *not* being processed only for the special purposes, then he may make a written determination and the data controller may appeal to the Information Tribunal. If the Commissioner considers that personal data *is* being processed only for the special purposes, then he has no duty (or indeed power) to make a written determination to that effect. A person (for example a data subject) who considers that the Commissioner ought to have made a determination under section 45 has no right of appeal to the Information Tribunal against the Commissioner's failure to do so. His only recourse would seem to be to apply for judicial review, seeking an order that the Commissioner make a section 45 determination.

Section 44 of DPA 1998, empowers the Commissioner to serve a 'special information notice' on a data controller.[107] This is to enable him to obtain information to assist him in ascertaining whether personal data is being processed only for the special purposes, or with a view to the publication by any person of any journalistic, literary, or artistic material which has not previously been published by the data controller. In other words, section 44 assists the Commissioner in deciding whether to make a section 45 determination.

The question whether or not the Commissioner has made a determination under section 45 is relevant in two ways. First, where an action has been stayed under section 32(5) then a determination by the Commissioner under section 45 will bring the stay to an end. Secondly, section 45 interacts with section 46, which imposes significant limitations on the Commissioner's enforcement powers in respect of media organizations.

Section 46 provides that the Commissioner may not serve an enforcement notice on a data controller with respect to the processing of personal data for the special purposes unless two conditions are satisfied. The first is that a determination under section 45(1) with respect to that data has taken effect. The second is that the court has granted leave for the notice to be served. Before granting leave, the court must be satisfied (section 45(2)) of two matters:

- that the Commissioner has reason to suspect a contravention of the data protection principles which is of substantial public importance; and
- except where the case is one of urgency, that the data controller has been given notice in accordance with the rules of court of the application for leave.

Moreover, under section 46(3) the Commissioner may not serve an information notice (as opposed to a special information notice) on a data controller with respect to the processing of personal data for the special purposes, unless a determination under section 45(1) with respect to that data has taken effect.

---

[107] The Commissioner may do so only where he has received a request for assessment under DPA 1998, s 42, or in certain circumstances where there has been a stay of proceedings under s 32. The special information notice must contain a statement that these statutory preconditions have been satisfied: s 44(3).

Section 46 significantly limits the scope for using the Commissioner's enforcement powers against media organizations. For instance, consider the following scenario. An individual is concerned that a story about his private life will be published by a newspaper, and so asks the Commissioner to carry out an assessment (under section 42) of the processing of his personal data by the newspaper. The individual hopes that the Commissioner will use his enforcement powers under section 40 to direct the newspaper to delete any information that it holds, on the basis that the data processing is unfair. This will effectively prevent the newspaper from publishing the story. The individual faces serious difficulties. The Commissioner is unlikely to be able to make a section 45(1) determination on these facts. Even if he did so, he would require leave of the court before serving an enforcement notice, and the stringent conditions in section 46(2) would need to be satisfied. What this scenario illustrates is that there is a clear policy behind sections 45 and 46 that the Commissioner's enforcement powers should not operate as a prior restraint on publication.

On the other hand, if a newspaper had published a story but retained its research material thereafter, then the Commissioner might well be able to make a determination under section 45(1), on the basis that the personal data was not being processed with a view to the publication of hitherto unpublished material. That would potentially enable him to take enforcement action requiring the information to be deleted (but subject to obtaining the leave of the court under section 46(2)). So although section 46 limits the Commissioner's enforcement powers in relation to media organizations, it does not exclude them altogether.

Note that the Commissioner has the power to give assistance in certain specified proceedings under DPA 1998 relating to personal data processed for the special purposes, and this may include bearing the costs of legal advice or representation. The Commissioner cannot assist unless in his opinion the case involves a matter of substantial public importance. See section 53 of, and Schedule 10 to, DPA 1998.

7.4.2.5 *Section 55 and the media: unlawful obtaining of personal information*
Section 55 of DPA 1998 is a very important provision as far as information gathering by the media is concerned. The section creates a criminal offence of unlawfully obtaining personal data. Currently there is no exception for media organizations; for example, there is no provision modifying or excluding section 55 where data is processed for the 'special purposes'.[108]

Under section 55(1), a person must not knowingly or recklessly, without the consent of the data controller:

- obtain or disclose personal data or the information contained in personal data; or
- procure the disclosure to another person of the information contained in personal data.

---

[108] See, however, Criminal Justice and Immigration Act 2008, s 78, discussed below, which is not yet in force.

Contravention of section 55(1) is a criminal offence (see section 55(3)).

Section 55(1) does not apply to a person who shows:

* that the obtaining, etc, was necessary for the prevention or detection of crime or was required or authorized by any enactment, rule of law, or court order;
* that he acted in the reasonable belief that he had in law the right to obtain, etc;
* that he acted in the reasonable belief that he would have had the consent of the data controller had the latter known of the obtaining, etc, and the circumstances; or
* that the obtaining, etc, was justified in the particular circumstances as being in the public interest.

There are also offences of selling, offering to sell, or advertising for sale personal data obtained in breach of section 55(1): see section 55(4) to (6).

The offence under section 55(1) may be committed where an employee abuses his access to his employer's computer system by looking up information for his own purposes.[109] The offence may also be committed where the data controller is deceived into disclosing information (for example where a third party passes himself off as the data subject).[110]

Two reports from the Information Commissioner have focused attention on the illicit trade in personal data: see 'What Price Privacy? The unlawful trade in personal data' (May 2006),[111] and 'What Price Privacy now? The first six months progress in halting the unlawful trade in confidential personal information' (December 2006).[112] According to the May 2006 report the suppliers of personal information almost invariably worked within the private investigation industry;[113] the buyers included journalists, and in one major case investigated by the Commissioner the records included information supplied to 305 named journalists working for a range of newspapers.[114] The main methods used for obtaining information were corruption and deception ('blagging'). The May 2006 report included fascinating details of the techniques used, including extracts from a 'blagger's manual' recovered from the office of a private investigator.[115]

One issue addressed in these reports is the penalty for offences under section 55. Under DPA 1998 as originally enacted, individuals who are guilty of an offence under

---

[109] See *R v Codrington*, November 2002, unreported but referred to in Jay (n 52 above) paras 20–51 (Benefits Agency employee abusing access to employer's computer to obtain personal data about friends and family); *R v Rooney* [2006] EWCA Crim 1841 (police civilian employee using access to police records to obtain address of sister's ex-partner).

[110] See the authorities in relation to sexual offences, that fraud as to identity of person or nature of act will vitiate consent: eg *R v Linekar* (1995) 2 Cr App R 49, CA. See also Jay (n 52 above) paras 20–48.

[111] 10 May 2006, HC 1056

[112] 13 December 2006, HC 36.

[113] See May 2006 report, para 1.10.

[114] See December 2006 report, para 1.8; paras 5.6–5.11. Further details are given in the December 2006 report, at pp 8–9.

[115] May 2006 report, paras 5.30–5.34 and Annex B.

section 55 can be fined, but not imprisoned (see section 60(2)). The central recommendation of the May 2006 report was that these penalties should be increased to a maximum of two years' imprisonment.[116] The Commissioner also called for the Press Complaints Commission to take a much stronger line to tackle press involvement in this illegal trade.[117]

Subsequently, section 77 of the Criminal Justice and Immigration Act 2008 was enacted, which empowers the Secretary of State, by order, to increase the penalty for offences under section 55, to a maximum of two years' imprisonment. At the same time, section 78 of that Act provides for a new defence[118] where a person can show:

that he acted—

(i) for the special purposes,

(ii) with a view to the publication by any person of any journalistic,
literary or artistic material, and

(iii) in the reasonable belief that in the particular circumstances the obtaining,
disclosing or procuring was justified as being in the public interest

Neither section 77 nor section 78 has yet been brought into force.

7.4.2.6 *Application of DPA 1998 to internet-based publication*

How does DPA 1998 apply in relation to web-based media? Very many broadcasters and newspapers now have an internet presence, and DPA 1998 is likely to apply to their web-based activities in the same way as to their other activities. However, the internet also enables individuals to publish material with hitherto unprecedented ease, by way of personal websites, blogs, entries on social networking sites, and so forth. Some of this material is accessible to anyone with an internet connection. Other material may be accessible on a more limited basis: for instance, material posted by a user of a social networking site[119] may be accessible to all other members of the site (which may mean many millions of individuals), or may be accessible to only a few individuals selected by that user. Much will depend on the range of privacy settings offered by the site, and on how the individual uses those settings. A great deal of the information that individuals publish on the internet will consist of personal data, about themselves and other people. Two questions arise: to what extent this kind of activity comes within the scope of the DPA 1998 at all; and, where it does, to what extent it is covered by the 'special purposes' exception in section 32 of the Act.

Section 36 of DPA 1998 provides an exemption from most of the substantive provisions of the Act, in respect of personal data processed by an individual only for the purposes of that individual's personal, family, or household affairs (including

---

[116] May 2006 report, para 1.13. The recommendation was reiterated in the December 2006 report.
[117] May 2006 report, paras 1.15 and 7.21.
[118] To be inserted as section 55(2)(ca) of DPA 1998.
[119] At the time of writing (March 2009) the leading sites for UK users are Facebook and MySpace: see *The Observer*, 29 March 2009, available at <http://www.guardian.co.uk/technology/2009/mar/29/myspace-facebook-bebo-twitter>.

recreational purposes). This reflects the limitation as to the scope of the Data Processing Directive set out in Article 3.2 of that Directive, which provides that the Directive does not apply to data processing by a natural person in the course of a purely personal or household activity.

In the *Lindqvist* case[120] the European Court of Justice held that a personal website maintained by a Swedish woman in relation to her part-time work as a parish catechist fell within the scope of the Directive, notwithstanding Article 3.2. The material on the website was accessible to an indefinite number of people (essentially, anyone with an internet connection, anywhere in the world) and so the processing of that material could not be a purely personal or household activity.[121]

The *Lindqvist* case would suggest that personal blogs (if they are generally accessible and not password-protected) come within the scope of DPA 1998, at any rate where they include personal data. Potentially the same would apply to pages maintained on social networking sites, at any rate where those pages are very widely visible.[122] It would appear to follow, in the light of *Lindqvist*, that there are many millions of individuals (including a high proportion of the teenage population) who ought to be notifying the Information Commissioner under section 18 that they are processing personal data.

It is suggested that the *Lindqvist* approach does not take proper account of modern social conditions. For many people, their use of the internet is an extension of their family and social life rather than a way of communicating with the world in general. Their use of the internet can properly be seen as personal, domestic, or recreational, even though the material they post may in theory be very widely accessible.

However, even if the *Lindqvist* decision goes too far, there is undoubtedly a great deal of internet-based activity carried out by individuals that is not personal or domestic in nature. Websites or blogs focusing on matters of general interest (such as politics, religion, sport, or celebrity gossip) would, it is suggested, fall outside section 36 and thus would come within the scope of the Act. The question that then arises is whether activity of this nature comes within the scope of the 'special purposes' and is therefore potentially protected by section 32 of DPA 1998.

Given that the purpose of section 32 is to reconcile data protection with freedom of expression, it is suggested that the special purposes (journalism, artistic purposes, and literary purposes) should be widely interpreted. For instance, blogging about current affairs and the events of the day can properly be described as journalistic in nature (even if the blogger earns nothing for his work[123]). Much blogging is a form of amateur creative writing, and can properly be described as literary (there is no test of literary merit in DPA 1998).

---

[120] Case C-101/01, [2004] QB 1014.

[121] See paras 29–48 of the decision.

[122] eg a Facebook user might join the London network and make their profile visible to all other members of that network. As at 29 March 2009 the London network had 3,578,679 members: see <http://www.facebook.com>.

[123] There is nothing in DPA 1998 to indicate that journalism only covers paid activities. In any event, a distinction between paid and unpaid blogging would be unworkable. Would one have to consider whether the blogger was an Amazon affiliate, for instance, and if so how much revenue they generated?

This approach to section 32 does not give individuals *carte blanche* to publish personal data about others on the internet. The control mechanism is section 32(1)(b), whereby the section 32 exemption is available only if the data controller reasonably believes that publication would be in the public interest. Where no question of public interest arose, the disclosure by a blogger of the personal information of other people could contravene DPA 1998 (for example as being unfair processing of personal data, in breach of the first data protection principle), and could lead to a claim for compensation under section 13. Moreover, if the blogger's activities came within the 'special purposes' then (unlike in the usual run of cases) compensation would be available for distress alone, even in the absence of damage.[124]

7.4.2.7 *Conclusion: how significant for the media is DPA 1998?*

One possible view is that, whatever may have been the fears at the point when the Act was introduced, DPA 1998 has turned out to be of relatively little importance for the media. In the three leading cases discussed above in relation to breach of confidence—the *Douglas*, *Campbell*, and *Murray* cases—the claimants relied both on breach of confidence and on DPA 1998. The DPA claims added little of practical value. In the *Douglas* case the individual claimants were awarded nominal damages at trial for breach of their rights under DPA 1998. In *Campbell* by the time the case reached the House of Lords the debate was about breach of confidence, not data protection. In the *Murray* case, although there was a claim under DPA 1998, the Court of Appeal did not find it necessary to discuss it in any detail.[125] It is tempting to conclude that, in cases concerning the publication of private information by the media, claims under DPA 1998 will do nothing except add to the costs of the litigation.[126]

It is suggested, however, that it would be a mistake to treat DPA 1998 as an irrelevance. Even confining one's attention to claims brought by individuals before the civil courts, the Act has the potential to add something to the post-*Campbell* law on breach of confidence. For instance, the first data protection principle includes both a highly generalized concept of fairness, and a requirement of notification to individuals about data processing; these go beyond the requirements of breach of confidence. Looking beyond the field of civil litigation, under DPA 1998 there is the possibility of enforcement action by the Information Commissioner. For those who are not wealthy celebrities, a complaint to the Commissioner is likely to be far more attractive than facing the costs and risks of High Court litigation.[127] And finally, the Act has the potential to criminalize some intrusive or dishonest forms of media investigation.[128] In short, the

---

[124] See DPA 1998, s 13(2)(b). This is a respect in which a data controller is potentially worse off if his activities fall within the special purposes.

[125] See paras 62–63 of the judgment.

[126] See the discussion in M Warby 'Privacy and the Media—data protection impacts', a paper for the JUSTICE/Sweet & Maxwell Data Protection and Privacy Conference, December 2008.

[127] Note, however, the important limitations on the Commissioner's enforcement powers, under DPA 1998, s 46.

[128] See ibid s 55.

legislation is complex and difficult, and the temptation to treat it as peripheral is therefore considerable; but it is a temptation that should be firmly resisted.

7.5 FREEDOM OF INFORMATION

7.5.1 Access rights and the media

From the point of view of the media, information law is double-edged. It is a fetter on how information can be obtained and what can be published. At the same time it is potentially a source of positive rights of access to information.

Although DPA 1998 does confer a right of access to information (under section 7 of the Act), this only entitles individuals to obtain their own personal information; it is therefore of very limited value to media organizations as an information-gathering tool.[129] The various statutory provisions conferring rights of access to public sector information are a great deal more important in this context. The main provision is the Freedom of Information Act 2000 (FOIA 2000), discussed in this section. Section 7.6 below, goes on to consider the Environmental Information Regulations 2004 (EIR 2004), as well as various sector-specific provisions for access to information (for instance, in relation to local government).

Mention should also be made of the separate Scottish legislation in relation to freedom of information, namely the Freedom of Information (Scotland) Act 2002 (FOISA 2002). This applies to the various public authorities listed in Schedule 1 to that Act, which operate solely in or in relation to Scotland; UK-wide public authorities, even in relation to their activities in Scotland, are covered by FOIA 2000. The Scottish legislation is enforced by the Scottish Information Commissioner[130] (established under section 42 of FOISA 2002). Although FOISA 2002 is similar to FOIA 2000 in its general structure, there are some important differences. Space does not permit a detailed comparison of the two Acts in this chapter. The provisions of FOISA in relation to personal data were considered by the House of Lords in *Common Services Agency v Scottish Information Commissioner*,[131] discussed further at sections 7.5.3.3 and 7.5.6 below.

None of these enactments is tailored specifically for media organizations. For the most part they confer rights of access in general terms, without specific reference to the identity of the person seeking the information, the purpose for which it is sought, or the connection between the requester and the body that holds the information. Nevertheless, in some respects media organizations are in a special position when it comes to making use of statutory information access rights. In the first place they are

---

[129] The scope for making subject access requests to media organizations was discussed in the previous section.

[130] Note that enforcement of DPA 1998 throughout the UK is the responsibility of the Information Commissioner and not the Scottish Information Commissioner.

[131] [2008] UKHL 47, [2008] 1 WLR 1550.

often regular users of the legislation, and therefore in a position to develop an expertise in using it effectively. Secondly, journalists with specialist knowledge of a particular subject matter may be well placed to identify what information is worth requesting, and where it is likely to be held. And thirdly, media organizations (unlike the majority of requesters) may have the resources to instruct legal representatives in appeals to the Information Tribunal or the courts.

At times the use made of FOIA 2000 by media organizations has been politically controversial. On 21 March 2007, Lord Falconer (the then Lord Chancellor) gave the Lord Williams of Mostyn Memorial Lecture, on the subject of open government. He said this: 'The Government approaches openness on the basis of improving how government operates, for the benefit of the public. Many sections of the press do not approach it in that way. Instead, many approach it on the basis of what gives them most information exclusive to their journalistic outlet.' He added: 'The job of the Government is not to provide page leads for the papers, but information for the citizen. Freedom of information was never considered to be, and for our part will never be considered to be, a research arm for the media.'

The antithesis between 'page leads for the papers' and 'information for citizens' is highly questionable. Inevitably, those with an interest in public affairs will be dependent on the media for much of their information. A number of high-profile FOIA cases have involved requests made by the media. Consider, for example, the request by *The Guardian* newspaper for disclosure by the BBC of the minutes of the Governors' meeting at which the Hutton Report was discussed.[132] It could not possibly be suggested that a request of this kind was in some way an abuse of FOIA 2002, because made by a newspaper, but would have been legitimate if made by a private individual. Nor is there anything in the terms of the Act itself that is capable of supporting a distinction of that kind.

Although rights of access to information are potentially of considerable value to the media, their limitations also need to be appreciated. There are restrictions as to the *amount* of information that can be obtained: see for instance the provisions in section 12 of FOIA 2000, limiting the amount of time that public authorities can be required to spend in locating information. There are limitations as to the *speed* with which information can be obtained: in the context of a 24-hour rolling news cycle, the time limits under FOIA 2000 can appear very leisurely indeed. And there are limitations as to the requester's *control* over the information that is disclosed. Information may be disclosed to the general public (for example via an online disclosure log)[133] at or about the same time as it is given to the requester. For a journalist hoping for an exclusive news story, this may not be particularly welcome.

Successful journalistic use of the information access legislation will require careful thought and planning. Wide-ranging requests that are no more than a fishing

---

[132] This request was the subject of the Information Tribunal decision in *Guardian Newspapers and Brooke v Information Commissioner and BBC* EA/2006/0011 and EA/2006/0013.

[133] For an example of a disclosure log maintained by a government department, see <http://www.mod.uk/DefenceInternet/FreedomOfInformation/DisclosureLog>.

expedition, embarked upon in the hope that something of interest will turn up, may well be frustrated by the costs limits in section 12 of the Act. By contrast, a series of carefully focused FOIA requests addressed to different organizations will often assist in building up an overall picture, and there is then scope to 'add value' by detailed analysis of the information obtained. A good example is a story published in *The Times* in November 2005,[134] using data obtained under FOIA 2000 in order to show that there was a wide difference in conviction rates as between different parts of the UK. Another example of this kind of approach, in a non-journalistic context, is the work of the Taxpayers'Alliance[135] in using FOIA 2000 to assemble an annual 'Rich List' of the highest-paid public sector executives. FOIA 2000 can also be used effectively by journalists who familiarize themselves with the information that is in the public domain, and then use the Act to try to fill in any apparent gaps in the record.[136]

Section 7.5.2 below, gives a general introduction to FOIA 2000. The subsequent sections outline the main provisions of the Act, and the decision-making mechanism that it establishes. Section 7.5.8 looks at the position of certain public authorities (in particular, the BBC) as public authorities under FOIA 2000 in their own right. Finally, section 7.5.9 looks at the potential for future amendment to the Act. Section 7.6 goes on to consider other enactments giving a right of access to public sector information.

7.5.2 Introduction to the Freedom of Information Act 2000

In international terms, the UK was a latecomer in introducing freedom of information legislation. The Swedish Freedom of the Press Act (introduced in 1766) is often referred to as the world's first freedom of information statute.[137] The US introduced freedom of information at federal level in 1966; Australia did likewise in 1982; and the New Zealand Official Information Act also dates from 1982. By contrast, until FOIA 2000 there was no general statutory right of access to public sector information in the UK—there was merely a non-statutory Code of Practice on Access to Government Information, introduced in 1994 by the Conservative Government under John Major.

The BBC political comedy series *Yes Minister*, broadcast in the early 1980s, illustrates the perception that there was at that time an entrenched culture of secrecy within the UK's political institutions. The very first episode[138] was entitled 'Open Government', this being an enthusiasm of Jim Hacker, the (newly-appointed) Minister in question. Sir Arnold Robinson, the Cabinet Secretary, was not enthusiastic: 'My dear boy, it is a contradiction in terms: you can be open or you can have government.'

---

[134] See <http://www.timesonline.co.uk/tol/news/uk/article593173.ece> (site accessed 21 March 2009).

[135] See <http://www.taxpayersalliance.com>.

[136] For an example of a successful request of this nature, see *Foreign and Commonwealth Office v Information Commissioner* EA/2007/0047 (request for disclosure of an early draft of the September 2002 dossier on Iraq's Weapons of Mass Destruction).

[137] Though it has been suggested that the legislation was in turn inspired by certain features of Chinese government under the Tang Dynasty (AD 618–907): see S Lamble (2002) 97 *Freedom of Information Review* 2.

[138] First broadcast on 25 February 1980.

Sir Arnold would not have been at all surprised that the genesis of FOIA 2000 was in a White Paper published in December 1997,[139] by a Labour government newly elected after eighteen years in opposition. Nor would he have been surprised that the experience of holding power seemed to reduce the government's enthusiasm for freedom of information. When the Bill that subsequently became FOIA 2000 was introduced in 1999, a number of commentators expressed disappointment that the proposals in the White Paper had been diluted.[140] Although the Act was passed in 2000, its central provision—the right of access to information, under section 1—did not come into force until 1 January 2005. The timing suggested a certain lack of enthusiasm for the provision, even within the government that had introduced it.

The Act has now been fully in force for over four years. There have been a number of high-profile disclosures. For instance, successive decisions of the Information Tribunal[141] (one of which was unsuccessfully appealed to the High Court) have required greater openness in relation to MPs' expenses. Policy-related information has been disclosed in relation to matters such as the ID cards scheme,[142] tax changes affecting pension funds,[143] and education funding.[144] A decision of the Information Commissioner requiring disclosure of Cabinet Minutes relating to the Iraq War was upheld by the Information Tribunal[145] but was then overruled by ministerial veto.[146] In the light of developments such as these, suggestions that the Act would have no real impact[147] have been shown to be too pessimistic.

Although FOIA 2000 has altered the balance between government and the individual (or the media) in terms of access to information, the shift towards greater openness is not universal. The Official Secrets Acts 1911 and 1989 remain in force.[148] These criminalize the disclosure by civil servants of various kinds of official information 'without lawful authority'. A civil servant who leaks official information to a journalist may still be liable to prosecution, therefore; and there is no defence available that disclosure was in the public interest.[149]

---

[139] *Your Right to Know—the Government's Proposals for a Freedom of Information Act* Cm 3818 (1997)

[140] See eg the article by Maurice Frankel of the Campaign for Freedom of Information in *The Guardian*, 11 October 1999, at <http://www.guardian.co.uk/politics/1999/oct/11/freedomofinformation.uk1> (site accessed 21 March 2009).

[141] See *Corporate Officer of the House of Commons v Information Commissioner and Norman Baker MP* EA/2006/0015 and 0016; *Corporate Officer of the House of Commons v Information Commissioner* EA/2006/0074 (and others); *Corporate Officer of the House of Commons v Information Commissioner, Ben Leapman, Heather Brooke and Michael Thomas* EA/2007/0060 (and others), [2008] EWHC 1084 (Admin).

[142] *OGC v Information Commissioner* [2008] EWHC 737 (Admin), EA/2006/0068 and 0080.

[143] *HM Treasury v Information Commissioner and Times Newspapers Ltd* EA/2006/0041 (appeal withdrawn: Information Tribunal decision relates only to question of costs).

[144] *DfES v Information Commissioner and Evening Standard* EA/2006/0006.

[145] *Cabinet Office v Information Commissioner and Christopher Lamb* EA/2008/0024 and 0029.

[146] See <http://www.justice.gov.uk/news/announcement240209a.htm> (site accessed 22 March 2009).

[147] See eg T Cornford in [2001] 3 Web Journal of Current Legal Issues, suggesting that the Act was closer to being a sham than to being genuine, at <http://webjcli.ncl.ac.uk/2001/issue3/cornford3.html> (site accessed 21 March 2009).

[148] The very wide offence of 'disclosure of any official information, without authority' created by s 2 of the 1911 Act was repealed by the 1989 Act and replaced by a number of more specific restrictions.

[149] See *R v Shayler* [2003] 1 AC 247.

Even in relation to FOIA 2000 itself, there are some serious practical concerns. For example, the limited resources available to the Information Commissioner's Office in dealing with freedom of information have led to a backlog in dealing with complaints under the Act.[150] Nor can it be assumed that the Act will remain in its current form indefinitely; there have already been various proposals for the scope of the Act to be restricted, though so far none of these has been implemented.[151]

7.5.3 The right of access to information in outline

7.5.3.1 *The right of access to information under section 1*

The key provision in FOIA 2000 is section 1, providing a general right of access on request to information held by public authorities. A person making a request for information to a public authority[152] is entitled to two things (subject to the limitations and exemptions discussed below). He is entitled to be informed in writing whether the public authority holds information of the description specified in the request; if yes, he is entitled to have that information communicated to him. The public authority's duty to say whether it holds the information sought is referred to in the Act as the 'duty to confirm or deny'. The duty to provide that information is referred to in this chapter as the 'duty to disclose', though this term does not appear in the Act itself. Of the two duties, the duty to disclose is usually much the more significant.

7.5.3.2 *What is a 'public authority'?*

The FOIA 2000 imposes duties on *public authorities*. Defining the boundary between public and private bodies is a notoriously difficult legal issue.[153] Rather than leaving the question at large, the Act seeks to define in exhaustive terms what counts as a public authority for the purposes of the Act. Any body, person, or office-holder listed in Schedule 1 to the Act is a 'public authority': see section 3(1)(a) of the Act. The Secretary of State can extend the coverage of the Act by order, provided certain conditions are met, under sections 4 and 5 of the Act. Publicly-owned companies, as defined by section 6, are also public authorities for the purpose of the Act (see section 3(1)(b)).

If a body is not a public authority as defined in FOIA 2000, then it will fall outside the Act (whether or not it is treated for other legal purposes as being public in nature).

---

[150] See the House of Commons Justice Committee's Report on the work of the Information Commissioner, published on 9 February 2009 (HC 146). Annexed to this is a memorandum from the Information Commisisoner prepared in January 2009. Paragraph 3.2 of the memorandum indicates that the ICO is now closing over 50% of straightforward cases within 30 days, but most of the remaining cases now have to wait 6 months before the ICO can start on them. The same paragraph states that the ICO has an establishment of only 52 staff devoted to some 2,500 FOI cases a year, involving the entirety of the public sector.

[151] See further section 7.5.9 below.

[152] The Act refers to the person seeking information as an 'applicant', or (in the context of a complaint to the Information Commissioner under section 50) as a 'complainant'. For clarity this chapter also uses the word 'requester' to cover both applicants and complainants, though this term is not found in the Act itself.

[153] cf the case law as to whether particular bodies are public authorities for the purposes of HRA 1998, s 6(3): see eg *Wallbank v Parochial Church Council of Aston Cantlow* [2003] UKHL 37, [2004] 1 AC 546.

For instance, the Security Service (MI5), the Secret Intelligence Service (MI6), and the Government Communications Headquarters (GCHQ) are not public authorities under the Act, and hence there is no right of access under FOIA 2000 to information held by those authorities.[154]

When Northern Rock plc was taken into public ownership, there was considerable controversy as to whether it should come within FOIA 2000. The transfer to public ownership was brought about by the Banking (Special Provisions) Act 2008, and the Northern Rock plc Transfer Order 2008, made under that Act. A House of Lords amendment to the Banking (Special Provisions) Bill,[155] providing that FOIA 2000 should extend to Northern Rock, was rejected in the House of Commons.[156] The effect of Article 18 of the Transfer Order is that Northern Rock is deemed not to be a publicly-owned company under section 3(1)(b) of FOIA 2000 while it is in public ownership.[157] Hence information held by Northern Rock falls outside the scope of the Act.

Some authorities are listed in Schedule 1 only in relation to information held for specified purposes. The BBC, for instance, is a public authority only in respect of information held for purposes other than those of journalism, art, or literature.[158] Where a public authority is listed in Schedule 1 only in relation to information of a specified decription, then the Act is disapplied (save in certain minor and technical respects) in respect of any other information held by that authority.[159]

Section 7(3)(a) of FOIA 2000 empowers the Secretary of State to amend Schedule 1 by order, so as to limit to information of a specified description the entry in Schedule 1 relating to any public authority. This is potentially a very important provision. It makes it possible to reduce the coverage of the Act by order, without the need for primary legislation.[160] Section 7.5.9 below, discusses a recent proposal to use this section so as to take certain information about MPs' expenses outside the scope of the Act.

7.5.3.3 *When is information held by a public authority?*

The Act confers rights in relation to *information* that is *held* by a public authority. Information for this purpose is defined in section 84 as being 'information that is recorded in any form'. Information is *held* by a public authority if it is held by the authority itself (other than on behalf of another person) or if it is held by another person on behalf of the authority.[161] The duty to confirm or deny and the duty to disclose apply to information that is held by the public authority at the time that the request is received,

---

[154] FOIA 2000, s 23 deals with information held by public authorities that relates to or is supplied by these three bodies (along with other security bodies).

[155] See *Hansard*, HL, vol 699, 21 February 2008, cols 315–323.

[156] See *Hansard*, HC, vol 472, 21 February 2008, cols 634–654.

[157] Nor can information held by Northern Rock be treated as information held on behalf of the Treasury, for the purposes of FOIA 2000, s 3(2)(b): see the Transfer Order, art 18(2)(b).

[158] See FOIA 2000, Sch 1, Part VI; and see also section 7.5.8 below.

[159] See ibid s 7(1), which disapplies Parts I to V of the Act in relation to such information.

[160] As mentioned above, the coverage of the Act can be *increased* by order, under ss 4 and 5 of the Act.

[161] FOIA 2000 s 3(2).

although account may be taken of any amendment or deletion made between the receipt of the request and the statutory deadline for responding to the request, provided that the amendment or deletion would have been made regardless of the request.[162]

Sometimes a request for information will require a public authority to collate information from a variety of different sources. This may give rise to an issue as to whether the request is truly for information that is held by the authority, or whether instead it is a request for the authority to create new information that it does not currently hold. The House of Lords considered a similar issue arising under FOISA 2002, in *Common Services Agency v Scottish Information Commissioner*.[163] The Scottish Commissioner had required disclosure of information about childhood leukaemia in a particular locality, in 'barnardised' form. Barnardisation is a technique for the random modification of small numbers, intended to allow health statistics to be disclosed while minimizing the risk that there will be any resulting disclosure of individual identities. It was argued that the Scottish Commissioner had gone beyond the requirements of FOISA 2002[164] by requiring the public authority to create new information that it did not hold at the time of the request. The House of Lords rejected this: barnardisation did not involve the creation of new information, but was similar to a process of redaction.[165]

In *Johnson v Information Commissioner and Ministry of Justice*[166] the Information Tribunal considered a request for information about decisions by High Court Masters to strike out claims. In order to answer the request the Ministry of Justice would have had to collate information manually from a large number of individual paper files. The Tribunal considered that the requested information was 'held' by the Ministry; collating it manually from the paper files, although time-consuming, would have been a mechanical process involving minimal skill and judgment. However, the Ministry was not required to answer the request, because the cost of doing so would exceed the appropriate limit in section 12 of FOIA 2000 (see section 7.5.3.7 below).

7.5.3.4 *Format of requests under FOIA*

A request for information under FOIA 2000 may be informal, and does not need specifically to mention the Act. The request must be in writing (see section 8(1)), but this includes e-mail (see section 8(2)). There is no requirement to explain why the information is being sought.

It is, however, advisable in the requester's own interests to give as much detail as he can about the information that is being sought, if only so as to assist the public authority in locating and retrieving the information. In cases where a qualified exemption is likely to be engaged (thus requiring the public interest to be considered),[167] it may also

---

[162] ibid s 1(4).

[163] [2008] UKHL 47, [2008] 1 WLR 1550.

[164] For the purposes of this issue there is no material difference between FOIA 2000 and FOISA 2002.

[165] See [2008] UKHL 47, paras 14–16 (Lord Hope).

[166] EA/2006/0085.

[167] See further the discussion of the qualified exemptions at section 7.5.4 below.

be advisable for the requester to set out any factors that he thinks relevant to the public interest in disclosure. Where requests are made for media purposes, it may be important to obtain the information as quickly as possible: focused requests (for example for 'the document dated 1 March 2008, referred to in the minutes of the meeting of 1 February 2008') are more likely to achieve this than are wide-ranging requests (for example for 'any information about why the Chief Executive was dismissed').

The request must give the applicant's name and address, and hence requests made anonymously are invalid.[168]

7.5.3.5 *Assistance for requesters*
FOIA 2000 recognizes that requesters have the difficulty that they may not know what information a public authority holds, or how it is stored. Hence, under section 16, public authorities have a duty to provide requesters with reasonable advice and assistance. Any public authority which conforms with the relevant provisions of the code of practice issued by the Secretary of State under section 45 of the Act is to be taken to comply with this duty (see section 16(2)).

A code was issued under section 45 in November 2004, by the Secretary of State for Constitutional Affairs. Part II of the Code deals with advice and assistance. It states that the purpose of assistance is to clarify the nature of the information sought, not to determine the requester's aims and motivations (see paragraph 9 of the Code). Paragraph 10 gives examples of appropriate assistance (for instance, providing an outline of the different kinds of information which might meet the terms of the request).

The distinction drawn in paragraph 9 between the nature of the information sought, and the requester's aims and motivations, will often, in practice, be an elusive one. In order to understand what someone is asking for it is usually helpful to know why they are asking for it. For this reason, unless there is some particular reason not to do so, it may well be in the interests of requesters to make clear, from the outset, the purpose of their request.

7.5.3.6 *Time limits under the Act*
Public authorities must answer requests promptly, and in any event within twenty working days (see section 10(1)). If a public authority is relying on an exemption then within that same period it must give the applicant a notice which specifies the exemption in question, state (if not otherwise apparent) why it applies, and give various other specified information: (see section 17). If a public authority is relying on a qualified exemption under Part II of the Act then it is entitled to reasonable further time in order to consider whether the balance of public interest is in favour of maintaining the exemption.[169] It must, however, inform the applicant of any exemption on which it relies, within the primary time limit (ie twenty working days). If the public authority's

---

[168] For guidance by the ICO in dealing with anonymous requests, see <http://www.ico.gov.uk/upload/documents/library/freedom_of_information/detailed_specialist_guides/name_of_applicant_fop083_v1.pdf>.

[169] See FOIA 2000, s 10(3).

decision is that the balance of public interest is in favour of maintaining the exemption, it must inform the applicant of the reasons for this conclusion, either within twenty working days or within such further time as is reasonable in the circumstances.[170]

Where a freedom of information, request is controversial, its resolution may take a great deal longer than twenty working days. The request may go to internal review, followed by a complaint to the Information Commissioner, with perhaps an appeal to the Information Tribunal and possibly to the High Court thereafter (these various further stages are discussed below). Where information is needed urgently in relation to a breaking news story, FOIA 2000 will often be of little practical help.

7.5.3.7 *Costs limits, vexatious and repeated requests, and charges*
Although the main provisions about exemptions are in Part II of FIOA 2000 (discussed below), Part I contains two important general limitations on the right of access conferred by section 1, relating to the cost of compliance and to vexatious or repeated requests.

Under section 12 there is no obligation to comply with a request if the authority estimates that the cost of compliance exceeds the 'appropriate limit'. This provision is designed to limit the amount of work that public authorities are required to do in answering requests made under the Act.[171] Section 12 provides a framework only; the Freedom of Information (Appropriate Limit and Fees) Regulations 2004[172] supply the necessary details.

The appropriate limit is currently £600 for central government and Parliament, and £450 for other public authorities.[173] In calculating whether this figure has been exceeded the public authority can attribute £25 an hour to the time spent in complying with the request.[174] Hence a public authority can refuse to comply with a request if to do so would take more than 24 hours' work (for central government and Parliament) or 18 hours' work (for other public authorities). However, in estimating whether the cost of compliance would exceed the appropriate limit the public authority can only take account of costs incurred (or time spent) in: determining whether it holds the information; locating the information or a document which may contain it; retrieving the information or a document which may contain it; and extracting the information from a document containing it.[175] The public authority cannot, therefore, take account of costs incurred (or time spent) in considering whether the information is exempt from disclosure under FOIA 2000, or in applying the public interest test where a qualified exemption is engaged. Nor can the public authority take account of the cost of obtaining legal advice about the request.

---

[170] ibid s 17(3).
[171] See section 7.5.9 below for discussion of proposals to change the operation of the costs regime (these proposals were not pursued).
[172] SI 2004/3244.
[173] See ibid, reg 3.
[174] This figure is set by ibid, reg 4(4).
[175] ibid, reg 4(3).

In estimating the costs of compliance, there are some circumstances in which separate requests can be aggregated rather than being treated individually. Aggregation is potentially an important limitation on requesters' rights, as it significantly increases the chance that the appropriate limit will be exceeded. Regulation 5 of the 2004 Regulations allows two or more requests to be aggregated if the following three conditions are all met:

(1) the requests are made to a public authority by the same person, or by different persons who appear to the public authority to be acting in concert or in pursuance of a campaign;

(2) the requests relate to any extent to the same or similar information; and

(3) the requests are received by the public authority within any period of sixty consecutive working days.

These provisions are important for media organizations that make frequent or extensive use of FOIA 2000. One important point to note is that the provisions do not provide for aggregation of requests made to *different* public authorities. If a newspaper makes a similar request for information to every local authority in the country, section 12 will be applied to each local authority separately, in respect of that authority's costs in complying with the request.[176] Another point is that, in order for aggregation to be permitted, there must be some overlap as to the subject matter of the requests. Wholly unrelated requests, even if made to the same public authority, cannot be aggregated.

Section 14 of FOIA 2000 deals with vexatious or repeated requests. Under section 14(1), a public authority is not obliged to comply with a request if it is vexatious. By section 14(2), if a public authority has previously complied with a request for information then it is not obliged to comply with a subsequent identical or substantially similar request from that person unless a reasonable interval has elapsed between compliance with the previous request and the making of the current request. The Information Commissioner has given detailed guidance about vexatious requests, last updated on 3 December 2008.[177]

In deciding whether a request is vexatious, inevitably the purpose for which the information is sought will be material. For instance, one factor that has been treated as relevant by the Information Tribunal is whether the request is likely to lead to distress or irritation without justification or proper cause;[178] and this issue is likely to depend partly on the requester's purpose in seeking the information. Where a request is genuinely made for journalistic purposes, it is suggested that it would take very unusual

---

[176] The Information Commissioner issued guidance about 'round robin' requests on 13 March 2009: <http://www.ico.gov.uk/upload/documents/library/freedom_of_information/practical_application/round_robins_v1.pdf> (accessed 22 March 2009).

[177] See <http://www.ico.gov.uk/upload/documents/library/freedom_of_information/practical_application/awareness_guidance_22_vexatious_and_repeated_requests_final.pdf> (accessed 22 March 2009).

[178] See *Hossack v Information Commissioner and DWP* EA/2007/0024, paras 24–27.

circumstances for the request to come within section 14(1). Section 14(2) may be of more concern to media organizations, as it is a potential constraint on using FOIA 2000 in order to follow up a story on a continuous basis. Media organizations may need to resist an unduly wide reading of the provision. Take the example of a local newspaper that makes a freedom of information request each month for information about restaurant inspections carried out by a local authority's environmental health officers during the previous month. It is suggested that section 14(2) would not apply: 'What inspections did you carry out in February?' is not identical with or substantially similar to a request for the same information for January.

A public authority is entitled to charge a fee under FOIA 2000 (see sections 9 and 13). Where the appropriate limit is not exceeded, then the public authority may only charge a very limited fee, and may not take account of staff time.[179] If the appropriate limit is exceeded, the public authority may nevertheless be willing to provide the information in return for payment, in which case the fee charged may include an element for staff time, again at the rate of £25 per hour.[180] However, if the appropriate limit under section 12 is exceeded, the requester cannot compel the public authority to provide the information, even if he makes it clear that he is willing to pay.

7.5.3.8 *Publication schemes*

The right of access to information under section 1 is clearly at the heart of FOIA 2010. However, it is important not to overlook the other route whereby information can be obtained under the Act. Section 19 requires public authorities to adopt, maintain, and implement a publication scheme for the disclosure of information. Schemes require the approval of the Information Commissioner (section 19(1)), though public authorities may have the option of adopting a model publication scheme approved by the Commissioner (section 20).

Section 19 therefore requires public authorities to consider the proactive disclosure of information, rather than simply responding to requests under section 1 when they are received. In practical terms, before making a request under section 1 it is advisable to find out whether the requested information is disclosed under the publication scheme and can be obtained by that route.

7.5.4 Exemptions in Part II of FOIA 2000

Part II of the Act provides for a number of exemptions to the right of access under section 1. The most difficult legal questions under FOIA 2000 relate to the operation of these provisions. The exemptions have also been a focus of political controversy. Section 7.5.2 above, referred to criticisms that were made of the perceived weakness of the Freedom of Information Bill while it was before Parliament. Many of these criticisms focused on the range and breadth of the exemptions under the Act.

---

[179] See SI 2004/3244, reg 6.
[180] See ibid, reg 7.

This section gives a general outline of the exemptions in Part II. There is a more detailed discussion below of the exemptions that apply in respect of two specific types of information likely to be of particular interest to media organizations: personal data (section 7.5.6 below); and policy-related information (section 7.5.7 below).

7.5.4.1 *Different types of exemption*

The exemptions fall into two principal groups. Some are absolute: if information falls within one of these categories then it will be exempt from disclosure.[181] Others are qualified, and are subject to a public interest test.[182] If in all the circumstances of the case the public interest in maintaining a qualified exemption outweighs the public interest in disclosure then the information need not be disclosed; otherwise, the duty of disclosure still applies. Hence in relation to the qualified exemptions there are two separate (but closely linked) questions to consider. The first is whether the information comes within the scope of the exemption or, as it is sometimes put, whether the exemption is 'engaged'.[183] The second is whether the balance of public interest is in favour of maintaining the exemption.

A different distinction can be made, between those exemptions that are class-based and those that are prejudice- or harm-based. A class-based exemption applies to all information of a particular category or description. A prejudice- or harm-based exemption applies to information if its disclosure would or would be likely to lead to prejudice or harm to a specific interest (for example to the prevention or detection of crime). Almost all of the prejudice- or harm-based exemptions are qualified rather than absolute.[184]

A further complication is that in theory one must consider separately whether any exemption excludes (a) the duty to confirm or deny, and (b) the duty to disclose. In practice, in most cases the real issue is whether the duty to disclose is excluded.

(a) *The absolute exemptions* The following provisions create an absolute exemption from disclosure:

- section 21: information that is reasonably accessible to an applicant by other means;
- section 23: information supplied by, or relating to, one of certain specified bodies dealing with security matters;
- section 32: information held in certain court records;

---

[181] The absolute exemptions are listed at FOIA 2000, s 2(3).

[182] See ibid s 2(1)(b) (in relation to the duty to confirm or deny) and s 2(2)(b) (in relation to the duty to disclose).

[183] The Act itself does not use this term. When discussing qualified human rights under the European Convention—eg the privacy right under Art 8—lawyers often distinguish between the question whether the right is 'engaged', that is to say whether there is some *prima facie* interference with the substance of the right, and whether the interference can be justified.

[184] FOIA 2000, s 36 is harm-based, and is absolute in relation to information held by either House of Parliament.

- section 34: information the disclosure of which would infringe Parliamentary privilege;
- section 36: information the disclosure of which would prejudice the effective conduct of public affairs (this is an absolute exemption only in relation to information held by either House of Parliament);
- section 40: personal information: (a) in cases where the information sought is personal information about the applicant; and (b) in cases where the information sought is personal information about a third party, and disclosure would breach one of the data protection principles;
- section 41: information obtained by the public authority from another person, if disclosure would constitute a breach of confidence actionable by that or any other person;
- section 44: information the disclosure of which is prohibited by or under any enactment, is incompatible with any Community obligation, or would be a contempt of court.

(b) *The qualified exemptions* The following provisions create a qualified exemption from disclosure:

- section 22: information intended for future publication;
- section 24: information that is required to be exempt for the purposes of safeguarding national security (note, however, that if the information falls within section 23 then the exemption is absolute);
- section 26: information the disclosure of which would or would be likely to prejudice certain defence interests;
- section 27: information the disclosure of which would or would be likely to prejudice certain aspects of international relations;
- section 28: information the disclosure of which would or would be likely to prejudice relations between any of the 'UK administrations', that is to say, the UK government, and the devolved governments operating in Scotland, Wales, and Northern Ireland;
- section 29: information the disclosure of which would or would be likely to prejudice certain economic interests;
- section 30: information that has at any time been held for the purpose of certain investigations and proceedings conducted by public authorities;
- section 31: information the disclosure of which would or would be likely to prejudice the prevention or detection of crime or certain other interests related to law enforcement;
- section 33: information the disclosure of which would or would be likely to prejudice the exercise of certain public sector audit functions;
- section 35: information relating to the formulation of government policy, Ministerial communications, and other similar matters;

- section 36: information the disclosure of which would or would be likely to prejudice the effective conduct of public affairs (except in the case of information held by the House of Commons or the House of Lords, where this exemption is absolute, not qualified);
- section 37: information relating to communications with Her Majesty, the conferring of honours, and related matters;
- section 38: information the disclosure of which would or would be likely to endanger physical or mental health or safety;
- section 39: environmental information—the purpose of this exemption is so that disclosure of this information can be considered instead under the Environmental Information Regulations 2004 (discussed at section 7.6.1 below);
- section 40: personal information, in circumstances where the information is about a third party not the requester, and: (a) disclosure would contravene section 10 of DPA 1998 (the right to prevent processing likely to cause damage or distress), or (b) the information is exempt from the third party's own right of subject access by virtue of any provision of Part IV of DPA 1998;
- section 42: information that is subject to legal professional privilege;
- section 43: trade secrets, and information the disclosure of which would or would be likely to damage certain commercial interests;

(c) *Harm- or prejudice-based exemptions* The following exemptions specifically require consideration of the harm or prejudice that would result from disclosure of the information in question:

- section 26: defence;
- section 27: international relations;
- section 28: relations within the UK;
- section 29: the economy;
- section 31: law enforcement;
- section 33: audit functions;
- section 36: prejudice to effective conduct of public affairs (except information held by the House of Commons or the House of Lords);
- section 38: health and safety;
- section 43: commercial interests.

It is also arguable that section 24 of FOIA 2000 should be regarded as a harm-based exemption. Information is exempt under section 24 if exemption is requiring for the purpose of *safeguarding* national security; this is tantamount to saying that information is exempt if its disclosure would prejudice national security.

7.5.4.2 *Interpreting the harm- or prejudice-based exemptions*

The prejudice-based exemptions are phrased in similar terms. The question is usually whether disclosure under the Act of the information sought would or would be likely to, prejudice some specified matter. For instance, section 33 of FOIA 2000 creates an exemption for information the disclosure of which would or would be likely to prejudice the exercise of certain public sector audit functions. A variation on this theme is section 38, using the language of endangering rather than of prejudice: information is exempt under that section if its disclosure under the Act would or would be likely to endanger the physical or mental health, or safety, of any individual. There is yet another variation in section 36(2)(b): the question under that provision is whether disclosure would or would be likely to *inhibit* the free and frank provision of advice or the free and frank exchange of views for the purposes of deliberation

The Information Commissioner's general guidance about the application of the prejudice-based exemptions suggests that the term 'prejudice' is equivalent to 'harm'.[185] The Commissioner's guidance also indicates that although prejudice need not be substantial he would expect it to be more than trivial. The Information Tribunal has upheld this approach: *Hogan and Oxford City Council v Information Commissioner*,[186] paragraph 30.

The formula used repeatedly in the Act is whether disclosure under the Act *would* or *would be likely* to prejudice the specified interest. Disclosure *would prejudice* the specified interest, if prejudice is more probable than not: see the *Hogan* case, above, at paragraph 35. There has been a considerable amount of discussion in the Tribunal case law as to the standard to apply in deciding whether disclosure *would be likely* to prejudice the specified interest. In a number of decisions, the Tribunal has stated that what is required is a significant and weighty chance of prejudice,[187] albeit that this may fall short of establishing that prejudice is more likely than not. This approach has recently been endorsed by the Information Tribunal in *Office for Government Commerce v Information Commissioner* (see paragraphs 120 to 136).[188]

7.5.4.3 *Qualified exemptions and the public interest test*

If a qualified exemption is engaged then the duty to disclose does not apply if 'in all the circumstances of the case, the public interest in maintaining the exemption outweighs

---

[185] See the Commissioner's FOIA Awareness Guidance No 20, last updated on 6 March 2008, and available at <http://www.ico.gov.uk/upload/documents/library/freedom_of_information/practical_application/round_robins_v1.pdf> (accessed 22 March 2009).

[186] EA/2005/0026 and 0030.

[187] See *John Connor v Information Commissioner* EA/2005/005; *Guardian Newspapers and Brooke v Information Commissioner and the BBC* EA/2006/0011 and 0013; and *Hogan and Oxford City Council v Information Commissioner* EA/2005/0026 and 0020. This approach draws on a decision of Munby J in relation to the construction of similar language in DPA 1998, in *R (Lord) v Home Secretary* [2003] EWHC 2073 (Admin), paras 99–100.

[188] Decision promulgated 19 February 2009, on remission from the High Court: EA/2006/0068 and 0080.

the public interest in disclosing the information'.[189] The application of this test is one of the most difficult aspects of FOIA 2000. It is necessary to identify the respects in which there is a public interest in maintaining the exemption, and in disclosing the information sought; and it is then necessary to assess the respective weight of those public interests. The exercise must be carried out having regard to *all the circumstances of the case*. The test will need to be applied by the public authority itself (both when the request is first considered, and in carrying out any internal review); by the Information Commissioner (in considering a complaint under section 50 of the Act); and by the Information Tribunal (in determining an appeal against the Commissioner's decision notice, under section 57).[190]

Is this exercise to be carried out on the basis that there is any presumption in favour of disclosure? Or does the exercise begin with the scales equally balanced between the competing public interests?

FOIA 2000 does not include any general provision that there is a presumption in favour of the disclosure of information held by public authorities. In that respect it is different from the Environmental Information Regulations 2004, discussed at section 7.6.1 below.[191] Nor does FOIA 2000 include any purpose clause to assist in determining the respective weight of the competing public interests.[192]

On the other hand, in one important respect FOIA 2000 does contain a presumption in favour of disclosure. The duty to communicate is displaced by a qualified exemption only if the public interest in maintaining the exemption *outweighs* the public interest in disclosure of the information sought. So if the competing interests are equally balanced, then the public authority must communicate the information sought.

There is also a wider point. In *Office of Government Commerce v Information Commissioner and anor*[193] Stanley Burnton J (as he then was) approved of the following statement from the Information Tribunal decision in *Secretary of State for Work and Pensions v The Information Commissioner*:[194]

It can be said, however, that there is an assumption built into FOIA that the disclosure of information by public authorities on request is in itself of value and in the public interest, in order to promote transparency and accountability in relation to the activities of public authorities. What this means is that there is always likely to be some public interest in favour of the disclosure of information under the Act. The strength of that interest, and the strength of the competing interest in maintaining any relevant exemption, must be assessed on a case by case basis: section 2(2)(b) requires the balance to be considered 'in all the circumstances of the case'.

What this passage recognizes is that in applying the public interest test it is necessary to have regard to the purpose of the Act. The whole premise behind the Act is that it

---

[189] FOIA 2000, s 2(2)(b).
[190] See section 7.5.5 below for a discussion of the respective roles played by these bodies.
[191] See EIR 2004, reg 12(2).
[192] As is found, for instance, in New Zealand's Official Information Act 1982, s 4.
[193] [2008] EWHC 737 (Admin) para 71.
[194] EA/2006/0040.

is in the public interest for public authorities to be transparent and accountable. Of course, the extent to which a particular disclosure will contribute to these objectives, and the weight of any competing public interest considerations in favour of maintaining an exemption, will need to be assessed on a case-sensitive basis. What ought not to happen, however, is that the application of the public interest test turns into what is in substance a debate about whether FOIA 2000 ought to have been introduced in the first place.

7.5.4.4 *Public interest in the disclosure of information*
The Commissioner's guidance about the public interest test[195] refers to five general public interest factors that may favour the disclosure of information:

(1) furthering understanding of and participation in public debate about issues of the day;

(2) promoting accountability and transparency in respect of decisions taken by public authorities;

(3) promoting accountability and transparency in the spending of public money;

(4) allowing individuals and companies to understand decisions made by public authorities that affect their lives; and

(5) bringing to light information affecting public health and public safety.

These considerations are not exhaustive. The Guidance itself suggests some additional factors that may be relevant: for instance, the disclosure may contribute to scientific advancements, ensure the better operation of financial and currency markets, or assist in access to justice and other fundamental rights.

The mere fact that a substantial section of the public is interested in a subject does not, of itself, mean that disclosure of information about that subject is in the public interest.[196] For example, there may be widespread and prurient interest among members of the public in the private life of a celebrity; this does not of itself mean that disclosure of relevant information would be in the public interest. Essentially, to say that disclosure of information is in the public interest is equivalent to saying that disclosure is for the public benefit, or that it serves the common good.[197]

What is relevant is the *public* interest in disclosure, as opposed to any private interest. So, for example, the fact that disclosure of a piece of information would be to the financial benefit of an individual or organization is not, in itself, a public interest factor in favour of disclosure. On the other hand, sometimes interests that appear at first sight to be private may turn out to have a public element. Take a case where a public authority is investigating an individual on the grounds of suspected misconduct, but has not disclosed the reasons for its investigation. The individual seeks disclosure of

---

[195] Freedom of Information Act Awareness Guidance No 3: the Public Interest Test.
[196] See eg *Lion Laboratories Ltd v Evans* [1985] QB 526, 537.
[197] See *DTI v Information Commissioner* EA/2006/0007, para 50.

information that would reveal those reasons. It might be argued that the individual's interest in disclosure of the information, so as to be able to answer the allegations against him, is a purely private one. However, if disclosure of the information would enhance the fairness of the investigation, then it is suggested that this is a matter of public, not merely private, interest.

In *Scotland Office v Information Commissioner*[198] the Information Tribunal recognized that similar arguments (based on transparency, accountability, etc) were likely to be put forward in favour of disclosure in very many freedom of information cases. This did not in any way diminish their importance, though the weight to be attached to these considerations would vary depending on the circumstances of the case. The question to be considered is in what way will disclosure of this information, at this specific point in time, foster the desired objectives such as accountability or transparency.[199]

Articulating the public interest in favour of disclosure can often be a challenging task. For example, explaining how disclosure of particular information would contribute to informed public debate on a particular subject may require both a knowledge of the subject matter concerned, and an understanding of how much information about that subject is already in the public domain. Media organizations will often be in a stronger position than other requesters, at any rate in cases where they have expertise in the subject matter to which the request relates. However, there is a practical problem that affects all requesters (however well-resourced and well-informed), which is that they are seeking to identify the public interest in disclosure of information of which (inevitably) they do not know the actual content. This is where the role of the Information Commissioner is crucial,[200] not merely as a decision-maker in complaints under the Act, but also as a party to proceedings in the Information Tribunal or the courts. The Commissioner has the advantage that he is likely to have seen the actual content of the disputed information, and that he can articulate the public interest in disclosure by reference to that content.

7.5.4.5 *Public interest in maintaining the exemption*
The first point to note is that the statute refers to the public interest *in maintaining the exemption*, not *in withholding the information*. It is suggested that this means the focus should be on the public interest as it is reflected in the particular exemption. The question is not: would harm flow from the disclosure of the information? The question, rather, is whether disclosure would lead to the sort of harm that comes within the scope of the FOIA 2000 exemption on which the public authority seeks to rely.

Where the exemption is a harm-based or prejudice-based exemption, then the same considerations are likely to be relevant both to determining whether the exemption is engaged and to identifying the public interest in maintaining the exemption. At both

---

[198] EA/2007/0128: see paras 57–60.

[199] See *OGC v Information Commissioner* EA/2006/0068 and 0080 (19 February 2009, on remission from High Court) para 149.

[200] See section 7.5.5 below for more detailed discussion of the role of the Commissioner in enforcing the Act.

stages of the analysis, the focus will be on identifying any harmful consequences of disclosure, and assessing their weight.

When considering the class-based qualified exemptions there is a somewhat different approach. Here the exemption will be engaged merely because the information is of a particular description. At the first stage of the analysis, when considering whether or not the exemption is engaged, there will be no need to consider the consequences of disclosure. However, when considering the public interest in maintaining the exemption, the consequences of disclosure will be highly relevant. Take the case of a public authority that is claiming an exemption under section 30(1), on the basis that the information is held for the purpose of a criminal investigation that the authority has a duty to conduct. At the first stage of the analysis, in deciding whether or not the exemption is engaged, the only issues will be whether the public authority has the duty to conduct such investigations, and if so whether the information is held for that purpose. Usually these questions will not be difficult to resolve. Moving on to the balance of public interests, the public interest in maintaining the exemption requires a consideration of whether disclosure will damage the public authority's ability to carry out this particular investigation, or other similar future investigations. It might be suggested by the authority, for instance, that disclosure of the information sought would enable the person under investigation to conceal or destroy relevant documents, or that disclosure would make it harder for the authority to secure cooperation from potential witnesses in the future.

The public interest in maintaining an exemption is to be assessed 'in all the circumstances of the case'. This means that, whether the exemption is class-based or prejudice-based, the public authority is not permitted to maintain a blanket refusal to disclose all information of a particular type or nature. The question is not, is the balance of public interest in favour of maintaining the exemption in relation to this type of information? The question is, is the balance of public interest in favour of maintaining the exemption in relation to *this* information, and in the circumstances of *this* case?[201] The public authority may well have a general policy that the public interest is likely to be in favour of maintaining the exemption in respect of a specific type of information, but such a policy must not be inflexibly applied and the authority must always be willing to consider whether the circumstances of the case justify a departure from the policy.[202] The issue is whether there is a public interest in maintaining the exemption, and so any private interests in maintaining the exemption should be disregarded. For instance, it is not relevant that the disclosure of the information would embarrass particular individuals.

---

[201] See eg *DfES v Information Commissioner* EA/2006/0006, para 75(i); *ECGD v Friends of the Earth and Information Commissioner* [2008] EWHC 638 (Admin) paras 25–28 (this is a case under EIR 2004, but also relevant to the construction of FOIA 2000).

[202] In relation to policies or guidelines about FOIA disclosure, see *OGC v Information Commissioner* EA/2006/0068 and 0080 (19 February 2009, on remission from High Court) paras 165–169 (relevance of 'working assumption' about the disclosure of OGC Gateway Reviews).

Where a number of different exemptions are engaged, then there is Court of Appeal authority (*Ofcom v Information Commissioner*)[203] that the public interest should be assessed by reference to the exemptions in aggregate and not simply by reference to each exemption viewed separately. The case relates to the 2004 Environmental Information Regulations (EIR 2004), but if it is correctly decided then the same approach would probably apply in relation to FOIA 2000. The Information Commissioner has lodged a petition with the House of Lords seeking permission to appeal against this decision.

7.5.5 Decision-making under FOIA 2000

The decision-making structure established by FOIA 2000 is complex. Public authorities, the Information Commissioner, the Information Tribunal, and the courts all have a role to play.

Applications for information under section 1 of FOIA 2000 are made directly to the public authority that holds the information. In the first instance it is for the public authority to make a decision under the Act. There is no statutory duty to consult with third parties that have an interest in whether the information should be disclosed, although such consultation is good practice and is recommended in the Code of Practice made by the Secretary of State under section 45 of the Act.[204] Nor is there any statutory duty on public authorities to operate an internal review procedure, though again the section 45 Code recommends this.[205]

A dissatisfied requester can apply to the Information Commissioner under section 50 of FOIA 2000 for a decision as to whether his request has been dealt with in accordance with the Act. The requester is the only person who can complain to the Commissioner under section 50; if the public authority agrees to provide the information requested then a third party who is affected by the disclosure cannot complain to the Commissioner.[206] There are various grounds under section 50 on which the Commissioner may refuse to make a decision[207]—for instance, that the complainant has not exhausted any internal complaints procedure provided by the public authority. Except in these specified circumstances the Commissioner has a duty to reach a decision on the complaint. Where the Commissioner makes a decision he may order the public authority to disclose information, and if so he must set a time within which this must be done.

The Commissioner's decision notices are published on his website at <http://www.ico.gov.uk>. It is important not to treat them as if they were a series of binding precedents; each case must turn on its own facts, and neither the Information Tribunal nor

---

[203] [2009] EWCA Civ 90.
[204] See section IV of the Code, paras 25–30.
[205] See section VI of the Code, paras 36–46.
[206] The only recourse for the third party would be to seek judicial review of the decision to disclose, and/or an injunction to restrain disclsosure.
[207] See FOIA 2000, s 50(2).

the courts are in any way bound by the Commissioner's interpretation of the legislation. That said, the decision notices are a very useful and interesting source of information about the practical application of FOIA 2000, and about the sorts of requests for information that are being made.

Either the public authority or the complainant may appeal to the Information Tribunal against the Commissioner's decision. Note that these are the only parties who can appeal. Where an appeal is brought by a person seeking information, the public authority may be joined as a party, and vice versa. A third party affected by the disclosure has no right of appeal. However, third parties (for example a private sector body that was the original source of the information in dispute) can be added to Information Tribunal appeal proceedings as interested parties.

In formal terms the Information Tribunal is hearing an appeal against the decision notice issued by the Information Commissioner, though in practice the underlying dispute is likely to be between the requester and the public authority from which information is sought. The Commissioner's position is an unusual one; in considering a complaint under section 50 he is an adjudicator, but then when his decision is appealed to the Information Tribunal he becomes a litigant, defending the decision that he reached. The Commissioner's role is particularly important in cases where the public authority is appealing against his decision that information ought to be disclosed. If the Commissioner were not a party then it would be left to the requester to defend his decision; many requesters would lack the resources or expertise to do this effectively. Even where the requester is a media organization (and perhaps willing and able to engage specialist legal representation) it has the disadvantage that it will not have seen the disputed information; the Commissioner will usually have done so, and will be able to make submissions about the public interest in disclosure by reference to the specific content of that information.

The Tribunal considers whether the Commissioner's decision notice was not in accordance with the law, or whether the Commissioner ought to have exercised any relevant discretion differently.[208] It has the power to review any finding of fact on which the decision notice was based.[209] It can make its own findings of fact and substitute them for the Commissioner's findings; it is not confined to considering whether there was material capable of supporting the Commissioner's findings.[210] The Tribunal may allow an appeal (in which case the decision notice issued by the Commissioner no longer stands), or it may substitute another decision notice for the Commissioner's decision.[211]

The Tribunal is currently governed by its own procedural rules,[212] which are applicable to appeals under DPA 1998, FOIA 2000, and EIR 2004. Appeals are considered

---

[208]   ibid s 58(1).

[209]   ibid s 58(2).

[210]   See *Hemsley v Information Commissioner* [2006] UKITEA 2005 0026, EA/2005/0026.

[211]   See FOIA 2000, s 58(1).

[212]   Information Tribunal (Enforcement Appeals) Rules 2005 (SI 2005/14), as amended by Information Tribunal (Enforcement Appeals) (Amendment) Rules 2005 (SI 2005/450) There is a separate set of rules in relation to appeals to the National Security Panel of the Information Tribunal: see the Information Tribunal (National Security Appeals) Rules 2005 (SI 2005/13).

either on paper or at an oral hearing. If there is an oral hearing, the Tribunal can hear evidence from witnesses (in complex cases there may be extensive evidence, over several days). If necessary the Tribunal will sit in private, or in the absence of a party, in order to hear evidence or argument about the actual content of the disputed information (ie the information sought by the requester and withheld by the public authority).[213]

With effect from January 2010 the work of the Information Tribunal will transfer to the General Regulatory Chamber of the First Tier Tribunal.[214] This is part of the new unified tribunal structure established under the Tribunals, Courts and Enforcement Act 2007. At the time of writing a consultation is in progress on draft procedural rules for the General Regulatory Chamber.[215]

Decisions of the Information Tribunal are a very important source of guidance on the operation of FOIA 2000. They are available on the Tribunal's website.[216] The Tribunal received ninety-nine appeals in the course of calendar year 2008,[217] and the Tribunal's website shows eighty-six decisions that were issued during the course of that year. The great majority of Tribunal appeals are brought under FOIA 2000 or EIR 2004, with only a few appeals a year under DPA 1998.

There is a right of appeal from the Information Tribunal to the High Court on a point of law (section 59 of FOIA 2000). According to the Information Tribunal's website, by the end of March 2009 there had been twelve cases in which appeals had been brought to the High Court against Tribunal decisions under FOIA 2000 or EIR 2004. Some of those appeals have not yet been determined.

Given that there is a right to complain to the Commissioner under section 50 of FOIA 2000, and then a further right to appeal to the Tribunal under section 57, it is most unlikely that the court will grant permission for judicial review of a refusal by a public authority to disclose information under FOIA 2000.[218]

Finally, section 53 of the Act gives the government a power of veto over decisions of the Information Commissioner or the Tribunal. The section applies to a decision notice or enforcement notice of the Information Commissioner which is served on a government department, the National Assembly for Wales, or any public authority designated by order for the purposes of this section, and which relates to a failure to comply with

---

[213] See Information Tribunal Rules, rule 22 and 23; and Information Tribunal Practice Note (No 1), available at <http://www.informationtribunal.gov.uk/Documents/formsguidance/InformationTribunal PracticeNotes_191208.pdf> (accessed 29 March 2009).

[214] See <http://www.tribunals.gov.uk/Tribunals/PlannedChanges/generalregulatorychamber.htm> for further explanation (accessed 29 March 2009).

[215] The consultation paper is available at <http://www.tribunals.gov.uk/Tribunals/Documents/Grc/ GRConsultationPaper.pdf> (accessed 29 March 2009).

[216] <http://www.informationtribunal.gov.uk/>. There is a considerable amount of useful information on the site, including a guide for litigants in person at the Tribunal: <http://www.informationtribunal.gov.uk/ Documents/LIPguidancenotesV1.pdf> (accessed 29 March 2009).

[217] The Tribunal numbers its appeals by order of receipt: the last appeal for 2008, received on 31 December 2008, was EA/2008/0099.

[218] *R on the application of Carruthers v South Norfolk District Council and ors* [2006] EWHC 478 (Admin).

the duty to confirm or deny or with the duty to disclose. Any such decision notice or enforcement notice shall fail to have effect if the 'accountable person' in relation to that authority certifies to the Commissioner that he has formed the opinion on reasonable grounds that there was no failure to comply with the duty to confirm or deny or with the duty to communicate. Such a certificate may be issued after the Commissioner's decision notice or enforcement notice was issued, or after an appeal to the Information Tribunal has been determined. An 'accountable person' would be a Cabinet Minister, the Attorney-General, the Advocate-General for Scotland or the Attorney-General for Northern Ireland.[219] The certificate must be laid before Parliament,[220] and the accountable person must inform the applicant of his reasons for issuing the certificate.[221]

The power of veto has so far been exercised only once. On 24 February 2009 the Secretary of State for Justice, Jack Straw, announced in the House of Commons[222] that he was vetoing the Tribunal decision[223] requiring disclosure of Cabinet minutes relating to the decision to go to war in Iraq.[224]

7.5.6 Personal data under FOIA 2000

Requests by media organizations under FOIA 2000 will often be for the disclosure of personal data about identifiable individuals. For instance, there may be requests for information about the salaries of individual public sector employees,[225] their job titles and position within their organization,[226] or the circumstances in which their employment came to an end.[227]

There is a complex exemption under section 40 of FOIA 2000 in relation to requests for personal information. This exemption cross-refers to DPA 1998; and where section 40 refers to 'personal data', the term bears the same meaning as in DPA 1998.[228]

---

[219] See FOIA 2000, s 53(8). In relation to a Northern Ireland department or any other Northern Ireland public authority the term 'accountable person' means the First Minister and Deputy First Minister in Northern Ireland acting jointly. In relation to the National Assembly for Wales the term 'accountable person' means the Assembly First Secretary.

[220] ibid s 53(3). In certain cases involving Northern Ireland the certificate would instead be laid before the Northern Ireland Assembly, and in certain cases involving Wales the certificate would be laid before the National Assembly for Wales.

[221] See ibid s 53(6). The provision in fact refers to 'the complainant' rather than 'the applicant', because a certificate will only be issued after the applicant has made a complaint to the Commissioner under s 50 about the way in which the public authority has dealt with his request for information.

[222] *Hansard*, HC, vol 488, 24 February 2009, col 153.

[223] *Cabinet Office and Dr Christopher Lamb v Information Commissioner* EA/2008/0024 and 0029.

[224] Further details of the basis for the veto are available at the Ministry of Justice website, at <http://www.justice.gov.uk/news/announcement240209a.htm> (accessed 29 March 2009).

[225] See Decision Notice FS50062124, Corby Borough Council (request for information about payments made to local authority's Temporary Finance Officer).

[226] See eg *Ministry of Defence v Information Commissioner and Rob Evans* EA/2006/0027 (request by *Guardian* journalist for disclosure of internal directory of Defence Export Services Organization).

[227] cf *Salmon v Information Commissioner and King's College Cambridge* EA/2007/0135 (request for information about circumstances in relation to resignation of Provost of a Cambridge college).

[228] See FOIA 2000, s 40(7).

There is an absolute exemption under FOIA 2000 where the requested information is for personal data of which the applicant is the data subject: (section 40(1)). The purpose of this provision is to ensure that requests by individuals for their own personal data are dealt with as subject access requests under section 7 of DPA 1998 rather than as requests under section 1 of FOIA 2000. Hence this provision is a piece of legal traffic flow management; it is not intended to prevent individuals from obtaining their own personal data from public authorities. Media organizations are unlikely to use subject access requests as an information-gathering tool, and so this exemption is of relatively little interest to them.

There are also three exemptions in relation to requests for third-party personal data (ie personal data of individuals other than the requester):

(1) There is an absolute exemption where disclosure to a member of the public otherwise than under FOIA 2000 would contravene any of the data protection principles.[229] For this purpose, manual data held by public authorities[230] is treated as being covered by the data protection principles.[231]

(2) There is a qualified exemption where disclosure of the information to a member of the public otherwise than under FOIA 2000 would contravene section 10 of DPA 1998 (right to prevent processing likely to cause damage or distress).[232]

(3) There is a qualified exemption where the information is exempt from the data subject's own right of subject access.[233]

So far, most of the Tribunal case law under section 40 has been about the exemption relating to breach of the data protection principles. At first sight it may be surprising that this exemption is absolute rather than qualified. Does this mean that a policy choice has been taken that considerations of personal privacy (reflected in the data protection principles) should take priority over the interest in promoting open government? It is suggested that this would be a superficial reading of FOIA 2000, and would disregard the fact that the data protection principles themselves seek to balance competing considerations, as is illustrated by the Tribunal's decisions under this section.

The Tribunal's approach to section 40 of FOIA 2000 is illustrated by a series of three cases involving the disclosure of information about MPs' expenses, the third of which was the subject of an unsuccessful appeal to the High Court by the House of Commons.[234] In all these cases the Tribunal required disclosure of information (and in the third case, it went further than the Information Commissioner had done).

---

[229] ibid s 40(2), read with s 40(3)(a)(i) and (3)(b).

[230] ie data falling within limb (e) of the definition of data in DPA 1998, section 1(1).

[231] See FOIA 2000, s 40(3)(b), which provides that the exemptions in DPA 1998, s 33A are to be disregarded for this purpose.

[232] FOIA 2000, s 40(2), read with s 40(3)(a)(ii).

[233] ibid s 40(2), read with s 40(4).

[234] The House of Commons is a public authority under FOIA 2000, Sch 1, Part 1, para 5. Individual MPs are not themselves public authorities under the Act.

The first case in the series,[235] the *Baker* case, arose out of requests made by the Liberal Democrat MP, Norman Baker, and a *Sunday Times* journalist, for information about MPs' travel expenses. These expenses were already published in aggregate form (showing how much was claimed by each MP, in total, each year); the request was for the annual figure for each MP, broken down by mode of transport. The Information Commissioner ordered the information to be disclosed, and the Information Tribunal upheld his decision on appeal.

The House of Commons argued that the information was exempt from disclosure under section 40. Disclosure would breach the first data protection principle (it would be unfair to individual MPs, and would not satisfy any of the conditions in Schedule 2 to the Act); it would also breach the second data protection principle. Individual MPs had an expectation that disclosure would not go beyond the terms of the publication scheme adopted by the House of Commons (under section 19 of FOIA 2000), which envisaged that travel expenses would be disclosed annually on an aggregate basis.

The Tribunal accepted that the requested information was personal data. However, in assessing fairness for the purpose of the first data protection principle, the interests of the individuals MPs were important but were not the first and paramount consideration, given that the allowances were paid from public money and related to the performance of public duties.[236] On this basis, disclosure would not be unfair to MPs. The Tribunal's approach, therefore, indicates that personal data in relation to an individual's public life carries a lower expectation of privacy than would data in relation to domestic or private matters. Clearly, this approach is of general importance in applying the section 40 exemption.

As to whether any of the conditions in Schedule 2 to DPA 1998 were satisfied, the Tribunal considered the application of condition 6. This is satisfied if: 'The processing is necessary for the purposes of legitimate interests pursued by the data controller or by the third party or parties to whom the data are disclosed, except where the processing is unwarranted in any particular case by reason of prejudice to the rights and freedoms or legitimate interests of the data subject.'

The Tribunal considered[237] that the application of this paragraph involved a balance between competing interests, broadly comparable, but not identical, to the balance that applies under the public interest test for qualified exemptions under FOIA 2000. Paragraph 6 required a consideration of the balance between: (a) the legitimate interests of those to whom the data would be disclosed, which in this context were members of the public; and (b) prejudice to the rights, freedoms and legitimate interests of the data subjects (in this case, MPs). However, because the processing must be 'necessary'

---

[235] *Corporate Officer of the House of Commons v Information Commissioner and Norman Baker MP* EA/2006/0015 and 0016.

[236] The Tribunal therefore distinguished *CCN Systems Ltd v The Data Protection Registrar* (DA/90 25/49/8) and *Infolink Ltd v The Data Protection Registrar* (DA/90 25/49/6), earlier Tribunal decisions under the Data Protection Act 1984 to the effect that the interests of the data subject were the first and paramount consideration in assessing fairness.

[237] See para 90 of the decision.

for the legitimate interests of members of the public to apply, the Tribunal considered that only where (a) outweighs or is greater than (b) should the personal data be disclosed. Applying this approach, the Tribunal considered that the legitimate interests of the public in receiving this information outweighed any prejudice to MPs. Finally, the Tribunal considered that the publication of this information did not amount to its use for a purpose incompatible with the purpose for which it had been obtained; so there was no breach of the second data protection principle.

The approach taken in the *Baker* case was followed in the second case in the series,[238] the *Moffat* case, which related to the travel expenses of Anne Moffat MP. A number of requests for information were made, seeking more detailed disclosure than had been ordered in the *Baker* case. The Information Commissioner required the information to be disclosed, and again the Tribunal upheld the decision. It appears that the reason why this particular MP was targeted was that she was in the highest 5 per cent of travel expenders among MPs, and for one year she made the highest claim for travel expenses of any MP; there were however good reasons for this, as she was in a largely rural constituency a long way from Westminster.[239] The only issue considered by the Tribunal was the application of paragraph 6 of Schedule 2 (applying a similar approach to that adopted in the *Baker* case), and the Tribunal considered that the balance came down in favour of disclosure.

The third case in the series, the *Brooke* case,[240] unlike the *Baker* and *Moffat* cases, was not concerned with travel expenses. This case arose out of requests for information about the claims made by various MPs under the Additional Costs Allowance (ACA). This is intended to defray the costs incurred by MPs representing constituencies outside Inner London, in residing in two different places (ie in Westminster and in their constituencies). Three journalists sought full details of the ACA claims made by various MPs. The Information Commissioner did not uphold the requests in full. He required disclosure to be made of the total sum claimed under the ACA by each MP in each year, broken down into a number of different headings.

The Tribunal upheld an appeal by the requesters, and dismissed an appeal by the House of Commons. It required disclosure (with very limited exceptions) of all of the documentation submitted by these MPs in respect of their claims for ACA. The Tribunal applied the same principles as in the *Baker* case, and was clearly heavily influenced by its view that the ACA system was highly unsatisfactory, being both unclear in its rules and lax in its controls.[241] The *Brooke* case received a considerable amount of media attention, not least because it brought into the public domain the existence of the so-called 'John Lewis list', setting out the maximum permissible claim by way of ACA for various standard domestic items.

---

[238] *Corporate Officer of the House of Commons v Information Commissioner* EA/2006/0074 (and others).

[239] See para 19 of the Tribunal's decision. The constituency in question was West Lothian.

[240] *Corporate Officer of the House of Commons v Information Commissioner, Leapman, Brooke and Thomas* EA/2007/0060 (and others).

[241] See decision at para 33.

On appeal, the Divisional Court of the High Court upheld the Tribunal's decision.[242] The main ground of appeal was that the Tribunal had failed to give adequate weight to the expectations of MPs (derived from the publication scheme) as to how much information about the ACA would be made public. The Court considered that the Tribunal had taken this argument into account and rejected it, and that there was no error of law. In any event, the Court could not discern any basis for an expectation by MPs that the requested information would not enter the public arena.

The House of Lords has considered the provision in FOISA 2002 that is equivalent to section 40[243] (see *Common Services Agency v Scottish Information Commissioner*).[244] The Scottish Information Commissioner ordered the disclosure in 'barnardised' form of statistics about the incidence of leukaemia in a particular area. As explained above, barnardisation is a statistical technique intended to allow statistics to be disclosed in cases where the individual numbers are very small, without giving away information about identifiable individuals. The House of Lords considered that the crucial question was whether barnardisation effectively removed the risk of disclosing information about identifiable individuals. If yes, then the information would not constitute personal data, and could be disclosed. If no, then it would be necessary to consider whether disclosure would breach any of the data protection conditions. The case was remitted to the Scottish Information Commissioner for reconsideration in the light of the House of Lords decision.

7.5.7 Policy-related information under FOIA 2000

When FOIA 2000 first came into force, there was considerable interest in how it would apply to policy-related information. How far, if at all, would it alter established understandings about the confidentiality of civil service advice? Would it bring documents that were at the heart of the policy-making process into the public domain?

The framework within which FOIA 2000 deals with policy-related information is set by sections 35 and 36. Section 35 provides as follows:

(1) Information held by a government department or by the National Assemby of Wales is exempt information if it relates to—

    (a) the formulation or development of government policy,

    (b) Ministerial communications,

    (c) the provision of advice by any of the Law Officers or any request for the provision of such advice, or

    (d) the operation of any Ministerial office.

---

[242] *Corporate Officer of the House of Commons v Information Commissioner, Brooke, Leapman and Thomas* [2008] EWHC 1084 (Admin).
[243] FOISA 2002, s 38.
[244] [2008] UKHL 47, [2008] 1 WLR 1550.

(2) Once a decision as to government policy has been taken, any statistical information used to provide an informed background to the taking of the decision is not to be regarded—

(a) for the purposes of subsection (1)(a), as relating to the formulation or development of government policy, or

(b) for the purposes of subsection (1)(b), as relating to Ministerial communications.

Section 35(4) provides that in assessing the public interest regard is to be had to the particular public interest in the disclosure of factual information which has been used to provide an informed background to decision-taking.

The leading Tribunal case on section 35 is *Department for Education and Skills v Information Commissioner and the Evening Standard* EA/2006/006, where the Tribunal required disclosure of information contained in the minutes of the DfES Board (the most senior committee in the DfES) and the Schools Directorate Management Group (the next most senior committee). The Tribunal heard evidence from senior civil servants about the implications of disclosing policy-related information, including from Lord Turnbull (the former Cabinet Secretary) and Paul Britton (Director-General of the Domestic Policy Group in the Cabinet Office). That evidence included material about the indirect implications for future policy-making if the requested information were disclosed: it was argued that disclosure would inhibit the frankness and candour of policy advice by civil servants, and would interfere with the 'safe space' needed by government in order to develop policy without the pressure of publicity. The case for the government was essentially that any disclosure of policy-related information, even if the information itself appeared innocuous, was inherently damaging and a threat to good government.[245]

The Tribunal accepted that all of the requested information came within section 35(1)(a) as relating to the formulation or development of government policy. In relation to the public interest test, the Tribunal accepted that it was relevant to consider the indirect consequences of disclosure.[246] However, when it came to assessing what those consequences would be the Tribunal was not bound to accept the evidence of the witnesses called, however eminent, but was entitled and indeed bound to reach its own conclusions. The Tribunal set out[247] some guiding principles in relation to the disclosure of policy-related information. These included the following points.

• Every decision was specific to the actual content of the particular information in question. Whether there might be significant indirect or wider consequences from disclosure had to be considered case by case.

• No information was exempt from disclosure simply by virtue of its status (for example by being classified as advice to a minister).

• The purpose of confidentiality was to protect civil servants, not ministers, from compromise or unjust public opprobrium.

---

[245] See para 48 of the Tribunal decision.
[246] See para 70 of the decision.
[247] See para 75 of the decision.

- The timing of a request was of paramount importance. Disclosure of discussion of policy options while policy was in the process of formulation was unlikely to be in the public interest unless, for example, it would expose wrongdoing. Disclosure after policy formulation had been completed was, however, a different matter.

- Whether formulation or development of a particular policy was complete was a question of fact. The Act itself (see section 35(2) and (4)) assumed that policy was formulated, announced, and in due course superseded; policy-making was not a 'seamless web'. However, this did not mean that any public interest in maintaining the exemption disappeared immediately the policy had been announced; everything would depend on the particular facts of the case.

- In judging the likely consequences of disclosure, the Tribunal was entitled to expect of civil servants 'the courage and independence that has been the hallmark of our civil service since the Northcote-Trevelyan reforms'.

The Tribunal has endorsed and applied these principles in a number of cases, while recognizing that they are guidelines only and not a binding statement as to the law.[248] In *OGC v Information Commissioner*, a High Court appeal from the Information Tribunal, Stanley Burnton J (as he then was) discussed these principles without disapproval.[249]

The case-sensitive approach set out in the *DfES* case has been applied in a number of subsequent cases. For instance, the Tribunal has required disclosure of two OGC Gateway Reports regarding the ID cards scheme.[250] On the other hand, the Tribunal refused to order disclosure of information about the decision as to which sporting events should be protected under the Broadcasting Act 1996 from having television rights sold for exclusive viewing by subscription or pay-per-view.[251] The Tribunal considered that the value of the requested information in informing public debate was very limited, and that any public interest in disclosure was outweighed by generalized 'good government' considerations in favour of maintaining the confidentiality of advice given by civil servants. The High Court has emphasized (in a case about the comparable exemption in regulation 12(4)(e) of EIR 2004) that the considerations in favour of maintaining the confidentiality of advice within and between government departments are likely to be material in every case when assessing the public interest, albeit that the weight to be given to those considerations will vary from case to case.[252]

If the submissions made for the government in the *DfES* case had been accepted in their entirety, the practical effect could well have been to turn section 35 into a

---

[248] See eg *Secretary of State for Work and Pensions v Information Commissioner* EA/2006/0040, para 110; *Scotland Office v Information Commissioner* (EA/2007/0128, at paras 49–53.

[249] [2008] EWHC 774 (Admin), paras 68–102.

[250] *OGC v Information Commissioner* EA/2006/0068 and 0080 (19 February 2009, on remission from High Court).

[251] *DCMS v Information Commissioner* EA/2007/0090.

[252] *Export Credit Guarantee Department v Friends of the Earth and the Information Commissioner* [2008] EWHC 638 (Admin), para 38.

quasi-absolute exemption, with policy-related information being disclosed only where an exceptionally strong public interest case could be made out. The case law has not taken this course. It is clear that any adverse consequences of disclosure, both in relation to the particular policy-making exercise concerned and in respect of policy formation in general, must be taken into account in applying the public interest test. However, the content of the information sought and the timing of the request are both highly material in determining how much weight to give those considerations in any individual case.

Section 35 only applies in relation to information held by a government department or the National Assembly of Wales. Other public authorities wishing to resist disclosure of policy-related information are likely to rely on the qualified exemption[253] in section 36.[254] This applies where in the reasonable opinion of a qualified person[255] disclosure of the information under the Act would or would be likely (among other matters) to inhibit the free and frank provision of advice[256] or the free and frank exchange of views for the purpose of deliberation,[257] or would otherwise prejudice or be likely otherwise to prejudice the effective conduct of public affairs.[258]

The leading Tribunal case on this section is *Guardian Newspapers & Brooke v Information Commissioner and BBC*,[259] where the Tribunal required the BBC to disclose the minutes of a BBC Governors' meeting at which it considered the Hutton Report into the death of Dr David Kelly. The Director-General of the BBC, Greg Dyke, had resigned on the day following the meeting.

The Tribunal considered that in order for the exemption to be engaged, the relevant opinion of the qualified person (ie his opinion that the specified adverse consequences would or would be likely to occur) must be both reasonable in substance and reasonably arrived at.[260] If the exemption was engaged, then the public interest test fell to be applied. In relation to that test, the opinion of the qualified person was an important piece of evidence, but the person applying the test needed to form his own view on the severity, extent, and frequency with which the specified adverse consequences would occur.[261]

7.5.8 Media organizations as public authorities under FOIA 2000

Although the main relevance of FOIA 2000 from a media point of view is as a means of obtaining information, some media organizations are themselves FOIA

---

[253] The s 36 exemption is absolute so far as relating to information held by the House of Commons or the House of Lords, but is otherwise qualified: FOIA 2000, s 2(3)(e).

[254] This section also applies to information held by a government department or the National Assembly of Wales which is not exempt information under s 35.

[255] FOIA 2000, s 36(5) makes provision as to who is the appropriate 'qualified person' in respect of various public authorities.

[256] ibid s 36(2)(b)(i).

[257] ibid s 36(2)(b)(ii).

[258] ibid s 36(2)(c).

[259] EA/2006/0011 and 0013.

[260] See para 64 of the decision.

[261] See para 92 of the decision.

public authorities. Notably, the BBC is a public authority 'in respect of information held for purposes other than those of journalism, art or literature'(see Schedule 1, Part VI to FOIA 2000).

The application of FOIA 2000 to the BBC was considered by the House of Lords in *Sugar v BBC and anor* [2009] UKHL 9. The case arose out of an application for disclosure of the Balen Report (a report commissioned by the BBC in relation to its coverage of the Middle East). The BBC contended that the report was held for the purposes of journalism, so that it fell outside the Act.

The House of Lords considered how FOIA 2000 was to apply in respect of 'hybrid authorities',[262] that is to say, bodies that were public authorities within the Act in respect of some, but not all, of the information that they held. By a majority (3–2) they held that the Information Commissioner had jurisdiction to entertain an application under section 50 of the Act from an applicant who had made a request to a hybrid authority for information, which was rejected on the ground that the authority was not a public authority in respect of that information. It followed that the Information Tribunal had jurisdiction to entertain an appeal from the Commissioner's decision in such a case. The House of Lords did not itself consider the question whether the Balen Report was held for the purposes of journalism.

7.5.9 The future of FOIA 2000

Since FOIA 2000 came fully into force in January 2005, there have been a number of proposals to restrict its scope. So far these have not been put into effect, but they do demonstrate that it cannot be taken for granted that the Act will remain in its current form for the indefinite future.

On 16 October 2006 an independent review of FOIA 2000 was published, commissioned by the Department for Constitutional Affairs and carried out by a company called Frontier Economics.[263] The key elements of the report were as follows:

• the cost of dealing with FOIA requests across central government was £24.4 million per year;

• the cost to the wider public sector was an additional £11.1 million per year; and

• there were various possible options for reducing these costs (for example introducing a flat rate fee for FOIA requests, or changing the way of determining whether a request exceeded the 'appropriate limit' under section 12 of FOIA 2000).

On 14 December 2006 and 29 March 2007 the Department for Constitutional Affairs published consultation papers setting out possible changes to the calculation of the appropriate limit. The proposals would have widened the circumstances in which

---

[262] See para 7 (Lord Phillips); para 73 (Lord Neuberger). Lord Hope (para 52) thought it preferable not to use this expression, as it does not appear in the statute.

[263] The review is available at <http://www.foi.gov.uk/reference/foi-independent-review.pdf> (accessed 21 March 2009).

different requests could be aggregated for the purposes of section 12: the practical effect could have been to ration individual newspapers, or even the BBC, to making one request every three months to bodies such as government departments. The proposals were extremely controversial, and on 25 October 2007 it was announced that they had been abandoned.[264]

In January 2009, Harriet Harman MP, Leader of the House of Commons, announced a proposal whereby information about MPs' expenses would be published in summary form rather than item by item. FOIA 2000 would be amended so as to negate the effect of the earlier Tribunal and High Court decisions (discussed above).[265] On 21 January 2009 it was announced that the proposed amendment would not be pursued.

The mechanism to be used for the proposed amendment was very striking. As explained above, the public authorities covered by the Act are listed in Schedule 1; and section 7(3) allows the Secretary of State by order to amend Schedule 1, *inter alia*, so as to limit to information of a specified description, the entry relating to any public authority. The proposed order would have provided that the Houses of Parliament were not 'public authorities' in relation to information about MPs' expenses, save to a very limited extent. In other words, section 7(3) effectively allows the scope of the Act to be reduced, without the need for primary legislation.

Finally, Jack Straw MP's House of Commons statement (24 February 2009) about the veto on disclosure of the Iraq War Cabinet minutes[266] includes the following passage:

Shortly after he became Prime Minister, my right hon. Friend the Prime Minister established a high-level inquiry into the 30-year rule under the chairmanship of Mr. Paul Dacre of the Daily Mail. That report, published last month, proposed a reduction from 30 to 15 years of the time after which Cabinet minutes and other papers would automatically be released. I have already told the House that the Government favour a substantial reduction in the 30-year limit. In that context, the report also recommended that we consider protection under the Act for certain categories of information.

The Dacre Report into the future of the 30-year rule was published on 29 January 2009.[267] The reference in Jack Straw's statement relates to the following section in chapter 8 of the Report:

8.7 As we noted in Chapter Five, there are genuine concerns among some ministers and civil servants about the early release of particularly sensitive types of papers . . . Given that we are recommending a substantial reduction to the 30 year rule, we believe that the government may wish to look again at the exemptions set out in the FoI Act.

8.8 We therefore recommend that, in parallel with the adoption of a 15 year rule, the government, in consultation with interested parties, may wish to consider whether there is a case for enhanced protection of such categories of information.

---

[264] See <http://www.justice.gov.uk/news/newsrelease251007c.htm> for the press release issued by the Ministry of Justice (accessed 29 March 2009).

[265] See section 7.5.6 above.

[266] *Hansard*, HC, vol 488, 24 February 2009, col 153.

[267] The report is available at <http://www.30yearrulereview.org.uk/> (accessed 29 March 2009).

So what may be under consideration is a change along the following lines. The 30-year rule would be replaced by a 15-year rule; and at the same time some categories of information that are at present covered by a qualified exemption under FOIA 2000 would become subject to absolute exemption. Possible candidates for this treatment might be Cabinet minutes, or some forms of policy advice in central government. If the same technique were to be adopted as in relation to the proposals about MPs' expenses, the change could be brought about without the need for primary legislation.

7.6 OTHER RIGHTS OF ACCESS TO INFORMATION

7.6.1 Environmental Information Regulations 2004

The Environmental Information Regulations 2004 (EIR 2004) came into force at the same time as FOIA 2000. The Regulations provide for a right of access on request to environmental information held by public authorities. The intention of FOIA 2000 appears to be that requests for environmental information (as defined in the Regulations) should be dealt with under EIR 2004 and not under FOIA 2000.[268]

In many respects FOIA 2000 and EIR 2004 can be considered side by side, as part of a single package. One significant difference between them should, however, be mentioned at the outset. FOIA 2000 does not implement an EU obligation; it is an entirely domestic piece of legislation. EIR 2004 gives effect in UK law to Council Directive (EC) 2003/4 on public access to environmental information. The language of EIR 2004 in many respects reflects the language of the Directive. This difference is important in two respects. It means that, applying normal principles of European law, the domestic provisions must be construed so as to give effect to the Directive, as far as it is possible to do so.[269] It also means that the scope to amend EIR 2004 is much more limited than is the case with FOIA 2000. If in the future the scope of FOIA 2000 is restricted in any way, the question whether a particular request falls within the Act or EIR 2004 may become of considerable significance.

EIR 2004 applies to 'public authorities'. The term does not bear exactly the same meaning as in FOIA 2000. Under regulation 2(2), a public authority means a government department, or a public authority as defined in section 3(1) of FOIA 2000, disregarding the exceptions in paragraph 6[270] of Schedule 1 to the Act. However, any body or office-holder listed in Schedule 1 to FOIA 2000 only in relation to information of a specified description is not a 'public authority' under EIR 2004;[271] and nor is any person designated by order under section 5 of the Act. In two respects, however, the definition of public authority under EIR 2004 is wider than under the Act. EIR 2004 applies

---

[268]   See FOIA 2000, s 39, which in effect exempts information from FOIA 2000 if it falls within EIR 2004. However, the s 39 exemption is qualified, not absolute: FOIA 2000, s 2(3).

[269]   See eg *Von Colson* [1984] ECR 1891.

[270]   FOIA 2000, Sch 1, para 6 excludes certain aspects of the armed forces from the scope of the Act.

[271]   Thus the BBC is not a public authority within EIR 2004.

to any body or person that carries out functions of public administration;[272] and also to any body or person that carries out various environmental functions, and that is under the control of another body that is itself a public authority within EIR 2004.[273]

EIR 2004 applies to 'environmental information', which term has the same meaning as in Article 2(1) of Directive (EC) 2003/4 (see regulation 2(1)). It covers any information in written, visual, aural, electronic, or any other material form on a number of matters, including the state of the elements of the environment, and factors likely to affect the elements of the environment. The definition is complex and needs to be considered in full when applying it to the facts of any specific case.

The core of EIR 2004 is regulation 5(1), which creates a general duty on a public authority that holds environmental information to make that information available 'on request'. A request under EIR 2004 does not even have to be made in writing. The information is to be made available within twenty working days (regulation 5(2)), though where the public authority reasonably believes that the complexity and volume of the information make it impracticable to comply within that period, it can extend the period to forty working days (see regulation 7(1)). There is no separate provision in EIR 2004 for a duty to confirm or deny: the only duty is to make available the information that is requested.

Under regulation 12(4) and (5), there are a number of exceptions to the right of access conferred by regulation 5(1). These are all qualified exemptions: disclosure may only be refused if in all the circumstances of the case the public interest in maintaining the exceptions outweighs the public interest in disclosing the information. Moreover, regulation 12(2) specifically provides that a public authority is to apply a presumption in favour of disclosure.

The exceptions in regulation 12(4) apply in the following circumstances:

- where the public authority does not hold the information in question when the applicant's request is received (regulation 12(4)(a));
- where the request for information is manifestly unreasonable (regulation 12(4)(b));
- where the request for information is formulated in too general a manner and the public authority has provided advice and assistance[274] (regulation 12(4)(c));
- where the request relates to material still in the course of completion, to unfinished documents, or to incomplete data (regulation 12(4)(d)); or
- where the request involves the disclosure of internal communications (regulation 12(4)(e)).[275]

---

[272] See EIR 2004, SI 2004/3391, reg 2(2)(c).
[273] See ibid reg 2(2)(d).
[274] As it is required to do by ibid reg 9.
[275] For discussion, see *Export Credits Guarantee Department v Friends of the Earth and Information Commissioner* [2008] EWHC 638 (Admin).

The exceptions in regulation 12(5) are all based on the concept of 'adverse effect'. A public authority may refuse to disclose information to the extent that its disclosure would adversely effect:

- international relations, defence, national security, or public safety (regulation 12(5)(a));[276]
- the course of justice, the ability of a person to receive a fair trial, or the ability of a public authority to conduct a criminal or disciplinary inquiry (regulation 12(5)(b));
- intellectual property rights (regulation 12(5)(c));
- the confidentiality of the proceedings of any public authority (not limited to the authority that received the request) (regulation 12(5)(d));
- the confidentiality of commercial or industrial information where such confidentiality is provided by law to protect a legitimate economic interest (regulation 12(5)(e));[277]
- the interests of a person who provided the information, where that person did not and could not have had a legal obligation to disclose it, did not supply it in circumstances such that any public authority is entitled to disclose it apart from the Regulations, and has not consented to its disclosure (regulation 12(5)(f)); or
- the protection of the environment to which the information relates (regulation 12(5)(g)).

It is interesting to note the relative simplicity of the drafting of regulation 12. There is a distinct contrast with the elaborate exemptions in Part II of FOIA 2000. Regulation 12(5) covers similar ground to Part II of FOIA 2000, but there are interesting contrasts. One is that there is no equivalent to the provision in section 40, whereby requests for access to the claimant's own personal data are treated as subject access requests under DPA 1998 rather than as requests under FOIA 2000. So it would appear that where personal data of the applicant is also environmental information, the request would constitute both a subject access request under section 7 of DPA 1998 and a request for environmental information under regulation 5. The advantage for the applicant of relying on EIR 2004 as opposed to DPA 1998 is that the applicant would be able to make use of the enforcement mechanisms under EIR 2004, which are essentially the same as under FOIA 2000 (see below), rather than having to go to court to enforce his subject access right.

Regulation 13 deals with requests under EIR 2004 for personal data of third parties; it does not apply to personal data of which the applicant is the data subject. Disclosure is prohibited in any of the following cases:

- disclosure would contravene any of the data protection principles (see regulation 13(2)(a)(i) and 13(2)(b));

---

[276] For discussion see *Ofcom v Information Commissioner* [2008] EWHC 1445 (Admin), [2009] EWCA Civ 90.
[277] For discussion see ibid.

- disclosure would contravene section 10 of DPA 1998, *and* in all the circumstances of the case the public interest in not disclosing the information outweighs the public interest in disclosing it (regulation 13(2)(a)(ii)); or

- the information is exempt from the data subject's own subject access right under section 7 of DPA 1998, *and* in all the circumstances of the case the public interest in not disclosing the information outweighs the public interest in disclosing it (regulation 13(3)).

Regulation 13 is thus couched in very similar terms to section 40 of DPA 1998 (so far as that section relates to personal data of third parties rather than of the applicant himself). As will be apparent, some parts of regulation 13 create absolute rather than qualified exemptions to the general duty of disclosure under regulation 5.

Where a number of different qualified exemptions are engaged, there is Court of Appeal authority (*Ofcom v Information Commissioner*)[278] that the public interest should be assessed by reference to the exemptions in aggregate and not simply by reference to each exemption viewed separately. As indicated at section 7.5.4 above, the Information Commissioner has lodged a petition to the House of Lords seeking permission to appeal against this decision.

EIR 2004 uses the same enforcement mechanisms as the Act.[279] A dissatisfied applicant may make representations to a public authority seeking a reconsideration of its decision, if it appears to him that the authority has failed to comply with a requirement of EIR 2004 in relation to his request (see regulation 11(1)). Thereafter the applicant may apply to the Commissioner for a decision as to whether the public authority has complied with EIR 2004 in relation to his request; and either the public authority or the applicant may appeal to the Information Tribunal against the Commissioner's decision. There is no equivalent in EIR 2004 to the power of executive veto under section 53 of FOIA 2000.

There is a power to charge for making environmental information available under EIR 2004 (see regulation 8(1)). By regulation 8(3), the charge 'shall not exceed an amount which the public authority is satisfied is a reasonable amount'. The Tribunal considered this provision in *Markinson v Information Commissioner*.[280] It took the view that in general a guide price for providing photocopied information was 10p per sheet, and a public authority that wished to charge a higher figure would need to show specific justification.

7.6.2 Access to local authority information

Local authorities are public authorities under FOIA 2000 and so are subject to the duty to confirm or deny and the duty of disclosure, under section 1 of that Act. In addition

---

[278] [2009] EWCA Civ 90.
[279] See EIR 2004, reg 18 extending those enforcement mechanisms but with certain minor modifications.
[280] EA/2005/0014.

there are a number of statutory provisions that create rights of access specifically relating to information held by public authorities. Two types of provision are discussed here: (a) provisions relating to access to local government meetings and to the accompanying documentation; and (b) provisions relating to the audit of local authority accounts.

As far as the first group of provisions is concerned, the position is made more confusing as a result of the changes to local authority governance introduced by the Local Government Act 2000 (LGA 2000). There are now two parallel regimes existing side by side; and the two may well be relevant to different meetings of the same local authority. The provisions are complex, and the account given below is a brief summary.

One of the two parallel regimes is set out in Part VA of the Local Government Act 1972 (LGA 1972). Part VA of the 1972 Act governs full council meetings, and meetings of committees of the council. Under section 100A(1) of LGA 1972, these meetings must in general be held in public. However, the public *must* be excluded if 'confidential information' is likely to be disclosed in the discussion. For these purposes 'confidential information' means information furnished to the council by a government department upon terms forbidding its disclosure to the public, and information the disclosure of which to the public is prohibited by enactment or court order.[281] The public *may* be excluded by resolution under section 100A(4) in circumstances where 'exempt information' is likely to be disclosed by the discussion. 'Exempt information' is defined in Part I of Schedule 12A to LGA 1972.

Members of the public have a right of access in advance to copies of agendas and of reports prepared for the meetings,[282] but these papers may be excluded from publication if they relate to items that are not likely to be open to the public.[283] After a meeting has been held there is an entitlement, for a period of six years beginning with the date of the meeting, to have access to the agenda, minutes, and reports.[284] but again there is no entitlement in relation to documents that would disclose exempt information.

The second regime, in LGA 2000 and regulations made under that Act,[285] applies to meetings of the executive of a local authority, and committees of the executive. In certain circumstances these meetings must be held in public,[286] including when the meeting is likely to make a 'key decision'.[287] Where a meeting will be held in public, then in general the agenda and reports for that meeting must be available for public inspection in advance of the meeting: however, confidential and exempt information[288]

---

[281] LGA 1972, s 11A(3)(a).

[282] ibid s 100B.

[283] ibid s 100B(2).

[284] ibid s 100C.

[285] The Local Authorities (Executive Arrangements) (Access to Information) (England) Regulations 2000, SI 2000/3272 (hereinafter 'the Access Regulations 2000').

[286] Access Regulations 2000, reg 7.

[287] As defined by Access Regulations 2000, reg 8. Key decisions are defined by reference to their financial significance or their impact on communities living or working in the local authority's area.

[288] These terms are defined as in LGA 1972, above.

and the advice of political advisers or assistants need not be disclosed.[289] There are additional requirements for advance publicity in respect of key decisions.[290] Executive decisions made after a private or public meeting of a decision-making body must be recorded, and the record open to public inspection along with any relevant report and background papers.[291] The same applies to executive decisions made by individual council members, and key decisions made by officers.[292] However, again there is no requirement to disclose confidential or exempt information or the advice of a political adviser or assistant.[293]

These various rights of access are less important now than they were before the right of access under FOIA 2000 came into force. There are two general issues as to the relationship between these provisions and FOIA 2000. One arises out of section 21 of FOIA 2000: information that is available under any of these local government provisions may be exempt from disclosure under section 21 of FOIA 2000 on the ground that it is reasonably accessible to the applicant other than under section 1 of FOIA 2000. The second issue is whether any of the provisions in the local government legislation amount to a prohibition on disclosure giving rise to an absolute exemption under section 44 of FOIA 2000. Here, it is very important to distinguish between: (a) provisions that *prohibit* disclosure; and (b) provisions that merely set a limit to a duty of disclosure that would otherwise exist. It is only the first type of provision that can be a prohibition for the purposes of section 44. Thus, for instance, the mere fact that information comes within Schedule 12A of LGA 2000 does not mean that it is exempt from disclosure under section 44 of FOIA 2000. If information falls within Schedule 12A then the duty of disclosure that would otherwise arise under Part VA of LGA 1972 is excluded, but this does not mean that there is any prohibition on disclosure.

As to information relating to the audit of local authorities, this is governed by the Audit Commission Act 1998. Under this Act, a local government elector for the area of a body subject to audit by the Audit Commission is entitled to inspect and make a copy of any statutory statement of accounts prepared by the body under the Act.[294] At each audit under the Act a 'person interested'[295] may inspect the accounts to be audited, and all books, deeds, contracts, bills, vouchers, and receipts relating to them.[296] There is an exception in relation to certain information regarding local authority staff.[297]

---

[289] See Access Regulations 2000, regs 11 and 21.
[290] See ibid regs 12–16.
[291] See ibid regs 3 and 5.
[292] See ibid regs 4 and 5.
[293] ibid reg 21.
[294] Audit Commission Act 1998, s 14.
[295] *R on the application of HTV Ltd v Bristol City Council* [2004] EWHC 1219 (Admin) for a discussion of what is meant by this.
[296] Audit Commission Act 1998, s 15.
[297] ibid s 16. In the *HTV* case, above, the Court left open the question whether HRA 1998 and ECHR, Art 8, read together, permitted a local authority to withhold personal information not mentioned in s 16.

7.7 CONCLUSION

As the discussion in this chapter demonstrates, information law is developing at considerable speed. Recent changes in this area have principally been driven by HRA 1998 and FOIA 2000, two of the main legal legacies of the first Blair government.

From the point of view of the media, developments during the last decade have been a mixed blessing. On the one hand the right of access to public sector information has expanded considerably, giving the media a valuable tool for researching the activities of central and local government. At the same time there have been some startling developments in the protection of individual privacy, suggesting that in some circumstances even the publication of apparently innocuous photographs taken in public can give rise to legal liability. A crude summary would be that the last decade has been—in terms of information law—good for the broadsheets, and bad for the *paparazzi*. The former are more likely to be interested in FOIA 2000; the latter are likely to be concerned by the implications of cases such as *Campbell* and *Murray*. Inevitably, though, this is something of a caricature. Restrictions on the disclosure of personal information have the potential to affect serious journalism on matters of public concern, not just the dissemination of gossip about supermodels and minor royalty. Celebrity journalism sells newspapers, and enables us to enjoy the variety of media that are available in the UK.[298]

For the future, there are two obvious questions of importance. One is whether there will be any serious attempt to reduce the scope of FOIA 2000, and if so to what extent this will be matched in practical terms by an increase in the volume of requests made under EIR 2004. The second is whether the courts will continue along the path exemplified by the *Campbell* and *Murray* case, or whether they will take the view that the pendulum has now swung too far in favour of the protection of individual privacy. This complex and fascinating area of the law will undoubtedly continue to generate questions of great interest for many years to come.

---

[298] cf *Campbell v MGN Ltd* [2004] UKHL 22; [2004] 2 AC 457, para 143 (Baroness Hale).

8

BROADCASTING

Tony Ballard

8.1 THE MEANING OF BROADCASTING

As a legal concept, the meaning of broadcasting has always been somewhat elusive. There is no single definition or accepted understanding of its meaning. Its origins lie in agriculture, describing the scattering of seeds over the whole surface of a field.[1] In the early twentieth century, this pastoral image must have appealed to those who saw the opportunities of the new radio technology as a means of disseminating information, music, and other material to the general public. To do so involved a host of activities including production, editing, and distribution of the material to radio masts, any one of which might have provided a name for the new activity. But it was the final delivery stage, the act of transmission from the masts, which gave us 'broadcasting' as the name for the whole. The industry itself was characterized by the technology used in the final stage in the delivery of the material to the recipient. It remains so to this day. The BBC is the British Broadcasting Corporation notwithstanding that it sold its transmission masts years ago. But by characterizing an industry by a particular historic delivery technology, the seeds of future confusion were sown. The result is a diverse crop of meanings through which the draftsman, whether of legislation or contracts, is well advised to pick his way with care.

---

[1] 'Broadcast' as an adjective is dated from 1767 as follows in *The Shorter Oxford Dictionary* of seed, etc: 'Scattered over the whole surface. Of sowing: Performed by this method.'

8.1.1 Broadcasting as provision of a programme service

In 1988, the government published a White Paper setting out its proposals 'for broadcasting in the UK in the 1990s'. It was followed by the Broadcasting Act 1990, which implemented those proposals by introducing a radically new regulatory scheme for the sector (the main features of which are still in place today). Instead of regulation being focused on the person controlling the distribution or delivery technology, it was applied to the provider of the programme service, irrespective of whether the service was distributed or delivered over the air or by cable. It was a first step towards technological neutrality. It was a regulatory scheme for programme provision but it was still expressed in terms of implementing the government's 'broadcasting policy'. Indeed it was a 'Broadcasting' Act. One could be forgiven for thinking that the word itself, consistent with the new regime, had been separated from its historical roots in the transmission technology of the 1920s and would be used in the new Act to denote the provision of a programme service, irrespective of the transmission technology. But on the contrary, not only does the Act not attempt to define what broadcasting means, it says that, in that Act, 'broadcast' means broadcast by wireless telegraphy.[2] So within the Act itself, the word is used in that limited sense even though in the underlying policy documents and indeed in the title of the Act it is used in a new and much wider sense.

8.1.2 Broadcasting as use of an allocated frequency

The Radio Regulations of the International Telecommunication Union set out the international framework for the use of the radio frequency spectrum, allocating particular bands to particular uses. Some bands are allocated to broadcasting. When the Astra satellite system, whose downlinks were originally not in bands allocated to broadcasting, offered service providers the opportunity to deliver programme services direct to the home, the Independent Television Commission, which was then the broadcasting regulator, did not treat those services as broadcasts even though they were delivered (to use a neutral term) by wireless telegraphy. It divided licences under the 1990 Act into broadcast and non-broadcast categories, classifying those using bands not allocated to broadcasting as non-broadcast. The UHF bands which carried channels 3 (ITV), 4, and 5 were allocated to broadcasting and therefore those channels fell into the ITC's broadcast category. Licences granted in relation to services delivered on frequencies allocated to other uses, such as Sky which utilized bands allocated to telecommunications under the Radio Regulations, were categorized as 'non-broadcast' services. The division reflected a conventional UK regulatory perception that those parts of the spectrum which were allocated to broadcasting were scarce while those which were not allocated to broadcasting were somehow plentiful and should be regulated more lightly. It also reflected the underlying statutory scheme in the 1990 Act as originally enacted which drew a distinction between what were called domestic and

---

[2] Broadcasting Act 1990, s 202 (1).

non-domestic satellite services (something of a misnomer). The distinction led to controversy on more than one occasion, particularly in the late 1980s when competing satellite services, BSB and Sky, fell on either side of the line and were subject to different regulatory regimes as a result. These arrangements were re-regulated in 1997[3] and the distinction has not been carried forward in the Communications Act 2003. This particular development of the meaning of broadcasting, which would have limited it to transmissions on particular frequencies, has fallen by the wayside.

8.1.3 Broadcasting as transmission

Another tailored meaning is given to 'broadcasting' in section 1 of the Broadcasting Act 1996. This is a section which deals with the meaning of 'multiplex service' in Part 1 of the Act, which in turn deals with digital terrestrial television (DTT). Section 1(7) says that, in that section, 'broadcast' means broadcast otherwise than from a satellite. This itself must be read with the definition in the 1990 Act of 'broadcast' as broadcast by wireless telegraphy.[4] Within that broader meaning, section 1(7) carves out a local meaning for the word broadcast as terrestrial broadcasting by wireless telegraphy. In context, it plainly means the act of transmission itself.

None of the providers of the mainstream terrestrial and satellite programme services now run their own transmission systems for the delivery of their main services. The transmission system for the independent television sector was in effect privatized pursuant to the Broadcasting Act 1990 and the BBC subsequently sold off its own transmission infrastructure. BSkyB sold its satellites after the merger between BSB and Sky and used the Astra system operated by a Luxembourg company, SES. Insofar as they remain 'broadcasters', the link with their delivery systems has been decisively broken.

8.1.4 Broadcasting as Ofcom's regulatory arena in television and radio

Like the 1990 Act, the Communications Act 2003 defines 'broadcast' as broadcast by wireless telegraphy (and cognate expressions are to be construed accordingly)[5] except insofar as the context otherwise requires.[6] The exception creates an opportunity for the draftsman, which is exploited revealingly in sections 316 to 318 of the 2003 Act. Section 316 deals with competition between providers of licensed services and services connected with them. A 'licensed service' is defined as a service licensed by a Broadcasting Act licence, ie any licence granted under the relevant parts of the 1990 and 1996 Acts.[7] But in section 318, under which a duty is imposed on Ofcom to review

---

[3] SI 1997/1682.
[4] Broadcasting Act 1996, s 147(2).
[5] Communications Act 2003, s 405(1).
[6] ibid ss 316(4) and 405(1).
[7] ibid s 405(1).

its codes, guidance, and directions so far as they may have effect for a competition purpose, it was necessary or at least convenient for the draftsman to find some generic expression to refer to the whole range of regulatory provisions relating to television and radio—ie the provisions of Part 3 of the 2003 Act, the whole of the 1990 and 1996 Acts, and the provisions of licences granted under the latter Acts. The expression that the draftsman alighted upon was a 'broadcasting provision', conveniently capturing Ofcom's regulatory arena which is not, of course, limited to services broadcast by wireless telegraphy but extends to other services. A 'broadcasting provision' might therefore be concerned as much with services delivered by cable or fibre as with services broadcast by wireless telegraphy.

Unlike the limited meaning given to 'broadcast' elsewhere in the 2003 Act, it is used here to convey a quite different meaning. The expression means, in short, a provision which concerns the regulation of television or radio, irrespective of the means of transmission.

8.1.5 A new consensus?

The Broadcasting Act 1990 introduced a regulatory scheme for television and radio that extended beyond services delivered by traditional wireless-based systems to services provided for delivery by means of any telecommunications system, including cable, and (although not in the mind of the draftsman at the time) the internet. Having at least to some extent loosened the link between broadcasting and its roots in wireless transmission, the emergence of on-demand services prompted a new use of the word in official policy documents to denote a service of programmes intended for simultaneous reception by an audience as distinct from one where programmes were sent on demand. In 'Broadband Britain', for example, a government policy document published in 1998, 'broadcast' is used throughout the document to indicate services delivered for simultaneous reception in two or more dwelling-houses, as distinct from on-demand services such as video-on-demand (VOD), which are described as non-broadcast services.[8] The delivery technology, be it wireless telegraphy, cable, or the twisted pairs of copper wire that connect the home to the local telephone exchange, was not relevant.

Building on this usage, a new consensus is emerging, which is that broadcasting is not limited to wireless telegraphy but extends to the dissemination of material to the public by electronic transmission on any network, whether wireless or otherwise. The concept of broadcasting is, in effect, being separated from its historical roots in the transmission technology of the 1920s and is increasingly being used to denote any service delivered to audiences over electronic networks, irrespective of the transmission technology. It is a development which has been more or less confirmed or blessed by the decision of the European Court of Justice in the *Mediakabel* case

---

[8] See eg para 15.

(see section 8.3.7 below)[9] to treat television broadcasting as limited to simultaneous transmissions of programme material to an indeterminate audience and by the approach adopted by the subsequent Audiovisual Media Services Directive, both of which are discussed further below.

A similar trend is discernible in copyright law. Until 2003, the acts restricted by copyright in the UK as exclusive rights in a work included broadcasting the work (defined as certain transmissions by wireless telegraphy) and including it in a cable programme service, reflecting the technologies of the 1980s.[10] Fitting the new digital world into these categories was not easy, as was illustrated by the *Shetland Times* case[11] where the court held that newspaper headlines were arguably cable programmes and that a website was a cable programme service. In October 2003, the old restricted acts were replaced by the generic expression 'communication to the public' by electronic transmission, of which broadcasting was retained as a subset but redefined in terms which embraced both wireless, cable, and (to some extent) internet delivery.[12] The details are slightly complex, with internet transmissions counting as broadcasts only in certain circumstances, but the link with wireless telegraphy had gone. Where a reference to broadcasting by wireless telegraphy is to be made, the 1988 Act now uses the expression 'wireless broadcast'.[13]

8.2 THE RATIONALE FOR REGULATION/REGULATORY POLICY

8.2.1 Why regulate?

The regulation of radio and television broadcasting is so entrenched a feature of the media landscape that it seems unremarkable. And yet other forms of distribution or publication of similar content, such as newspapers, books, and theatre productions, are subject to little or no regulation beyond what is generally called the law of the land. There is, in other words, little or no sector-specific regulation that applies to them or at least to the content of the medium. Why should the distribution or publication of the same content by electronic transmission over telecommunications networks attract state intervention when distribution by other means does not?

8.2.2 Spectrum scarcity and the power of the medium

The conventional rationale for the control of broadcasting, at least until the development of multi-channel cable and satellite television and the rise of the internet, was from the

---

[9] Case C-89/04 *Mediakabel BV v Commissariaat voor de Media* ECR I–4891.
[10] Copyright, Designs and Patents Act 1988, ss 6 and 16(1)(d) as originally enacted.
[11] *Shetland Times Ltd v Wills and anor* [1997] FSR 604.
[12] The Copyright and Related Rights Regulations 2003 (SI 2003/2498).
[13] See Copyright, Designs and Patents Act 1988, s 178 as amended.

earliest days based on two principal props.[14] On the one hand, the radio frequency spectrum was regarded as a scarce resource. On the other, the medium was thought to be one of great power and intimacy, capable of addressing a mass audience in the privacy of their own homes. These two considerations underpinned what came to be called the public service principle in broadcasting policy, whereby broadcasting was regarded as a national asset to be used for the national good. Responsibility was to lie with one or more broadcasting authorities appointed as trustees for the national interest in broadcasting. Viewers or listeners should pay the same for reception and the broadcasting authorities should be free of government intervention in their day-to-day affairs.[15]

This public service principle was implemented by what was in effect a deal: the broadcasters accepted public service obligations to inform and educate as well as to entertain, to maintain high standards, wide range and balance, to present news with due impartiality, and so forth in return for the allocation of scarce frequencies within the radio frequency spectrum. Those obligations were accepted in exchange for the specially privileged position that they obtained from access to the airwaves. The two issues of spectrum scarcity and the power of broadcasting were therefore central to the regulatory arrangements that were adopted, whereby broadcasting was reserved to national institutions designed, in one form or another, to promote the national interest.[16] Thus the BBC in its original incarnation was designed to be a trustee for the national interest, an evergreen feature underlying the recent formation of the BBC Trust.

With the rise of multi-channel television, particularly the use of satellites and cable, a distinction was drawn in official thinking between the public service obligations of the main broadcasters who had access to the frequencies reserved for broadcasting, such as obligations to inform and educate as well as to entertain, and consumer protection obligations, such as that programmes should not offend against good taste and decency and that there should be special rules applying at times when large numbers of young children could be expected to be in the audience. Spectrum scarcity was no longer considered a sustainable rationale for the regulation of these new services but the public still needed protection against the power of the medium. It was thought appropriate to require them to accept at least the consumer protection obligations.

At the same time, especially as some of the new services did not use the radio frequency spectrum and were not therefore amenable to regulation through the wireless telegraphy licensing regime, a new regulatory scheme was introduced by the Broadcasting Act 1990 whereby the provision of programme services was made to be subject to a licensing regime, irrespective of the nature of the network over which the services were conveyed. The provision of such services was prohibited without a licence from the appropriate regulator.

---

[14] See eg the Report of the Broadcasting Committee chaired by Sir Frederick Sykes, 23 August 1923.
[15] See the summary in section I of the Home Affairs Committee Third Report on the Future of Broadcasting, June 1988.
[16] Minutes of Evidence taken before the Home Affairs Committee, 20 January 1988, Memorandum submitted by the Home Office.

Further, a key feature of the new regime was that the licensing requirement applied not to the person providing the means of distribution (such as the cable operator in relation to cable services) but to the person providing the programme service itself. Novel at the time of the 1990 Act, this innovation laid the foundations for what has turned out to be a resilient regulatory regime which has been adaptable to technological change because it focused not on the technology used to deliver the service but on the activity of making available programmes for reception by the general public irrespective of the means used for its delivery. The intensity of regulation could be and was graded to reflect the ongoing public service principle and the use made by the service provider of scarce spectrum resources but all were subject to the consumer protection requirements, reflecting the perceived need to regulate the service in the light of the power and intimacy of the medium.

8.2.3 The internet

Digital television and the emergence of the internet presented a new challenge to these arrangements. It became apparent in particular that programme services would become available on the internet that were not or not readily amenable to regulation because of the impracticality of bringing the service providers under regulatory control.[17] This led to the emergence in official thinking in the late 1990s of the view that content regulation might be abandoned altogether. The Culture Minister at one point spoke somewhat theatrically of digital television bringing about the end of television as broadcasting and the beginning of electronic communications as a seamless web which transcended the old distinctions between television, computer, and the telephone. He said he could imagine a future where broadcasting regulation was based in the first instance on competition law with a reduced set of distinctive media rules added only where strictly necessary.[18] The trend in this direction was brought to at least a temporary halt, however, by a reassertion of the public service principle in the government's White Paper in 2000 on the pragmatic ground that it worked.[19] As for consumer protection requirements, there was a perception that, while there remained among the general public an expectation of what would or would not appear on television, that expectation ought not to be disappointed and regulation should support that expectation.[20] Policy therefore settled on regulation being carried forward in relation to the familiar television channels and also new television services, albeit at diminishing levels, but with regulation ceasing for on-demand programming of the kind that

---

[17] See eg Government recognition that specific regulation of internet content was in practice probably impossible: *Regulating Communications: The Way Ahead* (Cm 4022, 1999) para 3.20.

[18] Chris Smith, Secretary of State for Culture, Media and Sport, speech to the Royal Television Society, September 1998.

[19] *A New Future for Communications* (Cm 5010, 2000) para 5.3.1.

[20] This is reflected in the Secretary of State's reserve powers to modify the meaning of the key expressions defining the scope of regulation in the Communications Act 2003, ss 234, 249, and 361(7) where he may have regard to public expectations as to content protection.

was expected to characterize the internet. This was characterized in the White Paper as a 'tier zero', below the tiers of specific regulation, governing material on the internet and via telephony where only so-called basic laws of the land, such as obscenity and defamation, and self-regulation apply.[21]

The result was a series of amendments to the 1990 and 1996 Broadcasting Acts in the Communications Act 2003 under which, among other things, sector-specific regulation of on-demand services was withdrawn. Only linear services were to be subject to regulation, with the boundaries between them and on-demand services carefully drawn (see below).

8.2.4 Legacy regulation of one-to-one communications

A remarkable feature of the new regime under the Communications Act 2003 and the amended Broadcasting Acts is that sector-specific regulation of on-demand services has been withdrawn altogether.[22] Previously, on-demand services were in principle regulated under the Broadcasting Act 1990 (although in practice the then television regulator, the ITC, declined to do so and contributed instead to a self-regulatory system established by the Video on Demand Association).[23] Other communications over public networks were subject to penalties for what was called improper use, which were set out in section 43 of the Telecommunications Act 1984 and are now in section 127 of the Communications Act. Those sections have carried forward what might be called a default regulatory regime for broadcasting, at least to the extent of the consumer protection obligations. This was a legacy of the old Post Office Acts. Section 127 makes it an offence among other things to send by means of any public electronic communications network (ECN) any matter that is grossly offensive or of an indecent, obscene, or menacing character. This is plainly a kind of consumer protection requirement but quite what policy objective it is now intended to serve is unclear.[24] Whatever it is, it does not apply to anything within the ambit of the Broadcasting Acts: section 127 expressly provides that it does not apply to anything done in the course of providing a programme service within the meaning of the Broadcasting Act 1990.

While on the face of it this seems straightforward enough, it creates a regulatory gap because of the meaning given to the expression 'programme service' in the 1990 Act. That meaning does not coincide with the boundaries of content regulation under that Act. Some programme services fall outside those boundaries and are unregulated, with the result that the consumer protections under the 1990 Act, on the one hand, and

---

[21] *A New Future for Communications* (n 19 above) paras 5.5 and 5.9.1.

[22] See Communications Act 2003, ss 233(3) and 361(2).

[23] The Video on Demand Association Code of Practice is available at <http://www.culture.gov.uk/images/publications/VoDCodeofPractice.pdf>.

[24] See what would be, but for the seriousness of the matter, the almost comical misunderstanding of their Lordships in *DPP v Collins* [2006] UKHL 40 where its purpose was held, at para 7 of the leading speech, to be to prohibit the use of a service provided and funded by the public for the benefit of the public for the transmission of communications which contravene the basic standards of our society.

section 127 of the 2003 Act, on the other, do not apply to them. This is because the expression 'programme service' has more than one meaning under the Broadcasting Act 1990. Section 201 of that Act, as amended by the 2003 Act, defines programme service so as to include not only regulated services but also any other service consisting of the sending, by means of an ECN, of sounds or visual images for reception at two or more places in the UK, whether they are so sent for simultaneous reception or at different times in response to requests made by different users of the service. This is a legacy from the 1990 Act as originally enacted. It excludes from the ambit of section 127 not only those programme services that are now regulated under the post-2003 regime (which applies the consumer protection requirements) but also on-demand services other than purely one-to-one services. Whether the reference to two or more 'places' in the UK means that it relates only to fixed and not mobile services is not clear. Subject to the doubt about mobile services there is, therefore, currently no sector-specific regulation that applies to the sending of sounds or visual images for reception at two or more places in the UK where they are sent at different times in response to requests from different users.

These arrangements are no doubt intended to give effect to the policy principle that content regulation should not apply to services provided on the internet but it has the odd consequence that it is, for example, an offence to send indecent material to a single recipient over a public network but it is not an offence to send the material on-demand to more than one recipient or indeed to the general public.

There are traps here for the unwary, at least for those who send anything that might be treated as offensive, indecent, obscene, or menacing over a public network. Section 127 will bite unless the material is either part of a licensed programme service or for reception at two or more places in the UK. An adult service consisting of content tailored to the wishes of a particular customer, for example, would be caught by section 127 unless it was for reception at two or more places. An e-mail containing offensive material that would be caught by section 127 if sent to a single person would not be caught if it was copied to another. The boundaries of this regulatory gap are as obscure as the policy objective that it is meant to serve.

8.2.5 The AVMS Directive

Directive (EC) 2007/65 has amended what was called the Television without Frontiers (TWF) Directive.[25] The amendments include replacing that name with 'Audiovisual Media Services Directive' as its new title[26] and extending its scope beyond what it calls television broadcasting to on-demand audiovisual media services. Specific regulation is justified on the ground of the growing importance of audiovisual media services for societies, democracy—in particular by ensuring freedom of information, diversity of opinion, and media pluralism—education, and culture.[27] Each Member

---

[25] Directive (EEC) 89/552 as amended by Directive (EC) 97/36.

[26] Directive (EC) 2007/65, Art 1(1).

[27] ibid Recital (3).

State is obliged to ensure that all audiovisual media services transmitted by media service providers under its jurisdiction comply with the rules of the system of law applicable to such services intended for the public in that Member State.[28] The changes are loosely modelled on the new (2002) regulatory framework in telecommunications, which seeks to create a level playing field among competitive providers of networks and network services. They are designed to ensure that a basic tier of coordinated rules should apply to both television broadcasting (ie linear audiovisual media services) and on-demand (ie non-linear audiovisual media services) so as to avoid distortions of competition, improve legal certainty, help to complete the internal market, and facilitate the emergence of a single information area. They are also designed to retain the country of origin principle and common minimum standards (to which we return below), which are regarded as having worked well in relation to television broadcasting.[29] The UK therefore now has no alternative but to regulate these services in accordance with the AVMS Directive to the extent that they are transmitted by media service providers under its jurisdiction.

This European initiative has sharply reversed the trend in policy towards withdrawing from regulation of on-demand services. In pursuit of a level playing field and a true European market for audiovisual media services, it requires Member States to extend regulation to on-demand services.[30] A vigorous campaign by the UK government within Europe against the European Commission's original proposals has limited the final scope of the extension to mass-market, television-like, video-on-demand services that compete with conventional television but the boundaries have nevertheless been moved. At the time of writing, the government has consulted on the changes, which have to be implemented by 19 December 2009,[31] and is planning to do so by way of Regulations under section 2(2) of the European Communities Act 1972.

At the heart of the TWF Directive, the predecessor to the AVMS Directive, was a deal whereby each Member State in effect guaranteed the freedom of reception on their territory of television broadcasting services emanating from another Member State so long as those services complied with certain basic content requirements. This was called the country of origin principle and it has been carried forward into the AVMS Directive in relation to both television broadcasting and the newly regulated on-demand services that are within its scope, albeit with different rules as to derogation (as to which more below). At least in principle, a service provider whose service complies with the requirements of its country of origin (and there are detailed rules about this) and is available for reception in other countries in the European Union generally does not need to find out whether the service complies with local regulatory requirements in other Member States. The objective is to promote a single European television market. The country of origin principle offers service providers

---

[28] Directive (EEC) 89/552, Art 2(1).
[29] Directive (EC) 2007/65 Recital (7).
[30] ibid Recital (6).
[31] <http://www.culture.gov.uk/reference_library/consultations/5309.aspx>.

the significant advantage of being able to market their services in other Member States without the burden of separate compliance requirements in each of them.

The advantage for on-demand service providers is, however, tempered by the fact that the provisions in the Directive for Member States to derogate from the country of origin principle are not the same as those applicable to television broadcasting but instead have been modelled on the looser provisions of the e-Commerce Directive, which may lead to practical problems in future.

At all events, insofar as it is an effective mechanism, the underlying deal provides a further practical rationale for content regulation.

8.3 THE RIGHT TO BROADCAST

8.3.1 Liberalization

The broad framework of the regulatory scheme established by the Broadcasting Act 1990 swept away the old arrangements whereby broadcasting services were provided exclusively by the great monolithic broadcasting authorities, the BBC, on the one hand, and the Independent Broadcasting Authority (IBA), on the other. Those arrangements were replaced by a licensing regime for most forms of independent (ie non-BBC) services. The BBC retained its position as a self-regulatory broadcaster pursuant to its Charter and Agreement but the old arrangements whereby programme contractors supplied programmes for the IBA to broadcast were abolished. In their place the 1990 Act created a licensing regime administered by independent regulators, the Independent Television Commission (ITC) and the Radio Authority, under which programme services were provided under licences granted by the appropriate regulator and which contained regulatory provisions in accordance with the framework set by the Act. The details of that framework were changed considerably by the Communications Act 2003 but the main feature, whereby service providers are regulated by means of licensing conditions imposed by a statutory regulator, is still in place.

Perhaps the most significant effect of the change was to create a framework in which anyone with access to a distribution or delivery network could provide programme services so long as they accepted the consumer protection obligations and other requirements of the regulatory framework. This was a profoundly liberalizing change.

8.3.2 The regulatory scheme for television and radio

Unlike the new regulatory scheme for telecommunications in Part 2 of the Communications Act 2003, the regulatory scheme for television and radio is adapted to, rather than driven by, the underlying Directives. Part 3 of the Act sets out the details of that scheme, building on the foundations of the 1990 and 1996 Acts, which are extensively amended. In particular it establishes the regulatory structure for independent television (Chapter 2) and radio services (Chapter 3) and Ofcom's functions as regulator of them within certain overarching duties imposed on Ofcom under Part 1. There are different regulatory regimes for different categories of service and they are applied to service providers by means of the licensing regime established under the 1990 and 1996 Acts. It is Ofcom's duty to secure that the holders of licences granted under those Acts do so on the conditions included in the relevant regulatory regime and to do all that it can to secure that they comply with those conditions.[32]

8.3.3 The prohibition

Section 13 of the Broadcasting Act 1990 contains a prohibition on providing certain television services without a licence. In particular, any person who provides what the Act calls a relevant regulated television service without being authorized to do so by or under a licence under Part I of either the 1990 Act or the 1996 Act is guilty of an offence.[33] No proceedings may, however, be instituted in England and Wales or Northern Ireland except by or with the consent of the relevant Director of Public Prosecutions.[34] Similar provisions in section 97 prohibit the provision of independent radio services without a licence.

The effect of the prohibition is to ensure that the right to provide a relevant regulated service is exercisable only through the licensing regime. It makes the licensing system work.

8.3.4 Who 'provides' a service?

One of the principal innovations of the 1990 Act was to apply regulation to the provider of the programme service and not, for example, to the person who was responsible for its delivery. Thus it is the service provider to which the prohibitions in sections 13 and 97 apply and therefore the service provider who needs a licence. But what, then, amounts to 'providing' a service of the relevant kind? This is now explained in section 362(2) of the 2003 Act. In the case of any such service, the person (and the only person) who is to be treated as providing the service is the person with general control over which programmes and other services and facilities are comprised in the service (whether or not that person has control of the content of individual programmes or of the broadcasting or distribution of the service). In short, the person who provides the service is the person who is in a position to decide what is to be included in it. It is this person who must obtain a licence from Ofcom if an offence under sections 13 or 97 is to be avoided.

In relation to television, the UK will have to consider whether this formulation is consistent with the requirements of the AVMS Directive (the Directive does not cover radio). The Directive is concerned with audiovisual media services transmitted by

---

[32] Communications Act 2003, s 263.
[33] Broadcasting Act 1990, s 13(1).
[34] ibid s 13(4).

media service providers, and a media service provider is defined as the person who has editorial responsibility for the choice of the audiovisual content of the service, and determines the manner in which it is organized. 'Editorial responsibility' is the subject of a specific definition in terms of the exercise of effective control both over the selection of the programmes and over their organization either in a chronological schedule, in the case of television broadcasts, or in a catalogue, in the case of on-demand services. So there are in effect three elements of control in the definition of a media service provider in the Directive—the selection of the programmes, their organization into a schedule or a catalogue, and the manner in which the service is organized.[35]

This definition of control may be more challenging to apply in the case of on-demand services than television broadcasting, and in particular in the treatment of service aggregators where the various elements may be shared between the original service provider and the aggregator, making it difficult to know who should hold a licence. The government has consulted on the difficulties here but at the time of writing has reached no clear conclusion.[36]

8.3.5 What services are regulated?

One might expect that there would be some generic description in the legislation of a relevant regulated television or radio service, but there is none. For television, instead of a single definition, there is a description of six different kinds of service, some based on historical categories and others on technology.[37] One of them, a television licensable content service (TLCS), is a residual catch-all category and it is sometimes (but not always) helpful to think that the others are subsets of that category.

The practical upshot is not, however, that every television service provided within the UK must be licensed under the 2003 Act. There is a jurisdiction test for certain services. Thus, for example, the provider of a TLCS is within the scope of the prohibition only to the extent that the provider is under the jurisdiction of the UK for the purposes of the TWF Directive.[38] On the other hand, a foreign provider which is beyond the reach of section 13 may yet be regulated by Ofcom by virtue of being under the jurisdiction of the purposes of the Directive.[39]

8.3.6 Jurisdiction

The Directive contains detailed rules to ascertain which Member State has jurisdiction over a particular service. The application of these rules is often of considerable

---

[35] AVMS Directive, Art 1(c) and(d).
[36] DCMS consultation document of July 2008 on proposals for implementation in the UK, paras 34–39.
[37] Communications Act 2003, s 211 and Broadcasting Act 1990, s 13(1A), which excludes a television multiplex service from the meaning of a 'relevant regulated television service'.
[38] Communications Act 2003, s 211(2)(b).
[39] ibid s 211.

commercial importance since they determine the compliance regime for the service provider. The compliance regime may differ significantly between different Member States because the requirements of the AVMS Directive are minimum standards only. Member States are entitled to require media service providers under their jurisdiction to comply with more detailed or stricter rules in the fields coordinated by the Directive, provided that such rules are in compliance with Community law.[40] Differences between national rules create conditions in which there may be a commercial advantage for service providers to go forum shopping, ie a service provider may so arrange its affairs as to bring its service under the jurisdiction of a state which has less detailed or less strict rules.

Jurisdiction over a media service provider falls to be determined in the first instance by reference to one or more of three factors—where it has its head office, where editorial decisions are taken, and where its workforce operates.[41] If jurisdiction cannot be determined by reference to them, it depends on where its satellite uplink is situated or what country's satellite capacity it uses.[42] Failing that, the competent Member State is the one in which the provider is established within the meaning of Articles 43 to 48 of the Treaty.[43]

Where, however, the service is intended exclusively for reception in countries other than Member States and is not received with standard consumer equipment directly or indirectly by the public in one or more Member States, the Directive does not apply.[44]

A media service provider will be deemed to be established in a particular Member State if the service provider has its head office and the editorial decisions about the service are taken in that Member State.[45] Where, however, it has its head office in one Member State but the editorial decisions are taken in another Member State, it will depend on where the workforce involved in the pursuit of the audiovisual media service activity operates. In particular:

• it will be deemed to be established in the Member State where a significant part of that workforce operates;

• if a significant part of that workforce operates in each of those Member States, it will be deemed to be established in the Member State where it has its head office;

• if a significant part of that workforce operates in neither of those Member States, it will be deemed to be established in the Member State where it first began its activity in accordance with the law of that Member State, provided that it maintains a stable and effective link with the economy of that Member State.[46]

---

[40] Directive (EC) 2007/65, Art 3(1).
[41] These are what Directive (EC) 97/36, Recitals (12) and (13) call practical criteria.
[42] AVMS Directive, Art 2.
[43] ibid Art 2(5).
[44] ibid Art 2(6).
[45] ibid Art 2(3)(a).
[46] ibid Art 2(3)(b).

Quite what is meant by the workforce or a significant part of the workforce is not explained in the Directive.

Where the media service provider has its head office in a Member State but decisions on the service are taken in a third country (ie a country which is not a Member State), or vice versa, it is deemed to be established in that Member State, provided that a significant part of the workforce involved in the pursuit of the service activity operates in that Member State.[47] It is odd that the decision-taking criterion here is any kind of decisions on the service and not editorial decisions, if only because it undermines the logic of the scheme for determining the place of establishment and it may be that it should be construed as meaning editorial decisions.

There is a fall-back for any case where the foregoing factors or criteria do not apply. Media service providers to whom those factors are not applicable are to be deemed to be under the jurisdiction of a Member State if:

- they use a satellite uplink situated in that Member State;
- if not, they use satellite capacity appertaining to that member state.

Thus, for example, a media service provider might have its head office in Moscow, take editorial decisions there, and use an uplink there. If it used Eutelsat satellite capacity and the service was received in a Member State with standard consumer equipment, it would be under the jurisdiction of France for the purposes of the Directive, since Eutelsat's frequency assignments are administered by France.

In practice these rules do not work well. They are designed to determine which Member State has jurisdiction by identifying the Member State in which the broadcaster is established and to ensure that one Member State and one only has jurisdiction.[48] It is not always easy for the national regulatory authority to establish the facts and it is not clear what should happen under the rules if it is unable to do so. Further, even if it is clear that jurisdiction cannot be determined by reference to the location of a television channel's head office, workforce, or editorial decision-making and it is necessary to fall back on where the uplink is situated or what satellite capacity is used, the rules assume that the channel will be delivered to viewers in Europe on only one satellite. If, as is not uncommon, the channel is carried on more than one satellite, these rules do not enable a jurisdiction to be determined if the uplinks are in (or the frequencies appertain to) different Member States. In these circumstances, it is necessary to fall back on general Treaty and case law principles that apply to determine the place of establishment.[49]

These rules determine jurisdiction only for the purposes of the Directive. They do not determine jurisdiction for other purposes. For example, under English law a company will normally be treated as resident for tax purposes in the country in which its central management and control is exercised. That may not be the same country as the

---

[47] ibid Art 2(3)(c).
[48] Directive (EC) 97/36, Recital (13).
[49] ibid Recital (11).

country in which its head office is located, where editorial or other decisions on the service are taken, or where the workforce is located. For these and other reasons, such as those mentioned above arising from Member States' freedom to apply more detailed or stricter rules to providers under their jurisdiction, providers may go forum shopping, seeking to establish themselves in the country in which the lightest regulation applies.

There are, however, limits to the extent that a provider may do so. Where a Member State has adopted more detailed or stricter rules of general public interest and assesses that a broadcaster under the jurisdiction of another Member State provides a television broadcast which is wholly or mostly directed towards its territory, that the results of an inter-state cooperation procedure designed to find a solution are not satisfactory, and that the broadcaster has established itself in that Member State in order to circumvent the stricter rules which would otherwise be applicable, it may adopt measures against the broadcaster concerned. The measures must be objectively necessary, applied in a non-discriminatory manner, and be proportionate to the objectives that they pursue.[50] Furthermore, the Member State may take the measures only if it has notified the European Commission and the other Member State of its intention to take the measures while substantiating the grounds on which it bases its assessment and the Commission has decided that the measures are compatible with Community law and the assessments are correctly founded.[51] The Commission has three months within which to decide.[52] These arrangements are designed to codify case law of the European Court of Justice (ECJ) and to provide an efficient procedure to deal with circumvention issues without calling into question the country of origin principle.[53] Examples of indicators of whether a particular service is wholly or mostly directed at a particular Member State are given in the Recitals to the 2007 Directive, including the origin of the television advertising and/or subscription revenues, the main language of the service, and the existence of programmes or advertisements targeted specifically at the public in that Member State.[54] These rules apply only to television broadcasting.

In the absence of specific rules dealing with circumvention by an on-demand provider, a Member State could in some cases (depending on what the more detailed or stricter rules might be) achieve a similar result in practice under the provisions for derogation from the country of origin principle. The provisions are different as between television broadcasting and on-demand services. Those applicable to on-demand services are similar to those applied in relation to services under the e-Commerce Directive, permitting Member States to take measures to derogate in respect of a given service for reasons of public policy, the protection of public health, public security, and the protection of consumers.[55] Before taking the measures, the Member

---

[50] AVMS Directive, Art 3(2) and (3).
[51] ibid Art 3(4).
[52] ibid Art 3(5).
[53] Directive (EC) 2007/65, Recital (32).
[54] ibid Recital (33).
[55] Directive (EC) 2000/31.

State must have attempted to get the other Member State to take measures and have notified it and the Commission of its intention to take them, save in urgent cases, and the Commission may ask the Member State to refrain or put an end to them.[56] Alternatively the Member State might seek to rely on the existing case law concerning circumvention of the television broadcasting rules which might be applied by analogy to the new rules for on-demand services.

To the extent that different Member States apply more detailed or stricter rules, it can be expected that there will be cases where service providers will seek to bring themselves under the jurisdiction of a more benign regime, restrained only by the rules relating to circumvention and derogation. In doing so, however, they will not have the benefit of any translation of these jurisdictional rules into English law. The draftsman of the 2003 Act simply refers to the Directive. Thus a TLCS is regulated by Ofcom only if it is provided by a person 'under the jurisdiction of the United Kingdom for the purposes of the Television Without Frontiers Directive'.[57]

8.3.7 The boundaries of television regulation

With the emerging consensus that 'broadcast' includes distribution of programme material over any network platform, there has grown a perception that there is a fundamental difference between conventional scheduled or linear services and new on-demand or non-linear services. 'Broadcast' has come to be associated with linear services and to be distinct from non-linear services. On this basis, the 2003 Act might be characterized in very broad terms as applying regulation to broadcast services and withdrawing from regulation of non-linear services. The trend in that direction was no doubt encouraged by the decision of the ECJ in the *Mediakabel* case in 2005. The main issue before the Court in that case was whether a near video on demand (NVOD) service provided by Mediakabel in Holland was a television broadcasting service within the meaning of the TWF Directive. Television broadcasting was defined in the Directive in terms of the transmission of programmes intended for reception by the public and excluding services providing information or messages on individual demand. The service was a pay-per-view film service accessible by subscribers using a PIN to select and view films which were transmitted at scheduled times. The Court did not accept that the NVOD service was an on-demand service. On the contrary, it said that PIN access was not relevant because the subscribing public all received the broadcast at the same time. It was a broadcast because it was intended for reception by the public, ie by an indeterminate number of potential viewers to whom the same images were transmitted simultaneously. It was this feature, the simultaneous transmission to an audience, that characterized television broadcasting—and it did not matter how the transmission was effected and therefore covered cable transmissions as well as those made over the air.[58]

---

[56] AVMS Directive, Art 2a (4)–(6).
[57] Communications Act 2003, s 211(2)(b).
[58] Case C-89/04 *Mediakabel BV v Commissariaat voor de Media*, n 9 above.

The decision was consistent with the approach taken in the Communications Act 2003 to the drawing of the boundary between relevant regulated television services and on-demand services.

The legislative formulation of the boundary is to be found in section 361 of the 2003 Act, which concerns the meaning of the phrase 'available for reception by members of the public'. That is a phrase which is used in the Act to describe an essential quality of the main regulated television services—television broadcasting services,[59] television licensable content services,[60] and digital television programme services,[61] which together encompass the mainstream services such as ITV and Channel 4, cable and satellite channels such as Sky, and DTT services such as those available on Freeview. It is widely used throughout the 2003 Act in substitution for the expression 'for general reception' in relation to programme services. Section 361 offers no definition as such of the phrase. Subsection (1) says, in effect, that it includes services available only to subscribers, so long as the facility to subscribe is offered or made available to members of the public. Subsections (2) to (5) say that certain services are not to be treated as so available (these are the on-demand services to which we will return). And subsection (7) says that the Secretary of State may by order modify any of the provisions of the section if it appears to him appropriate to do so having regard to any one or more of a number of matters. So the section offers a gloss about subscription services, excludes on-demand services, and confers powers on the Secretary of State to rewrite it.

The importance of the section lies in subsections (2) to (5) which are, in effect, a definition of on-demand services and set a boundary beyond which those services fall outside the regulatory net of the Act. In the laborious prose that is a feature of much recent legislation, subsection (2) says that a service is not to be treated as available for reception by members of the public if each of the following conditions is satisfied:

• first, the service must be confined to the provision of a facility for the making by users of the service of individual selections of the material to be received and for receiving whatever is selected;

• secondly, it must be only in response to a selection made by a user of the service that anything (whether encrypted or not) is transmitted by means of an ECN;

• thirdly, the individual selections do not include any that are limited to electing to be one of the recipients of material offered for reception on the basis that, in short, it has been selected by the service provider and will be distributed simultaneously, or virtually so, to every user who has elected to receive it—in other words, accessing scheduled material as in an NVOD service.

If those conditions are satisfied, the service is not available for reception by members of the public and therefore falls outside those principal categories of regulated service.

---

[59] Communications Act 2003, s 362(1)(b), definition of television broadcasting service.

[60] ibid s 232(2).

[61] Broadcasting Act 1996, s 1(4).

The conditions describe, in effect, an on-demand service where the material that is transmitted is selected by the user for viewing at a time chosen by the user. It is against these conditions that the facts relating to a particular service have to be tested to ascertain whether a licence from Ofcom is required. Thus an IPTV service in which a user selects and downloads a programme on demand would normally fall on one side of the line and an NVOD service, such as that in the *Mediakabel* case, would fall on the other side of the line (having failed to satisfy the third condition described above).

There are, in addition to the on-demand boundary, other boundaries. Excluded from the definition of a TLCS are:[62]

• a service which is part of another service provided for purposes that do not consist wholly or mainly in making television or radio programmes available for reception by members of the public (an exception whose boundaries are obscure but include internet-only services, which are discussed further below);

• a two-way service, ie a service provided by means of an ECN an essential feature of which is that it involves transmissions of visual images and/or sounds both by the service provider and by the user for reception by the service provider or other users;[63]

• a service on a single set of premises, where it is distributed by means of an ECN only to persons on those premises and the ECN is within the premises and is not connected to an ECN any part of which is outside the premises;

• a business service, where in short it is for reception only by those with a business interest in the programmes or who show them to those with such an interest or who are on the business premises of the recipient.

It is a feature of the first of these exclusions that an IPTV television channel or other television programme service that would otherwise be subject to content regulation as a TLCS, falls outside the regulatory net if or to the extent that it is distributed over the internet (or indeed over any other network, such as a mobile network, which does not consist wholly or mainly of programmes). This feature, which reflects the underlying policy with respect to not regulating content on the internet, is no longer regarded as consistent with the requirements of the TWF Directive as clarified by the recent amendments[64] and is to be abolished with effect from 19 December 2009 when section 233(3) of the Communications Act 2003 is to be repealed.

8.3.8 Restrictions on the holding of licences

Not everyone may provide a regulated service. The licensing regime is designed to exclude certain categories of person. Whether this makes sense in a world in which those excluded categories have unrestricted access to the internet to provide on-demand

---

[62] Communications Act 2003, s 233.
[63] ibid s 232(5).
[64] DCMS, 'Consultation on implementing the AVMS Directive' (July 2008) Part 2, para 4.

or other material outside the regulated net is a moot point, and raises questions about the sustainability of the restrictions. The main restrictions are as follows.

• Any holder of a licence must be a fit and proper person to hold it.[65]

• Local authorities and bodies whose objects are wholly or mainly of a political nature are disqualified from holding a licence.[66] Also disqualified are certain bodies and individuals linked with them. A person is also disqualified if, in Ofcom's opinion, they exert influence over the activities of that person, whether by the giving of financial assistance or otherwise, and that influence has led, is leading, or is likely to lead to results which are adverse to the public interest. The undue influence test is no doubt designed among other things to be a safeguard against the dissemination of propaganda for unacceptable political groups or countries. There is a special exception in relation to a service provided by a local authority exclusively for the purposes of the carrying out of its functions under section 142 of the Local Government Act 1972, which have to do with the provision by local authorities of information about their activities.[67]

• Bodies whose objects are wholly or mainly of a religious nature[68] are also disqualified, together with certain persons linked with them, such as a parent, a 5 per cent subsidiary, or an individual who is an officer of the body. But unlike the disqualifications based on political connections, which apply across the board, those based on religious connections apply only to certain specified licences, including those for Channels 3 and 5 and national sound broadcasting licences. Where such a person is not disqualified, however, that person is still not entitled to hold any other category of licence unless that person has applied for and Ofcom has made a determination in that person's case as respects a description of licences applicable to that licence and the determination remains in force. Ofcom may make such a determination if, and only if, it is satisfied that it is appropriate for that person to hold a licence of a particular description. Ofcom must publish guidance as to the principles that it will apply when determining what is appropriate, and has done so.[69]

• Advertising agencies are disqualified (and for this purpose an advertising agent is someone who carries on a business involving the selection and purchase of advertising time or space for persons wishing to advertise),[70] together with certain bodies and individuals linked with them.

• There are some disqualifications of broadcasting bodies and their subsidiaries. The BBC and Sianel Pedwar Cymru are disqualified persons generally. Companies in which they, Channel 4, and companies controlled by them have any participation are

---

[65] Broadcasting Act 1990, s 3.
[66] ibid sch 2, Part II, para 1(1)(c) and (d).
[67] ibid para (1A).
[68] ibid para 2(1)(a).
[69] Communications Act 2003, Sch 14, part 4; the published guidance is available at <http://www.ofcom.org.uk/tv/ifi/tvlicensing/guidance_notes_and_apps/guide_rel_bod>.
[70] Broadcasting Act 1990, s 202(7).

disqualified in relation to Channel 3 and Channel Five licences. BBC companies are disqualified in relation to national, local, and restricted radio services.

• There are also some media ownership rules restricting cross-interests between newspapers and Channel 3 services and restricting the numbers of radio muliplex and local sound broadcasting licences that may be held by a person and the number of local digital sound programme services that may be provided.[71]

These carefully crafted restrictions do not apply to services outside the regulatory net. They can readily be circumvented by providing a service exclusively on an on-demand basis. There is no indication from government that it intends to extend the restrictions to those services that will fall into the net when the AVMS Directive is implemented.

8.3.9 The right to call for a licence

In relation to certain categories of licence, Ofcom must grant the licence if certain conditions are fulfilled. Where an application for a licence is made in accordance with the relevant requirements, Ofcom may refuse the application only if:

• the applicant is not a fit and proper person to hold the licence;

• the applicant is a disqualified person in relation to the licence or would not comply with the relevant media ownership rules; or

• Ofcom is satisfied that if the application were to be granted, the provision of the service would be likely to involve contraventions of Ofcom's codes of standards for the content of programmes or its code of practice in relation to unjust or unfair treatment or interference with privacy.[72]

A similar pattern is followed in relation to digital programme services,[73] digital additional services,[74] and their DTT radio equivalents, [75] although without the third of the above items.

The grant of a licence does not confer any right of access to any communications network or spectrum. The holder of a licence must make its own arrangements in this respect and, if necessary, observe any application conditions and secure any necessary spectrum licence to do so (or contract with another person who is appropriately authorized). What a licence under the Broadcasting Acts confers is a right to 'provide' a service within the special meaning explained above. It is for the holder of the licence to secure the means of making the service available to the public, whether by broadcasting (ie transmitting) it from a satellite or distributing it by some other means involving an ECN.[76]

---

[71] Communications Act 2003, Sch 14. See further Ch 2 above.
[72] ibid s 235(3).
[73] Broadcasting Act 1996, s 18(4).
[74] ibid s 25(4).
[75] ibid ss 60(6) and 64(4).
[76] See the Communications Act 2003, s 232(1) for a convenient formulation of this proposition.

8.3.10 The nature and function of a licence

General provisions about licences granted under the Broadcasting Acts are set out in section 3 of the 1990 Act in relation to television programme services (other than digital) and section 3 of the 1996 Act in relation to multiplex and digital programme services. The main features of any such licence are that it must be in writing, that its duration is determined by the provisions of the relevant Part of the relevant Act, and that it is granted for the provision of such a service or description of service as is specified in the licence. Ofcom may vary its duration with the licence-holder's consent. Any other variation requires that the licence-holder be given a reasonable opportunity of making representations to Ofcom about it. A licence is not transferable without the previous consent in writing of Ofcom.

Licences are the means by which the statutory requirements for the regulation of television and radio are passed on to service providers. Few requirements apply to service providers direct. The scheme of the legislation is to give statutory functions, powers, and duties to Ofcom and it is for Ofcom to give effect to those requirements by including appropriate conditions in the licences that it grants and by doing all that it can to ensure that licences comply with them.[77]

In general, a licensee is answerable to Ofcom for any failure to comply with a licence condition. Unlike conditions applicable to providers of electronic communications networks and services under Part 2 of the 2003 Act, a breach of a licence condition is not actionable by any other person.[78]

Although licensees must look to the conditions of their licences to ascertain their regulatory obligations rather than to the legislation, departures by Ofcom from the requirements of the legislation are likely to be amenable to review by the courts through an application for judicial review. A licensee could expect to be able to challenge Ofcom's decisions if it acted outside the scope of its statutory powers, if the decision was made using an unfair procedure, if the decision was beyond the bounds of reasonableness, or was otherwise unlawful.

8.4 REGULATION OF NETWORKS AND NETWORK SERVICES

8.4.1 Introduction

Whatever meaning is attributed to the broadcasting of programmes, it involves distribution or delivery by means of electronic transmission. The networks over which transmissions pass, and the services provided by those who convey or route them over those networks, are regulated under a separate regulatory framework set out in Part 2

---

[77] ibid s 263.
[78] See ibid s 104.

of the Communications Act 2003. Part 2 also deals with some aspects of radio frequency spectrum management. In case there should be any doubt, the Broadcasting Acts expressly provide that the holding of a licence under those Acts does not relieve the holder of any obligation to comply with requirements imposed by or under the relevant Chapter of Part 2 of the 2003 Act or any liability in respect of a failure to hold a licence under section 8 of the Wireless Telegraphy Act 2006.

The regulatory framework for provision of networks and network services is best understood by reference to the package of Directives that were adopted in 2002 for the regulation of the telecommunications sector. These were the so-called Framework, Access and Authorisation Directives and the Directive on privacy and electronic communications.[79] They were supplemented by a Commission Directive on competition in the markets for electronic communications networks and services[80] and a Decision of the European Parliament and Council on a regulatory framework for radio spectrum policy in the European Community.[81] They were designed to respond to the convergence of the telecommunications, media, and information technology sectors by covering all transmission networks and services by a single regulatory framework.[82] The Framework Directive establishes a harmonized framework for the regulation of electronic communications services (ECSs), electronic communications networks (ECNs), associated facilities, and associated services but without prejudice to measures taken at Community level or national level, in compliance with Community law, to pursue general interest objectives, in particular relating to content regulation and audiovisual policy.[83] The new regulatory framework does not therefore extend to regulation of the content of services delivered over ECNs using ECSs, it being considered necessary to separate the regulation of transmission from the regulation of content.[84]

Regulating transmission separately from the regulation of content and applying common rules to all transmission networks and network services represents a decisive shift away from the earlier regime of telecommunications regulation, which did not (at least at the European level) include broadcasting networks.[85] Under the new regulatory framework, broadcast transmission networks and services are (subject to one caveat)[86]

---

[79] Respectively Directive (EC) 2002/21 of 7 March 2002 on a common regulatory framework for electronic communications networks and services [2002] OJ L108/33; Directive (EC) 2002/19 of 7 March 2002 on access to, and interconnection of, electronic communications networks and associated facilities [2002] OJ L108/7; Directive (EC) 2002/20 of 7 March 2002 on the authorisation of electronic communications networks and services [2002] OJ L108/21; and Directive (EC) 2002/22 of 7 March 2002 on universal service and users' rights relating to electronic communications networks and services [2002] OJ L108/51.

[80] Directive (EC) 2002/77.

[81] Decision No 676/2002/EC.

[82] Framework Directive, Recital (5).

[83] ibid Art 1.

[84] ibid Recital (5).

[85] See the definition of 'telecommunications services' in Council Directive (EEC) 90/338 which expressly excludes 'radio-broadcasting and television'.

[86] The caveat is discussed below in relation to spectrum licensing and Directive (EC) 2002/20, Art 5(2) (the Authorisation Directive).

regulated in the same way as any other networks and network services. The direct practical effects of this change are limited in the UK, where national law had effectively anticipated it by treating the transmission companies as subject to licensing under the Telecommunications Act 1984 (now repealed), but it may have had some indirect effects in bolstering the trend towards separating the concept of broadcasting from its roots in the transmission technology.

The main features of the new regulatory framework established by the Directives were implemented in the UK by Part 2 of the Communications Act 2003. Those who find it easier to follow the Directives than its UK statutory implementation will find the official Explanatory Notes helpful, especially as they contain a table identifying which sections of the Act implement which Articles of the Framework, Authorisation, Access, and Universal Service Directives and transposition tables identifying how the requirements of each of those Directives has been dealt with in the Act.[87]

8.4.2 Abolition of licensing

Licensing procedures for telecommunications operations were meant to have been harmonized and simplified by the Licensing Directive[88] but it did not work out that way and there was a perceived need for a more harmonized and less onerous market access regulation.[89] The Authorisation Directive therefore obliges Member States to guarantee the freedom to provide ECNs and ECSs subject to a 'general authorisation' the definition of which in effect requires that sector-specific obligations be imposed on the providers of all or specific types of ECNs or ECSs, and to make commencement of activities subject to a notification procedure and not subject to any decision or administrative act.[90] These arrangements are without prejudice to the separate imposition of specific regulatory obligations, such as those imposed on operators with significant market power, and the grant of individual rights of use of radio frequencies and numbers.[91] In other words, the Directive, in effect, abolishes licensing in the sector except for spectrum and numbers, which makes sense as they are a scarce resource, and requires a general authorization subject only to certain conditions which are set out in an Annex to the Directive (including payment of administrative charges).

These arrangements have been carried into effect by the abolition of the old telecommunications licensing regime under the Telecommunications Act 1984 and its replacement by the statutory regime under Part 2 of the Communications Act 2003,

---

[87] The Explanatory Notes can be accessed at <http://www.opsi.gov.uk/acts/acts2003/en/ukpgaen_20030021_en.pdf>.

[88] Directive (EC) 97/13 of 10 April 1997 on a common framework for general authorisations and individual licences in the field of telecommunications services [1997] OJ L117.

[89] Authorisation Directive, Recital (1).

[90] ibid Art 3. Art 3(1) does, however, permit Member States where necessary to prevent a foreign national from providing ECNs and ECSs for reasons based on public policy, public security, or public health.

[91] ibid Art 3(2).

which confers power on Ofcom to set conditions, including general conditions, but only within the limits set by the Directive.[92] The Act provides for a notification procedure, although only in relation to designated services, and in practice Ofcom has chosen to make no designation. The result in the UK is that a new entrant need observe no formalities under the Act before commencing operations in the UK, save in respect of spectrum and numbering.[93] Spectrum licensing is dealt with separately under the Wireless Telegraphy Act 2006.

It is perhaps important to appreciate that conditions set under the general authorization could have been included in a licence. The difference is not in the substance of the regulatory conditions but in the procedure. Removing the requirement of a prior licence as a condition of starting operations in a Member State avoids the inconvenience of a multinational operator having to secure as many licences as there are Member States and the creation of barriers to entry in some states by the imposition of prior conditions. But it is perhaps a model that might be used in other sectors, such as broadcasting, in place of the prohibition/licensing model that is currently in use, at least for the vast majority of licensees who currently have to seek and hold licences setting identical conditions. Indeed the government at the time of writing proposes that on-demand programme services that are to be regulated pursuant to the AVMS Directive should be subject to a version of this model whereby the requirements of the Directive would be imposed on service providers as statutory duties which would be enforceable by Ofcom.

8.5 REGULATION OF SPECTRUM USE

8.5.1 Introduction

The broad framework for the regulation of access to and use of the radio frequency spectrum is set out in the Wireless Telegraphy Act 2006. Like the Broadcasting Act 1990, there is a general prohibition and a licensing scheme. Section 8 of the Act makes it unlawful to establish, install, or use wireless telegraphy stations or apparatus except under and in accordance with a wireless telegraphy licence granted under that section by Ofcom. This does not, however, apply in relation to the use of a television receiver for receiving a television programme or to the installation of a television receiver solely for that purpose. And Ofcom may exempt the establishment, installation, or use of stations or apparatus of such kinds as it may specify. Ofcom may also make a grant of what is called recognized spectrum access in respect of use of anything for wireless telegraphy that is specified in the grant. In effect, these provisions create or facilitate the creation of four mutually exclusive regimes—regimes for exemption, television licensing, wireless telegraphy licensing, and recognized spectrum access.

---

[92] Communications Act 2003, s 45.
[93] ibid s 33.

8.5.2 The exemption regime

The power to exempt the establishment, installation, or use of stations and apparatus is exercisable by regulations. The exemption is subject to such terms, provisions, or limitations as Ofcom may specify in the regulations. So Ofcom has a wide power to confer licence-exempt status on stations and apparatus. In some cases, thanks to Article 5(1) of the Authorisation Directive, Ofcom is bound to exercise that power. In particular, if Ofcom is satisfied that the use of stations or apparatus of a particular description is not likely to involve undue interference with wireless telegraphy, it must make regulations exempting the establishment, installation, and use of a station or apparatus of that description.[94]

A wide range of items, particular passive receivers, and low power transmitters, are exempt pursuant to regulations made under this power.

8.5.3 The television licensing regime

The regime for television licensing is not in the 2006 Act. It is in Part 4 of the Communications Act 2003, which makes it an offence to install or use a television receiver without a licence under that Part of that Act (known as a TV licence), subject to such exemptions as the Secretary of State may make by regulations. The Act confers powers on the BBC to issue TV licences, a statutory arrangement reflecting the fact that the BBC is in effect funded out of the proceeds of the grant of TV licences. 'Television receiver' means apparatus installed or used for the purpose of receiving any television programme service[95] which (almost certainly)[96] means only the main regulated television services.[97] Consequently the installation or use of apparatus to receive only on-demand services would not require a TV licence.

8.5.4 The wireless telegraphy licensing regime

Apart from cases within the exemption or television licensing regimes, access to and use of the radio frequency spectrum is in effect prohibited without a wireless telegraphy licence granted under section 8 of the Wireless Telegraphy Act 2006 by Ofcom. Section 9 provides that such a licence may be granted subject to such terms, provisions, and limitations as Ofcom thinks fit, a formulation inherited from earlier Acts which conferred a very wide discretion on the grantor. The exercise of that discretion is now limited by Article 6 of the Authorisation Directive and section 9(7) of the 2006 Act, which limits Ofcom to imposing terms, provisions, or limitations that it is satisfied are objectively justifiable, non-discriminatory, proportionate, and transparent.

---

[94] Wireless Telegraphy Act 2006, s 8(4).
[95] Communications (Television Licensing) Regulations 2004, SI 2004/692, reg 9.
[96] The definition of this expression strictly speaking applies only to Part 3 of the 2003 Act whilst the TV licence regime is in Part 4.
[97] Communications Act 2003, s 362(1).

8.5.5 'Recognised spectrum access' (RSA)

A novelty of the Communications Act 2003 was the creation of a new right called 'recognised spectrum access'. By section 159 of the Act, Ofcom was given power in certain circumstances to make a grant of recognized spectrum access to a person in respect of any use by that person of anything for wireless telegraphy that is specified in the grant. The effect of the grant is to impose on Ofcom a duty to take into account the existence of the grant and the restrictions and conditions subject to which the grant has effect to the same extent as it would take into account a wireless telegraphy licence with terms, provisions, or limitations making equivalent provision.[98]

Some explanation is necessary to understand what this means. The licensing regime seeks to limit harmful interference by controlling emissions through the grant of wireless telegraphy licences. Where, however, the emissions cannot be licensed, because, for example, they emanate from beyond the jurisdiction, Ofcom may have no means of taking account of them to seek to protect their reception in the UK from harmful interference. An example is radio astronomy, in relation to which Ofcom has made regulations which enable applications to be made to protect reception by radio telescopes.[99] Another example is satellite broadcasting, although Ofcom has made no such regulations. Where, for example, satellite broadcasts are made on frequencies assigned by another country for broadcast transmissions that are capable of reception in the UK, Ofcom would not necessarily be under any duty with respect to the prevention of harmful interference with respect to the reception of the broadcasts. An example is transmissions intended for reception by a UK audience from a Luxembourg satellite on a frequency allocated within the UK to other purposes, such as fixed terrestrial telecommunications links. Any satellite receiver in the path of the terrestrial links would be likely to suffer harmful interference. To avoid this, it could be open to those concerned with the broadcasts to apply for a grant of recognized spectrum access in respect of that frequency, the practical result of which ought to be that reception would enjoy a measure of protection from harmful interference. Some years ago Ofcom indicated that, in the absence of any means of formally recognizing such use for spectrum planning purposes or indeed of applying market mechanisms to encourage efficient use, it intended to consider and consult on the introduction of RSA for satellite services.[100] No public consultation has yet emerged.

8.5.6 Spectrum management

Access to and use of the radio frequency spectrum is regulated internationally as a limited natural resource to be used efficiently and economically and on the basis that

---

[98] Communications Act 2003, s 160(2).
[99] Wireless Telegraphy (Recognised Spectrum Access) Regulations 2007, SI 2007/393.
[100] 'Recognised Spectrum Access as applied to Radio Astronomy,' Ofcom consultation document (April 2005) para 3.5.

all stations must be established and operated in such a manner as not to cause harmful interference to services or communications operating in accordance with the Radio Regulations of the International Telecommunication Union.[101] In the UK, this broad requirement was traditionally implemented by the government or its agencies managing access to and use of the spectrum through a licensing system by which users were subject to detailed control through the wireless telegraphy licensing system, under which the establishment, operation, or use of stations and apparatus was tightly controlled. In recent years, this approach has been characterized as a command and control system of such rigidity that comparisons were made with Soviet administration. Users paid fees for their licences that were designed to cover the cost of administering the system.

In the 1990s, proposals were put forward by the Radiocommunications Agency, an executive agency of the government, to introduce spectrum pricing as an aid to effective spectrum management and in particular to promote spectrum efficiency (as well as to promote and accelerate the transition from analogue to digital broadcasting services).[102] The proposals were intended as a step towards a more effective market-based form of spectrum management. These proposals were implemented in the Wireless Telegraphy Act 1998, a short measure (of 10 sections) which swept away the link between the licence fee and administrative costs. Instead, in setting licence fees, there was to be a duty to have regard to supply and demand as well as spectrum efficiency and the like. The Act also established a novel alternative framework for the allocation of spectrum by auction, which notoriously led to the extraordinary auction of 3G mobile spectrum in 2000 where five bidders secured licences for a total of £22.4 billion. It marked the end of an era in which regulation, rather than price, was the *quid pro quo* for spectrum access. There followed, in March 2002, an influential review of radio spectrum management by Professor Martin Cave, an economist, advocating the use of market mechanisms in spectrum management.[103] The recommendations of the review were largely accepted by government. At the same time, the 2002 package of Directives assimilated spectrum management to the overarching policy objectives and regulatory principles of the new European regulatory framework for electronic communications, including permitting spectrum trading and pricing.[104] The Communications Act 2003 contained provisions carrying forward the use of spectrum pricing and conferring on Ofcom powers by regulation to authorize transfers of the rights and obligations arising by virtue of a wireless telegraphy licence or a grant of RSA—in other words, to establish a system of spectrum trading.[105] This set the scene for Ofcom to establish a new strategy for spectrum management based on three principles— spectrum pricing, spectrum trading, and liberalization—liberalization meaning the

---

[101] International Telecommunication Convention, Nairobi 1982, Arts 33(1) and 35(1).
[102] *Spectrum Management: into the 21st Century* (Cm 3252, 1996).
[103] DTI, 'Review of Radio Spectrum Management' (March 2002).
[104] Framework Directive, Art 9 and Authorisation Directive, Art 13.
[105] Communications Act 2003, s 168.

removal of the restrictions on use of particular frequency bands for particular purposes so long as harmful interference was not thereby caused or increased.

The new market-based approach to spectrum management has its limits at the international, European, and national levels, however, particularly in relation to broadcasting.

For example, an international agreement has been made within the framework of the Radio Regulations for a plan for the transition from analogue to digital broadcasting in Europe and some other regions.[106] This so-called Geneva 2006 Agreement contains a plan for the assignment of frequencies in the UHF bands hitherto occupied by analogue television services, under which the UK may operate up to eight digital multiplexes at particular locations and power levels. At the national level, the government has decided that, at each UK location, six multiplexes will be reserved for the existing DTT operations (three for public service broadcasters, three for commercial), leaving the other two for other purposes (known as the digital dividend). The plan in the Geneva 2006 Agreement was devised on the assumption that all of the multiplexes would be used for digital broadcasts but so long as transmissions stay within the interference parameters of the plan they may be used nationally for other purposes, such as mobile.[107]

At the European level, where the allocation and assignment of frequencies are meant to be based on objective, transparent, non-discriminatory, and proportionate criteria,[108] and the scope for imposing conditions or obligations on users is limited to those set out in the Directive,[109] there is an exception for broadcasting. The exception arises under the second paragraph of Article 5(2) of the Authorisation Directive, which provides that the procedures for the grant of rights of use are to be without prejudice to specific criteria and procedures adopted by Member States to grant use of radio frequencies to providers of radio or television broadcast content services with a view to pursuing general interest objectives in conformity with Community law. Some commentators have suggested that this is perhaps not intended, as it is inconsistent with the general approach in the Framework Directive to the separation of the regulation of transmission from the regulation of content, providing a cultural exception which blemishes the intellectual purity of the new framework.[110] It seems, however, to have been deliberate, the European Commission's current proposals for amendment being designed to strengthen and clarify the exception in favour of broadcasters to the extent even of an express exception from the requirement of openness where it can be shown to be essential to meet a particular obligation defined in advance by the Member State

---

[106] Regional Agreement GE06 governing the use of frequencies by the broadcasting service and other primary terrestrial services in the frequency bands 174–230 MHz and 470–862 MHz contained in the Final Acts of the Regional Radio Conference, Geneva, 2006.

[107] For a more detailed summary, see Ofcom's consultation document, 'Digital Dividend Review', 19 December 2006, paras 3.8–3.17.

[108] Framework Directive, Art 9.

[109] ibid Art 6.

[110] W Maxwell (ed), *Electronic Communications: the New EU Framework* (Oceana Publications, 2002) booklet 1.2, para 5.2.1.1.

which is necessary to achieve a general interest objective in conformity with Community law.[111] Furthermore, the proposals would amend Article 5 so that individual licensing would be permitted where it is justified in order either to avoid a serious risk of harmful interference (as before) or to fulfil other objectives of general interest (which is new, although perhaps implicit).

At the national level, Ofcom's independence of action and its aspirations to a market-based approach to spectrum management are circumscribed by section 5 of the Wireless Telegraphy Act 2006 which reserves to the Secretary of State powers by order to give general or specific directions to Ofcom about the carrying out of its functions, including directions to secure that specified frequencies should be kept available for specified uses or users. The government therefore retains powers of command and control and is in a position to determine, as it has done, the uses to which the eight internationally agreed multiplexes are to be put. In much the same way, the Secretary of State has wide powers to modify the licensing provisions of the 1996 Act in relation to DTT licensing, an illustration of which is the order under which one of the DTT multiplexes, known as Multiplex B, is to be cleared of its existing services and upgraded to the more efficient 64-QAM, MPEG4, and DVB-T2 technologies and to be allocated partly to a BBC company and partly to bidders in a comparative selection process or beauty contest in pursuit of government policy objectives.[112]

The practical upshot is that, at least in relation to television broadcasting, the government remains in control of the allocation of spectrum notwithstanding the trend towards market-based mechanisms in spectrum management.

8.5.7 Spectrum rights

It has been a feature of some recent consultations about spectrum trading and liberalization that rights under a wireless telegraphy licence are commonly referred to as if they were in the nature of property. Whilst this may be a convenient shorthand to assist debate it can also be misleading, especially if it is supposed that a user suffering interference would be entitled to take private legal action in the civil courts for infringement of his supposed right. The existence of any such right is at best doubtful.[113] Section 8 of the Wireless Telegraphy Act 2006 provides that use of stations and apparatus otherwise than under and in accordance with a licence is unlawful, and section 35(1) makes it an offence. By section 108(2), compliance with section 8 is enforceable in civil proceedings by the Crown or by Ofcom for an injunction or any other appropriate relief. As a general rule, a statute may be enforced only by means of the enforcement mechanisms set out in it but there are exceptions, one of which is to the effect that a statute containing only criminal enforcement provisions for the purpose of protecting

---

[111] European Commission proposals for the review of the telecoms regulatory framework 13 November 2007, COM (2007) 697 final.
[112] The Television Multiplex Services (Reservation of Digital Capacity) Order 2008 (SI 2008/1420).
[113] See <http://www.ofcom.org.uk/consult/condocs/sfr/responses/ballard>.

a particular class of persons may be enforced in civil proceedings by members of that class who suffer loss arising from a contravention of the statute.[114] If spectrum users could be said to be a particular class within the scope of the exception, then it would be open to a spectrum user to take civil proceedings against an interferer who was committing an offence under the Act. There may also be other ways in which to frame the argument. Support for the proposition that a civil right arises in these circumstances comes from section 108(1) of the 2006 Act, which somewhat enigmatically provides that the fact that the doing of a thing is an offence does not limit a person's right to bring civil proceedings in respect of the doing or the apprehended doing of that thing. In other words, if there is a civil right, it is not over-ridden by the criminal enforcement provisions in that section, but the question remains whether there is a civil right in the first place.

It is remarkable that there should be doubt about this. It is, of course, widely understood that one of the functions of a national regulatory authority is to protect authorized stations from harmful interference, having regard to the provisions of the International Telecommunication Convention and the Radio Regulations made under it, but the extent to which the user is entitled to require protection is by no means clear. It is not even clear whether the holder of a licence is entitled to protection from Ofcom granting a further licence to another person in relation to the same frequency in circumstances in which mutual interference may arise. It is submitted, however, that, in at least some cases, to do so would be inconsistent with the Convention which, as noted above, requires that all stations must be established and operated in such a manner as not to cause harmful interference to services or communications operating in accordance with the Radio Regulations.

8.5.8 The scope of a wireless telegraphy licence

The scope of the rights conferred by a wireless telegraphy licence were recently the subject of litigation before the Competition Appeal Tribunal in the *Floe Telecom* case.[115] The case was decided under the earlier Wireless Telegraphy Act 1949 but nothing turns on this. A question arose as to the meaning and effect of a wireless telegraphy licence granted under the 1949 Act to Vodafone, a mobile network operator (MNO). The licence authorized the MNO to establish, install, and use the radio transmitting and receiving stations and/or radio apparatus described in a schedule to the licence. The only relevant apparatus described in the schedule was base transceiver stations forming part of a network in which approved users' stations communicate by radio with the MNO's equipment to provide a telecommunications service for customers. The question that arose was whether the licence meant what it said and extended only to the defined radio equipment, ie the base transceiver stations, or whether it extended

---

[114] *Lonrho Ltd v Shell Petroleum Co Ltd (No 2)* [1981] 2 All ER 456.
[115] *Floe Telecom v Ofcom* [2006] CAT 17.

to other equipment, specifically GSM gateway equipment, which met relevant European technical standards.[116] The tribunal rejected such a literal interpretation. It held that the licence (and related exemption regulations) had to be construed against the relevant European legislative background and in conformity with Community law, if possible. The European legislative background included Directive (EC) 1999/5 on radio equipment and telecommunication terminal equipment and the mutual recognition of their conformity (the RTTE Directive). Among other things, the Directive requires Member States to allow radio equipment to be put into service if it complies with certain technical standards subject only to restrictions related to the effective and appropriate use of the radio spectrum, avoidance of harmful interference, or matters relating to public health which, being restrictions on free movement, had to be construed strictly.[117] The evidence was that the equipment was compatible with the relevant standards and that no relevant restriction was justified. It followed that the licence could not be construed so as to restrict the putting into service of compatible equipment.

The consequence of this decision, if it had been followed by the higher courts, would have been that a wireless telegraphy licence would have had to be construed against the background and as an integral part of the European legislation, including in particular the RTTE Directive, and would have severely limited the extent to which Ofcom could restrict a grant of rights by reference to descriptions of equipment. In effect, the rights granted by such a licence would have been wider than appeared on its face. The decision was, however, overturned by the Court of Appeal, which rejected the Tribunal's construction of the licence, holding that the wording of the licence should be given its ordinary and natural meaning and that, as a bilateral transaction between the parties, the licence did not need to be given any enlarged meaning by reason of the background Directives.[118]

The tribunal considered but did not decide whether or not the licence was granted on an exclusive basis. The evidence was that the Radiocommunications Agency, Ofcom's predecessor, regarded Vodafone and the other MNOs as having been licensed on an exclusive basis, but Ofcom submitted that there was nothing in the licence itself which would suggest that it was exclusive. It had not in fact granted any other licence to use the same frequencies but submitted that there was nothing to prevent it from doing so and it was perfectly possible under section 1 of the 1949 Act to issue more than one licence covering use of the same frequencies.[119]

---

[116] A GSM gateway is apparatus designed to enable communications from a private fixed network, by the use of SIM cards, to be made to a mobile network as if they were calls from a mobile device on the same mobile network, thereby attracting the lower on-net tariff applicable to mobile to mobile calls instead of the higher fixed to mobile tariff.

[117] RTTE Directive, Art 7.

[118] *Office of Communications and T-Mobile (UK) Ltd v Floe Telecom Ltd (in liquidation)* [2009] EWCA Civ 47.

[119] *Floe Telecom* (n 115 above) judgment, para 78.

It is suggested that it would not now be open to Ofcom to grant an exclusive licence in relation to any frequency. Section 8(4) of the 2006 Act obliges Ofcom by regulations to exempt stations and apparatus whose use is not likely to involve undue interference with wireless telegraphy and an exclusive grant would be inconsistent with that section. On the other hand, the holder of the licence would (at least in principle) not be prejudiced because there should be no undue interference. Equally it would not be open to Ofcom to grant another licence to use the same frequency if that use were likely to involve undue interference because that would be inconsistent with the requirement of the Convention to avoid harmful interference.

8.6 THE CHANGING NATURE OF BROADCASTING

8.6.1 The Audiovisual Media Services Directive

The AVMS Directive applies, obviously enough, to audiovisual media services. What such a service consists of is set out in a definition in Article 1. Apart from an audiovisual commercial communication, which is itself defined in terms of images accompanying a programme, an audiovisual media service is defined in terms of a one-to-many commercial service. It must fall within Articles 49 and 50 of the EC Treaty as a service normally provided for remuneration and its principal purpose must be the provision of programmes to the general public in order to inform, entertain, or educate. It is a definition which reflects the nature and use of conventional networks and is not apt to assimilate new forms of content and its dissemination on the internet. That may, of course, be deliberate but in considering the changing nature of broadcasting in its widest sense it is helpful to bear in mind that the AVMS Directive, for all that it extends regulation to on-demand content, does so only in relation to the standard model of television distribution, which is a one-way commercial service delivered to an audience.

Even within the area that it carves out for regulation, the Directive is conventional in the distinction that it draws between television broadcasting and on-demand services, or between linear and non-linear services. What it says in the definition is that, apart from an audiovisual commercial communication, an audiovisual media service is either a television broadcast (defined in terms of simultaneous viewing on the basis of a programme schedule) or an on-demand audiovisual media service (defined in terms of the viewer selecting the time of viewing on the basis of a catalogue). This distinction has hitherto been consistent with the devices commonly used to access programming—a television receiver on the one hand and a PC on the other. As these devices converge, and as the capacity of networks to distribute and deliver data increases, it is likely that the distinction will be increasingly descriptive of the means by which viewers find the programmes rather than the services themselves. This is because, with the widespread uptake of broadband access and reception devices able to store, process, and transfer large data files, the viewing of programmes is increasingly under the control of the viewer irrespective of whether the programmes are delivered in a linear schedule or accessed on demand from a catalogue. The instrument that enables the viewer to choose is a search engine, ie a device or process by which a programme can be found. Seen in these generic terms, even a programme schedule is a search engine—less advanced perhaps than Google, but well understood and effective. But it is not a means to characterize the underlying service itself, which is the provision of programmes and which is the same whatever the engine that is used to find them. On that view, the distinction between linear and non-linear services is unlikely to be sustainable, since it relates to the means of access and not to the services themselves.

Further, the Directive suggests that what is in scope should change over time. Whether or not the distinction between linear and non-linear is useful, a service is in scope only if its principal purpose is the provision of programmes, ie a set of moving images with or without sound constituting an individual item within a schedule or catalogue and whose form and content is comparable to the form and content of television broadcasting.[120] The comparability with television broadcasting is emphasized by Recital (17) which states that it is characteristic of on-demand audiovisual media services that they are 'television-like', ie they compete for the same audience as television broadcasts, and the nature and the means of access to the service would lead the user reasonably to expect regulatory protection within the scope of the Directive. It goes on to say that, in the light of this and to prevent disparities as regards free movement and competition, the notion of 'programme' should be interpreted in a dynamic way taking into account developments in television broadcasting. So what is television-like will likely change over time depending on competition conditions and user expectation arising from the nature,[121] and the means, of access to the service.

A model for how this might work from a legislative point of view already appears in the Communications Act 2003. The current boundary between regulated programme services and unregulated on-demand services appears in section 361, subsection (7) of which confers power on the Secretary of State by order to redraw the boundary if it appears to him appropriate to do so having regard, among other things, to the protection which, taking account of the means by which the programmes and services are received or may be accessed, is expected by members of the public as respects the content of the programmes. Any such order would require a positive vote from both Houses of Parliament, which restrains over-enthusiastic use of this order-making power,[122] but the trend towards governments adopting an active approach to redefining the boundaries is unmistakable. Such a development could, in practice, discourage investment because of the high degree of regulatory uncertainly that it would introduce.

---

[120] See the definition of 'programme' in the AVMS Directive, Art 1.

[121] Strictly speaking, the grammar of Recital (17) indicates that 'nature' refers to the means of access and not to the service itself. This does not make sense because the use of the word adds nothing to 'the means of access'. It is probably a mistake.

[122] Communications Act 2003, s 361(8).

8.6.2 Beyond the AVMS Directive

Beyond the boundary of matters within the scope of the Directive, wherever it may be set, there lie such activities as social networking, the exchange of user-generated content, video games, virtual worlds, and other internet applications which have some but not all of the characteristics of an audiovisual media service. The Directive does not require them to be regulated. It is open to Member States to impose regulation on providers in their territory. The UK Government has made it clear that it does not intend to do so, at least in response to the Directive. Other Member States may, however, do so. Where those activities amount to information services within the e-Commerce Directive, Member States which impose regulation will be obliged, unless they derogate, to apply the country of origin principle to services provided from other Member States by not restricting their freedom to provide information society services. What amounts to an information society service will therefore be of some importance. Like an audiovisual media service, this too is defined in terms of a service normally provided for remuneration and consequently some internet activities will be outside the scope of that Directive as well.[123]

It may be that the range of activities on the internet is such that a new approach to regulation is needed. Certainly in the UK, concern about making the internet and video games safer for children has led to the government accepting a set of recommendations for regulation which owe little or nothing to conventional regulatory models. They include a recommendation that there should be a self-regulatory system for protecting children from potentially harmful or inappropriate material. This is a step away from the regulatory model that seeks to impose requirements on service providers to protect consumers or other users. It would include opportunities for service providers to take credit for signing up to self-regulatory standards but it would not be limited to this, extending, for example, to a voluntary code of practice on the moderation of user-generated content and the rollout of approved parental control software.[124]

Another approach towards establishing a self-regulatory scheme has been taken by the Broadband Stakeholders Group, an industry body, which in February 2008 launched a code of good practice principles.[125] It is limited to commercially produced or acquired content and therefore does not extend to such things as user-generated content. Its main approach is to encourage members of the scheme to enable users to manage potentially harmful or offensive content by ensuring that they have the information available to make an informed choice about the content that they watch or listen to. This may include use of schemes for classifying material, such as the BBFC scheme for films, the IMCB scheme for mobile content, and the PEGI scheme for electronic games, as well as codes such as Ofcom's Broadcasting Code and the ATVOD Code of Practice.

---

[123] Directive (EC) 2000/31. The definition of information society service appears in Directive (EC) 98/34 as amended by Directive (EC) 98/48.

[124] The Byron Review Action Plan, Ch 2.

[125] Good Practice Principles in Audiovisual Content Information.

To what extent is it helpful to treat any of these activities as broadcasting, within the most flexible meaning of that word? It is not obvious that to limit broadcasting to conventional linear programming in the manner adopted by the *Mediakabel* case and the AVMS Directive will give it a future as a useful descriptive term unless perhaps it is assimilated to a new understanding of what it means, and reflects an absolute technological neutrality. Material which is available to the public by electronic transmission, whatever the platform and however it is accessed, would be within the old metaphor of agricultural dissemination, would encompass most of the activities with which regulation might be concerned, and, for want of a better generic term, might conveniently be regarded as broadcast.

9

REGULATION AND EXTRA-LEGAL REGULATION OF THE MEDIA SECTOR

Lorna Woods

9.1 INTRODUCTION

It is commonly suggested that the 'old' system of media regulation is inadequate or inappropriate, especially given the 'needs' of the new media and the 'necessity' to ensure that ever more channels of communication are filled with content,[1] whatever that content's worth. To encourage industry, 'better regulation', often equated to self-regulation, is suggested, with the possibility of co-regulation for more sensitive areas.[2] Against this background, this chapter is concerned with two linked issues. The first is the identification of the various regulatory systems in place, though the chapter will not involve itself with the technicalities of taxonomy and categorizing the various

---

[1] A Burnham, MP, Convergence Think Tank Launch, Opening Address, 7 February 2008, available at <http://www.culture.gov.uk/Convergence/submissions/seminar1/CTT-one.pdf>.

[2] European Parliament, Council and Commission, Inter-institutional Agreement on Better Law-Making [2003] OJ C321/1, paras 17 *et seq.*

systems,[3] and the assessment of their structures from the perspective of the viewer. The second is the question of whether the system of media regulation in the UK is, in its totality, coherent and workable.

The assumption that regulation is in some way a 'bad' thing is linked to a view that sees regulation only as limiting freedom of activity, and correspondingly infringes the right to freedom of expression. While regulation undeniably does limit freedom of action and, in the context of the media sector, operate to limit some bodies' freedom of expression, it is also linked with a view of the public interest. Even fundamental rights, such as freedom of expression, may be limited in the public interest.[4] Alternatively, regulation can level the playing field between those with power and those without. Regulation could require those with dominant voices occasionally to hand over the 'megaphone' to others who would otherwise not be heard, or to say things that they might not have otherwise chosen to say. On this basis, regulation facilitates freedom of expression.[5] Furthermore, given the commonly accepted idea about the importance of the media to public discourse and to democracy,[6] there are rights also to receive information, held by the audience. Here, the media's right to freedom of expression is primarily instrumental, justified by reference to its role in protecting democracy and the functioning of the public sphere, not an end in its own right. Whilst there may be differences between the media,[7] an audience should have an expectation of a certain range and quality of programming, information, or content,[8] an expectation regulatory authorities should take into account.[9]

The question becomes how to regulate, and in this there are two aspects: policy formation or standard setting; and monitoring and enforcement. A linked question is who regulates. Self-regulation and co-regulation are claimed to have fewer costs and the consequence that the industry members, in 'owning' the system, are more likely to comply with it.[10] The reverse side of this is that there are costs inherent in determining standards and monitoring and enforcing them; the key must be to ensure

---

[3] See eg Hans Bredow Institut, 'Co-regulatory Measures in the Media Sector in the EU', commissioned by the European Commission, 2005, available at <http://ec.europa.eu/avpolicy/info_centre/library/ studies/ index_en.htm>.

[4] Not all rights may be so limited: see eg Arts 2 and 3 ECHR.

[5] E Barendt, 'Press and Broadcasting Freedom: Does Anyone Have Any Rights to Free Speech?' (1991) 44 Current Legal Problems 63, 65–6.

[6] E Barendt, *Freedom of Speech* (OUP, 2nd edn, 2005) 18.

[7] This chapter will not review the different justifications for each of the media, nor the explanations for their being treated differently. See eg L Hitchens, *Broadcasting Pluralism and Diversity: A Comparative Study of Policy and Regulation* (Hart Publishing, 2006) Ch 2.

[8] These principles have been accepted: see 'Political Declaration of the 7th European Ministerial Conference on Mass Media Policy' (Kyiv, 10 and 11 March 2005), with respect to ensuring pluralism and diversity, respect for human rights and non-discriminatory access not just to the existing media but also to new communication services. The role of digital broadcasting has also been noted: Council of Europe, Council Recommendation on measures to promote the democratic and social contribution of digital broadcasting, Rec (2003) 9.

[9] Council of Europe, Declaration of the Committee of Ministers on the independence and functions of regulatory authorities for the broadcasting sector, adopted 26th March 2008, point IV.

[10] See eg Ofcom, 'Self or Co-regulation Consultation'.

adequate resources. Further, industry may have heterogeneous interests: quite apart from an analysis which sees citizen/viewer interests in an opposing position to those of industry, there is the possibility that all industry interests are not the same. Such differing interests may skew the standard-setting process, undermine the funding arrangements, and adversely impact on the compliance and enforcement of the system. A further issue is that of legitimacy. Policy formation requires some claim to legitimacy, as it affects society in general; it is most often the role of Parliament, as the government seemed recently to recognize.[11] Thus, when policy in the form of standard-setting is carried out, we need to ensure that this is not something that industry determines in its own interest, but that the needs and expectations of society as a whole are taken into account.[12] Given the power of those setting standards, and the opportunity in some cases for *ex ante* control, it is crucial that the decision-making be open, neutral, and transparent. The independence and effectiveness of the regulator, as well as the resources available to the regulator, are key, as is the scope of the regulator's remit.

At no point is there an absence of law; even self-regulation takes place within the framework of the general law. Whilst we might ascribe to the media standards of speech (and behaviour) more stringent than that applied to the general populace, both because one-to-many speech cannot be tailored in the way individual speech can and because of the role of the media in society, the law will in certain cases step in. Self-regulation thus operates in the shadow of the law and, indeed, under the threat of statutory intervention. Further, whilst codes of conduct are likely to inculcate standards higher than those required by law, there may be cases of overlap between the regulatory and the legal. This has two aspects: public and private. The law may prohibit certain behaviour, such as incitement to racial hatred, reflecting societal values on this point, but it may also protect rights benefiting individuals. Such rights are normally enforced through private law mechanisms. We might question whether the systems in view will be assessed differently depending on whether we see them as enforcing standards in the public interest or as mechanisms for individuals to seek redress.

These are the underlying issues as we assess the regulatory system, starting with the approach taken towards the press and moving through the audiovisual sector in its various forms chronologically by reference to the introduction of the relevant technology and service. Secondly, in doing so, this chapter will consider the system as a whole. The discussion will bear in mind the needs of the audience, but crucially the audience is seen in the context of public debate and democratic concerns, as these are the key issues which make the media more than just an industrial sector.

---

[11] BERR, Government's Response to House of Lords Select Committee on Regulators Inquiry, UK Economic Regulators (January 2008) para 1.14.

[12] Contrast the views of Ofcom, which, somewhat worryingly, seems to think that standard-setting is for industry alone to determine, and the industry's view of citizen interest is without more ado, to be accepted: Ofcom, 'Self and Co-regulation Consultation', para 2.24.

9.2 PRINT MEDIA

The press is the most notorious example of self-regulation. On one view the system is the embodiment of freedom of expression, essential for the functioning of the press as 'watchdogs'. According to commentators in this broad camp, editors take the views of the current self-regulatory body, the Press Complaints Commission (PCC), seriously.[13] Conversely, critics see the press as concerned, not with matters of public moment, but with gossip and trivia, the self-regulatory system failing to set and enforce standards.[14] Whilst Lord Wakeham thought that it had transformed standards in newspapers since its establishment,[15] Barendt noted that PCC decisions in the area of privacy are 'far from impressive'.[16]

The history of the development of the PCC is instructive, as the resistance to any form of control suggests a minimalist approach at best to the protection of citizens' interests, and one that possibly does not take these interests seriously. The PCC was set up, under threat of government intervention, to replace the Press Council, itself established in 1953 to divert government intentions to regulate the press.[17] The Calcutt Review[18] recommended the introduction of a new body and the industry established the PCC in 1991, broadly in line with the Calcutt recommendations. Calcutt, in 1993, was unimpressed and recommended a statutory body.[19] Again the government stopped short, despite many claims for such action and yet another private member's Bill.[20] Not much has changed in the PCC, although in 1995 a separate membership committee was established as a step to increase independence from industry interests. Both Conservative and Labour governments have favoured strengthening self-regulation; some have suggested because the government feared the power of the press.[21] The principle, in accordance with the fashions of the moment, has now become more accepted by the select committees,[22] although the Committee's recommendations indicate that the system is far from perfect. Repeated attempts to introduce private

---

[13] See eg T Jaffa, 'Adjudications are a truly serious matter for editors' (2006) 65 MLN 29–30.

[14] S Smith, 'Why PCC gives no real protection to privacy' (2006) 65 MLN 28–30; N Hanson, 'Papering over Cracks' (2004) 101(29) Law Society Gazette 22–4.

[15] Lord Wakeham, 'Press, privacy, public interest and the Human Rights Act' in D Tambini and C Heyward (eds), *Ruled by Recluses* (IPPR, 2002) 25.

[16] E Barendt, 'Media Intrusion: The case for legislation' in *Ruled by Recluses* (n 15 above) 17.

[17] In this, the UK's experience is not unique: see D Tambini, D Leonardi, and C Marsden, *Codifying Cyberspace: Communications Self-regulation in the Age of Internet Convergence* (Routledge, 2008) 66.

[18] *Report of the Committee on Privacy and Related Matters* (Cmnd 1102, 1990).

[19] Calcutt, *Review of Press Self-Regulation* (Cm 2135, 1993).

[20] Consultation Paper issued by Lord Chancellor's Department (July 1993); Report on Privacy and Media Intrusion, 1992–3, HC 294-1.

[21] G Robertson, and A Nicol, *Media Law* (Penguin, 5th edn, 2007) 762.

[22] Select Committee Report on 'Privacy and Media Intrusion' Fifth Report 2003, HC 458-1.

members' Bills[23] suggest that not all MPs share the faith of whichever government is in power in self-regulation.

The first issue concerns the scope of the PCC's remit. This is particularly problematic when we look at the position of internet content. The PCC extends no control over the communication by one-to-many by 'citizen journalists': wikis, blogging, and other forms of user-generated content, unless adopted by the press (which raises its own questions), are unregulated. The issues raised by these new forms of journalism pose challenges not just to the press but to broadcasters also. Both broadcasters and newspapers have internet presence, but since the PCC has exercised jurisdiction over press-disseminated content, are subject to markedly different regimes. Such a distinction becomes hard to justify when the press are now making public on those sites audiovisual content. The approach of the PCC is that the press is different from the broadcast media, seemingly because the press is not regulated. Self-regulation, assuming this is the same as the mediation service the PCC provides, is seen as necessary to ensure freedom of expression. This argument constitutes a somewhat simplistic analysis, which ignores the complexity of newspapers as institutions[24] as well as the rights of the audience, although it was accepted by the government during the adoption of the Human Rights Act 1998 (HRA 1998).

The membership and funding of the PCC will affect the way in which it fulfils its functions. Although the PCC includes lay members, as part of the appointment criteria the PCC requires any such lay members to be in favour of press self-regulation. Whilst one would not want lay members who had sought the role merely to disrupt the system, requiring such a positive mindset might well encourage deference towards industry views. There is no reference to the Nolan Committee standards in Public Life (discussed further below), which contain standards of behaviour, for instance with regard to conflicts of interest. Should we expect the PCC, as an industry body, to adhere to such standards or their equivalent? Insofar as the PCC claims to represent the public interest, or to be a substitute for regulation, the answer must be 'yes'. There is a potential conflict, found in most self-regulatory systems, between industry values and the public interest. As far as the PCC is concerned, there is a worry that the driving motivation of the PCC is not the serving of the public interest. Rather, the PCC adopts—or continues—the proselytizing approach towards freedom of the press. Thus, whilst the formal removal of the 'dual mission' of the Press Council has been seen as significant in terms of distinguishing between the PCC and the Press Council,[25] this distinction may be more apparent than real.

---

[23] See Right of Reply and Press Standards Bill 2005, put forward by Peter Bradley MP, discussed by J Coad in 'The Press Complaints Commission—Are We Safe in its Hands?' [2005] Entertainment Law Review 167.

[24] E Barendt, *Broadcasting Law: A Comparative Study* (Clarendon Press, 1993) 32–3.

[25] See S Shivakumar, Press Council of India, background Paper for the workshop on Press, Ethics and Law, 23 and 24 March 1998, cited by Tambini *et al* (n 17 above) 66.

Furthermore, the PCC is funded by industry, raising questions about its independence from that industry. This, though, is a common model, which can work well, as the example of the Advertising Standards Authority (ASA) shows. More worrying in the context of the press, is the degree to which it is funded. Lack of resources not only indicates a lack of commitment on the part of the press, but limits the ability of the PCC to engage in wider projects. Beyond the terms of the code of conduct itself, the PCC engages in little standard-setting activity, although research suggests that guidance, for example on the acceptability of the use of the term 'asylum seeker', can have an impact.[26] Furthermore, strong guidance can support journalists against the commercial pressures of the newspaper environment; the 2003 Select Committee recommended that journalists be allowed to refuse assignments which breached the code, but this suggestion has not been implemented.

The PCC adjudicates on the industry code of conduct, which is drafted by the Code Committee made up of senior editors. The PCC argues that such an approach gives the code legitimacy, but this legitimacy is from the perspective of industry alone and may be overstated as industry standards tend to be set by the big players in any given sector. The 'self' in self-regulation may not reflect the views of the sector as a whole. This is not a problem unique to the press but it does undermine the legitimacy argument here. Another potential weakness is that standards are set at a level which reflects the preference of certain sectors of the industry (or its dominant elements), rather than at the optimum level for protection of whichever public interest is in issue. Since 1993, however, the Code has been subject to ratification by the PCC, thus giving some claim to the Code representing interests other than those of the industry. It is, however, far from clear that the lay members of the PCC could introduce provisions into the Code with which the Committee of Editors did not agree.

In some respects, the remit of the PCC is somewhat limited. Complaints from third parties are not accepted, even if there is a clear violation of the Code. The Code does not deal with matters of taste, nor is there an impartiality requirement. In terms of serving democracy, this latter point might cause concern, although the partisan nature of the press has long been accepted. There are no positive obligations on the press as to the type of content that newspapers should carry, nor are there quantitative requirements. Given the significance of these sorts of requirements for the continued existence of public service broadcasting, this is a weakness if the media, including the press, have a role in the functioning of democracy. Here, the function of the Code is to identify the limits of acceptable press behaviour. In this, the Code outlines ethical aspirations, which also have a role in ensuring the quality of reportage and protecting the rights of others. Although some elements of such codes do not operate within the field of law, clearly there are places of overlap. The courts post-*Reynolds*[27] have seemed to take the PCC Code as a baseline, and thus expect journalists, editors, and newspapers

---

[26] See eg Report by ICAR, *Reporting Refugees and Asylum Seekers* (PressWise, 2003), available at <http://www.mediawise.org.uk/display_page.php?id=776>.
[27] *Reynolds v Times Newspapers* [2001] 2 AC 127.

to comply with their own industry standards.[28] In this, there seems to be divergence between the approach of the courts and that of the PCC,[29] which rarely finds a violation of the accuracy provisions and ascribes privacy a narrow scope.[30] For those that rely on the PCC for the protection of their rights, this means there is a chance that their claim will not be upheld when a legal action could have been won.[31]

There have been further criticisms of the PCC adjudicatory process, and the effectiveness of PCC rulings and sanctions. The PCC, however, claims its activities to be a success as the number of complaints have gone up, showing that the Code and the PCC's mission have become well known among the general public. Likewise, the PCC has been commended for the transparency of its website and for the range of information available on it.[32] The information can, however, be read in another, less positive way. One practitioner notes that although the PCC publishes summaries of its decisions, the hearings are not open: the only source of information about the decisions comes from the summaries themselves, which tend to be brief and phrased in such a way as to support the PCC's conclusions.[33] Further, the increase in complaints suggests the ineffectiveness of the PCC system. Indeed, given its emphasis on mediation, the PCC only adjudicates in a small number of cases, leading to very few complaints being upheld. This trend continues: the summary of complaints for April–September 2007 showed that of 1,845 complaints, 16 were adjudicated, and 9 upheld; for the six months prior to that, of 1,647 initial complaints, 16 were adjudicated, and 2 upheld.[34] It is also hard to identify why some complaints were excluded; this is hardly transparent.

There are criticisms of the PCC's system of mediation, in particular the PCC's preference for mediation over adjudication. It is the PCC which decides if mediation is successful; ie if the newspaper in the PCC's opinion has offered sufficient amends, the PCC will inform the complainant of this fact.[35] Such a view might not accord with that of the complainant.[36] Further, the fact that the same officers are involved raises problems in terms of the flow of information and the neutrality of the adjudication process. There is also an underlying question as to whether mediation is appropriate in a

---

[28] D Bloy, 'What price irresponsible journalism? Reflections on the Galloway litigation?' (2006) 11(1) Communications Law 13.

[29] Note *Ewing v News International* [2008] EWHC 1390 (QB), which commended the thoroughness of the PCC's analysis in the context of a vexatious litigant.

[30] See eg JK Rowling's experience before the PCC and before the courts: *Murray v Big Pictures (UK) Ltd* [2008] EWCA Civ 446.

[31] It is still possible to bring a legal action after complaining to the PCC: in the Sara Cox case an apology appeared after she complained to the PCC about a breach of the code but she then brought a legal action, which resulted in a payment of £50,000 to settle the claim. See <http://www.pcc.org.uk/news/index.html?article=MTk=> for the PCC's view, and for some other views <http://www.guardian.co.uk/print/0,,4689055-103683,00.html>; <http://news.bbc.co.uk/1/hi/uk/2971330.stm>.

[32] Tambini *et al* (n 17 above) 69.

[33] Coad (n 23 above)168.

[34] PCC Complaints Summary Reports 75 and 74 respectively. Note that the total complaints include complaints where the complainant did not subsequently formalize the complaint.

[35] Coad (n 23 above).

[36] J Rozenberg, *Privacy and the Press* (OUP, 2004) 159.

regulatory context. The answer to this question depends on what the function of the system is. If we are concerned about redress in individual cases or the enforcement of an individual's rights, mediation as a mechanism for resolving the dispute is appropriate. If the concern is the enforcement of standards, it may be less so. There is a public interest in the finding of a breach which goes beyond providing redress for individuals which is not served if the question, 'was this acceptable behaviour', is not answered. A cynic could suggest that such a system has value to the industry in showing a better compliance record. There are further weaknesses in the system: there is no right of appeal as to the substance of the decision, only limited procedural rights, and the decision is made by the same body. This is problematic in terms of the requirements of Article 6 of the European Convention on Human Rights (ECHR). Although judicial review is possible, it focuses more on procedural rather than substantive issues.[37]

The content of the PCC website is not neutral about the benefits of using the system as opposed to bringing a legal action: legal action before the courts is not a perfect system but the PCC overstates its difficulties.[38] This is particularly worrying given the divergence in outcomes noted above and the fact that complainants who use lawyers are more likely to win their claim than those without. The PCC has refused to contemplate the possibility of fining its recalcitrant members, the only remedy being the finding of a breach and the publishing of an apology. It has ignored the suggestions of the 2003 Select Committee that fees be geared by reference to adverse holdings and that in extreme cases a fixed scale of awards be paid to complainants.[39] These, by contrast to the other regulators, are the weakest of sanctions and do not seem to constitute much in the way of a disincentive to violating the rules. Despite some steps to improve the legitimacy of the PCC, it is 'an ineffective regulator which fails to offer adequate redress in a great many cases'.[40] Whilst we could argue that regulation is not about providing a remedy in individual cases but enforcing standards in the public interest, it seems the PCC does neither, but it has little incentive to change its approach given the government's current commitment to self-regulation.[41]

9.3 FILMS AND CINEMAS

The regulatory system for films has one of the longest histories in the audiovisual sector, pre-dating that of broadcasting. The licensing powers were introduced

---

[37] See *R v PCC, ex p Ford* (unreported, 29 July 2001), which challenged a decision on its substance and failed, although of course this decision was pre-HRA, which may affect the courts' understanding of what a rational decision-maker may decide.

[38] Robertson and Nicol (n 21 above) 769.

[39] Rozenberg (n 36 above) 161.

[40] M Feintuck and M Varney, *Media Regulation, Public Interest and the Law* (Edinburgh University Press, 2nd edn, 2006) 195.

[41] Rozenberg (n 36 above) 161.

following concerns for public safety: early films were flammable,[42] although subsequently other rationales, such as public morality, were introduced.[43] The British Board of Film Classification (BBFC) was established in 1912 as the British Board of Film Censors to provide guidance to local authorities which licensed cinemas and films for distribution. It was established by the film industry on the basis that it was better to censor its own products, than to have local councils do it.[44] Some similarities in motivation can therefore be discerned with the establishment of the PCC and ATVOD (see below). A practice developed whereby councils required BBFC certification of a film as a prerequisite to its showing, a practice which was approved by the courts[45] and then found recognition in statute: the Cinematographic Act 1952. This 'curious arrangement'[46] continues to this day. The current regime is found in the Licensing Act 2003. Like its predecessors, the Licensing Act 2003 obliges local authorities to impose a condition prohibiting the admission of children to 'unsuitable' films[47] and they may rely on the decisions of the BBFC in this regard, or their own recommendations.[48] Even where certification has been granted, however, the final decision remains with the local authorities, which means that different authorities (even adjoining authorities) may take different views as to the acceptability (or not) of a given film. Since the Licensing Act 2003, the Secretary of State suggests that the licensing authority should not duplicate the BBFC's efforts without good reason.[49] The Licensing Act 2003 thus strengthened the role of the BBFC.

The current BBFC guidance identifies seven categories of film, determining which age of children, if any, should be permitted to see the film.[50] The licensing regime itself specifies that it should not be used for censorship purposes; the only restrictions are those related to access of children.[51] Nonetheless, failure to grant a classification means that the film cannot be shown. The BBFC will give advice as to cuts that must be made to obtain classification, or even to obtain a particular category of classification. This is clearly a form of prior censorship, even if the term 'classification' sounds benign, and the film industry will prioritize profits over principle.[52] The public interest requirements met here are limited and negative in form; cultural policy or concern for

---

[42] A Hunt and C Manchester, 'The Licensing Act and its Implementation: Nanny knows the "Third Way" is best' [2007] 1 Web Journal of Current Legal Issues, available at <http://webjcli.ncl.ac.uk/2007/issue1/hunt1.html>.

[43] Under the current system, the Licensing Act 2003, s 4(2) specifies four 'licensing objectives': prevention of crime and disorder, prevention of public nuisance, public safety, and protection of children from harm.

[44] N March Hunnings, *Film Censors and the Law* (Allen & Unwin, 1967) 51.

[45] *Mills v London County Council* [1925] 1 KB 213.

[46] H Morrison, (1952) 385 HC Debs 504.

[47] Licensing Act 2003, s 20(1).

[48] Cinemas Act 1985, s 1(3), the obligation was formerly found in the Cinematographic Act 1952, s 3.

[49] DCMS Revised Guidance under section 182 Licensing Act (June 2007) 79.

[50] The categories are described on the BBFC website <http://www.bbfc.co.uk/policy/policy-thecategories.php>.

[51] DCMS, Revised Guidance under section 182 Licensing Act (June 2007) 74.

[52] Robertson and Nicol (n 21 above) 822.

matters of public interest have no role; in this, there are similarities with the concerns of the video regime, ATVOD and the IMCB. Further, as regards the criminal law, a film which has obtained a classification is unlikely to be prosecuted for obscenity, showing yet another example of the interplay between (self) regulation and law. The role of the BBFC is therefore significant; it is unclear whether the views of other self-regulatory bodies will have a similar status.

The BBFC claims to be independent: its website claims: 'We are open and accountable. As an independent, self-financing regulator, we are mindful of our unique position and proud of the trust that our expertise and integrity have built with the industry and public.'[53] The BBFC's income is derived solely from the fees it charges for its services, calculated by measuring the running time of films or video works submitted for certification. Industry therefore supports this body, rather than government, giving it some degree of independence from government. This income seems to be sufficient for its activities, and because films cannot be marketed legally without classification, this is a strong compliance mechanism for payment; it is not dependent on the goodwill of the film industry, suggesting a degree of independence from industry too.

Although the BBFC aims for impartiality, as with the PCC, there is no express reference to the Nolan statements on public life, nor is it clear how the key figures are appointed. Given the claims to impartiality, it may be that the reference to Nolan would add little to existing practice. Nonetheless, this is an interesting omission which underlines the inherent conflict in a self- or even co-regulatory model. The BBFC has a Council of Management, comprising leading figures from the manufacturing and servicing sections of the film industry, which appoints the presidential tier comprising one president and two vice-presidents. In effect, the Home Secretary has the right of approval in respect of these appointments. There are three advisory committees: the Advisory Panel on Children's Viewing (established 1999); the Consultative Council (formerly the video consultative council and responsible for BBFC policy and practice generally); and a committee advising on packaging. Post-Nolan, the BBFC noted the desirability of advertising positions on the Consultative Council rather than operating by invitation. More recently, a private member's Bill suggested that the power of scrutiny for the appointment of the four principal officers of the BBFC should be given to the Home Affairs Select Committee of the House of Commons, rather than allowing unsupervised internal selection.[54] If we apply the standards applicable to broadcasting regulators here, the BBFC would undoubtedly fall short.[55]

The Council of Management also controls business affairs and finances, but takes no part in policy development, which is formulated by the Management Team. This is in marked contrast to the PCC, where the PCC Code is drawn up by editors. Here, not only are the industry representatives not involved directly in code setting, but they are

---

[53] See BBFC webpage <http://www.bbfc.co.uk/about/vsindex.php>.

[54] British Board of Film Classification (Accountability to Parliament and Appeals) Bill 2007–08, see summary at <http://www.julianbrazier.com/type3.asp?id=105&type=3>; the Bill was ultimately talked out.

[55] Council of Europe, Council Recommendation, Rec (2000) 23, and see appendix section II, para 5.

drawn from the elements of the industry that have less direct interest in the outcome of particular decisions. Standard-setting, as we shall see below, involves the views of the public much more than the standards incorporated into the press code. In a sense, however, the standard-setting is more limited, as the BBFC does not set ethical standards for the industry—for example a classification decision could not be withheld because of the way the film had been made (unless illegality was involved). The president and vice-presidents are consulted in the case of works that raise particular questions of policy. Day-to-day decisions on film content are made by the 'examiners', who are appointed after positions are publicly advertised.

Accountability is via the publication of an annual report, which has been made available generally on the BBFC website since 1999 and placed in the libraries of the Houses of Commons and Lords. The BBFC also publishes its guidelines (since 1998) and decisions on its website, and indeed has recently developed specialist sites to provide advice to parents and to children. In this, there are parallels with the broadcasting regulators, and again it would seem to satisfy concerns regarding transparency and the communication of information, with the exception of its complaints procedure (see below).

The BBFC does not attempt representation of the population but acts in the capacity as 'expert' or 'judge', although the Consultative Council does include a 'wide range of representatives of relevant interests and expertise and a number of independent members of experience and distinction'.[56] Whilst there might be concerns about the standards applied, over the years the BBFC has moved to a system of greater consultation. The 2000 Guidelines were the first to be prepared following extensive public consultation.[57] In its 2007 Annual Report, the BBFC noted that the current Guidelines (2005), on which all decisions are based, were drafted following consultation with over 11,000 people in the UK. New Guidelines are planned for 2009, which means that the BBFC will embark, during 2008, on a new programme of consultation.[58] The BBFC has also commissioned research to inform its policy and its approach to regulation. In this, the voice of the public is having some say in the determination of public interest standards.

The BBFC accepts complaints about its classifications, though it receives fewer complaints than comparable organizations. Whether this is because the BBFC decision-making process is better than those of the other bodies, or because its complaints procedure is less well known is debatable. Given that there is no separate or identifiable system for viewers to complain, the latter possibility seems likely. Although there is an appeal committee, the right of appeal is limited to those submitting videos, thereby excluding complaints regarding films and from the general public. A failure to have a grievance or appeal procedure is a weakness in the accountability system in place; essentially the BBFC is judge in its own case. We have noted this situation is problematic in the context of the PCC. Decisions under the informal film complaints system are not published either, which compounds the problems. Although

---

[56] BBFC, *Annual Report 2007*, 6.
[57] ibid 5.
[58] ibid 10.

interested parties may make representations under the Licensing Act 2003, this relates to the decision to grant a licence to the premises and not to questions relating to the suitability or classification of any given film. The licensing authority cannot use its powers to influence the content of films, nor the range of films shown.

In terms of the classification process, the BBFC gives reasons for its decisions, and specifies whether cuts have been made, satisfying requirements for transparency. We have noted that in defining its guidelines, the BBFC takes account of consumer views. It has also had regard to the impact of the Human Rights Act 1998.[59] Following Fenman's retirement, the guidelines were revised, the new guidelines incorporating more objective tests rather than the somewhat vague and certainly subjective approach used previously. The changes suggest that the views of the president are influential.[60] In this the BBFC might not be alone: Ofcom's tone was set initially by the view that it should be aiming to do itself out of a job.

Despite its function as a censorship body, the BBFC emphasizes its role as informing consumers (and there is no discussion as to whether the BBFC should take into account citizenship concerns), so that parents in particular may make choices about issues of particular concern to them. The BBFC also engages in outreach and education work, to a marked degree that exceeds the work done by the other bodies. However, as suggested above, there are limits on the BBFC's remit. In particular, there are no positive requirements on film-makers or cinemas to show particular ranges of films; this then (with the exception perhaps of the European Union via its MEDIA support programme) is a free market environment concerned more with entertainment than enlightenment or the public sphere, though admittedly it makes no such claims.

9.4 BROADCASTING

Broadcasting has been the subject of state intervention almost since public radio broadcasting was introduced.[61] The current legislation provides a complex structure. Radio and television are subject to separate regimes,[62] reinforced by their different treatment under EU law.[63] Our understanding of the scope of television will be

---

[59] ibid 2.

[60] Duval implicitly noted this possibility: BBFC, *Annual Report 1999*, 4.

[61] Originally, radio licences were held by private companies, then consolidated into the British Broadcasting Company, which then, following two government reviews (*Sykes Committee on Broadcasting* (Cmd 1951, 1923) and *Crawford Committee on Broadcasting* (Cmd 2599, 1925) became the British Broadcasting Corporation. For more on the history of broadcasting, see A Briggs, *The History of Broadcasting in the United Kingdom* (Oxford University Press, 1961–79) and J Harrison and L Woods, *European Broadcasting Law and Policy* (Cambridge University Press, 2007) Ch 2.

[62] The ECtHR has not distinguished between radio and television in its jurisprudence: see eg *Murphy v Ireland* 44179/98 [2003] ECHR 352, 10 July 2003 and *Autronic AG v Switzerland* 15/1989/175/231 [1990] ECHR 12, 22 May 1990.

[63] The print media are likewise outside the AVMS Directive, although where radio stations are providing audiovisual messages across the internet, the exclusion from the AVMS Directive is not self-evident.

influenced by the AVMS Directive when it comes into force. Other distinctions in the current UK regime[64] comprise the distinction between the BBC, which operates within the framework imposed by its Charter and Agreement, and the other broadcasters, which all operate under licence from Ofcom; as well as the distinction between broadcasters subject to public service broadcasting obligations and those which are not.

9.4.1 BBC

Despite the distinctions in the Communications Act 2003 and at EU level, television and radio fall within the same framework as regards the BBC services. The BBC finds its powers and limitations in its Charter and Agreement, which is reviewed from time to time. Between the 1996 Charter and the current Charter (effective from 1 January 2007), the BBC has been the subject of a number of reports and investigations. Additionally, the position of the BBC was considered as part of the discussions leading to the enactment of the Communications Act 2003. In 2004, the government published a consultation document on the renewal of the BBC's Charter, the results of which were published, and commissioned two independent reports: the Burns Report and the Graf Report, followed by two more reviews by Barwise and Gardam and a Green Paper[65] and a White Paper.[66] Both Houses of Parliament established committees to consider the future of the BBC. At the same time, Ofcom reviewed public service broadcasting, resulting in three phases of documentation. The BBC issued its own report, 'Building Public Value'. The government responded to the reports from the Houses of Parliament, and the BBC to the government's Green Paper. During this period, the Hutton Report, and the Neil Report on journalism standards were published. Although not connected directly to the the Charter renewal, Tessa Jowell accepted that both reports would have an impact on the renewal process; certainly the whole Kelly affair resulted in the resignation of the Director-General and the Chairman of the BBC. The outcome of all this scrutiny was the renewal of the BBC's Charter, a statement as to continued licence fee funding for the medium term, an attempt to find a more precise definition of the BBC's remit, and a new structure for BBC internal governance, the BBC Trust. Nonetheless, concerns remain. The semi-constant state of review can lead to uncertainty, inimical to long-term planning, and opens the BBC to the threat of political pressure. Indeed, the Council of Europe Parliamentary Assembly described the BBC as having been attacked by the government for its coverage on the war in Iraq[67] and in the view of the House of Lords, the Hutton Inquiry and the approach of the government, 'suggest that the BBC's current constitutional and funding

---

[64] Note the Isle of Man and the Channel Islands have separate regulatory systems.
[65] DCMS, 'A Strong BBC, independent of Government' (May 2005).
[66] DCMS, *A public service for all: the BBC in the digital age* (Cm 6763, 2006).
[67] Council of Europe, Parliamentary Assembly, Recommendation 1641 (2004) 'Public Service Broadcasting', 27 January 2004 (3rd Sitting), para 9.

arrangements are not sufficiently robust to prevent unease within the BBC about its future should it upset the Government of the day'.[68]

There are strong links between the concerns which justify a right to receive information and the function of the press as a watchdog, and those underpinning the role of public service broadcasting. Given this role, the independence of the BBC is central.[69] In addition to concerns about the renewal process, it is unclear whether the charter form is satisfactory in ensuring independence and it has been suggested that some other form, such as a statutory corporation as is used for Channel 4, might be better. The government, however, resisted the suggestion, arguing that the use of the charter form removes the BBC from the political arena, where putting the BBC on a statutory footing would require the approval of the Houses of Parliament, and thereby subject it to ad hoc intervention.[70] Conversely, the use of the charter form can be seen as putting the BBC at the whim of the relevant Secretary of State.[71] As the House of Lords noted, 'the fact is the Government do not have to listen to anyone and can draw up the new Charter and Agreement as they please—indeed this is what they seem to be doing'.[72] The choice of Charter has some other, odd consequences the most striking of which is that if the Charter is at any time not renewed, the BBC will cease to exist. Thus, the BBC is inherently temporary, dependent on political activity for its continued existence. Whilst Channel 4 may be subject to interference or be dismantled, political action is required. Even if its broadcasting licence is ever not renewed, it would still exist and could remain involved in the broadcasting industry at other points in the value chain: not so the BBC. It is unfortunate that tradition rather than a concern for independence informed the Charter Review. Long-standing practice seems to be the guarantee for the BBC's continued existence.

Further, although the BBC derives additional income from commercial exploitation of its resources, its main funding lies in the hands of the government. In the view of the Council of Europe, PSB and regulators should be financially independent of government.[73] The BBC may be in a better position than other public service broadcasters here. On the one hand, the renewal and size of the licence fee is controlled by the executive, giving rise to possibility that a broadcaster, especially when the fee is

---

[68] House of Lords, Select Committee on the BBC's Charter Review, 'The Review of the BBC's Royal Charter', 1 November 2005, HL Paper 50-I, 15.

[69] Recommendation 1641 (2004) (n 67 above). *Public Service Broadcasting*.

[70] DCMS, *Government Response to the Lords Committee Report on Charter Review* (Cmnd 6739, 2005). This view was apparently also that of the then Chairman of the BBC, Michael Grade, House of Lords, Select Committee on the BBC's Charter Review, 'The Review of the BBC's Royal Charter', 1 November 2005, HL Paper 50-I, 18.

[71] ibid, 17–18.

[72] ibid 17.

[73] Council of Europe, 'Council Recommendation on the independence and functions of regulatory authorities for the broadcasting sector', Rec (2000) 23, Declaration on the Guarantee of the independence of public service broadcasting in the Member States (27 September 2006), Declaration of the Committee of Ministers on the Independence and Functions of Regulatory Authorities for the Broadcasting Sector, (26 March 2008).

due for renewal, might become more cautious of antagonizing the current executive. Conversely, the licence fee tends to be settled for some years at a time, thus allowing some stability and even some immunity from market forces. One must also recognize that nothing is ever perfectly independent, so the question is, whether the licence fee arrangement allows the BBC to be independent enough.[74]

Originally, the BBC was controlled through its Board of Governors, and the terms of its Agreement with the relevant minister. The BBC might be seen as an example of self-regulation, although questions about its independence arose as the BBC seemed cautious of criticizing authority. It was only in the 1960s that a more critical stance was adopted and the BBC was obliged to accept conditions comparable to those imposed on commercial television so as to avoid broadcasting material viewed as offensive or politically undesirable. Even so, the BBC was not subject to an external regulator, but continued to be guided by the Board of Governors. More recently, the BBC has been the subject of government complaints from both sides of the political spectrum, suggesting that the overly deferential days have gone. Nonetheless, Robertson and Nicol note the level of detail in the BBC Producer Guidelines,[75] based on the principle that, 'the more important or contentious the issue, the higher up the referral needs to be'.[76] They note the extent of the control in that even queries about how to interpret the guidelines must be referred up the BBC hierarchy. On one view, this might just be a system established to ensure good practice; a more sinister interpretation suggests that the more sensitive a matter is, the more likely a political decision will be made about its acceptability.[77] Whichever view is taken, it should be noted that the system was criticized by Hutton, resulting in the introduction of the new system, whereby the governance of the BBC was split and the BBC Trust was introduced.

The new system is found in the 2006 Charter and Agreement, which proclaims the BBC's independence.[78] The Charter outlines the constitution of the BBC, splitting the running of the BBC into an Executive Board, responsible for day-to-day running of the BBC, and the Trust, which has responsibility for setting the overall strategic direction including a general oversight of the Executive Board.[79] In carrying out these tasks, the Trust is to act in the public interest, especially the interest of the licence fee-payer.[80] The Trust is stated to remain independent of the Executive and is the 'sovereign body' within the BBC.[81] Crucially, the Trust has the task of issuing the licences

---

[74] The House of Lords expressed some scepticism on this point: House of Lords, 'The Review of the BBC's Royal Charter', 17.

[75] Robertson and Nicol (n 21 above) 934.

[76] BBC Editorial Guidelines, 10.

[77] Robertson and Nicol (n 21 above) 871 suggest that the BBC was cowardly in its compliance with the Attorney-General's injunction with regard to the cash for peerages investigation, in contrast to the 'brave' *Guardian* newspaper, which ran the front page and won the legal case. In this context note subsequent challenge: *Attorney-General v BBC* [2007] EWCA Civ 280.

[78] *BBC Charter, 2006* (Cm 6925, 2006) art 6.

[79] ibid art 7.

[80] ibid.

[81] ibid art 9, subject always to the role of Ofcom and general law.

for the various BBC services, rather than the Department for Culture, Media and Sport (DCMS) as previously,[82] and must assess them in accordance with the public interest and, in particular, in the light of a public value test (PVT).[83]

The new arrangements were not universally well-received on the basis that the proposals conflated two types of responsibility, those of a governing body and those of a regulator. The Burns Panel suggested that regulation of the BBC be entrusted to an independent body, whilst the BBC Board would be modelled on unitary corporate practice (as Ofcom is). This proposal had the advantage of delineating a clear boundary between the subject of regulation and the regulator—or ensuring that 'the BBC would no longer be seen as judge and jury in its own cause',[84] arguably increasing accountability to the licence fee payer. There are, however, weaknesses, notably the resource implications of yet another regulatory body; and the difficulties of sorting out the demarcation between the multiple regulators. The problem of demarcation is not unique to the Burn Panel's proposals. One criticism of the government's proposal was that some of the regulatory functions held by the BBC Trust overlap with responsibilities held by Ofcom—for example the Trust is to review BBC services in the public interest and for compliance with its public service obligations whilst Ofcom has a responsibility for public service broadcasting as a whole (see below).[85]

A further concern relates to the appointment and membership of the Trust: essentially these are government appointees. The threat to independence from government is unlikely to be significant, however. Following concerns about appointments to public bodies during the early 1990s, the Committee on Standards in Public Life (Nolan Committee) made recommendations about behaviour in public life, and the appointment process follows them. Thus vacancies are advertised and appointments are made on merit, following a process regulated by the Office of the Commissioner for Public Appointments (OCPA), itself an independent body. This is a much more clearly open process than that adopted by the PCC and BBFC. Whilst the result may constitute a gathering of the 'great and the good' rather than reflecting the make-up of society, it can still work.[86] The members of the Trust itself are bound by a Code and by the Nolan Principles.[87] Whilst the intentions of the Trust members may not be in issue, the decisions of the Trust will reflect its membership, whose experience and values need not necessarily reflect those of current society: the Code of Practice for OCPA

---

[82] *BBC Charter, 1996* (Cm 3248, 1996) art 3(b).

[83] *BBC Charter, 2006* (Cm 6925, 2006) art 24. Further details on the public value test are set out in clauses 24 *et seq* of the Agreement (Cm 6872, 2006). Clause 17(2) of the Agreement specifies that each licence granted by the trust must contain provisions setting out how the service will contribute to the promotion of the Public Purposes and of relevant priorities set out in purpose remits, and each licence must also include indicators against which the Trust can monitor performance.

[84] House of Lords, 'The Review of the BBC's Royal Charter', 25.

[85] Ofcom and the BBC Trust have entered into an MoU to deal with this problem, March 2007.

[86] It has been accepted by Council of Europe, Recommendation, Independence and Functions of Regulatory Authorities, Rec (2003) 23.

[87] <http://www.public-standards.gov.uk/about_us/the_seven_principles_of_life.aspx>.

expressly states that: 'In making appointments departments must guard against positive discrimination'.[88] The Trust may therefore be independent but not representative.

The Trust is responsible for issuing the licences for the various BBC services, all of which were re-issued following a public consultation in April 2008 to implement the BBC Trust's six-year plan.[89] The BBC Trust—indeed the BBC as a whole—has made its work plans available generally, thereby showing a broader openness and accountability than the formal structures require. Licences operate within a framework comprising the public purpose remits found in the Charter and Agreement. Although the purpose remits themselves are subject to major review after five years, the service licences will be reviewed periodically and will, together with any major change to the service, be subject to a PVT.[90] The licences are one of the Trust's main tools of governance. They are significant because they go to the general framework of broadcasting and comprise positive obligations, rather than focusing on individual instances of breach at programme level, which seems more the concern of a complaints system; they are thus primarily a regulatory mechanism rather than part of a system of enforcement for individual rights. Licences cover four areas for each service: a statement as to the range and type of output; high level scheduling commitments; commitments to search and navigation; and commitments to programme commissioning. More detailed obligations, such as commissioning obligations and detailed scheduling commitments are found in statements of programme policy (SOPPs), revised annually. As in the case of commercial television, licences and SOPPs provide a benchmark against which BBC provision can be measured.[91] In addition to having concern for the provision of public service, the BBC Trust is concerned to have regard to the competitive impact of the BBC's activities on the wider market, reinforced by the use of PVT. This is worrying, as services in the citizen's interest may be withdrawn or not provided out of concern for commercial interests.[92] It is too soon to gauge how stringent it will be in its approach, although the new licences adopt a simplified approach with the more detailed operational conditions removed.[93] Putting these sorts of obligations in the SOPP framework, allows a broadcaster more flexibility, which can be beneficial but can also remove safeguards for the public interest. In this, there are parallels with the changes introduced for commercial television, although as we shall see, that change has not been without difficulties.

---

[88] The Commissioner for Public Appointments, 'Code of Practice for Ministerial Appointments to Public Bodies' (2005) section 2.04.

[89] BBC Trust, 'Delivering the Creative Future' (October 2007).

[90] The changes incorporated in the 2008 re-issues were not judged significant enough to warrant a PVT.

[91] BBC Charter, art 22c.

[92] This was the concern behind the withdrawal of BBC Jam, despite the fact that the European Commission cleared it under the state aid rules.

[93] The licences will no longer contain conditions reflecting statutory obligations, although these will be monitored: BBC Trust, 'Service Licence Reissue, April 2008: Explanatory Note on the Variations', 3.

The Trust has not been in existence long, having made just one annual report (previously reports were made by the governors). Within its report were the results on a group of studies/surveys on the public service remit, as well as a study on trust in broadcasting (concerning the use of artifice). During its existence it has already commissioned a number of studies on the BBC's performance, notably the report on bias in the news, which revealed that the BBC's coverage was focused towards London. Another report on editorial standards focused on the premium phone and quiz debacle. Whilst the BBC should deal with this matter, and indeed suggests a sensitivity to ethical standards, it is to be hoped that the sum of the editorial issues to be dealt with is not limited to this point.

The Trust has another role: that of 'final court of appeal' for editorial complaints, although this system operates against the backdrop of the general law.[94] Following a consultation, the Trust published a new complaints framework effective from 1 August 2008, which envisages the possibility of complaints against the Trust itself. For all complaints against the BBC, the first step is to complain to the BBC management. It is only if the response is inadequate that the Trust gets involved and it has expressed a preference for leaving non-editorial matters (scheduling, production values, etc) to the BBC management. Currently, the BBC management operates a two-stage process, with a third stage comprising a complaint to the BBC Trust. The first is a response to editorial complaints from the department responsible for the programme; if this is deemed unsatisfactory, then the Editorial Complaints Unit (ECU) will look at the matter independently. If its conclusions are disputed, the matter then goes to the BBC Trust's Editorial Standards Committee (ESC). A complaint to Ofcom is also possible (see below).

In terms of accountability, the BBC makes public responses to recent issues of wide audience concern if they cause a significant number of complaints or involve a significant issue;[95] this can be contrasted with the BBFC, which does not provide such public responses. The decisions of the ECU are likewise made available before being archived. There are monthly summaries of complaints and all responses are published in quarterly reports, also available on the BBC website.[96] ECU reports are found on the same site. The Trust publishes its complaints on a separate site. The system would at least seem to satisfy requirements of transparency. A brief review of the decisions show that the BBC receives a wide range of complaints, and deals with a broader range of issues than those covered by Ofcom, which is itself a broader regime than that of the PCC. It receives complaints about the quality of programmes and the range of programmes broadcast, as well as on issues such as bad language and impartiality. According to the BBC Trust, the new framework will allow consideration by the Trust

---

[94] The new framework recognizes that individuals might have rights to bring action through the courts; in such cases, the BBC and the BBC Trust may decide not to deal with the complaint. Where a case has been adjudicated upon, the BBC will not re-open those decisions.

[95] <http://www.bbc.co.uk/complaints/read_responses.shtml>.

[96] <http://www.bbc.co.uk/complaints/review_reports.shtml>.

of a far greater range of complaints than it has handled in the past, apparently thereby strengthening its role in safeguarding licence fee payers' interests. It should be noted that the issues dealt with here cover both concerns for standard setting, and for the enforcement of individual rights (privacy and fairness), although there is no formal mechanism for redress for an individual seeking to enforce rights. In this, the role of general law and recourse to the courts remains an options for some individuals, though it seems far fewer feel the need to bring legal action against the BBC (or other television companies) than against the newspapers. Furthermore, the guidelines allow the Trust to take all appropriate appeals, and in determining the appropriateness of an appeal, the BBC Trust seems to have a wide discretion. This compounds the obvious structural problem that all routes of complaint and appeal fall within the BBC, even if the various bodies are differently constituted. While the procedures allow for a range of review mechanisms, the fundamental question of the extent to which they are truly independent of one another, as would seem to be required by Article 6 ECHR jurisprudence, and of government influence, remains. This weakness may be a common problem in self-regulatory systems; certainly the position here would be no worse than that found in the PCC. A weakness specific to the BBC's regulation arises from the overlap with Ofcom, which allows for the possibility of confusion between the two systems. This fact may prove problematic from the perspective of the viewer complainant. It therefore remains to be seen how effective these procedures are in ensuring accountability.

9.4.2 Commercial broadcasting

Commercial television and radio have, since their inception,[97] been regulated via an independent regulator, although the nature of such regulation has varied over time showing a trend to less direct control. The current regulator for both television and television is Ofcom, which also has some powers vis-à-vis the BBC. It was created to cover the communications sector generally, replacing not only all the previous broadcasting regulators but Oftel and the Radiocommunications Agency. The fact that Ofcom has some regulatory responsibilities over the BBC has been seen as bringing some coherence to the regulation of broadcast content, reinforcing a view of the commercial and public service elements of the system as complementary, rather than as competing or even as separate systems.[98] Nonetheless, the extent to which we now have a single coherent regulatory system is debatable. Television on the internet is not

---

[97] Commercial television was introduced in 1954; it was not until the 1970s that we see the introduction of commercial radio. Until that point, the BBC had a monopoly on radio broadcasting in the UK—with the exception of pirate radio stations.

[98] Barendt (n 5 above) 82.

(directly) regulated.[99] Additionally, given that the main focus of the Communications Act 2003 was to deregulate or co-regulate,[100] there is a fragmented patchwork of co-regulation based on non-legally binding memoranda of understanding in addition to numerous self-regulatory bodies. The lack of transparency is exacerbated by the fact that the review of the sector resulting in the 2003 Act did not replace the pre-existing regime comprising the Broadcasting Acts of 1990 and 1996, but amended them. It is therefore necessary to consult all three acts to understand the 'unified' system. This system is most un-user friendly and Ofcom does not yet seem to appreciate the need, from the viewers' perspective, of some form of coordination, coherence, and publicity in a devolved system of regulation.

Within the broadcasting sector, Ofcom is responsible for licensing, competition, and economic regulation as well as content concerns. Although it may delegate functions, as in the case of broadcast advertising and the ASA, it remains ultimately responsible. This chapter will focus on content regulation apart from broadcast advertising. Ofcom's specific obligations as broadcasting regulator must be understood in the light of Ofcom's general duties set out in section 3 of the Communications Act 2003. These duties have a schizophrenic, or at least bifurcated, quality to them.[101] Whilst section 3(1)(a) refers to the interests of citizens, section 3(1)(b) refers to those of consumers.[102] Ofcom is under a duty to ensure the availability of a wide range of television and radio services of high quality, appealing to a wide range of tastes and interests, and maintaining a plurality of suppliers, whilst at the same time it is under pressure to move towards lighter regulation and devolved regulation.[103] On the one hand, we can see that there is the possibility of regulation in the interests of the public sphere and of citizens. This approach ties in with a view of the role of the media as the fourth estate, providing information to facilitate more rational discourse taking into account a variety of views. Implicit is the possibility of ensuring that not only purely populist or 'easy' programming is available. Significantly, the Communications

---

[99] Communications Act 2003, ss 232 and 233 define the scope of Ofcom's regulatory remit by reference to the transmission of television programmes, but exclude 'two-way services' thereby excluding on-demand services. This position will change following the AVMS Directive, which extends negative regulations to all audiovisual media service providers irrespective of platform.

[100] Communications Act 2003, s 6(2). Ofcom has recently consulted on reviewing its approach to co- and self-regulation: Ofcom, 'Initial Assessments of When to Adopt Self or Co-regulation: Consultation' (27 March 2008), available at <http://www.ofcom.org.uk/consult/condocs/coregulation/condoc.pdf>. Note that the DCMS in its consultation on implementation of the AVMS Directive took a broader range of factors into account for assessing whether self-regulation, co-regulation or regulation would be appropriate.

[101] On the different interests of citizens and consumers, see eg Harrison and Woods (n 61 above) Ch 1. It has also been suggested that the true tension in Ofcom's duties lies in the conflict between Ofcom's obligations to individuals and the need to create a dynamic and robust industry: Ofcom, 'A case study on public sector mergers and regulatory structures', available at <http://www.ofcom.org.uk/about/accoun/case_study/case_study.pdf>, 66.

[102] The Communications Bill referred to 'customers'; the references to citizens were introduced by the House of Lords.

[103] Communications Act 2003, s 3(3)(a) and (4)(c).

Act 2003 does not specify how the interests of the citizen are to be provided for, giving Ofcom a degree of latitude in this regard which may not be beneficial.[104] The other theme underlying the 2003 Act is broadcasting as a commodity, that is aimed at consumers, and for their needs to be satisfied by the operation of competition. Although consumers must have choice, it is less clear what content will be found in this choice. This view tends towards the majoritarian, the populist, and the saleable. It is clearly difficult to identify how the choices of citizen and consumer overlap, which takes priority in the case of a conflict,[105] or how we identify when they are satisfied. With the reference to competition, we can question whether the view of what consumers want is to be found from the perspective of the market. Market choice thus becomes what the consumer is offered to choose from rather than viewer choice, as we will see in the case of children's television. Despite clear demand, provision of children's stations on commercial stations is dropping. The weakness is compounded where we have a system favouring light regulation, or self-regulation, which allows the public interest in large part to be defined by those subject to regulation.

As with the BBC, there are two broad approaches to regulation of content: one concerns itself with minimum standards (negative content regulation); the second concerns types of programming and relates more to diversity and pluralism (positive content regulation). Negative content regulation is referred to as tier 1; positive content obligations comprise quotas (tier 2) and public service broadcasting requirements (tier 3). The main mechanism for control of content is through the use of codes with which broadcasters must comply, although positive content obligations (for example regional programming, amount of news, etc) may be contained in the broadcasters' licences.[106] Compliance with the codes is required by the terms of the Communications Act 2003; compliance is also ensured by virtue of terms inserted in the operators' licences. As we will see below, the scope of these obligations, specifically positive qualitative obligations (public service broadcasting), may not be without weaknesses. There are a range of sanctions such as fines, but in some instances a broadcasting licence may be revoked.[107]

In terms of structure, many of the complaints made about the BBC Trust do not arise in relation to Ofcom. It is a statutory corporation and structurally independent of government, although it is required to report annually to Parliament. This is the basis

---

[104] Note economic regulators should not trespass on Parliament's policy-making prerogative as far as citizens' needs are concerned: BERR, 'Response to the House of Lords Select Committee on Regulators Inquiry UK Economic Regulators' (January 2008) para 1.14.

[105] Ofcom is to make this decision on a case-by-case basis: Ofcom's own in-built preferences would seem therefore to influence this decision.

[106] Note the difference between television licensable content services (TLCS) (defined in the Communications Act 2003 s 232) and television broadcast services; a similar distinction may be made for radio (ibid s 247). The former licences are required for the provision of content organized into channels, and are essentially available on demand, subject to payment of a fee and compliance with relevant content requirements (ibid s 235(2)). TLCS does not give the holder a right to a frequency to broadcast.

[107] Revocations occur most frequently in relation to TLCS, often for non-payment of fees; Ofcom will give a statement of reasons where revocation is due to non-compliance with the licence: see <http://www.ofcom.org.uk/tv/ifi/tvlicensing/tvupdates/>.

on which it is found accountable.[108] One difficulty with this system was, given the range of issues in which Ofcom is involved, that no structures were put in place for coordination of parliamentary accountability. Ofcom generally has made its plans open to scrutiny and, as with the BBC, could thus be seen to be accountable more widely, even if informally, than just via Parliament.

The main decision-making body of Ofcom is its Board, which is a unitary board with a mix of executive and part-time members. The executive and non-executive members have equal weighting (save in audit and governance matters) and the non-executive board members operate on the basis of collective responsibility. The chair was appointed after a full Nolan-compliant appointment process. The appointment of senior executives deliberately focused on private sector experience, thus reinforcing choices about the sort of regulator Ofcom would be that were implicit in its structure. The structure is different from the structures established for the previous regulators and from that used for the BBC;[109] it has been deliberately established in this manner to replicate the boards of the companies that Ofcom regulates and it is claimed that this structure has given Ofcom the ability to act swiftly.[110] Within Ofcom, there are a number of committees which have relevance for broadcasting: the Ofcom Content Board;[111] the Content Sanctions Committee; the Radio Licensing Committee; the Fairness Committee; and the Elections Committee.[112] There is additionally the Ofcom and BBC Joint Steering Committee[113] and a number of advisory committees required by the Communications Act 2003.[114] It has been remarked that these committees were introduced in a fairly haphazard manner,[115] although practice (see below) seems to minimize some of the potential difficulties of overlap.

The Content Board is, according to Ofcom, the 'primary forum for the regulation' of television and radio and its role is 'understanding, analysing and championing the voices and interests of the viewer, the listener and the citizen'. It considers those issues that would be unprotected from a purely market-based and economic analysis and is therefore a significant element in the protection awarded to viewers and listeners, particularly in their capacity as citizens. Thus, it is the Content Board which should be protector of the public sphere, insofar as there is one within the current regime. In its early days, the Content Board was concerned with establishing the framework for content regulation, moving to a lighter touch approach to the Broadcast Code. In this context, it has been noted that the Content Board's activities are different in scope from

---

[108] This is acceptable for the terms of Council of Europe Recommendation, Rec (2003) 23.
[109] At one end of the scale was the single Director-General as in Oftel's case; and at the other the commission structure of the ITC and the Radio Authority.
[110] Ofcom, 'A case study on public sector mergers' (n 101 above) 14.
[111] Communications Act 2003, s 12(1).
[112] ibid s 333.
[113] BBC Agreement 2006, cl 29.
[114] See Communications Act 2003, ss 20 and 21.
[115] Ofcom, 'A case study on public sector mergers' (n 101 above) 15.

what might have been originally envisaged.[116] Subsequently, it seems to have focused on dealing with complaints about particular programmes, rather than more general concerns about overarching programme provision: these issues fall within general public sector broadcasting (PSB) review, or are to some extent picked up by the Consumer Panel. The Content Board was subject to criticism by the House of Lords, which suggested that the Ofcom Content Board be strengthened; by contrast to the Consumer Panel, it does not have an independent budget or independent staff[117] and might therefore be seen as a weak body, with expertise or interest only in matters economic. This proposal was rejected, as the Content Board, unlike the Consumer Panel, has executive functions within Ofcom and is not just an advisory body.[118]

The Advisory Committee on Older and Disabled People provides advice where requested to the Ofcom Board and, sometimes, to the Ofcom Content Board on matters found in section 3 of the Communications Act 2003 as they affect older people and those with disabilities. In practice, its focus seems to have been on technical rather than content-related matters, and it claims it has succeeded in getting its concerns regarding digital switchover and accessible television absorbed into the mainstream of Ofcom's work plan. Likewise, the Committees for the Nations so advise on matters related to the nations. Both have reporting obligations. Nonetheless, it should be noted that these are advisory committees which cannot enforce their views on Ofcom.[119]

The Communications Act 2003 also stipulated that a consumer panel should be established.[120] By contrast to the other advisory committees, it is intended to operate at arm's length from Ofcom and, in the terms of the Act, identify issues from the consumers' perspective and to Act as a 'critical friend'. To this end, it has its own budget to commission research and there is a memorandum of understanding establishing the working relationship between it and Ofcom. Given its significance to Ofcom, Ofcom was heavily involved in its recruitment process, opening the question of whether Ofcom's influence has affected the Panel's ability to do its job. On one level this seems unlikely. Although in the terms of the Communications Act 2003, the Panel has responsibility only for consumer interests, the memorandum of understanding and the terms of its research make it clear that it has broader concerns, notably the interests of the citizen. In this sense, we can suggest that to some extent the practice is overcoming some of the weaknesses of the regulatory system. Indeed it is arguable that the Consumer Panel has been more proactive in this regard than the Content Board.

Despite the potentially broad scope of activities with which the Ofcom Content Board might concern itself, after its activities reviewing the Broadcast Content Code, its main public focus seems to be adjudicatory, responding to the breaches of the

---

[116] ibid 66.
[117] House of Lords, 'The Review of the BBC's Royal Charter' (n 68 above) 33.
[118] DCMS, *Government Response* (n 70 above) 4.
[119] Contrast the position in the Broadcasting Act 1981, ss 16–18.
[120] Communications Act 2003, s 16.

broadcast Code and section 319 of the Communications Act 2003,[121] as well as the impartiality requirement in section 320. Like the PCC and BBC (including the Editorial Complaints Unit and Trust) and its predecessor the ITC, the Ofcom Content Board makes its decisions available publicly, thus satisfying standard concerns about transparency. Over the years, the Ofcom Content Board seems to have become more confident in explaining its reasoning; its decisions have a more judgment-like quality to them. Three issues stand out. As with the PCC, the Ofcom Content Board does not explain the basis on which complaints are deemed to be out of remit; indeed, it mixes them in with cases not in breach and those resolved. The majority of impartiality cases suggest deference to the broadcaster's judgment,[122] although there have been a couple of cases in which the Content Board has made the decision that there has been a violation. Finally, Ofcom will impose sanctions, including in some instances significant fines. Nonetheless, there is a suspicion that except in extreme cases, broadcasters may choose to ignore the decision, even though it is made public: some long-running shows fall foul of the same provisions in the same way, series after series.[123]

It is in terms of the positive content requirements, contained in tiers 2 and 3 and which are central to the audience's right to receive (and central in an instrumental view of the broadcaster's freedom of expression), that particular weaknesses show. The Communications Act 2003 specifies certain conditions governing what is required by public service broadcasters but the Act also brought in a change of emphasis in PSB review and enforcement. There are two aspects to this change: the approach to review and the increased emphasis on self-assessment. Ofcom is under a duty to review at regular intervals the provision of PSB, but in doing so it focuses on the public services broadcasting provided by television services as a whole.[124] This is a more general and environmental assessment than the licensee-by-licensee assessment found in the ITC reports. In its first review of PSB, Ofcom moved to an approach which identified broad characteristics of PSB and how it might be attained; the second review followed a broadly similar format. Thus, Ofcom seemed to suggest that the main focus of PSB was the BBC and that the other public service broadcasters defined under the 2003 Act had narrower, more specific roles. The consequences of this can be seen in the fact that Ofcom accepted a weakening of the PSB obligations on ITV in respect of non-news regional programming and in children's programming, the latter because of provision elsewhere. ITV then proposed in its statement of programme policy (SOPP) for 2008 to reduce its commitment to children's programming still further, despite Ofcom's concerns. ITV took account of Ofcom's representations and then effectively ignored

---

[121] This replaces Broadcasting Act 1990, s 6 and it is drafted in similar terms, though the 'good taste requirement' derived from the 1954 Act has been replaced by a requirement that broadcasters should not broadcast material which is offensive and harmful. This is arguably more objective than 'good taste'.

[122] See eg Ofcom Content Bulletin 111, Dispatches: The Court of Ken—Channel 4, 22 January 2008, 20:00, though it is interesting to note that Ofcom looked at what was actually broadcast rather than assessing the programme in the light of 'journalistic practices'—contrast the approach of the PCC.

[123] See eg 'Wire in the Blood', 'Big Brother'.

[124] Ofcom suggests it has an overarching duty under the Communications Act 2003, s 264.

them, claiming that it had satisfied its obligations under the Communications Act 2003 merely by 'listening'.[125] It seems that with market forces determining programming choices within commercial television, the overarching television environment will be served in the main by the BBC, a development which Ofcom itself seems to recognize. Whether this is desirable, Ofcom also questions: there are issues about diversity of suppliers and the position of independent producers of such programmes, as well as the fact that the UK television environment will become increasingly dependent on support for the BBC.[126]

Secondly, there has been a move to self-reporting, the television companies being under a duty to provide SOPPs and to produce reports (SAR) annually on whether they have met their own self-imposed targets.[127] This system parallels the approach for the BBC within the Trust system. Such a form of organization is part of a move to lighter regulation. As noted, the Communications Act 2003 envisages that broadcasters may make significant changes to their SOPP, provided Ofcom is consulted; this is weaker than the role of the Trust for BBC services which may undertake a PVT. Thus, the provisions which allow for Ofcom's involvement in significant changes are merely legitimating the renegotiation of broadcasters' obligations. As noted above, they have not operated to stop a relaxation of genre-specific PSB obligations. Nonetheless Ofcom does have fall-back powers to act to introduce detailed regulation in the case of system failure, where a particular broadcaster with public service obligations has failed to fulfil the public service remit for that channel or has failed, in any respect, to make an adequate contribution towards the fulfilment of the purposes of public service television broadcasting.

There are weaknesses in this provision, as illustrated by the fact that, despite Ofcom's obvious concern about the level of provision of children's programmes, it took no action. The first is that the failure of provision (or otherwise) is assessed by reference to the broadcaster's public service remit as defined in the Communications Act 2003. These have moved to a broader, almost functional definition, rather than being based on genres specifically. Thus the remit of Channels 3 and 5, in that it requires 'the provision of a range of high quality and diverse programming', does not specify any particular type of programming. Looking at the rights of audiences, it may not necessarily relate to the wider democratic participation of individuals.[128] Furthermore, Ofcom may only interfere if a two-stage test is passed, not only that it is the failure of the provider but also that it is not excused by economic or market conditions, both conditions being matters of Ofcom's opinion. It has rightly been suggested that this

---

[125] ibid s 267(2).
[126] Ofcom, 'Ofcom's Second Public Service Broadcasting Review. Phase One: The Digital Opportunity' (April 2008).
[127] Communications Act 2003, s 266 and with regard to the BBC, see terms of Charter and Agreement at s 21.
[128] Contrast the role of the BBC: in s 6 of the BBC Agreement one of the BBC's purposes is stated as 'sustaining citizenship and civil society'. This, of course, is equally open to definition on the part of the broadcaster.

second condition drives a coach and horses through the obligations imposed on licensees.[129] If Ofcom does not have discretion enough in this section a final condition is imposed: that Ofcom determines that the situation requires the exercise of their powers under this section. To return to the case of ITV and children's programmes, ultimately it seems that Ofcom chose not to exercise its discretion here, raising the question of when Ofcom would think a threat serious. This assessment relates back to Ofcom's stated preference for not intervening. Perhaps part of the problem lies in Ofcom's approach: with its research and study-based approach, some have suggested that it is acting more like a think-tank developing policy than a regulator with enforcement powers. In this case, it might be looking forward to its assessment of the market in terms of provision of PSB, and trying to get the market to work, rather than protecting the viewer in the meanwhile. This essentially is a restatement of the tensions in the 2003 Act itself. In sum, although Ofcom would satisfy most tests for independence and transparency, there are serious shortcomings in the system for enforcing public sphere-related positive obligations.

9.5 VIDEOS, DVDS, AND VIDEO GAMES

The Video Recordings Act 1984 (VRA 1984) introduced the regime for audiovisual content on storage media:[130] the content could have been released in a cinema, broadcast on television, or been released straight to video/DVD. Thus, content can be subject to overlapping regimes. The system introduced by VRA 1984 is a classification system similar to that operated in relation to films by the BBFC. Although primarily concerned with programming style content, the terms of VRA 1984 potentially cover software and computer games, provided that there is a 'series of visual images'. The VRA system exempts certain categories from the classification regime, but then limits the exception. Thus, video games are an exempted class provided they do not depict human sexual activities; mutilation, torture or acts of gross violence; or human genital organs or human urinary or excretory functions.[131] VRA 1984 specifies that it is an offence to distribute a video which has not been awarded a classification, which effectively gives the classifying body the possibility of banning a video by refusing it a classification. Local trading standards departments are the enforcement authority for VRA 1984, rather than the BBFC, introducing yet another set of actors into the regulation of the media. The 1984 Act gives the BBFC statutory powers (ie it is the body designated for this purpose by the Secretary of State) to determine the classification of videos.

---

[129]   Hitchens (n 7 above) 163.

[130]   Amended by the Criminal Justice and Public Order Act 1994, VRA 1984 is expressed to include any other device capable of storing data electronically. The Act is therefore no longer limited to video tape or disc, but also content released on cartridge and, probably, any other device used now or in the future. VRA 1984 was also amended in 1993.

[131]   VRA 1984, s 2.

Although the age-rating guidance is not set down in statute, the legislation forming the video framework identifies the criteria which the BBFC must bear in mind, taking into account the viewing audience likely to be found in homes.[132]

As required by the VRA 1984, there is a right of appeal from BBFC decisions to the Video Appeals Committee (VAC), but this right is limited to the person submitting the video for classification; it does not extend to the general public. Whilst this may have the advantage of excluding pressure groups, it may also limit legitimate public concern. There is no other complaints procedure, although the BBFC will respond to letters (or e-mails) of complaint. The VAC has other weaknesses. One particular concern relates to appointment of members. As the 2000 Consultation on the 18R classification category noted, although VRA 1984 requires the BBFC to have an appeal system in place, it is silent as to membership. The assumption underlying the passage of the Bill was that the Committee's membership would consist 'of people of distinction and integrity, wholly independent of the industry and the BBFC'.[133] The same consultation procedure subsequently noted that, 'the Committee is unrepresentative and unaccountable'.[134] There is no mention of Nolan principles. A number of proposals were put forward to make the appointments more transparent. Against this background, without explanation seven new members of the VAC were appointed and some commentators have suggested that the those appointed were chosen specifically because they were less likely to have liberal views.[135] This does not ameliorate the underlying concerns (indeed the response might seem further to undermine independence) and a recent private member's Bill suggested that VRA 1984 be amended to establish a new independent body.[136]

The relationship between the BBFC and the VAC has not been without conflict: although not many appeals are taken to the VAC, the BBFC has brought judicial review proceedings against the decision of the VAC in a couple of cases, most recently in respect of the decision in Manhunt II. Although the VAC had misdirected itself as to law,[137] on reconsidering the case by a 4–3 decision it still overturned the BBFC's decision to ban the game. It would seem from this that the VAC is independent of the BBFC, as should be the case in an appeal body. Indeed, the somewhat unlikely element of these cases is the BBFC's attitude to the VAC, as exemplified by the bringing of judicial review actions. Of course, the position is somewhat tricky as there is no formal route of appeal from the VAC and judicial review would seem the only option

---

[132] ibid s 4; VRA 1984; the Criminal Justice and Public Order Act 1994 introduced further criteria that the BBFC should also take into account.

[133] BBFC, 'Consultation on 18R' (2000) para 1.7.

[134] ibid para 3.17

[135] Robertson and Nicol (n 21 above) 860.

[136] British Board of Film Classification (Accountability to Parliament and Appeals) Bill, available at <http://www.publications.parliament.uk/pa/cm200708/cmbills/016/en/2008016en.pdf>.

[137] *R (on application of BBFC) v Video Appeals Committee* [2008] EWHC 203 (Admin); see previously *R v VAC, ex p BBFC* [2000] EMLR regarding hardcore porn.

where the BBFC believes there has been an error or misdirection, as was the case in Manhunt II.

Subject to the operation of section 2(2) and (3) of VRA 1984, video games fall outside the Act's regime; video games played in amusement arcades do not require licensing as films and cinemas do. Two points should be noted. First, the VRA system will not cover online games at all, as they are not stored on digital media; and BBFC-commissioned research suggested that this was a concern for members of the public not just as regards games, but all content. Secondly, the boundary between games which have to be classified by the BBFC and those which do not can be seen as introducing a discrepancy between the system used for films (which distinguishes between classifications for younger children) and games in terms of having statutory back-up in place for the rules. Otherwise, there are no codes of conduct relating to the content contained in the games, though there is a classification system. This, on the whole, is dealt with in a self-regulatory manner.[138]

Until 2003, the system in place was Entertainment Leisure Software Publishers Association (ELSPA). The system was administered by the Video Standards Council (VSC), a body which was established in response to government concerns about the video industry. It manages a code of practice, last updated in 2003, agreed by the industry and concerned with the supply and distribution of videos and DVDs. There are some weaknesses in its system in terms of independence and accountability. First, membership is voluntary and the VSC cannot impose sanctions on its membership; secondly, the VSC is funded by industry, raising questions about independence (though we have noted that this is a common 'problem');[139] and thirdly, the VSC is managed by a twenty-one member committee comprising representatives from the different groups making up its membership. There is no lay representation, although the VSC has established its own VSC Consultative Committee, to advise on issues of taste and decency and prevailing attitudes in society. Members of this committee include not only members of the VSC committee but also representatives of religious and child protection communities, presumably acting as experts. The public at large does not seem to be represented and, unlike the BBFC, the VSC does not engage in research into public expectations. Although there is a complaints system, it is not immediately obvious, and the Complaints Board seems to made up of the main board members. There seems to be no further right of appeal. Additionally, there is no obvious accountability mechanism to the public (or their representatives), meaning it is difficult to assess the operation of the system. In general terms, the body (like the IMCB) seems to be industry facing rather than concerned with citizens, which is problematic if it is to have a role in enforcing public values.

This system has been replaced by the European PEGI system as of spring 2003. It is run by the Dutch authority, NICAM, which has appointed the VSC as its agent.

---

[138] Note there are also rules relating to packaging.

[139] Contrast the level of funding to the PCC, on the one hand, and the ASA and the BBFC, on the other, and also their respective approaches to the industries they regulate.

The system is different both as to the age categories and the descriptors used and, given the fact that it is a pan-European system, it does not reflect the idiosyncrasies of the British public. It appears to be the result of industry agreement, rather public consultation. PEGI has extended its system to games on the internet. Currently, the PEGI Online logo appears on those websites that have been checked by the VSC and found to comply with minimum safety standards to protect minors and their privacy. Game publishers provide NICAM with necessary materials so it can examine the content of all games applying for a 12+ rating. Random checks of games rated at the 3+ and 7+ levels may be carried out. Given that games may lose exemption under VRA 1984, those games applying for a 16+ or 18+ rating will be examined by the VSC to ensure that they do still fall within the terms of section 2(1)(c). There is, however, little in the way of sanction; certainly there is no statutory point of sale enforcement as there is for the BBFC. Nonetheless, if there is a conflict between the assessment of PEGI/VSC and the BBFC (for instance, if in the view of BBFC the game falls within section 2(3) of VRA 1984), then the view of the BBFC will take priority. The BBFC has further expressed concern regarding confusion between the two ratings systems, that of the BBFC—according to BBFC research—being better understood.[140] Whilst this may be a consequence of the relative newness of the PEGI system, the understanding or recognition of the system by the audience is a weakness of a number of systems relating to new services.

Against this backdrop we come to the Byron Report, which concerned children's safety on the internet, and particularly online games. Her report contained several suggestions, including the lowering of the standard which would trigger review by the BBFC, which would lead to more games being reviewed under the co-regulatory system, rather than just the self-regulatory system. Although both are classification systems, it may be that the BBFC is more rigorous on the boundaries between different classifications. The Report also suggest using the BBFC ratings system in addition to the PEGI system, as the BBFC symbols and categories are more familiar to parents.[141] Additionally, this would introduce greater commonality into the systems across games, videos, and films. Finally, a strategy to empower parents and to encourage better codes of conduct would be adopted.[142] In the light of the challenge to industry, the BBFC suggested a scheme for providing age ratings for downloaded video content and video games.[143] The system would also require such services and video-on-demand schemes

---

[140] This was noted in the Byron Report, T Byron, 'Safer children in a Digital World' (March 2008) para 7.24.

[141] The European Commission has suggested that Member States do more to avoid confusion arising from dual systems: a single Europe-wide system is, of course, easier from the perspective of ensuring free movement of goods and services (22 April 2008), although the ECJ has been sympathetic to national concerns regarding the protection of minors and age-based classifications, as *Dynamic Medien Vertriebs GmbH v Avides Media* (Case C-244/06, judgment of 14 February 2008), especially para 44, illustrates.

[142] See eg the Good practice guidance for the providers of social networking and other user interactive services (2008), available at <http://police.homeoffice.gov.uk/publications/operational-policing/social-networking-guidance>.

[143] See <http://www.bbfc.org.uk/bbfcOnline/bbfcOnline.php>.

to have age verification or other gate-keeping technologies so that parents could monitor and, it is to be hoped, control under-age viewing.

The BBFC proposal is interesting for a number of reasons. The timing was fortuitous, coinciding with the release of the Byron Report. The system is, by comparison with the system in place for film and video, voluntary; there is no obligation to comply. Nonetheless, a number of major industry players have, according to the BBFC, signed up. Indeed the degree of choice operators have in the light of the Byron Report to avoid any similar scheme is limited. The BBFC states that it takes compliance with the rules of this scheme[144] seriously, the voluntary nature of the system notwithstanding, and reserves the right to terminate membership for non-compliance. If the BBFC sign is seen as a trust mark, then this could be an effective sanction. Using the same scheme has a couple of other advantages. It treats products which are similar from the perspective of the viewer alike. It also relies on an established support system, which is well funded, thus avoiding problems that other self-regulatory bodies (the PCC and ATVOD, for example) have run into. Interestingly, there is a potential for overlap with other bodies such as ATVOD for content other than games, which may lead to regulatory competition; it is unlikely that more than one regulator is viable.

The government has recently issued a consultation paper on ways to improve the way in which video games are classified.[145] Although it notes that its starting point is the Byron recommendations, it is also aware that Byron's focus was children's safety and that there may be other considerations, such as the economic well-being of companies, that trump child safety. There are four models put forward. The first, taken from the Byron Report, is that there should be a dual model based on the BBFC plus PEGI, together with an extension of the BBFC's statutory powers to 12+ games. The second enhances the BBFC's powers, applying its ratings from U to 18. The third option would give statutory powers to a body (such as the VSC, although the VSC poses obvious problems in terms of independence, given its funding and the make-up of its board) to apply PEGI. The final possibility is to leave the legislative framework unchanged and to ask retailers to sign up to a code of conduct. The games industry supports PEGI, despite the lack of general understanding of the system by parents. Whichever system is adopted, it should be a coherent one. In terms of coherency between converged industries and coherency between geographical territories, given language differences, industry convergence is more likely to occur. On that basis, coherence between film, video, and games would suggest that the BBFC's system should be adopted, whether alone or in conjunction with PEGI; this appears to be the preference of the House of Commons Select Committee on Culture, Media and Sport.[146]

---

[144] <http://www.bbfc.org.uk/downloads/pub/BBFConline/BBFC.online_Scheme_Rules%20Edition_1.1.pdf>.

[145] DCMS, 'Video games classification: a consultation' (July 2008).

[146] House of Commons, Select Committee on Culture, Media and Sport, 'Harmful content on the Internet and in video games', HC 353-I, 31 July 2008.

9.6 VIDEO-ON-DEMAND

Video-on-demand can be provided over a number of different networks, including mobile phones and the internet. Whilst the content may be the same as that provided over broadcasting networks (including near video on demand), two-way services lie outside the broadcasting regime. Ofcom has not stepped in; instead, a number of self-regulatory bodies have been established—notably ATVOD and, specifically regarding content over mobile phones, the IMCB. We have also noted the possible involvement of the BBFC in classifying downloads. ATVOD and the IMCB are both industry bodies, effectively established (like the PCC and the VSC) to avoid the threat of direct regulation. Both have small memberships and limited resources, which may hinder their effectiveness. Equally, both are dependent on funding from the industry, which, as noted above, brings difficulties as far as independence from that industry is concerned.

The IMCB was appointed pursuant to a code of practice agreed by a number of mobile operators, known collectively as the Mobile Broadband Group (MBG); the code of practice is currently under review and for the first time MBG has decided to open the process to consultation.[147] The IMCB is a subsidiary of the premium rate phone regulatory body (PhonepayPlus (PPP), formerly ICSTIS) and the IMCB's Board is drawn from that of PPP. PPP's appointment of lay members is open, seemingly designed to comply with Nolan standards. The IMCB operates a classification system according to which its commercial content providers self-classify their content; mobile operators according to the code will impose access controls on material classified as 18, and unclassified material will be treated as 18. Although there was no consultation on the classification system, the terms of the classification system broadly reflect those of the BBFC, which did take public expectations into account, and are set independently of the MBG and, crucially, content providers.

The mobile operators will enforce the terms of the code through their contractual arrangements with the content providers. It is this aspect which would give the determinations by the IMCB (if it ever made any) bite, as content providers are dependent on the mobile companies to access the audience. In this regard, the effectiveness has some similarity to the system adopted in relation to advertising and the film industry. By contrast with the BBFC, review is not carried out by the classification body, which implies a weakness in the system. This point should not be overstated; reliance on complaints is a mechanism by which many of the contents standards systems operate and, by contrast with the PCC, for example, there is some degree of review in that the mobile content operators will monitor the classification of content.[148] As with other systems, complaints must be brought to the service provider first.

---

[147] MBG, 'Consultation on the review of the "UK code of practice for the self-regulation of new forms of content on mobiles"' (8 August, 2008). See also Ofcom, 'UK Code of Practice for the Self-regulation of new forms of content on mobiles: Review' (11 August 2008).

[148] MBG, 'Consultation on Code' (n 147 above) 5.

Ofcom believes the code to be working well, being well understood by industry members, even given the inactivity of the IMCB.[149]

There are a number of points to note about this system. In one sense, this is not true self-regulation, but rather a case of one industry (the mobile companies) requiring another industry (content) to comply with standards; it works because of the commitment of the MBG, which gives its determinations (and the mobile companies' determinations about content) their bite. The mobile operators operate a 'yellow' and 'red' card system, where the yellow card is a warning and a take down notice, whilst red cards will lead to the content producer (or possibly the content aggregator) being barred. According to Ofcom, the mobile operators informally share information about yellow and red cards.[150] While this might result in consistent application, there is a risk that content providers are barred without due warning. As with the Internet Watch Foundation (IWF), it also constitutes the transfer of control of content to a private party, meaning the transparency and fairness of its systems are crucial and it is here that the IMCB comes into play. Interestingly, the MBG also relies on the IWF list of unacceptable content, which has been criticized for not respecting human rights as far as freedom of expression and natural justice are concerned.[151]

There are some limitations on the system too. The first group relates to scope: the MBG notes that it cannot control content on the internet,[152] nor is material transferred via Bluetooth technology covered by the code.[153] In a converged environment, it is somewhat surprising to see limits of protection depending on means of transfer. This difficulty reflects the system overall which has developed. Further, the boundary between content which is accessible or not lies at the 18 classification. Given that children much younger have mobile access, the system may not offer adequate protection to the younger children; indeed this is the sort of complaint levelled at the video games system also. The MBG notes this difficulty, though it believes its signposting of which content is appropriate is sufficient,[154] but has raised the question as to whether there is sufficient 'granularity' in the content classification system. At the very least, there is a tension in the MBG's comments, which underscores concerns about the level of protection really offered, especially to young children. As a final point, it should be noted that this system, in focusing on the protection of children, is narrow in scope (there are, for example, no accuracy or impartiality requirements) and central concerns to society, such as the prohibition of hate speech, must be left to the general law. The system is also essentially negative. Nonetheless, in that its focus is the setting of

---

[149]   Ofcom, 'Self-Regulation of new forms of content on Mobiles' (n 147 above) 2.
[150]   ibid 14.
[151]   D Wall, 'On the Politics of Policing the Internet: Striking the right balance', 14th BILETA Conference, 'CYBERSPACE 1999: Crime, Criminal Justice and the Internet' (1999), available at <http://www.bileta.ac.uk/Document%20Library/1/On%20the%20Politics%20of%20Policing%20the%20Internet%20-%20Striking%20the%20Right%20Balance.pdf>, 5.
[152]   MBG, 'UK Code of Practice for the Self-Regulation of New Forms of Content on Mobiles' (2004) cl 2.
[153]   MBG, 'Consultation on Code' (n 147 above) 5.
[154]   ibid.

standards, it is aimed at protecting at least some aspect of public interest, albeit in narrow terms. The system does not provide individual rights, which perhaps lessens the need for individual rights of access to an independent tribunal, but would not lessen concerns about transparency (discussed below).

ATVOD likewise aims to ensure that unsuitable material is not available to children (and in doing so may have reference to classification by other bodies such as the BBFC and Ofcom); information is to be given regarding content which may cause harm or offence, so adults may make their own choices.[155] This is essentially a form of labelling which is akin to a classification system and so similar comments may be made about its scope as were made about the IMCB classification code. As regards ATVOD, it is interesting to note that it has moved from a code which was based on the broadcasting code, a basis which makes sense given the likely similarity of content, to the less demanding system. There are no provisions prohibiting particular types of content or material (for example pornography or hate speech), although where ATVOD members have editorial control, they should attempt to ensure that the use of material which infringes human dignity is justified.[156] It is questionable whether such systems would satisfy the negative content requirements in the AVMS Directive. From the perspective of the citizen, neither system operates so as to ensure civil society involvement, diversity of content, or the protection of the public sphere.

The IMCB (as a body separate from the MBG) is problematic in ways similar to ATVOD; neither appears to do much and there are real issues of transparency. The IMCB has published one adjudication in 2005, which was held to be out of remit. Although publication is in principle good, as with the PCC, concerns might arise regarding summaries of facts which cannot be independently verified and which are drafted so as to justify the conclusion. There have been no subsequent rulings, suggesting a perfect industry or a lack of public profile. From the Ofcom review, it seems that lack of public profile is a real issue.[157] Worryingly, in terms of both transparency and activity, the IMCB has not published a separate annual report, despite claiming it was going to in 2005, its report instead apparently forming part of the annual report of PPP (formerly ICSTIS). As Ofcom noted, this is not adequate. It further noted that the IMCB saw itself as an industry-facing body, rather than one with responsibility to the public, which explains the lack of outreach work. The lack of transparency extends into the operation of the code by the MBG: the operators keep no records of complaints and the low level of recorded complaints is not a reliable indicator of the actual access of children to unsuitable content; such children are unlikely to report it.[158] Despite these problems, the government sees the IMCB as one possible plank of the system.[159]

[155] ATVOD Code (October 2007), para 8.
[156] The previous version of the ATVOD Code borrowed from the Broadcasting Codes and therefore did contain such obligations.
[157] Ofcom, 'Self-Regulation of New Forms of Content on Mobiles' (n 147 above) 12.
[158] ibid 3 and 8.
[159] DCMS, 'Public Consultation on implementing the EC Audiovisual Media Services Directive' (July 2008); see also Ofcom, 'Self and Co-regulation Consultation'.

Although ATVOD was put forward as an exemplar of desirable new-style regulation by politicians, independent studies for the European Commission[160] have been more critical, suggesting that the body is not well-resourced, and that it is not well known by the public. Despite its claims to inform the public, it seems to do little regarding public awareness. Although changes have been made to the ATVOD website giving some contact details, as is the case with ATVOD and the BBC, members of the public have to complain first to their service provider before bringing a complaint to ATVOD. Complaints can be made via e-mail, online, or by letter; it is not possible to telephone ATVOD. Although remedies are available such as publicity of the decision or, in severe cases, suspension of membership, it is difficult to assess their effectiveness since no complaints seem to have been brought, or at least not those that fall within ATVOD's remit. This point is difficult to assess, as there is no section on the ATVOD website dealing with decided complaints, which is a weakness in the transparency of the system. Although other bodies use similar mechanisms, there is a particular problem as far as ATVOD is concerned in that membership is voluntary and key members of the industry have not joined. It is possible to do well in this sector without the imprimatur of ATVOD. Furthermore, although the BBC is a member, complaints about the BBC on-demand service should be taken to the BBC; this duplication as regards the BBC may lead to confusion.

The IMCB Framework also introduces the Classification Framework Appeals Body, which is a body of persons independent of the IMCB appointed to hear appeals against decisions made by the IMCB under the IMCB Complaints and Dispute Procedures. Since 2007, there has at least been the possibility of a further level of appeal, to an independent adjudicator, which is an improvement on the BBFC as regards films. Both systems in this respect make some effort to comply with natural justice concerns (and Article 6 ECHR) regarding the impartiality of appeal bodies, which is an improvement on the Ofcom and PCC systems. Whether the IMCB and ATVOD will end up bringing judicial review actions, as the BBFC has, remains to be seen.

As already noted, the government recently issued a consultation paper on the implementation of the AVMS Directive, which will affect on-demand services. A new regulatory structure will be required.[161] The consultation document envisages three possible models. The first is co-regulation with a co-regulator designated by the Secretary of State, with Ofcom holding backstop powers. The co-regulator would then be responsible for drawing up and maintaining a standards code in conjunction with industry, and for monitoring compliance, complaints handling, and enforcement (covering a range of sanctions). Although the consultation paper suggests that the industry would own this model, there are questions of independence arising from a system in which the co-regulator was designated by the Secretary of State. The second model is effectively that in use with the ASA regarding broadcast advertising: the responsibilities lie

---

[160] On ATVOD see Rand, Commissioned study for the European Commission: Self and Co-Regulation on the Internet (2008); Hans Bredow Institut, 'Co-Regulation of the Media: UK Country Report 2'.

[161] DCMS, 'Public Consultation' (n 159 above) para 8.

with Ofcom, but Ofcom may devolve them to an appropriate designated body. The third model assigns regulatory responsibility to Ofcom. While the consultation paper suggests that the existing bodies (ATVOD and the IMCB) already have codes in place on which they could build, it should be noted that neither code would satisfy the requirements of the Directive as they currently stand, and there is no commonality between the two codes. The savings in effort thus identified are more apparent than real. The government's preference is for model 2, which does work well with the ASA. Caution should be exercised here. The ASA was already well established and well funded, with an experienced staff when it took over responsibility for broadcast advertising; it is hard to avoid the implication that the system worked so well because of the strength of the ASA. The question then is, which body does the government envisage in the equivalent role to the ASA? The government has since confirmed that the ASA will be responsible for advertising content on VOD services. ATVOD has not got the resources or the commitment of the industry; the IMCB from the perspective of the viewer is unsatisfactory; does this leave the BBFC as a serious contender? Although a ministerial statement has confirmed that it intends to adopt model 2, the statement was silent as to the body to be designated as co-regulator. It is not clear whether an entirely new body is envisaged, or whether one of the existing bodies could be adapted to take on this responsibility. With the implementation date for the AVMS Directive fast approaching, some doubt may be expressed as to whether all the details of the body and of its responsibilities will be fleshed out in time, although it is possible that Ofcom (assuming the necessary statutory instrument to give it the powers to regulate is passed in time) could act as a temporary, caretaker regulator. At a stakeholder meeting, DCMS indicated that much of the work will be done by a steering group of industry representatives. Such an approach excludes other stakeholders and is consequently worrying from the perspective of viewers' interests, and arguably that of the public interest generally.

9.7 CONCLUDING REMARKS

It is self-evident that the media sector comprises a range of regulatory systems which enjoy varying degrees of public confidence, to the extent that it is hard to draw generalizations. Certainly, it is not possible to conclude that self-regulation or co-regulation are better than traditional regulation, or vice versa. Not only are there different types of self-regulation, co-regulation, and traditional regulation, but institutions do not constitute the complete picture—the context in which the system operates, including the nature and maturity of the industry, as well the pressures or safety-valves provided by other legal measures. Consider the cases of self-regulation: the PCC, the IMCB, and ATVOD. Why is the PCC so problematic? Clearly, the system was set up under duress; but then that was the case for a number of other regulators, from the BBFC to the IMCB and ATVOD. Some distinctions between the PCC and the other systems can be noted. Although statutory regulation for the press has been frequently suggested, there is currently government commitment to self-regulation in this area. As recent consultation suggests, the reverse is true for on-demand audiovisual content, currently subject to the classification systems of ATVOD, the IMCB, and, to some extent, the BBFC. This suggests that the intensity of the threat has an impact on resistance to external pressure.

Further, the scope of the codes is very different: the PCC (along with the broadcasters' codes) contain protection for individual rights which are justiciable; the classification codes do not. It is less likely that an individual would bring actions before the courts in respect of matters dealt with by those codes than, for example, privacy: judicial review of a regulator's decision would be the extent of possible action. The fact that an alternative course of action exists allows a path for aggrieved individuals to show their dissatisfaction with the system which effectively does not exist for a classification system. This does, however, raise the question, relevant also for the BBC and for Ofcom, of which type of values we expect regulation to protect and whether a regulatory system provides—or should provide—adequate redress for individuals.

There is another distinction between the PCC and the other self-regulating bodies. The PCC is set up by the press to deal with press ethics: the IMCB was set up by the MBG to classify content provided by others (and to an extent likewise with ATVOD). This is a different form of self-regulation in that, although government is not involved, it is not regulation by 'self' either; it is one industry regulating another. The sanction for non-compliance is strong too: failure means no access to the audience. In this there are similarities to the co-regulator, the BBFC (and the ASA). There is no such mechanism for ensuring compliance within the press. Sanctions and industry structure together have a significant impact on how effective the system is.

Similar points can be made within the context of a statutory regulator. The way in which Ofcom works is programmed by the terms of the Communications Act 2003, which we might say define its intent. We have noted the impulse towards market analyses, with the role of the citizen to some extent underdeveloped, and the move towards co-regulation and self-regulation. This tendency has been re-affirmed by the institutional frameworks in place, and by the attitudes of those in charge. Ofcom is comparatively weak on the protection of the public interest in broadcasting, partly because of the terms of the Communications Act but partly because it does not seem to want to take action. The BBC Trust, despite reservations about the introduction of PVT, has at its heart a different view of broadcasting, as, presumably, does the BBC Executive. These two are the creatures of the documents framing them: the Charter and the Agreement, which aim to ensure that the BBC provides a public service.

We noted that there are arguments to suggest that audiences have a right to receive information. Overall, the codes do not ensure that the public receives a range and quality of programming, information, or content; insofar as they extend beyond classification they are negative in formulation, with the exception of the provisions relating to the broadcasters. It could be argued that the remit of the regulators, other than those concerned with broadcasting, is focused on entertainment and that therefore diversity and even impartiality arguments are not relevant. Not only is this not true for the press, but entertainment material can influence our view of the world just as much as factual material, so surely there is a case for diversity here too.

In terms of the substance, the codes vary. This creates not only an uneven playing field, but is somewhat surprising if we are looking at similar, if not the same, material just on a different platform. This is particularly problematic if the delivery platform looks similar: the boundary between near video-on-demand and video-on-demand, given the likely similarity in content, looks arbitrary and certainly does not operate to protect the unwary viewer. Whilst the classification systems of the self-regulators may start from the system used by the BBFC, they lack the ability to distinguish, in terms of barring access, between categories of children, the main group supposedly protected by the system thus relying once again on parents' ability to understand and to police the system. In these contexts, the profile of the regulator and the system acquires significance and it is here that the self-regulatory systems seem to fall down; they are, in effect, industry facing, by contrast to the co-regulatory (such as the BBFC) and the regulatory. This weakness is significant if we view the systems from the perspective of the audience, as a badly explained system undermines the audience's ability to choose or to access appropriate content. Further, assuming that the classification approach to regulation ensures that standards are upheld, it does not protect individuals' rights, such as privacy. Although we could suggest that the nature of the content seen by the BBFC, for example, is unlikely to infringe privacy, such an argument overlooks the development of television on demand in which a broader range of programming, including that which might infringe privacy rules, will be available through these systems. Recourse to the courts is available, but this point highlights the shortcomings in the classification system if we accept that regulation should protect individual rights as well as maintaining standards.

Whilst we have noted that structures alone to not determine effectiveness, this does not mean that they do not have a significant role to play. The bodies have power both in terms of standard-setting and enforcement. We have noted the impact of regulatory intent. There must then be systems in place to ensure independence and accountability; this is true of Ofcom and the BBC as well as the other bodies. All the regulatory models are in some respect deficient here, which could raise problems in terms of natural justice and access to justice, although the BBC and Ofcom probably satisfy concerns about transparency and standard-setting. Crucially, the public interest should reflect standards held by the public (insofar as these can be reduced into a single body of standards); certainly they should not constitute the determination by industry of what it thinks the public interest is. There is a marked difference between the bodies in terms of outreach and consultation, which may reflect the motives of the body but also its resources. Small bodies are unlikely to be able to undertake such work. Whilst self-regulation may seem to save costs, it might not provide a very good level of service.

Finally, we should consider the system as a whole. This can be described, briefly, as a mess. While the co-regulatory choice may be described as government choosing to co-ordinate rather than command, there seems to be little consistency or coherence here. There are overlapping systems and gaps between the systems, as well as differing standards. The situation makes the system difficult to understand and not at all accessible, which is hardly in the public interest, despite industry claims for different and flexible treatment. As noted, it runs the risk that the same content will be treated differently depending on the medium used, leading to potential viewer confusion. The gaps, which are based on the technology used, are particularly worrying given the growth in content available over the internet, for example, and do not reflect a converged approach to regulation. In the long term, common sense would suggest that the system is not viable.

There is also an element of competition between the regulators; they are likely to seek to expand their remit rather than be subsumed or merged, especially if they have a strong independent existence, as does the BBFC. Ofcom has noted that where the service market is fragmented, there is unlikely to be effective self-regulation; too many disparate voices; the difficulty of establishing a trust mark which has public recognition; and the problem of resourcing. A contrast here may be made between the code of practice established by the MBG, which has the backing of the major mobile operators who impose their standard on suppliers, and ATVOD, where membership is missing a crucial player. A way round the problem of different standards, and poorly resourced, small regulators would be to require consolidation, a single regulator with a coherent set of standards. Such a system is more comprehensible from the viewers' perspective. But, when we say a single system, the consequence is removing content regulation from Ofcom, abandoning the BBC Trust and, finally, getting rid of the PCC as well as a host of smaller bodies. The concern is that there would then be no safeguards for positive and public service-related obligations—unless, that is, a statutory instruction were enacted to that effect, backed up with effective sanctions.

10

DEFAMATION

Gavin Sutter

10.1 INTRODUCTION: WHAT IS DEFAMATION?

> He that filches from me my good name,
> robs me of that which not enriches him,
> but makes me poor indeed.
>
> *Othello*
> Act III Scene III

Defamation law is about the protection of reputation, an intangible thing which nevertheless can be of considerable value, both personally and commercially. Shakespeare was certainly correct in his estimation of the value of one's own good name to the individual, if not the value of besmirching it to another; perchance the playwright was simply unable to foresee the extent to which celebrity tittle-tattle would come to form such an economically significant chunk of our contemporary media in the early twenty-first century. The law protects a person's 'good name' from being unfairly maligned. Defamation law is clearly a form of restriction upon freedom of speech and expression—one that is recognized as a legitimate exception by, for instance, the European Convention on Human Rights (ECHR). The Convention provides a right to freedom of expression under Article 10(1), which states: 'Everyone has the right to freedom of expression. This right shall include freedom to hold opinions and to receive and impart information and ideas without interference by public authority and regardless of frontiers.' This is not an unfettered right, as Article 10(2) makes clear: 'The exercise of these freedoms, since it carries with it duties and responsibilities, may be subject to such formalities, conditions, restrictions or penalties as are proscribed by law and are necessary in a democratic society, in the interests of national security, territorial integrity or public safety . . .' The Convention clearly states that the purposes for which such exemptions may be made include 'the protection of the reputation . . . of others'.

Even the First Amendment to the Constitution of the United States of America, which provides the broadest protection for its citizens' free expression of any major nation state, exempts defamation from its ambit.[1]

So how exactly is defamation to be defined? Despite its importance as a legal concept, English law provides no formal, statutory definition. Instead, it has been left to the courts to establish its boundaries. In *Parmiter v Coupland*[2] the Court ruled that defamation required: 'A publication, without justification or lawful excuse, which is calculated to injure the reputation of another, by exposing him to hatred, contempt or ridicule.'[3] In this instance, the Court intended 'calculated' to mean 'likely to', as opposed to indicating that there must be a malicious motive behind the defamatory publication.

The bounds of defamation were broadened considerably by two cases in the early mid-twentieth century. *Youssoupoff v MGM*[4] arose from the portrayal of a particular character in MGM Studios' *Rasputin, the Mad Monk*, a film based on the historical person of Grigori Rasputin and his position of influence in the court of the last Russian Tsar. In the course of the film, a character called Princess Natasha is raped by Rasputin. The plaintiff in this case claimed that she could be identified with the character of Princess Natasha, and as a result persons who knew her would believe that she had actually been the victim of a sex crime perpetrated by Rasputin, something which did not happen in reality. The Court ruled that the film did not expose the plaintiff to hatred, contempt, or ridicule, as required under *Parmiter*, as the seduced character was portrayed as an innocent victim of the evil Rasputin. However, the Court also found that the association drawn by others between the plaintiff and the fictional events shown in the film had the effect of tending to cause her to be shunned and avoided by others. This being so, the Court was prepared to rule that the plaintiff had indeed been defamed. *Sim v Stretch*[5] extended the boundaries of defamation yet further, Lord Atkin stating that the test should be 'would the words tend to lower the plaintiff in the estimation of right-thinking members of society generally?'[6]

---

[1] See eg *Milkovich v Lorain Journal Co* 497 US 1 (1990).
[2] (1840) 6 M & W 105.
[3] ibid 108.
[4] (1934) 50 TLR 581.
[5] [1936] 2 All ER 1237.
[6] ibid 1240.

In 1975, the *Report of the Faulks Committee on Defamation*[7] recommended that a statutory definition of defamation should be adopted. The Committee suggested that defamation should be defined thus: 'The publication to a third party of matter which in all the circumstances would be likely to affect a person adversely in the estimation of reasonable people generally.'

In effect, this would have placed Lord Atkin's *Sim v Stretch* definition on a statutory footing. Despite this recommendation, Parliament has to date chosen not to follow this course of action; notably, the Defamation Act 1996, designed to clarify certain matters and address new legal issues which had arisen, would have been an ideal opportunity to include a statutory definition, but none such appears in the statute as passed. Nevertheless, the basic elements of defamation are clear:

(1) the actual words used must be defamatory;

(2) they must refer to an identifiable person;

(3) they must be published;

(4) there must be a tendency for them to have one or more of the following negative impacts:

    (a) exposure of the plaintiff to hatred, contempt, or ridicule, or

    (b) causing the plaintiff to be shunned and avoided by others, or

    (c) lowering the plaintiff in the estimation of ordinary, 'right-thinking' people.

10.1.1 Classification

There exist two distinct species of defamation: slander, and libel. As a general rule of thumb, slander constitutes the spoken word, while libel[8] requires that publication involves the defamatory words being recorded in a permanent form. The vast majority of defamation cases involving the media are likely to fall under libel. The distinction between these two categories is of no little significance: while libel is actionable *per se*, in order to succeed in a suit involving slander, the claimant must prove to the court's satisfaction that there has been *actual* damage to reputation as a result of the published defamation. Distinguishing between the two is relatively straightforward for the most part: books, newspapers, magazines, and other written forms of communication are all clearly recorded in a permanent form, more than merely transitory, and therefore a defamation thus published would be libel. Some forms of spoken word are considered to have sufficient permanency to constitute libel. For example, words spoken in the course of a performance in a theatre will, under the Theatres Act 1968, constitute libel if they are defamatory. Rehearsals are exempted from this (thus in that context they would be slander), as are performances in private homes. Performances given with the sole or primary intention that they be recorded for broadcast are also excluded, although of course recordings made of them would be in a form with the

---

[7] (Cmnd 5909, 1974).
[8] from the Latin, 'libellus'—'little book'.

requisite permanency for libel.[9] Spoken words which are included in a broadcast will also be sufficiently permanent to be libel.[10]

The first of several challenges which the internet presented to traditional English defamation law was the question of how material published in that arena should be classified. As a general rule of thumb, this will come down to the application of the common law test: is there a sufficient permanent recording of the defamatory statement for it to constitute libel? If not, it will be slander. The test for permanency is not especially high—something as ultimately ephemeral as a handwritten holiday postcard will be libel, if defamatory. English courts have also shown themselves to be open to a wide range of possibilities for recording in a permanent form; in the old case of *Monson v Tussauds Ltd*[11] the Court ruled: 'Libels are generally in writing or printing, but this is not necessary; the defamatory matter may be conveyed in some other permanent form. For instance, a statue, a caricature, an effigy, chalk marks on a wall, signs or pictures may constitute a libel.'[12] It is no great leap of logic to add being recorded in binary digits or some other machine coded form upon an internet server. This might include an e-mail stored in an online account, an article on a web page, or a log of an online chatroom.[13] The definition given to 'programme' and 'programme service' under the Broadcasting Act 1990, as revised by the Communications Act 2003, is also sufficiently broad to cover much internet content[14] (although this remains untested in the courts). The redefinition of the concept of broadcasting under the European Audio Visual Media Services Directive[15] will further broaden the scope of material considered to be recorded in a permanent form for defamation purposes under the auspices of broadcasting legislation.

Online bulletin boards, newsgroups, and other internet pages where individual users can carry on asynchronous discussions of their own are fertile sources of defamation. The prevailing culture of many online bulletin boards is one of regular 'flame wars', with increasingly vicious insults being traded, and a robust style of debate that would be frowned on as unacceptably impolite in the 'real' world. Unsurprisingly, such exchanges frequently sink to the level of base, *ad hominem* attacks which are likely to be defamatory. This is increasingly a source of concern for the media as the trend towards increased interactivity with its audience progresses. Some insight into the classification of online discussion newsgroups was given by Ipp J in the Australian

---

[9] See Theatres Act 1968, s 7.

[10] See Broadcasting Act 1990, s 166(1), which provides that 'the publication of words in the course of any programme included in a programme service shall be treated as publication in permanent form'.

[11] [1894] 1 QB 671.

[12] ibid *per* Lopes CJ, 692.

[13] A defamation made available in a chatroom in which the typed discussions are completely unlogged is likely to be classified as slander, unless perhaps the size of the audience for a live chat session is such that a court might consider it to be analogous to a broadcast interview. For instance, a tabloid such as *The Sun* running a chat session via its website with a pop star or a glamour model might well draw an audience of a size comparable to some broadcasts.

[14] See further M Collins, *The Law of Defamation and the Internet* (Oxford University Press, 2nd edn, 2005) para 4.07.

[15] Directive (EC) 2007/65.

case of *Rindos v Hardwick*:[16] 'The messages that appear on the bulletin board can remain on the computer of a subscriber or participant for a number of days, or weeks, depending on the storage capacity of the computer in question . . . Items of interest on the bulletin board can be printed on hardcopy.'[17] In Ipp's judgment, this was a sufficient level of permanency to constitute libel.

10.1.2 Other species of related actions

10.1.2.1 *Criminal libel*

This chapter is concerned with libel as a tort, but there also remains in English law an offence of criminal libel. A key distinction between the two is that while the tort of defamation is focused upon compensating the party whose reputation has been injured, criminal libel is primarily concerned with punishing the publisher. Under section 5 of the Libel Act 1843: 'If any person shall maliciously publish any defamatory libel, every such person, being convicted thereof, shall be liable to fine or imprisonment or both, as the court may award, not to exceed the term of one year.'

The 1843 Act further provides that where such a publication is made in the knowledge that it is false, the publisher will be liable on conviction to pay an unlimited fine, and/or be imprisoned for up to two years.[18] While this offence remains on the statute books, recent years have seen only a very few private prosecutions, with none on behalf of the state. The view has long been expressed that it is something of an anachronism, though calls for repeal were rejected by the Faulks Committee.[19] During debate on the Coroners and Justice Bill in the House of Lords in early July 2009, a proposed amendment to the Bill, which would have provided for the abolition of this offence, was withdrawn following an indication by the Government of a specific intent to rescind the offence in England and Wales, and Northern Ireland, at a later stage in the progress of the Bill through Parliament.[20]

10.1.2.2 *Trade libel*

Trade libel, as distinct from regular libel, is properly a subspecies of malicious falsehood. It may be made orally, hence its alternative nomenclature of 'slander of goods'. The similarity to defamation is that an action for trade libel also arises from harm to reputation, occasioned by a false statement. The key difference is that rather than the company or any of its employees being the subject of the libel, it is the product they produce which has its reputation maligned. Any actual damage caused to the reputation of the company or those it employs is irrelevant to the trade libel action.[21]

---

[16] No 1994 of 1993, Western Australian Supreme Court, 31 March 1994.
[17] ibid 4.
[18] Libel Act 1843, s 4.
[19] On the subject of criminal libel, see further G Sutter, 'Defamation on the Net' in *Encyclopaedia of Ecommerce Law* (Sweet & Maxwell, 2004) paras 17.005–17.006.
[20] See House of Lords Hansard, 9 July 2009, cols 843–857.
[21] On the subject of trade libel see Sutter (n 19 above) para 17.007.

10.2 DEFAMATORY MEANING

In order for an action to lie in defamation, the actual words of the statement complained of must be defamatory. While it may well often be obvious that this is so, it can be difficult to determine whether this is the case. In *Berkoff v Birchall*[22] the defendant, a journalist, had written a newspaper column in which she stated that the plaintiff, actor Steven Berkoff, was 'hideously ugly', comparing him unfavourably to Frankenstein's monster. While a majority ruled in Berkoff's favour, the Court of Appeal was split as to whether Birchall's article was indeed defamatory. Dissenting, Millett LJ considered that Birchall's words were not defamatory:

The line between mockery and defamation may sometimes be difficult to draw . . . A decision that it is an actionable wrong to describe a man as 'hideously ugly' would be an unwarranted restriction on free speech. And if a bald statement to this effect would not be capable of being defamatory, I do not see how a humorously exaggerated observation to the like effect could be. People must be allowed to poke fun at one another without fear of litigation. It is one thing to ridicule a man; it is another to expose him to ridicule.[23]

In Millett's opinion, then, Birchall's words were an attack on the actor's physical appearance, rather than his reputation, did not make him look ridiculous, and did not lower his standing in the eyes of ordinary people. The majority opinion, as expressed by Neill LJ, disagreed:

. . . it would in my view be open to a jury to conclude that in the context the remarks about Mr Berkoff gave the impression that he was not merely physically unattractive in appearance but actually repulsive. It seems to me that to say this of someone in the public eye who makes his living, in part at least, as an actor, is capable of lowering his standing in the estimation of the public and of making him an object of ridicule.[24]

Clearly as far as the majority were concerned, the nature of the plaintiff's occupation was instrumental in the finding of a defamatory meaning: had his profession not been reliant upon his looks—were he, say, a builder, estate agent, or even an academic, or a lawyer, it seems that the Court of Appeal would not have ruled that the words could have a defamatory meaning.

What the defamatory meaning of a statement may be is to be determined by the standard of the likely reaction of the ordinary, reasonable, fair-minded reviewer—in practice, the members of the jury at first instance. The actual meaning intended by the publisher or author is here irrelevant; over the years, many defendants have found, much to their cost, that they are liable for defaming unawares, or even that they have defamed someone other than the person to whom they intended the article to refer.[25]

---

[22] [1996] 4 All ER 1008.
[23] ibid 153.
[24] ibid 151.
[25] See eg *Hulton v Jones* [1910] AC 20 and *Newstead v London Express* [1940] 1 KB 331; see seven 10.3 below.

The 'natural and ordinary meaning,' the sole meaning which the statement in question will be considered to have for the purpose of determining whether it is in fact defamatory, will in practice fall to be decided by the jury. In determining this meaning, the words are not to be strained or twisted in order to impose a derogatory meaning, but neither are they to be taken solely at face value. The 'natural and ordinary meaning' may include implications or inferences that a reasonable reader with an average general knowledge would draw from the words. It is the broad impression conveyed by the words used that is at issue; the average man on the street (or, more to the point, in the jury room) is not expected to over-analyse in the manner of a Machiavellian lawyer.

Mapp v News Group Newspapers[26] concerned an article which appeared in Sunday tabloid *The News of the World* under the heading 'Drug quiz cop kills himself'. The article stated:

Police Sergeant Gerry Carroll killed himself after being ordered to provide information about ex-colleagues accused of peddling drugs. Sergeant Carroll, 46, shot himself through the head in a cell. He was custody officer with the drugs squad in Stoke Newington, north London, when eight fellow officers were alleged to have been involved in drug dealing and bribery. The accused officers have been transferred to other police stations while an investigation is carried out.

The claimants were among the officers transferred to other police stations during a major police investigation into corruption in the Stoke Newington area. They argued that the article carried the defamatory meaning that they were guilty of involvement in drug dealing and other criminal activity, that the dead man had been in a position to know this as he had worked alongside them, and that he had committed suicide rather than be forced to confirm that his colleagues had been involved in criminality. The question as to whether the article was capable of bearing this claimed meaning came before the courts as a preliminary issue. The Court of Appeal ruled that this was not so, Hirst LJ stating:

. . . it would be virtually unarguable to suggest that the words complained of here imputed actual guilt as contrasted with a reasonable suspicion of guilt unless, as Mr Shields suggests, their meaning is transformed by the prominent reference to Sergeant Carroll's suicide. I do not think it has this effect since, to my mind, Sergeant Carroll's suicide could be interpreted by the reasonable reader in a number of different and perhaps more plausible ways; for example, that he himself had something to hide which would come out if he had to respond to his superior's order, or that he was overwhelmed by stress or depression.

The words complained of were, in the opinion of the Court of Appeal, capable of suggesting that there were reasonable grounds to suspect that the claimants were guilty of the offences under investigation, and thus the claimants were permitted to amend their pleadings to refer to this lesser allegation.

Goldsmith v Bhoyrul[27] gives another example of how the courts consider that the 'natural and ordinary meaning' of a statement is to be determined. In this case, the

---

[26] [1997] EMLR 397.
[27] [1998] QB 459.

claimant was the founder of the Referendum Party, a political organization which sought election to Parliament on a manifesto consisting chiefly of opposition to the UK's involvement in the European Union. In the run-up to the 1997 general election, for which the party was officially fielding 550 candidates, the *Sunday Business* published an article under the headline 'Goldsmith looks for "dignified exit" from election race'. The article stated: 'Sir James Goldsmith has begun to pave the way for pulling his Referendum Party completely out of the general election . . . Goldsmith is understood to be disenchanted by the lack of popular support for the party and preparing the way for a "dignified exit" before the deadline to declare candidates . . .'

Accompanying the article was a photograph of the claimant, which was captioned 'Goldsmith: ready to pull out of May's general election'. The claimant argued that the natural and ordinary meaning of this article, taken as a whole, was that he had lied to the electorate, misleading them about his true intentions by campaigning on the basis that the party would participate fully in the election when, in fact, it was already planning to withdraw from the proceedings. The Court, however, held that while the article did indeed attribute a change of attitude to the party, it also outlined reasonable grounds for this change, such as a lack of popular support. The reasonable reader, not being minded to read between the lines looking for a scandal, would not construe the article to mean that the claimant had acted dishonestly. The article was capable of much less serious meanings, for instance, that the Referendum Party was not willing to risk humiliation at the ballot box, but none of these alternative 'natural and ordinary' meanings had been put forward by the claimant.

In *Charleston v Newsgroup Newspapers*[28] the courts made it abundantly clear that an article must be taken as a complete whole when determining the meaning: claimants cannot simply take action in relation to a carefully isolated part thereof. This case concerned an article which appeared in the *News of the World* tabloid newspaper. Under the headline 'Strewth, what's Harold up to with our Madge?' there was printed a photograph which appeared at first glance to be two actors, who portrayed the named characters in popular, Australian soap opera *Neighbours*. The controversy surrounded the fact that, in the words of Lord Bridge:

Immediately beneath this [headline] is a large photograph of a man and a woman nearly naked. The woman is leaning forward over some piece of furniture and the man is standing behind her apparently engaging in an act of intercourse or sodomy with her. Superimposed over the lower part of their bodies is an outline map of Australia bearing the words 'Censored Down Under'. To the right of this is another smaller photograph of a woman wearing a tight-fitting blouse or jacket with holes cut to expose her bare breasts. The face of the man in the large photograph is the male plaintiff's and the face of the woman in both photographs is the female plaintiff's.[29]

The accompanying text went on to explain that, in fact, the published photograph was a fake, created by super-imposing the claimants' faces onto an existing pornographic picture; part of a pornographic computer game that the newspaper had discovered for sale. Counsel for the claimants sought to base their case on an argument that the photograph and headline should be considered as a 'stand-alone' publication, independent of the text, as the average *News of the World* reader would be unlikely to read more than the headline and look at the photo. Thus, the argument ran, the average reader of the newspaper would blithely assume that it was indeed the claimants in the pornographic photograph. This contention was soundly rejected by the Court, which ruled that the article must be taken as a whole. That being so, it was found that the text adequately explained away the potential defamatory sting of the headline and photograph to the extent that no defamatory meaning would arise in the mind of the reasonable reader.

Following the *Charleston* case, a potentially defamatory statement made in one part of an article which is sufficiently explained away elsewhere within the same article will not be considered to have a defamatory meaning. This is commonly referred to as the 'bane and antidote'. If the antidote is sufficient to counteract the bane, a defamation claim can be avoided. This is of great significance to the media. In tabloid newspapers terms, the article in *Charleston* was a hot story; given the rapid growth of celebrity culture since, accompanied by a seemingly insatiable public appetite for celebrity gossip in any form,[30] it could only be more so over a decade later. The *Charleston* decision effectively confirmed that such stories are free from the threat of libel action provided that they are worded so as not to mislead the reader as to the true nature of what appears, *prima facie*, to be happening. Of course, the media must still ensure that any such story is presented in such a way that the 'antidote' is sufficient to balance the 'bane'. This will include not only ensuring that the explanation that all is not as it may at first seem is sufficiently clear, but also such simple factors as the way in which the story is presented on paper—location and layout, for instance. An explanation buried on page 53, between the obituaries and the horse racing fixtures, will not be sufficient to counteract an apparently defamatory story splashed all over the front page. Here one must also consider the nature of online media publications where, instead of flicking through a paper copy, the reader is instead presented with a series of links and so is unlikely to see anything beyond the headline (and possibly accompanying photograph) of stories which do not sufficiently catch the individual reader's attention to follow the link to the full text.[31]

Nevertheless, the courts have clearly indicated that claimants who seek to cherry pick potentially defamatory statements outwith the context of an article as a whole will not succeed. For instance, the case of *Norman v Future Publishing*,[32] in which the

---

[30] Following in the wake of the success of *Heat* magazine, there has been an apparently endless wave of popular magazines which seem to consist of little more than photographs of individuals of varying levels of celebrity (reality television 'stars' for the most part) going about their day-to-day lives—even activities as mundane as grocery shopping, eating in a restaurant, or simply walking in the street.

[31] See further the discussion of *Buddhist Society of Western Australia v Bristle* [2000] WASCA 210, 10.4 below; see also Sutter (n 19 above) paras 17.008–17.009.

[32] [1999] EMLR 325.

claimant, a well-known opera singer, took action over an article which she felt portrayed her as either conforming to or encouraging an offensive, racial stereotype of lower class African-Americans. The article in question appeared in *Classic CD* magazine. Referring to the claimant's 'statuesque figure', the article went on to state: 'This is the woman who got trapped in swing doors on her way to a concert and, when advised to release herself by turning sideways replied "Honey, I ain't got no sideways." '

It was this portrayal of the claimant's use of language that gave rise to her case. In effect, ran the argument, the natural and ordinary meaning of this statement was that she spoke in a crass, undignified manner, either conforming to a racial stereotype herself, or using such dialect in a patronizing mockery of cultural stereotypes of lower class African-Americans. The Court of Appeal, finding against the claimant, considered that the statement complained of could not bear the alleged defamatory meaning when taken in the context of the article as a whole. In the context of a piece which was on the whole actually rather flattering in its portrayal of the claimant, her claims were considered to be unsustainable.[33]

By way of contrast, *Cruise v Express Newspapers*[34] indicates that the context of the statement will not extend to other, separate articles within a newspaper. In this case, the *Express on Sunday* failed to persuade the Court of Appeal that an article which repeated defamatory rumours speculating about the state of Hollywood actors Tom Cruise and Nicole Kidman's marriage was completely 'cured' by an article on the previous page, which presented an idealized view of the relationship. Rather than attempt to mount this defence in front of a jury, the publishers settled out of court.

A further context which must be considered in determining the natural and ordinary meaning of a statement is the meaning likely to be attributed to it by the reasonable reader or viewer likely to encounter it. For instance, where a statement might be made in the context of an advertisement, its meaning must be construed as if seen through the eyes of the reasonable viewer or reader to whom it is addressed.[35] The expectations of such an audience will be borne in mind: those exposed to an advertisement will be credited with sufficient intelligence to understand that a certain level of hyperbole in marketing must be expected, and know whether to take statements made seriously.[36] Similarly, the reader of a fictional story, or a satirical piece, might be presumed to understand not to take the piece seriously, provided the nature of the article is readily apparent.[37] It must be stressed that such audience considerations are in the objective. The meaning of the article in question must always be determined on the basis of the

---

[33] See also *Bookbinder v Tebbit* [1989] 1 All ER 1169, in which the Court of Appeal ruled that where the words complained of had been spoken in the course of a public meeting, their meaning might be affected by the general course of a speech of which they formed a part. Thus, the Court held, the natural and ordinary meaning had to be determined with reference to the words in the context in which they appeared, not in isolation.

[34] (1998) EMLR 780.

[35] *Emaco v Dyson Appliances The Times*, 8 February 1999.

[36] See eg *Vodafone v Orange* [1997] FSR 34.

[37] See also, in relation to fictional stories, section 10.3 below; in particular, see the discussion of *Hulton v Jones* [1910] AC 20.

article itself, and the court will not hear anything relating to how the actual audience understood it. For example, in the *Charleston* case, the claimants were forbidden to produce evidence which they contended would prove that, in fact, many of the newspaper's readers did indeed only read the headlines and look at the pictures accompanying most stories. Had such evidence been permitted it would have assisted the claimants in that case, though it is easy to imagine circumstances in which it would be of benefit to a media defendant to be able to produce information suggesting that the audience had interpreted the article in a way favourable to them. The Faulks Committee Report specifically rejected calls for a change in the law to permit such evidence, the Committee opining that such a move would only make libel proceedings longer, more expensive, and more confusing.

Once the natural and ordinary meaning of a statement or article has been determined, it is up to a jury to determine whether that meaning is defamatory. A judge may direct the jury that the words complained of are *capable* of being defamatory, but the decision as to whether they *are* is for the jury alone. When considering whether the statement is defamatory, a jury will be required to consider the statement in the context of its subject. For instance, in the *Berkoff* case, calling the claimant 'hideously ugly' was sufficient because he was an actor in the public eye; there was no need for him to prove that such an allegation would have been defamatory of any individual person. Similarly, in *Winyard v Tatler Publishing*[38] it was found to be defamatory to refer to a beautician as a 'boot', as it was considered that this would damage the claimant's professional reputation: no one, it seems, was thought likely to want to be attended by an ugly beautician. In other professions where one might expect such negative analyses of physical attractiveness to be broadly irrelevant, such as the position of a university law lecturer, for example, it would be extremely unlikely that being labelled 'ugly' would be capable of causing sufficient damage to reputation to be considered defamatory.

The interpretation of whether an article is defamatory is to reflect that of right-thinking, reasonable members of society in general; it is not to be coloured by the views of any specific group. For instance, the claimant in *Byrne v Dean*[39] filed suit over the claim that he had been the member of a golf club who had reported the presence of an unlicensed fruit machine in the clubhouse. Despite the fact that this had damaged considerably his standing in the eyes of fellow golf-club members, it was found that respectable members of society in general would not have thought less of him for bringing the matter to the attention of the police. The statement, therefore, could not be defamatory.

English defamation law also takes account of the fact that a statement may be worded so as to provide a double meaning for those who are aware of certain other facts or information. These additional factors giving rise to the innuendo meaning must be known to at least some of the audience at the time of publication: if knowledge of this further information is not gained until later, the defamation will not be actionable.[40]

[38] *The Independent*, 16 August 1991.
[39] [1937] 2 All ER 204.
[40] *Grappelli v Derek Block* [1981] 2 All ER 272.

In *Cassidy v Daily Mirror*[41] the defendant newspaper published a photograph of a racehorse owner standing with a young woman. The photograph, which appeared under the headline 'Today's Gossip', was captioned 'Mr MC, the race horse owner, and Miss X, whose engagement has just been announced'. Nothing appeared amiss; there seemed nothing objectionable in the photograph or in its caption, and the man himself had told the newspaper it was welcome to print the news of the engagement. The plaintiff in this case was neither the racehorse owner nor his new fiancée—rather, it was his existing wife. This lady claimed that she had suffered damage to her reputation as several people to whom she had been represented as Mr MC's wife saw the article and assumed that she had been lying about their marriage and had in fact been merely living with him in what was, in 1929, considered to be a state of immoral cohabitation. This meaning was not apparent from a reading of the article alone; indeed, the claimant was not even mentioned in the article, nor had the newspaper been at all aware that Mr MC was already married when it went to print with this story. The Court of Appeal reached a conclusion that a defamation had indeed been published in this case, this despite the fact that the defendants had been ignorant of the true facts of the case, and that the defamatory meaning was apparent to only a small number of persons who had met the claimant as Mr MC's wife.

Following the *Cassidy* case, a party wishing to claim an innuendo is required to establish all the facts which are relied upon to support the innuendo meaning. It is not required that the claimant show those persons who were aware of sufficient facts and circumstances to understand the innuendo did indeed do so, merely that they were aware of all the facts that might have led them to that conclusion. It is then up to the jury to decide whether the statement did indeed carry this innuendo meaning. Slang meanings can also be pleaded as innuendo where slang meaning gives that spin to the small off-mainstream group that use the slang before it has entered broad usage.

Given that an innuendo meaning can be wholly unintentional, as in the *Cassidy* case, an argument might be made that this places an unfair burden on the defence, over and above the usual challenge of strict-liability defamation. The issue was raised at the Court of Appeal in that case, but the Court held that there had been no injustice, liability arising here from the newspaper's own failure to double-check its own story before publication. While certainly circumstances may arise in which that could well be the case, the author would suggest that to even think of investigating a story such as Mr MC's would necessitate some degree of paranoia on the part of the journalist (or sub-editor) concerned.

10.3   IDENTIFICATION

In order to be entitled to bring an action in respect of a defamatory publication, the would-be claimant must be able to show that he is the person referred to by the

---

[41] [1929] 2 KB 331.

statement in question. Again, whether this is so is a matter to be determined in court, and the intentions of the publisher are irrelevant to this decision.[42] This is a simple matter where the claimant is referred to by name; however, simply avoiding using a name is not sufficient. Referring to a known person by a nick-name such as 'Posh', or otherwise describing them in a way such that they will be identifiable to the reasonable reader or viewer, will be sufficient for defamation purposes. For this reason, the sort of tabloid newspaper or website which indulges in 'wicked-whispers'-type articles must tread a fine line between making their story interesting to the reader while still avoiding potential liability arising from printing a story they cannot prove about an identifiable individual.[43] Much like innuendo meanings, identification can also be dependent upon special knowledge about the claimant which may only be known to a few people. The burden in that case falls to the claimant to show that at least some of the audience had a sufficient level of knowledge in order that they would be able to appreciate that the article referred to him. It then becomes a matter for the jury to decide whether the reasonable reader or viewer, in possession of the requisite knowledge, would have understood the article to refer to the claimant. Again, as with innuendo meanings, it does not matter that this may be only a very small group, although in such a case the reduced scope of publication will of course result in a lower award of damages being made should the claimant's case succeed.

It is also possible for an individual to be sufficiently identified for libel purposes as a member of a group. The key test was formulated by the House of Lords in *Knupffer v London Express*:[44] 'Are the words such as would reasonably lead persons acquainted with the claimant to believe that he was the person referred to?' A statement about a group or class of persons can be actionable, provided the words used could reasonably be understood to refer to each member of the group individually. In practice, the size of the group will be an issue. Where it is very large—such as a contention that all Irish people are intellectually inferior[45]—is unlikely to be considered specific enough in the absence of a further qualifying statement which points to the plaintiff in particular. The simple fact that an individual may be one of the six million who fall into the class of persons about which the above derogatory remark has been made is wholly insufficient

---

[42] *Hulton v Jones* [1910] AC 20.

[43] A 'Wicked Whisper' essentially involves publishing a salacious gossip story, generally about a celebrity, who if named would leave the publication open to a defamation action. The journalistic trick is to give just enough information that the audience is able to begin to speculate as to whom the story might refer, while at the same time maintaining a plausible argument that the story is about someone else should anyone attempt to sue. Some outlets have raised this to an art form, not least website and e-mail list HolyMoly.co.uk, which even invites its readers to post to the website their guesses as to the identity of the story's subject. Of course, this has the potential to render them open to strict, editorial liability in respect of third-party material thus uploaded and published via their servers.

[44] [1944] AC 116.

[45] The author, being Irish himself, considers this not to be an insensitive example for illustrative purposes.

for identification in defamation.[46] On the other hand, were the grouping much smaller, the outcome might be very different. For example, a bold statement such as 'all academics working at the Centre for Commercial Law Studies are incompetent academics and should not be allowed to teach' refers to a sufficiently narrow class of persons that identification would be possible. The *Knupffer* case concerned an article about a pro-Hitler movement of Russian migrants trying to infiltrate the USSR in the early 1940s. The article described the group in loose terms as being 'established in France and the USA', with secret agents who could enter and leave the USSR at will. The claimant, a Russian living in London, launched libel proceedings, claiming that he, as a Russian migrant, had been personally defamed. The House of Lords disagreed, finding that this was too wide a group for a reasonable reader to believe that the claimant individually was identified by the story.

Cases can and do arise where the courts have ruled that a particular claimant has been identified, despite this being counter to the intentions of the publisher. This is, of course, wholly consistent with the principle that the 'natural and ordinary meaning' of a statement is to be determined by the jury, and does not take account of the intention of the author or publisher. Such identification can come about as a result of association with a particular story, as happened in the *Cassidy* case, the claimant being identified by the association with her husband whose picture appeared in the newspaper—the defence being wholly unaware of her existence. In *Hulton v Jones*[47] the claimant coincidentally happened to be known by the same name as a character in a fictional story. An action was brought alleging that acquaintances of the claimant had believed it was a story about him. The House of Lords considered that the proper test was to determine whether sensible and reasonable people reading the article would think that it was about a real or imaginary person. If the audience believed the character to be fictional, then it would be impossible for them to also think that the story referred to the claimant. It is for this reason that works of fiction so often carry a disclaimer along these lines: 'This is a work of fiction, and any similarity to persons either living or dead is entirely coincidental.'

In *Newstead v London Express*[48] a newspaper was found liable for defaming a claimant who shared a name with the bigamist whom the article was intended to be about. Commenting on the perceived difficulty this caused for defendants in such cases, Sir Wilfred Greene MR said: 'If there is a risk of coincidence it ought, I think, in reason to be borne not by the innocent party to whom the words are held to refer, but by the party who puts them into circulation.' In order to avoid liability in such cases, the media now typically give a fair degree of information about the subject of the report.

---

[46] 'Assuming the article to be libellous, it is not a libel on the plaintiff; it only reflects on a class of persons . . . If a man wrote that all lawyers were thieves, no particular lawyer could sue him unless there is something to point to the particular individual, which there is not here. There is nothing to show that the article was inserted with any special reference to the plaintiff. It does not appear that the defendant knew of his existence'. *Eastwood v Holmes* (1858) 1 F & F 349, *per* Willes J.

[47] [1910] AC 20.

[48] [1940] 1 KB 331.

Most commonly this will constitute name, age, and address, although a photograph or, if broadcast, whether in the traditional sense or online,[49] other details of appearance may also be included. The intention is, obviously, to make it as clear as possible that they are referring to that particular person, and not anyone else whom the audience may mistakenly believe the story to be about.

In *Kerry O'Shea v MGN Ltd and Free4Internet.net Ltd*[50] Morland J explicitly refused to follow the rule in *Hulton*, ruling that in placing too heavy a burden on the publisher to avoid mistaken identity, it breached the Article 10 right to free expression. The case concerned an advertisement for a pornography service offered by an online service provider which specialized in 'adult' services. This service provider was the second named defendant, the first was the publisher of the newspaper in which it appeared. This advertisement contained a photograph of a young woman who resembled the claimant to such a degree that a number of her acquaintances, including friends and family members, believed that it was actually her in the photograph. The claimant argued that this publication had the defamatory meaning that she 'was appearing or performing on a highly pornographic website containing material of an explicit, indecent and lewd nature and had shamelessly agreed to promote this website and her own appearance on it in a national newspaper'.

The defence countered that this was a step too far, taking the rule in *Hulton* into a wholly new factual situation, one in which the paper had simply published a photograph of another actress in an advertisement for a lawful business. Further, the defence also argued that this would be a breach of the Article 10 right. Morland J held that while it would be entirely reasonable, given the resemblance, that those who saw the advertisement and knew the claimant might believe that she was the person in the photograph, the advertisement in question fell under the ambit of Article 10 protection. No pressing social need such that would justify derogation under Article 10(2) from the right could be found in applying the *Hulton* strict-liability position for the protection of the reputation of the claimant who looked like the person in the photograph. On this basis, the claimant's case had no realistic prospect of succeeding, and so was dismissed. In the judge's opinion, persons in the claimant's position would still be able to pursue a case based on the tort of malicious falsehood in order to prevent deliberate and dishonest use of a lookalike.[51]

Morland's decision, insofar as it might mark a turning point in defamation law on this issue, is one that is clearly favourable to the media, who would no doubt strongly agree with his assessment that strict liability would 'impose an impossible burden on

---

[49] Regarding the changing nature of broadcasting, see Ch 8 above.

[50] [2001] EMLR 40.

[51] As the genre of 'lookalike' pornography continues to expand, the most recent phenomenon being lookalikes of unsuccessful US GOP Vice-Presidential candidate Sarah Palin (see eg 'Larry Flynt is Hustling up an Ala-skin flick with Sarah Palin look-alike' in *New York Daily News*, 2 October 2008, available at <http://www.nydailynews.com/gossip/2008/10/02/2008-10-02_larry_flynt_is_hustling_up_an_alaskin_fl.html>), this decision can only assume greater importance for that significant, if not entirely conventional, section of the media.

a publisher if he were required to check if the true picture of someone resembled someone else who because of the context of the picture was defamed'.[52]

Critics of the decision would no doubt argue that the net result is the even less palatable situation in which the individuals who have been caught up in such a 'lookalike' situation find imposed upon them the burden of proving that the publisher has acted in bad faith. It remains to be seen whether Morland's approach will in future be applied to other circumstances in which libel suits for mistaken identification arise. In particular, it would seem difficult to distinguish credibly between the hardships that strict liability à la *Hulton* might impose upon a media outlet inadvertently responsible for an identification by association, as happened in the *Cassidy* case, and that which gave rise to Morland's decision regarding the application of Article 10(2).

10.4 PUBLICATION

The final essential element of building a case in defamation is also an extremely logical one: the defamatory statement about the claimant must be published. A claimant's rights under defamation law are ultimately aimed at compensating for, and repairing, damage caused to reputation. A statement without an audience, however defamatory its meaning, cannot be the cause of any such damage; as Lord Esher MR put it in *Hebditch v MacIlwaine*:[53] 'The material part of the cause of action in libel is not the writing, but the publication of the libel.'

As a general rule, publication for libel purposes requires the communication of the statement or article in question to at least one person other than the subject.[54] Communication to the subject may, however, be sufficient where the subject is bound by duty (such as a contract of employment) to others, or where such a communication is standard procedure and therefore would have been reasonably foreseeable.[55] For publication to take place, the statement must be in a form in which the person to whom it is communicated will be able to understand it. In both *Jones v Davers*[56] and *Price v Jenkings*[57] the respective claimants' cases failed, owing to the courts ruling that as the letter which they claimed had defamed them had been written in French, a language which the recipients could not understand, no publication had taken place.

---

[52] *Kerry O'Shea v MGN Ltd and Free4Internet.net Ltd* [2001] EMLR 40, para 43.

[53] [1894] 2 QB 58, 61.

[54] 'The making known of the defamatory matter after it has been written to some person other than the person of whom it is written.' *Pullman v W Hill & Co Ltd* [1891] 1 QB 524, *per* Lord Esher. There are very limited exceptions to this general rule where publication of the defamation only to the subject of it will be sufficient. These include cases involving criminal libel (see *Gleaves v Deaken* [1980] AC 477) and defamation under Scottish law (*MacKay v M'Cankie* (1883) 10 R 537); note, however, that in the absence of communication to a third party, damages for actual economic loss will not be recoverable—only damages for insult will be available. Collins (n 14 above) para 5.02.

[55] *Theaker v Richardson* [1962] 1 All ER 229.

[56] (1596) Cro Eliz 496.

[57] (1601) Cro Eliz 865.

There is no *de minimus* standard for publication in English law, publication to a single third party being sufficient for an action to lie. In practice, however, the court retains its discretion to decide not to hear a case where publication has been so limited that its impact upon the claimant's reputation is minimal.[58]

Contemporary rules on publication must also take account of the impact of the internet and online publishing. Where a defamatory statement has been published via an e-mail list that automatically forwards it to the accounts of all those who subscribe to that list, it would seem a logical step for the courts to accept evidence of the number of subscribers as an indication of the scope of publication. For instance, in the Australian case of *Rindos v Hardwick*[59] a judge was prepared to set damages based on an estimate that there were 23,000 subscribers signed up to the e-mail group at issue. Online bulletin boards can generally be set up such that it is possible to track the use made of the system, and thus tell how many members have accessed particular threads. In either case, it should be fairly certain that those who post a reply to a defamatory posting have actually read it.

Where a defamation is made available via a website, it might seem, *prima facie*, logical to assume that it has been published to all persons who visit the website. Yet, as has already been discussed above, the average person views a website in a different way than they might read a newspaper. The upshot of this is that the readership of a website is far more likely to be selective, following only select links which appear of interest, and therefore less likely to follow a particular link which leads to a defamatory story. On a technical level at least, every separate page on a website is a different file—to what degree does this render them sufficiently separate publications for libel purposes? In *Buddhist Society of Western Australia v Bristle*,[60] the Western Australian Supreme Court explicitly refused to assume that for publication purposes all visitors to a particular website had viewed all parts of that site. Separate letters and other articles on a website, the Court held, could constitute separate publications in their own right where the form, purposes and 'substantive identity' of different areas of the website are sufficiently distinct.[61] Such an approach, if taken by the English courts, would certainly help to clarify not only to how many persons publication had been made, but also the limits of the article 'as a whole': clearly, the articles in the *Cruise* case would still fall to be treated separately, while most likely that at issue in the *Charleston* case would still require to be taken as a whole—photograph, headline, *and* accompanying text even if the text was located on a linked page, as a clear hyperlink indicating there was more to the story than at first appeared would, the author submits, be sufficient to indicate that there were no separate, substantive identities sufficient to require them being treated separately in the way that the claimants wished.[62]

---

[58] See eg *Jameel v Dow Jones Inc* [2005] EWCA Civ 75.
[59] *Rindos v Hardwick* No 1994 of 1993, Western Australian Supreme Court, 31 March 1994. An unverified copy of the judgment was available at <http://www.law.auckland.ac.nz/research/cases/Rindos/html>.
[60] [2000] WASCA 210.
[61] ibid para 10.
[62] See discussion of *Charleston v Newsgroup Newspapers* [1995] 2 All ER 313 at section 10.2 above.

Liability for publishing a libel does not arise solely where the publication containing the defamatory statement has been made deliberately. It is sufficient for the publisher to negligently allow a statement which is defamatory to be published where it is reasonably foreseeable in all the circumstances, or that that will be the natural and probable result of his actions. In *Pullman v William Hill*[63] Lord Esher stated: 'If the writer of a letter locks it up in his own desk, and a thief comes and breaks open the desk and takes away the letter and makes its contents known, I should say that would not be a publication.'[64] By the same logic, where a sealed letter is opened and read by someone other than the addressee, it would seem unlikely that there would be a publication. In *Slipper v BBC*,[65] the broadcaster had screened a television programme relating to Ronald Biggs and the 1963 'Great Train Robbery', which included certain defamatory allegations about the claimant. Not only were the BBC found liable in respect of the initial publication by broadcasting the programme; the Court of Appeal also held the broadcaster liable in respect of onward publication of the allegations made in newspaper review columns the following day as these onward publications were clearly reasonably foreseeable at the time the broadcast was made. By the same logic, an e-mail, sent in the knowledge that it was likely to be published or forwarded onwards could render the sender liable for any defamation contained therein. If nothing else, following the urban legend of Claire Swire[66] and the many column inches devoted to it, it is doubtful that anyone within the English jurisdiction could be so naive as to believe that an e-mail always ends with the intended recipient—even if quite that level of global phenomenon is not anticipated. Equally, if an e-mail is sent to someone in their business capacity, especially if to a generic address such as themanager@companyx.com, or helpdesk@companyx.com, then it could be said to be reasonably foreseeable that the communication might be opened by someone else—a personal assistant, for example. Indeed, Lord Esher in the *Pullman* case referred to it being reasonably foreseeable that a letter sent to a person in their business capacity might be opened by a clerk or secretary.[67]

An e-mail being intercepted by a hacker, on the other hand, would not be so foreseeable, not least given the sheer volume of traffic on the internet. This would fall to be treated in the same manner as the letter in a locked drawer, broken into by a thief. Internet security experts often advise 'never write anything in an email that you wouldn't put on a postcard'. This is a not a suitable analogy for libel law, however.

---

[63] [1891] 1 QB 524.

[64] ibid 527.

[65] [1990] All ER 165.

[66] This was the young lady whose e-mail to her boyfriend praising his sexual prowess on the previous evening became a global phenomenon after being forwarded by the latter to a number of his acquaintances, who proceeded to send it on to many others. While there are those who have suggested the whole episode to be a hoax, it nevertheless illustrated very publicly just how rapidly an e-mail can spread—especially one containing juicy gossip. See further <http://en.wikipedia.org/wiki/Claire_Swire>; for those so motivated, a Google search will no doubt turn up the full text of the original email which Ms Swire is said to have sent.

[67] *Pullman v W Hill* [1891] 1 QB 524, 528; see also *Powell v Gelstone* [1916] 2KB 615, *per* Bray J, 619.

The 'postcard rule' in *Huth v Huth*[68] states that where a postcard has passed through the mail system, it is to be presumed until proven otherwise that it has been read by a third party. This presumption does not apply where a letter is posted in an unsealed envelope, a situation in which the claimant must still prove that a third party did indeed read the letter. The latter situation seems a much better parallel to a message sent via e-mail. Even an unencrypted, unsecured e-mail requires some level of effort to be expended in order to be read by a person other than the intended addressee, wholly comparable with that required to remove a sheet of paper from an unsealed envelope.

It is a general rule of English defamation law that each re-publication of a defamatory article constitutes a new publication in its own right, and a new limitation period begins to run. Publication occurs at the time and place at which it is received and understood, therefore each copy of a newspaper is a separate publication.[69] This rule was first applied to archives in the mid-nineteenth century case of *Duke of Brunswick v Hamer*.[70] In this case the Duke had heard that he had been defamed in an old issue of a journal, and sent out his servant to acquire a copy of this publication to see for himself. The servant managed to acquire two copies: one from the British Museum, the other from the distributor. The Duke proceeded to launch libel proceedings, despite the fact that this was some seventeen years following date of original publication, and yet the limitation period was in those days only six years (over time further reduced, it now stands at twelve months).[71] Nevertheless, the Court held that the multiple publication rule applied in this situation such that the delivery of copies of the article to the Duke's servant was a new act of publication, thus a new limitation period had begun to run and the claimant was entitled to sue in libel.

The additional burden that the multiple publication rule places upon those who maintain archives which others may access may be, at least in the physical world, somewhat alleviated by the nature of those archives, which tend to be mere distributors and therefore subject to a lower level of liability.[72] Its application online,[73] however, raises further difficulty for many archivists, as often these archives are maintained by the original publisher rather than a third party. Also significant is the sheer convenience of online archives as compared to the physical equivalent, meaning that many more people are likely to access the former. It has been recorded that 90 per cent of UK regional newspapers have a web-presence with some degree of archiving of past stories online. Some online media outlets offer access to their archives only on

---

[68] [1915] 3 KB 32.
[69] See eg *Pullman v W Hill* [1891] 1 QB 524; *Shevill v Press Alliance SA* [1995] 2 AC 18, 41.
[70] [1849] 14 QB 185.
[71] Limitation Act 1980, s 4A.
[72] See section 10.7.6 below.
[73] That the rule applies equally to the internet was confirmed in *Godfrey v Demon Internet Ltd* [1999] EMLR 542.

payment of a subscription, while many others, such as *The Times*,[74] *The Guardian*,[75] and the BBC[76] offer free access to theirs. The multiple publication rule was applied to online archives for the first time in *Loutchansky v Times*.[77] The claimant had already brought an action against the newspaper in respect of two articles published in the print edition, which had alleged that he was involved in organized crime. These articles were also published online on the same dates, and continued to be available over a year later when Loutchansky made them the subject of a second action against *The Times*. The limitation period in respect of the original print publications, currently set at twelve months,[78] had expired, and the defence tried to argue that the claimant was therefore blocked from suing over the internet publication of the same articles. The Court of Appeal, however, held that the rule in *Duke of Brunswick* applied equally online as to print publications, finding that each time an article is downloaded to a third party's browser in an intelligible form, a new publication takes place and so a new limitation period commences. The Court of Appeal also denied the defendant's request for leave to appeal to the Lords. In any case, the Appeal judgment was approved by the Lords in the later case of *Berezovsky v Michaels*.[79] Counsel for the defence had attempted to convince the Court of Appeal that applying the multiple publication rule online would be in breach of the Article 10 right to freedom of expression, as it would have a chilling effect, discouraging those who maintain archives from offering them to the public online. The Court agreed that archives serve a valid and useful social purpose, but it also considered that any chilling effect would be minimal as any damages in respect of an old article would be likely to be modest. The Court appears not to have given such heed to the issue of costs, which are highly unlikely to diminish over time. An appeal to Europe was similarly unsuccessful, the European Court of Human Rights ruling that the application of the multiple publication rule to internet archives in this manner did not constitute a breach of the defendants' Article 10 right.[80] Notably, however, the Court did indicate that had a longer period of time elapsed between the date of first publication and the date of publication giving rise to an action under the multiple publication rule, it would have been prepared to reach a different conclusion:

While an aggrieved applicant must be afforded a real opportunity to vindicate his right to reputation, libel proceedings brought against a newspaper after a significant lapse of time may

---

[74] <http://www.thetimes.co.uk>.
[75] <http://www.guardian.co.uk>.
[76] <http://www.bbc.co.uk>.
[77] [2002] 1 All ER 652.
[78] Limitation Act 1980, s 4A.
[79] [2001] 1 WLR 1004.
[80] *Times Newspapers Limited (Nos 1 and 2) v UK* (Application Nos 3002/03 and 23676/03) 10 March 2009.

well, in the absence of exceptional circumstances, give rise to a disproportionate interference with press freedom under Article 10.[81]

The Law Commission, in the consultation ahead of its 2002 report on internet defamation,[82] received a number of responses which were very critical of the application of the multiple publication rule in this way, arguing that it effectively defeats the very purpose of the limitation period. Other criticisms raised the practical difficulties involved in defending a libel action arising out of an old story, when the journalists who wrote it may no longer be available, or may have forgotten the details, having long ago destroyed their notes. There are those who would argue that not only is the rule a challenge to Article 10, but also Article 6 (fair trial). The Law Commission noted calls for change in the law, but declined to commit itself to any of the alternatives suggested and discussed in the report without further research being undertaken. The most radical alternative proposed was the wholesale replacement of the multiple-publication rule with a US-style single publication rule. Set out in the US Restatement (Second) of Torts 1976, this provides that 'any one edition of a book or newspaper, or any radio or television broadcast . . . is a single publication'.[83] Under this approach, publication occurs only once, at the time of first publication and the limitation period runs from that point only.[84] The rule was originally formulated in *Wolfson v Syracuse Newspapers Inc*,[85] later to be applied to archives in *Gregoire v GP Putnam & Sons*.[86] The *Gregoire* case concerned a book originally published in 1941, and in its seventh reprint by 1946, when the suit was filed. The Court specifically rejected the rule in *Duke of Brunswick*, as being antiquated and unsuited to modern mass-publishing, further noting that a multiple publication rule would thwart the purpose of having a limitation period.[87] The offending publication in *Firth v State of New York*[88] was a report which had been launched at a press conference. On the same day, it had also been placed on the website, but the suit was filed only after the limitation period in respect of the original publication to the press conference had expired. The issue before the Court was when the limitation period in respect of the online publication expired. Following the earlier case law, in particular *Gregoire*, the Court held that the limitation period had begun to run from the moment the report was first placed on the website, and so the claimant was out of time to bring a case.

---

[81] ibid para 48.
[82] Law Commission, *Defamation and the Internet: A Preliminary Investigation*, Scoping Study (Law Com No 2, 2002).
[83] Section 577A.
[84] This also has implications for jurisdiction within the US, as the rule is also applied such that the point of first publication geographically dictates the place of publication.
[85] (1938) 279 NY 716.
[86] (1948) 298 NY 119.
[87] ibid 125.
[88] (2002) NY Int 88.

The New York Court of Appeal also considered whether an article would qualify as the same publication or a new one in the event of unrelated alterations being made to other parts of the website. This was crucial as it goes to the issue of what constitutes a separate publication. In the offline world, the morning and evening editions of a newspaper are separate publications,[89] as are (more significantly in relation to limitation periods, as they typically are published months, rather than hours, apart) the hardback and paperback editions of a book.[90] The Restatement of Torts gives the following example:

• A defamatory article appears in a magazine. The same article is reprinted in the next issue of the magazine. This constitutes a new publication, and a new limitation period begins to run.

• A defamatory article appears in a magazine. The issue sells very well, and so the following month the same issue is reprinted and offered for sale. This constitutes the same publication, and no new limitation period arises.[91]

In the *Firth* case the Court ultimately decided that unrelated changes elsewhere in the website were not to be relevant in respect of the application of the single publication rule. Online content is by its very nature in a state of flux, with website change occurring on a very regular basis. Applying the spirit of the single publication rule was thus considered to be even more important in this context, as constantly triggering new limitation periods—effectively defeating the very point of the latter—would, in the view of the Court, lead to chaos. Further, the multiple publication rule was considered too apt to leave an individual defendant open to multiple suits, with implications for freedom of expression.

It can certainly be said that a single publication rule would be easier to apply. Not only does it avoid effectively emasculating the very point of the limitation period, but also it avoids a situation where a defendant finds himself attempting to construct a defence to an allegation of libel relating to an article which was originally published many years ago. Critics of the single publication would counter-argue that it is unfair to a claimant who may not be made aware of the defamatory publication in sufficient time to mount a case, although this contention might as readily be made in respect of any area of civil law. Referring to the limitation period for libel, in its 2001 report, *Limitation of Actions*, the Law Commission suggested lengthening the limitation period to three years, as it was between 1985 and 1996.[92] The basic proposal made here was that the three-year limitation period would begin to run from the point in time at which the claimant could reasonably be expected to have been aware of the existence of the defamatory publication, the identity of its source (anonymity being a somewhat easier state to maintain in the online environment), and that the damage caused to his

---

[89] *Cook v Conners* (1915) 215 NY 175.
[90] *Rinaldi v Viking Penguin Inc* (1981) 52 NY 2d 422.
[91] Section 577A, Illustrations 5 and 6.
[92] Prior to 1985, the limitation period for bringing a defamation action stood at 6 years.

or her reputation is significant. A further and final element of this proposal was that if these conditions have not been met and no limitation period commenced on the expiry of a ten-year period following first publication, then no action may be brought.[93] It should be noted, however, that this was not considered within the context of the point in time at which the limitation period began to run, nor did this report consider the potential benefits (or otherwise) of introducing a US-style single publication rule. The 2002 study did recognize that any such tampering with the limitation period would be broadly inconsequential as regards the libel defendant, assuming it was not also accompanied by change to the multiple publication rule.[94]

An inevitable result of the growth of the internet and its increasingly widespread use as a distribution channel for media content has been the rapid increase in commonality of international defamation disputes. Previously, only very large-scale print-publishers might have been involved in defending such actions, however, in the online world, no matter how small the publishing organization, it can have an international reach. Even an individual's blog posting, comments on a BBS, or eBay feedback[95] might result in them becoming a defendant in a libel case. It is a simple fact of the operation of the internet that an article uploaded in one country is instantly available globally. The question of place of publication as a geographical issue is thus raised. Clearly the appropriate law and jurisdiction under and in which a case is to be heard will be the law of the locality in which the article is published. So, where is the place of publication? Traditionally, tort law would hold that the appropriate place in which to bring a case is that in which the damage caused has been suffered. When dealing with internet content, however, the range of options for the forum-shopping claimant, seeking a favourable jurisdiction in which it is easiest to bring a case, are limited only by the claimant's pockets and scope of reputation. Where both parties to such a dispute are located within the European Union, the Brussels Regulation 2002 (which succeeded the Brussels Convention 1968) applies. The implications for defamation cases were outlined by the European Court of Justice in *Shevill v Press Alliance SA*.[96] The claimant in this case was an English student, who had spent some time working for a bureau de change in France. A French newspaper printed a story accusing her of abusing her position by using it to launder money. The vast majority of copies of the particular issue of the newspaper in which the article appeared were sold in France; some 237,000 in comparison to a mere 230 copies sold in England. Nevertheless, the claimant wished to sue in England in order to protect her reputation in her home country. The Court held that, under the Brussels Convention, as then

---

[93] Law Commission, *Limitation of Actions* (Law Com No 270, 2001).

[94] See Law Commission, *Defamation and the Internet: A Preliminary Investigation*, Scoping Study (Law Com No 2, 2002) para 3.11, n 10. For further comparison and analysis of the multiple and single publication rules, including jurisdictional implications, see G Sutter, 'One way, or another? Is it time for the introduction of the single publication rule in English defamation law?' (2005/06) 7(4) Contemporary Issues in Law 375.

[95] 'eBay buyer faces libel action after leaving negative feedback' *The Times*, 24 October 2008.

[96] [1995] ECR I-415.

was,[97] the claimant had the choice of whether to sue in the jurisdiction in which the defendant was domiciled, or in each individual Member State in which the defamatory publication had been made. If she took action in France, where the defendant was based, she would be able to sue in respect of the total number of publications made, whereas if she chose the second option, she could sue only in each individual state in respect of the damage to her reputation which had been caused within that territory. The upshot of this decision was that the claimant was entitled to bring a case in the English courts, though any damages awarded would be in respect of the 230 publications made in England only.

Where a cross-border defamation dispute arises between a party in England and one based outside the European Union, the situation falls to be resolved under the traditional rules of private international law. In essence, the English courts maintain a broad discretion to decide whether or not to hear a case based on a consideration of whether the claimant has a sufficient connection with the jurisdiction, and whether there has been a publication there. The number of copies published in England may also be significant; if a court considers the circulation of the article to be negligible, and therefore harm to reputation unlikely, it can decline to hear the case.[98] In *Berezovsky v Michaels*[99] the claimant was a Russian businessman whom a US publication had alleged to be involved with the Russian Mafia. While the bulk of copies published, some 785,000, had been circulated in the US, there were 2,000 copies circulated in England, and only 19 in Russia. The claimant wished to bring a case before the English courts. The House of Lords, finding in favour of the claimant being permitted to bring his case in England, considered that there was clearly a sufficient circulation of the defamatory article within England. A sufficient connection with the jurisdiction was also held to exist as the claimant had been a regular visitor to England for several years before commencing the action, and had both personal and professional contacts in England.

Prior to the application of these principles by the English courts to defamation cases involving publication online, there was some indication as to how this might be done in the Australian case of *Gutnick v Dow Jones*.[100] Gutnick was a prominent, if somewhat controversial, businessman who lived in the Australian State of Victoria. The defendants, a publisher based in the US, published a magazine which contained an article that the plaintiff believed defamed him. In addition to the physical print run, only a very small fraction of which was sold in Australia, the article was also made available on the defendants' website. The website content was accessible only to subscribers, of which there were 550,000 globally, 1,700 of those being based in Australia. Gutnick wished to sue in Australia rather than the US, but this was contested by the defendants, who

---

[97] Despite the Convention later being replaced by the Brussels Regulation of 2002, the equivalent provisions in each of these are sufficiently similar that *Shevill*'s authority remains unchanged.
[98] See eg *Jameel v Dow Jones Inc* [2005] EWCA Civ 75.
[99] [2000] 1 WLR 1004.
[100] [2002] HCA 56 (Aus).

clearly wished to be sued in the US courts, they being generally considered to be rather more sympathetic to the defendant. Gutnick brought proceedings seeking the permission of the courts in the State of Victoria to file suit there. The Supreme Court of the State of Victoria determined that the appropriate jurisdiction in which the case should be heard was that in which the article was published, and the judgment turned on the Court's consideration of this issue. The defendants argued that the articles were published in the US, as that was where they had been uploaded, and the server on which they were stored was located there. On policy grounds, they argued, there should be a single geographical point of publication[101] as otherwise publishers would be bound to abide by all laws globally, which would be both impractical (not least given incidences of conflicting laws) and unfair. This argument was soundly rejected by the Australian court. The focus of defamation law, it was found, is upon damage caused to reputation. Such harm can only be caused when the defamatory article is successfully communicated to the audience. Internet publication, therefore, is a two-step process, only complete when the article has been made available by the publisher *and* the reader has downloaded it in a form which they can read and understand.[102] The place of publication of the article in question in respect of those copies published to Australian subscribers, and consequently the appropriate place for the action to be taken, was therefore the State of Victoria.

The *Gutnick* decision caused much wringing of hands in certain quarters, as apocalyptic scenarios predicted doom for international and online publishers involving suits coming from all corners of the globe, even multiple suits across different jurisdictions from the same claimants, in respect of the same publication. The reality appears somewhat less dystopian. Certainly this approach leaves the door open for forum shopping by claimants with sufficiently deep pockets to be able to afford to bring cases in a more favourable jurisdiction. There are, for example, Hollywood celebrities who prefer to sue in the more claimant-friendly English courts rather than the courts of their native US where such rules as that in *New York Times v Sullivan*,[103] *inter alia*, make it somewhat more difficult to succeed. As discussed below, however, there are limiting factors within English defamation law which should mitigate against this becoming a particular problem.

The *Gutnick* line of reason is clearly directly applicable to the English multiple publication rule, and it would appear that in *Harrods v Dow Jones*[104] Eady J did just that. While merely a passing mention of *Gutnick* is made,[105] Eady's judgment suggests at least a tacit approval of the Australian Court's identification of place of publication as the place at which material is downloaded and viewed. Specific reference

---

[101] This is consistent with the application of the single publication rule in US law; see Sutter (n 93 above) 387–90.

[102] This is wholly consistent with traditional concepts of when publication occurs, see section 10.4 above.

[103] 376 US 254 (1964).

[104] 2003 WL 21162160, [2003] EWHC 1162.

[105] 2003 WL 21162160 (QBD), [2003] EWHC 1162, para 36.

is made to the multiple publication rule, to the effect that even if the publication's primary circulation is in a foreign jurisdiction, there can still be separate publications in other jurisdictions, each sufficient to found a separate action. However limited the circulation might be, there would still be publication in England. Eady also referred to the presumption of damages in libel cases. In the immediate case, which again involved a US-based website, there were very few publications into England, however, there being no *de minimis* principle as regards establishing publication beyond the one communication to a single third party, the judge held that this was no bar to an action being brought and so the case could be heard under English law.[106]

This seemingly liberal approach in the *Harrods* case is tempered by two later decisions in the English courts. First, in *Don King v Lennox Lewis*[107] the Court of Appeal emphasized that while a *Gutnick*-style rule on the place of publication was correct, the traditional rules of private international law on determining the appropriate forum must also be considered.[108] Secondly, in *Jameel v Dow Jones*[109] the Court of Appeal placed a significant restriction upon the right to bring a case before the English courts. Following the *Harrods* case, online publishers were potentially at the mercy of any would-be libel claimant who could establish some form of connection with England and show that there had been at least one publication into the jurisdiction: the virtually perfect forum-shopper's paradise. The *Jameel* decision indicates that the English courts will not permit this to go unfettered. The claimant here was a Saudi businessman suing a US-based website. He sought to sue in England on the basis that there had been publications made there. On the facts, it transpired that only five persons had downloaded and read the offending article from England, one of those being the claimant himself, and another two his lawyers. The Court of Appeal declined to allow this case to be heard in England on the basis that publication and therefore damage to reputation was so limited that the cost of proceedings would be wholly disproportionate to any damage actually suffered by the claimant and any consequent redress available. While these decisions certainly do not put a complete stop upon libel actions being brought in England by non-nationals who have a significant connection with the jurisdiction and can show more than a minimal number of publications took place, they certainly indicate that the courts will not take lightly any decision to permit an action. This should, at least in theory, allay fears that the libel courts will be swamped by foreign claimants on a forum-shopping spree.

---

[106] 2003 WL 21162160 (QBD), [2003] EWHC 1162, para 39.
[107] [2004] EWCA Civ 1329.
[108] The situation was, of course, somewhat different in *Harrods v Dow Jones*, as the claimant was domiciled in England.
[109] [2005] EWCA Civ 75.

10.5 POTENTIAL LIBEL CLAIMANTS:
WHO MAY SUE FOR LIBEL?

An oft-repeated saying, assumed by many to be a truism, is 'don't speak ill of the dead'. Libel lawyers will tell you, however, that this is in fact the best time to speak ill of anyone, as not only are they less likely to take offence, but they (or, more accurately, their estates) are barred from suing for libel. Only living individuals and existing legal persons may file a suit in defamation. The reputation of a company as a legal person has been held to exist separately to that of the individual employees, executives, and so on. A corporation can thus sue as a person where its reputation has been damaged, although damages will only be recoverable in respect of harm to goodwill, a company having no feelings which need compensation for emotional upset.[110] One example of a corporation suing to protect the reputation of its brand was *McDonalds Corp v Steel and anor*,[111] more popularly known as the 'McLibel' case; the longest libel trial in English legal history. A charity, although non-commercial, could similarly sue in libel. For instance, a charity collecting money to provide aid to Palestinian refugees would be able to sue in libel the publisher of a newspaper article which made the defamatory allegation that the charity was a front for fundraising for Hamas. The exact nature of the allegations made in a defamatory article will be important in such cases: the corporation will not be permitted to sue where it is an individual employee who is defamed, nor will employees be able to successfully sue if the court decides that it is the company which has been defamed rather than its employees.

Certain bodies are forbidden from suing in libel: these include government bodies and local authorities,[112] political parties,[113] and nationalized industries.[114] The courts have held that there is a legitimate public interest in the uninhibited public criticism of bodies that put themselves forward for public office or who are democratically elected to govern, or are responsible for public administration. This rationale was succinctly put by Lord Bridge in *Hector v AG of Antigua and Barbuda*:[115] 'Any attempt to stifle or fetter such criticism amounts to political censorship of the most insidious and objectionable kind.'[116]

It must be noted that even where an organization is barred from filing suit, it is possible for an individual within that group to bring proceedings in libel provided that he has been sufficiently identified.[117] For example, a local newspaper in the East End of London publishing an article stating that 'All Family Party members on the East End

[110] *Lewis v Daily Telegraph* [1964] AC 234.
[111] *The Times*, 14 April 1994.
[112] *Derbyshire CC v Times Newspapers* [1993] AC 534.
[113] *Goldsmith v Bhoyrul* [1998] QB 459.
[114] *British Coal Corp v NUM* 28 June 1996, unreported.
[115] [1990] 2 All ER 103.
[116] ibid 106.
[117] *Derbyshire CC v Times Newspapers* [1993] AC 534.

Council are corrupt and fiddle their expenses' could not be sued by the Family Party as a corporate body. The individual East End councillors belonging to that party, however, would in all probability be considered members of a sufficiently small group such as to be identified by the article and therefore able to sue.[118]

One might assume that a fugitive from justice might not be permitted to being a libel case, however, in *Polanski v Conde Nast Publications*[119] the Court facilitated just such a situation. In 1977, Roman Polanski, a well-known film director and widower of actress Sharon Tate who was murdered by the infamous Manson family, in a US Court entered a guilty plea to charges of unlawful sexual intercourse with a minor, a girl of 13. While awaiting trial, Polanski absconded to France, where he held citizenship, and has been able to remain ever since. The US did not request that the French authorities prosecute Polanski, nor have they ever tried to extradite him from France. In 2004, Polanski launched a libel action against Conde Nast Publications, the publishers of *Vanity Fair* magazine, in London.[120] This case concerned a 2002 article in the magazine, which recounted a claim made by an editor of *Harper's Magazine* that, while en route to his murdered wife's funeral, Polanski had made sexual advances towards a young model travelling with him, telling her that she could be 'the next Sharon Tate'. After expressing a concern that, were he to enter the UK, he might be arrested and extradited to the US to face the outstanding criminal charges against him, the Court permitted Polanski to give his evidence via a video link from France. Indeed, not only was Polanski permitted to bring his case in this manner, but he was also ultimately awarded £50,000 upon winning the case.

10.6 POTENTIAL LIBEL DEFENDANTS: WHO MAY BE SUED FOR LIBEL?

There is a range of persons against whom an action in libel action may be taken. Potential defendants might include the author of a defamatory article, for example a journalist. If the article in question happens to be an interview and the interviewee makes defamatory allegations in the course of the interview, then that individual may also be sued. Naturally, it would not only be 'reasonably foreseeable' but blindingly obvious that words spoken during the course of an interview might be repeated in the subsequent publication, and so the rule in *Slipper v BBC* would clearly apply in such a situation.[121] The editor of a newspaper, book, or magazine, or any publisher thereof, is a valid target for a libel suit, as would be the broadcaster of a television programme containing a defamation. These persons may be sued in relation to a libel distributed online just as in the offline world. An individual who posts a comment on a bulletin

---

[118] See section 10.3 above.
[119] [2005] 1 WLR 637.
[120] *Polanski v Conde Nast* [2005] 1 WLR 637.
[121] See section 10.4 above.

board, for example the *Daily Mirror*'s 'Have your say', is open to primary liability as a publisher if the uploaded text contains a defamatory statement. Equally, the newspaper may be liable for publishing that statement, either strictly, as a publisher or editor, or possibly as a distributor where no editorial control is exercised over uploaded comments. An internet service provider (ISP) hosting third-party content which is defamatory may also be liable as a distributor, given sufficient awareness. It is possible for there to be several different defendants in one libel case, who might be any of those already discussed. In practice, however, claimants are less likely to adopt the scattergun approach of suing all possible defendants. More commonly, the defendants tend to be the publishers, or, in the case of an internet-based defamation, the service provider responsible for hosting or otherwise providing the facility by which it is made available. It is often suggested, somewhat cynically, that such parties tend to be the defendant as they are likely to have the deepest pockets. It must be noted that these are the parties most likely to have a greater level of control over the onward distribution of the libel in question. An ISP can have it deleted from their servers, while a newspaper publisher is best placed to call to account the decisions of the paper's editorial staff. In the case of online defamation, the responsible service provider, whether the host in the traditional sense or the operator of a bulletin board service, may be the only source of information leading to the identity of an otherwise anonymous libeller. Clearly where protection of reputation rather than mere damages is the aim of an action, these are very significant factors.

10.7 DEFENCES TO LIBEL

10.7.1 Justification

Libel law presumes that a defamatory statement is false, but this is a rebuttable presumption. It is a complete defence for the defendant to show that the article complained of is in fact true, or substantially true. This defence will be available even where the publication has been made purely for financial gain, spitefully, or otherwise with malicious intent. A defendant seeking to establish a justification defence must further prove the truth of any reasonable interpretation of the article in question, as well as the truth of any innuendo meaning. Justification can be a difficult defence to run successfully. Juries can be unpredictable, and the defence can suddenly find itself faced with a defamatory meaning completely other than that which it is able to justify. Justification can be a deceptively challenging defence as it is not always so easy to prove an allegation in court on the basis of admissible evidence a story that the defendant 'knows' to be true. The classic illustration of this lies in *Liberace v Daily Mirror Newspapers*.[122] The claimant, a famous American pianist who popularized classical music by, in his own words, 'cutting out the boring bits', was visiting London in order to give a series

---

[122] *The Times*, 18 June 1959.

of performances. An article about the shows in the *Daily Mirror* described the claimant as 'the summit of sex—the pinnacle of masculine, feminine and neuter. Everything that he, she or it can ever want' and as a 'deadly, winking, sniggering, snuggling, chromium-plated, scent-impregnated, luminous, quivering, giggling, fruit-flavoured, ice-covered heap of mother love'.

In an action for libel against the newspaper's publishers, Liberace contended that the natural and ordinary meaning of this article was that he was homosexual. Salmon J agreed that the words were capable of this meaning, and the jury in due course decided that to be the meaning of the article, finding that it was indeed defamatory.[123] The twist to the story is that now, many years after his death, it is a matter of public record that Liberace was indeed homosexual. The defendant newspaper knew this, but fell foul of the libel laws because they were simply unable to prove it in court. By extension of this principle, we have the so-called 'repetition rule'. The repetition rule provides that when the defamatory statement purports to report a statement made by a third party, or to report on rumours and gossip circulating generally, it is not sufficient to prove merely that the third party did indeed make that statement, or that the rumour is in circulation. Even where the defamatory allegation has been generated by a third party source and is merely reported by the media, the truth of the statement must be proven in fact, otherwise a justification defence is unavailable.[124]

For justification, the defence must prove the truth of the substance of the allegations on the balance of probabilities. *Irving v Penguin Books*[125] was a case launched by the historian David Irving against two Jewish academics, who had written a book about holocaust denial, and their publisher. Irving argued that he had been defamed by being labelled a 'Holocaust denier' as, while a self-confessed revisionist who argues that the extent of the genocide carried out by the Nazis has been exaggerated by Jewish interests over the years, he claimed that he has never denied the events entirely. Gray J ruled that where a libel defendant's allegations are of a serious nature, the standard of proof

---

[123] It should be borne in mind that in the late 1950s, the liberalization introduced by the Sexual Offences Act 1967 had yet to take place, and homosexual activity between consenting male adults was a criminal offence. That being so, suggesting that Liberace was homosexual was to some degree implying that he indulged in criminal behaviour. The allegation of homosexual orientation alone was sufficient to mark out an individual as a 'deviant' in the eyes of the average person in those more conservative times. In more recent years, it has been a matter of some debate and no little controversy whether being mistakenly referred to as being homosexual is in fact or should be libellous. The actor and singer Jason Donovan was much criticized by interested parties for (successfully) suing *The Face* magazine for labelling him gay in an article: *Jason Donovan v The Face* (1992, unreported). It can now be said that, in the early twenty-first century, society in general is rather less conservative than would have been the case in the late 1950s, to the point where it might be considered that a simple allegation of homosexuality alone would no longer be enough to amount to a libel within the *Sim v Stretch* [1936] 2 All ER 1237 parameters. If, on the other hand, such sexuality-related allegations imply, on the facts, an impropriety of some sort, an action may be possible. For example, an allegation that a married celebrity is actually homosexual may be interpreted by a jury to mean that his marriage is a dishonest sham, which certainly could cause those who read or hear such a story to think less of the individual concerned.

[124] See eg Lord Devlin's comments in *Lewis v Daily Telegraph* [1964] AC 234, 283.

[125] 2000 WL 362478.

required should be proportionately higher. Ultimately, the defence were able to adduce sufficient evidence to justify their serious allegations, and Irving's case failed.

In order for a justification defence to succeed, it is the natural and ordinary meaning attributed to the statement by the jury which must be proven. This, of course, may be wholly different from the meaning intended by the person responsible for publishing the article. It may even be an innuendo meaning the existence of which the publisher could not possibly have been aware, as was the case in *Cassidy*.[126] When preparing a justification defence, the defendant will seek to justify the meaning they believe that the words had, which may be entirely different from the meaning put by the claimant. The final decision as to the natural and ordinary meaning will remain with the jury, which will also determine whether a successful justification has been made. The difficulties for the media here are obvious, given that they must in effect guess at the meaning that the jury is likely to ascribe to the words, and then build their defence in the hope that they are correct. Mitigating this somewhat is the fact that it is not necessary to prove the truth of every single factual allegation, provided that the overall impact, or the 'defamatory sting', can be satisfactorily proven. Under section 5 of the Defamation Act 1952, where an action for defamation concerns two or more distinct charges against the claimant, a defence of justification will not fail by reason only that the truth of every charge is not proven, provided that the words which are unproven do not materially injure the claimant's reputation in the light of the truth of the remaining charges. For example, if it can be proven that a married family values campaigner whom a newspaper article has accused of secretly using pornography and employing the services of prostitutes, were to be proven to be a regular client of a prostitute, the newspaper's justification defence would not fail simply because it could not prove that he regularly viewed pornography. This provision means that justification can be a defence worth raising even where there are defamatory allegations which cannot be proven, on the proviso that these are of a lesser level of seriousness than those which can be justified.

In order to prove the truth of an allegation, the defendant will have to raise the right evidence before a jury. The issue of evidencing justification was addressed in *McDonalds Corp v Steel and anor*, the so-called McLibel Trial.[127] This case was brought against two unemployed environmental campaigners who had produced and distributed a leaflet entitled 'What's wrong with McDonalds?'. The leaflet made various allegations about the company, including that eating McDonalds' food carried serious health risks. The claimants applied to have various parts of the justification defence struck out. This application was granted by the High Court, on the basis that there was no evidence before the Court supporting the allegations in question. This decision was reversed by the Court of Appeal, which ruled that it was perfectly proper for the defendants to plead particulars of a justification in anticipation of being able to adduce sufficient evidence to do so by the date of the trial. The judges found that it was

---

[126] See section 10.2 above.
[127] *The Times*, 14 April 1994.

inappropriate to strike out the defence as requested before the trial unless it was clear at the time such an application was made that no other admissible evidence was going to become available.

Thus, in order for a successful justification defence to be mounted:

- the defendant must have an honest belief in the truth of the article in question;
- the defendant must intend to support the justification at the trial;
- the defendant must either be in possession of reasonable (and admissible) evidence to support the defence, *or* have reasonable grounds to believe that such evidence will be available by the date of the trial.

These requirements are not to be taken lightly: it would be a very unwise defendant indeed who, in circumstances where that was uncertain, gambled on being able to scrape together sufficient evidence for a justification by the time of the trial. Nevertheless, it has been held that a justification may be based upon evidence arising *after* publication has occurred. In *Moss v Channel 5 Broadcasting*[128] the claimant sued over a documentary broadcast by the defendant in 2005, and in which it was alleged that in one incident in 2001 she had taken so much cocaine that she had rendered herself comatose. Following the launch of the action, tabloid newspaper the *Daily Mirror* ran an article about Ms Moss's use of the drug, and she issued a public apology for her behaviour. This admission of use of the illegal substance was a big news item which caused not a little controversy, with several major brands gaining much free publicity as they cancelled (later to renew) her modelling contracts. The defendant broadcaster in the immediate case sought to reply upon this new information to justify their allegations. The claimant applied to have the defence struck out, arguing that this would be a justification of a more general charge rather than the claim of a specific event in 2001. Eady J, however, ruled that the defendant could enter a plea of justification of any meaning that the words complained of were capable of bearing. The allegations made in the broadcast were capable, in the context of the programme, of having the meaning that the claimant was a serious cocaine abuser, and the defence was permitted to rely upon the events which had taken place since the time of the broadcast in order to justify that meaning. Here again we see the court setting parameters to the defence that make it somewhat easier for a media defendant to succeed in a plea of justification, although as already noted it would still be unwise to take the risk of relying on such evidence being forthcoming by the time of the trial, as opposed to being open to it as a fortuitous additional plank in support of the defence should it happen to arise in time.

A further advantage for the media is that the mere fact that the defendant may be acting out of ill-will towards the plaintiff will generally not be relevant to justification. Provided that the statement is true or substantially true and that this can be proven, any motive behind the publication being made will be irrelevant. The sole exception to this rule is provided under the Rehabilitation of Offenders Act 1974. Certain previous criminal convictions are considered to be 'spent' after a set number of years following

---

[128] 3 February 2006.

the date of conviction; the length of this period will vary according to the nature of the offence. If a conviction is spent, it is never mentioned in court. The media are permitted to publish the details of spent criminal convictions; however, where such information is published maliciously, the defence of justification will not be available.

10.7.2 Fair comment on a matter of public interest

In *Telnikoff v Matusevitch*,[129] Lord Ackner outlined the purpose of the fair comment defence as being to protect 'the right of the citizen honestly to express his genuine opinion on a matter of public interest, however wrong or exaggerated or prejudiced that opinion may be'.[130]

This defence shields a genuine opinion, honestly given, from being unfairly subject to liability for libel, thus striking a delicate balance between the freedom of expression right in Article 10(1) ECHR, and the permitted derogation for protection of the reputation of others in Article 10(2) of the Convention. In *Burstein v Associated Newspapers*[131] the claimant was a composer who had brought a libel suit over a bad review of his new opera. The Court of Appeal confirmed that provided the critic was not motivated by malice, had actually seen the opera, and had honestly formed a very low opinion of it, he was entitled to write a severely critical review. There is no requirement of reasonableness here—as Lord Ackner said in the *Telnikoff* case, an honest opinion is valid 'however wrong or exaggerated or prejudiced that opinion may be'.

Determining whether an article is an expression of opinion or a mere statement of fact is not always straightforward. There may be indicators in the actual words used, for instance 'I think that', or 'in my opinion', but this is not necessary. It may also be an expression of an opinion, for example a statement that a minor member of the royal family behaved in a disgraceful manner, falling out of a nightclub drunk on a Monday evening. In *Keays v Guardian Newspapers*[132] the claimant was a known public figure as a result of her affair with, and subsequent child by, a Conservative politician. Sunday newspaper *The Observer* ran a story about the claimant in its 'Comment' section, which made various speculations about the claimant's motives for selling her story and thus placing not only herself but also her young daughter under public scrutiny. The judge held that it was clear that the article was a statement of opinion: it did not claim to be anything else (indeed, its positioning in the 'Comment' section of the newspaper suggested it was intended to be opinion), there was no way that the author could have actually known the claimant's state of mind and motives, and so the reader would understand that it was intended to be an opinion rather than a statement of fact. In *Silkin v Beaverbrook Newspapers*[133] the fact that offensive language was used in the expression of the opinion in question was no bar to the defence being available.

---

[129] [1991] 4 All ER 817.
[130] ibid 826.
[131] [2007] EWCA Civ 600.
[132] [2003] EWHC 1565.
[133] [1958] 1 WLR 743.

The defendant does not have to convince the court that his opinions are correct, or even reasonable, but the comments must be based upon true facts which are known to the defendant at the time of publication. The reason for this is simple: one cannot legitimately hold an opinion on factual circumstances of which one is not yet aware. Further, however, the defence is not available where a comment is based upon 'facts' which turn out to be incorrect—even where the comments have been made in the honest belief that they are true facts. The defence must prove that the facts commented on are substantially true. While in other respects fair comment is an easier defence for the media to make than justification, the requirement that the true facts be proven on the basis of evidence that was available at the time of publication may be somewhat more challenging in the context of a particular story.

The onus is also upon the defendant to show that the article at issue was concerned with a matter of public interest. In *London Artists v Littler*[134] Lord Denning indicated that it will be in the public interest if the story concerns people at large such that they might have a legitimate interest in or concern about the story and how it might affect them. This will include, for instance, opinions about the conduct and behaviour of public figures, those involved in local and national government, and public and private companies insofar as these affect people or the administration of justice. The general rule of thumb is that should someone place themselves in the public eye, they open themselves to public comment, although of course their private life will be considered to be private save where it is relevant to their public existence. In practice, the courts appear to set the bar for 'public interest' rather low. In the *London Artists* case, an article giving an opinion about a West End theatre production which was threatened with closure when three of the actors withdrew from performing was considered to be in the public interest. The public's opportunity to go and see the production being under threat was enough for public interest to be present: its parameters are much broader than, say, matters of state or politics. More recent cases have continued the trend towards a liberal interpretation of what is in the public interest, Eady J, a leading member of the judiciary in the area of libel, having stated:

In a modern democracy all those who venture into public life, in whatever capacity, must expect to have their motives subjected to scrutiny and discussed. Nor is it realistic today to demand that such debate should be hobbled by the constraints of conventional good manners—still less of deference. The law of fair comment must allow for healthy scepticism.[135]

The defence of fair comment may be defeated by the presence of malice in the statement of opinion. Malice is interpreted widely in this context: a simple lack of honest belief in the opinion being expressed will be sufficient. Once the defence has been raised, the true facts proven, and it is found that a matter of public interest is in fact at stake, it is up to the claimant to prove a lack of honest belief in the opinions stated on the part of the defendant. Clearly this is favourable to the defence, balancing out any

---

[134] [1968] 1 All ER 1075.
[135] *Branson v Bower* [2001] All ER (D) 159, para 25.

potential difficulties involved in establishing to the satisfaction of the court the true facts upon which the defence is proven.

10.7.3 Consent

Where a person has consented to the publication of defamatory material, that consent will provide a complete defence. This consent may be express or implicit, but it must also be both specific and informed. Were the Mayor of London to consent to appear on a television programme to be interviewed about his love of dining and fine wine, for example, this would not constitute consent for the purposes of broadcasting in the course of that programme a defamatory allegation that he had an alcohol dependency problem. Further, if the claimant has in a private context disclosed information about himself which is then published by the media to the world at large, such limited disclosure is unlikely to be taken as having been consent to this wider publication. [136] It is clear, then, that the media must be careful when seeking consent from an individual to the publication of material which might otherwise occasion liability in libel. While an implied consent is sufficient at law, a clearly expressed, explicit consent in writing will always be preferable from the point of view of evidencing that consent. The most likely form for this to take is that of a signed consent form, setting out all relevant details relating to the programme or article. Given the widespread use of consent forms for copyright and other purposes in the media already, this would not be a difficult thing to incorporate in practice.

10.7.4 Privilege

There are two key types of privilege: absolute, and qualified (a third form, parliamentary privilege, although to be treated separately here is really a distinct sub-grouping of absolute privilege). The key distinction between types is that while absolute privilege is absolute, qualified privilege may be defeated by a finding that the publication in question has been made with malice.

10.7.4.1 *Absolute privilege*
Absolute privilege is a complete defence to any defamation action, even where the statement complained of is indeed libellous, and it cannot be defeated by the presence of malice. It applies to statements made in the course of court proceedings by any participant in those proceedings, whether witness, judge, counsel for either side, or even the parties to the actions themselves. There is no statutory definition *per se* of what constitutes 'court proceedings', although section 14 of the Defamation Act 1996, which extends absolute privilege to cover *reports* of court proceedings, defines what is meant by proceedings in that context. This includes any UK court, the European Court

---

[136] *Cook v Ward* (1830) 6 Bing 409.

of Justice or the Court of First Instance of the European Union, the European Court of Human Rights, and any international criminal court under the auspices of the United Nations or any international agreement to which the UK is a party. This protection applies to: 'A fair and accurate report of proceedings in public before a court to which this section applies, if published contemporaneously with the proceedings, is absolutely privileged.'[137]

The determination of whether a publication is contemporaneous will be influenced by the nature of the publication. A newspaper report, for instance, will be published contemporaneously if published in the next available issue after the court proceedings which it concerns. The precise timeframe may be influenced by such factors as whether it is a weekly newspaper, in which case a publication made the following week may be contemporaneous, or an evening or morning newspaper, in which case the following morning, or (depending upon the time of day the proceedings occur) the same evening, or the following evening's report will be covered. In the case of a monthly magazine, the period can be longer, depending upon the lead time to the next available issue, while it might be very narrow indeed where the report is broadcast on a 24-hour rolling news television channel. Where a court exercises its discretion to postpone the reporting of certain details of proceedings, or such is required by statute,[138] any such report will be published contemporaneously if it is published as soon as is reasonably practicable following the lifting of these restrictions.

10.7.4.2 *Parliamentary privilege*

Under parliamentary privilege, there is a complete bar on bringing an action against a Member of Parliament or a Member of the House of Lords which is aimed at finding him liable in either criminal or civil law in respect of anything said or done by him in the course of proceedings in Parliament. This parliamentary privilege, rooted in Article 9 of the Bill of Rights 1689, long pre-dates more modern conceptions of freedom of expression. Rather than being designed to protect an individual freedom as such, its intent is to free those in Parliament from any fear of liability in order that debates leading to new laws are sufficiently unfettered so as to result in the best possible scrutiny of provisions passed by either House. In *Prebble v Television New Zealand*[139] the Privy Council confirmed that this privilege extends to any party to an action. In other words, it not only prevented proceedings from being launched against an MP, it also meant that an MP could not bring proceedings in relation to allegations about his conduct in Parliament. The practical effect of this is to preclude MPs from bringing defamation proceedings against anyone who alleges some professional impropriety on the part of the MP. In 1994, Neil Hamilton, then a Conservative MP, filed suit against a story in *The Guardian* which alleged him to be one of several Conservative MPs who had taken money and other benefits from Mohammed Fayed, the owner of Harrods, in exchange for asking

---

[137] Defamation Act 1996, s 14(1).
[138] See Ch 4 above.
[139] [1995] 1 AC 321.

questions in Parliament. The newspaper claimed that it could justify the report. Parliamentary privilege prevented the parties from bringing into court evidence about Hamilton's conduct in Parliament, and so the newspaper was prevented from showing a link between payments supposedly made by Fayed to Hamilton with services rendered in return. In 1995, the Court stayed Hamilton's action on the grounds that in order for a defence to be viable, it would have to infringe the privilege to such a degree that a fair trial was not possible. In 1996, however, the Defamation Act amended the law to introduce a new concept. Where previously parliamentary privilege had been conceived of as a collective entity, it was now something that attached to each MP individually, and could be waived by each individual for himself alone.[140] When the case resumed, the newspaper was still prevented from bringing a large quantity of its evidence as this related to another MP who had not waived his privilege; the defence was still hampered to some degree[141] and the case was settled out of court. In *Hamilton v Al Fayed*[142] the defendant had appeared in a television documentary, claiming that he had given the claimant cash on a number of occasions. Concurrent with these new proceedings, an internal parliamentary committee on standards and privileges had found against Hamilton. The defendants tried to have Hamilton's case struck out, claiming it to be a 'collateral attack' on the internal findings and thus an infringement of the privilege in those proceedings. In making this argument, the defence stressed that the Court might come to a different conclusion than that reached in the internal proceedings. The Court of Appeal declined to strike the case out, holding that it would only infringe the proceedings if the case was clearly a threat to undermine the authority of Parliament; the mere possibility of a conflicting conclusion was no such threat. The Lords, however, disagreed,[143] ruling that Hamilton's waiver of his own privilege did not affect any privilege enjoyed by Parliament as a whole. The findings of the Committee could therefore be considered by the Court insofar as they related to Hamilton alone. It should also be noted here that this decision applies only in respect of parliamentary proceedings, and does not address the effect of waiver on another MP.

10.7.4.3 *Qualified privilege*
As already stated, the key distinction between absolute and qualified privilege is that the latter will be defeated where the defendant published the article in question with a malicious motive. The burden of proof to show the existence of such malice rests with the claimant. As with fair comment, malice here has a broad meaning, incorporating statements made by someone who does not have a positive belief in the truth of the same. The test for malice is subjective, and it is sufficient to be reckless, or indifferent as to the truth of a statement.[144] A statement may also be made maliciously where the defendant

---

[140] See Defamation Act 1996, section 13.
[141] Arguably this raises questions in relation to the Art 6 ECHR right to a fair trial.
[142] [1999] 3 All ER 317, CA.
[143] [2000] 2 All ER 224, HL.
[144] *Horrocks v Lowe* [1975] AC 135.

honestly believes it to be true, but misuses it for a purpose other than that for which the publication is granted.[145] A misuse here might include, for example, the publication of the statement for the purpose of attacking the character of the person it concerns. In order to establish malice here, the claimant must be able to prove that the defendant's improper motive was the dominant one when the latter made the publication. The existence of malice is a question of fact for the jury. While the question of whether malice is present is subjective, the natural and ordinary meaning of the statement is still to be judged objectively by the jury. This being so, it is possible that the jury may find that a statement has a meaning which differs from that intended by the defendant, and in the truth of which he believed. In such a case, the courts have decreed that there can be no malice in an unintended meaning.[146] Where there is more than one defendant in an action, the defence must be established separately for each defendant.[147]

Schedule 1 of the Defamation Act 1996 lists a number of types of statement which are protected by qualified privilege, either automatically,[148] or 'subject to explanation or contradiction'.[149] 'Explanation or contradiction' refers to the right of the claimant to the publication of a reasonable letter or statement by way of explanation or contradiction of the report. Qualified privilege will not be a defence to the publication of any type of statement listed in Part 2 of Schedule 1 if it can be proven that the defendant had been asked by the claimant to publish in the same place and with the same prominence as the original story a reasonable response to the original statement, and refused so to do. Where a response is published, but it is not adequate or reasonable in all the circumstances, or is not given the necessary level of prominence, the defence will not be available.

There are also, at common law, limited types of report to which qualified privilege will attach. These do not form a closed, exclusive list, but any new instances will have to fall within the established parameters of the defence.[150] Some types of statement listed in Schedule 1, such as a report of court proceedings, can also attract qualified privilege at common law if they are 'fair and accurate'. This is an important defence as it applies where qualified privilege is not available under statute as the report has not been made contemporaneously. A verbatim report of the proceedings in question is not required; as Lord Denning noted in *Cook v Alexander*,[151] a case concerning a report of parliamentary proceedings, selective reporting is important to the media, which is interested in publishing only the elements of proceedings that the public is interested in reading. This, according to Lord Denning, is perfectly acceptable, provided the

---

[145] ibid.

[146] *Loveless v Earl* [1999] EMLR 530.

[147] *Egger v Chelmsford* [1964] 3 All ER 406.

[148] For example, a 'fair and accurate report of [court proceedings, or proceedings in a legislature] anywhere in the world' (Part 1).

[149] eg 'a fair and accurate copy of or extract from a notice . . .' issued by EU Parliament or Member State Legislature (Part 2).

[150] *Watts v Times Newspapers* [1996] 1 All ER 152.

[151] [1974] QB 279.

report gives 'a fair presentation of what took place so far as to convey to the reader the impression which the debate itself would have made on the hearer of it'.[152]

Where a statement made to rebut or defend from a defamatory attack is published, qualified privilege will be available as a defence. The court in *Turner v MGM*[153] drew a comparison with the criminal law on self defence: in both, there is the right to defend oneself, a protection which will be lost if the defendant oversteps the mark and moves from defence to a position of attack. Where such a reply is published by the media, the outlet publishing the reply—whether newspaper, broadcaster, or other—is protected by qualified privilege when it publishes the reply. This applies where the publicity given to the reply is equivalent to that given to the original defamatory statement, and as far as it sticks to the defamatory allegations made therein. In *Adam v Ward*[154] the claimant, an MP, made a defamatory statement in the House of Commons about a high-ranking officer in the army. This statement was not true; when the army investigated the allegations, they were found to be baseless. The MP was, however, protected by parliamentary privilege. Following the military investigation, the Army Council's secretary was instructed to write a letter to the officer, exonerating him. This letter contained certain statements which defamed the claimant; when it was later released to the press, the Court found that the media were entitled to rely on qualified privilege. *Regan v Taylor*[155] confirmed that where a response to a defamatory allegation is published by an agent such as a solicitor on behalf of the person defamed, qualified privilege will apply equally as if it had been published by the latter. As increasingly not only celebrities but regular persons pushed, by circumstances, into the media limelight (for example the parents of missing child Madeline McCann) employ spokespeople to deal with the media for them, this is an important point for the media.

Common law also provides a qualified privilege defence where there can be demonstrated a duty (legal or moral) to communicate the statement to someone who has a material interest in receiving the statement.[156] Both the duty and interest elements must be proven, and the position of both the publisher and the person to whom the publication has been made will be considered when the court is deciding whether qualified privilege applies. A major question which arises here is whether and to what extent the duty and interest form of qualified privilege provides, or should provide, a public interest defence for the media. Such a defence would be highly attractive to the media, as it would be easier to establish than either justification or fair comment. Traditionally

---

[152] ibid 288.
[153] [1950] 1 All ER 449.
[154] [1917] AC 309.
[155] [2000] 1 All ER 307.
[156] See, for instance, *Beach v Freeson* [1972] 1 QB 14, in which the claimants were a firm of solicitors, and one of the constituents of an MP had asked that MP to request that they be investigated by the Law Society. The MP duly wrote to the Law Society and the Lord Chancellor, setting out the allegations as passed to him by the constituent. The Court found that this was a privileged communication: as a general rule, an MP who is requested by a constituent to pass on a serious complaint to the appropriate body has a duty to comply.

the courts considered this a step too far, as it would bias libel law too far in favour of the defendant, who would not be required to prove the truth of anything published in order to successfully mount a defence.[157] In 1991, The Neil Committee considered that 'the media are adequately protected by the defences of justification and fair comment at the moment, and it is salutary that these defences are available to them only if they have got their facts substantially correct'. The committee did not approve of the idea of a public interest defence. In recent years, the media have attempted to argue the existence of a *de facto* public interest defence by stressing the duty and interest test for qualified privilege, but to date the courts have resisted developing the law along these lines.

The bounds of qualified privilege were reconsidered in *Reynolds v Times*.[158] This was brought by Albert Reynolds, a former Taioseach of the Republic of Ireland, against the *Sunday Times* newspaper, which had published an article claiming he was guilty of malpractice in carrying out his duties in that office. These allegations had led to the collapse of his government and loss of office. The Court of Appeal expanded the traditional duty and interest test to incorporate a third leg: were the nature, status, source, and all circumstances of the story such that publication in the public interest should be protected in the absence of malice? This third element was based upon earlier case law, but represented a significant new development as it required the consideration of circumstantial issues for the sole purpose of considering the status of the publication in order to facilitate a decision as to whether the publication qualified for protection. The Court of Appeal considered it to be the duty of the news media to inform the public and discuss issues which are of public interest. These were said to include not only political issues such as conduct of government and elections, but also issues relating to the operation of public bodies, institutions, and companies. The Court did specifically exclude personal and private matters. As a general rule, it was found that the public has an interest in receiving information the media publishes: where the subject matter of a report is in the public interest, the duty and interest test should be satisfied. This represented a narrowing of the concept of public interest via the circumstantial test. Under this, the courts would scrutinize all steps taken to verify the truth of a story. The reliability of any source would be considered, as would be the matter of whether the subject was given any opportunity to reply to or rebut the allegation. The primary purpose of this test, according to the Court, was to maintain a proper balance between claimant and defendant, rather than to regulate journalism. It might reasonably be asked how the Court of Appeal expected this to be possible without doing exactly that. Applying its three-step test, the Court concluded that the duty and interest steps had indeed been satisfied. The circumstances in which the former Taioseach had fallen from power were of public interest to UK citizens: the newspaper thus had a duty to inform the citizens, who had a reciprocal interest in receiving that information. This third,

---

[157] See eg Canter J in *London Artists v Littler* [1968] 1 All ER 1075.
[158] [1998] 3 All ER 961, CA, [1999] 4 All ER 609, HL.

circumstantial leg of the test had not been satisfied, however. The defendants had not given Reynolds' side of the story, nor had they informed him of their conclusions prior to publication. In all the circumstances of the publication, the Court considered that it would be inappropriate to allow qualified privilege protection to apply.

The circumstantial test in application would raise a number of significant difficulties for the media. Not least of these would be additional delay until publication, necessitated by the need to ensure that the Court would accept the story as being sufficiently in the public interest. All the value of news media lies in its currency: too long a delay before a story is reported, and it is of no interest to its audience. Requiring the media to provide the subject with an opportunity to rebut an allegation could in some cases tip off the latter, allowing him the opportunity to apply for an injunction to prevent publication, or at least delay it long enough for it to be of no value. Prior notice might also afford an unscrupulous subject the opportunity to destroy evidence, perhaps also to fabricate an alibi. This would certainly be bad for investigative journalism. Equally serious for the media was the likelihood of a clash with the right of a journalist, under section 10 of the Contempt of Court Act 1981, to withhold the identity of his sources in certain circumstances.[159] The Court of Appeal's circumstantial test would require the identity of a source to be revealed so that its reliability could be verified. A few months after the *Reynolds* case this issue came before the Court of Appeal in *Gaddafi v Telegraph Group*,[160] when the defence sought to rely upon qualified privilege but wished to avoid naming the source in case the latter was thus endangered. Concern over this conflict was expressed by the judge.

The *Reynolds* case was appealed to the House of Lords, which overturned the Court of Appeal's creation of the circumstantial test.[161] The finding that qualified privilege might be available for publication of material which is in the public interest was approved, however, the Lords held that while circumstantial factors could be taken into account in deciding whether the duty and interest tests were satisfied, they should not constitute a separate test in themselves. Reinforcing the traditional resistance to the introduction of an all-out public interest defence by the back door, the Lords confirmed that the duty and interest tests would not automatically be satisfied simply because the subject matter of the publication was in the public interest. The value to the public of the information depends also on its quality: there is neither a duty in publishing nor an interest in receiving misinformation. The defence, according to the Lords, is required to show that it acted responsibly in relation to the publication. It is clear from both the Lords' judgment in the *Reynolds* case, and subsequent decisions, that the watchwords for the media in this context are: *responsible journalism*.

---

[159] See Ch 3 above.
[160] (1998, unreported).
[161] [1999] 4 All ER 609, HL.

Giving his judgment in the Lords, Lord Nicholls suggested an illustrative, non- exhaustive list of factors that a court should consider when determining whether a publication is privileged. These were:

- The seriousness of the allegation
- The nature of the information—is the matter of public concern?
- The source of the information
- Any steps taken to verify information
- The status of the information
- The urgency of the matter
- Was any response sought from the claimant?
- Did the article include the gist of the claimant's case?
- The tone of the article
- The circumstances of publication—including timing.[162]

Lord Nicholls was also clear that the importance of these and any other relevant factors will vary from case to case.[163] The Lords also noted, and approved of, the European Court of Human Rights case law, which has held that Article 10 of the Convention protects a journalist's right to communicate information on matters of general interest, provided that he is acting in good faith and on an accurate factual basis. Journalists are not subjected to an onerous duty to guarantee the truth of their stories, but they are expected to act within the bounds of responsible journalism. *Per* Lord Nicholls, where there is 'any lingering doubt' as to whether a publication is in the public interest, the courts should err on the side of the press and find that such exists. Less encouraging for the media was a lack of a definitive answer to the question of the conflict between evidencing the quality of a story by divulging its sources, and the right to withhold such information. Lord Steyn acknowledged that this was an issue of concern for the media, but held that if a defendant wishes to rely upon that right, he voluntarily assumes the risk of leaving a gap in his evidence before the court, and what the judge and jury may infer from that. Lord Nicholls, on the other hand, considered that a newspaper's unwillingness to disclose its sources should not weigh against it. It remains to be seen whether and how the courts will resolve this issue in future.

With respect to the requirement of balance in news reports, the Lords held that in normal circumstances, it would be required that the subject's side of the story is included. If this is not present, the absence will have to be justified. One potential circumstance in which the lack of a response might be acceptable would be where publication is a matter of urgency: for example the story must go to press within the hour, or is to be included in a breaking news broadcast, and there is simply no way of getting in touch with the subject. Lord Nicholls' inclusion of this consideration in his

---

[162] ibid 626.
[163] ibid.

guiding factors reflects the jurisprudence of the European Court of Human Rights, which has stated that 'news is a perishable commodity and to delay its publication, even for a short period, may well deprive it of all its value and interest'.[164]

The *Reynolds* decision has been considered by its critics to blur unacceptably the distinction between the defence of qualified privilege, and malice. In order to defeat the defence, the burden is upon the claimant to prove that the defendant acted with a malicious motive, yet a number of Lord Nicholls' factors are issues which a claimant might take into account when trying to establish malice. The majority opinion in the Lords might be argued to have shifted the burden of proof of malice from claimant to defendant: bad news for the media. This remains to be fully clarified in future. The Law Lords unanimously rejected the notion of a generic right to privilege for all political statements made in the absence of malice. The defence had suggested that the Lords introduce to English libel law a 'public figure' defence, along the lines of that available in the US under *New York Times v Sullivan*.[165] The Lords rejected this for two key reasons. First, in English law, journalists have a general right to refuse to divulge their sources: this is not the case in the US, where the claimant is entitled to a pre-trial inquiry into the sources of information and editorial decision-making. Without the defence being obliged to disclose the identities of their sources, it would be too hard for claimants to establish malice. Secondly, the Lords considered that such a generic right to qualified privilege would be counter to European Court of Human Rights jurisprudence, which is rooted in the concept of a balance of rights, as opposed to providing that one right will automatically cancel out the other.

Overall, *Reynolds* can be said to be broadly pro-press, or rather, pro-*media* (as the Lords gave no indication that they intended this decision to be limited to the newspaper industry, or that any specific type of media should be treated differently). It must be noted that the notion of 'responsible journalism' required to be further clarified, although since 1999 some indication of its parameters of responsible journalism can be seen in subsequent judgments. *Galloway v Telegraph Group Ltd*[166] concerned a series of allegations about George Galloway, made in the *Daily Telegraph*. Galloway, an MP on the old left of the Labour Party, was extremely vocal in his opposition to the 2003 military invasion and subsequent occupation of Iraq by the UK and US. The newspaper claimed to have seen papers, gathered from a bombed-out Iraqi office, which proved that Galloway had been involved in various unscrupulous activities, including siphoning off money from various charities to himself, accepting money and other benefits from Saddam Hussein, and so on. Galloway claimed that the documents were either faked or at least partially forged. Eady J, having already dismissed fair comment as a potential defence in this case, considered whether the defence should be

---

[164] *Oberschlick v Austria* (1991) 19 EHRR 389.

[165] (1964) 376 US 254. In essence, this provides that where the claimant is a 'public figure', in order to succeed in libel he must not only prove the publication of a statement which defames him, but also that this publication was made maliciously.

[166] [2004] All ER (D) 33.

allowed to claim qualified privilege. The defendant claimed that it had merely been engaged in 'neutral reporting', responsible journalism in the public interest. Eady J, however, came to a very different conclusion. Following Lord Nicholls' guidelines, the judge looked at the tone of the articles and the attitudes expressed therein, considering the articles to be far from neutral, instead embracing the allegations 'with relish and fervour'.[167] Further, some of the more serious allegations, such as that he had accepted money from Saddam Hussein, were not put to Galloway for a response. None of the documents on which these allegations were based were shown to Galloway, and any denials he did express were put in the articles in such a way as to make them seem unreliable. The newspaper's editor claimed this to be 'a blow to the principle of freedom of expression in this country'. Eady J denied leave to appeal, and so the *Telegraph* announced its intention to appeal directly to the Court of Appeal for the case to be heard. The Court of Appeal, however, endorsed Eady's findings.[168]

In February 2002, the *Wall Street Journal Europe* published an article under the headline 'Saudi Officials Monitor Certain Bank Accounts' with a smaller sub-heading 'Focus Is on Those With Potential Terrorist Ties'. The thrust of this article, published within a few months of 9/11, was that the Saudi Arabian Monetary Authority was, at the request of US law enforcement, monitoring the bank accounts of certain influential Saudis in order to make sure that they were not being used either deliberately or without the holders' knowledge to transfer money to terrorists. The article said that this information came from 'US officials and Saudis familiar with the issue'. In the second paragraph, a particular group of companies was mentioned, along with the statement that they 'could not be reached for comment'. The president of that particular trading conglomerate and one of the companies belonging to the group launched a libel action against the newspaper.[169] The newspaper did not attempt to claim justification, seeking to rely entirely on a defence of *Reynolds* privilege. At first instance, the judge directed the jury to consider, in deciding whether the defence was satisfactorily made out, the sources that the reporter relied upon, and any attempt made to elicit a response from the claimants. The journalist who had written the article stated in court that he had relied upon a prominent businessman and several other sources. The jury found that as a matter of fact he did get the information he claimed from the former, but it was not proven that he did from the other four sources claimed. The judge informed the jury that this was significant, as the reporter would not have written the article based on the one source alone. This direction was criticized by the Court of Appeal. The judge also directed the jury that, as there was no plea of justification, if they found that the article was defamatory then they should assume that it was untrue. The journalist made a number of attempts to elicit a response from the claimants. He had left an answerphone message, and later spoke to an employee who had no authority to issue an official response, and who asked the journalist to wait until the next morning when there would

[167]   ibid para 159.
[168]   [2006] All ER (D) 178.
[169]   *Jameel v Wall Street Journal Europe* [2006] 4 All ER 1279.

be someone present who would be able to comment. The journalist claimed that he had not been asked to wait until the next day, but the Court of Appeal found that he was and on this ground decreed that *Reynolds* privilege was not available.

The House of Lords found that *Reynolds* did not reject the duty and interest test. The nature and source of the information should be considered as part of a decision as to whether this test was satisfied and, as a necessary precondition, the material must be in the public interest. In the immediate case, the Lords clearly considered this to be so, though they were careful to point out that material being in the public interest is not necessarily the same thing as information the general public is interested in. The Lords, referring back to Lord Nicholls' guidelines in *Reynolds*, found that core to this is the question of what constitutes responsible journalism: there can be no duty to publish, and the story will not be in the public interest, if there have been no reasonable steps taken to verify the story. In this case, the Court of Appeal had discounted qualified privilege on very narrow grounds; indeed, Lord Bingham noted that this subverted what he considered to be the liberal intentions of *Reynolds*. On the facts, the story was on a matter of great public interest; it had been written by an experienced, specialist reporter; was approved by senior *Wall Street Journal* staff; there had been at least an attempt to verify it and to solicit a response from the claimants; and the report itself was unsensational, and factual in nature. This was no hysterical tabloid story. Regarding the absence of a response from the claimants, Lord Bingham considered that any comment would be unlikely to be revealing as they would be unlikely to be aware that they were being watched, given the nature of the covert surveillance operation. Bingham also praised the article as 'the sort of neutral, investigative journalism *Reynolds* privilege exists to protect'.[170] The Lords allowed the appeal unanimously.

10.7.5 Offer of amends

The defence of offer of amends is an innovation of the Defamation Act 1996. Under section 2(4), a defendant to defamation proceedings may offer to make 'a suitable correction of the statement . . . and a sufficient apology' and 'pay . . . such compensation (if any) and such costs, as may be agreed or determined to be payable'. Where such an offer is made and rejected by the claimant, provided the offer is not withdrawn, the fact that it has been made is a valid defence. Where the offer is qualified in that it relates only to a particular meaning, it will only provide a valid defence in respect of the meaning to which the offer relates.[171] The defence is also subject to the proviso that the offeror neither knew nor had any reason to believe that the statement in question referred to the defendant or was likely to be interpreted as doing so, and 'was both false and defamatory of that party'. The burden of proof falls to the claimant to rebut the presumption that the defendant lacked such knowledge.[172] Crucially, where a defendant

---

[170] ibid 1292.
[171] Defamation Act 1996, s 4(2).
[172] ibid s 4(3).

wishes to use this defence, it must be the sole defence relied upon, although where the offer is qualified, this exclusivity requirement will apply only in relation to the meaning to which the offer related.[173] Whether or not the offer is relied on as a defence, it can be taken into account in mitigation of any damages awarded.[174]

10.7.6 Innocent dissemination

This final defence is alone provided not for authors, editors, publishers, or anyone else directly responsible for the publication of a defamation, but exclusively for subordinate distributors who merely pass on material published by others. Examples include a newsagent selling a newspaper which contains a defamatory article, or a library which stocks a book that contains a defamation. The defence is based on awareness: a distributor who is, or should be, aware of the defamatory nature of the publication yet fails to withdraw it will be equally liable for the publication as if he had been the actual author. This so-called defence of innocent dissemination, long established at common law,[175] was placed on a statutory footing by section 1 of the Defamation Act 1996. Under section 1(1), a person who is not the 'author, editor or publisher' of the defamatory statement will be entitled to a defence, provided that he had neither actual nor constructive knowledge of the defamatory nature of the statement in question, and that he had taken 'reasonable care' in relation to its publication. Section 1 was drafted with the then still fairly new world wide web very much in mind, and this is reflected in the definitions given for 'editor'[176] and 'publisher',[177] both clearly defined so as to exclude an internet intermediary who merely provides the facility by which a defamatory article is made available. As the online world increases in importance for the traditional media, this defence becomes increasingly significant not only for regular ISPs, but also any media entity involved in making available third party content which it does not actively monitor or edit. This might include, for instance, bulletin board services, provided by many newspapers and intended for discussion of news items carried on the website, or consumer reviews provided by third parties, for example Amazon's user reviews.

Section 1 was first applied to the online context in *Godfrey v Demon Internet*.[178] Here the claimant had been defamed in a posting made to a usenet newsgroup dedicated to the discussion of Thai culture. He had informed the defendant ISP, which hosted but did not edit the newsgroup, of the existence of the defamatory posting, but Demon had failed to remove it until it was automatically deleted by the system some ten days later. In a preliminary hearing to determine whether the section 1 defence

---

[173] ibid s 4(4).

[174] ibid s 4(5).

[175] See *Emmers v Pottle* (1885) 16 QBD 354.

[176] '... a person having editorial or equivalent responsibility for the content of the statement or the decision to publish it'. Defamation Act 1996, s 1(2).

[177] '... a commercial publisher, that is, a person whose business is issuing material to the public, or a section of the public, who issues material containing the statement in the course of that business'. Defamation Act 1996, s 1(2).

[178] [1999] EMLR 542.

would be available, the Court found that the defendant would be liable for the defamation from the point in time at which they were in receipt of actual notification of the defamation and failed to act expeditiously to remove it. Significantly, the Court noted that the defendant would not be held liable for publishing the defamation prior to the receipt of actual knowledge, as it would be unreasonable to expect the ISP to have been aware that a defamation would be contained in an otherwise innocent group discussing Thai culture and society. This aspect of the decision, indicating the nature of the website to which a defamation is posted by a third party, is of great significance to the media. It is easy to imagine other circumstances, such as a tabloid newspaper-run bulletin board designed to discuss celebrity gossip, in respect of which a court might consider that an awareness of the very nature of the website alone is sufficient to count towards constructive knowledge.[179]

A distributor may further be required to hand over any information in its possession which may help to identify the source of a defamation. In *Totalise v Motley Fool*[180] the defendant ISP had complied fully with the requirements of section 1, and evaded liability for publishing a series of defamatory postings made by one of its subscribers who went by the screen-name of Z-Dust. The claimants in this case sought to oblige the ISP to hand over such information as it had which might lead to the identification of this subscriber, so that a case might be pursued against the source of the defamation. The ISP unsuccessfully attempted to raise defences based on data protection and contempt of court, and the Court ordered the handover of the information sought. Significantly, it was found that this was the only way in which the source of the defamation might be identified, and so the claimants would be denied justice in respect of what the Court considered to be a sustained campaign of defamation.

This line was softened somewhat in *Sheffield Wednesday FC v Hargreaves*,[181] resulting in a somewhat more favourable position for the defence. This case involved a fan-run bulletin board, on which there had been a large number of postings which were defamatory of the board of directors and others responsible for running the football club in a way which displeased its followers. The claimants sought a court order obliging those responsible for running the club to hand over any details in their possession which could help discover the real world identities of those screen-names which had posted the defamatory comments. In a move very favourable to defendants, the Court agreed to issue an order for the handover of information relating to some, but, crucially, not all, of those responsible for the defamatory postings. The Court specifically declined to order the handover of details relating to a number of postings which, while technically defamatory, were only minor defamations. In these specific instances, it was held that

---

[179] See, for instance, Holy Moly <http://www.holymoly.co.uk>, which publishes lurid gossip stories on its website, not naming the subject but inviting the reader to guess about whom they might be, posting suggestions to a bulletin board on the same page. Should anything posted to this bulletin board give rise to a libel suit, it would seem unlikely that, even in the absence of any editorial control or actual knowledge of the defamatory posting, those responsible for the website would be considered not to have sufficient constructive knowledge to lose the protection of section 1.

[180] [2001] All ER (D) 213 (February).

[181] [2007] EWHC 2375.

the protection of these individuals' privacy should be paramount over the claimants' interest in bringing a libel suit. If this line of reasoning is followed by the courts in future, it will be very attractive from the point of view of the defendant online discussion forum provider, an environment in which so-called 'flame-wars' are rife, and every abusive posting may be a libel case in waiting. Of course, it is clear that such an approach would not be favoured in a situation where an individual has mounted a 'sustained campaign' of defamation, as was the case in *Totalise*.[182]

Critics of section 1 have suggested that it places distributors in something of a Catch 22: too little attention paid to the material which they publish and they will fall foul of the 'reasonable care' requirement; too much, and they will be classified as an editor, losing the availability of the defence while simultaneously finding themselves in a position of much greater liability. The *Godfrey* case also sparked fears for the future of freedom of expression: surely this would lead to services providers, when faced with claims of defamation, meekly acquiescing to a request for removal of material, rather than first making an effort to determine whether the complaint is vexatious, or in bad faith. Thus much legitimate, free expression could be crushed. In practice, this appears much less of a problem than some anticipated.

Since 2002, the impact of the Electronic Commerce (EC Directive) Regulations must also be considered in this context. These regulations, which enact in UK dometic law the provisions of the Electronic Commerce Directive, in Articles 17 to 19 provide a similar awareness-based defence to that in section 1, the difference being that here it applies to all forms of third-party-provided content, and its availability is limited to online service providers. To date, there is no case law discussing the application of the Regulations in the defamation context, nor their relationship with section 1. They were referred to obiter in *Bunt v Tilley*,[183] although Eady J's judgment in that case merely mentions the provisions, with no new analysis. The common question as to whether, in relation to online service providers, the Regulations would supersede section 1 was not addressed. A further open question which remains is in relation to the timeframe in which an intermediary, once aware of a defamatory posting, can be expected to have the material removed or face liability. Very large international organizations may have sufficient staffing capabilities to be able to remove material within a narrow window, but smaller operations, which perhaps only have limited office opening hours and may close at weekends, might reasonably be expected to require a little longer. Some idea may be given by comparison with material of another kind entirely under the Terrorism Act 2006. Section 3 of that statute gives a set time limit of 'two working days' for compliance with an order to remove third-party material in breach of either section 1 (encouragement of terrorism) or section 2 (dissemination of terrorist publications). 'Working days' is defined in section 3 as 'any day other than' a Saturday or Sunday, Christmas Day, Good Friday, or 'a day which is a bank holiday under the Banking and Financial Dealings Act 1971'.

---

[182] *Totalise plc v Motley Fool* [2001] All ER (D) 213, at 214 per Lord A'dous.
[183] [2006] EWHC 407.

By way of comparison, internet intermediaries in the US enjoy, by virtue of section 230 of the Communications Decency Act 1996, a complete freedom from liability for third-party-provided material which is defamatory, even where the service provider had actual and direct knowledge of the libel.[184] Such a broad immunity is unlikely ever to be introduced into English law, not least as in the US context it has patently failed in its original intent.[185]

10.8 REMEDIES

There are two key remedies potentially available to libel defendants: damages and injunctions. Typically, these will go hand in hand, as most claimants will be seeking not only compensation for damage to reputation, but also an assurance that the libel will not be repeated.

10.8.1 Damages

Libel is the sole remaining area of civil law in England which at first instance involves a jury trial. This is a significant factor when it comes to damages, as juries can be notoriously overgenerous, especially where a celebrity claimant is involved. Following much controversy during the 1980s, Parliament responded by passing the Courts and Legal Services Act 1990, section 8 of which empowers the Court of Appeal to change the figure awarded. This may be done only where the award made by the jury is so high that it is 'divorced from reality', and no reasonable jury could have considered it to be appropriate. The Court of Appeal exercised its new power in numerous cases throughout the 1990s. In *Rantzen v Mirror Group Newspapers*,[186] the Court of Appeal found a jury award of £250,000 to be excessively disproportionate to the damage to the claimant's

---

[184] *Zeran v America Online Inc* 129 F 3d (4th Circuit 1997), 524 US 937 (1998). See further, G Sutter, 'Online Intermediaries' in C Reed and J Angel (eds), *Computer Law* (Oxford University Press, 6th edn, 2007) 260–5. Note, however, the impact of the Supreme Court of the State of California's decision to overturn the decision of the Appeal Court in *Barett v Rosenthal* 51 Cal Rptr 3d 55 (Cal Sup Ct, 20 November 2006), ruling that *Zeran* is the correct interpretation of s 230, and that the immunity should continue to be so applied.

[185] This immunity was originally passed by Congress in the context of new offences relating to making indecent material, ie pornography, available to minors online, and the provision of service to another knowing that it will be used for the same. Section 230 was intended to immunize service providers from liability for defamation should they adopt an editorial role over content on their servers, thus encouraging them to play good citizen and help to drive pornography off the internet. When the US Supreme Court in *Reno v American Civil Liberties Union* 521 US 844 (1997) found the CDA unconstitutional on First Amendment grounds, s 230 remained in law divorced of its original context. Far from encouraging service providers to play editor, its application in *Zeran v America Online Inc* 129 F 3d 327 (4th Circuit 1997), 524 US 937 (1998) and subsequent cases seems merely to have encouraged a very *laissez-faire* approach. See especially, eg *Blumenthal v Drudge* 992 F Supp 44 (DDC 1998), in which the ISP, despite exercising editorial control over a gossip columnist, declined to do anything about a defamation published by him on their servers, secure in the knowledge that they were shielded by the s 230 immunity.

[186] [1993] 3 WLR 953.

reputation, reducing it to £110,000. Damages in *John v MGN*,[187] a case surrounding allegations of bulimia, were reduced from £350,000 to £75,000, the Appeal Court commenting that it was offensive to public opinion that a far higher award of damages be made over a slighted reputation than would be in a case of serious personal injury. The Court went on to propose several guidelines that should be given to the jury, including details of awards previously approved by the Court of Appeal, information about compensation available for personal injury for comparison purposes, and also some indication by the presiding judge of an appropriate bracket for an award. Despite these guidelines, difficulties remain. For example, in *Kiam v MGN*,[188] despite a judicial indication that an award of between £40,000 and £80,000 would be appropriate, the jury settled on £105,000. The Court of Appeal was powerless to intervene, as the jury's award, although beyond that indicated by the judge as appropriate, was not outside what a reasonable jury would have awarded. Worth noting is the dissenting opinion of Sedley LJ, in particular paragraph 70:

> To be sure, this was a spiteful, insolent and damaging story, based on slapdash research, published without any justification and without even asking the claimant about it. It was repeated more than once and was defended in one way or another until the end of the trial. All of this I accept and so, clearly, did the jury. It was their verdict in his favour which vindicated Mr. Kiam's good name. There was no ongoing damage that anybody could point to, except no doubt that some of the mud would have stuck in some people's minds. But substantially it was all over within 14 months of the original publication. To put this, by an award of £105,000, on a compensatory par with the wreckage of a human life by brain damage or the loss of both legs below the knee is, in my opinion, indecent. Even a sum of £60,000 represents considerably more than, for example, a young woman would get for severely disfiguring facial scarring.

Alongside the guidelines offered by the Court of Appeal in the *John* case, there is a range of other factors which may influence damages. For instance, there is the size of the audience to whom publication has been made: a local newspaper selling 200 copies of a defamation will be required to pay out much less than a national tabloid selling perhaps hundreds of thousands more. It is entirely logical that libel damages—which are, after all, intended to compensate for damage to reputation—will be affected by the number of persons in whose eyes the claimant's reputation has been damaged. An unsuccessful plea of justification can also lead to a higher award, while the identification of a malicious motive on the part of the defendant can lead to higher, punitive damages. On the flipside, where a claimant's name has been publicly cleared prior to the action being brought, or where he has succeeded in actions against other defendants regarding the same or similar allegations, damages are liable to be lower. In more recent years, it would appear that there is a trend away from the excessive awards of the past. In *Nail v News Group Newspapers*,[189] Eady J made reference to 'the current

---

[187] *The Times*, 14 December 1995.
[188] [2002] All ER (D) 235 (January).
[189] [2005] 1 All ER 1040.

conventional overall ceiling for damages of £200,000'.[190] The highest award of damages to date in respect of an online defamation was made in *Gentoo Group & Walls v Henratty*,[191] and amounted to £100,000. Of course, it should not be assumed that damages are always apt to be on the high side: a jury, or indeed the Court of Appeal, can as well indicate moral disapproval of a nevertheless successful claimant by awarding a derisory figure, frequently, as was the case in *Reynolds*, £1.

10.8.2 Injunctions

Injunctions, whether to prevent re-publication or, more rarely, publication of a libel at all, may be granted at the court's discretion. It is fairly common, following the conclusion of a libel trial in which the claimant has succeeded, for not only damages to be awarded, but also an injunction against any repeated publication of the allegations at issue in the trial. Under section 12 (4) of the Human Rights Act 1998, where a court is considering the grant of an injunction:

The court must have particular regard to the importance of the Convention right to freedom of expression and, where the proceedings relate to material which the respondent claims, or which appears to the court, to be journalistic, literary or artistic material (or to conduct connected with such material), to—

   (a) the extent to which—

      (i)   the material has, or is about to, become available to the public; or

      (ii) it is, or would be, in the public interest for the material to be published;

   (b) any relevant privacy code.

Interim injunctions for defamation are extremely rare. The Court of Appeal noted in *William Coulson & Sons v James Coulson & Co*[192] that the power to grant an interim injunction should be exercised only sparingly, and only in 'the clearest cases, where any jury would say that the matter complained of was libellous and where if the jury did not so find the court would set aside the verdict as unreasonable'.

The trend in recent years has been for the courts to err on the side of freedom of expression, with the courts only granting an injunction in very rare cases where the article is clearly defamatory and there is no possible arguable defence. Even in such apparently open and shut cases, the court retains its discretion to decide whether to grant the injunction. A court may also take into consideration evidence produced by the claimant which indicates that the defendant intends to make a further publication of the article, or of another article carrying the same or similar allegations. Even if a claimant succeeds in convincing the court to grant a preliminary injunction, this can be a risky strategy, as should the defence prevail at trial, the claimant may be obliged to

---

[190] ibid 1051.
[191] [2008] EWHC 2328 (QB).
[192] [1887] 3 TLR 846.

cover all costs incurred by the defendant in complying with the order. Due to the difficulty of acquiring an interim injunction in libel to prevent publication ahead of a trial, it is common for claimants to apply instead under breach of confidence, or breach of contract, where an interim injunction may be granted even where the defendant has a defence which may succeed at trial.

10.8.3 Corrections, apologies, and statements in open court

Damages offer some form of compensation for injury to reputation and hurt feelings which flow therefrom, but in terms of clearing an individual's good name, a published correction and apology will go a long way. Indeed, many cases are settled on this basis long before they reach a courtroom. An alternative is for the claimant in an impending or ongoing case to require as part of a settlement that the defendant make a statement to that same effect in open court. For instance, in March 2003, the *Daily Mail* published an article which claimed that actor Jude Law had had an on-set affair with his co-star Nicole Kidman at a time when he was still married. In part satisfaction of an agreed settlement, the *Daily Mail* made a statement in open court, apologizing for any distress and embarrassment caused by its untrue allegations.[193] This approach has two key advantages which makes it attractive for claimants. First, it means that it will be formally noted in court records that the allegations were untrue, as admitted by the defence. Secondly, in particular where a celebrity claimant who will attract news media coverage is involved, it provides an opportunity for other media outlets to publicize the statement, allowing for a much wider dissemination of the correction and apology than would be the case were it simply to be published by the defendant alone.

10.9 CONCLUSION

English defamation law is an ever-evolving beast; the number of grey areas and open questions raised in this chapter suggest that this is unlikely to change any time soon. It remains to be seen, for instance, whether Morland J's deviation from the *Hulton* strict liability rule in *Kerry O'Shea v Mirror Group Newspapers Ltd and Free4Internet.net Ltd* will be extended by the courts to apply in other factual circumstances. It is probable that the internet will continue to present difficult challenges for libel law into the foreseeable future. It seems highly unlikely that in the longer term the UK will reverse its legal tradition so totally as to opt for a US-style single publication rule; however, it may well be that some form of legal amendment, such as the Law Commission's proposed 'archive defence', will be considered by Parliament. Some form of amendment to the rule in its application to online archives seems marginally more likely as of

---

[193] *Kidman v Associated Newspapers* (2003, unreported).

March 2009, when the Minister for Justice, Jack Straw, announced his intention to review this area in the wake of the European Court of Human Rights ruling against *The Times*.[194] The timely decision by the Court of Appeal in *Jameel v Dow Jones* should help to stem the tide of libel tourists attracted to England while on a forum-shopping expedition. Regarding defences, it is likely that the next several years will see some further refinement of *Reynolds* qualified privilege, with emphasis on both the Article 10 right, and the corresponding duties of 'responsible journalism'.

The details of the defence of innocent dissemination as applied to those who make third-party content available in the online environment require to be developed further, clarifying such nebulous concepts as 'actual notice', and 'acting expeditiously'. As concerns remedies, we can confidently predict that there will be no return to the heady days of the 1980s when juries were prone to awarding what one judge referred to as 'Mickey Mouse money'.[195] However, following the *Gentoo* case, it is possible that we will see damages awarded in respect of online libels rising, particularly as the main-stream media place increasing emphasis on the internet as an alternative to traditional publishing and broadcast channels. Whatever new developments are to come, one need only glance across the shelves of any local newsagents, in the direction of the dozen or so weekly celebrity gossip magazines, stimulated in large part by the explosion of so-called reality television in the early twenty-first century, at the many more 'real-life' magazines with their lurid headlines such as 'swinging turned my hubby into a woman', or even in the direction of the ever-popular tabloid press, to know that libel law has a long future ahead of it.

[194] 'Jack Straw to probe internet libel law' *The Times*, 11 March 2009, available at <http://business.timesonline.co.uk/tol/business/law/article5889539.ece>.

[195] Ignoring the words of the judge, the jury proceeded to award £1.5m in damages, an amount later found by the European Court to be so excessive as regarded the potential damage posed to the claimant's reputation by the libel in question as to constitute a breach of Article 10 of the European Convention on Human Rights. See *Tolstoy Miloslavsky v UK* (1996) EMLR 152.

11

CRIMINAL CONTENT AND CONTROL

Ian Walden

11.1 INTRODUCTION

Media law is primarily concerned with controlling content. As illustrated throughout this book, the justifications for such control are varied, from the promotion of pluralism to the protection of privacy. The legal mechanisms by which content is controlled in media law are also varied, from licensing regimes for broadcasters to civil suits against those making defamatory statements. This chapter is concerned with another category of controlled content, criminally illegal content. Such content will often overlap with regulated content and that which results in civil liability, but is rendered distinct and worthy of separate treatment by its designation as criminal and the consequences that flow from that.

The availability of criminalized content has tended to differ between written and visual media, specifically film and television, due to the fact that the regulatory regimes governing the latter[1] generally provide an effective filter and buffer preventing the public from being exposed to such content. This distinction is being eroded, however, and the comparative importance of criminal content within media law has consequently risen as the internet has developed, offering a proliferation of media outlets or channels through which criminally illegal content may be communicated. In particular, three aspects of internet usage have driven this change: the ease with which

---

[1] ie film classification (see Ch 9 above) and broadcast licensing (see Ch 8 above).

content can be reproduced and distributed; the greater degree of interactivity between the provider and consumer of media content; and the increasingly transnational nature of modern media. The first and second factors mean an enhanced opportunity for criminal content to be made available through media or media-like outlets. The third factor results in more frequent jurisdictional conflicts over content considered permissible in one country, while unacceptable in another.

When considering criminally illegal content, a distinction needs to be made between the criminal nature of the content itself and the conduct that is carried out in relation to that content. Classifying certain subject matter as criminally illegal can be a highly contentious matter, raising complex definitional issues, questions of causation, and human rights concerns, especially rights to freedom of expression. Illegal content is also often tied, both at a policy level and in the minds of the general public, with the broader topic of harmful content; that which certain persons, such as parents, may consider undesirable, but which is not itself illegal.[2] This blurring of subject matter further exacerbates debate and polarizes views about the right approach to addressing criminally illegal content in the media. In terms of conduct, we are primarily concerned with the media law aspects of publishing or distributing illegal content, rather than its possession; although modern media techniques blur the line between acts of supply and possession. Criminalizing possession is also being promoted as a necessary tool in the fight against illegal content originating outside the jurisdiction.

This chapter focuses on two broad categories of content or speech crimes of relevance to the media sector: hate speech and obscene or indecent material. Other types of speech examined in this book may be subject to criminal law sanctions, including contempt, defamation, and intellectual property infringement, but are not examined further in this chapter.[3] We are also concerned with the challenges and issues surrounding the control of criminally illegal content in our modern media environment, specifically foreign content, which has required governments to shift their attention to other points of control within the media supply chain, from that of creator, editor, or publisher.

11.2 ILLEGAL CONTENT AND HUMAN RIGHTS LAW

Under the European Convention on Human Rights (ECHR), restrictions on freedom of expression must fall within one of the Article 10(2) recognized interests 'in the interests of national security, territorial integrity or public safety, for the prevention of disorder or crime, for the protection of health or morals, for the protection of the reputation or rights of others, for preventing the disclosure of information received in confidence, or for maintaining the authority and impartiality of the judiciary'.

---

[2] eg Commission Communication 'on illegal and harmful content on the Internet' COM (1996) 487, Brussels, 16 October 1996.
[3] See further Chs 4, 6, and 10 above, respectively.

Of the types of media content examined in this book that are subject to criminal law sanction, the applicable interests clearly differ. Intellectual property laws and defamation protect the rights of others, although by criminalizing certain instances the state is recognizing a broader harm to the nation than the private interests of a rights-holder or individual. Under Convention jurisprudence, hate speech is sometimes treated as expression that is not protected under Article 10(1) at all, because it goes against the Convention's underlying values.[4] Where it has been engaged, however, it is seen as being both a threat to public safety, and as endangering the rights of others.[5] For obscene and indecent material, the protection of morality is the primary justification, although protecting the rights of others would also be relevant to certain categories of material, particularly where children are the subject matter. Finally, criminal contempt is concerned with maintaining the authority of the judicial system.

Identifying the applicable interest justifying a restriction is, however, only one element of the European Court of Human Rights (ECtHR) jurisprudence on freedom of expression. A second element is the differential treatment given by the Court to different types of expression, with political speech and public interest media claims being given strong protection, in contrast to artistic speech, such as pornographic material, and commercial speech, which is afforded weaker protection.[6] This reflects the fact that the Court tends to be less willing to interfere with state measures relating to issues of morality, granting them a more liberal 'margin of appreciation' than that offered for political speech.

Any restriction in furtherance of an applicable interest must of course be 'necessary', which means both that there is a 'pressing social need'[7] and that the response of the state is proportionate to that need.[8] The former places an evidential burden upon the state to indicate what the need to be protected is and, more importantly, the relationship between the imposition of the restriction and addressing that need; although in practice the ECtHR has imposed 'widely varying standards' upon states.[9]

The difficulty of evidencing the causal relationship between certain content and individual and societal harms has always been a challenge for policy-makers and legislators, and one which is at the forefront of current debates in the UK about criminalizing content, particularly sexually explicit material.[10] Justifications for criminalizing such content generally include the vulnerability of certain audiences, primarily

---

[4] *Lehideux and France v France* (2000) 30 EHRR 665, para 53. See also *Jersild* (1995) 19 EHRR 1, para 35.

[5] As such, hate speech will also often engage Art 17, prohibiting an abuse of rights.

[6] See H Fenwick and G Phillipson, *Media Freedom under the Human Rights Act* (Oxford University Press, 2006) 56–60.

[7] *Handyside v UK* (1979–80) 1 EHRR 737, in particular para 49.

[8] *Sporrong and Lonroth v Sweden* (1982) 5 EHRR 35, para 69; *Soering v UK* (1989) 11 EHRR 439, para 89.

[9] Fenwick and Phillipson (n 6 above) 87.

[10] eg Human Rights Joint Committee, Eighth Report 'Legislative Scrutiny: Coroners and Justice Bill' HL 57/HC 362, 17 March 2009, para 1.178: 'we are disappointed that the Government has failed to provide sufficiently weighty reasons for the need of the new offence that they propose in this Bill.'

children; the protection of those that participate in the creation of the content, especially children and women;[11] and the link that consumption of such material has to the commission of further sexual offences. This last claim is generally and more appropriately couched in terms of concerns about encouraging a culture that legitimates and reinforces inappropriate views, such as the acceptability of rape, rather than directly resulting in criminal conduct; reflecting in part the weak evidential basis for the latter.[12] Direct crime prevention arguments are also being increasingly countered by claims that pornographic material may tend to reduce rather increase the likelihood of further offences being committed; the availability of such material acting as a substitute[13] or release[14] for potential offenders.

In terms of proportionality, a continuum of state responses to criminally illegal content can be seen to exist, from the imposition of controls over the availability of material; through penalties for publishing illegal material, to the prior restraint of speech through the exercise of seizure and forfeiture powers. Prior restraint is widely seen as the most onerous form of state interference with freedom of expression, demanding 'the most careful scrutiny' by the courts.[15]

From a human rights perspective, one critical difference between criminally illegal content and other unlawful content lies in the nature of the state's response. In civil proceedings, the remedies granted are generally preventive (eg injunctions) or compensatory (eg damages). By contrast, the sanctions imposed for an offence are punitive in nature (eg fines and imprisonment). As such, the impact in terms of acting as a *de facto* prior restraint over speech is likely to be greater in a criminal context compared with civil proceedings, which is relevant when evaluating proportionality. Both civil and criminal proceedings permit of actual prior restraint to the extent that the courts grant injunctive relief to the claimant, forfeiture powers to law enforcement, or the right to proscribe broadcasters.[16]

Another element of the inquiry into criminalizing media content concerns the extent to which statutory provisions are drafted in sufficiently clear terms, on the one hand, to clearly identify the illegal expression subject to the prohibition but, on the other, not so broadly as to create legal uncertainty in the minds of potential speakers that restrains their legitimate expression through self-censorship; such collateral interference being

---

[11] eg Home Office, 'Consultation: On the Possession of Extreme Pornographic Material' (2005) 2 and para 34.

[12] See eg Ministry of Justice, 'The evidence of harm to adults relating to exposure to extreme pornographic material: a rapid evidence assessment (REA)', No 11/07 (September 2007).

[13] T Kendall, 'Pornography, Rape and the Internet' (September 2006), available at <http://www.idei.fr/doc/conf/sic/papers_2007/kendall.pdf>.

[14] Jenny Willott MP: 'If the evidence showed that having images that were not photographic acted as a release, and therefore reduced the risk of harm to children, legislating could increase the risk of harm'. Public Bill Committee Debate, *Hansard*, 3 March 2009, col 482.

[15] *The Observer and the Guardian v UK* (1992) 14 EHRR 153, para 60.

[16] See further section 11.5.1 below.

generally referred to as the 'chilling effect'.[17] The evolving nature of modern media, as described in Chapter 1 above, requires us to re-examine whether substantive and procedural rules drafted for traditional media remain 'fit for purpose' in an online media context.

11.3 HATE SPEECH

For those that are intent on spreading hatred against others, the media provides an obvious platform for disseminating such messages. Publishing and distributing material that is considered capable of either generating 'hatred against a group of persons' by reference to their colour, race, nationality, ethic origin, or religious beliefs, or advocating acts of violence. Such conduct is viewed as an offence against public order, under English criminal law.[18] Historically, governments have been cautious about criminalizing such material. However, as part of the 'war on terrorism', coupled with growing public disquiet about the availability of dangerous content over the internet, the government has recently introduced new hate speech offences.

At a European level, there have been a range of initiatives addressing hate speech, from both the European Union and the Council of Europe, some of which are specifically targeted at the media industry. At a general level, the European Council has adopted a measure criminalizing certain forms of racist and xenophobic conduct.[19] This has a relatively broad remit, including 'publicly condoning, denying or grossly trivialising' crimes against humanity and war crimes;[20] although Member States may criminalize only that conduct which is 'likely to disturb public order or which is threatening, abusive or insulting'.[21] It is also expressly stated that the measure should not contradict fundamental rights and principles, whether based in substantive or procedural law, concerning 'the press or other media where these rules relate to the determination or limitation of liability'.[22] The UK government has stated that compliance with this measure does not require a change to domestic legislation.[23]

The Television without Frontiers Directive (TWF Directive) obliges Member States to ensure that broadcasts do 'not contain any incitement to hatred on grounds of

---

[17] See eg F Schauer, 'Fear, Risk and The First Amendment: Unravelling the "Chilling Effect"' (1978), 58 Boston University Law Review 685 and E Barendt, *Libel and the Media—The Chilling Effect* (Clarendon Press, 1997).

[18] See generally M White, 'Far right extremists on the Internet' in D Thomas and B Loader (eds), *Cybercrime: Law Enforcement, Security and Surveillance in the Information Age* (Routledge, 2000). 234–50.

[19] Council Framework Decision 2008/913/JHA of 28 November 2008 'on combating certain forms and expressions of racism and xenophobia by means of criminal law' [2008] OJ L328/55.

[20] ibid Art 1(1)(c).

[21] ibid Art 1(2).

[22] ibid Art 7(2).

[23] Baroness Scotland of Asthal, Home Office Minister, written answer, *Hansard*, 22 May 2007, col WA89.

race, sex, religion or nationality'.[24] The provision was repealed as a stand-alone provision by the AVMS Directive;[25] although it appears instead as a legitimate justification for a Member State to derogate from its obligation not to restrict television broadcasts or on-demand audiovisual services from other Member States.[26] The original reform proposal would have included incitement of hatred based on 'sex, racial or ethnic origin, religion or belief, disability, age or sexual orientation',[27] which reflected the wording used in the Treaty establishing the European Community in respect of discrimination.[28] There was concern, however, that the proposal might have an unduly adverse effect on freedom of expression, which was considered both unjustifiable and undesirable; the final version therefore returned to the more limited list used under the TWF Directive. For UK-based broadcasters, the Broadcasting Code obliges compliance with 'generally accepted standards' in respect of such material, which would clearly encompass content not considered criminally illegal.[29] The AVMS Directive will also enable control to be exercised against non-EU television channels that are uplinked to satellites from the UK.[30]

Within the Council of Europe, a Committee of Ministers adopted a recommendation on hate speech in 1997.[31] In January 2003, a Treaty-based instrument was adopted, as an Additional Protocol to the Convention on Cybercrime (2001)[32] 'concerning the criminalisation of acts of a racist and xenophobic nature committed through computer systems'.[33] Such issues were considered during the drafting of the main Convention, but consensus could not be reached, therefore the approach of drafting a separate instrument was agreed.[34] As at February 2009, 29 Member States had signed the Protocol, as well as 2 non-Member States, Canada, and Montenegro; this entered into force in March 2006 with the fifth ratification.[35] However, the UK is not, and does not intend to become, a signatory, with the government believing that existing law 'strikes the right balance' between protecting individuals from violence and hatred and freedom of expression', which the Additional Protocol 'does not allow us to maintain'.[36]

---

[24] Directive (EEC) 89/552, Art 22 originally, although it became a separate article, Art 22a, following an amendment in 1997 (Directive (EC) 97/36).

[25] Directive (EC) 2007/65, para 24.

[26] ibid Art 2(a)(4)(a)(i) for on-demand services and Art 2(a)(2)(a) and (a)(3)(b) for television broadcasts.

[27] COM (2005) 646 final, 13 December 2005, Art 3e.

[28] TEC, Art 13.

[29] Ofcom Broadcasting Code, para 2.3.

[30] See further section 11.5.1 below and Ch 8 above.

[31] Recommendation Rec (97) 20 on 'Hate Speech'.

[32] European Treaty Series No 185.

[33] European Treaty Series No 189 ('Additional Protocol').

[34] Explanatory Report, available at <http://conventions.coe.int/Treaty/en/Reports/Html/189.htm> para 4.

[35] European Treaty Series No 189, Art 10(1).

[36] Vernon Coaker, Home Office Minister, in a written answer, 29 January 2008, *Hansard*, col 209W.

The Additional Protocol requires the establishment of a range of substantive offences concerning 'racist or xenophobic material', including the dissemination of such material, threats and insults, and denial of genocide and crimes against humanity. The scope of content covered by the Protocol includes material that promotes or incites 'discrimination', as well as hatred and violence, which is a more expansive concept of hate speech than that recognized under English law. However, due to the complexities of legislating against such material, Member States have considerable autonomy not to adopt such measures, where, for example, issues of freedom of expression conflict by preventing effective remedies.[37] As such, the government's blanket refusal to be associated with the measure seems somewhat disingenuous and difficult to reconcile with its approval of the largely similar EU Framework Decision noted above.

Under English law, hate speech is categorized as an offence affecting public order, under the Public Order Act 1986. As such, the law is concerned with behaviour as much as words. Part 3 of the Act criminalizes speech intended to stir up racial hatred or where it 'is likely to be stirred up' (section 18(1)); although for the latter offence to be made out it must be shown that the speaker did intend and was aware that his words were at least 'threatening, abusive or insulting' (section 18(5)). However, the link with public order has been substantially diluted over the years, with the original offence being directly concerned with a 'breach of the peace'.[38] This lowering of the threshold for hate speech can be criticized as a disproportionate restriction of freedom of expression; although it should also be noted that prosecutions under Part 3 will often also involve charges relating to the solicitation of murder,[39] which can be viewed as an indirect reassertion of the threshold concerning the serious nature of the expression.[40]

'Racial hatred' is defined by reference 'to colour, race, nationality (including citizenship) or ethnic or national origins'.[41] Although concerned with public order, the use of 'threatening, abusive or insulting words'[42] or displays of 'written material' may be committed in a public or private place.[43] In a media context, therefore, an offence could be made out whether the environment, such as a bulletin board or chatroom, was subject to access controls or not.[44] It is an offence to publish or distribute racial hatred material,[45] perform a play,[46] distribute a recording,[47] or broadcast within a

---

[37] ie Art, 3(3), 5(2)(b), and 6(2)(b).

[38] POA 1936, s 5. The direct precursor of the current offence was included in the Race Relations Act 1965.

[39] Offences Against the Person Act 1861, s 4.

[40] See *R v El-Faisal* [2004] EWCA Crim 456 and *R v Saleem (Abdul)* [2007] EWCA Crim 2692.

[41] POA 1986, s 17.

[42] Not defined in POA 1986, but is a question of fact to be determined (see *Brutus v Cozens* [1973] AC 854).

[43] POA 1986, s 18(2).

[44] The only defence based on location is when the act is between persons in a 'dwelling' (s 18(4)), which would not be applicable to such examples.

[45] ibid s 19.

[46] ibid s 20.

[47] ibid s 21.

programme service.[48] The latter offence extends liability to the broadcaster and the programme producer or director, as well as the speaker themselves.[49] Imposing criminal liability upon persons within the media supply chain presents an obvious threat of collateral interference with freedom of expression. In *Jersild*,[50] the ECtHR was required to consider this issue in respect of the prosecution of a Danish journalist and the head of the news section of a radio station that had broadcast a programme containing racist remarks made by some youths. The Court held that the prosecution was an unnecessary interference with the right of the press to discuss matters of public interest.

To limit the scope for the provisions to be abused, unduly restricting free speech, a prosecution can only be brought with the consent of the Attorney-General.[51] As with the other content-related offences examined in this chapter, the maximum tariff has recently been raised substantially, from two to seven years' imprisonment.[52] However, the paucity of prosecutions for racial hatred, a total of sixty-five over a twenty-year period,[53] would not seem to justify such a shift. Such low levels of prosecutions are despite claims from both government and the police, over recent years, that they are targeting action against the publishing of racist material on the internet.[54] As with other illegal content, perpetrators will often utilize online resources located outside the jurisdiction, leaving law enforcement with no option other than simply to pass information on to the relevant national authority in countries where both the law and policing priorities may be significantly different.

In 2006, the Public Order Act 1986 was amended by the Racial and Religious Hatred Act 2006, to insert a new offence of stirring up 'religious hatred', defined by reference to 'religious belief or lack of religious belief'.[55] The provisions came into force on 1 October 2007.[56] In response to concerns about the 'chilling effect' that the amendment could have on free speech, in addition to the requirement for consent from the Attorney-General for prosecutions, the following provision was inserted:

Nothing in this Part shall be read or given effect in a way which prohibits or restricts discussion, criticism or expressions of antipathy, dislike, ridicule, insult or abuse of particular religions or the beliefs or practices of their adherents, or of any other belief system or the beliefs or practices

---

[48] ibid s 22.

[49] ibid s 22(2).

[50] (1995) 19 EHRR 1.

[51] POA 1986, s 27(1). This would also extend to charges of conspiracy to commit such offences, see *R v Pearce* (1981) 72 Cr App R 295.

[52] POA 1986, s 27(3)(a), amended by the Anti-Terrorism Crime and Security Act 2001, Part 5, s 40.

[53] House of Lords *Hansard*, HL statement by the Attorney-General, Lord Goldsmith, 31 January 2005, col WA5.

[54] See BBC News, 'UK crackdown on Internet racism', 15 September 1998, available at <http://news.bbc.co.uk>.

[55] Racial and Religious Hatred Act 2006, Schedule, inserting a new Part 3A in POA 1986, ss 29A–29N.

[56] Racial and Religious Hatred Act 2006 (Commencement No 1) Order 2007, SI 2007/2490, the provisions of the Act came into force on 1 October 2007. On the same date, the Electronic Commerce Directive (Racial and Religious Hatred Act 2006) Regulations 2007, SI 2007/2497.

of its adherents, or proselytising or urging adherents of a different religion or belief system to cease practising their religion or belief system.[57]

This qualifying provision was added against the wishes of the government, who felt it would generate unnecessary uncertainty in the application of the offence.

Experience to date in respect of the offences relating to racial hatred does not augur well for the application of the new offence; although a government minister has noted that lack of prosecutions is not necessarily indicative of bad law-making, but rather reflects the law as an effective mechanism for changing people's behaviour.[58]

With the extension of the hate speech offences to encompass religious belief, the government has subsequently abolished the common law offences of blasphemy and blasphemous libel;[59] thereby bringing to an end a notorious area of English criminal law that has been the subject of rare but passionate legal dispute between free speech advocates and those concerned to control the publication of content perceived as damaging to the Christian religion.[60] The common law offence had seemingly fallen into abeyance during the latter half of the twentieth century, before being successfully revived in the *Lemon* case.[61] The case concerned the publication of a poem and picture that purported to detail certain acts of sodomy and fellatio being carried out against a dead Jesus. The defendants were convicted, with the Appeal Court upholding the lower court's direction that subjective intention to commit the blasphemous libel was not an essential element of the offence. The revival of the offence was subsequently and controversially endorsed both by the European Commission of Human Rights[62] and the ECtHR[63] as a legitimate restriction on the Convention right to freedom of expression; although its recent abolition has been welcomed by the UN Human Rights Committee.[64]

In October 2007, the government announced its intention to criminalize incitement to hatred based on one's sexuality, which would encompass the most extreme forms of homophobic behaviour. Provision was made to amend the Public Order Act 1986 to criminalize 'hatred on the grounds of sexual orientation', which 'means hatred against a group of persons defined by reference to sexual orientation (whether towards persons of the same sex, the opposite sex or both)'.[65] The government intends to bring the provisions

---

[57] POA 1986, s 29J.

[58] Comment by Paul Goggins, then a Home Office Minister, quoted in *The Telegraph*, 'Now you face jail for being nasty to Satanists', 10 June 2005.

[59] Criminal Justice and Immigration Act 2008, s 79.

[60] See *R v Bow Street Magistrates' Court, ex p Choudhury* [1990] 91 Cr App R 393, where it was held that the offence of blasphemy only extends to Christianity.

[61] *Lemon and Gay News Ltd* (1978) 67 Cr App R 70.

[62] *Gay News Ltd and Lemon v UK* (1983) 5 EHRR 123.

[63] *Wingrove v UK* (1997) 24 EHRR 1.

[64] United Nations CCPR: Consideration of Reports Submitted by States Parties under Article 40 of the Covenant Concluding Observations of the Human Rights Committee United Kingdom of Great Britain and Northern Ireland; (2008) 47 EHRR SE19, 4.

[65] Criminal Justice and Immigration Act 2008 (CJIA 2008), s 74 and Sch 16, inserting s 29AB in the POA 1986.

into force in autumn 2009.[66] As with the amendment for religious hatred, there was concern that this new offence could have an unnecessary 'chilling effect' on speech in relation to sexual orientation. As a consequence, an amendment was introduced in the Lords, in the face of government opposition, inserting the following qualification: 'In this Part, for the avoidance of doubt, the discussion or criticism of sexual conduct or practices or the urging of persons to refrain from or modify such conduct or practices shall not be taken of itself to be threatening or intended to stir up hatred.'[67] The government has subsequently proposed, in a recent Bill, that this provision be removed from the Act.[68]

Words themselves are sometimes capable of causing actual harm to a person, so the idea that words that advocate violence may be criminalized as a form of hate speech would seem reasonable in certain circumstances. Words or written material are capable, for example, of causing fear of, or provoking, 'immediate unlawful violence'.[69] In such cases, however, there is a strong temporal relationship between the speech and the possible violence. Under the Terrorism Act 2006, a new offence has been established of publishing a statement 'as a direct or indirect encouragement or other inducement to them to the commission, preparation or instigation of acts of terrorism or Convention offences'.[70] The provision was introduced to implement the requirements of Article 5 of the Council of Europe Convention on the Prevention of Terrorism, which requires states to criminalize 'public provocation to commit a terrorist offence'.[71] However, the tenuous nature of the causal and temporal relationship between the speech and any eventual terrorist conduct would seem to challenge traditional principles of English criminal law.[72]

Under the provision, a person publishing such a statement must either intend to encourage or induce, or be reckless as to such a consequence.[73] During its parliamentary passage and subsequently, considerable concern was expressed about what comprises 'indirect encouragement',[74] with the standard being that which 'members of the public could reasonably be expected to infer that what is being glorified is being glorified as conduct that should be emulated by them in existing circumstances'.[75] It is also an offence to disseminate terrorist publications.[76] The acts of terrorism being encouraged may occur anywhere in the world, not just in the UK. The maximum tariff for both offences is seven years' imprisonment. Where a person is being prosecuted for being

---

[66] Telephone call with Diana Symonds, Ministry of Justice, 21 January 2009.

[67] POA 1986, s 29JA.

[68] See Coroners and Justice Bill 2009, cl 58.

[69] POA s 4.

[70] Terrorism Act 2006, s 1.

[71] Council of Europe Convention on the Prevention of Terrorism, No 196 (2005).

[72] See A Ashworth, *Principles of Criminal Law* (Oxford University Press, 4th edn, 2003) para 4.6.

[73] Terrorism Act 2006, s 1(2).

[74] See Fenwick and Phillipson (n 6 above) 529–30; A Hunt, 'Criminal Prohibitions on Direct and Indirect Encouragement of Terrorism' [2007] Criminal Law Review 441 and the UN Human Rights Committee (n 64 above) 26.

[75] Terrorism Act 2006, s 1(3).

[76] ibid s 2. See *Abdul Rahman and Bilal Mohammed v R* [2008] EWCA Crim 1465.

reckless in respect of such material, it is a defence to show that the statement did not represent the person's views or have his endorsement and that this is clear for 'all the circumstances of the statement's publication',[77] which would be relevant for media organizations and their staff.

Both offences are also subject to an additional provision in respect of so-called 'internet activity',[78] which establishes a procedure for the removal of material falling under sections 1 and 2. Under the procedure, a police constable can issue a notice to persons responsible for the provision of 'a service provided electronically' through which the material is published and who can, if the person fails to comply with the notice within two working days by ensuring that it is no longer 'available to the public', be deemed to be endorsing the content of the material and therefore liable.[79] It is a defence to show a 'reasonable excuse' for a failure to comply with a notice or that the person has 'taken every step he reasonably could'[80] to prevent republication or dissemination of the statement. Although the section refers to 'internet activity', such as websites, the breadth of the phrase 'electronic service' would be equally applicable to internet service providers (ISPs) and radio and television broadcasters offering on-demand programme services.

11.4 OBSCENE AND INDECENT MATERIAL

While the publication of hate speech is criminalized conduct, the act of publication is perhaps more appropriately characterized as a preparatory act likely to result in a disturbance to public order committed by others, the central mischief being addressed by such laws. By contrast, for obscene and indecent material, the publication of such material is the perceived harm, by damaging the person receiving such material, in the case of obscene material, or by perpetuating the sexual abuse, in the case of indecent images of children.

While publication has generally been the focus of laws criminalizing obscene and indecent material, the possession of such material may also be an offence. The traditional rationale for treating possession as criminal conduct is the belief that exposure to the material results in long-term harm to the person consuming it;[81] although the evidence to support this contention is generally scant and unclear. However, as the internet has facilitated access to pornographic material, circumventing traditional controls over physical material exercised by Customs authorities,[82] criminalizing

---

[77] Terrorism Act 2006, ss 1(6) and 2(9), (10).
[78] ibid s 3.
[79] ibid s 3(2), (3).
[80] ibid s 3(2), (5)(a) and (6)(b).
[81] eg 'there is concern that these images fuel the abuse of real children by reinforcing potential abusers' inappropriate feelings towards children', Home Office Consultation 'on possession of non-photographic visual depictions of child sexual abuse' (April 2007) 6.
[82] ie Customs Consolidation Act 1876 and Customs and Excise Management Act 1979.

possession has been seen as a valid policy response to the fact that enforcement against the supplier of the material is difficult, if not impossible, in a transnational context.[83]

From a media law perspective, the relevance of offences of possession may not be immediately obvious. However, the nature of internet-based communications means the distinction between acts of publication and possession has become blurred, extending potential liability and creating legal uncertainty. The particular problem has been identified in the field of child sexual abuse, but would seem equally applicable in other areas. First, the act of obtaining possession of information in an internet environment is generally, as a matter of fact, an act of copying, replicating the original information. As such, it results in a proliferation of the illegal content, a mischief against which the criminalization of supply or publication is directed.[84] Secondly, where the act of obtaining possession involves some form of conduct by the recipient above and beyond the mere act of establishing a communication session, such as some form of exchange of value,[85] then the process of obtaining may be characterized as a form of incitement to publish or supply.[86] Thirdly, once the information is possessed, it may reside or be placed in a public or quasi-public environment, such as a website[87] or a person's P2P folder,[88] conduct which itself would enable further copying by others, again akin to supply or publication. As a consequence of one or all of the preceding points, where a person's conduct in respect of illegal content is identified primarily through evidence of his online activities, prosecutors may be able to charge on the basis of supply/publication rather than possession.

11.4.1 Obscene publications

The primary statute governing obscene material is the Obscene Publications Act 1959. Under the Act, it is an offence to publish an obscene article or to have an obscene article for publication for gain, which can attract a maximum tariff of five years (section 2(1)).[89] In the alternative, any such material may be subject to seizure and forfeiture (section 3), which is obviously a form of prior restraint of speech.

Although primarily used in respect of pornographic or sexually explicit material, an article may be considered obscene without having a sexual context, as the test for determining whether an article is obscene is wider in scope: '. . . if its effect or (where the article comprises two or more distinct items) the effect of any one of its items is,

---

[83] See Home Office Consultation 'on the possession of extreme pornographic material' (August 2005) paras 32–35.

[84] *R v Bowden* [2000] 1 Cr App R 438.

[85] eg payment or other content, as is common in cases of child sexual abuse images.

[86] *R v Goldman* [2001] EWCA Crim 1684. The inchoate offence of incitement was placed on a statutory footing under the Serious Crime Act 2007, Part 2, as 'encouraging or assisting an offence'.

[87] eg a subscriber's page on a social networking site.

[88] *R v Dooley* [2005] EWCA Crim 3093.

[89] As amended by CJIA 2008, s 71, which raised the maximum tariff from 3 to 5 years' imprisonment.

if taken as a whole, such as to tend to deprave and corrupt persons who are likely, having due regard to all relevant circumstances, to read, see or hear the matter contained or embodied in it'.[90] The intention of the author or publisher is irrelevant to a finding of obscenity. However, a lack of knowledge is a defence that can be argued by the defendant. The defendant must prove that he had 'not examined the article in respect of which he is charged and had no reasonable cause to suspect' its obscene nature (section 2(5)).

Over the years there has been much criticism made against the 'deprave and corrupt' formulation, from all sides of the free speech debate.[91] The threshold has been viewed as breaching the principle of legal certainty and fair warning, or as having the necessary flexibility to evolve 'with contemporary moral standards'.[92] However, reform has not been seriously pursued within government and, recently, the Home Office stated about the Act that they 'are satisfied that it continues to provide a benchmark for society's tolerance of certain material at a given time, as expressed through the courts . . .'.[93]

Determining whether material is obscene is for a jury to decide, without the admission of expert testimony. As such, it would also be impossible for the state, or an individual, to obtain a civil injunction to prevent the publication of obscene material, since a civil court would not have the power to decide whether the material was obscene.[94] While the threshold of obscenity is higher than that for indecency, applicable to child sexual abuse images, the obscenity threshold is based on the likely audience for the material. Where that audience comprises children, the threshold is likely to be met more easily, on the basis that children are more vulnerable to being corrupted and depraved. As noted by Lord Wilberforce in *DPP v Whyte*,[95] 'to apply different tests to teenagers, members of men's clubs or men in various occupations or localities would be a matter of common sense'.

The issue of child access to obscene material may not be a major issue in an environment where physical access controls can be exercised by those operating an outlet, such as a newsagents; but control is obviously more difficult in a media environment where the obscene material is made available directly into the home, either through television or the internet, particularly where the material originates outside the jurisdiction. For domestic television broadcasts, subject to the Broadcasting Code,[96] a tiered approach is adopted, which reflects the UK's transposition of its obligations under the Television without Frontiers Directive.[97] The default position is a prohibition for material that 'might seriously impair the physical, mental or moral development'

---

[90] OPA 1959, s 1(1). See *John Calder (Publications) Ltd v Powell* [1965] 1 QB 509, as an example of a non-sexual obscene publication.
[91] See generally Fenwick and Phillipson (n 6 above) 385–480.
[92] D Ormerod, *Smith & Hogan Criminal Law* (Oxford University Press, 11th edn, 2005) 947.
[93] Home Office, Consultation 'on the possession of extreme pornographic material' (August 2005) para 21.
[94] *Gouriet and ors v A-G* [1978] AC 435, 471.
[95] [1972] AC 849, 863B.
[96] Ofcom, October 2008.
[97] TWF Directive, Art 22.

of under-18s (section 1.1 of the code), which would cover obscene material. At a second level, 'unsuitable' material should be subject to 'appropriate scheduling', which for television is known as the 'watershed', from 9.00 pm until 5.30 am (section 1.5 of the code).[98] A third level of control is the use of a 'protection system (a mandatory PIN or other equivalent protection)', which controls access to classified material[99] on premium subscription film services.[100] Finally, for adult-sex material on premium subscription services, pay per view/night services, there is both a scheduling restriction, commencing at 10.00 pm, and a requirement for the use of a 'mandatory PIN protected encryption system' (section 1.24 of the code). International broadcast services are subject to a special prohibition regime, discussed further below.

In an internet context, it could be envisaged that a site which aggressively promoted pornographic material to internet users, through search engines and associated techniques such as meta-tags, without placing controls on access to its material, could be found liable on the basis that children are 'likely' to be visitors attracted to the site. Such an argument would seem even stronger in the case of those that send unsolicited emails that contain potentially obscene material.

The likelihood of children being the audience for obscene material is an objective issue for the jury to decide, not a quantitative issue, the prosecution not being required to show how many and what types of persons actually visited the site, but rather that vulnerable people such as children are 'likely' to have visited the site. However, this still raises the question of what numerical threshold the jury should have in mind when deciding whether children would be 'likely' to constitute the audience? In *Calder and Boyars Ltd* Salmon LJ felt that it required 'a significant proportion';[101] although such an approach was rejected by Lord Pearson in *DPP v Whyte*, who felt that it was sufficient that 'some persons' were affected, subject to a *de minimis* principle.[102] In *Perrin*,[103] a case involving material depicting coprophilia and coprophagia in the form of a preview page made available to anyone with access to the internet from a web site based in the US (sewersex.com), the court rejected a claim based on 'significant proportion' in favour of a 'more than a negligible number' standard.[104]

---

[98] However, in the 'Red Hot Dutch' case, *R v Secretary of State for National Heritage, ex p Continental Television BV* [1993] 2 CMLR 333, Court held that material broadcast between midnight and 4.00 am would make it more likely that the programmes are recorded, which in itself poses a greater likelihood that children may obtain access to such material (at 33). See further 11.5.1 below.

[99] Other than R18-rated films or their equivalent, which are prohibited from being broadcast (Broadcasting Code, section 1.25).

[100] Although for premium subscription film services not protected by level 3 mechanisms the watershed commences at midnight.

[101] [1969] 1 QB 151, 168.

[102] [1972] AC 849, 866. See also *R v O'Sullivan* [1995] 1 Cr App R 455, where the two were conjoined: 'such as to tend to deprave and corrupt a significant proportion, that is more than a negligible number of those who were likely' (at 466).

[103] [2002] EWCA Crim 747.

[104] ibid para 31.

Subsequent to the *Perrin* case, the government contended, in response to a parliamentary question, that they considered the threshold for obscenity where children are likely to access material to be a 'degree of sexual explicitness equivalent to what is available to those aged 18 and above in a licensed sex shop'; while such access is considered 'likely' where material is 'not behind a suitable payment barrier or other accepted means of age verification, for example, material on the front page of pornography websites and non-commercial, user-generated material'.[105]

The sheer scale of the potential audience in cyberspace effectively increases the risk that a publication may be held to be obscene in respect of a particular societal group, whether determined by age, culture, or other relevant characteristic. In such a case, expert evidence may be submitted in respect of the nature of the audience that is likely to view particular material, even though the only the evidence before the jury of someone having actually seen it may be from the law enforcement officer involved in the investigation, who is not susceptible to corruption and depravity.[106]

Publication of an obscene article is defined in the following terms:

(a) distributes, circulates, sells, lets on hire, gives, or lends it, or who offers it for sale or for letting on hire or;

(b) in the case of an article containing or embodying matter to be looked at or a record, shows, plays or projects it, or, where the matter is data stored electronically, transmits that data.[107]

Originally, the 1959 Act expressly excluded television and radio broadcasting from the concept of publication, but this was repealed by the Broadcasting Act 1990 and obscene material contained in a programme included in a programme service is a form of publication (section 162). A 'programme service' is broadly defined to include a service comprising the sending of sounds or visual images for reception by persons either simultaneously or on individual demand (section 201(1)(c)), although this is subject to limitations, specifically for 'two-way' services[108] where there is an exchange of images between the service provider and user, as would be the case with YouTube, for example. The Broadcasting Act 1990 also provides that 'ownership, possession or control' of an obscene article that is intended to be included in a programme shall be taken to be possession for the purposes of 'publication for gain' (paragraph 3 of Schedule 15).[109]

What constitutes an act of publication in an internet context? Does making an obscene article available for download from a website, or transfer via a P2P network constitute 'transmission'? Transmission has connotations of information being pushed from the sender to the recipient, while in the examples given the process is more akin to information being pulled by the recipient from the sender. A similar semantic issue

---

[105] Vernon Coaker, Home Office Minister, in a response to a question from Dr Iddon MP, on 13 December 2006.

[106] *Perrin* (n 103 above) para 22.

[107] OPA 1959, s 1(3). The latter words were inserted by the Criminal Justice and Public Order Act 1994, Sch 9, para 3.

[108] Communications Act 2003, s 232(5).

[109] The prohibition on such articles is specified in OPA 1959, s 2(1).

has arisen in the copyright field, giving rise to legal reform making it clear that the exclusive right to communicate a copyright work to the public included 'the making available to the public of their works in such a way that members of the public may access them from a place and at a time individually chosen by them'.[110] The courts have taken a robust approach to interpretation on this point in *Fellows and Arnold*,[111] rejecting an argument that publication requires some form of active conduct, rather than the passive conduct of making information available for access.

In the *Waddon* case[112] the defendant operated a website entitled 'xtreme-perversion', which was accessed by a police officer through subscription, enabling material to be downloaded that was considered obscene. In the course of appeal proceedings, defence counsel conceded that the defendant was responsible for the transmission of the material to the website, as well as its subsequent transmission to the police officer. However, the court was also asked to rule on what the position would be were the person uploading the material not to have the intention to enable subsequent downloading into the jurisdiction. While the Court refused to rule, it did opine that publication should not be considered as a single act, but multiple acts, further acts of publication taking place each time the material was downloaded. As such, the *actus reus* of the offence is carried out by the perpetrator in the first instance, when uploading the material; but subsequently by the victim(s), or jointly with the perpetrator, when downloading the material. In addition, by conceiving the act broadly, the obiter in the *Waddon* case consequently multiplied the possible places of publication and therefore the jurisdictional scope of the offence.

Subsequently in the *Perrin* case,[113] in accepting the *Waddon* position, the Court drew further support from the different forms of publications recognized in section 1(3)(a) of OPA 1959, specifically the reference to 'offers it for sale', which as a passive form of 'publication' has obvious parallels with the establishment of a website (paragraph 18). The defendant was a French citizen and claimed that 'where sites were developed abroad they were legal where they were managed' (paragraph 4). However, such an approach was ignored by the Court, finding guilt on the basis that the publication through downloading occurred in England.

The issues raised in the *Waddon* and *Perrin* cases contain interesting parallels with the *Yahoo!* case in France.[114] In *Yahoo!* one of the determining factors in attributing liability was the perceived targeting of French citizens. Counsel in both English cases raised the issue of jurisdiction. In *Waddon* the Court declined a request to rule on a situation where material was placed on a website with no intention for subsequent transmission back to England; although they did opine that it would be likely to 'depend

---

[110] Directive (EC) 2001/29 on the harmonisation of certain aspects of copyright and related rights in the information society [2001] OJ L167/10, Art 3(1).

[111] [1997] 2 All ER 548.

[112] [2000] All ER (D) 502.

[113] *R v Perrin* [2002] All ER (D) 359.

[114] *League Against Racism and Antisemitism (LICRA), French Union of Jewish Students, v Yahoo! Inc (USA), Yahoo France* Tribunal de Grande Instance de Paris, 20 November 2000; EBLR (2001).

upon questions of intention and causation in relation to where publication should take place' (paragraph 11). In *Perrin* counsel for the defendant suggested that 'a prosecution should only be brought against a publisher where the prosecutor could show that the major steps in relation to publication were taken within the jurisdiction of the court'—a suggestion dismissed by the Court.

The *Perrin* decision has been criticized for being 'extremely harsh',[115] potentially extending English obscenity laws to all foreign-hosted websites. Alternative approaches would seem to be either no liability for such foreign sites, even if the site seeks to attract English subscribers—a possibly 'unpalatable conclusion',[116] but perhaps best suited to the nature of cyberspace; or the imposition of liability based on localization factors such as whether the publisher directs his activities to English subscribers, similar in kind to defamation cases and the US 'minimum contacts' doctrine in an internet context.[117]

In respect of the offence of having an article that is 'for publication for gain', a preparatory offence of prospective publication introduced by the Obscene Publications Act 1964, reference should be made 'to such publication for gain of the article as in the circumstances it may reasonably be inferred he had in contemplation and to any further publication that could reasonably be expected to follow from it'.[118] In the case of digital information, especially where it could be shown that a person was intending to distribute the obscene material via a file-sharing application, such as KaZaA, the extent of further publication that could be 'reasonably expected' must be of a different degree in terms of propagation than that for a physical text.

The main statutory defence under the Obscene Publications Act 1959 is one of 'public good'; being 'in the interests of science, literature, art or learning, or of other objects of general concern' (section 4(1)). One of the best-known cases illustrating the successful deployment of this defence arose in respect of the publication of DH Lawrence's *Lady Chatterley's Lover*,[119] which has been seen as a turning point in terms of literary freedom in the UK.[120] The defence is not available where the obscene article is a moving picture, film, or soundtrack, where the defence of 'public good' is recast to be in 'the interests of drama, opera, ballet or any other art, or of literature or learning' (section 4(1A)).[121] While expert testimony is not admissible in respect of the test of obscenity, it may be presented as to merits of the article in terms of these various

[115] Ormerod (n 92 above) 952.

[116] See M Hirst, 'Cyberobscenity and the ambit of English criminal law' (2002) 13(2) Computers and Law, available at <http://www.scl.org/site.aspx?=is9160>.

[117] See eg the Australian defamation case, *Dow Jones & Co Inc v Gutnick* [2003] 1 LRC 368, Aus HC, and the US contacts case, *Zippo Mfg Co v Zippo Dot Com Inc* 952 F Supp 1119 (WD Pa 1997). See generally, C Reed, *Internet Law: Text and Materials* (Cambridge University Press, 2nd edn, 2004) para 7.1.3.

[118] OPA 1964, s 1(3)(b).

[119] *R v Penguin Books* [1961] Crim LR 176.

[120] Fenwick and Phillipson (n 6 above) 439.

[121] This provision was inserted by the Criminal Law Act 1977, s 53(6), and is taken from the Theatres Act 1968, s 3.

stated interests (section 4(2)). The defence would only need to be argued once it had been held that the article is obscene and would require the defendant to convince a jury that, on a balance of probabilities, the merits outweigh the obscenity. As clearly stated in *Calder and Boyars Ltd*:

> . . . the jury must consider on the one hand the number of readers they believe would tend to be depraved and corrupted by the book, the strength of the tendency to deprave and corrupt, and the nature of the depravity or corruption; on the other hand, they should assess the strength of the literary, sociological or ethical merit which they consider the book to possess. They should then weigh up all these factors and decide whether on balance the publication is proved to be justified as being for the public good.[122]

Whether a jury is capable of engaging in such a complex balancing exercise has been widely questioned;[123] as has the absence of a general defence based on a right to freedom of expression, without the need to fall under one of the headings specified in section 4.[124]

Reference must also be made to the common law offences of conspiracy to corrupt public morals and outraging public decency. The former was established by the House of Lords in *Shaw v DPP*,[125] which concerned the publication of a 'Lady's Directory', detailing the services of certain 'call-girls'. It was applied again a decade latter in *Knuller v DPP*,[126] but in a more restrictive manner.[127] The *actus reus* of the offence is the agreement to lead people 'morally astray', while the *mens rea* is intention to achieve such corruption. While the latter is more narrowly conceived than the intention required under the Obscene Publications Acts, the former is much broader.[128] While the 1959 Act expressly prohibits proceedings for an offence at common law, where the issue in question is whether the material is obscene,[129] this does not extend to offences of conspiracy. In addition, the court in the *Shaw* case suggested that a defence of public good was not applicable, which could enable the OPA 1959 to be circumvented. The offence of outraging public decency was revived in the *Gibson* case,[130] when an artist and the proprietor of an art gallery were convicted in respect of some earrings made from human foetuses. Were either offence to be charged today, however, it is considered likely that both would struggle to survive intact, if at all, in the face of a challenge under the Human Rights Act 1998.[131]

---

[122] See n 101 above, 172.
[123] eg G Robertson, *Obscenity* (Wiedenfeld, 1979).
[124] Fenwick and Phillipson (n 6 above) 441.
[125] [1962] AC 220.
[126] [1973] AC 435.
[127] G Robertson and A Nicol, *On Media Law* (Sweet & Maxwell, 5th edn, 2007) para 4–061.
[128] Fenwick and Phillipson (n 6 above) 444.
[129] OPA 1959, s 2(4), (4A), and the Broadcasting Act 1990, Sch 15, para 6.
[130] [1990] 2 QB 619.
[131] Fenwick and Phillipson (n 6 above) 447 and Robertson and Nicol (n 127 above) paras 4–062 *et seq*.

While the Obscene Publication Acts may be seen as standing the test of time, including the emergence of cyberspace, supplementary statutory regimes have been established to address the supply of certain forms of pornographic material in different contexts.

11.4.2 Video recordings[132]

In addition to the Obscene Publications Acts, there are other offences that may be applicable to the provision of pornographic material over the internet or via other communications services, such as mobile. The Video Recordings Act 1984, for example, establishes a classification system for video recordings and a number of offences relating to their supply, including supplying unclassified videos[133] and supplying video recordings classified as 'R18'[134] material except from licensed premises.[135] As well as being applicable to the distribution of pornographic material, the Video Recordings Act 1984 has also been relevant in intellectual property counterfeiting cases[136] and child abuse images.[137]

Under the 1984 Act, a 'video recording' is defined is defined in the following terms: 'any disc, magnetic tape or any other device capable of storing data electronically containing information by the use of which the whole or part of a video work may be produced'.[138] While this would clearly seem to capture the shift from video cassettes to DVDs, and the distribution of such material through web-based transaction engines,[139] the focus on the existence of a 'device' would seem to preclude pure digital video products, where the 'video work' is downloaded as a stream of data to the customer's equipment, such as a computer or mobile handset. In the latter scenario, however, the data may instead fall under broadcasting law, depending on the manner in which it is distributed, ie simultaneously or on-demand through selections made by customers.[140]

The application of the 1984 Act in a distance-selling context was examined in *Interfact Ltd and ors v Liverpool City Council*,[141] which has implications for web-based transaction sites distributing physical products. Here the defendants operated licensed sex shops, but also supplied such products in response to orders received by post, telephone, or e-mail. On appeal, the issue for the Court was the meaning of 'supply'

---

[132] See also section 9.5 above.
[133] VRA 1984, s 9.
[134] ibid s 7(2)(c), as classified by the British Board of Film Classification.
[135] ibid s 12(1).
[136] eg *R v Passley* [2004] 1 Cr App R (S) 70.
[137] eg *R v Farquhar* [2002] EWCA Crim 1633.
[138] VRA 1984, s 1(3). A 'video work' is 'any series of visual images (with or without sound)—(a) produced electronically by the use of information contained on any disc magnetic tape or any other device capable of storing data electronically, and (b) shown as a moving picture' (s 1(2)).
[139] eg from <http://www.amazon.co.uk> and <http://www.blockbuster.co.uk>.
[140] Communications Act 2003, s 361.
[141] [2005] EWHC 995 (Admin).

and offering to supply under the Act. The defendants argued that since the process of supply commenced in a licensed shop, the fact that the person was not required to be physically present in the shop to receive the goods was not relevant. The Court rejected this interpretation, holding that the requirement for persons to be supplied at a specific physical location was a critical aspect of the control regime established under the Act. However, the purposive approach taken by the Court towards 'supply' would not be likely to enable the scope of the Act to be extended beyond device-based distribution schemes.

The Video Recordings Act 1984 provides a defence where the commission of the offence was due to the act of another person and the defendant has taken 'all reasonable precautions and exercised all due diligence' to avoid the offence.[142] Despite the wording, the standard of care that an innocent reputable retailer is required to exercise has been held to be relatively minimal.[143]

Certain types of 'video works' are exempt from the regime, such as educational videos and video games.[144] However, a work is not exempt where it depicts '(a) human sexual activity or acts of force or restraint associated with such activity; (b) mutilation or torture of, or other acts of gross violence towards, humans or animals; (c) human genital organs or human urinary or excretory functions';[145] or 'criminal activity which is likely to any significant extent to stimulate or encourage the commission of offences'.[146] The breadth of the phrase 'human sexual activity' means that the certification scheme and related offences are applicable even where the images would not be considered obscene, indecent, or even necessarily pornographic![147]

11.4.3 Extreme pornography

In August 2005, the Home Office published a consultation paper 'On the possession of extreme pornographic material'. The initiative was driven, in part, by some disturbing evidence presented in the *Coutts* case.[148] One element of the evidence presented against Graham Coutts in his trial for the murder of Jane Longhurst was that, around the relevant time, he had visited various websites concerned with sexual violence related to rape, murder, and necrophilia.[149]

In the consultation paper, it noted that while the Obscene Publications Act 1959 was applicable to such material, its focus on those that supply such material was problematic in an internet era, where publishers are generally located abroad. Therefore, it put forward proposals to mirror the arrangements for child pornography, by criminalizing

---

[142] VRA 1984, s 14A.
[143] eg *Bilon v WH Smith Trading Ltd* [2001] EWHC 469 (Admin).
[144] VRA 1984, s 2(1).
[145] ibid s 2(2).
[146] ibid s 2(3). See also the Terrorism Act 2006, s 2 ('Dissemination of terrorist publications').
[147] See *Kent CC v Multi Media Marketing (Canterbury) Ltd The Times*, 9 May 1995.
[148] [2005] EWCA Crim 52.
[149] ibid 39–43.

possession of such material; thereby attempting to address the demand-side of the industry.

The proposal also differs from the Obscene Publications Act approach of examining the effect such material may have on the viewer, criminalizing instead specific types of content, similar to the Video Recordings Act 1984. Given the vague nature of the 'deprave and corrupt' standard, the addition of a possession offence to the 1959 Act would lack sufficient clarity and certainty.[150] It was proposed to criminalize, through a separate offence, possession of material containing actual or 'realistic depictions' of the following:

- intercourse or oral sex with an animal;
- sexual interference with a human corpse;
- serious violence in a sexual context; and
- serious sexual violence.[151]

However, this change of focus creates problems for legislators in terms of adequately defining such content without encroaching on existing legitimate activities, such as certain sadomasochist practices and the film industry. The proposal has generated particular controversy in respect of the last two categories of content. The maximum penalty for possession is three years, although a distinction has been maintained from that of publication, by raising the tariff under the Obscene Publications Act to five years.

In August 2006, the government published its response to the consultation process.[152] Despite opinion among respondents being 'sharply divided', the government decided to proceed with its proposals for a new offence, which were then presented in a Bill that became the Criminal Justice and Immigration Act 2008 (CJIA 2008). The new offence addresses four categories of content considered to be an 'extreme image':

(a) an act which threatens a person's life,

(b) an act which results, or is likely to result, in serious injury to a person's anus, breasts or genitals,

(c) an act which involves sexual interference with a human corpse, or

(d) a person performing an act of intercourse or oral sex with an animal (whether dead or alive), and a reasonable person looking at the image would think that any such person or animal was real.[153]

In addition, the 'extreme image' must be 'grossly offensive, disgusting or otherwise of an obscene character'.[154] During the passage of the Bill, considerable concern was

[150] J Rowbottom, 'Obscenity Laws and the Internet: Targeting the Supply and Demand' [2006] Criminal Law Review 97, 102.
[151] Such violence would be subject to prosecution for grievous bodily harm in England and Wales.
[152] Home Office, Consultation on the possession of extreme pornographic material: Summary of responses and next steps (August 2006).
[153] CJIA 2008, s 63(7).
[154] ibid s 63(6)(b).

expressed that the provisions could inadvertently criminalize the possession of images that were taken from material, specifically film, which was already available to the public, the so-called 'Casino Royale' issue.[155] To address this concern, provision was made to exclude 'classified works', which would include those subject to the BBFC regime.[156]

In an August 2006 response, the government accepted that the phrase 'in a sexual context' was confusing and unnecessary, given the formulation of the offence. At that time, the proposed alternative was 'serious violence', defined as images of acts appearing 'to be life threatening or likely to result in serious, disabling injury'.[157] As for the nature of the material, it will be for a jury to find that the material is 'pornographic', as well as involving real acts or a depiction of apparently real acts.[158]

The use of the term 'pornographic' would seem to create unnecessary uncertainty by creating a third category of subject matter distinct from obscene and indecent material. While obscene material would appear to have the highest threshold, it is unclear what the relationship between indecent and pornographic is intended to be.[159] Whereas for obscenity and indecency, the intent of the maker is irrelevant, the Bill initially provided that the criteria for determining whether material is pornographic is whether it 'appears to have been produced solely or primarily for the purpose of sexual arousal',[160] which would have required consideration of the intent of the supplier, when considering the guilt of the person in possession. This suggests that 'extreme pornography' could be seen not as a subset of obscene material, but a distinct category in its own right, although extensively overlapping with obscene material. The final provision, however, states that material is pornographic if 'it must reasonably be assumed to have been produced solely or principally for the purpose of sexual arousal';[161] an objective determination to made by a tribunal of fact.

Although primarily aimed at consumers of such material, the offence could obviously be used to prosecute a publisher or distributor of such material, since they will be, or will have been, in possession of the material. Indeed, prosecuting under the proposed offence would be likely to be easier than an action under the Obscene Publications Acts, since there is no requirement to show that someone would have been depraved or corrupted.

The general statutory defences mirror those available under the Criminal Justice Act 1988 in respect of child abuse images.[162] There is an additional defence where the

---

[155] At one moment in the recent remake of *Casino Royale*, James Bond is subject to interrogation involving the beating of his genitals.

[156] CJIA 2008, s 64.

[157] Home Office Survey (n 152 above) para 14.

[158] ibid paras 8 and 10.

[159] Regarding the relationship between indecent and obscene, see *R v Stanley* [1965] 2 QB 327, 333: 'The words "indecent or obscene" convey one idea, namely, offending against the recognised standards of propriety, indecent being at the lower end of the scale and obscene at the upper end of the scale.'

[160] Criminal Justice Act 1988, s 64(3).

[161] CJIA 1998, s 63(3).

[162] ibid s 65(2).

person charged with possession was actually a participant in the acts portrayed and those acts did not involve the infliction of non-consensual harm[163] on any person.[164] The three-year maximum prison tariff will only be sought for material depicting serious violence, with lesser maximums for the other categories. A prosecution can only be initiated, however, by or with the consent of the DPP.[165]

11.4.4 Protecting children

Protecting children from harmful content is a central component of media law and regulation in most jurisdictions.[166] The TWF Directive,[167] for example, contains provisions enabling derogation from the freedom of reception principle where it is necessary for the protection of minors (Article 2a(4)(a)(i)); controlling advertising to minors (Article 3e(1)(e) and (g)); and requiring that television broadcasts and on-demand content are not made available to minors where this may be harmful (Articles 22 and 3h). Similarly, the Press Complaints Commission Code contains two sections devoted to the protection of children.[168] In terms of criminally illegal content, a distinction must be made between content that is considered to be harmful to minors, obscene material, and content that contains images of child abuse, indecent material.

As noted in section 11.4.1 above, the Obscene Publications Act 1959 is applicable to material that would 'deprave and corrupt' those likely to view it, which would include children, were access to that material not to be controlled. In addition, there is the little known and little used statute, the Children and Young Persons (Harmful Publications) Act 1955. This criminalizes the printing, publication and sale of 'any book, magazine or other like work' that portrays the commission of crimes, acts of violence or cruelty, or incidents of 'a repulsive or horrible nature' (section 1), with a maximum tariff of four months' imprisonment (section 2).

If any topic is unequivocally associated in the minds of politicians, the media, and the public with the 'dark side' of the internet, it is that of the indecent images of children. The internet has facilitated the supply of this form of illegal content to such an extent that it is now considered a multi-billion dollar industry,[169] primarily through a proliferation of pay-per-view sites. As a consequence, child protection is currently at the forefront of government policy on cybercrime.[170] Some indecent images are taken surreptitiously without direct interference with the child; however, the vast majority of

---

[163] ie that which in law a person can consent to; which reflects the decision in *R v Brown* [1994] 1 AC 212.

[164] CJIA 1998, s 66.

[165] ibid s 63(10).

[166] See generally, A Millwood Hargrave and S Livingstone, *Harm and Offence in Media Content* (Intellect, 2006).

[167] As amended.

[168] Press Complaints Commission Code, ss 6 and 7. See further Ch 9 above.

[169] National Center for Missing and Exploited Children (NCMEC), Press Release: 'Financial and Internet Industries to combat Internet child pornography', 15 March 2006, available at <http://www.missingkids.com>.

[170] See eg HM Government, 'The Byron Review Action Plan' (June 2008).

hard core images involve the direct abuse of children. Indeed, use of the phrase 'child pornography' is considered inappropriate in the context of children, since pornography embraces a semi-legitimate industry and creates confusion in the minds of the public, especially where the images involve pubescent children.[171] The more appropriate term is simply child sexual abuse images.

The two principal statutory provisions under UK law in respect of child pornographic images are in relation to the supply of such images, under the Protection of Children Act 1978, and the possession of such images, under the Criminal Justice Act 1988.[172] Supply is distinguished into four different types of activity: (a) taking and making; (b) distributing or showing; (c) possession with a view to distribution; and (d) publishing an advertisement suggesting that the advertiser distributes or shows indecent photographs.[173] The prohibition relates to an indecent 'photograph', including 'film', 'pseudo-photograph', or a 'tracing or other image' derived from a photograph or pseudo-photograph.[174]

While the possession of obscene material has only recently been criminalized, in large part as a response to the internet, the possession of 'indecent images' of children pre-dates such developments and is indicative of the broader consensus that exists around the suppression of this form of expression. However, in an attempt to counter the growth in availability of such material over the internet, successive governments have steadily raised the maximum tariff that such offences attract. The maximum penalty for the section 1 offences under the Protection of Children Act 1978 has been raised from three years to ten years; while the tariff for possession under section 160 of the Criminal Justice Act 1988 was raised from six months to five years.[175]

'Indecent' is not defined in the legislation, but is a question of fact to be determined by the jury, applying normal standards of propriety,[176] which may include account of the age of the child, where known.[177] In the *Land* case[178] the Court held that the determination of the age of a child in an image was to be made exclusively by the jury, and was something for which expert testimony was not normally required. However, in reality, prosecution activity tends to focus on pre-pubescent children, thereby avoiding any significant argument about age.[179] As with obscenity, the intention of the person making the image is irrelevant to a finding of indecency.[180]

---

[171] Stated by Jim Gamble, Deputy Director-General, National Crime Squad, at a conference, 'Child Pornography on the Internet: Investigation and Prosecution', London, 19 October 2005.

[172] CJA 1988, s 160.

[173] PCA 1978, s 1(1)(a)–(d) respectively.

[174] ibid s 7, as amended.

[175] Inserted by the Criminal Justice and Court Services Act 2000, s 41.

[176] *R v Murray* [2004] EWCA Crim 2211, [2005] Crim LR 386.

[177] *R v Owen* (1986) 86 Cr App R 291.

[178] (1998) 1 CAR 301.

[179] See AA Gillespie, 'Child pornography: Balancing substantive and evidential law to safeguard children effectively from abuse' (2005) 9(1) International Journal of Evidence & Proof 36.

[180] *R v Smethurst* [2002] 1 Cr App R 50, [2001] 1 Crim LR 657.

In terms of what constitutes a child, the Protection of Children Act 1978 states that 'a person is to be taken as having been a child at any material time if it appears from the evidence as a whole that he was under the age of 18'.[181] The age threshold was raised from 16 by the Sexual Offences Act 2003,[182] which was designed in part to assist law enforcement in bringing prosecutions against those distributing images of children aged 16 and below, on the basis that borderline cases are often ignored. However, it has also created a risk for those involved in film and video, who may previously have used actors aged 16 or 17 in sexual-related material.

Until 2003, the only express defences available in respect of supply applied to distribution and showing or possession with a view to distribution.[183] A defence could be made out if the defendant could prove either a 'legitimate reason', or that he had not seen the photographs and did not know, or have any cause to suspect their nature, ie an absence of knowledge. However, when 'making' a photograph was inserted into the 1978 Act in 1994,[184] no similar statutory defence was provided for, leaving a defendant with only the possibility of showing an absence of the necessary *mens rea*.

However, as a consequence of the courts more broadly defining the concept of 'making' to something akin to simple possession, they inadvertently criminalized a range of activities and actors beyond that anticipated by Parliament when the legislation was adopted. For example, an editor of a website containing user-generated content may discover an indecent image and decide to report its presence to the law enforcement authorities. However, the act of reproducing the image to make the report was itself a criminal offence. While a prosecution would be unlikely to result, as the prosecution authorities would exercise their discretion, this exposure to liability was perceived as an unsatisfactory state of affairs. To remedy this situation, the Sexual Offences Act 2003 establishes a new defence that the defendant is not guilty if he can prove that 'it was necessary for him to make the photograph or pseudo-photograph for the purposes of the prevention, detection or investigation of crime, or the purposes of criminal proceedings, in any part of the world'.[185]

The operation of this provision has been the subject of a Memorandum of Understanding between the Crown Prosecution Service (CPS) and the Association of Chief Police Officers (ACPO).[186] In it, major factors are listed that shall be taken into account when considering the intentions of an individual who has 'made' an image and wishes to rely on the section 46 defence, including how the images were handled, the number of copies 'made', and the timeliness of the reporting.

---

[181] Protection of Children Act 1978, s 2(3).
[182] Sexual Offences Act 2003, s 45.
[183] Protection of Children Act 1978, s 1(4).
[184] By the Criminal Justice and Public Order Act 1994, s 84(2)(a), (b).
[185] Sexual Offences Act 2003, s 46, inserting a new section '1B Exception for the criminal proceedings, investigations etc.' in the PCA. Other defences are available for those working in the Security Service and GCHQ.
[186] October 2004, available at <http://www.iwf.org.uk/documents/20041015_mou_final_oct_2004.pdf>.

In March 2007, the government issued a consultation paper[187] proposing the criminalization of other forms of visual images of child abuse, specifically computer generated images (CGIs), such as avatars in a virtual world, as well as cartoons, such as Japanese Manga comics. The government's proposed offence has been published in the Coroners and Justice Bill 2008. The offence would criminalize the possession of any 'image', excluding those already covered under existing law, which would include a 'moving or still image (produced by any means), or . . . data (stored by any means) which is capable of conversion into an image'.[188] While the subject matter is child sexual abuse, the provisions are a stand-alone possession offence, rather than an extension of the existing provisions, and are modelled on the extreme pornography provisions discussed above, which are concerned with obscenity rather than indecent material.

11.5 CONTROLLING FOREIGN ILLEGAL CONTENT

A third factor resulting in the heightened importance of illegal content within media law, noted in the introduction, is the more frequent jurisdictional conflicts over content considered permissible in one country, while unacceptable in another. While the internet is the most prominent environment in which such conflicts arise today, the introduction of satellite television in the 1970s is an earlier example of the problems of regulating illegal content originating on media services provided from outside the jurisdiction.

11.5.1 Foreign television and radio services

The regulation of satellite television under European law is discussed elsewhere in the book.[189] Of particular interest to the issue of criminally illegal content, however, is the recent jurisdictional amendment under the AVMS Directive. The effect of this amendment is to shift the default jurisdictional position from being the state under whose jurisdiction the satellite resides to the state where the content is uploaded to the satellite (Article 2(4)(a)). For the UK, this represents a significant change, as the two main satellite operators operate under French (ie Eutelsat) and Luxembourg (ie SES Astra) law, while there are significant numbers of UK-based uplinks.[190] As a consequence, this will enhance the UK's ability to control broadcasts into the UK of criminally illegal material.

---

[187] Home Office, 'Consultation on possession of non-photographic visual depictions of child sexual abuse' (March 2007).
[188] Coroners and Justice Bill 2009, cl 52(2).
[189] See further Ch 8 above.
[190] See DCMS, 'The Audiovisual Services Directive: Consultation on Proposals for Implementation in the United Kingdom' (July 2008) Part 5.

Currently, if Ofcom considers a foreign satellite service to be of 'unacceptable quality', it can notify the Secretary of State, who can issue an order proscribing the service.[191] To be of 'unacceptable quality', the subject matter must offend 'against good taste or decency or [be] likely to encourage or incite to crime or to lead to disorder or to be offensive to public feeling' (section 177(3)). The first component is the wording present in the old Broadcasting Code standard, now replaced by 'generally accepted standards'.[192] The second is also present in the Broadcasting Code. The third component has no equivalent in the current rules and seems potentially over broad. When deciding to make an order, the Secretary of State should consider whether it satisfies the public interest and is compatible with the UK's international commitments (section 177(4)), which would include EU law.

An offence is committed when a person engages in conduct considered to support the proscribed foreign satellite service (section 178(2)). Such conduct is widely drawn to include the supplying of equipment capable of receiving the service, including decoders;[193] supplying programme material to be included in the service; arranging or inviting others to so supply (a form of incitement); advertising within the programme service, or advertising the proscribed service or the times of programmes within the service (section 178(3)). The maximum penalty is two years' imprisonment (section 178(5)).

Since 1990, six proscription orders have been issued.[194] The Broadcasting Act 1990 provisions were subjected to the scrutiny of the English courts in *R v Secretary of State for National Heritage, ex p Continental Television BV* [1993] 2 CMLR 333, generally known as the 'Red Hot Dutch' case. The case concerned the transmission of hardcore pornography from the Netherlands and then Denmark, which was receivable in the UK between midnight and 4.00 am. The then Broadcasting Standards Council considered that some of the material would have been in breach of the Obscene Publications Act 1959 were it to have been published on a domestic service,[195] and reported it to the Secretary of State. The Secretary of State announced his intention to proscribe the service under the Broadcasting Act procedure, which was challenged by judicial review by the broadcaster on the grounds that it would breach the UK obligations under the freedom to provide services provisions of the TWF Directive.[196] The High Court made a reference to the European Court of Justice (ECJ) on two points: (a) whether direct broadcasting by satellite fell within the concept of 'retransmission' under Article 2(2); and (b) whether the state can prevent such broadcasts where measures have been taken to ensure that minors 'will not normally hear or see such

---

[191] Broadcasting Act 1990, s 177. The order can be annulled by Parliament (s 177(5)(b)).

[192] Ofcom Broadcasting Code, s 2.

[193] See 11.3 above.

[194] ie SI 1024/1993 (Red Hot Television); SI 2917/1995 (XXX TV Erotica); SI 2557/1996 (Rendez-Vous); SI 1150/1997 (Satisfaction Club); SI 1865/1998 (Eurotica Rendez-Vous); SI 220/2002 (Extasi TV).

[195] Although transmission (ie a downlink) into the UK should have been sufficient to have prosecuted the English company, Continental Television plc, that was licensed to market the service in the UK.

[196] TWF Directive, Art 2(2).

broadcasts'.[197] Unfortunately, from a media law perspective, the broadcaster later ceased operations and the points were never argued before the ECJ.[198]

During the proceedings, counsel for the defence raised a 'proportionality' argument under Community law, but founded in ECHR jurisprudence, on the basis that prior to the issuance of the proscription order, the concerns about access by minors should have been put to the broadcasters, who would have been able to suggest measures to prevent such access. The Court was not, however, prepared to entertain any such conception of proportionality as embracing a 'duty to consult' with the speech maker; this despite the fact that meetings between the parties were apparently proposed,[199] while in a subsequent case, 'an exchange of observations' took place between the government department and the party subject to the proscription order.[200]

While satellites represent the first technology to enable wide-scale circumvention of national broadcasting controls, the proliferation of alternative communications platforms has presented many further opportunities to provide services from outside the jurisdiction. In response, the government has established a concurrent proscription regime for all other radio and television services, covering the same 'objectionable matter'.[201] Where such an order is made, the proscribed service should not be included in a 'multiplex service' or 'cable package' (section 330(2)). As the proscribed service can only be received through a regulated service, the enforcement provisions target the regulated service provider, rather than criminalizing a range of conduct related to the proscribed service, as for proscribed foreign satellite services. Ofcom has the power to issue a notification to the regulated service provider requiring the removal of the proscribed service, which is enforceable through civil proceedings (section 331(5)). Failure to comply with a notification can result in the imposition of a penalty of up to £5,000 (section 332).[202] To date, however, no proscription order has been issued.

A cable package is defined with the intention of excluding television and radio services received via the internet,[203] by stating that a programme service does not form part of a cable package where the service is 'only part of a service provided by means' of an electronic communications service (ECS) and the service does not consist 'wholly or mainly' in the provision of programmes for reception by the public

---

[197] Such controls were discussed at section 11.5.1 above, in respect of considerations about the likely audience for obscene publications.

[198] The High Court refused to lift the proscription order pending the outcome of the reference, which was upheld on appeal: *R v Secretary of State for National Heritage* [1993] 3 CMLR 387.

[199] *R v Secretary of State for National Heritage, ex p Continental Television BV* [1993] 2 CMLR 333, paras 35–36. See also comment at n 98 above.

[200] Case T-69/99 *Danish Satellite TV A/S (Eurotica Rendez Vous Television) v Commission of the European Communities* [2000] ECR II-4039, para 6.

[201] Communications Act 2003, ss 329–332.

[202] A separate contravention occurs every day the proscribed service is included, which would appear to enable Ofcom to impose multiple £5,000 penalties (ibid s 332(9)).

[203] Communications Act 2003, Explanatory Note, para 693.

(section 330(5)). This formulation is both problematic in itself, as well as out-of-step with the recent reforms made to the TWF Directive, which were expressly designed to capture certain programme services made available over the internet. In terms of the former, the manner in which online services are provided may make it difficult to identify the 'service' that the programmes form part of. Yahoo!, for example, provides a range of television-related services, including the 'BBC on Yahoo! Video', but access to these are not dependent on the persons receiving any other Yahoo! service, such as e-mail. The phrase 'wholly or mainly' is the same wording used for establishing the regulatory boundary between ECSs and 'information society services', and is likely to generate the same legal uncertainties.

11.5.2 Internet media

An early story from the 2008 Beijing Olympics concerned the problems visiting journalists were having accessing certain material over the internet. The phenomenon, referred to widely as the 'Great Firewall of China', was not a new story, but was given fresh impetus both by the numbers of foreign journalists present for the Olympics and because the Chinese authorities had given certain assurances to the International Olympics Committee, prior to being awarded the right to stage the Games, that such controls would no longer be present. The indignation generated from the Western media coverage demands examination of the situation in our own jurisdiction concerning controls over illegal content, where such content emanates from outside the UK. The issue extends beyond the concern of mainstream media, raising wider issues about internet censorship.

For the traditional mass media provider of print publications, television, and radio, the exercise of editorial control over the content they publish, broadcast, or distribute, coupled with establishment or some presence within the jurisdiction, enables regulatory regimes, whether statutory or otherwise, to impose sanctions where illegal content is made available, whether under criminal or civil law or regulatory rules.

For criminally illegal material published or made available in a foreign jurisdiction and accessible via an internet service, there are three potential points of control. First, domestic law enforcement agencies could notify a foreign law enforcement agency in the jurisdiction where the illegal material is located (if that can be successfully identified). The foreign law enforcement agency would then be in a position to take enforcement action against the place of publication. The viability of such an option obviously depends on a range of factors, from the need for harmonized legal treatment of the identified content to the necessary law enforcement resource. Secondly, the consumption or possession of such material could be the criminalized conduct in the domestic jurisdiction, as well as the initial publication, making available, expression, or speech. As discussed above, this approach has been taken in respect of certain obscene or indecent material. The third point of control is the ISP, the entity providing connectivity to the internet. It is this third category where significant legal developments are taking place and are of concern to us in this section.

11.5.2.1 *Intermediary liability*

As seen throughout this book, media law and regulation is predominantly concerned with two areas, the content and the outlet, platform, or means by which that content is made available to the public. In a traditional media environment, the distribution of content generally involves one or more intermediaries, from the newsagent to the set-top box required for digital television.[204] The legal responsibility such intermediaries attract for the content they make available varies according to the knowledge and control that they are perceived to have in respect of such content. A newspaper, for example, is held to be liable for the defamatory articles it publishes, while the newsagent from which the paper is sold has a defence to liability where it can show a lack of knowledge.[205] A broadcaster may be liable for any breach of the Broadcasting Code,[206] but not the provider of a broadcast transmission service or the set-top box supplier.

In an internet environment, issues of knowledge and control have generated new uncertainties about where liability for criminally illegal content may lie. On the one hand, the nature of the access and communication services provided by an ISP go beyond the simple carriage of third-party content that occurred when using traditional voice telephony services. Internet protocol networks and internet services involve acts of reproduction, storage, and distribution that can be construed as more akin to that of supplier or publisher, rather than as 'common carrier'.[207] On the other hand, the increasingly interactive nature of online media services, encouraging consumers to post comment and content in response to the material they have received,[208] challenges traditional concepts of editorial control.

To address the role of ISPs, new rules have been widely adopted around the world to protect these intermediaries from liability for third party content. Under European law, three activities carried out by providers of 'information society services'[209] have been subject to *sui generis* liability rules, 'mere conduit', 'caching', and 'hosting'.[210] Under the UK regulations transposing these provisions, it is made clear that an ISP shall 'not be liable for damages or for any other pecuniary remedy *or for any criminal sanction*'.[211] To endow procedural support to such protection, it is provided that in any criminal

---

[204] For the regulation of set-top boxes, see further 2.5.3 above.

[205] Defamation Act 1996, s 1(1). See further 10.7.6 above.

[206] eg Communications Act 2003, s 237(1).

[207] While originating in England, the application of the 'common carrier' doctrine to the telecommunications sector has been a US development. See generally, E Noam, 'Beyond liberalization II: The impending doom of common carriage' (1994) 18(6) *Telecommunications Policy* 635.

[208] eg 'Have Your Say' on the BBC site.

[209] ie 'any service normally provided for remuneration, at a distance, by electronic means and at the individual request of a recipient of services', Directive (EC) 98/34 of 22 June 1998 laying down a procedure for the provision of information in the field of technical standards and regulations [1998], OJ L204/37, as amended by Directive (EC) 98/48 of 20 July 1998 [1998] OJ L217/18, at Art 1(2).

[210] Directive (EC) 2000/31 on certain legal aspects of information society services, in particular electronic commerce, in the Internal Market [2007] OJ L178/1, at Arts 12–14 (hereinafter 'eCommerce Directive').

[211] Electronic Commerce (EC Directive) Regulations 2002, SI 2002/2013, regs 17–19.

proceedings against an ISP, where any of the defences made available under the 2002 Regulations is raised, with sufficient evidence adduced, 'the court or jury shall assume that the defence is satisfied unless the prosecution proves beyond reasonable doubt that it is not'.[212]

To the extent that a media outlet can be characterized as a provider of 'information society services', rather than as a provider of an 'audiovisual media service', it will be able to claim defences against liability that may not be available to the latter. So, for example, an electronic newspaper that provides a message board for its readers may be able to assert the 'hosting' defence on the basis of an absence of knowledge, which would place the burden of proof on the prosecution to prove otherwise,[213] which would not be available to a broadcaster, where the presumption would be one of editorial control over the content and thereby knowledge.[214]

For each activity, the protection from liability is subject to certain conditions, designed to reflect the absence of knowledge or control.[215] Upon becoming aware of the illegal content, the ISP is obliged to take action to remove or disable access to such material, in order to be able to continue to rely on the statutory protections; a process generally referred to as 'notice-and-take-down' (NTD).[216] Under the Terrorism Act 2006, in respect of the encouragement of terrorism,[217] a failure to remove content upon notification may render the ISP directly liable for that content. The provisions do not affect the ability of a court or administrative body to issue an order requiring the removal of the illegal content.[218]

These 'safe harbour' liability provisions can be seen as supportive of freedom of expression, to the extent that they reduce the liability risks for intermediaries and the consequent controls over illegal content that may have been implemented to reduce such liability risk. However, an NTD regime in isolation is likely to lead to excessive removal of content, reflecting the economic self-interest or incentive of the intermediary.[219] As this is likely to have a detrimental impact on freedom of expression, it begs the question whether governments have an obligation to address this concern, in their role as protectors and promoters of individual rights. One possible solution is the requirement to implement a statutory 'take-down and put-back' regime, as provided for in the US under the Digital Millennium Copyright Act 1998.[220]

---

[212] ibid reg 21.

[213] ibid reg 21(2).

[214] AVMS Directice, Art 1(d), although it is arguable that such control would only be presumed in respect of audiovisual content.

[215] ibid Recital (42).

[216] See eg Reed (n 117 above).

[217] Terrorism Act 2006, s 3. See further 11.3 above.

[218] eCommerce Directive (n 210 above) Arts 12(3), 13(2), and 14(3) respectively.

[219] See eg C Ahlert, C Marsden, and C Yung, 'How "Liberty" Disappeared from Cyberspace: The Mystery Shopper Tests Internet Content Self-regulation' (2004) available at <http://pcmlp.socleg.ox.ac.uk/text/liberty.pdf>.

[220] 17 USC § 512(g).

11.5.2.2 *Monitoring and filtering*

By contrast, online media entities that are responsible for the content they make available are increasingly keen to encourage user interactivity as a part of their services, enabling users to submit content, for example posting text messages or video clips, which are then available for viewing by other users. Such user-generated content (UGC) obviously generates a new dimension of liability risk for the media entity. While they may potentially be able to rely on the same *sui generis* defences as ISPs, their greater control over the core content being made available under the service, as editors, may limit the scope for claims about lack of knowledge. In particular, online media entities are likely to consider implementing some form of moderation or monitoring of UGC as a risk mitigation strategy. For the purposes of this chapter, moderation means the active or passive review of UGC by persons acting on behalf of the editorial entity; while monitoring involves the use of technical mechanisms, such as hardware or software-based filtering applications, implemented by the editorial entity to automatically review UGC against certain criteria, parameters, or keywords. Moderation and monitoring may be carried out prior to the UGC being made publicly available or subsequent to its disclosure. As well as the cost implications for media entities of putting such systems in place, both moderation and monitoring are forms of review and censorship of a fundamentally different nature and scale from the traditional role of the newspaper or television 'duty' lawyer reviewing copy or items prior to publication or broadcast.

In terms of monitoring, it is not widely known among the UK general public that internet users already do not have unmediated access to web-based internet services in the UK, as nearly all broadband service providers filter URL requests against a list of addresses where 'potentially illegal child sexual abuse' content is located on foreign sites and services. The list against which such filtering is carried out is created and maintained by the Internet Watch Foundation (IWF), a self-regulatory body established in 1996.[221] Where such illegal material is found to be residing on domestic internet sites, it would be subject to an NTD procedure, with the IWF notifying the relevant hosting provider. Currently, the deployment of the filtering database is carried out purely on a voluntary basis by certain members of the IWF. Although deployment is not a requirement of IWF membership, in May 2006, the Home Office minister, Vernon Coaker, made the following statement:

> . . . we are setting a target that by the end of 2007, all ISPs offering broadband internet connectivity to the UK general public put in place technical measures that prevent their customers accessing websites containing illegal images of child abuse identified by the IWF . . . If it appears that we are not going to meet our target through co-operation, we will review the options for stopping UK residents accessing websites on the IWF list.[222]

---

[221] <http://www.iwf.org.uk>.
[222] House of Commons Written Answer from Home Office minister, Vernon Coaker, *Hansard*, 15 May 2006, col 716W.

As such, the IWF approach must be viewed as a form of 'extra-legal' regulation.[223] Where moderation and monitoring is implemented as part of a process of exercising editorial control, concerns over freedom of expression must reside primarily with the operative impact of the liability regime, rather than the acts of the editorial entity themselves. However, such concerns are much more widespread where, as with the IWF filtering system, the monitoring is government sanctioned, whether directly or indirectly.

The IWF model has been perceived as so successful that there have been numerous calls for further such controls against other forms of illegal content. In January 2008, the Home Secretary, Jacqui Smith, announced the government's intention to use similar techniques against terrorist websites that 'groom' potential terrorists.[224] At the end of July 2008, the House of Commons Committee on Culture, Media and Sport published a report on harmful content on the internet that included in its recommendations that action be taken to 'block access to websites which assist or encourage suicide'.[225] In response, the government has already proposed an amendment to the Suicide Act 1961, creating a new offence of conduct capable of intentionally 'encouraging or assisting' a suicide act; which could include conduct by a UK-established information society service provider.[226]

The moderation and monitoring of communications obviously involves an act of interception, looking into the content of a communication, which is widely recognized as one of the more egregious forms of privacy intrusion, particularly when carried out by the state.[227] To the extent that we consume more of our media through on-demand communication techniques, such as the internet, legal regimes governing interception may therefore become an element in the governance of online media content. Interception laws currently tend to reflect the bilateral nature of traditional communications, and do not adequately address one-to-many forms of communication. Under the Regulation of Investigatory Powers Act 2000, interception is expressly stated not to include 'the interception of any communication broadcast for general reception',[228] which is intended to cover television and radio, but not pager and mobile phone signals,[229] although neither 'broadcast' nor 'general reception' are further defined. It is arguable therefore that many websites could be viewed as falling within this exception. In this regard, 'broadcast' would seem the more problematic term since, as a verb, it could be interpreted narrowly as requiring conduct beyond that of making content

---

[223] See further Ch 9 above.
[224] 'Home Secretary gives major counter-terrorism speech', 17 January 2008, available at <http://www.homeoffice.gov.uk>.
[225] 'Harmful content on the Internet and in video games' HC 353-I, 31 July 2008, para 117.
[226] Coroners and Justice Bill 2009, cs 46–48 and Sch 10, which exempts such service providers where they are from an EEA state other than the UK, or are acting as 'mere conduits', 'caching', or 'hosts'.
[227] *Malone v UK* (1985) 7 EHRR 14.
[228] Regulation of Investigatory Powers Act 2000, s 2(3).
[229] Explanatory Notes to the Regulation of Investigatory Powers Act, para 29.

available, while reference to statutory definitions would further limit the activity to the use of wireless telegraphy.[230]

From a privacy perspective, automated monitoring systems for identifying illegal content are often seen as preferable to moderation, because ongoing human review of communications content is not required.[231] However, from a freedom of expression perspective, automated systems give rise to concerns about over-blocking, resulting in collateral infringement of free expression, as a consequence of their automated nature. Such concerns are illustrated in a 2008 example concerning the operation of the IWF filtering system and the Wikipedia site. On the site was an image taken from a Scorpions' album, 'Virgin Killers', which was widely accepted as being indecent under the Protection of Children Act 1978.[232] As such, the image was entered into the IWF's database and was then incorporated into the filtering systems operated by IWF members that use the database. As a consequence, certain users of the Wikipedia site, those with editorial rights, began to experience certain problems accessing and using the site,[233] which became widely reported, and eventually led to the IWF removing the image from their database.[234]

The Wikipedia case raised numerous issues for the various parties involved, as well as broader matters of public policy, but four aspects are of concern to us in terms of overblocking and freedom of expression. The first component of a filtering system is the building of the data list, identifying the location of the illegal material in an online environment, for example the Uniform Resource Locator (URL). To ensure that the image was blocked, the IWF listed two locations, the page in which the image appeared and the location of the image itself. The consequence of listing the former location was to block access to the text on the page as well as the image, the text of which was not illegal, resulting in collateral damage to freedom of expression. The second aspect was the implementation of the filter within the network of the ISP. To render the filtering manageable, ISPs have implemented a two-stage process, first identifying and re-routing traffic going to the same domain (for example <http://www.wikipedia.com>) as the listed location through a proxy server, which then identifies whether the request is going to the specific listed location.[235] This first stage can result in the emerging user request having its attributes altered, reflecting its routing through the proxy. In the

---

[230] eg Communications Act 2003, s 405(1). This definition ties the act of broadcasting to the use of wireless telegraphy, limiting it to the satellite and terrestrial platforms, and excluding cable, internet, or mobile platforms (the latter because only the final access aspect is wireless).

[231] See eg Office of the Information Commissioner, *The Employment Practices Code*, para 3.2.2 and the Article 29 Data Protection Working Party, 'Working document on the surveillance of electronic communications in the workplace' (WP 55, 29 May 2002), para 3.1.7.

[232] See further section 11.4.4 above.

[233] See Wikipedia:Administrators' noticeboard/2008 IWF action, available at <http://en.wikipedia.org/wiki/Wikipedia:Administrators%27_noticeboard/Major_UK_ISPs_reduced_to_using_2_IP _addresses>.

[234] See 'IWF statement regarding Wikipedia webpage', 9 December 2008 available at <http://www.iwf.org.uk/media/news.archive-2008.251.htm>.

[235] See R Clayton, <http://www.lightbluetouchpaper.org/2008/12/11/technical-aspects-of-the-censoring-of-wikipedia>.

Wikipedia case, this minor alteration had serious implications for users, as the manner in which the Wikipedia site operated meant that certain editorial rights granted to Wikipedia users were dependent on such meta-data being unique for each user, rather than common for all filtered requests. As a consequence, until the location was removed from the IWF list, the recipient Wikipedia site could not distinguish authorized editors from other visitors, including potential site vandals, which meant that all users were restricted. Another form of collateral interference therefore was the impact that filtered traffic may have on the site which is being communicated with. A final aspect of the Wikipedia case concerned the information given to users when their access was blocked. A user who tries to access an IWF URL may either receive an http://404 error response or a message from the ISP indicating why the requested page is inaccessible. The former approach lacks transparency, reducing the likelihood that such prior restraint will be subject challenge and review.

Each aspect of the Wikipedia case may be capable of being addressed from a technical or operational aspect to reduce or prevent future such overblocking arising. However, what the case illustrates is that automated monitoring systems may operate in unintended ways, particularly in a networked environment, which can result in collateral interference with lawful conduct and freedom of expression.

11.6 CONCLUDING REMARKS

This chapter argues that criminally illegal content has become an increasingly important constituent of media law in an online environment, as traditional regulatory schemes controlling content prove incapable of preventing the exposure of the UK media consumer to both UGC and foreign sourced material. One consequence is the need to focus attention on the intermediaries in the online media supply chain, the access and transmission providers, as well as the creators, editors, or distributors of criminally illegal material. Such attention is likely to comprise the implementation of technical schemes that monitor and filter such material.

In our internet era, where all information seems to be out there and available, legal debate and disputes about criminally illegal content seem less likely to be couched in the traditional language of freedom of expression and publication, as exemplified in the 1960s and 1970s trials of *Oz*[236] and *Gay News*,[237] but rather in terms of the right to monitor our consumption of such content and the potential encroachment on our rights to privacy. As a consequence, we perhaps need to shift our attention from the freedom to 'impart information' element of Article 10(1) ECHR to the right to 'receive' information. As the ECtHR noted in the *Leander* case, 'the right to freedom to receive information basically prohibits a Government from restricting a person from receiving

---

[236] *R v Anderson* [1971] 3 All ER 1152.
[237] *R v Lemon and Gay News* [1978] 3 All ER 175.

information that others wish or may be willing to impart to him'.[238] While Articles 8 and 10 have often been portrayed as representing conflicting objectives within a media context,[239] the use of filtering and blocking techniques as a means of controlling illegal content represents an area where privacy and freedom of expression have common cause.

Another consequence of this shift of focus from impart to receive is likely to be the nature of the cause of action in media cases. Historically, freedom of speech cases have usually been initiated by the party, whether state or private claimant, wishing to suppress the offending publication in question. In a receipt-based environment, we are increasingly likely to see actions brought by those wishing to preserve the freedom to receive information without oversight and review, based in privacy-related claims. While actions against government measures will be led by Article 8(1) ECHR assertions, private claims will be likely to be couched in terms of non-compliance with data protection rules and unlawful interception.

---

[238] *Leander v Sweden* (1987) 9 EHRR 433, para 74.
[239] See further Ch 7 above.

12

CULTURAL DIVERSITY IN BROADCASTING

Irini Katsirea

12.1 INTRODUCTION

In 1987, the Parliamentary Assembly of the Council of Europe issued Recommendation 1067 (1987) which focused on the cultural dimension of broadcasting in
Europe.[1] This Recommendation identified opportunities for cultural creation as a
result of the introduction of new transmission techniques such as satellite and cable
broadcasting. At the same time, it expressed concern about the likely 'reduction in
programme diversity and the erosion of socially accepted standards of behaviour', 'the
undermining of the cultural identity of smaller language groups and of the cultural
diversity of Europe as a whole', and the 'economic and thereby cultural dependence on
outside (largely commercial) factors' that might ensue from these new developments.[2]

Twenty years later, technology has moved on, but the threats to the cultural dimension of broadcasting remain. Digitalization and convergence as well as the globalization and progressive concentration of media markets mean that programme content

---

[1] Recommendation 1067 (1987) on the cultural dimension of broadcasting in Europe, 8 October 1987.
[2] ibid points 6(b), 6(c), 6(e).

becomes increasingly homogenized and is traded like any other goods by media moguls interested solely in the extension of their market shares. The Council of Europe's vision of television as a powerful cultural medium, perhaps the most powerful one, contrasts sharply with that of Dan Glickman, the President of the Motion Picture Association of America, that films have nothing to do with culture but are mere commodities.[3] One side believes that specific measures are needed to protect national and regional forms of expression, in television as much as in film and music, while the other argues that free trade—also in audiovisual goods and services—'opens minds as it opens markets, encouraging democracy and greater tolerance'.[4]

The clash between the two fronts is not merely ideological given that the wholesale inclusion of audiovisual goods and services in world trade talks has the capacity to undermine a great deal of national cultural policies such as quotas, media ownership regulations, and state aids. The proponents of cultural diversity added a new string to their bow on 18 March 2007, when the UNESCO Convention on the Protection and Promotion of the Diversity of Cultural Expressions entered into force.[5] The Convention is by no means the only source in international law backing up the protection of cultural diversity.[6] Its enactment is, however, of considerable importance given that the Convention is a binding legal instrument which was adopted with 148 countries voting in favour, with only the US and Israel voting against.

In its preamble, the Convention reaffirms that 'freedom of thought, expression and information, as well as diversity of the media, enables cultural expressions to flourish within society'.[7] It recalls further that 'linguistic diversity is a fundamental element of cultural diversity' and takes into account 'the importance of the vitality of cultures, including for persons belonging to minorities and indigenous peoples, as manifested in their freedom to create, disseminate and distribute their traditional cultural expressions'.[8] Cultural diversity of the media, especially linguistic diversity at national and regional level, will also be central to the analysis in this chapter. The emphasis will, however, be on measures for promoting cultural diversity in broadcasting adopted at European rather than international level.[9]

This chapter will first examine relevant Council of Europe standards for the protection of the linguistic identity of minorities in the media. These standards are of interest since they also—to a greater or lesser extent— inform the regulation of minority language broadcasting in the Member States of the European Union considered in the

---

[3] C Tongue, 'Who's afraid of WTO? Cultural trade and diversity', Université Libre des Bruxelles (7 May 2008) 2.

[4] ibid quoting R Zoellick, US trade representative.

[5] UNESCO Convention on the Protection and Promotion of the Diversity of Cultural Expressions, 20 October 2005 (hereinafter 'UNESCO Convention').

[6] See also the UNESCO Universal Declaration on Cultural Diversity, 2 November 2001; the Council of Europe Committee of Ministers' Declaration on Cultural Diversity, 7 December 2000.

[7] UNESCO Convention, recital 12.

[8] ibid recitals 14, 15.

[9] For the protection of minorities in the framework of the UN and of the OSCE, see I Katsirea, *Cultural Diversity and European Integration in Conflict and in Harmony* (Sakkoulas, 2001).

final section.[10] Subsequently, the focus will be on the European broadcasting quota. Together with the quota for independent European works, these instruments 'tend to be regarded as the main provisions in the TWF Directive which, by design or in effect, serve the goal of promoting cultural diversity in broadcasting'.[11] Finally, the cultural remit of public broadcasting in six Member States of the European Union—France, Germany, Greece, Italy, the Netherlands, and the UK—will be outlined and the role of public broadcasting as an alternative mechanism for advancing cultural diversity will be assessed.

12.2 CULTURAL DIVERSITY OF MEDIA CONTENT AND THE COUNCIL OF EUROPE: REGULATION OF MINORITY-LANGUAGE BROADCASTING

12.2.1 European Convention for the Protection of Human Rights and Fundamental Freedoms

The European Convention for the Protection of Human Rights and Fundamental Freedoms (ECHR), influenced by the prevailing opinion after the Second World War that individual human rights and the prohibition of discrimination were sufficient for the protection of members of minorities, does not directly guarantee minority rights.[12]

Nevertheless, individual rights are included in the Convention which could be of some consequence for the cultural and linguistic identity of minorities: the freedom of expression under Article 10 ECHR, the right to education under Article 2 of the First Protocol to the Convention, and the prohibition of discrimination under

---

[10] Ratification of relevant Council of Europe Conventions. Except where otherwise indicated, all dates appearing in columns 2 to 4 are the dates of ratification of the international instruments in question. 'S' means 'signed' as opposed to ratified.

Country	European Convention on Human Rights	Framework Convention for the Protection of National Minorities	European Charter for Regional or Minority Languages
France	03-05-1974	—	07-05-1999 (S)
Germany	05-12-1952	10-09-1997	16-09-1998
Greece	28-11-1974	22-09-1997 (S)	—
Italy	26-10-1955	03-11-1997	27-06-2000 (S)
The Netherlands	31-08-1954	16-02-2005	02-05-1996
United Kingdom	08-03-1951	15-01-1998	27-03-2001

[11] T McGonagle, 'European-level measures for promoting cultural diversity in broadcasting: quixotic tilting in a new technological era?', at <http://www.ivir.nl/staff/mcgonagle.html> (accessed 12 March 2009) 2.

[12] G Gilbert, 'The Council of Europe and Minority Rights' (1996) 18 HRQ 160; N Lerner, 'The Evolution of Minority Rights in International Law' in C Broelman, R Lefeber, and M Ziek (eds), *Peoples and Minorities in International Law* (Martinus Nijhoff, 1993) 77.

Article 14 ECHR. Regrettably, the interpretation of these provisions in the well-known *Belgian Linguistics* case has not contributed to an improvement of the status of minorities in Europe.[13] It can be argued that Article 10 ECHR implicitly protects the right of minorities to media in their own language, and also to media content from kin or neighbouring states.[14] The Commission has, however, been reluctant to accept such an interpretation.[15] Likewise, Article 14 ECHR was interpreted as laying down no obligation to adopt positive measures. Such an obligation has only been recognized to a limited extent in connection with the language used in criminal proceedings.[16]

Consideration will now be given to the relevant provisions of the Framework Convention for the Protection of National Minorities (FCNM) and of the European Charter for Regional or Minority Languages ('the Charter') that deal specifically with minorities' access to the media.

12.2.2 Framework Convention for the Protection of National Minorities

The 1995 Framework Convention for the Protection of National Minorities, which entered into force on 1 February 1998, is the first comprehensive minority rights instrument adopted by the Council of Europe. Many of its provisions set out programmatic goals, leaving states some discretion as to how to achieve them. However, the FCNM, similar to Article 27 of the International Covenant on Economic, Social and Cultural Rights (ICCPR),[17] also accords to members of minorities

---

[13] *Case Relating to Certain Aspects of the Laws on the Use of Languages in Education in Belgium* (Merits), judgment of 23 July 1968, ECtHR (Series. A), Vol 6.

[14] K Jakubowicz, 'Persons Belonging to National Minorities and the Media' (2004) 10 International Journal on Minority and Group Rights 291, 297.

[15] B de Witte, 'Surviving in Babel? Language Rights and European Integration' in Y Dinstein and M Tabory (eds), *The Protection of Minorities and Human Rights* (Martinus Nijhoff, 1992) 277.

[16] Art 6(3)(e) ECHR. However, there is no right to a free interpreter if the defendant has sufficient knowledge of the language used in court. See App No 26891/95, *Lagerblom v Sweden*, 14 January 2003, ECtHR.

[17] Art 27 ICCPR provides that: 'In those States in which ethnic, religious or linguistic minorities exist, persons belonging to such minorities shall not be denied the right, in community with the other members of their group, to enjoy their own culture, to profess and practice their own religion, or to use their own language.' Art 27 ICCPR has been, at least until recently, the central provision for the protection of minority rights under general international law. It is an individualistically oriented provision with some elements of group protection. Even if judged from the wording of Art 27 it is fair to assume that states are not obliged to take affirmative action to support minority cultures, the provision has been given more positive content through interpretation in accordance with the principle of effectiveness. See P Thornberry, 'International and European Standards on Minority Rights' in H Miall (ed), *Minority Rights in Europe: The Scope for a Transnational Regime* (Pinter, 1994) 15; F Capotorti, 'Are minorities entitled to collective international rights?' in Y Dinstein and M Tabory (eds), *The Protection of Minorities and Human Rights* (Martinus Nijhoff, 1992) 505; R Stavenhagen, 'Cultural Rights and Universal Human Rights' in A Eide, C Krause, and A Rosas (eds), *Economic, Social and Cultural Rights* (Martinus Nijhoff, 1995) 63.

individual rights which shall be exercised in community with others.[18] Although certain provisions ensure only formal equality or repeat rights already afforded in the ECHR, others impose positive obligations on states. These obligations are, however, vaguely worded, being thus open to different interpretations by the parties.[19]

A significant contribution to the protection of the linguistic identity of minorities is the obligation under Article 9 FCNM to assist them in the creation and use of radio and television broadcasts. Article 9 FCNM reflects Article 10 ECHR, but adds new dimensions to the right of freedom of expression that are of particular interest to persons belonging to national minorities.[20] Under Article 9(1) states parties undertake to ensure that persons belonging to minorities enjoy linguistic freedom and are not discriminated against in their access to the media. Moreover, they are required to ensure, 'as far as possible', that persons belonging to minorities are granted the possibility of creating and using their own print and broadcast media.[21] The caveat 'as far as possible' is not a carte blanche for the legislator, but merely alludes to the fact that states parties have to act within the constraints of their financial resources.[22] Finally, Article 9(4) requires parties to 'adopt adequate measures in order to facilitate access to the media for persons belonging to national minorities and in order to promote tolerance and permit cultural pluralism'.

The term 'access to the media' that is prominent in Article 9 FCNM is unclear. It could be interpreted as 'passive access', meaning the availability of content in a minority's language or addressing issues of concern to that minority. A broader and more preferable interpretation would, however, be that of 'active access', enabling minorities to participate in mainstream media, to own their own minority media, and to influence media legislation, regulation, and policy.[23] Active access brings potentially greater benefits to minorities. Clarification of the term 'access to the media' is therefore desirable.

The FCNM also remains silent as regards two forms of positive state action to promote minority media rights. First, it enables minorities to create and use their own media, but does not directly address the right of minorities to participate in publicly-funded media or the provision of state support for minority language

---

[18] R Dunbar, 'Implications of the European Charter for Regional and Minority Languages for British linguistic minorities' (2000) European Law Review, 46, 49; Gilbert (n 12 above) 178, 183; Milivojevic, 'Yugoslavia and the Council of Europe's Framework Convention for the Protection of National Minorities' (1999) 50 Review of International Affairs 9, 10; contra A Van Bossuyt, 'Is there an effective European legal framework for the protection of minority languages? The European Union and the Council of Europe screened' (2007) European Law Review 860, 871.

[19] P Keller, 'Re-thinking Ethnic and Cultural Rights in Europe' (1998) 18 OJLS 29, 32.

[20] T McGonagle and A Richter, 'Regulation of Minority-Language Broadcasting' (2004) IRIS plus 1, 2.

[21] Art 9(3) FCNM.

[22] T McGonagle, B Davis Noll, and M Price (eds), 'Minority-Language Related Broadcasting and Legislation in the OSCE', Study commissioned by the OSCE High Commissioner on National Minorities (April 2003), at <http://www.osce.org/hcnm/item_11_13547.html> (accessed, 6 March 2009) 4.

[23] Jakubowicz (n 14 above) 311.

broadcasting.[24] The OSCE Oslo Recommendations Regarding the Linguistic Rights of National Minorities suggest, however, that minorities should not only have the right to establish private stations, but also to actively access public media.[25] The OSCE Guidelines on the use of Minority Languages in the Broadcast Media also highlight the importance of the existence of public service broadcasting in minority languages.[26] Moreover, they invite states to consider providing financial support for minority language broadcasting through 'direct grants, favourable financing/ tax regimes, and exemption from certain fees payable on award or alteration of a licence'.[27]

Secondly, the FCNM does not expressly mention the right of persons belonging to minorities to access broadcasts from other states in the minority language. It merely recognizes in Article 17(1) the right of minorities to maintain links with citizens of other states with whom cultural identity is shared. As stated in the 1999 Report on Linguistic Rights of Persons Belonging to National Minorities in the OSCE Area: 'It may be especially important for the maintenance and development of identity for such persons to have access to the usually more developed and fuller programming available from the kin state.'[28]

Despite these shortcomings, Article 9 FCNM is an innovative provision which attaches more weight than hitherto to the cultural identity of minorities. This positive aspect is, however, moderated by the reliance of the Convention for its implementation on national legislation and governmental policies. State compliance with the Convention is monitored by means of a system of state reporting under which state reports are scrutinized by a committee of independent experts, the Advisory Committee.

The Advisory Committee considers the state report and adopts an opinion that is transmitted to the state concerned to comment on. It subsequently transmits its opinion to the Committee of Ministers, which adopts conclusions concerning the adequacy of the measures taken by the contracting party concerned to give effect to the principles of the FCNM and may also adopt recommendations in respect of the party concerned, and set a time-limit for the submission of information on their implementation.

However, the Committee's role is narrowly construed, since it is only competent to assist the Committee of Ministers in 'evaluating the adequacy of the measures taken by the Parties', but cannot actively advise the parties themselves on what they need to do

---

[24] Report on Linguistic Rights of Persons Belonging to National Minorities in the OSCE Area (OSCE, March 1999), at <http://www.osce.org/documents/hcnm/1999/03/239_en.pdf> (accessed 6 March 2009) 25; Jakubowicz (n 14 above) 311.

[25] Oslo Recommendations Regarding the Linguistic Rights of National Minorities (February 1998), at <http://www.osce.org/documents/hcnm/1998/02/2699_en.pdf> (accessed 6 March 2009) para 9.

[26] Guidelines on the use of Minority Languages in the Broadcast Media (November 2003), at <http://www.osce.org/documents/hcnm/2003/10/2242_en.pdf> (accessed 18 March 2009) para 15B.

[27] ibid para 16.

[28] OSCE, 'Report on Linguistic Rights of Persons Belonging to National Minorities in the OSCE Area' (March 1999) 25.

to give effect to the principles of the FCNM.[29] This is regrettable, the more so given that the Resolutions of the Committee of Ministers rarely take up media-related issues raised in the Advisory Committee's opinions.[30]

Finally, the effectiveness of the Convention's implementation is undermined by frequent delays to the submission of state reports and by the lack of sanctioning powers of the Advisory Committee or the Committee of Ministers for parties' non-compliance with the recommendations.[31]

12.2.3 European Charter for Regional or Minority Languages

The 1992 European Charter for Regional or Minority Languages, which entered into force on 1 March 1998, contributes substantially to the preservation and development of the cultural identity of minorities through the obligation of states to adopt positive measures for the upgrading of the use of minority languages in important areas, including in the media. Because the Charter aims to promote regional or minority languages, not minorities, it does not establish any individual or collective rights for the speakers of these languages.[32] In this sense, the Language Charter falls behind the FCNM, which espouses a rights-based approach.

The relevant provision for the broadcasting sector is Article 11 which is also modelled on Article 10 ECHR. In the Charter's gradated approach, a wide discretion is given to the Member States to choose among a ladder of measures ranging from the very far-reaching ones, such as the creation, in public broadcasting, of at least one radio station and one television channel in the regional and minority languages, to more modest ones, such as the making of adequate provision so that broadcasters offer programmes in the regional or minority languages. Even if states resort to the lowest options to fulfil their obligations, a considerable improvement of the position of minorities will have been brought about.

However, the Charter's legal and political clout in the European Union is mitigated by the low number of ratifications, or even signatures, to date.[33] Also, the monitoring of the Charter—similar to that of the FCNM—has shown that states have often implemented the Charter in a formalistic and minimalist manner rather than taking positive, substantive measures, suitable to further the protection of minority languages in a meaningful way.[34]

---

[29] Art 26 (1) FCNM; Jakubowicz (n 14 above) 312.
[30] ibid 313.
[31] Van Bossuyt (n 18 above) 872.
[32] ibid 872, 873; Dunbar (n 18 above) 49.
[33] Only 23 states have ratified the Charter to date, of which 15 are Member States of the EU. Four Member States have only signed it. Eight of the 27 Member States have not even signed the Charter; for an update, see <http://www.conventions.coe.int> (accessed 18 March 2009).
[34] Van Bossuyt (n 18 above) 873, 874; Dunbar (n 18 above).

12.3 CULTURAL DIVERSITY OF MEDIA CONTENT AND THE EUROPEAN UNION: THE EUROPEAN BROADCASTING QUOTA

12.3.1 Television without Frontiers Directive

Chapter III of the Television without Frontiers Directive (TWF Directive) on the promotion of distribution and production of television programmes has proved to be one of the most controversial areas coordinated by the Directive.[35] Two different kinds of quota are laid down in Chapter III: the so-called 'European quota' in Article 4 in connection with Article 6; and the 'independent quota' in Article 5. Article 4 requires the reservation of a majority proportion of the transmission time for European works, while Article 5 orders the reservation of 10 per cent of the transmission time, alternatively of 10 per cent of the broadcasters' programming budget, to independent productions. The European quota is a pure broadcasting quota, while the independent quota is a hybrid between a broadcasting and a production quota. The European quota has been a bone of contention since the adoption of the Directive, not least because it is more difficult to achieve for broadcasters than the independent quota.[36]

The context in which the European quota has been adopted is all too well known: a European broadcasting services market increasingly dependent on imported films and serials, the great majority of which come from the US.[37] The dominance of the American film industry is attributed in general to the greater acceptance of its programmes by the viewers. Moreover, American programmes can be offered at more competitive prices overseas, given that their costs have already been amortized at home.[38] It has also been predicted that, paradoxically, this situation was likely to be accentuated by the creation of a single broadcasting market, which—in conjunction with the proliferation of channels—would enhance the competition among broadcasters for productions offering better cost/audience relations.[39]

---

[35] Council Directive (EC) 97/36 of 30 June 1997 amending Council Directive (EEC) 89/552 on the coordination of certain provisions laid down by law, regulation and administrative action in Member States concerning the pursuit of television broadcasting activities [1997] OJ L202/60.

[36] F Hurard, 'The Production Quota System of the EU-Television Directive' in *Europäisches Medienrecht—Fernsehen und seine gemeinschaftsrechtliche Regelung*, Schriftenreihe des Instituts für Europäisches Medienrecht, vol 18 (Jehle-Rehm, 1998) 35.

[37] R Frohne, 'Die Quotenregelungen im nationalen und im europäischen Recht' (1989) 8–9 *Zeitschrift für Urheber- und Medienrecht* 390; V Salvatore, 'Quotas on TV Programmes and EEC Law' (1992) 29 CML Rev 967, 974; A von Bogdandy, 'Europäischer Protektionismus im Medienbereich: Zu Inhalt und Rechtmäßigkeit der Quotenregelungen in der Fernsehrichtlinie' (1992) 1 *Europäische Zeitschrift für Wirtschaftsrecht* 9, 11.

[38] D Graham and Associates Ltd, 'Impact Study of Measures (Community and National) concerning the Promotion of Distribution and Production of TV Programmes provided for under Art. 25 (a) of the TV without Frontiers Directive'. Final Report (24 May 2005) 180.

[39] B de Witte, 'The European Content Requirement in the EC Television Directive—Five Years after' (1995) I *Yearbook of Media and Entertainment Law* 107; BJ Drijber, 'The Revised Television Without Frontiers Directive: Is it Fit for the Next Century?' (1999) 36 CML Rev 87, 107.

It becomes clear against this backdrop that the European quota emerged as a counterbalance to the expansion of the American programme industry. By promoting 'markets of sufficient size for television productions in the Member States to recover necessary investments'[40] it was hoped artificially to replicate US conditions in Europe. The Commission considered that the main causes for the decline in the market share of European films were the partitioning of national markets and the fragmentation of distribution structures.[41] Only 20 per cent of European films go beyond their national frontiers on account of cultural and linguistic diversity in Europe and the lack of an overall distribution strategy. The European quota was expected to remove barriers between national markets by encouraging the production and distribution of European programmes. This industrial policy objective was backed up by the cultural policy argument, mainly advocated by France, that European identity needed to be protected from US cultural imperialism.

However, a significant number of Member States of the European Community have not been sympathetic to these arguments, the UK, Germany, and Denmark being the fiercest critics, as well as the US itself. The criticism of the Member States has been directed at the inefficiency of the quota and at the lack of Community competence, while the US claimed its incompatibility with the GATT Agreement. A further issue, which has been extensively discussed in legal literature, is whether the quota unduly interferes with the broadcasters' freedom of expression and is, therefore, in breach of Article 10(1) ECHR.[42]

12.3.2 Audiovisual Media Services Directive[43]

These arguments have been rehearsed all over again in the framework of the 2003 consultation for the review of the TWF Directive. The findings of this consultation process were summarized by the Commission in an issue paper released in July 2005. The Commission held that 'there was no majority trend in favour of changing the present regulations in substance. Whereas producers, scriptwriters, and trade unions proposed raising the majority proportion for European works, some Member States and private broadcasters considered broadcast quotas to be 'an [sic] disproportionate

---

[40] Directive EEC 89/552, Recital (20).

[41] Commission of the European Communities, Strategy options to strengthen the European programme industry in the context of the audiovisual policy of the European Union (6 April 1994), COM (94) 96 final, 5 *et seq*, 21.

[42] de Witte (n 39 above) 128; Drijber (n 39 above) 111; Salvatore (n 37 above) 984 *et seq*; M Dolmans, 'Quotas Without Content: The Questionable Legality of European Content Quotas under the Television Without Frontiers Directive' (1995) 8 Entertainment Law Review 332; J Gundel, 'Nationale Programmquoten im Rundfunk: Vereinbar mit den Grundfreiheiten und der Rundfunkfreiheit des Gemeinschaftsrechts?' (1998) 12 *Zeitschrift für Urheber- und Medienrecht* 1008 *et seq*; von Bogdandy (n 37 above) 15.

[43] Council Directive (EC) 2007/65 of 11 December 2007 amending Council Directive (EEC) 89/552 on the coordination of certain provisions laid down by law, regulation and administrative action in Member States concerning the pursuit of television broadcasting activities [2007] OJ L332/27.

restriction of broadcasters scheduling freedom. A majority of Member State were in favour of keeping the status quo.'[44] Accordingly, the quota provisions have been incorporated *in toto* in the Audiovisual Media Services Directive (AVMS Directive) as far as linear services are concerned.

Recent Commission Communications on the application of the quotas indicate that scheduling of European works has risen throughout the European Union.[45] The independent impact study, carried out in accordance with Article 25a of the Directive, found that besides their impact on the scheduling of European works, the quotas have contributed to the cultural objective of creating new outlets for creative works and to the strengthening of the European audiovisual industry. Further, it concluded that the average proportion of European works has increased more in Member States that have placed significant additional cultural requirements on broadcasters and that have implemented Articles 4 and 5 in a prescriptive manner than in those that have implemented them flexibly.[46]

However, considerable doubts exist as to whether the increased scheduling of European works can really be attributed to the European quota. It has been argued that it is the preference of national audiences for domestically-produced content and the fact that such content is cheaper in the long run that have led to the increased transmission of European works.[47] The point has also been made that the market has changed since the 1980s, when the few existing private broadcasters were forced to cover their programming needs with inexpensive US productions. Producers can now offer their content to a plethora of broadcasters that prefer to broadcast domestic works.[48]

The consultation process, being part of the wider project of extending the TWF Directive to non-linear audiovisual services, also asked the question whether Articles 4 and 5 should cover such services. This extension of the scope of the quotas was seen as a move to create a more level playing field between broadcasters and service providers. While some stakeholders, especially producers, argued that non-linear service providers should also be obliged to transmit a majority proportion of European works, others feared that such a move would harm the development of a nascent sector and encourage delocalization.

---

[44] European Commission, Issues Paper for the Liverpool Audiovisual Conference, 'Cultural Diversity and the Promotion of European and Independent Audiovisual Production' (July 2005) 1 (hereinafter 'Issues Paper').

[45] Sixth Commission communication on the application of Articles 4 and 5 of Directive (EEC) 89/552 'Television without Frontiers', as amended by Directive (EC) 97/36, for the period 2001–2002, 28 July 2004, COM (2004) 524 final; Seventh Commission communication on the application of Articles 4 and 5 of Directive (EEC) 89/552 'Television without Frontiers', as amended by Directive (EC) 97/36, for the period 2003–2004, 14 August 2006, COM (2006) 459 final.

[46] Graham *et al* (n 38 above) 180.

[47] Written contribution of the Federal Republic of Germany, at <http://ec.europa.eu/avpolicy/reg/history/consult/consultation_2003/contributions/index_en.htm> (accessed 12 March 2009).

[48] Written contribution of the *Verband Privater Rundfunk und Telekommunikation* (VPRT), at <http://ec.europa.eu/avpolicy/reg/history/consult/consultation_2003/contributions/index_en.htm> (accessed 12 March 2009).

The Commission decided to strike a middle path. In its proposal for the AVMS Directive it did not impose a quota for on-demand services but asked Member States to ensure that such services provided by media service providers under their jurisdiction promote, where practicable and by appropriate means, production of and access to European works.[49] This provision has now been moved to Article 3i(1) of the AVMS Directive, which clarifies further that: 'Such promotion could relate, *inter alia*, to the financial contribution made by such services to the production and rights acquisition of European works or to the share and/or prominence of European works in the catalogue of programmes proposed by the service.' It is included in a separate Chapter IIB, which is entitled 'Provisions applicable only to on-demand audiovisual media services'.

Article 3i contains more than just a political signal to the effect that non-linear services will be expected to contribute to the promotion of European works.[50] The comparison with the wording of Articles 4 and 5 of the TWF Directive leaves no doubt that Article 3i is also intended to be binding, the qualification 'where practicable and by appropriate means' notwithstanding. Member States' reporting obligations under Article 3i(2) and the evaluation process under Article 3i(3) also support this conclusion.

Extending the obligation to promote European works to the non-linear sector seems like a precipitate move given that the European quota's expediency and legality were already heavily contested as far as the linear sector was concerned. And while the effect of the 1989 quotas on a mature broadcasting industry was foreseeable, the same does not apply to the rapidly growing non-linear sector. The Commission only states by way of explanation that non-linear audiovisual media services have the potential partially to replace linear services.[51] There is no certainty, though, that this will in fact happen. Moreover, while it is possible to steer viewing behaviour to some extent in traditional television broadcasting, this becomes quite impossible in an environment where there are no capacity constraints.[52]

The Commission assumes that the increased availability of European works will be of benefit to these new services. No evidence is, however, adduced that on-demand services will benefit from the obligation to promote European content nor that they will be prepared to observe it. It is possible that they, much like the private broadcasting sector in its beginnings, will prefer to transmit cheap, massively available

[49] Proposal for a Directive of the European Parliament and of the Council amending Council Directive (EEC) 89/552 on the coordination of certain provisions laid down by law, regulation or administrative action in Member States concerning the pursuit of television broadcasting activities, 13 December 2005, COM (2005) 646 final, Art 3f.

[50] See European Commission, 'Cultural Diversity' (n 44 above) 2; contra C Holtz-Bacha, 'Die Neufassung der europäischen Fernsehregulierung: Von der Fernseh- zur Mediendiensterichtlinie' (2007) 2 *Media Perspektiven* 113, 121.

[51] Amended AVMSD proposal, Recital (35).

[52] JW van den Bos, 'No Frontiers: The New EU Proposal on Audiovisual Media Services' (2006) 4 Entertainment Law Review 109, 111.

non-European material.[53] The concern that they might even leave the EU area so as to escape such obligations is more justified in their case than in the case of the traditional broadcasting industry.

The focus of the present analysis will, however, not be so much on the rules applicable to the non-linear services as on the European quota rule and its cultural policy rationale.[54]

12.3.3 The European quota's cultural conception

The quota's cultural policy rationale was at best implicit in the text of the original TWF Directive. Even though cultural policy objectives played an important role in the legislative history of the European quota, no word was said about them in the preamble to Directive (EEC) 89/552.[55] This omission was rectified in the amended Directive (EC) 97/36, which mentioned Article 128(4) (now Article 151(4)) EC in its preamble.[56] Without clearly saying so, the 25th recital suggested that there is a cultural agenda behind the quota.

The linkage between the quota and cultural diversity became even more explicit during the latest revision of the TWF Directive.[57] The preamble to the AVMS Directive contains numerous references in this direction. Recitals (1), (4), (5), and (8) highlight the cultural nature of audiovisual media services and their importance for the protection of cultural diversity. Recital (48) takes up this theme in the context of on-demand audiovisual media services by stating that: 'On-demand audiovisual media services have the potential to partially replace television broadcasting. Accordingly, they should, where practicable, promote the production and distribution of European works and thus contribute actively to the promotion of cultural diversity.'

In the following, the European quota's professed contribution to the objective of promoting cultural diversity in traditional broadcasting will be questioned. However, many of the criticisms of the quota's cultural policy conception are also highly relevant as far as Article 3i, the European quota's non-identical twin for the non-linear sector, is concerned.

There are three main criticisms of the European quota's purported relevance for the promotion of cultural diversity. First, the quota has been criticized by

---

[53] T Kleist, 'Fernsehrichtlinie: Konvergenz und Wettbewerb bei audiovisuellen Angeboten' (2006) 2 *Multimedia und Recht* 61, 62.

[54] For an analysis of the European quota's legitimacy in terms of its internal market and industrial policy rationales, see I Katsirea, *Public Broadcasting and European Law. A Comparative Examination of Public Service Obligations in Six Member States* (Kluwer, 2008) 279 *et seq.*

[55] Explanatory comment to the Commission's original proposal, 6 June 1986, COM (86) 146 final/2, point 30; Communication from the Commission to the Council and the European Parliament on the application of Arts 4 and 5 of Directive (EEC) 89/552 Television without frontiers, 3 March 1994, COM (94) 57 final, 4; K McDonald, 'How Would You Like Your Television: With or Without Borders and With or Without Culture—A New Approach to Media Regulation in the European Union' (1999) 22 Fordham International Law Journal 2004.

[56] Directive (EC) 97/36, Recital (25).

[57] See European Commission, 'Issues Paper' (n 44 above).

commentators for placing itself on the side of cultural protectionism without taking a definite stance towards the issue of the cultural implications of media flows. Secondly, small Member States have voiced concerns that the quota might fling the door of their audiovisual markets wide open to productions in one of the big languages. Lastly, the difficulties with the all-inclusive definition of a 'European work' in Article 6 will be highlighted.

12.3.4 The European quota as a means of cultural dissociation

The European quota's cultural conception has to be seen against the background of a heated dispute in communication studies[58] concerning the role played by transnational flows of television programmes in the formation and development of cultural identities. While liberal internationalists favour the cross-fertilization of ideas facilitated by means of transnational flows of television programmes, their opponents warn against the resulting erosion of cultural identity.

The latter view, based on theories of media imperialism, was espoused by UNESCO during the 1970s, when it proclaimed the need to establish a new world information and communication order (NWICO).[59] This new order would replace the present state of domination of the Third World by the developed countries, both in its economy and communications, by a more balanced flow of information. In order for vulnerable cultures to develop self-reliantly, they would need to dissociate themselves from the existing economic and political dependency structures. The theory of media imperialism has been criticized for its failure to grasp the complex process of reception by viewers of a television programme originating in a different culture.[60] It was argued that message reception is not a uni-dimensional process: audiences interpret programmes in the light of their own cultural background.

The European quota is designed to slow the stream of US programmes, contributing thus to the dissociation of the European audiovisual industry from American cultural dominance. At first sight, it may appear that the drafters of the quota endorsed the discourse of media imperialism and transposed the NWICO problematic from the developing world to Europe. Hence, criticism was levelled against the Community for not having taken divergent views into account and for not having provided a well-grounded analysis of the relationship of cultural identity to television viewing.

[58] See Ch 1 above, for a reference to the role of communications theory underlying media law and policy.

[59] See UNESCO, *Many Voices, One World: Towards a New, More Just and More Efficient World Information and Communication Order* (Kogan Page, 1980); CJ Hamelink, *Cultural Autonomy in Global Communications: Planning National Information Policy* (Centre for the Study of Communications and Culture, 1988).

[60] See C Sparks and C Roach, 'Editorial' (1990) 12 *Media, Culture and Society* 275; M Tracey, 'The Poisoned Chalice? International Television and the Idea of Dominance' (1985) 114(4) *Daedalus* 17.

A commentator remarked sharply that Article 4 'would appear to be, at best, an intuitive thrust in the direction of a culture policy'.[61]

Indeed, analysed along these lines, the European quota raises more questions than it provides answers. It conspicuously fails to answer the question as to why cultural identities in Europe are more affected by US productions than by European ones.[62] The assumption that European cultures share greater affinity is questionable. Europe embraces a multiplicity of very different cultures, which often display stronger ties with their non-European counterparts. Spanish culture is probably more akin to the Latin-American than to Northern European cultures and Great Britain may find itself to be culturally more related to other Commonwealth countries than to the Balkans.[63]

However, communication scientists have by no means reached definite conclusions about the impact of the exposure to mass-mediated material.[64] The capitulation of science to the intricate problem under discussion is best captured in the following passage: 'It is claimed that this mass of material coming in from outside is both erasing traditional cultures and inhibiting the emergence of authentic cultural changes. There is no clear evidence that this is in fact happening, nor indeed any that it is not.'[65]

In view of these uncertainties, it is understandable that the European Community did not attempt to tackle the problem of the cultural impact of television along these lines. It approached it from a different angle instead, based on the forceful idea that the control of broadcasting by foreign productions has an injurious influence upon indigenous cultural life, an idea that is attractive to both the supporters and the opponents of the cultural domination thesis. It is precisely the atrophy of the European audiovisual industry due to the withdrawal of resources from domestic production that the European quota aims to fight in the first place. This is a cultural as much as an economic objective.

12.3.5 The European quota: a poisoned chalice for small European states?

Not surprisingly, the adoption of the European quota brought to the fore the long-standing divide between large and smaller European countries. While large countries with a strong audiovisual industry aspire to the improved distribution of their programmes, small countries fear that the flow of English, French, and German

---

[61] P Keller, 'The New Television Without Frontiers Directive' (1997/98) III *Yearbook of Media and Entertainment Law* 183.

[62] See P Schlesinger, 'From Cultural Protection to Political Culture? Media Policy and the European Union' in L-E Cederman (ed), *Constructing Europe's Identity: The External Dimension* (Lynne Rienner, 2001) 91, 99.

[63] JD Donaldson, '"Television Without Frontiers": The Continuing Tension between Liberal Free Trade and European Cultural Integrity' (1996) 20 Fordham International Law Journal 150, 155.

[64] DG Carrie and ASC Ehrenberg, 'Is Television All that Important?' (1992) 20(4–5) *Intermedia*, 18; ME Price, 'Globalization and National Identity on Television' (1992) 20(4–5) *Intermedia* 9.

[65] T Hollins, *Beyond Broadcasting: Into the Cable Age* (Broadcasting Research Unit, 1984), cited in Tracey (n 60 above) 38.

programmes into their audiovisual markets will be one-way with no flow in the opposite direction taking place.[66] These fears seem justified at first sight in view of the low audiovisual production capacity of small European countries linked to their restricted cultural or linguistic area. Their markets are confined, so that funding available for domestic production is limited. Their programmes are rarely successful in foreign markets, whereas their viewers are greatly exposed to imported programmes by way of a dense cable network.

Ironically, if the European quota produced the intended result—the increased circulation of programmes between the Member States—larger states would probably be in a better position to reap the benefit. However, monitoring reports have painted a different picture. The Commission has admitted that prime-time viewing is still dominated by domestic and US productions.[67] Highest audience ratings are attained by the transmission of national material. The proportion of non-national material in the European works transmitted has stagnated at a low level. It grew from 10.4 per cent in 1993 to 11.9 per cent in 2002 on primary channels, mainly public ones.[68] However, the share of qualifying transmission time devoted to European works in general has grown at a faster rate during the same period. As a result, non-national material now forms a slightly smaller proportion of the totality of European works broadcast than in 1993.[69]

Admittedly, smaller Member States that share a language with a larger neighbouring Member State, such as Austria, Belgium, and Ireland, have larger proportions of imported European works shown on television. Larger Member States, such as France, Germany, Italy, Spain and the UK, have the smallest proportion. At one end of the spectrum is Ireland, where a majority proportion (53.3 per cent) of non-domestic European works is broadcast. At the other end of the spectrum is the UK, with virtually zero per cent of non-domestic European works.

Between 1993 and 2002, the share of non-domestic European works grew in those Member States where the proportion was already high, while it declined in those Member States where it was historically low.[70] Small Member States that do not share the same language with a larger state, such as Greece and Portugal, continue to broadcast only a small proportion of such works. Consequently, the divide between smaller and larger countries as regards the transmission of imported European works cannot be attributed to the European quota but to the linguistic and cultural affinity between

[66] J Drijvers, 'Community Broadcasting: A Manifesto for the Media Policy of Small European Countries' (1992) 14 *Media, Culture and Society* 194; JC Burgelman and C Pauwels, 'Audiovisual Policy and Cultural Identity in Small European States: The Challenge of a Unified Market' (1992) 14 *Media, Culture and Society* 177.
[67] COM (94) 96 final, 27.
[68] European Commission, 'Issues Paper' (n 44 above) 4.
[69] Graham *et al* (n 38 above) 183.
[70] ibid 108.

some of these countries, as well as the lower price and better quality of works from larger neighbouring countries.[71]

As the Commission admitted in its Issues Paper, these trends suggest that 'Article 4 may have reinforced national objectives to protect and encourage the domestic content sector rather than fostering a truly European market in programming and encouraging the exchange/circulation of European TV programmes within Europe.'[72] Findings of a considerable decrease in the programming of domestic films in the early years after the adoption of the Directive do not hold true anymore.[73] The total volume of European works has risen over the period from 1993 to 2002.[74] This growth is mainly attributable to a rise in domestic content. European programming is perceived to be too informed by a specific national culture and taste to appeal beyond its home market, while US programming tends to attract a global audience.[75] The substantial trade deficit between television companies in the European Union and North America remains. The impact study has not been able to prove that, in the absence of the quotas, the trade deficit with the US would have been larger nor that measures to promote the circulation of programmes within the European Union have also promoted exports.[76]

During the latest review process, the Commission envisaged the creation of incentives for the increased distribution of European co-productions so as to improve the exchange of European programmes within Europe. It was argued that such incentives would possibly lead to a more integrated and internationally competitive 'European' film industry and foster a deeper understanding of Europe's cultural diversity and a wider acceptance of the European integration process.[77] Only a minority of stakeholders, mainly film producers, were in favour of a sub-quota for non-domestic European works or of a recommendation to encourage the circulation of such works. These proposals found their way into Recital (50) of the AVMS Directive, which urges Member States, when implementing Article 4, to make provision for broadcasters to include an adequate share of co-produced European works or of European works of non-domestic origin.

It is submitted that engaging in more European co-productions would not necessarily enhance Europe's cultural diversity. Intervention of this sort would only favour those Member States best able to support co-production due to the size of

---

[71] Contra J Harrison and L Woods, *European Broadcasting Law and Policy* (Cambridge University Press, 2007) 253, who argue that the advantage enjoyed by large Member States over small ones in the same language group is also attributable to the conflation of the idea of 'European' with individual Member States as opposed to pan-European productions.

[72] European Commission, 'Issues Paper' (n 44 above) 4.

[73] See E de Bens, M Kelly, and M Bakke, 'Television Content: Dallasification of Culture?' in K Siune and W Truettzschler (eds), *Dynamics of Media Politics: Broadcast and Electronic Media in Western Europe* (Sage, 1992) 75, 91, 94.

[74] According to the impact study, the average proportion of qualifying transmission hours devoted to European works for the channels covered has risen from 52.1% in 1993 to 57.4% in 2002.

[75] Graham *et al* (n 38 above) 183.

[76] ibid.

[77] European Commission, 'Issues Paper' (n 44 above) 4.

their broadcasting industries.[78] The proposal that broadcasters should transmit an adequate share of European works of non-domestic origin is entirely consistent with the European quota's rationale. It signifies an effort to stimulate the cross-border movement of programmes, not just the transmission of a majority proportion of European works.

While the increased circulation of European works would also contribute to the filling of the European quota, causality does not work the other way round. Even though the European quota is overfilled in most Member States, viewers are not being exposed to foreign programmes but get to see more of the same home-grown material. The Commission noted in its Issues Paper that national language quotas may have acted as a barrier to intra-Community trade.[79] Indeed, the paradoxical coexistence of European and national quotas is the most eloquent admission of defeat in view of cultural segregation in Europe. It also brings the point home that filling the quota has little to do with the exchange of European programmes. The impact study suggests that Member States operating significant additional cultural requirements have attained higher percentages of European works in their schedules and yet such requirements obstruct intra-Community trade.

The Commission's admonition to Member States to bear in mind the quota's industrial policy rationale when implementing the Directive is understandable against this backdrop. However, the fact that this admonition only found its way into the Directive's recitals speaks volumes. Imposing an obligation on private broadcasters to transmit works from other Member States would go against their commercial logic and their need to prioritize audience share over programme choice. The public funding received by public broadcasters would perhaps allow them to carry such a public service obligation. However, this would only exacerbate the inroads made into the broadcasting sovereignty of the Member States by the already existing European quota rule. Obliging them to transmit non-national works would be quite incompatible with the pronouncement in the Amsterdam Protocol that Member States are responsible for conferring, defining, and organizing the public service remit.[80]

Given that there is little scope for the adoption of further, more binding measures at Community level to increase the circulation of European works of non-domestic origin, it becomes quite clear that cultural diversity should be protected otherwise. The preference of national audiences for domestically-produced content should be respected and content regulations at the national level should be accepted as the most efficient way of promoting the cultures of the Member States.

It is very doubtful whether the increase in the volume of European works in the last decade can be attributed to the European quota in the first place or rather to domestic measures and the viewers' preference for domestic content. Even if the European

---

[78] Written contribution of the Department for Culture, Media and Sport, at <http://ec.europa.eu/avpolicy/reg/history/consult/consultation_2003/contributions/index_en.htm> (accessed 12 March 2009).
[79] European Commission, 'Issues Paper' (n 44 above) 4.
[80] Protocol on the System of Public Broadcasting in the Member States [1997] OJ C340/109.

quota has had an impact on the European schedule output, it is even more doubtful that it has strengthened the European audiovisual industry. The many loopholes in Article 4 have rendered it powerless to improve the balance of trade with the US and to lessen the reliance on American programmes.

Consequently, even though the European quota is not the harmful device smaller countries have imagined, its potential for contributing to the invigoration of their programme industries and hence to the flowering of their audiovisual cultures is limited. Nor is it obvious that, in drafting the European quota, any consideration was given to regional and minority cultures in the European Union. Even though productions at regional or sub-regional level qualify as 'European works', certain genres that are particularly suitable for such productions, ie news and sports events, are excluded from the transmission time that counts towards the obligation to achieve the quota.[81] The next section will look at further shortcomings in the definition of a 'European work', betraying the quota's chief preoccupation with industrial policy rather than cultural concerns.

12.3.6 What is a 'European work'?

The cultural conception of the European quota is not only marred by the lack of commitment of governments and market players to overcome the entrenched partitioning of national markets. In view of the increasingly international character of the television business it is also unlikely that the definition of 'European works' under Article 1(n) of the AVMS Directive (ex Article 6 of the TWF Directive) can guarantee the expression of a European cultural identity.[82]

Article 6 of the TWF Directive distinguished in a rather complex way between European works *per se* and other works, which are deemed to be European works. The first category was divided into three sub-categories: works from the Member States, works from European third states party to the European Convention on Transfrontier Television, and works from European third countries with which the Community has concluded agreements relating to the audiovisual sector.

So as to determine when a work originates from a certain country, Article 6(2) stipulated rules of origin. Emphasis was placed on the country of residence of the authors and workers, who made the work, and on the establishment of the producer, who either made the programme or supervised and controlled it or made a preponderant contribution to the total co-production costs. The criterion of the producer's establishment, which is also taken up in Article 1(n) of the AVMS Directive, is responsive to industrial policy objectives, but does not guarantee the European character of a work. The term 'producer' is ambiguous since it could mean the production company or the individual

---

[81] Harrison and Woods (n 71 above) 254.
[82] J Harrison and L Woods, 'Television Quotas: Protecting European Culture?' (2001) 1 Entertainment Law Review 11.

who has the role of producer in respect of a specific programme.[83] If the former is the case, the criterion of the producer's establishment can also be fulfilled by American subsidiaries.

The criterion of the workers' residence, more sensitive to cultural considerations, is only half-heartedly committed to them, since it cannot guarantee a specifically European character of the works either. The workers' nationality might be more suitable a criterion for this purpose. Even so, one should not necessarily assume that authors and workers of a certain nationality would also produce works reflecting their cultural background.[84] Globalization and the pressures of the marketplace might mean that works with a universal outlook are more in demand. And there is nothing wrong with this if content is produced which, informed by a specific culture, contributes to defining a universal ethos, a collective imagination. Cultures need exchange and openness so as to develop. If they become insular and narrow-minded, they will fossilize and perish.[85] Unfortunately, programmes of cultural merit, combining the national, regional, or local with the universal, remain the exception. More often than not, homogenized, bland content of broad appeal is produced instead.

The second category in Article 6 of the TWF Directive, that of fictitious European works, comprised works fulfilling the criterion of the personnel's residence, but none of the conditions related to the producer. These were considered to be European works under Article 6(5) 'to an extent corresponding to the proportion of the contribution of Community co-producers to the total production costs'. The idea of measuring the European quality of a work by financial criteria alone was abstruse.[86] What is more, the said formula could not always account for the source of financing of an audiovisual work, given that co-producers do not always co-finance a production. The source of financing is hence not necessarily apparent from the production budget.[87]

The revised Directive (EC) 97/36 added a new category of international co-productions with third countries under a newly inserted fourth paragraph. This category differed from the European works *per se* under Article 6(1), in that the works did not have to be made with authors and workers residing in the Community or in European third states party to the European Convention on Transfrontier Television.

This short overview of the TWF Directive's requirements on the European origin of works falling under the quota demonstrates that an all-embracing definition was adopted, which tried to determine what is Europe along cultural rather than

---

[83] Harrison and Woods (n 71 above) 255.

[84] ibid 257.

[85] L Castellina, 'What future for European cultural policy? Summary of debates', a seminar jointly organized by Friends of Europe and Eurocinema with the support of the French Ministry of European Affairs and the Culture 2000 Programme of the European Union in co-operation with Vivendi Universal Paris, Centre des Conférences Internationales Kléber, 12 February 2002, quoted by Tongue (n 3 above) 14.

[86] Harrison and Woods (n 82 above) 12; and (n 71 above) 246.

[87] Commission of the European Communities, Commission staff working paper on certain legal aspects relating to cinematographic and other audiovisual works, 11 April 2001, SEC (2001) 619, 10.

geo-political lines.[88] Still, the outcome was rather bewildering, given that a work produced entirely in Vladivostock was considered to be European. While, however, the satisfaction of the quota requirement by films from Vladivostock was unlikely to make a difference in practical terms, the same did not apply to the inclusion of international co-productions between Member States and third countries.

This aspect of Article 6 has been fiercely criticized, not only because it diluted the notion of a European identity to be protected by the European quota, but also because it disguised films produced by the major US production and distribution companies as 'European works'.[89] The distinction between audiovisual material embedded in the multinational production and distribution chains and such that is not integrated in this structure is decisive, since only the latter provide a space for genuine, European cultural expression in the film sector. Article 6 dressed the wolf in sheep's clothing by putting more emphasis on the participation of European creative personnel than on European investment. These inconsistencies are indicative of the lack of political will behind the European quota.

The consultation process for the review of the Directive posed the question whether a more detailed definition of 'European works' was needed so as to increase legal certainty for operators, given that Member States have implemented this definition in many different ways. The views were sharply divided concerning the need for further harmonization of the definition of 'European works'. Some Member States perceived the current definition as being satisfactory, giving them sufficient flexibility to implement it in relation to their production landscape.[90] Others were in favour of harmonization and proposed following the definition contained in the European Convention on Cinematographic Co-production.[91]

In view of this controversy, the core of the current definition was left untouched. Its place was moved under the Common Position from Article 6 to Article 1(n) of Chapter I together with all the other definitions. The only two amendments of the 'European works' definition that were already suggested by the Commission in its initial Proposal and that were agreed upon in the Common Position are the following. First, the

[88] R Collins, *Broadcasting and Audio-Visual Policy in the European Single Market* (John Libbey, 1994) 71.

[89] S Venturelli, *Liberalizing the European Media: Politics, Regulation and the Public Sphere* (Clarendon Press, 1998) 204; see speech by J Dondelinger, 'Broadcasting in the Single Market' in D Goldberg and R Wallace (eds), *Regulating the Audiovisual Industry: The Second Phase*, Current EC Legal Development Series (Butterworths, 1991) 193: 'This so-called "quota system" has become much less controversial than it was at the time of the adoption of the Directive. Our American friends have learned to live with the idea. Indeed, transatlantic co-operation between companies has never been so great.'

[90] See, for instance, the written contributions of the Federal Republic of Germany and of the UK at <http://ec.europa.eu/avpolicy/reg/history/consult/consultation_2003/contributions/index_en.htm> (accessed 12 March 2009).

[91] See Communication from the Commission to the Council, the European Parliament, the European Economic and Social Committee and the Committee of the Regions, The future of European Regulatory Audiovisual Policy, 15 December 2003, COM (2003) 784 final, 13.

third category of European works, namely those originating from other European third countries with which the Community has concluded agreements related to the audiovisual sector, has been modified. Whereas Article 6(3) also applied to productions made exclusively by producers established in one or more of these European third countries provided that the authors and workers were resident in one or more European states, the new definition only applies to co-productions fulfilling the conditions defined in each of these agreements. Secondly, the last category of fictitious partially European works under Article 6(5) has been removed, presumably due to their very tenuous characterization as 'European'. However, the category of international co-productions of doubtful European credentials under Article 6(4) has found its way into the AVMS Directive.

All in all, it is questionable whether Article 1(n) is conducive to the protection of European cultural diversity. Neither this definition nor, for that matter, the European quota rule, promote programmes representative of European cultures.[92] The main concern of the Directive is the development of commercial large-scale productions appealing to an international audience.[93] In this context, the introduction of 'cultural' aspects in Article 6 has been contemplated. However, the adoption of cultural criteria would exacerbate the intrusiveness of the quota mechanism without succeeding in refining its coarse nature.

12.4 CULTURAL DIVERSITY AND THE PUBLIC SERVICE REMIT

Having examined the inherent conceptual limitations and contradictions of the European broadcasting quota, this section will turn its attention to alternative mechanisms for promoting cultural diversity in broadcasting. An often forgotten, yet ideal candidate to perform this task is public broadcasting. Its commitment to cater for the democratic order and for the cultural life of a nation without being dependent in the same way as commercial broadcasters on high viewing figures enable it to offer a wide range of subject matter.

Even though there is no generally recognized definition of public broadcasting, its essential characteristics can be summed up as universality of access, universality

---

[92] ARD and ZDF, 'EG-Politik im Bereich des Rundfunks', 91. cf the cultural quotas of the Australian Content Standard as interpreted in the judgment of the High Court of Australia, *Project Blue Sky v Australian Broadcasting Authority* (1998) HCA 28, 28 April 1998, S41/1997. The main criterion for Australian content is whether a programme reflects the Australian identity and culture, while the nationality of the actors, authors, or producers is less important. See CB Graber, 'The Stumbling Block of Trade Liberalisation' in D Geradin and D Luff (eds), *The WTO and Global Convergence in Telecommunications and Audio-Visual Services* (Cambridge University Press, 2004) 165, 183.

[93] See Directive (EC) 97/36, Recital (27).

of content, independence and quality of services and output.[94] Universality of content means the provision of programming that reflects the interests of all social groups and that includes the entire range of programme genres.[95] It therefore entails the obligation of public broadcasting to advance cultural diversity.

The role of public broadcasting as a vector for cultural diversity is emphasized in numerous Council of Europe Recommendations.[96] For instance, the Council of Europe's Committee of Ministers Recommendation on the remit of public service media in the information society stresses that: 'In their programming and content, public service media should reflect the increasingly multiethnic and multicultural societies in which they operate, protecting the cultural heritage of different minorities and communities, providing possibilities for cultural expression and exchange, and promoting closer integration, without obliterating cultural diversity at the national level.'[97] The UNESCO Convention on the protection and promotion of the diversity of cultural expressions also suggests that parties may adopt 'measures aimed at enhancing diversity of the media, including through public service broadcasting'.[98]

By focusing on language policy, high culture, regional programmes, and cultural quotas, this section illustrates the various ways in which cultural diversity in each of the Member States under examination reflects in the public service remit.

12.4.1 France

12.4.1.1 *Language policy*

All broadcasters in France are obliged to use the French language in their programmes and in all commercials included therein.[99] The law only makes certain exceptions for cinematographic or audiovisual works in their original version, for musical works in a foreign language, for programmes that are intended to be transmitted exclusively in a foreign language, for religious services, and foreign language programmes. When programmes other than the exempted ones include foreign words, a translation in French needs to be provided that is as legible and comprehensible as the foreign language version. It is the task of the CSA to 'ensure the defence and demonstration of the French language and culture'.[100] In order to disseminate French language and culture abroad, France Télévisions participates in channels with a European and international vocation such as Arte, TV5, and the programme bank Canal France

---

[94] Council of Europe, 'Report of the Committee on Culture, Science and Education: Public Service Broadcasting', Doc 10029 (Council of Europe, 2004) para 12.

[95] G Born and T Prosser, 'Culture and Consumerism: Citizenship, Public Service Broadcasting and the BBC's Fair Trading Obligations' (2001) 64 MLR 657, 676.

[96] McGonagle (n 11 above) 7.

[97] Recommendation Rec (2007) 3 on the remit of public service media in the information society (31 January 2007) para 23.

[98] UNESCO Convention, Art 6(h).

[99] Law 86-1067 of 30 September 1986, art 3(1).

[100] ibid art 3-1.

International (CFI). The latter supplies its programmes to partner channels in developing countries at no cost.[101]

12.4.1.2 *High culture*

The *cahiers des charges* of the public broadcasters include specific obligations concerning the transmission of 'cultural programmes' in a narrow sense, ie classical arts, theatre, etc. France 2 and France 3 must each air fifteen musical, dance, or drama performances per year.[102] They also need to broadcast at least two hours per month of musical programmes and at least sixteen hours per year of concerts.[103] Public broadcasters usually broadcast more cultural programmes than required by these quotas.[104] However, the creation of the cultural European channel Arte has meant that the generalist public channels have been increasingly inclined to marginalize culture, for instance by scheduling it late at night.[105] There are no such cultural requirements for private broadcasters except for TF1.[106]

12.4.1.3 *Regional programmes*

Catering for the needs of linguistic minorities is not a specific feature of French broadcasting policy. Nonetheless, public broadcasters have traditionally been entrusted with the task of representing minorities.[107] Article 43-11(2) of Law 86-1067 obliges public broadcasters to reflect the diversity of cultural heritage in its regional and local dimensions. Regional and local identity is mainly fostered in France by the national public broadcaster France 3. France 3 is required to contribute to the expression of the principal regional languages spoken in the metropolitan territory (mainly Breton, Alsatian, Occitan, and Corsican), to offer programmes of a regional and local character and to develop the provision of information on regional and local issues.[108] It may also diffuse the main debates of the regional Assemblies.[109] In practice, France 3 airs regional and local news bulletins and programmes produced by thirteen regional directorates and thirty-seven local bureaus on a daily basis.[110] However, France 3 regional

---

[101] P Marcangeo-Leos, 'France' in European Audiovisual Observatory (ed), *Iris Special: The Public Service Broadcasting Culture* (European Audiovisual Observatory, 2007) 89, 97.

[102] *Cahiers des missions des charges de France 2 et France 3*, art 24.

[103] ibid art 26.

[104] T Vedel, 'France' in *Television across Europe: Regulation, Policy and Independence* (Open Society Institute, 2005) 679.

[105] Marcangeo-Leos (n 101 above) 96.

[106] T Ader, 'Der kulturelle Auftrag und der Aspekt "Regionalität" im Pflichtenprogramm der Rundfunkveranstalter' (2006) 8 *IRIS plus* 1.

[107] McGonagle *et al* (n 22 above) 205.

[108] *Cahiers des missions des charges de France 2 et France 3*, arts 16, 22, 24.

[109] ibid art 14.

[110] Vedel (n 104 above) 667.

channels only cover large regions, while the few existing local channels only reach a small percentage of the population.[111]

12.4.1.4 *Cultural quotas*

Quotas are a favoured instrument for protecting cultural identity and for stimulating programme-making in France. Programming quotas go beyond the requirements of the TWF Directive. Broadcasters are required to reserve at least 60 per cent of their yearly audiovisual and cinematographic productions for European creations and at least 40 per cent for French language productions.[112] Interestingly, the French language quota was lowered from an initial 50 per cent as a result of an agreement reached with the Commission in the beginning of the 1990s, so as to allow a wider 'corridor' for European works. The European and French language quotas apply to the entire schedule and especially at primetime (between 8.30 pm and 10.30 pm for cinematographic works, between 6.00 pm and 11.00 pm for audiovisual works).[113] For cable and satellite channels and for digital terrestrial television (TNT) the thresholds can be reached incrementally within a greater time span. Moreover, the satellite and cable channels may see their European quotas lowered (although never below the threshold of 50 per cent fixed by the TWF Directive), provided that they invest more into independent French language productions.[114]

Moreover, broadcasters are obliged to invest in the production of European and French language audiovisual and cinematographic works. Investment quotas are also more far-reaching than is required by the TWF Directive. As far as audiovisual works are concerned, broadcasters have to invest at least 16 per cent of their turnover from the previous year in the production of French language audiovisual works (and to diffuse 120 hours of original European and French language works). Two-thirds of the investments must be devoted to independent productions.[115] As far as cinematographic works are concerned, all channels, whatever their support (terrestrial, cable, or satellite), whose principal object is not the diffusion of cinematographic works and that diffuse at least 52 cinematographic works of long duration per annum, must invest a minimum of 3.2 per cent of their turnover from the previous year in European films and

---

[111] M Bourreau, 'Digital Terrestrial Television in France: An Attempt to Enhance Competition in an Oligopolistic Market', 20 April 2007, at <http://www.ses.enst.fr/bourreau/Recherche/DTV.pdf> (accessed 6 March 2009).

[112] Law 86-1067 of 30 September 1986, art 27 and Decree 90-66 of 17 January 1990, arts 7, 13, 14. For the distinction between audiovisual and cinematographic productions, a number of criteria are laid down in arts 2, 3, 4 of Decree 90–66. French language productions are defined in art 5 of Decree 90–66, European productions in art 6 of the same Decree that implements TWF Directive, Art 6.

[113] Decree 90–66 of 17 January 1990, arts 7, 14.

[114] ibid art 13.

[115] Decree 2001–609 of 9 July 2001.

2.5 per cent in French language films.[116] Again, three-quarters of these investments must be devoted to independent productions.

12.4.2 Germany

12.4.2.1 *High culture*
The cultural mission of German public broadcasters is laid down in § 11(2)4 RStV.[117] This provision emphasizes the obligation of public broadcasters to broadcast cultural contributions. It becomes evident from the *travaux préparatoires* that culture is understood in a wide sense, encompassing both popular and more highbrow programme genres.[118] The ARD also sees itself obliged to cater by means of its cultural programming not only for a small elite, but for broad segments of the population.[119] Its participation in 3sat and Arte represents clearly the more intellectual and ambitious end of the spectrum. The German Constitutional Court has also developed the idea of a special cultural responsibility (*kulturelle Verantwortung*) of public broadcasting that has become particularly important with the extension of broadcasting on offer to privately produced and European programmes.[120] However, public broadcasters are often criticized for not adequately fulfilling their cultural mission. The low quality of cultural programming as well as its relegation to the late night hours or to thematic channels are denounced. It has been suggested that the Broadcasting Councils should entrust external bodies with the task of overseeing the quality of programming or that soft quotas for cultural programmes should be introduced.[121] Both proposals risk being contrary to the constitutional requirement of programming autonomy (*Programmautonomie*).

12.4.2.2 *Regional programmes*
The main legal obligation of public broadcasters to broadcast regional programmes is contained in § 11(2)1 RStV, which obliges them to 'provide a comprehensive overview of international, European, national and *regional* developments'. In its report on the obligation of its public service mission, the ARD also assumes the obligation to commission together with Degeto (the film acquisition and production arm of the ARD) around 70 per cent of its productions from independent companies so as to

---

[116] CSA, 'Les obligations de production d'oeuvres audiovisuelles et cinématographiques à la télévision', 18 July 2007, at <http://www.csa.fr/infos/controle/television_quotas_production.php> (accessed 12 March 2009).

[117] Staatsvertrag für Rundfunk und Telemedien (RStV) of 31 August 1991, last modified by the 9th Rundfunkänderungsstaatsvertrag of 1 March 2007.

[118] R H Weber, A Roßnagel, S Osterwalder, A Scheuer, and S Wüst, *Kulturquoten im Rundfunk* (Nomos, 2006) 262.

[119] ARD, *Die Programmgestaltung der ARD 2005/2006: Bericht der ARD über die Erfüllung ihres Auftrages, über die Qualität und Quantität ihrer Angebote und Programme sowie über die geplannten Schwerpunkte (§ 11(4)3 RStV)*, 27 <http://www.ard.de/intern/organisation/-/id=8036/nid=8036/did=197252/j92len/index.html> (accessed 12 March 2009).

[120] BVerfGE 73, 118, 158 (1986); BVerfGE 94, 297, 324 (1996).

[121] T Kleist and A Scheuer, 'Kultur und Quoten' (2006) ZUM 96.

strengthen the German film industry.[122] Given that ARD is a cooperation of nine regional broadcasters, this commitment benefits regional production directly.[123] Moreover, seven out of nine ARD broadcasters have committed themselves to substantially supporting the film industry of the *Länder*. ARD's structure also guarantees that its programming, especially its Third Programmes, takes regional interests sufficiently into account. According to Article 5(2) ZDF-StV, ZDF is also obliged to give appropriate coverage to events in the individual *Länder* and to Germany's cultural diversity.[124]

As far as minority language broadcasting is concerned,[125] public broadcasters offer certain special channels such as the channel 'Lužyka' broadcast by the broadcasting corporation RBB in the Lower Sorbian language.[126] Saxony and Brandenburg have provisions in place, obliging public service media to give appropriate coverage to the Sorbian (Wendish) culture and language.[127] However, the Advisory Committee on the FCNM has repeatedly bemoaned that the Frisian language is virtually absent from the media and that the needs of the Danish and Frisian minorities as regards broadcasting in their respective language need to be better accommodated, particularly by public television.[128]

12.4.2.3 *Cultural quotas*

The law does not contain any precise cultural quotas. This is hardly surprising if one takes the traditional German hostility towards quotas into account. Fixed quotas would also be problematic from the point of view of the programming autonomy of German broadcasters.[129] Article 4 of the TWF Directive, the European quota rule, has been implemented in § 6(2) RStV, which requires broadcasters to reserve the main part of their broadcasting time for European works. Instead of listing types of programmes that do not count towards this obligation, § 6(2) RStV explicitly mentions those genres that count towards the relevant broadcasting time, namely feature films, television plays,

---

[122] ARD, *Programmgestaltung*, 31.

[123] Ader (n 106 above) 5.

[124] ZDF-Staatsvertrag (ZDF-StV) modified by the 9th Rundfunkänderungsstaatsvertrag of 1 March 2007.

[125] Germany recognizes as national minorities the Danes of German citizenship and the members of the Sorbian people with German citizenship. The FCNM also applies to ethnic groups traditionally resident in Germany, the Frisians of German citizenship and the Sinti and Roma of German citizenship. See Declaration contained in a letter from the Permanent Representative of Germany, dated 11 May 1995, handed to the Secretary-General at the time of signature, on 11 May 1995—Or Ger/Engl—and renewed in the instrument of ratification, deposited on 10 September 1997—Or Ger/Engl.

[126] C Palzer, 'Germany' in European Audiovisual Observatory (ed), *Iris Special: The Public Service Broadcasting Culture* (European Audiovisual Observatory, 2007) 48.

[127] Gesetz zur Ausgestaltung der Rechte der Sorben (Wenden) im Land Brandenburg (Sorben [Wenden]-Gesetz-SWG of 7 July 1994, art 12; Gesetz über die Rechte der Sorben im Freistaat Sachsen (Sächsisches Sorbengesetz—SächsSorbG) of 31 March 1999, art 14.

[128] Advisory Committee on the FCNM, Second Opinion on Germany adopted on 1 March 2006, ACFC/OP/II (2006) 001, para 20.

[129] Ader (n 106 above) 5.

series, documentaries, and similar productions. This provision is thus framed in narrower terms than Article 4(1) of the TWF Directive.

As far as the independent quota is concerned, Germany has implemented it rather liberally in § 6(3) RStV. According to this provision, general interest channels are obliged to devote a substantial part of their transmission time to in-house as well as commissioned and joint productions. There is neither a reference to independent producers nor a fixed quota or a requirement to earmark an adequate proportion for recent works as in Article 5 of the Directive. Therefore, § 6(3) RStV can only achieve the result envisaged by the TWF Directive by means of its harmonious interpretation in the light of the Directive.[130] The federal government has expressed a preference for the promotion of independent production by means of commitments freely entered into by the public broadcasters as opposed to binding legal rules.[131] Indeed, we have seen that ARD has committed itself to commissioning, together with Degeto, around 70 per cent of its production from independent companies. ZDF's commitments to support the German film industry are less concrete.[132]

12.4.3 Greece

12.4.3.1 *Language policy*
ERT SA is subject to specific cultural obligations related to the protection of the quality of the Greek language and the defence, promotion, and dissemination of the Greek civilization and tradition.[133] ERT SA and the private channels are obliged to take all necessary steps, such as recruitment of specialists and of text editors, and organization of seminars, to ensure the correct use of the Greek language in information, education, and entertainment programmes, as well as in the dubbing or subtitling of foreign programmes.[134] The editing, presentation, and subtitling of programmes need to follow the generally accepted rules of grammar and syntax of the Greek language.[135] The same care needs to be taken in the use of foreign languages in the framework of Greek or foreign language programmes. Foreign language programmes need to be presented, if possible, by native language speakers.[136] Furthermore, ERT SA and the private channels have to reserve at least 25 per cent of their transmission time, excluding news, sports events, games, advertising, or teletext services, for works produced in the Greek language.[137] Finally, both ERT SA and the private channels are obliged to organize a

---

[130] Weber *et al* (n 118 above) 281.
[131] ibid.
[132] See ZDF, 'Programm-Perspektiven 2007–2008' 17 April 2007, at <http://www.unternehmen.zdf.de/fileadmin/files/Download_Dokumente/DD_Das_ZDF/Programm-Perspektiven__SVE_2007-2008_2.pdf>, 10 (accessed 6 March 2009) 10.
[133] Common Ministerial Decree (KYA) AP 24/1 of 2 January 1997, art 14(2)(δ), (στ).
[134] Law 2328/95, art 3(18).
[135] Code 2/1991 for Radio and Television Programmes, art 2(4); PD 77/2003, art 2(4).
[136] Code 2/1991 for Radio and Television Programmes, art 2(4).
[137] Law 2328/95, art 3(18).

series of at least fifteen seminars every six months, lasting at least thirty minutes each, on the correct use of the Greek language or on its learning by foreigners or by illiterates.[138]

12.4.3.2 *High culture*

The fulfilment of the cultural needs of society and the education of Greek people, both in Greece and overseas, are part of ERT SA's public service mission.[139] Its programming displays a traditional public service profile, encompassing educational and children's programmes, news and current affairs, Greek and foreign serials, and feature films, music, sport, and documentaries.[140] The duration of cultural programmes is not specified.[141]

12.4.3.3 *Regional programmes*

Regional programming is provided by the regional television station, ET3, which is located in Thessaloniki. The only minority acknowledged by Greece are the Muslims of Thrace. Greek legislation does not, however, expressly provide for minority media or access of minorities to the media.[142] Only Presidential Decree 77/2003 incorporating the 'Code of Conduct for News and other Political Programmes' states that special care is needed for minority groups (national or religious) and other vulnerable sections of society.[143]

12.4.3.4 *Cultural quotas*

Greece has implemented the 'European quota' and the 'independent quota' of the TWF Directive. Broadcasters need to reserve at least 51 per cent of their transmission time, except for news, sport events, games, advertisements, teleshopping, and teletext services, to European origin programmes.[144] They also need to reserve at least 10 per cent of their transmission time, excluding the time appointed to news, sport events, advertising, and teleshopping, for independent productions.[145] The Greek legislator has included the time devoted to games and teletext services in the time on the basis of which the independent quota is to be calculated in contravention of Article 5 of the TWF Directive. Also, broadcasters have to devote 1.5 per cent of their yearly net

[138] ibid art 3(19).

[139] Law 1730/87, art 2(1).

[140] P Seri, 'Mediensystem Griechenlands' in Hans-Bredow Institut (ed), *Internationales Handbuch Medien 2004/2005* (Nomos, 2004) 324.

[141] A Oikonomou, 'Ethniko Symvoulio Radioteleorases: treis aneklerotes proupotheseis gia ten apotelesmatike leitourgia tou os anexartetes arxes' (2004) 2 *Dikaio Meson Enemeroses kai Epikoinonias* 185, 191.

[142] McGonagle *et al* (n 22 above) 233.

[143] Presidential Decree (PD) 77/2003, art 4(2). See M Kostopoulou, 'New Code of Conduct for News and Other Political Programmes', at <http://merlin.obs.coe.int/iris/2003/7/article20.en.html> (accessed 13 March 2009).

[144] PD 100/2000, art 10(1).

[145] ibid art 10(7).

income—after deduction of taxes and other charges in favour of the public sector, public bodies, and local authorities—for the production or co-production of cinematographic movies (with a duration of 70 to 150 minutes) that are aimed to be shown on the big screen.[146]

12.4.4. Italy

12.4.4.1 *Language policy*
There are no specific obligations on RAI to watch over the use of the Italian language. RAI is only asked to promote and spread the knowledge of the Italian language as well as of the Italian culture and economy in the world, with the aim of guaranteeing Italian communities living abroad a suitable level of information on developments in Italian society.[147]

12.4.4.2 *High culture*
Culture and entertainment, especially live performances such as theatre, dance, opera, drama, and classical and light music feature among the genres to which RAI has to assign a large percentage of its annual programming schedule according to the RAI service contract.[148]

12.4.4.3 *Regional programmes*
The Broadcasting Act 2005 requires RAI to have an office in each region and in each of the Autonomous Provinces of Trento and Bolzano, which shall operate under a regime of financial and accounting autonomy, and to promote decentralized production centres.[149] Further, it provides that each region shall approve a regional law laying down obligations for public broadcasting and shall conclude specific regional service contracts with RAI.[150] The new RAI service contract also states that RAI may conclude agreements with the regions and autonomous provinces so as to promote regional and local culture.[151] However, no regional laws exist yet. At the moment, only a very small part of RAI 3's programme is dedicated to the regions. Probably more attention will be paid to regional and local issues once regional laws have been adopted.

   As far as regional languages are concerned, RAI is obliged to broadcast in German and Ladin in the Autonomous Province of Bolzano, in French in the Autonomous Region Valle d'Aosta, and in Slovene in the Province of Trieste, Gorizia, and Udine.[152] To this end, specific conventions have been concluded between RAI and the Italian

---

[146] Law 1866/1989, art 7(1).
[147] RAI Service Contract 2007–2009, art 9(1).
[148] ibid art 4(1)(f).
[149] Legislative Decree 177 of 31 July 2005, art 45(2)(p), (r), (3).
[150] ibid art 46.
[151] RAI Service Contract 2007–2009, art 11(1).
[152] ibid art 11(2); Legislative Decree 177 of 31 July 2005, art 45(2)(f).

Presidency of the Council of Ministers.[153] A considerable number of radio and television programmes in French, German, Ladin, and Slovenian have been broadcast by RAI for some time.

However, the Advisory Committee on the FCNM noted in its Second Opinion on Italy that the reception of existing programmes was not always possible in the entire traditional area of settlement of the minorities concerned, for instance by Ladins living in the Belluno province and Slovenians in the Udino province, even though it was technically possible.[154] It criticized further the fact that article 12 of Law 482/99, which introduced a legal basis allowing for significant development of programmes in other languages, had yet to be implemented so far. As a result, repeated requests for further programmes by large minorities, like the Friulans, had been turned down despite the fact that existing programmes in Friulan were extremely limited and did not comprise any news.[155]

12.4.5 The Netherlands

12.4.5.1 *Language policy*

The regulation of language use in public broadcasting aims mostly at the promotion of Dutch and of Frisian, which is recognized as the second national language in the Netherlands. Public broadcasters are obliged to devote at least 50 per cent of their television broadcasting time to programmes originally produced in Dutch or Frisian.[156] Notably, there are no specified percentages for each of the two languages.[157] The NPS is not bound by any express commitments concerning language, but is obliged to ensure that at least 20 per cent of its television programme service consists of programmes for or relating to ethnic and cultural minorities.[158] *Omrop Fryslân*, a regional public broadcaster, broadcasts one hour of television programming daily in the Frisian language, while *Nederland 1* transmits on its national network a subtitled documentary produced by *Omrop Fryslân* once a week.[159]

12.4.5.2 *High culture*

The provision of a variety of programme services in the fields of information, culture, education, and entertainment forms the core of the public service remit in the Netherlands. The total television broadcasting time for all national broadcasting

---

[153] M Cappello and R Mastroianni, 'Italy' in European Audiovisual Observatory (ed), *Iris Special: The Public Service Broadcasting Culture* (European Audiovisual Observatory, 2007) 125, 130.

[154] Advisory Committee on the FCNM, Second Opinion on Italy adopted on 24 February 2005, ACFC/INF/OP/II (2005) 003, para 16.

[155] ibid paras 15, 90.

[156] Dutch Media Act, art 54(a)(1).

[157] N van Eijk, 'The Netherlands' in European Audiovisual Observatory (ed), *Iris Special: The Public Service Broadcasting Culture* (European Audiovisual Observatory, 2007) 149, 157.

[158] Dutch Media Decree, art 15(2)(a).

[159] T MacGonagle, 'Regulating Minority-Language Use in Broadcasting: International Law and the Dutch National Experience' (2004) 16 *Mediaforum* 155.

companies is to be used to provide such a complete programme.[160] Minimum amounts for information, education, and culture are set out in article 50 of the Media Act. At least 35 per cent of the broadcasting time is reserved for information and education and 25 per cent of the broadcasting time is reserved for cultural programmes, of which 12.5 per cent is set aside for the arts.[161] A programme is considered 'cultural' when more than half of the content is of a cultural nature. No more than 25 per cent of the total broadcasting time may be devoted to entertainment. In respect of the NPS a different regime applies, since its task is to satisfy social, cultural, and religious or spiritual needs among the public. At least 40 per cent of its programming consists of, or relates to, the arts.[162]

To stimulate the production of cultural programmes, the Minister of Education, Culture and Science established the Dutch Cultural Broadcasting Fund in 1988 (*Stichting Stimuleringsfonds Nederlandse Culturele Omroepproducties*). Its aim is to provide funding to encourage the development and production of programmes of a cultural nature that cover, *inter alia*, art, cabaret, theatre, and music. Entertainment shows and quiz programmes are not eligible for financial support.

12.4.5.3 *Regional programmes*

The Dutch Media Authority can allocate broadcasting time for a five-year period to regional and local broadcasters that are independent from national broadcasting. Only one local or regional broadcasting organization may be allocated broadcasting time in each municipality or province. The Media Authority grants the licences in consultation with the local or regional authorities. There are currently 296 local broadcasting organizations and 13 regional ones. The Regional Broadcast Foundation for Consultation and Cooperation (*Stichting Regionale Omroep Overleg en Samenwerking*, ROOS) coordinates the regional public broadcasters.[163] Regional channels are not allowed to broadcast their programmes outside the borders of their regions. Half of their broadcasting time must consist of programmes of an informative, cultural, and educational nature which have particular relevance to the region for which the programme is intended.[164] The representative bodies of the local and regional broadcasters, which are entrusted with programme policy, consist of members representing the main social, cultural, religious, and other movements within the municipality or province.[165]

12.4.5.4 *Cultural quotas*

In addition to the above-mentioned language quotas, national and regional broadcasters are obliged to devote at least 50 per cent of their broadcasting time to European

[160] Dutch Media Act, art 50(1).
[161] ibid art 50(2).
[162] ibid art 51(b)(3).
[163] Van Eijk (n 157 above) 152.
[164] Dutch Media Act, art 51(e).
[165] Van Eijk (n 157 above) 152.

works.[166] Moreover, public broadcasters are obliged to devote at least 25 per cent of their broadcasting time to works by independent producers,[167] at least one-third of which must not be more than five years old.[168] The concepts of 'independent production' and 'independent producers' are defined in Policy Rules laid down by the Dutch Media Authority.[169]

12.4.6 United Kingdom

12.4.6.1 *High culture*

The stimulation of creativity and cultural excellence is one of the BBC's newly acquired public purposes. The BBC is asked to enrich the cultural life of the UK through creative excellence in distinctive and original content; to foster creativity and nurture talent; and to promote interest, engagement, and participation in cultural activity among new audiences. In doing so, the BBC Trust must have regard, among other things, to the need for the BBC to have a film strategy; and the need for appropriate coverage of sports, including sport of minority interest.[170] This public purpose is not specific to cultural programmes in a narrow sense but applies across a wide range of genres and output including entertainment programmes that remain a key priority for the BBC.[171] However, BBC 1 has committed itself to providing a minimum of 45 hours of arts and music in 2008/2009, BBC 2 a minimum of 200 hours, and BBC 4 a minimum of 100 hours of new arts and music programmes.[172]

12.4.6.2 *Regional programmes*

Representing the UK, its nations, regions, and communities is another BBC public purpose. The BBC is asked to reflect and strengthen cultural identities through original content at local, regional, and national level, on occasion bringing audiences together for shared experiences; and to promote awareness of different cultures and alternative viewpoints, through content that reflects the lives of different people and different communities within the UK. In doing so, the Trust must have regard, among other things, to the importance of reflecting different religious and other beliefs; and the importance of appropriate provision in minority languages.[173]

---

[166] Dutch Media Act, art 54(1).

[167] ibid art 54(2).

[168] Dutch Media Decree, art 16a.

[169] CvdM, Policy Rules for Programme Quotas, 1 December 2006.

[170] *Agreement Dated July 2006 Between Her Majesty's Secretary of State for Culture, Media and Sport and the British Broadcasting Corporation* (Cm 6872, 2006) (hereinafter the 'BBC Agreement') s 8.

[171] BBC Trust, 'BBC Public Purpose Remit: Stimulating creativity and cultural excellence' (January 2007) 2.

[172] BBC, 'BBC Statements of Programme Policy 2008/2009', at <http://www.bbc.co.uk/info/statements 2008/pdf/BBC_SoPPs_200809.pdf> (accessed 13 March 2009) 6.

[173] BBC Agreement, s 9.

The BBC is committed to the promotion of minority languages.[174] As far as the Irish speaking and the Ulster-Scots speaking communities in Northern Ireland are concerned, there is no dedicated Irish-language television service, but Irish-language television programmes are either transmitted on the BBC or on TG4, an all-Ireland television channel funded by the Irish Government. However, the Advisory Committee to the FCNM bemoaned that, even though the government had begun to fund the extension of reception of TG4 in Northern Ireland, this channel was still unavailable in some parts of Northern Ireland.[175] As regards the Welsh-speaking minority, the BBC has a long-standing commitment to provide 520 hours free of charge to the Welsh-language television channel S4C.[176] The latter has been very successful, giving a boost to the Welsh language and producing outstanding films.[177] Finally, there is a regular Thursday evening slot for Gaelic broadcasting on BBC 2. The BBC in partnership with MG Alba (Meadhanan Gàidhlig Alba, or Gaelic Media Scotland) also runs BBC Alba, a dedicated digital Gaelic language service for Scotland which launched on 19 September 2008. However, the Advisory Committee to the FCNM noted that there were concerns about the availability of funding and appropriate infrastructure for the Gaelic channel in the long term and urged that this channel should be given appropriate support.[178]

The importance given to the regional dimension in the UK is reflected in the governance of the BBC. Four ordinary members of the Trust are designated the Trust member for England, for Scotland, for Wales, and for Northern Ireland respectively.[179] They are assisted by four Audience Councils covering the same regions. Their role is 'to bring the diverse perspectives of licence fee payers to bear on the work of the Trust'.[180] The Council of England is the largest because it is supported by a network of regional Audience Councils, one for every broadcasting region in England. The BBC's current target for the provision of regional programming amounts to 6,580 hours per year. Moreover, the BBC is obliged to secure that a suitable proportion of its programmes is made outside the so-called M25 area, ie outside London.[181]

---

[174] Welsh, Gaelic, and Irish are so-called 'indigenous minority languages' in the UK. Cornish, Scots, and Ulster Scots, have been recognized as falling under Part II of the European Charter of Regional and Minority Languages.

[175] Advisory Committee on the FCNM, Second Opinion on the United Kingdom adopted on 6 June 2007, ACFC/OP/II (2007) 003, para 166.

[176] BBC Trust, '*Operating Agreement: BBC Programmes on S4C—"The Contributed Programming"*', June 2007, at <http://www.bbc.co.uk/bbctrust/assets/files/pdf/regulatory_framework/other_activities/s4c_operating_agreement.pdf> (accessed 13 March 2009) 2.

[177] T Prosser, 'United Kingdom' in European Audiovisual Observatory (ed), *Iris Special: The Public Service Broadcasting Culture* (European Audiovisual Observatory, 2007) 103, 111.

[178] Advisory Committee on the FCNM, Second Opinion on the United Kingdom adopted on 6 June 2007, ACFC/OP/II (2007) 003, para 171.

[179] *Royal Charter for the Continuance of the British Broadcasting Corporation* (Cm 6925, 2006) (hereinafter referred to as the 'BBC Charter'), art 14.

[180] ibid art 39.

[181] BBC Agreement, s 51. The M25 London Orbital Motorway is used as a geographical boundary for London.

The target is currently one-third of its programmes. The commissioning and production across the UK will increase over the coming years as significant parts of the BBC production base are set to be relocated to Greater Manchester.

12.4.6.3 *Cultural quotas*

The BBC, in agreement with Ofcom, must allocate a certain proportion of time to the broadcasting of original productions, split between peak viewing times and other times.[182] BBC 1 for instance committed itself to dedicating 70 per cent of hours, and 90 per cent of hours in peak, to originations (first shows and repeats) in 2006/2007.[183] The BBC is also obliged to use its best endeavours to ensure that 50 per cent of its airtime is reserved for programmes made by the BBC through its in-house production facility.[184] Conversely, it must secure that at least 25 per cent of the total broadcasting time allocated to qualifying programmes on BBC 1 and in BBC 2 is devoted to the broadcasting of a range and diversity of independent productions.[185] This quota exceeds the independent quota under Article 5 of the TWF Directive. The UK has not adopted any quota as regards the broadcasting of programmes of European origin. The Broadcasting Act 1990 only refers to a 'proper proportion' of programmes of European origin.[186] However, the BBC agrees targets with Ofcom regarding the programming of European output each calendar year. These targets are monitored by Ofcom and by the Trust.[187] BBC 3 and BBC 4 committed themselves to broadcasting at least 90 per cent and 70 per cent of programme hours of EU/EEA origin respectively in 2006/2007.[188]

12.5 CONCLUSION

This chapter has given an overview of measures adopted at Council of Europe, EU, and national level for the protection and advancement of cultural diversity in broadcasting. The Framework Convention and the European Charter for Regional or Minority Languages are useful tools for the protection of minority rights in Europe. They are both legally binding texts. The former is devoted to the protection of national minorities in general, while the latter is the first international treaty directed specifically at linguistic minorities. However, these treaties are only binding on ratifying states. While the vast majority of European states subscribe to the Framework

---

[182]   ibid s 49.
[183]   BBC, '*BBC Statements of Programme Policy 2006/2007*', 10.
[184]   BBC Agreement, s 56.
[185]   ibid s 52; Communications Act 2003, Sch 12, para 1(1).
[186]   For instance, Broadcasting Act 1990, s 25(2)(e) for Channel 4.
[187]   Ofcom and BBC Trust, 'Memorandum of Understanding between the Office of Communications (Ofcom) and the BBC Trust' (Ofcom, 2007) 5.
[188]   BBC, '*BBC Statements of Programme Policy 2006/2007*', 20.

Convention, the same does not hold true for the Charter. Also, the effective implementation of these instruments rests solely on the states concerned as there are no enforcement mechanisms.

The European broadcasting quota of the TWF (now AVMS) Directive does not suffer from the same weaknesses as the above-mentioned international conventions. It is automatically legally binding as to the result to be achieved upon all EU Member States.[189] The Commission can enforce it by bringing its infringement to the attention of the European Court.[190] However, the European quota is not specifically geared towards the promotion of regional or minority languages and cultures. Its underlying, ill-defined cultural policy objective is the protection of European audiovisual cultures from American cultural imperialism.

The idea that cultural identities in Europe stand to lose from their exposure to US film and to non-European audiovisual content in general is questionable. It implies that European audiovisual cultures share common features, that they are inherently superior and that they might be weakened by cultural exchange. The assumed affinity of European audiovisual traditions has been shaken by the strong preference of European audiences for domestically produced content. Paradoxically, the protectionism and isolationism espoused by the European quota rule became its own worst enemy. This insular outlook also contradicts the notion that 'cultural diversity is strengthened by the free flow of ideas, and that it is nurtured by constant exchanges and interaction between cultures'.[191] Moreover, the failure to craft a convincing definition of a 'European work' has defied all attempts to superimpose a constructed common European audiovisual culture. The concept of a 'European work' remains artificial as it employs formalistic criteria that do not say anything about the work's actual cultural content.

The final section of this chapter examined the way in which public broadcasting in selected EU Member States contributes to cultural diversity. Given that public broadcasting systems and organizations are creatures of the historical, social, and political context in which they were born, it is not surprising that different means are employed to this end. Cultural obligations and the protection of minorities are more pronounced in some Member States than in others.

France views film as the seventh art that needs to be protected from an onslaught of bland, uniform American or other international productions. To this end, programming and investment quotas are imposed that go beyond the requirements of the TWF Directive, and the mandatory use of the French language is rigorously overseen. However, France has not signed the European Charter for Regional or Minority

---

[189] Art 249(3) EC.
[190] Katsirea (n 54 above) 300 *et seq.*
[191] UNESCO Convention, Recital (11).

Languages and has not ratified the FCNM. Insufficient regard is paid to the needs of linguistic minorities, which are only catered for by France 3.[192]

German public broadcasters have been entrusted with a special cultural responsibility by the German Constitutional Court, and consider culture to be one of the most important aspects of their programming.[193] As in France, however, cultural programming is often relegated to the late hours of the day or to thematic channels. In Germany, there are no precise cultural quotas as they would go against the grain of the highly valued programming autonomy of broadcasters. The quota rules of the TWF Directive have been rather loosely transposed into German law, but are fully complied with in practice. Provision for minority languages, particularly Frisian and Danish, leaves much to be desired.

The main cultural concern of the Greek broadcasting system is the protection of the quality of the Greek language and the promotion and dissemination of Greek civilization and tradition. Besides certain obligations related to the editing, presentation, and subtitling of programmes, Greek broadcasters need to transmit a fixed percentage of works produced in the Greek language. Greece has not ratified the Framework Convention and has not even signed the Charter. Minority-language broadcasting in Greece is very underdeveloped.

The Italian public broadcaster RAI does not have particular obligations as far as the use of the Italian language is concerned, but is specifically obliged to broadcast in the languages of the Autonomous Regions and Provinces. A significant number of programmes in most, but not all, minority languages in Italy are broadcast by RAI.

In the Netherlands, language policy centres on the promotion of the two official languages, Dutch and Frisian. The cultural diversity of the country is also catered for by the establishment of a great number of local and regional broadcasting organizations. Besides the European quotas, specific quotas exist for informational, educational, and cultural programming.

In the UK, the cultural obligations of the BBC have been streamlined by means of its new public purposes. Great importance has always been accorded to the regional dimension of public broadcasting, as becomes evident from the BBC's organizational structure. Also, the BBC is committed to the promotion of minority languages. It supports dedicated channels and broadcasts minority language programming. While the law specifies the percentage to be reserved for independent productions, there is no set quota as regards the broadcasting of European works. The programming of European output is agreed between the BBC and Ofcom each calendar year. Specific targets exist also for original and in-house productions.

The overview of the cultural obligations of public broadcasting in the Member States under examination shows that there are effective content regulations in place for the promotion of national languages and cultures. National language quotas and quotas

---

[192] See European Bureau for Lesser Used Languages, 'NGOs at the UN denounce French discrimination against its "regional" languages', at <http://www.eblul.org> (accessed 23 July 2008).

[193] Palzer (n 126 above) 39, 47.

for the promotion of audiovisual and cinematographic production exist alongside the European quotas. They draw on real cultures and are hence not tainted with the disingenuousness of the latter. On the contrary, the public service remit does not always accurately reflect regional cultural diversity. However, accession to the relevant Council of Europe conventions gives minorities enhanced legal and political leverage for the advancement of their claims.

13

COMMERCIAL COMMUNICATIONS

John Enser

13.1 INTRODUCTION

The use of communications media for commercial messaging is nearly as old as the media themselves; adverts have been found among Egyptian papyrus scrolls and in the ruins of Pompeii, handbills and other printed advertisements followed soon after the invention of the printing press, and the same pattern followed for radio and television. The first banner advert appeared on the worldwide web in 1994.

This chapter sets out how commercial communications—namely, advertising and sponsorship messages and product placement—are the subject of a range of regulatory and self-regulatory systems which control the content of advertising and, in some instances, its amount and nature. As will be considered, historically, two quite different advertising regulatory regimes (at least in terms of their form and structure) have existed—one for television advertising and one for advertising in all other media. Television, because of its perceived ability to be a medium of particular influence on its audience, has been subject to a statutory regime, although that has more recently become a co-regulatory regime. In contrast, advertising in other media has been subject to a self-regulatory regime, with a back-stop of legal powers; principally, those wielded by the Office of Fair Trading (OFT) but also Trading Standards and other consumer representatives. It is the increasing convergence of the various forms of media that is driving the desire to reduce the differentiation between the different regulatory regimes. For example, it is hard to explain why adverts on the internet or in a cinema are subject to one regime, the same one that applies to print adverts, while an identical advert playing on television is subject to a different regime. As will be discussed towards the end of this chapter, a third regulatory (or co- or self-regulatory) framework may shortly be in place for non-linear TV-like services, following implementation in the UK of the Audiovisual Media Services Directive (AVMS Directive).[1]

13.2 ADVERTISING AND THE GENERAL LAW

While the regulations specifically developed for advertising constitute the principal legal regime which concerns advertising, those creating and publishing commercial communications need also to be aware of the broad range of other laws applicable to the content of their messages. Each of these disciplines is one which is best discussed within its own literature, rather than the present chapter, but the most relevant topics for consideration are noted below:

(1) *Intellectual property law*.[2] Both copyright law and trade mark law are very important for advertisers.

    (a) Advertisements are capable of infringing copyright in just the same way as any other form of creative content. Indeed, the fact that many within the creative communities are wary about permitting their name to be associated with a particular product means that an unlicensed use is more likely to be pursued than in cases where the infringer is undertaking a less commercial exploitation.[3]

    (b) Trade marks are also a common cause of controversy in connection with advertising, particularly where one company makes reference to the trade marks of another in its own advertising. European law contains a specific regime dealing with the lawfulness of comparative advertising and the conflicting interplay between that regime and trade mark law has recently been resolved by the European Court of Justice (ECJ).[4] In the *O2 Holdings*

---

[1] Directive (EC) 2007/65.

[2] See further Ch 6 above.

[3] See eg *Griggs v Evans* [2005] EWCA Civ 11 where the Court of Appeal considered the copyright ownership of a 'Doc Martens/Air Wair' logo as between a freelance graphic designer and the company that commissioned him; *Norowzian v Arks Ltd and ors (No 2)* [2000] FSR 363 where the Court considered whether an advert for Guinness using a particular jump-editing technique could infringe copyright in another work which 'inspired' it.

[4] Case C-533/06 *O2 Holdings Ltd and O2 (UK) Ltd v Hutchison 3G Ltd* judgment of 12 June 2008.

case, the phone company '3', in comparing its own prices to those of its competitor O2, was accused of trade mark infringement in respect of the 'bubbles' imagery used as part of O2's brand identity. The ECJ found that the use of the imagery was lawful. Where registered trade marks are not involved, the laws of passing off are also invoked in connection with advertising.[5]

(2) *Defamation law.*[6] The association of a person with a brand which he/she does not wish to be associated with can be defamatory. In the well-known case of *Tolley v Fry*[7] the plaintiff was an amateur golfer who was found to have been defamed by his picture appearing in an advertisement—the defamatory inference being that the amateur had accepted money in connection with such an advert.

(3) *Consumer law.* Consumer protection legislation includes certain provisions aimed principally, or in some instances entirely, at advertising and these are discussed below.[8] However, there are also more generic obligations concerning the way in which consumers are dealt with which have application to advertising. For example, under the Consumer Protection (Distance Selling) Regulations[9] consumers have the right, prior to deciding to buy goods or services to which the regulations apply, to receive certain information about those goods and services. That information may well be conveyed in the course of an advertisement (for example a page in a magazine including an order form for a product).

(4) *Criminal law.*[10] Speech which is criminal in other contexts, for example by virtue of it being obscene or likely to incite racial hatred, cannot be used in advertising.

(5) *Contract law. Carlill v Carbolic Smoke Ball Co,*[11] possibly the most cited case in contract in the common law world, shows the dangers of publishing marketing materials which can be construed as an offer capable of acceptance to create a binding contract. History repeated itself in 1992, when the Hoover Company launched its notorious 'free flights' promotion, where the purchase of £100 of Hoover products gave an entitlement to free flights worth materially in excess of that sum. The open-ended offer unexpectedly attracted over 600,000 customers, Hoover was bound

---

[5] See eg *Irvine v Talksport Ltd* [2003] EWCA Civ 423 where the defendant used in connection with trade advertising an image of the plaintiff holding a radio which had been altered so that it appeared to have the defendant's logo on it.

[6] See further Ch 10 above.

[7] [1931] AC 333 (HL).

[8] Such as the Consumer Protection from Unfair Trading Regulations 2008 and the Business Protection from Misleading Regulations 2008, the enforcement of which, by the OFT, is discussed at section 13.10.2.5 below.

[9] SI 2000/2334.

[10] See further Ch 11 above.

[11] [1893] 1 QB 256, Court of Appeal.

to honour the offer and the final bill (for a somewhat disastrous advertising campaign) was estimated at £50 million.

(6) *Human rights.* The European Court of Human Rights has consistently accepted that commercial speech benefits from freedom of expression under Article 10 ECHR.[12] This means that restrictions on commercial speech must be justified as being proportionate by reference to the operation of other human rights. Commercial speech is, however, considered less important than political or artistic expression, and therefore the threshold may be passed more easily than in these other instances.[13]

13.3 REGULATION OF TELEVISION AND RADIO ADVERTISING

13.3.1 Introduction and general scheme of regulation

The BBC's monopoly over television in the UK was broken in 1955 and, on 22 September, ITV was launched, initially in the London region. The first UK television advertisement which appeared was one for Gibbs SR toothpaste. The Independent Television Authority (later the Independent Broadcasting Authority (IBA)) was then, and remained until the end of 1990, both the regulator and the ultimate broadcaster of UK independent television. Following the Cable and Broadcasting Act 1984, the IBA was supplemented, in its capacity as broadcast regulator, by the Cable Authority. This body exercised control over the content of services distributed over cable television networks and was in many ways the closest forebear to the current regulators.

The Broadcasting Act 1990 introduced the structure of the statutory regime, which remains in place today, to control advertising on television. Under the Act, broadcasting obligations and responsibilities were devolved upon the individual licensees under the control of a statutory regulator, whose obligations include those connected with advertising and sponsorship. The statutory obligations imposed by the regulator included those arising from implementation in the UK of the UK's international obligations under the Television Without Frontiers Directive (TWF Directive).[14] One further important structural change was implemented by Ofcom in 2004 when it subcontracted certain of its advertising regulatory functions to a new set of organizations which mirror the structure of the self-regulatory regime for non-broadcast advertising.[15]

---

[12] See eg *Casada Coca v Spain* (1994) 18 EHRR 1, paras 35–36.
[13] See eg *Markt Intern v Germany* (1989) 12 EHRR 161.
[14] Directive (EEC) 89/552 as amended by Directive (EC) 97/36.
[15] See section 13.3.2.1 below.

13.3.2 Communications Act 2003

Section 319 of the Communications Act 2003 sets out the objectives which Ofcom is tasked with achieving as regards the standards of television and radio services. These are, as regards advertising:

(1) The duty to enforce a prohibition on political advertising.[16] Political advertising (which includes advertising designed to influence public opinion on matters of public controversy in the UK)[17] has always been banned from UK televisions—as a *quid pro quo*, there are strict rules of political balance in editorial matters[18] and political parties are provided with airtime during election periods to make party political broadcasts.

(2) The prevention of the inclusion in television and radio services of advertising which may be misleading, harmful, or offensive.[19] This is the head upon which most substantive advertising regulation is based—the concept that advertising should be 'legal, decent, honest and truthful'. Separately, but closely related to this objective is that of ensuring that persons under the age of 18 are protected.[20] Ofcom takes its obligations to protect minors particularly seriously.

(3) Compliance with the international obligations of the UK with respect to advertising included in television and radio services[21]—this is a reference primarily to the TWF Directive.[22]

(4) Prevention of unsuitable sponsorship of programmes included in television and radio services.[23] Sponsorship is seen as a form of advertising that requires particularly close attention, owing to the power that derives from the close association between the television programme and the sponsor's name.

(5) The duty to ensure that there is no undue discrimination between advertisers who seek to have advertisements included in television and radio services.[24] Recognizing that television advertising is still a (relatively) scarce resource, broadcasters are under a duty to make it available to advertisers on an even-handed basis.

(6) The duty to ensure that there is no use of techniques which exploit the possibility of conveying a message to viewers or listeners, or of otherwise influencing their minds, without their being aware, or fully aware, of what has occurred.[25] Surreptitious advertising techniques, including the ability to display a so-called subliminal image, which is shown for too short a time to be recognizable to the eye, but

---

[16] Communications Act 2003, ss 319(2)(g) and 321(2) and (3).
[17] ibid s 321(3)(f).
[18] See section 5.3.3.2 above.
[19] Communications Act 2003, s 319(2)(h).
[20] ibid s 319(2)(a).
[21] ibid s 319(2)(i).
[22] See n 14 above.
[23] Communications Act 2003, s 319(2)(j).
[24] ibid s 319(2)(k).
[25] ibid s 319(2)(l).

which is nevertheless embedded in the brain, are seen to be unfair, and potentially dangerous, and are therefore outlawed.

In addition to these objectives, Ofcom is also required[26] to give directions as to the amount and distribution of advertising (which can include the spacing between advertising breaks and which can also include blocks on advertising for certain periods or around certain types of programming).

13.3.2.1 *Delivery of Ofcom's objectives—subcontracting*
Ofcom was required, from its inception, to seek to move towards co-regulatory and self-regulatory regimes. Indeed section 6 of the Communications Act 2003 requires Ofcom to review its regulatory regime and seek to reduce the regulatory burden wherever possible. In pursuance of this and following a public consultation and parliamentary approval,[27] in November 2004, Ofcom transferred to the Committee on Advertising Practice (Broadcast Committee) (BCAP), to the Advertising Standards Authority (ASA) and to their related finance committees,[28] the obligations to define the regulatory codes for broadcast advertising and to enforce them. Certain obligations remain with Ofcom, in particular, those related to programme sponsorship (which form part of the standards regime for programming content referred to below), the decision as to how much advertising is permitted, and judgments about whether advertising is prohibited by virtue of being political.

Where the ASA considers there to have been a significant breach of the rules requiring a formal sanction, that decision is referred back to Ofcom, which alone can impose the statutory sanctions prescribed in the Communications Act 2003.

13.3.2.2 *Delivery of Ofcom's objectives—codes and licence conditions*
Pursuant to the contracting out described above, BCAP has now published a series of codes which set out what advertising is and is not permitted on television. These currently include the Radio Advertising Standards Code, the TV Advertising Standards Code, the Rules on the Scheduling of TV Adverts, and the Code for Text Services and Guidance on Interactive TV.[29]

In addition, Ofcom has published a series of codes relating to the matters for which it retains jurisdiction, in particular, the Code on the Scheduling of Television Advertising. Also of relevance is the Ofcom Broadcasting Code (relating principally to programming content), which contains rules concerning sponsorship[30] and relating

---

[26] Under ibid s 322.
[27] Under the Deregulation and Contracting Out Act 1994.
[28] The Broadcast Advertising Standards Board of Finance (Basbof), which is responsible for funding the operations of the ASA and BCAP through a 0.1% levy on advertising airtime revenues.
[29] All available from <http://www.cap.org.uk>.
[30] Ofcom Broadcasting Code, s 9.

to commercial references in programmes (including the rules relating to undue prominence and product placement).[31]

Most of the BCAP and Ofcom Codes derive from documents first published by the Independent Television Commission (one of the regulators replaced by Ofcom in 2003), although each has been amended over the years to reflect changes in the general law; to give two examples: the impact of the Gambling Act 2005 in liberalizing the UK gambling market and permitting it to advertise; and the introduction of the Consumer Protection from Unfair Trading Regulations 2008.

The area where there is the greatest cross-over between the role of Ofcom and the role of BCAP relates to the scheduling of television services. The role of BCAP and the ASA is limited to regulating the extent to which advertisements for particular products, or featuring actors or characters who appear in programming content, can be shown at particular times. For example, there is a general restriction on advertising condoms prior to the 9pm watershed and adverts for products such as gambling and alcohol cannot be shown during children's programming. On the other hand, Ofcom's power in the context of scheduling is to set, for example, the total amount of advertising which may appear in any hour.

The Codes derive their force from provisions set out in the licences issued to broadcasters by Ofcom. Each broadcaster's licence includes specific obligations to comply with all of Ofcom's Directions concerning advertising and to comply with the Advertising Standards Code.[32] Ofcom may impose sanctions for any breach of a licence condition.

13.4 TELEVISION WITHOUT FRONTIERS DIRECTIVE

Before examining in detail some of the key obligations of broadcasters, it is important to understand how the UK advertising regime derives certain of its principles and powers from the Television without Frontiers Directive (TWF Directive).

The TWF Directive, introduced in 1987 and revised in 1997, has in its overall scheme the introduction of minimum rules on television channels which every Member State is required to implement for broadcasters under their own jurisdiction. In return, broadcasters regulated in one Member State are free (with very limited exceptions) to have their signals received and retransmitted in all other Member States free of any regulatory intervention in the country of reception/retransmission. It is noteworthy that the TWF Directive does not apply to radio services; for the UK, radio advertising is subject to a slightly less restrictive regime than television advertising, but the rules are broadly similar.

---

[31] ibid s 10.
[32] See eg condition 8 of the standard form of Television Licensable Content Service licence, available from the Ofcom website.

The TWF Directive was further revised in 2007 and renamed as the Audiovisual Media Services (AVMS) Directive. The AVMS Directive is required to be implemented in UK law no later than 19 December 2009. This section will reference only those elements of the Directive's implementation which impact on advertising on linear television. Advertising on other forms of audiovisual media service (principally 'on-demand' services) is dealt with in section 13.9 below.[33]

Advertising is one of the five main areas regulated by the TWF Directive. The key obligations set out in the TWF Directive relating to advertising are as follows.

• The separation principle—that advertising and editorial content should be kept 'quite separate' by optical and/or acoustic means—is applied.[34] The AVMS Directive preserves this principle, while adding 'spatial' to the possible means of separation and making clear that new advertising techniques (such as 'virtual billboards') are not prohibited by this rule.

• There is a prohibition on surreptitious and subliminal advertising.[35]

• There are constraints on 'break patterns'—under the TWF Directive, breaks should normally occur between programmes. A programme may be interrupted by an advertising break once every 20 minutes, other than: (a) in respect of movies, where a break may only occur every 45 minutes; and (b) in respect of events with intervals, where advertisement breaks can only run during those intervals (such as at half-time in a football match). The AVMS Directive liberalizes these rules considerably: the only specific rules remaining (in addition to a general principle that break patterns should not undermine the integrity of the programme) are that movies may only be broken every 30 minutes and that children's programmes may only be interrupted once every 30 minutes. Advertisement breaks within religious services are and will remain outlawed.[36] Ofcom has already taken the opportunity to implement these new rules when it implemented its revised Code on the Scheduling of Television Advertising in September 2008.

• With regard to discrimination, Article 12 of the TWF Directive sets out general principles that advertising should not prejudice respect for human dignity; discriminate on grounds of race, sex, or nationality; or be offensive to religious or political beliefs. In addition, advertising should not encourage behaviour that is dangerous to health and safety or prejudicial to the protection of the environment. The AVMS Directive adds to the list of discrimination that is outlawed, that based on ethnic origin, religion or belief, disability, age, or sexual orientation. It also makes clear that only activities which are 'grossly' prejudicial to the environment are prohibited (rather than, for example, the sale of large, fuel-inefficient cars).

---

[33] See further Ch 8 above.
[34] TWF Directive, Art 10(1).
[35] ibid Art 10(3) and (4).
[36] TWF Directive, Art 11, including as varied by the AVMS Directive.

- The advertising of tobacco products[37] and prescription-only medicines[38] is prohibited, while alcohol advertising is subject to constraints.[39]

- Measures are taken for the protection of minors, including the outlawing of practices which take advantage of their credulity or exploit 'pester power' over parents.[40]

- Sponsorship is controlled, requiring transparency (so that the fact of a sponsorship must be made clear), as well as demanding that the sponsor cannot interfere with the broadcaster's editorial control. Sponsorship by tobacco companies and by brands connected with pharmacy-only medicines is prohibited (so, for example, Pfizer may be a sponsor in its own name, but may not sponsor a programme using the name of a brand such as Viagra). News and current affairs programmes may not be sponsored.[41] Under the AVMS Directive, two further discretions are given to Member States; the first is to permit a derogation that sponsor logos can be outlawed from children's, religious and documentary programmes.[42] The second, the power to permit product placement, is discussed in section 13.5 below.

- Advertising minutage is controlled. Under the TWF Directive, spot advertising is limited to 15 per cent of total broadcasting time during any day (ie an average of 9 minutes per hour) and never more than 20 per cent (ie 12 minutes) in any one clock-hour. Teleshopping spots can bring the combined percentage of broadcasting time devoted to advertising and teleshopping spots up to 20 per cent of the total daily broadcasting time.[43] Under the AVMS Directive, the only restriction is 12 minutes per clock-hour of advertising and teleshopping spots (ie the 15 per cent limit solely for advertising spots is dropped).[44] Teleshopping 'windows' (which must be devoted to teleshopping and clearly identified as such) by contrast are set at a minimum of 15 minutes and may last for up to three hours at a time (or indeed may constitute an entire channel).

13.4.1 Implementation of the TWF Directive into the obligations of broadcasters

The TWF Directive sets minimum standards in respect of each of the above obligations which must be implemented in each Member State. Member States are free to apply more onerous regulation in any of these areas. From the UK perspective, Ofcom has historically been a relatively 'light touch' regulator and has rarely seen fit

---

[37] TWF Directive, Art 13.
[38] ibid Art 14.
[39] ibid Art 15.
[40] ibid Art 16.
[41] ibid Art 17.
[42] AVMS Directive, Art 3F, para 4.
[43] TWF Directive, Art 18.
[44] AVMS Directive, Art 3K, para 18.

to implement more stringent regulations. Accordingly, each of the above obligations is set out in one or more of the Codes issued by Ofcom and BCAP without materially more onerous incremental restrictions.

However, in a couple of areas the UK rules for television *are* materially stricter than the EU baseline set by the TWF Directive:

• *Advertising minutage.* While digital broadcasters are subject to the same minutage rules as are set out in the TWF Directive, Ofcom has directed that ITV 1, Channel 4, and Five are subject to stricter rules, which limit these channels to an average of 7 minutes per hour across the entire transmission day and no more than 8 minutes per hour in peak time.[45] These channels are also limited to a maximum of 3 minutes 30 seconds of advertising in any one advertising break. However, while Ofcom has already implemented certain of the rules regarding when television programmes may contain scheduled breaks, it has not yet resolved how to implement the AVMS Directive's more radical changes to advertising minutage rules, described above.

• *HFSS food advertising.* Ofcom, under pressure from the UK government and health lobbies to take some action in respect of the problems of childhood obesity, introduced new rules, which came into effect in phases (commencing in April 2007), restricting advertisements for foods high in fat or salt or sugar ('HFSS' foods).[46] Under these new rules, such advertisements could no longer be shown around children's programmes or around other programmes which have a 'disproportionately' high audience of children.[47] Whilst undoubtedly a populist cause, within the industry this was controversial at the time. First, because of the feared impact on television channels dedicated to children and, secondly, because of some anomalies in the consequences (more children, in absolute numbers, will see an HFSS advertisement during 'Coronation Street' than during a niche ITV 2 programme aimed at 15-year-olds, but only the latter is banned). Ofcom will review the application of these rules in 2010. The UK's actions also influenced the introduction into the AVMS Directive of a provision relating to HFSS advertising, although this rule[48] is only advisory, requiring Member States and the Commission to encourage service providers to introduce codes of conduct regarding HFSS advertising and children's programming.

---

[45] Ofcom Code on the Scheduling of Television Advertising, para 4.
[46] Determined by reference to a nutrient profiling scheme set down by another governmental body, the Food Standards Agency.
[47] Calculated by using specific audience measurement metrics to look at the children watching TV at a given time, compared with the number watching a particular show. Children from 4 to 15 form the basis of the measurement.
[48] Set out in the AVMS Directive, Art 3(e)(1)(g).

13.5 PRODUCT PLACEMENT

Product placement is the practice of brand owners paying in order to secure that their branded products appear in a particular programme, with the intent of enabling the brand owner to communicate its brand values by association with that programme. Traditionally, product placement has been banned on UK television, with the exception that foreign television shows and movies which contain product placement may be shown, so long as the UK broadcaster is not deriving any financial benefit from the product placement. The ban on product placement is reinforced by a rule which prohibits 'undue prominence' being given to any product or service within any television programme and making clear that any reference (visual or aural) to a product or brand must be editorially justified.[49] The UK position reflects the law in most other European countries, although there has been some variation in application of the TWF Directive rules on separation which means that in some countries, product placement has been permitted.

Under the AVMS Directive, the generic ban on product placement is made explicit.[50] However, all Member States are offered the option[51] to liberalize, to some degree, the product placement rules, subject to strict conditions designed to ensure transparency, protection of editorial independence, and the requirement that there be no undue prominence of the placed items. At the time of writing, the UK government, while consulting on the matter and indicating that the door remains open, has indicated that its preference is not to liberalize product placement beyond its present scope and therefore to refuse to take advantage of this opportunity. Inevitably, this has been heavily criticized by broadcasters who, faced with falling advertising revenues, are keen to explore any chance of finding some alternative income sources.

13.6 CLEARANCE OF ADVERTISEMENTS

The Ofcom and BCAP Codes are enforced post-broadcast. Neither Ofcom nor the ASA offers any kind of pre-clearance of proposed advertisements. However, in order to take advantage of the economies of scale inherent in a single clearance process (as compared with every broadcaster showing a particular advertisement being required to undertake a compliance review of the same content), industry bodies have been set up, with the support of the broadcasters, which undertake the vetting of advertisements pre-broadcast. These bodies will, for example, decide whether advertisements

---

[49] The ban on product placement and the control on undue prominence can currently be found in the Ofcom Broadcasting Code, paras 10.5 and 10.4 respectively.

[50] AVMS Directive, Art 3G, para 1.

[51] Unusually for the provisions of a Directive, this is drafted as an opt-out—that Member States shall derogate from the blanket ban on product placement in the way described 'unless a Member State decides otherwise'.

are fit to broadcast at all times, or only after the 9 pm watershed. Two such bodies exist—Clearcast (formerly the BACC) undertakes clearance of television adverts (both at script stage and at 'final cut' stage), while the RACC (Radio Advertising Clearance Centre) handles the clearance of radio adverts. In practice, the use of these bodies is close to mandatory as many broadcasters will only air advertisements that have been approved by Clearcast/RACC and, for certain categories of radio advertising (including all national advertisements), the use of RACC is a mandatory requirement of the relevant BCAP Code. The only types of adverts regularly excluded from such review are those for Ofcom-licensed foreign language broadcasters and for teleshopping services (where the broadcasters typically undertake their own clearances). The fact that an advertisement has been approved by Clearcast/RACC does not absolve the broadcaster from subsequent responsibility should a breach of the rules be found, but it will be considered in mitigation when deciding the relevant penalty.

13.7 REGULATION OF NON-BROADCAST ADVERTISING

13.7.1 Introduction and general scheme of regulation

The regime for regulation of advertising outside television and radio is, in terms of the substantive rules which apply, similar to that of its broadcasting counterpart. Again, it is the Committee of Advertising Practice (CAP) which is the main industry body responsible for producing the code of practice which governs, primarily, the content of marketing communications for non-broadcast advertisements, sales promotions, and direct marketing in the UK.

However, the legal underpinning of the regime for advertisers operating in the non-broadcast arena is entirely different. Unlike broadcasters, players in this arena are not under any direct legal obligation to comply with the CAP Code. Instead it is a truly self-regulatory regime, deriving its strength from the force and weight of its membership (which consists of media owners, agencies, and representatives of large advertisers, as well as trade organizations and consumer interests). As a result, anyone who might seek to flout the Code would quickly find themselves unable to obtain media space on which to place the offending advertisements or professional support in creating those adverts or buying media on which to expose them.

The CAP was established and created the first version of its Code in 1961, largely as a pre-emptive measure to avoid the introduction of a statutory regime of advertising controls, which objective was achieved. However, while it is true that there is no direct statutory power underlying the CAP Code, as the principles espoused by the Code are often allied to the rights granted to consumers as a matter of general law, there are often parallel opportunities for those affected by misleading or other inappropriate advertising to seek recourse through the consumer protection powers of the Office of Fair Trading (OFT) and local Trading Standards officers. These powers, as well as the scope of the specific sanctions available for breach of the CAP rules, are discussed in section 13.10 below.[52]

13.7.2 The CAP Code

The British Code of Advertising, Sales Promotion and Direct Marketing, commonly referred to as the CAP Code, regulates advertisements in print, on posters, in new media (including the internet), and in the cinema and also covers sales promotions, the use of personal data for direct marketing, and the delivery of mail order goods or refunds.[53] The current edition of the Code (the eleventh) was adopted in 2003 and has been subject to only minor alterations since then.

The CAP Code is explicit in stating that it does not cover (among other things):[54]

- television and radio advertisements (these are covered by the BCAP Codes);
- claims made by companies on their own websites;
- the contents of premium rate services and phone lines (this is covered by PhonepayPlus and is discussed separately);
- most advertisements that originate outside the UK;
- private classified advertising;
- telephone selling; and
- editorial content (such as books or newspaper articles).

Like the BCAP Codes, the CAP Code is endorsed and administered by the Advertising Standards Authority (ASA). The ASA investigates and adjudicates on complaints and incidents of non-compliance with the CAP Code.

The CAP Code is split into four key sections: general rules (which apply to all forms of advertising activity which is covered by the Code); sales promotion rules (which apply, as might be inferred, only to sales promotions); direct marketing rules (which apply to all forms of direct marketing activity which is within the CAP's remit); and 'other specific rules' which apply to: advertising addressed to, targeted at, or featuring children (defined by the Code as those under 16); to the advertising of particular products (such as those relating to alcohol, gambling, weight control); and to particular types of claim (notably environmental claims).

13.7.3 CAP Code general rules

Like its sister code for broadcast advertising, the CAP Code is based on the general principles that advertisements should be *legal*, *decent*, *honest*, and *truthful*. They

---

[52] The CAP non-broadcast Code may be found at <http://www.cap.org.uk/cap/codes>.
[53] CAP Code, para 1.1.
[54] ibid para 1.2.

should be prepared with a sense of responsibility to consumers and society and should respect the principles of fair competition generally accepted in business.

The other CAP Code general rules are described below:

- Substantiation—advertisers must be able to substantiate any claims made about the products being advertised, with 'documentary evidence'. In limited situations, untruths or exaggerations that are unlikely to mislead are permitted provided these 'do not affect the accuracy or perception of the marketing communication in any material way'. Halfords was recently told by the ASA to cease publishing a leaflet advertisement that claimed Halfords' 'scratch, chip and dent repair services' were 75 per cent cheaper than body shop prices. After a complaint was made to the ASA by a competitor, Halfords was unable to provide adequate substantiation for the claims and ASA therefore concluded that the claims were likely to mislead customers. It is interesting to note that the burden of proof here is for the advertiser to show that something is supportable, before running an advertisement, rather than for a third party to show that an advert is untrue or misleading.

- Legality—communications should be legal and should not incite anyone to break the law. Advertisements should not present rights given to consumers as a matter of law (for example the right to cancel the purchase of goods bought by distance selling means)[55] as a distinctive feature.

- Decency—advertisements should not contain anything likely to cause serious or widespread offence (in particular in relation to race, religion, sex, sexual orientation, or disability).

- Honesty—'Marketers should not exploit the credulity, lack of knowledge, or inexperience of consumers'.

- Truthfulness—marketing communications should not mislead by 'inaccuracy, ambiguity, exaggeration, omission or otherwise'. They must not omit material information that would be likely to affect consumers' decisions about whether and how to buy an advertised product (unless the information is obvious from the context). In a recent ruling by the ASA, Estée Lauder Cosmetics was banned from continued publication of a skin product advertisement that stated 'Start to see your wrinkles disappear—INSTANTLY!'. The ASA held, first, that it was not clear whether the optical effect of the 'de-wrinkling' was significant enough to be detected by a human observer and, secondly, that whilst the product may be able to reduce the appearance of wrinkles (through a poly-filler type effect), it could not instantly reduce the wrinkles themselves as was suggested by the advertisement.

- Matters of opinion—marketers may give views about any matter including the quality or desirability of the product advertised so long as it is clear that they are stating a matter of opinion rather than a fact.

---

[55] Granted under the Consumer Protection (Distance Selling) Regulations 2000, SI 2000/2334, reg 10.

• Fear and distress—advertisements should not cause 'fear or distress' without good reason (use of fear to encourage prudent behaviour or discourage dangerous actions is permitted so long as it is not disproportionate). Shocking claims or images used to attract attention are prohibited. Marketers should not mislead about the nature or extent of the risk to personal security of consumers if they fail to purchase the product.

• Safety—marketing communications must not condone or encourage unsafe practices (such as drink-driving). Particular care should be taken in respect of advertisements addressed at children (discussed in section 13.7.6(1) below).

• Violence and anti-social behaviour—advertisements should not contain anything which condones or is likely to provoke violence or anti-social behaviour.

• Political advertising—advertisements 'published or distributed whose principal function is to influence voters in local, regional, national or international elections or referendums [are] exempt from the [CAP] Code'. This provides one area of distinction with broadcast advertising—political advertising on TV and radio is not permitted, while in non-broadcast media it is no longer controlled by the CAP Code and, within the confines of the general law and, in particular, election laws, is unrestricted.

• Protection of privacy—marketers should not 'unfairly portray or refer to people in an adverse or offensive way'. Permission should be sought before referring to or portraying members of the public and people with a public profile, or before implying personal approval of the advertised product. The Code also contains restrictions on referring to members of the Royal Family or using Royal Arms and Emblems.

• Testimonials and endorsements—testimonials must relate to the product being advertised and should not be presented as genuine if they are fictitious. 'Marketers should hold signed and dated proof, including a contact address, for any testimonial they use.' Permission must be sought to use a testimonial unless it is taken from a published source. Marketers should not display any trust or quality marks or claim any approval or endorsement by any body or claim to be a signatory to any code of conduct, unless they have the necessary authorization or approval.

• Prices—prices on all advertisements must be clear, relate to the product advertised, and include VAT and other non-optional taxes. Where prices are dependent on the purchase of another product, this must be made clear and price claims such as 'up to' and 'from' should not be exaggerated. Recommended retail prices should be genuine and should not differ significantly from the price at which the product is generally sold. Any additional prices that may apply, such as booking fees, must be made clear.

• Availability of products—advertisements for products which cannot be supplied should not be used as a way of assessing potential demand (unless it is clear that this is the purpose of the marketing communication). Products should not be advertised as ready for purchase unless the advertiser reasonably believes that it can satisfy demand. Marketers must not engage in 'switch selling' where advertising one product is used to promote another. False claims by marketers that a company is about to cease trading, move premises, or that a product is available for a very limited time only are prohibited. Marketers must not 'mislead consumers about market conditions or the possibility of finding the product elsewhere in order to induce consumers to buy the product at conditions less favourable than normal market conditions'.

• Guarantees—the word 'guarantee' should not be used in a way that could cause confusion about consumers' legal rights (ie consumers should be informed what additional rights are conferred on them). The full terms of a guarantee should be available to consumers prior to any commitment and any limitations should be clearly spelled out. Refunds should be provided promptly where a customer claims under a money back guarantee.

• Comparisons—comparative claims are permitted but should not mislead or be likely to mislead. The products compared must meet the same needs or be intended for the same purpose and material features of the products should be objectively compared. Comparisons must not mislead consumers by creating confusion with other products, trade marks, and brand names.

• Denigration and unfair advantage—whilst comparative claims are permitted, advertisements should not 'discredit, denigrate the products, trade marks, trade names . . . of competitors'. Marketing communications must not unfairly attack or take unfair advantage of the reputation of other businesses or their products.

• Imitation—advertisements must not mislead or cause confusion by closely resembling other marketing communications, including misleading consumers as to who manufactures the product. Marketers must not present products as imitations or replicas of other products protected by trade marks or trade names.

• Recognizing marketing communications and identifying marketers—advertisers must ensure that marketing communications are 'designed and presented in such a way that it is clear that they are marketing communications'. Where unsolicited e-mails are sent, they should be identifiable as marketing communications without the need to open them. Marketers must identify themselves in communications by providing their name and contact details. 'Marketers should not falsely claim or imply that they are acting as consumers or for purposes that do not relate to their trade, business, craft or profession.'

• Advertisement features—also known as 'advertorials', these must comply with the CAP Code if their content is controlled by marketers rather than the publishers and should be labelled as advertisements.

• After sales services—if after sales services are available in a language other than English, then the marketing communication should state before the contract is concluded if such services are not available in the language of the marketing communication. 'Marketing communications must not falsely claim or imply that after-sales service is available in an EU member state other than the one where the advertised product is sold.'

13.7.4 CAP Code sales promotion rules

The Sales Promotion Rules are designed primarily to protect the public and to regulate the nature and administration of promotional marketing techniques, such as the provision of direct or indirect additional benefits offered to consumers to make goods and services more desirable, for example 'free offers' or 'buy one get one free'. Underpinning the Sales Promotion Rules is the notion that sales promotions should be conducted 'equitably, promptly and efficiently and should be seen to deal fairly and honourably with consumers'.

Promoters must ensure that during promotions, consumers are protected and that product samples are safe and suitable; special care must be taken when promotions are aimed at children. Promoters should avoid causing unnecessary disappointment by ensuring they have made a reasonable estimate of the likely response to a sales promotion and that they are capable of meeting that response. They should offer refunds or substitute products if they are unable to meet unexpectedly high demand. Consumers should not have to make purchases as a precondition for applying for promotional items if the number of these items is limited. Where prize promotions are advertised, entry forms and goods needed for proof of purchase should be widely available.

Promotions must be resourced adequately to ensure smooth administration and proper supervision. Promoters should fulfil applications within thirty days and allow sufficient time for each phase of the promotion. The Sales Promotion Rules include several provisions regarding acceptable use of the term 'free'. Where a promotion includes 'free offers' or a 'free trial', promoters cannot recover costs by inflating the price of a product which must be bought as a pre-condition of obtaining the free item. In similar vein, items cannot be described as 'free' if their cost is included in the package price.

The rules state that sales promotions must clearly inform customers before purchase:

- how to participate (including costs);
- the start and closing date of the promotion;
- if proof of purchase is required;
- the nature and number of any prizes;
- any restrictions on entry;
- the availability of promotional packs; and
- the promoter's name and address.

The Sales Promotion Rules relating to prize promotions operate alongside all applicable laws, such as the Gambling Act 2005. The rules cover the definition of a prize and explain how to distinguish between a prize and a gift which is offered to all or most customers. They further include rules regarding the mechanics of running competitions, such as claims about the chances of winning prizes, deadlines for entry, supplementary conditions, independent supervision of draws, collection of winnings, and information which must be made available to participants prior to entry.

13.7.5 CAP Code direct marketing rules

The CAP Code Direct Marketing Rules apply alongside the CAP's other rules and address two key areas—distance selling and database marketing. In addition, a further trade body, the Direct Marketing Association, requires its members to observe the DMA Code of Practice, which covers some practices (for example telemarketing) that fall outside of the remit of the CAP. Many of the provisions of the CAP Code Direct Marketing Rules overlap with the Consumer Protection (Distance Selling) Regulations 2000, although, clearly, marketers must comply with the Regulations first and foremost.

The distance selling elements of the CAP Code Direct Marketing Rules deal with the type of information which distance selling marketing communications should include, for example a full description of the goods, an explanation of the nature and terms of the offer, payment details (including price, taxes payable, and delivery charges), the marketer's contact details, the customer's cancellation and refund rights, and after sales service and guarantees.

In addition, the Direct Marketing Rules state that marketers must inform consumers if they intend to call on respondents personally and must provide them with a mechanism to refuse a personal visit. Marketers must take particular care when packaging products which might fall into the hands of children (so that, for example, children cannot readily access something that is toxic or a choke hazard). They must not falsely imply that consumers have already ordered the marketed product and should not demand that consumers either pay for or return unsolicited products.

The database practice section of the CAP Code Direct Marketing Rules contains provisions similar to the requirements of the Data Protection Act 1998, albeit applicable only in relation to databases used for direct marketing. As with the distance selling elements, these rules do not replace the statutory provisions.

These database practice rules cover, among other matters, the information that marketers must provide to customers about what personal data is being collected, why it is collected (ie what it will be used for), and to whom it will be disclosed. Under the database practice provisions, marketers are obliged to seek consent from customers to:

- process their sensitive personal data;
- send marketing communications by e-mail, fax, mobile, or automated calling systems; and
- use personal information for purposes other than those under which the original consent was given.

Marketers must hold personal data securely and for purposes which are relevant and not excessive. They may not keep such data longer than necessary and must suppress the personal data if requested to do so by the consumer. Personal data must not be transferred outside the European Economic Area unless the destination country has equivalent data protection standards.

Finally, marketers should not 'make persistent and unwanted marketing solicitations by telephone, fax, email or other remote media' and should take necessary steps to ensure that all marketing communications are suitable for those targeted, are sent only to consumers where explicit consent is obtained (if required), and are not sent to those individuals who have asked not to receive them. Databases used by marketers must be kept up to date.

Bearing in mind that, in most respects, the CAP Code rules in respect of distance selling and databases are no more onerous than the corresponding obligations under the underlying legislation, it is perhaps unsurprising that the list of ASA adjudications reveals no activity at all in respect of this aspect of the Code between January 2005 and December 2008. It can be deduced that, where consumers (or others) have a grievance about how they have been treated with respect to matters of distance selling or data protection, they would rather take those matters up with the applicable statutory enforcement body (the OFT and local Trading Standards in respect of the former and the Information Commissioner in respect of the latter) than with the ASA. Indeed, they may well be less likely to become aware of the ASA's remit in this regard than that of the statutory enforcement bodies.

13.7.6 Other specific rules

Some of the most significant regulations under the CAP Code are contained in the 'Other Specific Rules' section. This part of the CAP Code contains, among other areas, provisions regarding marketing to children, the marketing of cars, health products, financial products, tobacco, alcohol and gambling. The key provisions are explored in further detail below:

(1) Children—the CAP Code considers children to be those aged under 16. It is noteworthy that different regulatory and self-regulatory bodies have different approaches to the question of what constitutes a minor. As discussed above, Ofcom has a statutory duty, in connection with the standards of television and radio programmes and advertising, to protect those under the age of 18,[56] while in its broadcast code it applies two thresholds, one to all under-18s and another to 'children', which it defines as under 15. Similarly, the DMA (mentioned above) regards a minor as anyone under 18, although it applies certain of its rules to different age groups so that, for example, it requires parental consent to any provision of personal data by those aged under 16 in relation to 'online' activity, but only those aged under 14 in relation to 'offline' activity.

---

[56] Communications Act 2003, s 319(2)(a).

The principal thrust of the CAP Code in relation to children is to ensure that 'marketing communications must not contain anything that is likely to result in their physical, mental or moral harm'. This includes a prohibition on encouraging or displaying children talking to strangers, behaving dangerously, being in close proximity to dangerous substances (such as petrol), or copying unsafe practices. An internet banner advertising the film *RocknRolla* and showing a character from the film with his arms spread wide and a gun in each hand was recently banned by the ASA on the grounds that it glorified guns and was not suitable in a medium where it might be seen by children. The advertisement was classified by the ASA as irresponsible and found to be in breach of the rules relating to responsible advertising and anti-social behaviour. Marketing communications addressed to, targeted at, or featuring children should not 'exploit their credulity, loyalty, vulnerability or lack of experience', for example by making them feel inferior, or lacking in courage if they do not buy the advertised product. Advertisements must not encourage children to pester their parents and should not exaggerate what is achievable by use of the advertised product. With regard to food and soft drink advertisements, these should not 'condone or encourage poor nutritional habits or an unhealthy lifestyle in children', for example by using high pressure selling techniques, appealing to children's emotions, or encouraging them to replace healthy meals with confectionary. Advertisements must not disparage good dietary practices or give children a misleading impression about the nutritional or health benefits of a particular food. Marketing communications featuring promotional offers or popular children's celebrities should be prepared with a sense of responsibly, ie they should not encourage the purchase of excessive quantities for irresponsible consumption or eating or drinking products only to take advantage of a promotional offer. Promotions aimed at children should make clear that adult permission is required where prizes and incentives may cause conflict, and should contain a prominent closing date, information on the realistic value of the prizes, and the chances of winning them.

(2) Motoring—advertisements for motor vehicles should not make speed or acceleration the predominant message and should avoid referring to practices that 'encourage or condone anti-social behaviour', including speeding or driving irresponsibly or dangerously. Prices quoted should correspond with the vehicles illustrated; environmental claims should conform with the Environmental Claims rules discussed below, and safety claims must be backed up by supporting evidence.

(3) Environmental claims—the increasing importance placed by the public on environmental matters has resulted in the introduction by the CAP Code of specific rules to try to eliminate the use by marketers of unjustified claims of the green credentials of their products or services, sometimes referred to as 'greenwash'. These rules provide that the basis of all such claims should be 'explained clearly and should be qualified where necessary' unless such claims can be substantiated, for example by provision of convincing evidence by marketers. 'Marketers should not suggest that their claims command universal acceptance if that is not the case.' Extravagant

language and confusing scientific terms should be avoided. Toyota was recently asked by the ASA to amend a national press advertisement which claimed that its RAV4 XT-R model was low in CO_2 emissions. Whilst the car in question had low emissions in comparison with other cars of its type, the CO_2 emissions were not low in comparison to those of cars in general.

(4) Health and beauty products and therapies—in general, claims made about health and beauty products should be backed by evidence, including, where appropriate, trials conducted on people. Marketers should not discourage essential treatments, invite consumers to diagnose their own ailments, offer advice on diagnosis or treatment of serious conditions, or encourage consumers to use products to excess. They must not suggest that products are 'guaranteed to work, are absolutely safe or without side-effects' unless they hold proof, for example unqualified or false claims such as 'cure' and 'rejuvenation' are unacceptable, as are implying that minor addictions can be treated without effort on the part of sufferers. Marketers should encourage consumers to take independent medical advice before committing themselves to significant treatment.

(a) Medicines—the Medicines Act 1968 and its regulations (as well as the regulations implementing Council Directive (EEC) 92/28) govern the advertising and promotion of medicines. Medicines must have authorization from the Medicines Control Agency before they can be marketed. Prescription-only medicines must not be advertised to the public. Non-prescription medicines may be advertised but are subject to provisions regarding the information which must be included on packaging and labels (such as ingredients) and the manner in which they can be advertised (for example celebrity endorsement is prohibited, use of fear or anxiety to promote products is forbidden, as is advertising medicines to children and comparisons against other medicines).

(b) Vitamins—marketers must hold scientific evidence for claims that vitamin or mineral products or other food supplements are beneficial to health and when advertising these products must not imply that they prevent or treat illnesses. Marketing communications must not encourage people to swap healthy diets for supplements.

(c) Cosmetics—'claims made about the action that a cosmetic has on or in the skin should distinguish between the composition of the product and any effects brought about by the way in which it is applied, such as massage'.

(d) Hair and scalp—marketers must be able to provide scientific evidence (on the basis of trials conducted on people) for any claims that their products can cure, prevent, or reverse baldness.

(5) Weight control—the promotion or advertisement of weight control products is strictly regulated. Any claims made regarding weight loss treatment must be backed up by rigorous trials on people, testimonials not supported by trials do not constitute substantiation. Obesity treatments must not be advertised to the public without

qualified supervision. Marketing communications for weight loss products must not be aimed at those aged under 18 and must not suggest that being underweight is desirable. This section also contains specific provisions on how it is acceptable to advertise dieting plans and products.

(6) Employment and business opportunities—these should be clearly distinguished in all marketing communications. Advertisements for employment opportunities must be genuine and state whether earnings are from a salary or commission. The rules include strict requirements regarding the information which must be provided to participants on all marketing communications for employment opportunities (especially in respect of home working schemes). Where business opportunities are advertised, a clear description of the work involved and investor commitments must be given. Vocational training must not make promises of employment unless it is guaranteed. Overall, 'marketing communications must not advertise schemes where consumers pay or give other consideration for the opportunity to receive compensation'.

(7) Financial products—the Financial Services and Markets Act 2000 (and supplemental legislation) together with the Financial Services Authority rules and guidance govern the marketing and advertising of regulated financial products. The OFT is responsible for regulating consumer loans under the Consumer Credit Act 1974. The provisions of these statutes are beyond the scope of this book. The CAP Code rules govern only the financial marketing communications which fall outside this legislation. The code states that 'offers of financial products should be set out in a way that allows them to be easily understood by the audience being addressed'. Furthermore, marketers must not 'take advantage of people's inexperience or credulity'. The code also provides rules on the type of information which must be provided to consumers, for example expenses, penalties or charges for withdrawal, rates of interest, and financial forecasts or projections. All marketing communications must make clear that the value of investments can go down as well as up and that past performance is not a guide to future performance.

(8) Tobacco, rolling papers, and filters—the Tobacco Advertising and Promotion Act 2002 prohibits the advertising of most tobacco products, but does not cover rolling papers or filters and permits limited tobacco advertising at the point of sale. The provisions of this section of the CAP Code mainly govern the content of marketing communications, which should not depict anyone smoking, encourage smokers to increase their consumption, target those aged under 18 and those particularly susceptible (such as the emotionally young and immature), or encourage the use of illegal drugs. Advertisements for tobacco must not be 'sexually titillating'; imply that smoking is glamorous, safe, or healthy; or that it is adventurous, rebellious, and enhances people's independence.

(9) Alcoholic drinks—the key provisions of this section of the CAP Code include the prohibition on marketing communications and sales promotions which encourage excessive, unsafe, and underage drinking. Advertising to people aged under 18 or the use in advertisements of people who look younger than 25 or who behave in a

juvenile or adolescent way is forbidden. Drinking alcohol must not be portrayed in a way that suggests it has inspirational, character-enhancing qualities or improves consumers' abilities or social standing.

(10) Gambling—is defined in the Gambling Act 2005 as including gaming, betting, lotteries, and spread betting. In similar vein to the restrictions on the advertising of alcoholic drinks, this part of the CAP Code is aimed a ensuring that marketing communications for gambling products are socially responsible; do not target people aged under 18 or the emotionally vulnerable; and do not link gambling with social, financial, and personal success.

The way in which all of these rules set out in the CAP Code are enforced is explored further below.

13.8 ADVERTISING AND PROMOTING PREMIUM RATE/ PHONE PAID SERVICES

In addition to the provisions specified in the BCAP and CAP Codes, the advertising of premium rate services (also known as phone paid services) is regulated by PhonepayPlus (formerly the Independent Committee for the Supervision of Standards of the Telephone Information Services, or ICSTIS).

Providers of premium rate services are obliged by Ofcom, under the Communications Act 2003, to comply with the Code of Practice issued by PhonepayPlus.[57] Among other things, the Code of Practice sets out rules relating to the promotion of premium rate services. These rules include obligations on promoters to provide transparent and clear pricing information, the contact details for the relevant service provider, and information which makes it clear to consumers that the service uses premium rate numbers. Customers must also be informed of instructions on how to make use of a 'STOP' facility if this is available.

The Code of Practice also contains further provisions regarding the promotion of phone paid services, including limitations on describing such services as 'free' and restrictions on inappropriate promotions (for example to people who may find services offensive or harmful).

Where advertisements for services appear in publications or other media with a shelf life of 3 months or longer, a statement that the information is correct at the time of publication must be included.

---

[57] Communications Act 2003, s 120 authorizes Ofcom to introduce obligations relating to premium rate services into the conditions under which providers of electronic communications services and networks operate. Under these powers, Ofcom has introduced a condition requiring those providers to comply with the PhonepayPlus Code.

13.9 REGULATION OF VIDEO-ON-DEMAND ADVERTISING—A NEW REGIME?

The AVMS Directive[58] introduces a new regulatory framework applicable to audiovisual media services which do not constitute linear television services. The scope of which non-linear services are encompassed within the AVMS rules is dealt with elsewhere;[59] here they will be referred to as video-on-demand (VOD) services. As with the TWF Directive (discussed above), the basic premise for the framework is that VOD services will be regulated in their home territory and then benefit from freedom of reception and redistribution throughout the European Union. So far as this regime relates to advertising and sponsorship, it contains the following key provisions:

• The separation principle which has always formed a cornerstone of television advertising will also apply to VOD services, as will the prohibition on surreptitious and subliminal advertising and the principle that there should be no discrimination based on race, ethnic origin, religion or belief, sex or sexual orientation, nationality, age, or disability.

• The ban on advertising of tobacco and prescription-only medicines, the controls on alcohol advertising and the duty to protect minors are imported from the rules of traditional television.

• The provision requiring Member States to encourage service providers to introduce codes of conduct regarding the advertising to children of foods high in fat or salt or sugar (HFSS foods) applies equally to VOD services.

• Most controversially, the rules on sponsorship and product placement will apply to VOD services as well as to linear television services. This means that the current controversy in the UK regarding the liberalization of product placement will impact not only on linear television services, but also on VOD services.

It is valuable to note that the elements of the television advertising rules from the TWF Directive that are not imported into the VOD provisions include those relating to break patterns and the controls over the volume of advertising permitted. This means that, for example, a VOD programme might (if consumers could be persuaded to tolerate it) include an advertising break every ten minutes, which would not be possible on linear television.

At the time of writing, the UK government had yet to conclude how it intended to implement the AVMS Directive (which must be done by 19 December 2009). However, in its consultation paper,[60] it indicated its preferred options.

---

[58] Directive (EC) 2007/65.
[59] See further Ch 8 above.
[60] DCMS, 'The Audiovisual Media Services Directive, Consultation on Proposals for Implementation in the United Kingdom' (July 2008).

First, while not directly relevant to advertising content, the government indicated that for VOD service regulation generally, they would like to see a solution where Ofcom becomes the back-stop regulator, while delegating the day-to-day regulatory regime to an industry-led co-regulator (with the existing self-regulatory body ATVOD being cited as an entity which might possibly evolve into that co-regulator). This is similar to the structure under which the ASA regulated television advertising under Ofcom's auspices.

Secondly, for the pure advertising elements of VOD services, the government would like to see a solution where, as with television advertising, Ofcom becomes the back-stop regulator in a co-regulatory regime with the ASA. This would mean that the ASA remains a one-stop shop covering all media, albeit with slightly different remits for broadcast, non-broadcast, and VOD advertising.

Thirdly, the government would wish sponsorship and product placement to fall within the remit of the content regulator, rather than the advertising regulator. That is consistent again with the broadcasting regime, where these matters are reserved to Ofcom and are not within the ASA's remit.

Finally, the government recognizes that there must be a clear division between which advertisements fall within the new regime and which fall to be regulated under the existing non-broadcast regime. It recognizes that there are limiting cases, such as a menu page on a VOD service which might not in itself constitute VOD content but which might most sensibly be dealt with alongside all of the other VOD content and advertising regulation.[61]

13.10 SANCTIONS FOR BREACH OF ADVERTISING REGULATIONS

One of the core functions of the ASA is to pass judgment on whether or not a marketing communication or advertisement has breached the provisions of the BCAP or CAP Codes. Where a breach has occurred, the CAP compliance team is responsible for enforcing ASA adjudications.

13.10.1 Broadcasting (television and radio)

In the context of broadcasting, it is the broadcaster rather than the advertiser or the advertising agency which is ultimately liable for sanctions following a breach of the BCAP Code. Broadcasters are ultimately accountable to Ofcom under their broadcast licences for transmitting infringing advertisements and are also obliged to enforce ASA rulings, although it is worth noting that the various sanctions discussed below, for

---

[61] Since this section was written, the government has published the outcome of its consultation, reaffirming its original proposals as set out here.

example adverse publicity, will predominantly take effect against the advertiser itself rather than the broadcaster.

In the event that a broadcaster persistently runs advertisements in breach of the BCAP Code, it can be referred to Ofcom by the ASA. Ofcom has the power to impose fines on broadcasters and in severe cases can even revoke its licence to broadcast. In practice, breaches of the BCAP Code are rare, largely as a result of the Clearcast/RACC pre-clearance regime discussed above.

As for the advertisers themselves, whilst they are not subject to the Ofcom statutory sanctions, an adverse ruling by the ASA against an advertiser will have a similar impact on it as it would have in a non-broadcast environment, discussed below.

13.10.2 Non-broadcast

In the first instance, where the ASA finds that a marketing communication breaks the CAP Code, the advertiser is told to either amend or withdraw the advertisement. In the vast majority of cases the marketer will willingly comply with this ruling and no further action or sanction will be necessary.

If an advertiser refuses to adhere to the ASA ruling, sanctions will then be applied by either the ASA or CAP. The purpose of these sanctions is to ensure that non-compliant marketing communications are amended, withdrawn, or stopped as quickly as possible. ASA's or CAP's decision to impose a particular sanction is based on ensuring that it is proportionate to the nature of the breach of the CAP Code.

Sanctions may be applied by the ASA or CAP regardless of whether an advertisement has been the subject of a formal complaint and investigation, this means that these bodies may take pre-emptive action against an advertiser before any complaint has been registered or any investigation concluded.

13.10.2.1 *Adverse publicity*
One of the most effective and widely used sanctions is the adverse publicity which is generated from rulings by the ASA against infringing advertisers. These rulings are published by the ASA on its website on a weekly basis and, in high-profile cases, usually receive a considerable amount of media coverage, both nationally and internationally. The adverse publicity is damaging to both the advertiser and its brand. It also serves as a warning to consumers and the general public about the product (and advertiser), which in turn undermines the desirability of the product or service being advertised and the effectiveness of the marketing campaign. Unsurprisingly, this type of negative media coverage is enough of a deterrent or sanction to prompt most advertisers to withdraw non-CAP Code compliant advertising.

13.10.2.2 *Ad Alerts*
The CAP itself is an organization which is made up of a combination of trade and industry bodies, broadcasters, and companies involved in the marketing process. These

include, among others, organizations such as the Direct Marketing Association, the Internet Advertising Bureau, the Institute of Practitioners in Advertising, the Outdoor Advertising Association, BSkyB, ITV, and the Royal Mail.

Because of the nature of CAP's membership and their collective support for the workings of the ASA and CAP, the CAP compliance team is able to impose sanctions which, without the CAP's unique characteristics, would otherwise be very difficult to enforce. Ad Alerts are an example of such a sanction.

Ad Alerts are applied by the CAP issuing an order to its members, advising them to withhold services from or deny advertising space to an advertiser in breach of the CAP Code. Ad Alerts can be issued at short notice and contain the name and contact details of the non-compliant marketer and a description of the compliance issue together with (if available) a copy of the infringing marketing communication. The use of Ad Alerts makes it very difficult for an advertiser to secure the services and advertising space it needs to publish its infringing marketing communication. As a result, compliance with an ASA ruling to withdraw an advertisement can be achieved by default through this method.

13.10.2.3 *Withdrawal or withholding of trading privileges and recognition*
In a similar vein to Ad Alerts, following a ruling from the ASA, the trade associations, and professional bodies which make up the CAP are able, permanently or temporarily, to withdraw or revoke from their infringing members any trading privileges or recognition that are conferred with such membership. Examples include agency recognition offered by the print media members of the CAP or direct mail discounts offered by the Royal Mail on bulk mailings. In exceptional cases of non-compliance, CAP members may expel companies from membership.

13.10.2.4 *Pre-vetting*
Where an advertiser persistently breaches the CAP Code, the ASA and CAP may decide to subject all of such an entity's future marketing communications to mandatory pre-vetting. Under this sanction an advertiser must check all future advertisements with the CAP Copy Advice team before publication. This sanction can be applied by the CAP until it is satisfied that future communications will comply with the CAP Code (although such a sanction is often for a fixed period, for example two years).

13.10.2.5 *Referral to the OFT for action*
Probably the most severe sanction available to the ASA and CAP for serious breaches of the CAP Code is referring the offender to the OFT for action.

If advertisements or marketing communications which infringe the CAP Code (including those that are misleading or contain impermissible comparisons) continue to be published after the ASA has ruled against them, then the ASA can refer the matter to the OFT for action under the relevant legislation or regulation, usually the Consumer

Protection from Unfair Trading Regulations 2008 and the Business Protection from Misleading Regulations 2008. The details of these regulations are outside the scope of this chapter but they are concerned with protecting consumers and businesses from being unfairly treated and from being subject to misleading advertising and aggressive selling techniques and commercial practices. Of course, the OFT is entitled to enforce these laws without any advice or recommendation from the ASA but, in practice, in the rare instances where it receives a complaint from the ASA, it is clearly inclined to act, as any decision not to do so might undermine the self-regulatory system, which the OFT strongly supports.

The OFT has broad powers to seek remedies where it considers advertising to be in breach of the legislation mentioned above (or a raft of other consumer protection legislation that might be relevant). For example, it might seek an undertaking from anyone responsible for commissioning, preparing, or disseminating a misleading advertisement that it will be stopped. If such an undertaking is not given or is not honoured, the OFT can then seek an injunction from the court to prevent its further appearance. Non-compliance with a court injunction would constitute a contempt of court punishable by a fine or even imprisonment.

13.10.3 Sanctions applicable to premium rate services

Breaches of the PhonepayPlus Code of Practice can result in the imposition of sanctions by the PhonepayPlus Tribunal. These sanctions are ultimately enforceable by Ofcom as a breach by the relevant communications service provider of its operating conditions.

Sanctions include a formal reprimand, a fine, a requirement for advertisements and promotional materials to be submitted for copy advice prior to publication, the withdrawal of the right to use the premium rate number, and in serious cases a requirement for the service provider to refund all sums received from customers who have used that particular phone paid service. In serious cases, fines of several hundred thousand pounds have been imposed.

Index

safe harbour 457
safety
advertising 515
CAP Code 513
criminal investigations 76
journalists' sources, protection of 76
sales promotion rules 517
sanctions *see also* **fines; imprisonment;
sanctions for breach of
advertising regulations**
criminal content and control 430
Ofcom 353–60
Press Complaints Commission code 340
video-on-demand, regulation of 365–9
Video Standards Council (VSC) 362–4
videos, DVDs and video games 360–4
**sanctions for breach of advertising
regulations** 525–8
ad alerts 526–7
adverse publicity 526
Advertising Standards Authority
(ASA) 525, 526–8
aggressive selling 528
BCAP (Broadcast Committee of
Advertising Practice) Code 525–6
CAP Code 525–7
fines 528
injunctions 528
misleading advertising 528
non-broadcast advertising 526–7
Ofcom 525–6, 528
Office of Fair Trading, referral
to the 527–8
premium rate services 528
pre-vetting 527
radio 506, 525–6
reprimands 528
television 506, 525–6
trading privileges and recognition, withdrawal
or withholding 527
satellite broadcasting 301, 325, 452–4, 486
Scoopt 6
Scotland
barnardisation 266, 286
contempt of court 98, 100–1, 102, 111,
113–14, 120–1, 139–41
discontinuance 101–2
freedom of information 260–2, 266, 282–6
Information Commissioner 260
injunctions 139–41
innocent publication and
distribution 120–1
photographs and identification 112–15
security 111
sculptures, copyright and 192
search and seizure 74–6, 77–81, 82–8
search and sift off premises 78

search warrants 78–81, 84–90
security *see* **national security**
security services 265
seizure 74–6, 78–81, 82–8, 438
**self-incrimination, privilege
against** 87, 88–90
self-regulation
advertising 501, 506
Audio Visual Media Services (AVMS)
Directive 11
broadcasting 333
computer games 333
drivers of media law 11
freedom of expression 11
Independent Mobile Classification Body
(IMCB) 365, 367–70
Press Complaints Commission 11, 338–42
print media 338–42, 369
right to broadcast 309
traditional regulation 335
**serious organized crime, protection of
journalists sources and** 92–3
service providers
browsing software 215
caching 215
compliance regimes 312
copyright 213, 216
criminal sanctions 215
damages 215
defamation 400–1, 418–21
definition 310
E-Commerce Directive 216
file sharing 216
foreign illegal content, controlling 456–7
hate speech 437
hosting 214
immunity 214
injunctions 215
journalists' sources, protection of 94
jurisdiction 311–15
limitations on immunity 215
Memorandum of Understanding 216
message boards 94
P2P 216
right to broadcast 310–15
**services of general economic
interest** 29–30, 40
**sexuality, incitement to hatred
based on** 435
**Sky Subscriber Services Limited
(SSSL)** 45–6
slander see defamation
small European states 476
social networking sites 214
social services records 242
socio-political communications media 5
software 194, 215 *see also* **computer games**